AF477403

STOBI

RESULTS OF THE JOINT AMERICAN–YUGOSLAV ARCHAEOLOGICAL INVESTIGATIONS, 1970–1981

•

James Wiseman, *General Editor*

VOLUME 1

Ceramic analysis at Stobi, 1973

STOBI

THE HELLENISTIC AND ROMAN POTTERY

•

Virginia R. Anderson-Stojanović

PRINCETON UNIVERSITY PRESS

Published by Princeton University Press, 41 William Street,
Princeton, New Jersey 08540
In the United Kingdom: Princeton University Press, Oxford

Library of Congress Cataloging-in-Publication Data

Anderson-Stojanović, Virginia R. (Virginia Ruth), 1945–
Stobi—the Hellenistic and Roman pottery / Virginia R.
Anderson-Stojanović.
p. cm. — (Stobi—results of the joint American-Yugoslav
archaeological investigations, 1970–1981 ; v. 1)
Includes bibliographical references and index.
ISBN 0-691-03605-5 (cloth : alk. paper)
1. Stobi (Ancient city) 2. Romans—Yugoslavia—Stobi (Ancient city)
3. Excavations (Archaeology)—Yugoslavia—Stobi (Ancient city)
I. Title. II. Series.
DR2285.S77A53 1992 939′.8—dc20 91-4480

This book has been composed in Palatino

Princeton University Press books are printed on acid-free paper,
and meet the guidelines for permanence and durability of the
Committee on Production Guidelines for Book Longevity of the
Council on Library Resources

Printed in the United States of America by Princeton University Press,
Princeton, New Jersey

10 9 8 7 6 5 4 3 2 1

Designed by Laury A. Egan

In Memoriam Patris

CONTENTS

•

LIST OF FIGURES xi

LIST OF TABLES xiii

LIST OF PLATES xv

FOREWORD *by James Wiseman* xxi

PREFACE xxvii

LIST OF ABBREVIATIONS xxxi

1. INTRODUCTION 3

The Site 3

Goals and Methods of Pottery Analysis 4

Explanatory Note for the Catalogue 6

2. THE LOCAL CERAMIC TRADITION 8

3. THE HELLENISTIC AND ROMAN POTTERY 13

Early Hellenistic Wheelmade Gray Ware (**1–19**) 13

Black-Gloss Wares (**20–54**) 17

Lagynoi (**55, 56**) 22

Black-Gloss Wares with Gray Fabric (**57–105**) 23

Hellenistic Moulded Relief Bowls (**106–146**) 29

Thin-Walled Wares (**147–224**) 35

Terra Sigillata 44

Eastern Sigillata A (**225–234**) 44

Italian Sigillata (**235–296**) 45

Other Western Sigillata (**297–302**) 50

Eastern Sigillata B (**303–340**) 50

Çandarli Ware (**341–345**) 53

Cypriot Sigillata Ware (**346**) 54

Red Slip Wares 55

Cypriot Red Slip (**347**) 55

African Red Slip Ware (**348–393**) 55

Phocaean Red Slip Ware (**394–417**) 59

Macedonian Gray Ware (**418–484**) 61

Miscellaneous Stamps (**485–510**) 72

Italian Mugs (**511–516**) 74

Marbeled Slip (**517–519**) 75

Lead-Glazed Wares (**520–531**) 75

Miscellaneous Imports (**532–541**) 77

Miscellaneous Vessels with Relief Decoration (**542–557**) 78

Imitation Çandarli (**558, 559**) 80

Unguentaria (**560–610**) 80

Mortaria (**611–614**) 86

Tan Micaceous Ware (**615–627**) 87

Red Micaceous Ware (**628–631**) 88

Mica-Dusted Ware (**632–638**) 88

Amphorae (**639–715**) 89

Pompeian Red Ware (**716–721**) 97

Campanian Cooking Ware (**722**) 99

Aegean Cooking Ware (**723, 724**) 99

Local / Regional Color-Slipped and Plain Wares 99

Hellenistic wares: Forms 1–23 (**725–767**) 101

Hellenistic wares: Other (**768–813**) 105

Early Roman wares: Forms 1–18 (**814–855**) 109

Early Roman wares: Other (**856–910**) 112

Middle Roman wares: Forms 1–34 (**911–1016**) 116

Middle Roman wares: Other (**1017–1074**) 124

Late Roman wares: Other (**1075–1081**) 127

Local / Regional Cooking Wares 128

Hellenistic cooking wares: Forms 1–13 (**1082–1109**) 128

Hellenistic cooking wares: Other (**1110–1131**) 132

Early Roman cooking wares: Forms 1–7 (**1132–1145**) 133

Early Roman cooking wares: Other (**1146–1161**) 134

Middle Roman cooking wares: Forms 1–4 (**1162–1175**) 135

Middle Roman cooking wares: Other (**1176–1209**) 136

Late Roman cooking wares: Forms 1–13 (**1210–1242**) 138

Late Roman cooking wares: Other (**1243–1292**) 140

4. CHRONOLOGY AND DEPOSITS 144

Introduction 144

Descriptions of Core Deposits 146

Civil Basilica 146
Central Basilica 146
Peristeria Court 147
Acropolis 148
Large Bath 150
Inner Wall West 150
East City Wall 153
Theater 154
Quantification of Pottery at Stobi 155
Deposit Lists 155

5. SUMMARY AND CONCLUSIONS 184

APPENDIX 1. THE POTTER'S SHOP 195
APPENDIX 2. PETROGRAPHIC ANALYSIS OF SELECTED CERAMIC SAMPLES, *by Georgeana Little* 197
CONCORDANCE 203
INDEX 215
Greek Words and Names 217
Latin Potter's Names 218
PLATES

LIST OF FIGURES

Figure 3.1. Hellenistic Gray Ware. Bar graph illustrating quantity of the various forms at Stobi 15

Figure 3.2. Macedonian Gray Ware. Bar graph illustrating quantity of the various forms at Stobi 62

Figure 3.3. Proportion of Macedonian Gray Ware RBH found in 5th-century deposits at Stobi 63

Figure 3.4. Bar graph illustrating quantity of the most popular Hellenistic Color-Slipped and Plain forms at Stobi 100

Figure 3.5. Bar graph illustrating quantity of the most popular Early Roman Color-Slipped and Plain forms at Stobi 100

Figure 3.6. Bar graph illustrating quantity of the most popular Middle Roman Color-Slipped and Plain forms at Stobi 101

Figure 3.7. Bar graph illustrating quantity of Hellenistic Cooking Ware forms at Stobi 129

Figure 3.8. Bar graph illustrating quantity of Early Roman Cooking Ware forms at Stobi 129

Figure 3.9. Bar graph illustrating quantity of Middle Roman Cooking Ware forms at Stobi 129

Figure 3.10. Bar graph illustrating quantity of Late Roman Cooking Ware forms at Stobi 130

Figure 4.1. Proportions of pottery types expressed as percentage of total RBH in Hellenistic core deposits 159

Figure 4.2 Proportions of pottery types expressed as percentage of total RBH in Early Roman core deposits 159

Figure 4.3 Proportions of pottery types expressed as percentage of total RBH in Middle Roman core deposits 159

Figure 4.4 Proportions of pottery types expressed as percentage of total RBH in Late Roman core deposits 159

Figure 5.1. Quantity of Italian pottery in total RBH of Hellenistic and Early Roman deposits at Stobi 186

Figure. 5.2. Quantity of Fine Ware RBH at Stobi divided according to origin 186

Figure 5.3. Quantity of Cooking Ware RBH at Stobi divided according to origin 186

Figure 5.4. Breakdown of various types among Italian imports at Stobi 186

Figure 5.5. Proportion of fine wares (excluding local Color-Slipped) expressed as percentage of total RBH of these wares in Hellenistic core deposits 187

Figure 5.6. Proportion of coarse wares expressed as percentage of total RBH of these wares in Hellenistic core deposits 187

Figure 5.7. Proportion of fine wares (excluding local Color-Slipped) expressed as percentage of total RBH of these wares in Early Roman core deposits 189

Figure 5.8. Proportion of coarse wares expressed as percentage of total RBH of these wares in Early Roman core deposits 189

Figure 5.9. Quantity of imported fine ware RBH in Early and Middle Roman core deposits 191

Figure 5.10. Proportion of fine wares (excluding local Color-Slipped) expressed as percentage of total RBH of these wares in Middle Roman core deposits 191

Figure 5.11. Quantity of pottery types in each chronological period 191

Figure 5.12. Proportion of coarse wares expressed as percentage of total RBH of these wares in Middle Roman core deposits 191

Figure 5.13. Proportion of fine wares (excluding local Color-Slipped Wares) expressed as percentage of total RBH of these wares in Late Roman core deposits 192

Appendix Figure 2.1a. Major mineral constituents of Fabric group 1, fine wares 199

Appendix Figure 2.1b. Particle-size distributions for Fabric group 1, fine wares 199

Appendix Figure 2.2a. Major mineral constituents of Fabric group 2, gray wares 200

Appendix Figure 2.2b. Particle-size distributions for Fabric group 2, gray wares 200

Appendix Figure 2.3a. Major mineral constituents for Fabric group 3, Coarse Wares, Hellenistic to Middle Roman periods 201

Appendix Figure 2.3b. Particle-size distributions for Fabric group 3, Coarse Wares, Hellenistic to Middle Roman periods 201

Appendix Figure 2.4a. Major mineral constituents for Fabric group 3, Coarse Wares, Late Roman period 202

Appendix Figure 2.4b. Particle-size distributions for Fabric group 3, Coarse Wares, Late Roman period. 202

LIST OF TABLES

Table 1.1. Chronological range of wares at Stobi 5

Table 2.1. Fabric groups of Stobi Local Wares 9

Table 3.1. List of Macedonian Gray Ware forms and deposits 64

Table 3.2. List of Unguentaria types in Stobi graves 82

Table 4.1. Summary of Core Deposits divided into chronological periods 145

Table 4.2. Quantity of RBH for pottery types in Lots 12–14, 608, 610. Civil Basilica 146

Table 4.3. Quantity of RBH for pottery types in Lots 87–89, 130–132, 134, 135, 140, 829, 831. Central Basilica. Potter's Shop 147

Table 4.4. Quantity of RBH for pottery types in Lots 547–552, 554, 555, 557, 558. Peristeria Court 147

Table 4.5. Quantity of RBH for pottery types in Lots 228–231, 248, 249, 257–261. Acropolis 149

Table 4.6. Quantity of RBH for pottery types in Lots 234–236. Acropolis 150

Table 4.7. Quantity of RBH for pottery types in Lots 924, 929–934, 936–942. Large Bath 151

Table 4.8. Quantity of RBH for pottery types in Lots 1306–1310, 1332, 1333. Inner Wall West 151

Table 4.9. Quantity of pottery types in Lots 1295, 1296–1304. Inner Wall West 152

Table 4.10. Quantity of pottery types in Lots 1407–1410. East City Wall. Paved street 153

Table 4.11. Quantity of pottery types in Lot 1404. East City Wall. Paved street 154

Table 4.12. Quantity of pottery types in Lots 274, 277, 278, 293–295, 297–308. Theater. East Parodos 154

Table. 4.13. Quantified list of RBH from Core Deposits with date 155

Table 4.14. Counts of RBH for all types of pottery in Core Deposits combined in broad chronological periods 160

Table 4.15. Core Deposit List. Description of Lots 160

Table 4.16. List of other deposits arranged by Lot number 163

Table 4.17. List of other deposits arranged by date 175

Table 5.1. Quantity of Fine Ware RBH in Core Deposits for each chronological period 187

Table 5.2. Quantity of Coarse Ware RBH in Core Deposits for each chronological period 187

Table Appendix 2.1. Ceramic samples by fabric group and period. 197

LIST OF PLATES

•

(All drawings at a scale of 1:2 unless otherwise indicated.)

Frontispiece. Ceramics analysis at Stobi, 1973

Plate 1. Map showing location of Stobi. By Dragan Stojanović and David Clayton. Names of ancient towns in capital letters

Plate 2. Map of Stobi

Plate 3. Pottery stamps and moulds (**2**, scale 1:1)

Plate 4. Early Hellenistic Wheelmade Gray Ware. Forms 1–5

Plate 5. Early Hellenistic Wheelmade Gray Ware. Forms 6–10

Plate 6. Early Hellenistic Wheelmade Gray Ware. Form 10, lids, bases. Lagynoi

Plate 7. Black-Gloss Wares. Campanian A, B

Plate 8. Black-Gloss Wares

Plate 9. Black-Gloss Wares

Plate 10. Black-Gloss Wares

Plate 11. Black-Gloss Wares with Gray Fabric. Campanian C

Plate 12. Black-Gloss Wares with Gray Fabric. Campanian C. Asia Minor Wares

Plate 13. Black-Gloss Wares with Gray Fabric. Terra Sigillata Derivatives (**67, 73**, scale 1:3)

Plate 14. Black-Gloss Wares with Gray Fabric

Plate 15. Black-Gloss Wares with Gray Fabric

Plate 16. Black-Gloss Wares with Gray Fabric

Plate 17. Black-Gloss Wares with Gray Fabric. Stamps (scale 1:1)

Plate 18. Hellenistic Moulded Relief Bowls

Plate 19. Hellenistic Moulded Relief Bowls. Local series. Thin-Walled beakers, Group I (**144** top, scale 3:2)

Plate 20. Thin-Walled Ware. Beakers and Jars, Group I

Plate 21. Thin-Walled Ware. Jars, Group I

Plate 22. Thin-Walled Ware, Groups I, III, and IV

Plate 23. Thin-Walled Ware with Sanded and Barbotine decoration, Groups IV and V

Plate 24. Thin-Walled Ware with Barbotine decoration, Groups V and VI

Plate 25. Thin-Walled Ware, Group VI and others

Plate 26. Thin-Walled Ware, Pitchers (scale 1:3)

Plate 27. Eastern Sigillata A

Plate 28. Eastern Sigillata A and Italian Sigillata

Plate 29. Italian Sigillata

Plate 30. Italian Sigillata

Plate 31. Italian Sigillata

Plate 32. Italian Sigillata

Plate 33. Italian Sigillata bases (scale 1:1)

Plate 34. Italian Sigillata stamps (scale 1:1; **287, 288, 289, 292, 294, 295**, scale 2:1)

Plate 35. Other Western Sigillata and Eastern Sigillata B

Plate 36. Eastern Sigillata B (**314**, scale 1:3)

Plate 37. Eastern Sigillata B

Plate 38. Eastern Sigillata B

Plate 39. Eastern Sigillata B (**339**, scale 2:1)

Plate 40. Çandarli Ware. Cypriot Sigillata. Cypriot Red Slip Ware

Plate 41. African Red Slip Ware

Plate 42. African Red Slip Ware (scale 1:3)

Plate 43. African Red Slip Ware (scale 1:3)

Plate 44. African Red Slip Ware

Plate 45. Phocaean Red Slip Ware (scale 1:3)

Plate 46. Phocaean Red Slip Ware (scale 1:3)

Plate 47. Phocaean Red Slip Ware (scale 1:3)

Plate 48. Macedonian Gray Ware. Form 1 (scale 1:3)

Plate 49. Macedonian Gray Ware. Forms 1 and 2

Plate 50. Macedonian Gray Ware. Form 2

Plate 51. Macedonian Gray Ware. Forms 2 and 3

Plate 52. Macedonian Gray Ware. Forms 3, 4, and 5 (scale 1:3)

Plate 53. Macedonian Gray Ware. Forms 6, 7, and 8

Plate 54. Macedonian Gray Ware. Forms 9 and 10 (scale 1:3)

Plate 55. Macedonian Gray Ware

Plate 56. Potter's Stamps (scale 1:1)

Plate 57. Potter's Stamps (scale 1:1; 495, scale 2:1)

Plate 58. Potter's Stamps (scale 1:1)

Plate 59. Potter's Stamps (scale 1:1)

Plate 60. Italian Mugs. Marbeled Slip

Plate 61. Marbeled Slip. Lead-Glazed Wares (scale 1:3)

Plate 62. Lead-Glazed Wares

Plate 63. Miscellaneous Imports

Plate 64. Miscellaneous Imports

Plate 65. Miscellaneous Relief Wares. Imitation Çandarli Ware

Plate 66. Fusiform Unguentaria. Types A–Ç

Plate 67. Fusiform Unguentaria. Types D, E, and G

Plate 68. Fusiform Unguentaria. Type F

Plate 69. Fusiform Unguentaria. Type G

Plate 70. Bulbous Unguentaria. Types A–E

Plate 71. Bulbous Unguentaria. Types F–N

Plate 72. Bulbous Unguentaria. Types M–Q

Plate 73. Mortaria. Red Micaceous Ware (scale 1:3)

Plate 74. Tan Micaceous Ware

Plate 75. Tan Micaceous Ware. Mica-Dusted Ware

Plate 76. Amphorae. Hellenistic and Early Roman types (scale 2:5)

Plate 77. Amphorae. Hellenistic and Early Roman types (scale 2:5; **650**, scale 1:4)

Plate 78. Amphorae. Hellenistic and Early Roman types (scale 1:3; **651**, scale 1:6)

Plate 79. Amphorae. Hellenistic and Early Roman types (scale 1:3)

Plate 80. Amphorae. Middle Roman types (scale 1:3)

Plate 81. Amphorae. Middle Roman types (scale 1:3)

Plate 82. Amphorae. Middle Roman and Late Roman types (scale 1:3; **700**, scale 1:6)

Plate 83. Amphorae. Late Roman types (scale 1:3)

Plate 84. Pompeian Red Ware. Campanian Cooking Ware (scale 1:3)

Plate 85. Aegean Cooking Ware. Hellenistic Color-Slipped Forms 1 and 2

Plate 86. Hellenistic Color-Slipped Form 3

Plate 87. Hellenistic Color-Slipped Forms 4–8

Plate 88. Hellenistic Color-Slipped Forms 10–12

Plate 89. Hellenistic Color-Slipped Forms 13–17

Plate 90. Hellenistic Color-Slipped and Plain Forms 18–22 (scale 1:3)

Plate 91. Hellenistic Color-Slipped and Plain Form 23 and Other Hellenistic bowls (scale 1:3)

Plate 92. Hellenistic Color-Slipped bowls, jars, and pitchers

Plate 93. Hellenistic Color-Slipped and Plain pitchers, jug, and basin

Plate 94. Hellenistic Color-Slipped and Plain kraters, jar, and other shapes (scale 1:3)

Plate 95. Hellenistic Lids. Early Roman Color-Slipped Forms 1–3

Plate 96. Early Roman Color-Slipped Forms 4–9 (scale 1:3)

Plate 97. Early Roman Color-Slipped Forms 10–12

Plate 98. Early Roman Color-Slipped Forms 11, 13, 14, and 16 (scale 1:3)

Plate 99. Early Roman Plain Forms 15–17 (**846**, scale 1:4)

Plate 100. Early Roman Plain Form 18 (**852, 853**, scale 1:4)

Plate 101. Early Roman Plain Form 18 and Other Color-Slipped dishes (scale 1:3)

Plate 102. Early Roman Color-Slipped and Plain dishes and bowls (scale 1:3)

Plate 103. Early Roman Color-Slipped and Plain plates and bowls

Plate 104. Early Roman Color-Slipped and Plain bowls and jars

Plate 105. Early Roman Color-Slipped and Plain bowls and pitchers

Plate 106. Early Roman Color-Slipped and Plain pitchers and jars (scale 1:3)

Plate 107. Early Roman Plain large jars and lids (scale 1:3)

Plate 108. Middle Roman Color-Slipped Forms 1–3 (scale 1:3)

Plate 109. Middle Roman Color-Slipped Forms 4–6 (scale 1:3)

Plate 110. Middle Roman Color-Slipped Forms 6 and 7 (scale 1:3)

Plate 111. Middle Roman Color-Slipped Forms 8 and 9 (scale 1:3)

Plate 112. Middle Roman Color-Slipped Forms 10–13

Plate 113. Middle Roman Color-Slipped Forms 13–17 (scale 1:3)

Plate 114. Middle Roman Color-Slipped Forms 17–19 (scale 1:3)

Plate 115. Middle Roman Color-Slipped Forms 19–22 (scale 1:3)

Plate 116. Middle Roman Color-Slipped Forms 22–25 (scale 1:3)

Plate 117. Middle Roman Color-Slipped and Plain Forms 25–27, 29 (scale 1:3)

Plate 118. Middle Roman Color-Slipped and Plain Forms 28, 30, and 31 (scale 1:3)

Plate 119. Middle Roman Color-Slipped and Plain Forms 31 and 33 (scale 1:3)

Plate 120. Middle Roman Color-Slipped and Plain Form 32 (scale 1:3)

Plate 121. Middle Roman Plain Form 34. Middle Roman Color-Slipped plates and dishes (scale 1:3)

Plate 122. Middle Roman Color-Slipped dishes and bowls (scale 1:3)

Plate 123. Middle Roman Color-Slipped bowls and jars (scale 1:3)

Plate 124. Middle Roman Color-Slipped jars and jugs (scale 1:3)

Plate 125. Middle Roman Color-Slipped and Plain jars, bowls, and jugs (scale 1:3)

Plate 126. Middle Roman Color-Slipped and Plain jugs and bases. Late Roman Color-Slipped dishes (scale 1:3)

Plate 127. Late Roman Color-Slipped and Plain jars. Hellenistic Cooking Ware Forms 1–4 (scale 1:3)

Plate 128. Hellenistic Cooking Ware Forms 5–10 (scale 1:3)

Plate 129. Hellenistic Cooking Ware Forms 10–13 (scale 1:3)

Plate 130. Hellenistic Cooking Ware pans, jars, and stewpots (scale 1:3)

Plate 131. Hellenistic Cooking Ware stewpots and lids (scale 1:3)

Plate 132. Early Roman Cooking Ware Forms 1–6 (scale 1:3)

Plate 133. Early Roman Cooking Ware Form 7 and Early Roman Cooking Ware casseroles and jars (scale 1:3)

Plate 134. Early Roman Cooking Ware jars and stewpots (scale 1:3)

Plate 135. Middle Roman Cooking Ware Form 1 (scale 1:3)

Plate 136. Middle Roman Cooking Ware Forms 2–4 (scale 1:3)

Plate 137. Middle Roman Cooking Ware dishes and jars (scale 1:3)

Plate 138. Middle Roman Cooking Ware stewpots (scale 1:3)

Plate 139. Middle Roman Cooking Ware stewpots, jars, and jugs (scale 1:3)

Plate 140. Middle Roman Cooking Ware stewpot, bases, and lids. Late Roman Cooking Ware Form 1 (scale 1:3)

Plate 141. Late Roman Cooking Ware Forms 2, 3, and 5 (scale 1:3)

Plate 142. Late Roman Cooking Ware Forms 4–7 (scale 1:3)

Plate 143. Late Roman Cooking Ware Form 8 (scale 1:3)

Plate 144. Late Roman Cooking Ware Forms 9–13. Late Roman Cooking Ware dishes (scale 1:3)

Plate 145. Late Roman Cooking Ware bowls and casseroles (scale 1:3)

Plate 146. Late Roman Cooking Ware jars and stewpots (scale 1:3)

Plate 147. Late Roman Cooking Ware jars and stewpots (scale 1:3)

Plate 148. Late Roman Cooking Ware jars, stewpots, and jugs (scale 1:3)

Plate 149. Late Roman Cooking Ware stewpot, bases, and lids (scale 1:3; **1288**, scale 1:4)

Plate 150. Pottery stamps and kiln furniture

Plate 151. Lion's head mould and bowl moulds

Plate 152. Bowl moulds. Early Hellenistic Wheelmade Gray Ware

Plate 153. Black-Gloss Wares (**45**, scale 1:1)

Plate 154. Black-Gloss Wares. Black-Gloss Wares with Gray Fabric (**93**, scale 2:1)

Plate 155. Black-Gloss Wares with Gray Fabric. Hellenistic Moulded Relief Bowls (**102, 103**, scale 1:1)

Plate 156. Hellenistic Moulded Relief Bowls (**112**, scale 3:2; **113**, scale 1:1)

Plate 157. Hellenistic Moulded Relief Bowls (**120**, scale 3:2; **121**, scale 1:1)

Plate 158. Hellenistic Moulded Relief Bowls

Plate 159. Hellenistic Moulded Relief Bowls

Plate 160. Hellenistic Moulded Relief Bowls

Plate 161. Hellenistic Moulded Relief Bowls

Plate 162. Hellenistic Moulded Relief Bowls

Plate 163. Thin-Walled Wares

Plate 164. Thin-Walled Wares. Italian Sigillata

Plate 165. Italian Sigillata. Other Western Sigillata

Plate 166. Italian Sigillata Stamps

Plate 167. Other Western Sigillata

Plate 168. African Red Slip Ware

Plate 169. African Red Slip Ware. Phocaean Red Slip Ware. Macedonian Gray Ware

Plate 170. Macedonian Gray Ware

Plate 171. Macedonian Gray Ware. Miscellaneous Stamps

Plate 172. Miscellaneous Stamps

Plate 173. Miscellaneous Stamps. Marbeled Slip. Lead-Glazed Ware. Miscellaneous Imports (**531**, scale 2:1)

Plate 174. Miscellaneous Imports. Miscellaneous Relief Wares

Plate 175. Miscellaneous Relief Wares

Plate 176. Miscellaneous Relief Wares

Plate 177. Miscellaneous Relief Wares. Unguentaria. Mortarium

Plate 178. Unguentaria. Mica-Dusted Ware

Plate 179. Unguentaria. Mica-Dusted Ware

Plate 180. Tan Micaceous Ware. Amphora Stamp

Plate 181. Amphora Stamps

Plate 182. Amphora Stamps

Plate 183. Amphorae

Plate 184. Amphorae

Plate 185. Amphorae

Plate 186. Hellenistic Color-Slipped and Plain Wares

Plate 187. Early Roman and Middle Roman Color-Slipped and Plain Wares

Plate 188. Middle Roman Color-Slipped Wares

Plate 189a. Potter's Shop, Walls 6 and 7, looking south

Plate 189b. Potter's Shop, Wall 7, looking north

Plate 190a. Potter's Shop, Wall 7, close-up of bricks, looking north

Plate 190b. Potter's Shop. Walls 6 and 7 with gravel in background, looking south

Plate 191. Potter's Shop. Deposits as seen in reconstruction of West profile of Central Basilica Narthex

FOREWORD

•

Stobi has long held for scholars a special position among the urban centers of the Roman Empire because of some unusual, even unique, features of its historical evolution. It is the only *oppidum civium Romanorum* recorded among the Greek-speaking provinces,[1] a special rank it may have achieved during the Civil Wars of the Late Republic.[2] It later was elevated to the rank of *municipium*,[3] an honored status shared in the Greek East, so far as we know, only with Coela in the Thracian Chersonesus.[4] What is more, among the *municipia* located outside Italy, only Stobi is known to have possessed the *ius Italicum*, a privileged status that carried with it exemption from certain taxes, including the *tributum soli*, or "land tax."[5]

There are few other direct references to Stobi in ancient literature that touch on events during the time of the late Republic and early Empire, although several authors mention its location in various ways. Livy, who repeatedly refers to Stobi as a town of Paeonia, informs us that Philip V carried out military operations in its region in 197 B.C.[6] Livy also, in a passage referring to the founding of the city of Perseis in 183 B.C., mentions Stobi as a *vetus urbs*, an "old city."[7] In 167 B.C., when Aemilius Paullus partitioned Macedonia into four *merides*, he directed that towns of the third *meris* send salt to Stobi, which was to be the only emporium in the region from which the Dardanians might purchase the commodity.[8]

Literature provides no testimony about life at Stobi during the early principate. Christian bishops of Stobi, however, are named in various documents and letters, beginning with Budius, who attended the Council of Nicaea in 325 A.C., and continuing until the late 7th century.[9] Theodosius I issued two edicts from Stobi in 388 A.C.[10] Also in the late 4th century, Stobi became a part of the short-lived province Macedonia Salutaris,[11] probably serving as its capital, as it did later in the 5th and 6th centuries

[1] Pliny *Nat. Hist.* iv.34.

[2] See Fanoula Papazoglou, "*Oppidum Stobi civium Romanorum* et *municipium Stobensium*," *Chiron* 16 (1986) 213–237.

[3] A fact that we know not from literature, but from coins minted at Stobi itself (from the time of Vespasian to Elagabalus) and from inscriptions. On the coins see S. Dušanić, "A Foundation-Type on the Coinage of the Municipium Stobi," *Revue Belge de Numismatique* 113 (1967) 11–29. Stobi is designated a *municipium* in three inscriptions: *CIL* III, 629; *BullEpig* 54 (1941), no. 86; Stobi inv. no. I-77-5 in Wiseman (1978) 427–428. The text of the latter two inscriptions is presented with a discussion of the readings and commentaries in Wiseman, *Stobi 3*, in entry no. 579.

[4] A.H.M. Jones, *The Cities of the Eastern Roman Provinces*, 2nd edn. (Clarendon Press: Oxford 1971) 16–18 and notes 24–25.

[5] *Digest* 1.15.8.8. On the exemptions, see e.g., A. N. Sherwin-White, *The Roman Citizenship*, 2nd ed. (Clarendon Press: Oxford 1973) 276.

[6] Livy xxxiii.19.3. He also set out from Stobi in 181 B.C for his expedition against the Thracian Maedi: Livy x1.21.1.

[7] Livy xxxix.53.15–16.

[8] Livy xlv.29.13.

[9] See the recent discussion of the bishops of Stobi and their sources in Fanoula Papazoglou, *Les Villes de Macédoine a l'Époque romaine. BCH Supp. XVI* (École française d'Athènes, diffusion de Boccard: Paris 1988) 321–323.

[10] *Codex Theodosianus* 16. 4.2, 16. 5.15.

[11] *Notitia Dignitatum, Or.* I, p.5, 14. On the creation, extent, and demise of Macedonia Salutaris, see especially the article (in Greek) by Angeliki Konstantakopoulou, Ἡ Ἐπαρχία Μακεδονία Salutaris. Συμβολὴ στὴ Μελετὴ τῆς Διοικητικῆς Ὀργανύσης τοῦ Ἰλληρικοῦ in Δωδὼνη 1 (Ἰωάννινα 1981) 85–100.

for the province Macedonia Secunda.[12] We hear also of a military disaster in 482, when the Ostrogoths captured the city and massacred its garrison.[13] From later times we learn only of the destruction of a military garrison at Stobi in 1014 by the Byzantine Emperor Basil II.[14]

The historical record thus is tantalizing but brief in the extreme. We must turn to archaeology and epigraphy if we are to understand anything of the city's cultural and socioeconomic history. That research may be said to have begun in the third quarter of the 19th century with the identification of the ancient city at the confluence of the Vardar and Crna rivers (the ancient Axius and Erigon) in what is now Yugoslavian Macedonia, ca. 150 km. north of Thessaloniki (ancient Thessalonica), Greece.[15] The valley of the Vardar now, as in antiquity, lies on the most frequently travelled route between the middle Danubian regions and the Aegean sea; the railway line of the Orient Express and the adjacent highway between Belgrade and Athens were actually cut through the northern edge of the ancient site. An important west-to-east route also passed through Stobi in Roman times, connecting Heraclea Lyncestis on the Egnatian Way (on the outskirts of Bitola, Yugoslavia) with Serdica (modern Sofia, Bulgaria). The location of Stobi at this strategic crossroads near an early frontier of the Roman Empire endowed the city with a commercial and military significance that is now confirmed in the archaeological and epigraphical record of late Republican and early Imperial times.

After its identification, Stobi was the subject of occasional interest to scholars who happened to pass that way over the next 50 to 60 years, and a number of inscriptions and other antiquities were noted by them or recovered by construction workers building the highway and the railway. During World War I the site was disturbed by military entrenchments, and parts of some buildings were even intentionally dug up by Bulgarian and German soldiers working under the direction of their officers. Chief among these was the principal Christian basilica of the city, which has come to be called the Episcopal Basilica. It was not until 1924, however, that archaeological excavations were undertaken. Sponsored by the National Museum of Belgrade, they continued until World War II engulfed Yugoslavia in 1941. The excavations were directed first by Balduin Saria (1924–1928) and V. R. Petković (1927–1934) and, beginning in 1935, by Jozo Petrović and Djordje Mano-Zissi. By 1941 part of the Roman theater and a broad expanse of buildings, mostly of the Late Antique city (4th–6th centuries), had been uncovered, including parts of five Christian basilicas, two baths, and several large residences. Most of the works of art, as well as many other artifacts and some of the inscriptions recovered in the excavations, eventually were placed in the National Museum of Belgrade and the Archaeological Museum of Skopje. Preliminary reports on the results of these investigations, mostly in Serbian, were published primarily in

[12] Hierocles, *Synecdemus* 7-8. For a recent discussion of Macedonia Secunda, see Papazoglou, *Les Villes*, 96–98.

[13] Malchus, Frag. 18 (C. Müller, *Fragmenta Historicorum Graecorum* [1841–1870] IV, 125); Jordanes, *Getica*, c.286. On the date, see Papazoglou, *Les Villes* 140, 322.

[14] Cedrenus, *Corpus Scriptorum Historiae Byzantinae* 2, 709A.

[15] J. G. von Hahn, "Reise von Beograd nach Salonik," *Österreichische Akademie der Wissenschaften, Wien, Philosophisch-historische Klasse. Denkschriften* 11, pt. 2 (1861) 175, 231–236; Léon Heuzey, "Découverte des Ruines de Stobi," *Revue archéologique* n.s. 26, pt. II (1873) 25–42.

Yugoslavian journals; no final publications were prepared. As a result of the relative inaccessibility of the published reports and, more importantly, the unfamiliarity of most Western scholars with the languages of Yugoslavia, the important discoveries of the Yugoslavian archaeologists were little known in the West until 1946 when Ernst Kitzinger published his review, "A Survey of the Early Christian Town of Stobi."[16] Between 1945 and 1969, work at Stobi was confined primarily to conservation activities, supplemented by narrowly focused excavations, all under the direction of Yugoslavian conservators and archaeologists.[17]

In 1970 a new project was inaugurated by a joint American-Yugoslav team of scholars who conducted archaeological excavations and research at Stobi each summer through 1981. The first Yugoslavian codirector of the joint project was Djordje Mano-Zissi, chief curator of Ancient Art at the National Museum of Belgrade, professor of Art History and Museology at the University of Belgrade, and one of the early excavators at Stobi. The author of this foreword, at that time professor of Classics at the University of Texas at Austin, later (beginning in 1973) professor of Archaeology, Art History, and Classics at Boston University, was the American codirector of the project and field director for the duration of the project. In 1975, for reasons of health, Mano-Zissi withdrew from active participation in the project, and his place as codirector was taken by Blaga Aleksova, former director of the Archaeological Museum of Skopje, and then professor in the Department of Art History and Archaeology at the University of Cyril and Methodius in Skopje. I am honored to have served as codirector with Professors Aleksova and Mano-Zissi, and I treasure the warm friendship we established while working together at Stobi.

The project was sponsored by the National Museum of Titov Veles, the University of Texas at Austin (1970–1973), and Boston University (1974–1981). The administrative directors of the project were the successive directors of the National Museum of Titov Veles: Todor Gruev (1970–1972), Tiho Najdovski (1973–1977), and Nikola Tripčev (1978–1981). The principal funding for the project was provided by the Foreign Currency Program of the Smithsonian Institution (the Yugoslav-United States Joint Fund for Scientific and Technological Cooperation), the National Endowment for the Humanities, the Ford Foundation, and the Socialist Republic of Macedonia. Additional funding came from a number of institutions, from the Kress Foundation, and from private individuals. The Luther I. Replogle Foundation has provided continuing support to the project, including annual, post-excavation grants for drawings, photographs, and other expenses involved in the preparation of manuscripts. The project also enjoyed the active cooperation and occasional support of the National Museum of Štip, the Archaeological Museum of Skopje, the Conservation Institute of Macedonia, the National Museum of Prilep, and the National Museum of Bitola. The Macedonian Stobi Committee, composed of representatives from the Republic of Macedonia and

[16] *DOP* 3 (1946) 83–161.

[17] A detailed account of the earlier investigations at Stobi, summarized briefly in this paragraph, will be included in Volume 7 (forthcoming) of the same series as the present volume.

the relevant academic and conservation groups, provided helpful guidance under its successive chairmen, Stojan Dimov and Dragan Nikolovski. The project benefited from the friendly support and encouragement of more individuals in Yugoslavia than there is space here to name. Four persons who were especially helpful to the project, however, deserve special mention: Stojan Dimov, who was always available to us for advice and support, even after other official duties carried him to new posts; Stevo Čulumov, the mayor of Titov Veles, for his active and congenial cooperation throughout the years of the Project; Mikhail Apostolski, the late director of the Macedonian Academy of Sciences and Arts; and Tiho Najdovski, a poet and an author of stories for children, whose warm humanity all who worked at Stobi have admired. To all these I express sincere thanks and appreciation on behalf of all the staff of the joint project.

The professional staff was made up primarily of Yugoslavians and Americans in approximately equal numbers. The intense personal pressures that invariably attend large-scale, long-term field projects never disrupted the harmonious working relationship that existed between the American and Yugoslavian staff members; innumerable, continuing friendships attest to that social harmony. The staff varied in size over the years, and its members came from numerous disciplines, as the research activities required. There were at times as many as 50 professional scholars, technicians, and artists at work with expertise in archaeology, architecture, art, art history, conservation, draughting, geochemistry, geology, numismatics, palaeozoology, physical anthropology, statistical analysis, topographical survey, and other disciplines and skills.

The project was as interdisciplinary in concept and conduct as we were capable of making it at the time. Not all our research, however, always involved the extent of staff interaction and integrated investigation that some scholars have considered essential, or ideal, in *inter*disciplinary research;[18] perhaps *multi*disciplinary is a more appropriate designation, at least insofar as practice rather than intent is concerned. The chief goals of the project, which have been stated in previous reports,[19] were

1) to establish the chronology and spatial limits of the successive phases of habitation at Stobi;
2) to provide through stratigraphic studies insight into the local evolution of arts and crafts, changes in living conditions, social structure, mercantile activities, and other human endeavors that may be deduced from the material remains and their context;
3) to complete the study of the architectural history of several specific areas of the city (public and private) and to provide a beginning for the study of changes in the urban design;

[18] See, for example, the rather technical description of interdisciplinary in W. A. McDonald and G. Rapp, Jr., *The Minnesota Messenia Expedition: Reconstructing a Bronze Age Regional Environment* (Minneapolis 1972) 7, 16.

[19] W-MZ (1974) 120. The slightly abbreviated form presented here follows James Wiseman, "Multidisciplinary Research in Classical Archaeology: An Example from the Balkans," in N. Wilkie and W. Coulson, eds., *Contributions to Aegean Archaeology: Studies in Honor of William A. McDonald* (Dubuque 1985) 259–261.

4) through the excavation of a large number of graves (between 300 and 400) and the analysis of their contents to trace the changes of burial customs, to learn something of the health of those who were buried at Stobi, and to provide some assistance in demographic studies;
5) to gain an understanding of ancient technology as represented at Stobi through field and laboratory analyses . . .
6) through a study of the macro- and microfauna to acquire some insight into the local diet and possible changes of climate;
7) through other special analyses . . . to provide a basis for further ecological studies.

In practical terms the excavation strategies were intended to balance three elements of investigation: (1) a more thorough examination of certain structures (e.g., the theater and the Episcopal Basilica) that were in large measure exposed by earlier work; (2) excavation of (or sometimes narrowly targeted probes into) the deposits and structures that underlay those structures; and (3) the excavation of several areas that had not been previously investigated.

A number of other, very specific aims were developed within the several areas of research, but it is not appropriate in this foreword to recount such detail. In any case, some have been dealt with in earlier publications, and others will be presented and examined in the volumes of this series. Nor shall I attempt here to analyze the extent to which the aims of the project were achieved but will reserve that analysis for a subsequent volume that will provide an overview of the results of the project, as well as of the theories, methodologies, and kinds of documentation involved in the investigations.[20] But the reader will perhaps find useful here the following summary comments. They illustrate some of the ways in which interdisciplinary (or multidisciplinary) archaeological research, including epigraphy, has contributed to our understanding of social, economic, and environmental changes at Stobi.[21]

The date of the earliest settlement at Stobi remains uncertain, but occasional finds of chipped stone and early handmade pottery, though never in primary context, suggest that human use of the site may have begun in prehistoric times. What is more, the massive scale of Roman and Late Antique construction renders obscure much of the Hellenistic settlement, which we are able only to glimpse by deep, narrow soundings. It is now possible, however, to document archaeologically an increasing Italic influence in the late 2nd and 1st centuries B.C.,and an urban expansion in the time of Augustus. We are able to explore some of the most important civic and social institutions of Stobi in the 2nd and 3rd centuries A.C. and even to consider the social stratification of hundreds of citizens whom we now know by name. Many facets of the archaeological record, ranging from a variety of burial customs to direct epigraphical testimony, reflect a mixed ethnic population in the early principate that included Ro-

[20] Planned for volume 7 of this series. The same volume will include both a history of Stobi and a history of investigations at the site.

[21] The most recently published overviews of the results of the Joint Project are James Wiseman, "Archaeology and History"; *idem*, s.v. "Stobi" in *Supplement* to the *Enciclopedia dell'Arte Antica Classica e Orientale* (in press, 1990).

mans, Greeks and Macedonians, native Illyric peoples, and immigrants from the East, including Jews. We may explore the planning, construction, and institutional history of a marble theater, large enough to seat some 7,600 persons, that was built in the mid-2nd century. Through the archaeological record we can trace the vicissitudes of life in the city as it suffered economic misfortunes, social disruption, and natural disasters in the 3rd century. For the 4th and 5th centuries the excavations reveal evidence of a number of major changes. The urban design is radically altered, a response in part to increasingly severe environmental constraints. The area of the city is reduced by a new fortification wall, even while some of the more luxurious private residences are built. Christian basilicas appear in the 4th century, and in the 5th one is even built atop a demolished synagogue, thereby implying ominous consequences for the Jewish inhabitants of the city. In the middle of the 5th century a new cathedral—the Episcopal Basilica mentioned earlier—is raised on a high artificial terrace, towering above the ruins of the theater, which had been closed and abandoned towards the end of the 4th century. Building material from the theater was reused not only in the cathedral but in other new constructions throughout the city. Colorful frescoes and mosaics adorn many religious buildings and private residences. In the later 5th and 6th centuries there is evidence of a new cycle of economic decline, and before the end of the 6th century the city was abandoned, and many of its buildings devastated by an earthquake. Wind-blown dust began to cover the ruins on the upper slope of the ridge on which the city had been built, and the Crna river in a series of floods left meters of sand and silt over the lower town. Stobi ceased to exist as a city, and there is no evidence of any later urban community at the confluence of the Vardar and Crna rivers.

This volume is the first in a series devoted to the presentation of the results of research conducted by a number of scholars over a period of some 20 years.[22] In closing this foreword, I want to express my gratitude to them all for their hard work, their devotion to scholarship, and their friendship. I feel privileged to have worked so long with so many people of such exceptional talent.

James Wiseman
General Editor

[22] The principal preliminary reports in English are W-MZ (1971), (1972), (1973), (1976) and Wiseman (1978). Three volumes containing important reports on some of the research activities at Stobi have also been published: *Studies in the Antiquities of Stobi I* (1973), *II* (1975), and *III* (1981). See the List of Abbreviations for the full references of these publications.

PREFACE

•

This study of the Stobi ceramics has been carried out over a number of years, beginning with my participation in the Stobi Excavation Project in 1971 and continuing through many years of responsibility for the processing of ceramics at the site.

For the privilege of studying the material at Stobi and permission to make use of excavation documentation and records, I am indebted to James Wiseman, codirector of the Stobi Project, and to his colleagues, Djordje Mano-Zissi, Yugoslav codirector until 1977, and Blaga Aleksova, the succeeding codirector.

Throughout my work at Stobi I was a recipient of the support and hospitality of the National Museum of Titov Veles and its many staff members. Among them, Mr. Tiho Najdovski, former director, and Mr. Djordje Petački, archaeologist, were especially helpful in my work at Stobi during 1975–1976 season and during later visits to the site after the excavations were completed.

The processing of large amounts of pottery during excavation seasons at Stobi was made possible by a number of competent staff members. I would like to thank my associate, Ankica Milošević, former librarian of the University of Belgrade, who provided not only friendship but many helpful suggestions, and Lynn Stowell who worked with both the inventory and the supervision of the system especially in 1977 when I was not at Stobi. Biljana Djordjević, Dimče Naumovski, and Blaže Djordjievski were invaluable as student assistants, learning the system quickly and working with good humor. Without the young women of Palikura and Gradsko, however, working diligently to wash the pottery, the rest of us would have had nothing to do. Among these, Bosiljka deserves special thanks for her many summers devoted to keeping tags and containers of pottery together and training the others.

As a member of the Stobi staff I have benefited from many discussions with other members of the project engaged in studying the results of excavations at the site, including, especially, Mott Davis, Elizabeth Gebhard, Fritz Hemans, Carolyn Snively, Al Wesolowsky, and of course, James Wiseman. The Stobi Inventory System supervised with great care by Lucy Wiseman was invaluable for my study of the ceramics and other related materials.

Other colleagues in this country and abroad who have generously exchanged information and provided helpful suggestions are Aleksandrina Cermanović-Kuzmanović, Howard Comfort, Barbara Johnson, Carolyn Koehler, Elica Maneva, Maria Teresa Marabini Moevs, Henry Robinson, Susan Rotroff, Kathleen Slane, and Homer Thompson.

I owe a special debt of gratitude to John Hayes for his willingness to share his encyclopedic knowledge and experience of ancient pottery with me. I have acknowledged other more specific contributions within the text.

For financial support I am indebted to the Stobi Project for funding throughout the years of the excavation and research at the site, including a stipend for computer analysis and research at Boston University during 1980. For the years 1975–1976, grants from the International Research and Exchanges Board and the Fulbright-Hayes Doctoral Dissertation Research Abroad Program of the Department of Health, Education, and Welfare supported research at Stobi and at the University of Belgrade. I am grateful to Wilson College for providing a year of sabbatical leave for 1985–1986, which enabled me to complete a large part of the work of organizing the material for this volume. To these institutions I offer my sincere thanks.

A number of museums and individuals in Yugoslavia and Greece made their collections of published and unpublished material available to me. I would like to thank Milutin Garašanin of the University of Belgrade; Saržo Saržoski and Viktorija Sokolovska of the Archaeological Museum in Skopje; Dušanka Koračević of the Museum of the City of Skopje; Blagoja Kitanoski and Kostadin Kepeski of the National Museum in Prilep; Tome Janakievski of the National Museum in Bitola; Vlada Malenko of the Archaeological Museum and Conservation Institute in Ohrid; the National Museum in Štip and its former director, Voislav Sanev; K. Rhomiopoulou of the Archaeological Museum in Thessalonica; T. Leslie Shear, Jr., director of the Agora Excavations in Athens; and Charles K. Williams, director of the Corinth Excavations. James McCredie, former director of the American School of Classical Studies in Athens, was most helpful in obtaining permission to look at pottery in several of the museums in Greek Macedonia. In brief stays in Athens I have made good use of the Blegen Library of the American School of Classical Studies in Athens, and I thank Nancy A. Winter, librarian, for her interest and assistance.

The drawings that form a major part of this volume are the work of a number of persons including Todor Maksimov, Diane Peck, and Anjela Spahr. Dragan Stojanović, in addition to completing most of the drawings, also brought the entire collection into as consistent a presentation as possible, given the long period over which they were drawn. The majority of the photographs come from the Stobi Photographic Inventory and are the work of many persons responsible for photography at the site. I would like to thank Michael Hamilton at Boston University for producing most of the fine prints in this volume. He did not always have the best negatives to work with, and the uneven quality of some prints is a result of poor negatives, not the photographer.

Various parts of the manuscript for this volume were improved by the suggestions of Raymond Cormier, John Hayes, Carolyn Snively, and Dragan Stojanović. I am especially grateful for the care and patience of the general editor, James Wiseman, and for the congenial hospitality of the Wisemans during the final preparation of the volume.

Preparation of the concordance is the work of Erin-Joi Collins, a student assistant at Wilson College. Others who have assisted in various ways in the preparation of this volume and to whom I owe thanks are Margaret Vanderau, Candice Boettcher, and

Janice Fetters. Mary Clawson of the Stewart Library of Wilson College was always helpful in obtaining necessary materials through Interlibrary Loan. The graphs were generated by Delta Graph on a MacIntosh computer by a most patient Todd Orner at Sunrise Computers.

I am grateful to Elizabeth Powers, the editor at Princeton University Press, for her assistance in the production of this volume, to Laury Egan for her careful work in layout and design, and to Nancy Moore who saved this work from many inaccuracies. Any remaining deficiencies must be acknowledged as the responsibility of the author.

Without the patience and support of my husband Dragan, who has been living with this volume and helping me carry it for so many years, and who has contributed much more to it than his fine drawings, this work would never have been completed. For her help with various tasks, I must also thank my daughter Anna, who was almost born at Stobi while her mother was working on the ceramics and who has been waiting much too long for me to finish this project.

LIST OF ABBREVIATIONS

•

Explanatory note: References cited in full in the footnotes of the text are not included here.

Agora *The Athenian Agora. Results of Excavations Conducted by the American School of Classical Studies at Athens.*

AJA *American Journal of Archaeology.*

Ampurias 1 M. Almagro, *Las Nekrópolis de Ampurias*, Vol. 1, *Monografías Ampuritanas* 3 (Barcelona 1953).

Ampurias 2 M. Almagro, *Las Nekrópolis de Ampurias*, Vol. 2, *Monografías Ampuritanas* 3 (Barcelona 1955).

Anderson and Anderson (1981) A. C. Anderson and A. S. Anderson, eds., *Roman Pottery Research in Britain and North-West Europe. Papers presented to Graham Webster. BAR International Series* 123 (Oxford 1981).

Anderson-Stojanović (1981) V. R. Anderson-Stojanović, "Cultural Implications of the Pottery at Stobi," *Studies III* 47–59.

Anderson-Stojanović (1982) ———, "Computer-Assisted Analysis of Pottery at Stobi, Yugoslavia," *JFA* 9 (1982) 335–348.

Anderson-Stojanović (1984) ———, "Macedonian Terra Sigillata Grise from Stobi: A New Typology for the Ware." *RCRFActa* 23/24 (1984) 99–109.

Anderson-Stojanović, "Italy and Macedonia" ———, "Italy and Macedonia in the 2nd and 1st Centuries B.C.: The Ceramic Evidence," *RCRFActa* 25/26 (1987) 383–401.

Anderson-Stojanović (1987) ———, "The Chronology and Function of Ceramic Unguentaria" *AJA* 91 (1987) 105–122.

ANRW H. Temporini and W. Haase, eds., *Aufsteig und Niedergang der römischen Welt. Geschichte und Kultur Roms im Spiegel der neueren Forschung* (Berlin and New York).

Antioch F. O. Waage, "Hellenistic and Roman Tableware of North Syria," *Antioch on the Orontes, IV, Part 1. Ceramics and Islamic Coins* (Princeton 1948) 1–60.

Apollonia I. Venedikov et al., *Les fouilles dans la Nekropole d'Apollonia en 1947–1949* (Sofia 1962).

AthMitt *Mitteilungen des Deutschen Archäologischen Instituts, Athenische Abteilung.*

BABesch *Bulletin Antieke Beschaving. Annual Papers on Classical Archaeology.*

BAR *British Archaeological Reports.*

BCH *Bulletin de correspondance hellénique.*

Bitrakova-Grozdanova (1987) V. Bitrakova-Grozdanova, *Monuments de l'époque hellénistique dans la république socialiste de Macédoine. Filosofski Fakultet, Kniga 3* (Skopje 1987) (In Macedonian with French summary).

Blake, "Ceramica paleo-italiana" H. Blake, "Ceramica paleo-italiana. Studio in onore di G. Liverani," *FAENZA* 67 (1981) 20–54.

Bojović, *Singidunum* D. Bojović, *Rimska Keramika Singidunuma. Muzej Grada Beograda Katalog 8* (Beograd 1977).

Broneer, *Corinth 4* O. Broneer, *Corinth: Results of Excavations Conducted by the American School of Classical Studies at Athens. Volume 4, Part 2, Terracotta Lamps* (Harvard University Press: Cambridge, MA 1930).

Brukner, *Rimska Keramika* O. Brukner, *Rimska Keramika u Jugoslovenskom Delu Provincije Donje Panonije. Dissertationes et Monographiae 24* (Arheološko Društvo Jugoslavije: Beograd 1981).

Bruneau, "Tombes d'Argos" P. Bruneau, "Tombes d'Argos," *BCH* 69 (1970) 437–531.

BSA *The Annual of the British School at Athens.*

Burnham and Johnson (1979) B. C. Burnham and H. B. Johnson, eds., *Invasion and Response. The Case of Roman Britain. BAR British Series 73* (Oxford 1979).

Charleston R. J. Charleston, *Roman Pottery* (Faber and Faber: London 1955).

Charlesworth, *Trade Routes* M. P. Charlesworth, *Trade Routes and Commerce of the Roman Empire* (The University Press: Cambridge, England, 1926).

CIL *Corpus Inscriptionum Latinarum.*

Coja M. Coja, "La céramique grise d'Histria à l'époque grecque," *Dacia* 12 (1968) 305–329.

Comfort, *EAA* H. Comfort, "Terra Sigillata," *Enciclopedia dell'arte antica, classica e orientale*, Supplemento (G. Treccani: Rome 1973) 803–835.

Conze, *Pergamon* A. Conze, *Altertümer von Pergamon, 1, 2. Stadt und Landschaft* (G. Reimer: Berlin 1912).

Courby, *Vases* F. Courby, *Les Vases grecs à reliefs* (de Boccard: Paris 1922).

Crawford, "Stobi Hoard" M. Crawford, "The Stobi Hoard of Roman Republican Denarii," *Studies I*, 1–21.

CVA *Corpus Vasorum Antiquorum.*

DOP *Dumbarton Oaks Papers.*

Dore and Greene (1977) J. Dore and K. Greene, eds., *Roman Pottery Studies in Britain and Beyond. Papers Presented to John Gillam, July 1977. BAR Supplementary Series 30* (Oxford 1977).

Dragendorff H. Dragendorff, "Terra Sigillata," *Bonner Jahrbücher* 96–97 (1895) 18–155.

Dragendorff-Watzinger (1948) ——— and C. Watzinger, *Arretinische ReliefKeramik mit Beschreibung der Sammlung in Tübingen* (Gryphius Verlag: Reutlingen 1948).

Drougou and Touratsoglou, *Veroia* S. Drougou and I. Touratsoglou, Ἑλληνιστικοί Λαξευτοί Τάφοι βέροιας (Athens 1980).

Duklja A. Cermanović-Kuzmanović, D. Srejović, and O. Velimirović-Žižić, *Antička Duklja Nekropole* (Cetinje 1975).

Duncan, "Sutri" G. C. Duncan, "Roman Republican Pottery from the Vicinity of Sutri," *Papers of the British School at Rome* 33 (1956) 134–176.

Dyson, Cosa S. L. Dyson, "Cosa: The Utilitarian Pottery," *MAAR* 33 (1976).

EAA 2 *Enciclopedia dell'arte antica classica e orientale. Atlante delle forme ceramiche 2 (tardo ellenismo e primo impero). Ceramica fine romana nel bacino mediterraneo*, G. P. Carratelli, ed. (G. Treccani: Rome 1985).

Edwards, *Corinth* G. R. Edwards, *Corinth: Results of Excavations Conducted by the American School of Classical Studies at Athens, Volume 7, Part 3. The Hellenistic Pottery* (American School of Classical Studies at Athens: Princeton 1975).

Edwards, *Pnyx* ———, "Hellenistic Pottery," *Small Objects from the Pnyx, 2. Hesperia Supplement 10* (Princeton 1956).

Ephesos I R. Heberdey, in O. Benndorf, ed., *Forschungen in Ephesos I* (A. Holder: Vienna 1906) 167–180.

"Fanagoria" M. Kobilima, ed., "Fanagoria," *Materialii Isledovanija Po Arheologia SSSR* 57 (Moscow 1956).

Forti L. Forti, "Gli unguentari del primo periodo ellenistico," *Rendiconti dell'Accademia di Archeologia di Napoli* 37 (1962).

Goudineau C. Goudineau, *Fouilles de l'Ecole française de Rome à Bolsena (Poggio Moscini) 1962–67, 4. La céramique arétine lisse. Ecole française de Rome. Mélanges d'archéologie et d'histoire. Supplément 6* (Paris 1968).

Goudineau (1970) ———, "Note sur la céramique à engobe interne rouge-pompéien," *MEFRA* 82 (1970) 159–186.

Greene (1977) K. Greene, "Legionary Pottery, and the Significance of Holt," in Dore and Greene (1977) 113–132.

Greene (1986) ———, *The Archaeology of the Roman Economy* (University of California Press: Berkeley and Los Angeles 1986).

Hayes, "Corinth" J. W. Hayes, "Roman Pottery from the South Stoa at Corinth," *Hesperia* 42 (1973) 416–470.

Hayes, "Knossos" ———, "Four Early Roman Groups from Knossos," *BSA* (1971) 249–276.

Hayes, *LRP* ———, *Late Roman Pottery* (British School at Rome: London 1972).

Hayes, "Paphos" ———, "Early Roman Wares from the House of Dionysos, Paphos," *RCRFActa* 17–18 (1977) 96–101.

Hayes, *ROM Pottery* ———, *Roman Pottery in the Royal Ontario Museum* (Royal Ontario Museum: Toronto 1976).

Hayes, "Villa Dionysus" ———, "The Villa Dionysus Excavations, Knossos: The Pottery" *BSA* 78 (1983) 97–169.

Howland, *Agora 4* R. H. Howland. *The Athenian Agora. Volume 4: The Greek Lamps and Their Survivals* (American School of Classical Studies: Princeton 1958).

Iliffe J. H. Iliffe, "Sigillata Wares in the Near East: A List of Potters' Stamps," *Quarterly of the Department of Antiquities in Palestine* 6 (1936) 4–53.

IstMitt *Istanbuler Mitteilungen.*

JFA *Journal of Field Archaeology.*

JHS *Journal of Hellenic Studies.*

Jones, "Popilius and Lapius" F. F. Jones, "Bowls by Popilius and Lapius," *Record of the Art Museum, Princeton University* 17 (1958) Number 1, 21–54.

Kenrick, *Berenice 3* P. M. Kenrick, "The Fine Pottery," in *Excavations at Sidi Khrebish, Benghazi (Berenice) 3. (Supplement to Libya Antiqua 5)* (Tripoli 1985).

Keramopoullos (1932) A. Keramopoullos, "Ανασκαφαὶ Καὶ ἔρευναι ἐν τῇ Ἄνω Μακεδονία," Ἀρχαιολογικὴ Ἐφεμερίς (1932) 48–133.

Labraunda P. Hellström, *Labraunda: Swedish Excavations and Researches 2, 1. Pottery of Classical and Later Date, Terracotta Lamps and Glass* (Lund 1965).

Lamboglia N. Lamboglia, "Per una classificazione preliminare della ceramica campana," *Atti della Congressa Internazionale di Studi Liguri I 1950* (Bordighera 1952).

Lamb, "Lesbos" W. Lamb, "Gray Wares from Lesbos," *JHS* 52 (1932) 1–12.

Laumonier, *Délos 31* *Exploration archéologique de Délos 31.* A. Laumonier, *La céramique hellénistique à reliefs,* 1, *Ateliers "ioniens."* Ecole française d'Athenes (de Boccard: Paris 1977).

MAAR *Memoirs of the American Academy in Rome.*

"Magdalensberg" S. Scheffenegger and E. Schindler-Kaudelka, "Ein Fruher Fundort am Ostrand des Handlerforums des Magdalensberges, OR/39," *RCRFActa* 17–18 (1977) 51–80.

Maneva (1979) E. Maneva, *Several Kinds of Hellenistic and Roman Ceramics from Heraclea* (Bitola 1979) (In Macedonian with English summary).

Mayet F. Mayet, *Les céramiques à parois fin dans la péninsule ibérique* (Paris 1975).

MEFRA *Melanges de l'Ecole française de Rome. Antiquité.*

Metzger (1984) I. Metzger, "Ein frühhellenistisches Keramikdepot in Eretria (Diateichisma E/II)," *Deltion* 33A (1978, publ. 1984) 198–239.

Metzger (1985) ———, *Das Thesmophorion von Eretria. Eretria Ausgrabungen und Forschungen 7* (Bern 1985).

Mikulčič, *Pelagonia* I. Mikulčič, *Pelagonia u Svetlosti Arheoloških nalaza. Dissertationes 3* (Arheološko Društvo Jugoslavije: Skopje 1966).

Mikulčič, *Štip* ———, "Ilirsko-arhajski grobovi iz okoline Štipa," *Starinar* 13–14 (1962–63) 197–209.

Mikulčič, *Studies III* ———, "Some New Factors in the History of Stobi," *Studies III,* 215–227.

Mikulčič and Jovanović, *Vranje* ——— and M. Jovanović, "Hellenistički Oppidum iz Krševice kod Vranja," *Vranjski Glasnik* 4 (1968) 355–375.

Mocsy, *Pannonia* A. Mocsy, *Pannonia and Upper Moesia: A History of the Middle Danube Provinces of the Roman Empire* (Routledge and K. Paul: Boston and London 1974).

Moevs, "Cosa" M.T.M. Moevs, "Cosa: The Thin-Walled Pottery," *MAAR* 32 (1973).

Morel, *Les Formes* J.-P. Morel, *Céramique campanienne. Les Formes* (Ecole française de Rome: 1981).

Morel, *Notes* ———, "Notes sur la céramique étrusco-campanienne. Vases à vernis noir de Sardaigne et d'Arezzo," *Ecole française de Rome. Mélanges d'archéologie et d'histoire* 75 (1963) 7–58.

Morel, *Palatin* ———, *Céramique à vernis noir du Forum Romain et du Palatin. Ecole française de Rome. Mélanges d'archéologie et d'histoire, Supplement 3* (Paris 1965).

Morel, "Petites estampilles" ———, "L'Atelier de petites estampilles," *Ecole française de Rome. Mélanges d'archéologie et d'histoire* 81 (1969) 59–117.

NSc *Notizie degli Scavi di Antichita.*

Oxé-Comfort A. Oxé, *Corpus Vasorum Arretinorum,* H. Comfort, ed. (Habelt: Bonn 1968).

Papazoglu, *Cities* F. Papazoglu, *Makedonski Gradovi u Rimsko Doba [Macedonian cities in the Roman period]. Živa Antika Supplement 1* (Skopje 1957).

Papazoglu, "Province" ———, "Quelques aspects de l'histoire de la province de Macédoine," *ANRW* II, 7.1 (Berlin 1979) 302–369.

Papazoglu, *Tribes* ———, *Srednjobalkanska plemena u predrimsko doba [The central Balkan tribes in the pre-Macedonian period]. Centar za Balkanološka Ispitivanja, Knjiga 1* (Akademija Nauka i Umjetnosti Bosne i Hercegovine: Sarajevo 1969).

Pasquinucci (1972) M. M. Pasquinucci, "La ceramica a vernice nera del Museo Guardnacci di Volterra," *MEFRA* 84 (1972) 269–498.

Peacock, *PRW* D.P.S. Peacock, *Pottery in the Roman World* (Longman Group: New York 1982).

Peacock (1977) ——— ed., *Pottery and Early Commerce* (Academic Press: New York 1977).

Peacock and Williams, *Amphorae* ——— and D. F. Williams, *Amphorae and the Roman Economy. An Introductory Guide* (Longman Group: New York 1986).

Pergamon *Deutsches Archäologisches Institut. Pergamenische Forschungen.*

Pergamon 2 J. Schafer, *Hellenistische Keramik aus Pergamon. Pergamon 2* (de Gruyter: Berlin 1968).

Pergamon 6 C. Meyer-Schlictmann, *Die Pergamenische Sigillata aus der Stadgrabung von Pergamon mitte 2. JH v. Chr.–mitte 2. JH n. Chr. Pergamon 6* (de Gruyter: Berlin and New York 1988).

Perlzweig, *Agora 7* J. Perlzweig, *The Athenian Agora. Volume 7: Lamps of the Roman Period* (American School of Classical Studies at Athens: Princeton 1961).

Priene R. Zahn, "Thongeschirr: Die Gefässe," in T. Wiegand and H. Schrader, *Priene* 1895–98 (G. Reimer: Berlin 1904) 394–448.

Radošević (1973) Z. Radošević, "The Stobi Bibliography," *Studies I* (1973) 233–268.

RCRFActa Rei Cretariae Romanae Fautorum, Acta.

RDAC Report of the Department of Antiquities, Cyprus.

RE Pauly-Wissowa, *Real-Encyclopädie der klassischen Altertumswissenschaft.*

Rigoir (1960) J. Rigoir, "La céramique paléochrétienne sigillée grise," *Province historique* 10 (1960) 1–93.

Rigoir (1968) ———, "Les sigillées paléochrétiennes grises et orangées," *Gallia* 26 (1968) 177–244.

Riley, *Berenice 2* J. A. Riley, "Coarse Pottery," in *Excavations at Sidi Khrebish, Benghazi (Berenice) 2 (Supplement to Libya Antiqua 5)* (Tripoli 1983) 91–466.

Robinson, *Agora* H. Robinson, *The Athenian Agora. Volume 5: Pottery of the Roman Period, Chronology* (American School of Classical Studies at Athens: Princeton 1959).

Robinson, *Diss.* ———, "Early Roman Red Wares from the Athenian Agora" (Ph.D. Dissertation. Princeton University 1941).

Rotroff, *Agora 22* S. I. Rotroff, *The Athenian Agora. Volume 22: Hellenistic Pottery. Athenian and Imported Moldmade Bowls* (American School of Classical Studies at Athens: Princeton 1982).

RStLig Rivista di Studi Liguri.

Samaria J. W. Crowfoot, G. W. Crowfoot, and K. Kenyon, *Samaria-Sebaste 3. The Objects from Samaria* (Palestine Exploration Fund: London 1957).

Schäfer (1962) J. Shäfer, "Terra Sigillata Keramik aus Pergamon," *Archäologische Anzeiger* (1962) 777–802.

SIMA Studies in Mediterranean Archaeology.

Slane (1986) K. W. Slane, "Two Deposits from the Early Roman Cellar Building, Corinth," *Hesperia* 55 (1986) 271–318.

Sokolovska (1986) V. Sokolovska, *Isar-Marvinci and the Vardar Valley in Ancient Times* (Skopje 1986) (In Macedonian with English summary).

Sokolovska, *Studies II* ———, "Investigations in the House of Peristerias," *Studies II,* 123–141.

Stobi Stobi. Results of the Joint American–Yugoslav Archaeological Investigations, 1970–1981, J. Wiseman, ed.

Stobi 2 Elizabeth R. Gebhard, *Stobi Volume 2: The Theater* (forthcoming).

Stobi 3 J. Wiseman, *Stobi Volume 3: The Inscriptions from The Theater* (forthcoming).

Stobi 4 Frederick Hemans et al., *Stobi Volume 4: The Residences* (forthcoming).

Stobi 5 A. B. Wesolowsky, *Stobi Volume 5: The Cemeteries* (forthcoming).

Stobi 7 J. Wiseman, *Stobi Volume 7: The Ancient City of Stobi* (forthcoming).

Strong D. E. Strong, *Greek and Roman Gold and Silver Plate* (Cornell University Press: Ithaca, New York 1966).

StEtr Studi Etruschi.

Studies I, II J. Wiseman, ed., *Studies in the Antiquities of Stobi I* (Beograd 1973) *II* (Beograd 1975).

Studies III B. Aleksova and J. Wiseman, eds., *Studies in the Antiquities of Stobi III* (Titov Veles 1981).

Swan (1984) V. G. Swan, *The Pottery Kilns of Roman Britain. Royal Commission of Historical Monuments. Supplementary Series 5* (London 1984).

Tarsus F. F. Jones, "The Pottery," in H. Goldman, ed., *Excavations at Gözlü Kule, Tarsus, 1. The Hellenistic and Roman Periods, Section VI* (Princeton University Press: Princeton 1950) 149–296.

Taylor, "Cosa" D. M. Taylor, "Cosa: Black Glaze Pottery," *MAAR* 25 (1957) 65–193.

Techau, "Heraion" W. Techau, "Griechische Keramik, im samische Heraion," *AthMitt* 54 (1929) 6–64.

Thompson, "TCHP" H. L. Thompson, "Two Centuries of Hellenistic Pottery," *Hesperia* 3 (1934) 311–480.

"Tschandarli" S. Loeschcke, "Sigillata Töpfereien in Tschandarli," *AthMitt* 37 (1912) 344–407.

Ulbert (1960) G. Ulbert, *Die römische Keramik aus dem Legionslager Augsburg-Oberhausen. Materialhefte zur Bayerischen Vorgeschichte* 14 (1960).

Vegas, *Cerámica común* M. Vegas, *Cerámica común romana del Mediterráneo occidental. Universidad de Barcelona. Instituto de Arqueologia y Prehistoria. Publicaciones eventuales No. 22* (Madrid 1973).

Vučković-Todorović (1961) D. Vučkoviíc-Todorović, "Antićka Demir Kapija," *Starinar* 12 n.s. (1961) 229–269.

Vučković-Todorović (1973) ———, "La céramique grecque et hellénistique dans l'est de la Yougoslavie," *Revue archéologique* 1 n.s. (1973) 39–52.

Wadsworth (1983) M. Wadsworth, "A Potter's Experience with the Method of Firing Buchero," *Opuscula romana* 14 (1983) 65–68.

Will (1983) E. L. Will, "Exportation of Olive Oil from Baetica to the E. Mediterranean," in J. M. Blazquez and J. Remesal, eds., *Prod y com del aceite en la antigüedad, II Congresso* (Madrid 1983) 392–440.

Wiseman, "Gods" J. Wiseman, "Gods, War and Plague in the Time of the Antonines," in *Studies I,* 143–183.

Wiseman, "Family" ———, "A Distinguished Macedonian Family of the Roman Imperial Period," *AJA* 88 (1984) 567–582.

Wiseman, "City" ———, "The City in Macedonia Secunda," in *Villes et peuplement dans l'Illyricum protobyzantin, Actes du colloque organisé par l'Ecole française de Rome (Rome 12–14 mai 1982). Collection de l'Ecole française de Rome 77* (1984) 289–314.

Wiseman, "Archaeology and History" ———, "Archaeology and History at Stobi, Macedonia," in C. McClendon, ed., *Rome and the Provinces: A Symposium* (Archaeological Institute of America, New Haven Society: New Haven 1986) 37–83.

Wiseman, *Guide* ———, *Stobi. A Guide to the Excavations* (Belgrade 1973).

Wiseman (1978) ———, "Stobi in Yugoslavian Macedonia: Archaeological Investigations and Research, 1977–78," *JFA* 5 (1978) 391–429.

W-MZ (1971) ——— and Dj. Mano-Zissi, "Excavations at Stobi, 1970," *AJA* 75 (1971) 395–411.

W-MZ (1972) ———, "Excavations at Stobi, 1971," *AJA* 76 (1972) 407–424.

W-MZ (1973) ———, "Excavations at Stobi, 1972," *AJA* 77 (1973) 391–403.

W-MZ (1974) ———, "Excavations at Stobi, 1973–1974," *JFA* 1 (1974) 117–148.

W-MZ (1976) ———, "Stobi: A City of Ancient Macedonia," *JFA* 3 (1976) 269–302.

Wright (1980) K. S. Wright, "A Tiberian Pottery Deposit from Corinth," *Hesperia* 49 (1980) 135–177.

STOBI

THE HELLENISTIC AND ROMAN POTTERY

1

INTRODUCTION

•

The Site

Stobi is located in the Vardar (the ancient Axius) river valley of northern Macedonia at the point where the Crna river (the ancient Erigon) flows into the Vardar (Pl. 1). It was an important center along this north-south route between Greece and central Europe from early times until it was abandoned late in the 6th century after Christ. The major highway to Greece still passes the site of Stobi today, and the Orient Express runs alongside.[1] The variety of imported ceramics at Stobi and the quantity of particular wares present at various periods in the city's history are reflections of her strategic location between east and west.

The earliest stratified levels encountered by the Stobi Project were tested in a very small area, but they did produce quantities of a wheelmade gray ware of the late 4th, early 3rd centuries B.C.[2] Other sherds ranging in date from Neolithic to Iron Age (Hallstatt), including Greek archaic and classical material, have also been found in various parts of the site but none in original context.[3]

Several substantial deposits of the 2nd and 1st centuries B.C. have been excavated in the central part of the ancient city, and graves of this period are plentiful in the cemeteries.[4]

Although we know that the city expanded and flourished in the Augustan period and during the 1st century, deposits of this date are small and widely scattered over the site. The greatest quantities of 1st century pottery come from houses on the Acropolis.[5]

From the 2nd through the 4th centuries, the city continued to grow in size and prosperity, as seen by the number of public buildings and large residences on the site. The largest deposits of pottery belong to this period.[6]

The Christian city of the 5th and 6th centuries was populous and wealthy enough to build no fewer than five basilicas, and deposits with large amounts of pottery are associated with the construction and remodeling of these structures.[7]

[1] See map, Pl. 1.

[2] Lots 842 and 843. See Early Hellenistic Wheel-made Gray Ware in Chapter 3.

[3] Wiseman, "Archaeology and History"; Mikulčić, *Studies III*, 216–217. The prehistoric material will be published by Voislav Sanev of the Archaeological Museum of Skopje. See section on Black-Gloss Wares, **50–54**, for earliest pieces.

[4] See Deposit Lists in Chapter 4. In the central city: Acropolis, Central and Civil Basilicas. Graves: Fuller's House Graves 312 (Lot 1637) and 313 (1637); W-MZ (1976) 281–282; Peristeria Court Graves 99–103; W-MZ (1973) 401–402; Sokolovska, *Studies II*, 135–137. The location of buildings is shown on Pl. 2.

Reports on excavations in the West Cemetery have appeared in each of the first five preliminary reports, and *Stobi 5*, the final publication, is being prepared by Al B. Wesolowsky, who supervised the work in the West Cemetery. See also Wesolowsky, "Burial Customs in the West Cemetery," in *Studies* I, 97–142, and, in the same volume, I. Mikulčić, "The West Cemetery: Excavations in 1965," 61–96, and S. Valastro and A. B. Wesolowsky, "The C-14 Dating Program of the West Cemetery," *Studies III*, 301–310.

[5] See Chapter 4 and Table 4.5.

[6] General discussions appear in Wiseman, "City," and "Archaeology and History." For deposits, see Chapter 4 and Tables 4.7–4.10.

[7] Wiseman (1978) 395–407 and "City"; and R. F. Kolarik, "Mosaics of the Early Church at Stobi," *DOP* 41 (1987) note 2 with bibliography.

Goals and Methods of Pottery Analysis

The primary aim of this study has been to establish a chronology for the pottery at Stobi that would in turn help to provide a chronological framework for the site and for the structures excavated at the site. The absence of any such comprehensive study for Macedonia made this a most urgent task. Because local/regional wares outnumber imports in all periods of the site, a typology has been established for these wares. The identification of imports at Stobi, including amphorae, has helped to define the trading connections of the ancient city before and after the Roman conquest (168 B.C.) and to put Macedonia on the economic map of the ancient world.

Most of the archaeological excavations in Macedonia that have produced ceramic material from the Greek and Roman periods have been small-scale salvage operations; cemeteries have frequently been the focus of excavation. Although some pottery has been found in such excavations, little material comes from the stratified levels that would be suitable for setting up a ceramic sequence. Excavation is currently in progress at the classical sites of Heraclea Lyncestis, Marvinci, and Scupi, among others, and publication of the ceramics from those sites will add to our knowledge of regional ceramic production.

Since an earlier, partial version of this study was completed, several publications have appeared that present a selection of pottery (and other objects) of the Hellenistic and Roman periods in Macedonia.[8] None of these studies has provided a chronological framework or presents quantitative data.

The importance of quantification for the reconstruction of the ancient economy, especially for our understanding of trade patterns, has been stressed recently by social and economic historians and archaeologists.[9] Without some idea of the quantities of various types, wares, or forms present in any assemblage, one cannot begin to reconstruct relative frequencies of items in any given layer or on the site as a whole, or to compare the frequency of types at different sites. In this volume, quantities of wares and forms appear in the catalogue of Chapter 3 and in the discussion of deposits in Chapter 4. Tables and pie charts have been used throughout for a visual presentation of the quantified data.

With the exception of some whole vessels from the cemeteries, most of the pottery at Stobi consists of sherds. Where possible these have been related to complete shapes.

Quantities illustrated in the tables and graphs are based on counts of rims, bases, and handles (RBH) as an approximate indication of minimum individual vessels.[10] Sherd weights that are of arguable value were not taken at Stobi. Since all the material was studied after completion of excavation in a given area and after mending was complete, the probability that rims or bases from the same vessel would be counted twice was minimal. Whole pots and partially complete vessels were counted as one vessel or RBH item. Catalogued pieces were included in the counts.

Because the identification and publication of regional wares, and thus of interregional trade, have not begun in Macedonia, it has been possible only in a very limited way to set the picture at Stobi within the larger regional view.

The pottery presented here falls into two sections: the first includes all imported pottery and other distinct wares or classes, some of which were produced at the site or in the region; and

[8] The author's Ph.D. dissertation "Pottery of the Hellenistic and Early Roman Periods at Stobi," Department of Classics, University of Texas at Austin, 1977; Anderson-Stojanović, (1981) 47–59.

On material from Veroia, see Drougou and Touratsoglou, *Veroia*. Maneva (1979) is an M.A. thesis at the University of Belgrade on the pottery from the fill beneath the nave of the mid-5th-century Large Basilica at Heraclea Lyncestis where the pottery ranges in date from the 3rd century B.C. to the 5th century A.C. For the Vardar area, especially Marvinci, see Sokolovska (1986), and for Macedonia in general, Bitrakova-Grozdanova (1987).

[9] Note the comments of Riley, *Berenice* 2, 99–100; Greene (1986); Peacock, *PRW* 169–172, and most recently, the review of A. Giardina, ed. *Società Romana e imperio tardoantico III. Le merci gli insediamenti* (Laterza: Roma 1986), by R. Hodges and J. W. Hayes, "Aspects of the Decline and Fall of the Roman Empire," in *Journal of Roman Archaeology* 1 (1988) 215–222, especially the comments of Hayes on quantification, p. 221.

[10] Quantitative studies that utilize body sherds, which normally cannot be associated with any particular shape, are of little value; for example, it is difficult to distinguish body sherds of amphorae from plain wares, thin-walled Cooking Ware from Thin-Walled wares. Some fine-ware closed vessels have a partial slip only on the exterior, so they may end up in two groups, plain, slipped, or partially slipped.

the second comprises the large corpus of local color-slipped tablewares, plainwares, and cooking ware. Only the local/regional wares and other types that have not been identified before have been put into new type series (including Early Hellenistic Wheelmade Gray Ware, Macedonian Gray Ware, and Unguentaria). Well-known imports have been assigned to published typologies rather than new ones created for the few examples that found their way to Stobi. For example, African Red Slip Ware is classified according to the typology of John Hayes in *Late Roman Pottery*. (See "Explanatory Notes for the Catalogue" at the end of this chapter.) Wares are presented in approximate chronological order (Table 1.1).

The local corpus has been divided into Color-Slipped and Plain wares on the one hand, and Cooking Ware on the other. Color-Slipped and Plain are both characterized by a fine, light fabric, whereas the Cooking Ware has a dark, coarse appearance (see Chapter 2 and Table 2.1). The local wares have been presented in the following broad chronological periods: Late Hellenistic (2nd and 1st centuries B.C.), Early Roman (1st century A.C.), Middle Roman (2nd to mid-4th centuries A.C.), and Late Roman (mid-4th to 6th centuries A.C.).

The fragmentary nature of most of the pottery at Stobi has made the creation of a local typology difficult, and the numbers of types are small for this reason. Unless a form was represented by several examples, it was not made a part of the typology but was included in a category of "other" or miscellaneous pieces.

Because local wares comprise the majority of pottery at Stobi, the local typology comprises a large part of this volume. It is hoped that it will serve as a reference for other sites in Macedonia.

The evidence for the production of ceramics at Stobi is presented in Chapter 2. Chapter 3 contains the catalogue of Hellenistic and Roman pottery.

Table 1.1. Chronological range of wares at Stobi

Ware	Date
Early Hellenistic Gray Ware	3rd–2nd c. B.C.
Black-Gloss Wares	2nd–1st c. B.C.
Black-Gloss Wares with Gray Fabric	2nd c. B.C.–2nd c. A.C.
Hellenistic Relief Bowls	2nd–1st c. B.C
Thin-Walled Wares	1st B.C.–1st c. A.C.
Eastern Sigillata A	2nd B.C.–1st c. A.C.
Italian Sigillata	lst c. A.C.
Other Western Sigillata	lst/2nd c. A.C.
Eastern Sigillata B	1st/2nd c. A.C.
Çandarli	2nd/3rd c. A.C.
Cypriot Sigillata	1st/2nd c. A.C.
Cypriot Red Slip Ware	5th c. A.C.
African Red Slip Ware	4th–6th c. A.C.
Phocaean Red Slip Ware	5th–6th c. A.C.
Macedonian Gray Ware	late 4th–5th c. A.C.
Italian Mugs	2nd–4th c. A.C.
Marbeled Slip	2nd–4th c. A.C.
Lead-Glazed Wares	3rd–4th c. A.C.
Unguentaria	2nd B.C.–1st c. A.C.
Tan Micaceous Ware	4th c. A.C.
Red Micaceous Ware	4th c. A.C.
Mica-Dusted Ware	5th–6th c. A.C.
Pompeian Red Ware	2nd B.C.–2nd c. A.C.
Aegean Cooking Ware	2nd–3rd c. A.C.

Explanatory Notes for the Catalogue

At Stobi all contextual material from an excavation unit is associated at the time of excavation with a Basket. Within each Field Notebook (NB) the Baskets are numbered sequentially and described on standardized forms. The location of the deposit, a description of the matrix, elevations, and lists of artifacts and features are recorded for each Basket; all other documentation of the unit of excavation also refers to the Basket. Since the Field Notebooks are also numbered sequentially, the citing of NB and Basket, therefore, provides the basic, and unique, reference to the archaeological context of all material recovered at Stobi. Units of excavation, however, may reflect either stratigraphic or arbitrary levels or other divisions, and may contain a small or large amount of contextual material. For logistical reasons, therefore, a Basket may represent either all or only a portion of the material from one deposit but should never include material from *more* than one deposit.

When excavation in an area was completed for the season, the uninventoried material from Baskets representing the same deposit was combined and is referred to as a Lot. The Lot is the unit of storage for each deposit or context. Lots have been numbered sequentially throughout the Stobi Project. A summary of the information about each Lot, including a description of the soil, location, conditions of deposition, a list of the Baskets subsumed in the Lot, a brief description of the artifacts and their inventory numbers, and the date of the deposit, is recorded in the Context Storage Notebook.[11]

Two inventory systems are seen in the catalogues of Chapters 2 and 3. Some ceramics have a separate inventory number beginning with the prefix C, then the year in which the object was excavated, and then a sequential accession number within that year, for example, C-74-21. These objects are part of a comprehensive inventory system at Stobi. Complete measurements, descriptions, photographs, and contextual associations of these objects exist on cards that are part of the permanent excavation records at the site. These inventoried objects are stored separately from other context material.

Other items have a numbering system related directly to archaeological context. Lot 610, No. 50, indicates that this piece is the fiftieth item numbered in Context Storage Lot 610. Such items are stored in trays with the remaining context pottery of the Lot. The Lot number that serves as the deposit reference is included with each catalogue entry. A list of these Lots or deposits together with their location and date may be found in Chapter 4.

Dates have been supplied for those items with reliable context. When the date has not been given in the text, the reader should consult the deposit lists in Tables 4.13 and 4.16 for a date of deposit.

Most items in the catalogue are accompanied by an illustration, either a drawing or a photograph, or both. Drawings are at a scale of 1:2 unless otherwise noted. Metric measurements are included for each piece as well as some indication as to whether there is only one fragment or a complete profile or a complete vessel preserved. The total number of examples of a given type or shape and the context of each is also included in the text. The format for these entries will be as follows: Lot 140:2, indicating that two additional, similar examples are to be found in Lot 140. Fabric color is described according to the Munsell Color Chart (Baltimore 1975).

All pottery presented in this study is stored at the site of Stobi, as is all documentation related to the Stobi Project Excavations.

Type or Form numbers from the following publications are frequently used in the text.

Antioch, 22–24, pls. 3–4.
Broneer, *Corinth 4*, pls. 3–29.
Dressel, *CIL* XV, pl. ii.
Goudineau.
Hayes, *LRP*.
Howland, *Agora 4*, pls. 36, 41–45, 51.
Lamboglia, pp. 143–200.
Moevs, "Cosa," form chart at back of volume.

[11] Both Baskets and Lots may also refer to groups of artifacts and other material with origins other than excavation units (e.g., surface collections). The designations then still serve as the basic references to the record of the circumstances of recovery (NB and Basket) and storage unit (Lot). For a full description and critique of the Stobi system of documentation, see Wiseman, *Stobi 7*.

Peacock and Williams, *Amphorae.*
Pergamon 6, figs. 39–48.
Perlzweig, *Agora 7*, pl. 2.
Riley, *Berenice 2*, pp. 119–232 for amphora types at Berenice.
Samaria, figs. 73, 77–82.
Will, E., *Stamped Roman Amphoras in the Eastern Mediterranean* (forthcoming, *Athenian Agora* series)

Abbreviations

Dimensions in meters

H. = Height
P.H. = Preserved height
M.P.Dim. = Maximum preserved dimension
D. = Diameter
Est. D. = Estimated diameter
Th. = Thickness
L. = Length
P.L. = Preserved length
RBH = Rims, bases, handles
r. = rim
b. = base
NB = Notebook

Chronological designations

Hell. = Hellenistic
ER = Early Roman
MR = Middle Roman
LR = Late Roman

Areas of the site

Acro. = Acropolis
A.G.S. = Small Bath
Bas.Cem. = Basilica Cemetery
Cent.Bas. = Central Basilica
Civ.Bas. = Civil Basilica
C.W.E. = City Wall East
E.Bas. = Episcopal Basilica
E.Res. = Episcopal Residence
Ext. = Extension
F.H. = Fuller's House
I.W.W. = Inner Wall West
L.B. = Large Bath
P.C. = Peristeria Court
Peristeria H. = Peristeria House
S.C.W. = South City Wall
Syn. = Synagogue
Tr. = Trench
W.C. = West Cemetery

Stobi Inventory Classes cited in this volume

C = Ceramics (Pottery)
G = Glass
L = Lamps
MF = Miscellaneous Finds

2

THE LOCAL CERAMIC TRADITION

•

The earliest evidence for local production of ceramics at Stobi comes from the Potter's Workshop excavated below the narthex of the Central Basilica.[1] The presence of moulds made of local clays (nos. 7–9 below), and of fragments of imported pottery (**49**, **222** in Chapter 3), along with local imitations in the fills asssociated with the kilnlike structure, suggests pottery manufacture by the late 2nd/early 1st centuries B.C.

There is evidence for continued local production throughout the city's history, as moulds and stamps (nos. 1, 2, 10–18) have been discovered in contexts of various periods. A small circular structure of stone with four small arches of brick on its interior exists in the Peristeria complex, discovered during earlier excavations conducted by the Archaeological Museum of Skopje.[2] The excavator suggests that this structure may have served as a kiln. In 1975 also in the House of Peristeria but rather distant from the kiln, several objects that may have been kiln pipes or spools were found (no. 6).

Stobi provides an ideal location for the production of pottery. Clay beds are located on the east bank of the Crna river. Both the Crna and Vardar rivers provided a source of water as well as unlimited amounts of sand suitable as tempering material. The only other requirement for production would have been fuel; wood, sheep dung, and charcoal are all possibilities.[3] With such resources an enterprising landowner might sponsor the production not only of pottery, but also of more lucrative materials on a larger scale, for example, brick, water pipes, and roof tiles, as well as amphorae and even coffins.[4]

The Stobi clay comes from a gray shale interbedded with sandstone and consists of illitic and montmorillonitic clays. The clay strata are part of a formation that extends a considerable distance to the south and east.[5]

A variety of analytical tests have been performed on Stobi samples of clay and ceramics, and results were helpful, if not conclusive. The primary results of these tests were to confirm our ideas about the nature of locally manufactured wares and to distinguish the various local fabric groups.

Petrographic analysis has proved to be the most useful in determining the composition of the local fabrics and in confirming the validity of our macroscopic sorting criteria. Analysis of the thin sections was carried out by Dr. Robert Folk of the Department of Geology of the University of Texas at Austin, Dr. Georgeana Little of Boston University, and Dr. Robert Wiebe of the Geology Department of Franklin and Marshall College.[6] Appendix 2 contains a report of the petrographic analyses of Dr. Little.

Several local ware fabric groups have been isolated on the basis of fabric and form (Table 2.1).

[1] W-MZ (1971) 408–411. See also Appendix 1 and Table 4.3 with discussion in Chapter 4.

[2] Sokolovska, *Studies* II, 128.

[3] Wadsworth (1983) 68, and A. O. Shepard, *Ceramics for the Archaeologist* (Washington, D.C., 1971) 77, discuss relative merits of these and other fuels for kiln use.

[4] Moses Finley cites the exploitation of clay beds by the upper classes in his discussion of the commodity-producing aspects of land ownership, "The Study of the Ancient Economy, Further Thoughts," *Opus* 3 (1984) 8–9.

[5] R. Folk, "The Geologic Framework of Stobi," *Studies* I, 43, 49. Bricks and tiles are still made from clay at Negotino, to the south of Stobi, and further south at Demir Kapija. See Pl. 1.

[6] The first study was undertaken by Dr. Tomislav Ivanov (1974) on a selection of Stobi sherds. Spectographic analyses were carried out in Belgrade at the Mining Geology Faculty by Docent Engineer C. Mudrinjica, M.A. Financial support for all of these analyses was provided by the Stobi Project.

Table 2.1. Fabric groups of Stobi Local Wares

	Paste	Color	Types
Fabric 1	Fine with little or no tempering material visible. Mineral inclusions are fine quartz/feldspar sand with mica. Core rare.	Munsell 5YR 6/6–7/6, reddish yellow, to 7.5 YR 7/4, pink, more rarely, 2.5 YR 6/6, light red, or 10YR 7/4, very pale brown.	Tableware, serving vessels, moulded bowls, unguentaria, loomweights.
Fabric 2	Fine with no tempering material visible. Mineral inclusions are quartz/ feldspar, mica minerals, fine-grained igneous and metamorphic rock fragments.	Various shades gray, brownish gray, grayish brown munsell 10YR 6/1, 5/1, 6/2, 5/2, 4/2, 7.5YR N7/, N6/, N5/, 6/2.	Tableware, serving vessels.
Fabric 3	Coarse, gritty with much visible tempering material. Mineral inclusions are quartz/ feldspar, metaquartzite, mica schist, gneiss, and mica.	Tan to gray, reddish brown, brown, gray, black.	Cook ware: pots, pans, bowls, dishes, pitchers, pithoi, tiles.

The first is a fine light ware falling in the range of reddish yellow (5YR 6/6–7/6) to pink (7.5YR 7/4), sometimes fired light red (2.5YR 6/6) or very pale brown (10YR 7/4). Rarely is a core present. Little tempering material is visible, except under close inspection or under a hand lens. Petrographic analysis shows the primary mineral inclusions to be fine quartz/feldspar sand with some mica. This fabric was used for a wide range of Color-Slipped and Plain forms suitable for the serving of food and drink, for moulded relief bowls, and for unguentaria.[7]

Local Fabric group 1 appears in the 2nd century B.C. and continues to be used until the second half of the 4th century A.C., when it disappears, replaced by coarser, grittier fabrics.[8]

The second fabric is a fine gray ware, varying in color from light to dark gray (10YR 6/1, 5/1, 4/1, 6/2, 5/2, 4/2, and 7.5YR N7/, N6/, N5, 6/2) with variations to brownish gray; a darker core is sometimes present. The gray color would appear to be a result of a reduced firing technique. An oxidized version of the ware also exists but in very small numbers. Thin sections of samples show the presence of quartz/feldspar, mica minerals (muscovite, biotite), and some fine-grained igneous and metamorphic rock fragments.

The gray-ware tradition, perhaps not local at

[7] Some years ago, a potter working in the nearby town of Titov Veles made several vessels from the local clay (with no added temper), finding it of good quality for pottery. The vessels were fired in a wood-burning kiln producing surface colors similar to the lighter (10YR 7/4) examples of local Fabric group 1.

[8] This change is dramatically illustrated by the two different clay fabrics seen on spools/pipes of the same form but different periods, cat. nos. 5 and 6. Although occurring somewhat earlier, the same phenomenon has been noted at Corinth by K. W. Slane, "Corinth: Deposits of ca. A.D. 200 and A.D. 300 from East of the Theater," in a paper presented at the 91st General Meeting of the Archaeological Institute of America, Boston, December, 1989, *AJA* 94 (1990) 334–335 (abstract).

first, appears in the Hellenistic period. With the exception of the incurved bowl, these Early Hellenistic Gray Ware forms do not seem to continue into the later Hellenistic period. Some of the gray wares of the succeeding period, such as Campanian C and Asia Minor platters, are certainly imports, but a number are found in identical forms as the most commonly found forms of the local Fabric group 1, namely Hellenistic Forms 3 and 12, and are probably locally produced.

In the lst century A.C., the gray wares imitate forms of terra sigillata, and it is probable that some of these pieces, too, are imports. The 2nd, 3rd, and most of the 4th centuries are marked by the complete absence of gray pottery at Stobi, and fine wares are seen almost entirely in the local Fabric group 1, with the number of imports quite small (Fig. 4.3). In the late 4th century, however, gray ware becomes the primary fabric for tableware forms, such as plates, bowls, and drinking cups, and pitchers, taking the place of the earlier light fabric 1. This late Roman gray ware has been called Macedonian Gray Ware.[9]

The third local fabric is a coarse, gritty cooking ware of numerous shades from tan to gray, reddish brown to brown. The mineral components of the fabric are those of a metamorphic terrain: quartz/feldspar, metaquartzite, mica schist, gneiss, and micas. A number of examples display an extremely illitic paste.

This fabric remains essentially the same in appearance from the 2nd century B.C. until the 4th century A.C., when an increasingly greater amount of mica is apparent on the surface and in cross-section as well as under the microscope.

Similar to this cooking-ware fabric is a somewhat finer ware, smoothed on the exterior, hard fired, and thin walled but not brittle or foliating like later cooking ware. Tan Micaceous, as I have called this ware, appears in a rather small number of characteristic forms in the 4th century. It is not known whether or not this ware was actually produced at Stobi.

It is probable that the illitic and montmorillonitic clays present in the Stobi area were the source for these local wares. The abundant sand from the banks of the Crna provided a ready source of tempering material, since the components of the sand (quartz grains, metaquartzite, schist, biotite, muscovite, and feldspar) and the three local fabrics are very similar. The gravels common at the site, consisting of quartz pebbles, granite, schist, chert, and volcanic rocks, were probably also used for the cooking ware. An additional tempering source may have been the greenish sandstone containing metaquartzite and volcanic rock fragments widely used as a building material at Stobi. Additional clay sources exist south of Stobi at Negotino and Demir Kapija and are used today for the production of bricks and tiles.[10]

Whereas most examples of Fabric groups 1 and 3 are presented in the second section of the catalogue under Local Color-Slipped, Plain, and Cooking wares, items in Fabric group 2 appear in the first section of the catalogue together with the traditions to which they belong (i.e., Early Hellenistic Wheelmade Gray Ware, Black-Gloss Wares with Gray Fabric, and Macedonian Gray Ware). Fabric 1 was used in the production of local unguentaria and moulded bowls, also found in the first part of Chapter 3.

[9] This term replaces "Macedonian terra sigillata grise" used in Anderson-Stojanović (1984). Reasons for the occurrence of reduced/gray wares in certain areas were explored by the author in paper entitled "The Problem of Roman Gray Wares," presented at the 91st General Meeting of the Archaeological Institute of America in Boston, December, 1989, *AJA* 94 (1990) 335 (abstract). For further discussion, note comments in Chapter 3, Macedonian Gray Ware.

[10] See note 5 above, and Folk, *Studies I*, 49. In April of 1989 in a ceramics course at Wilson College, I did some experimental firing of clays from Stobi and the surrounding area. I mixed clays from Demir Kapija, Negotino, Palikura, and Stobi with water, then made sample briquettes for bisque firing. Each was 1½" by 2½" thick. The kiln was fired to cone 6, or approximately 1800° F. The results are summarized below. I was, unfortunately, not able to refire any sherds. Colors of clays were as follows: *Palikura*: Raw clay was 5Y 5/2 (olive gray) to 5/3 (olive). Bisque fired clay was 7.5YR 7/6 on surface. Slightly micaceous with cracking and lime(?) eruptions on surface. Broke apart easily and in cross-section were dark spots (10 YR 6/4: light yellow). Probably not pure enough clay. *Negotino*: Raw clay was 2.5Y 6/4 (light yellowish brown) to 5/4 (light olive-brown). Bisque-fired clay was 5YR 6/6–5/6 (reddish-yellow to yellowish-red). Very micaceous with lime eruptions, only a bit of cracking where clay compacted at corners. Cannot break with hands. *Demir Kapija*: Raw clay was 7.5YR 3/4 (dark brown). Bisque fired clay was 2.5YR 6/6–5/6 (light red to red). Very micaceous, no visible lime eruptions. Cannot pull apart with hands. This color is the same as that of the modern bricks seen at the site of Demir Kapija. *Stobi*: Raw clay was 5Y 5/1 (gray) to 4/1 (dark gray). Fired clay was 10YR 8/3 to 8/3 (very pale yellow). Crumbled after a few days. No mica visible. This sample was not taken from a good source, nor was it ground or levigated sufficiently before firing.

The following stamps, kiln furniture, and moulds were associated with the production of ceramics at Stobi. The format of the entries below, including abbreviations, is explained in detail at the end of Chapter 1. The numbering of items in this chapter constitutes a separate seriation from those in the catalogue of Chapter 3.

Stamps

1. Inv. No. C-74-88. Lot 1403. Pls. 3, 150.
H. 0.052. W. of palmette 0.016. D. circle 0.024. Complete except for chip at one end. Very micaceous soft reddish yellow (5YR 7/6) fabric. Unslipped. One end is a palmette stamp and the other a spoked circle.

2. Inv. No. C-78-240. Lot 2407. Pls. 3, 150.
L. 0.040. L. foot stamp 0.022. Complete *planta pedis* stamp. Micaceous pink to light brown (7.5YR 7/4–6/4) fabric.

Vessel supports

3. Inv. No. MF-71-104. Lot 131. Pl. 150.
D. 0.021. Complete. Fine pink (7.5YR 7/4) fabric. Small circular object with flat bottom and single broad depression across surface. W-MZ (1972) fig. 5.
Three other almost identical examples from the same context of the destroyed potter's shop area below the narthex of the Central Basilica: MF 71-105 (Lot 135); MF-71-106 (Lot 135); MF-71-107 (Lot 132). See Appendix 1.

4. Inv. No. MF-71-170. Lot 88. Pl. 150.
L. 0.081. H. 0.024. Th. 0.020. Handmade. Angular object, perhaps a kiln support. Because of the roughness of the surface, it is difficult to tell if this piece was broken at the ends or this was its intended length. Reddish brown (5YR 5/4) fabric. A series of incised hatchings on one surface. W-MZ (1972) note 12.
One additional fragment, MF-71-171, from same Lot. Many other fragments were found in the area.

Pipes (for hot air in kiln) or Spools

5. Inv. No. MF-74-46. Lot 1407. Pl. 150.
L. 0.081. D. cylinder 0.041. D. opening 0.030. Complete except for one small chip. Fine, soft, reddish yellow (5YR 6/6) micaceous clay some with gray core. Surface varies from pink (7.5YR 7/4) to pale brown (10YR 7/4).
Other examples of the same fabric were found in Lots 1296, 1298, and 1404.

6. Inv. No. MF-75-7. Lot 1656. Pl. 150.
L. 0.097. D. cylinder 0.047. D. opening 0.021–0.023. Complete except for a few chips missing. Wire marks visible on ends and wheel marks on sides. Micaceous reddish brown cookware fabric.
Sixteen other examples found nearby. MF-75-24 was found with C-75-19, a kiln waster.

Moulds

A total of thirteen fragmentary moulds have been found at Stobi. Aside from the few found in the area of the potter's workshop, none was found in its original context. The fabric of all seems to be local. Many of the moulds are similar to fragments of bowls found at Stobi, but none has been identified as the mould used to produce a surviving fragment.

Lion's head mould

7. Inv. No. C-71-135. Lot 134. Pl. 151.
Complete except for small chip from edge. Reddish yellow (5YR 5/6) fabric. Although no relief bowls with lions head supports/feet have been found at Stobi, it is probable that this was the function of this mould and one other only partially preserved (C-71-152).

Bowl moulds

8. Inv. No. C-71-73. Lot 134. Pls. 3, 151.
P.H. 0.027. Est. D. rim 0.060. Almost complete; base missing. Sandy, soft pink (7.5YR 7/4) fabric. Hemispherical bowl with disc base and flanged rim. Unslipped. Interior surface is covered with incised decoration consisting of long petals with rounded ends. In between the petals are rows of irregularly placed dots. The petals are divided from the base by a single concentric groove. Directly on the other side of the groove is a row of half circles. W-MZ (1972) fig. 4.

9. Inv. No. C-71-49. Lot 127. Pls. 3, 151.
P.H. 0.022. Est. D. rim 0.080. Flanged rim fragment and part of body. Hard, pink (7.5YR 7/4)

fabric with many white particles (lime?). Unslipped. Decoration on the interior: a single long petal on either side of which are three wavy vertical lines. Above the lines is a single horizontal zigzag line. Within each zigzag is a single dot.

10. Inv. No. C-72-21. Lot 610. Pl. 151.

M.P.Dim. 0.057. Small fragment from near base. Pink (7.5YR) clay, unslipped. The interior decoration consists of six irregularly spaced, incised lines in a general vegetal pattern.

11. Lot 231, No. 16. Pl. 151.

M.P.Dim. 0.035. Small fragment of wall. Pink (7.5YR 7/4) fabric. Unslipped. Preserved decoration on interior consists of a single horizontal zone and part of another separated by rows of many small dots. Within the zone are very stylized plants.

12. Inv. No. C-74-515. Lot 1501. Pls. 3, 151.

M.P.Dim. 0.023. Fragment from slightly inturned rim. Soft, reddish yellow (5YR 7/6) clay. Unslipped. Stamped rosettes on rim portion of interior.

13. Lot 1501, No. 16. Pl. 3.

M.P.Dim. 0.017. Rim fragment. Reddish yellow (5YR 6/6) clay. Unslipped. Narrow horizontal band at rim filled with diagonally incised lines.

14. Inv. C-74-459. Lot 1501. Pl. 152.

M.P.Dim. 0.047. Side wall fragment. Reddish yellow (5YR 6/6) fabric. Unslipped. Only a very small part of incised foliage decoration is preserved.

15. Inv. No. C-75-66. Lot 1662. Pl. 152.

M.P.Dim. 0.038. Side wall fragment. Reddish brown (5YR 5/4) fabric at core and brown (7.5YR 5/4) at surface with sparse white inclusions. Fired very pale brown (10YR) at surface. Negative impressions made by stamps are preserved in three zones. The lower and largest zone consists of irregularly placed lozenge and oblong shapes. At the upper part of the lower zone is a row of circles. In the middle zone a single racket shape with incised vertical lines appears. One small circle is visible at the lower edge of the upper zone.

16. Inv. No. C-74-457. Lot 1314. Pl. 152.

M.P.Dim. 0.078. Fragment from wall. Pink (7.5YR 7/4) sandy clay with peeling self-slip. On interior, stamped decoration includes three palmettes; below, part of a lotus and an eight-petalled rosette circumscribed by a circle.

17. Inv. No. C-78-3. Lot 2111. Pl. 152.

M.P.Dim. 0.052. Est. D. base 0.055. One base fragment. Micaceous yellowish red (5YR 5/6) fabric. Incised petals on wall; remains of three petals of medallion.

18. Inv. No. C-78-189. Lot 2335. Pl. 152.

P.H. 0.028. Th. 0.007. One fragment of rim and wall. Micaceous reddish yellow (5YR 7/6) fabric. Unslipped. Rim with slight carination. One bit of floral pattern preserved.

3

THE HELLENISTIC AND ROMAN POTTERY

•

Note: Entries in the catalogue are numbered sequentially from 1, and the numbers are in boldface type. For ease of identification, all references in the text to these entries retain the boldface numbers. Catalogue numbers for the entries in Chapter 2 are in plain face.

Early Hellenistic Wheelmade Gray Ware (**1–19**)

The tradition of a gray wheelmade pottery can be traced back a long way—in fact, to the Minyan Ware of the Middle Bronze Age Aegean.[1] Gray pottery and bucchero are also found on Lesbos, in northwestern Asia Minor, and western Phrygia from the Early Bronze Age down through the early Roman period.[2] Excavations further to the west on the Black Sea, at Histria,[3] in Thrace,[4] and nearby Thasos,[5] and in Macedonia[6] show that gray wares appear sporadically in the Bronze Age, were popular in the Iron Age, and continued to be so down through the Hellenistic period. In Macedonia and Thrace, gray pottery reappears again during the Late Roman period.[7] Colonies from Asia Minor in the west, at Massalia, Ampurias, and Megara Hyblaea show significant quantities of this reduced wheelmade pottery from the period of their founding through the Roman period.[8] In fact, in this area, as in Macedonia, gray pottery was very popular in the Late Roman period.[9]

There is no particular series of shapes exclusive to the technique producing gray wares throughout its history. Rather, the technique is applied to those shapes popular at the time,[10] especially those of metal vessels, since gray wares may

[1] Gray pottery occurs even in the late Neolithic period in Greece; see R. E. Jones, *Greek and Cypriot Pottery* (Athens 1985) 373, 375. The origins of Minyan Ware are still being sought. Recent studies include: J. B. Rutter, "Fine Gray-burnished Pottery of the Early Helladic II Period: The Ancestry of Gray Minyan," *Hesperia* 52 (1983) 327–353; and O.T.P.K. Dickinson, *The Origins of Mycenaean Civilization. SIMA* 49 (Göteborg 1977), and Jones (*Greek and Cypriot Pottery*, above), 414–420.

[2] Aeolic Gray wares: Lamb, "Lesbos," 1–12; *Pergamon 2*, 13, 14, 29.

[3] Histria: Coja, 305–329.

[4] D. Tsontchev, "Sivata Trakiiska Keramika v Bulgaria," *Godišnik na Narodni Arheološki Musej, Plovdiv* 3 (1959) 93–135.

[5] L. Ghali-Kahil, *Céramique grecque. Etudes Thasiennes* 7 (Paris 1960) 45.

[6] Iron Age: W. A. Heurtley, *Prehistoric Macedonia* (Cambridge 1939) 106–107. Iron Age and later, Mikulčić, *Pelagonia*, 29, 30, 53, and note 15 below.

[7] See below, notes 94, 99, 104–107.

[8] See Coja, 325, and notes 21, 22, 23; Moevs, "Cosa," 211–212, 217. For the earlier tradition see A. Nickels, "Contribution à l'etude de la céramique grise archaique en languedoc-roussillon," *Les céramique de la Grèce de l'est et leur diffusion en Occident. Colloque international. Centre Jean Bérard. 6–9 juillet, 1976. Institut français de Naples*, 248–267; Rigoir (1960) 9. Mocsy, *Pannonia*, 27, discusses the connections between northwest Asia Minor and the Dardanians.

[9] Hayes, *LRP*, 402–404, 405.

[10] See Waage's sensible comments in *Antioch*, 59, 60.

have begun as an imitation of silver.[11] The polished or burnished surface, often covered with a lustrous micaceous slip, enhanced this effect.

In central Macedonia, that is, the Vardar (ancient Axius) valley and the Lankadas basin, wheelmade gray ware is found in levels as early as the early Iron Age (7th century B.C.). The principal forms are bowls with incised decoration on the rim and one-handled kantharoi.[12]

By the late Archaic and Classical periods (5th–4th centuries B.C.) there is a greater variety of forms that are imitations and adaptions of contemporary Greek shapes.[13] It is likely that firing vessels of Greek form in a reducing atmosphere was a method of producing a local substitute for expensive imported wares.[14]

Gray ware is found in varying quantities together with handmade wares and wares of Greek origin throughout Pelagonia, Paeonia, and among the Dardani as far north as Skopje, Kumanovo, and Vranje.[15] In Paeonia and Dardania the wheelmade gray ware is by far the most popular type of pottery from the Late Archaic through the Early Hellenistic periods.[16] In the earliest levels excavated by the Stobi Project, the pottery is similarly divided into handmade wares, wheelmade gray wares, and Greek imports.

The forms of the two regional wares suggest that the gray ware functions as a tableware and that handmade vessels are used for kitchen and household purposes.

At Stobi the ware varies in color from the light to dark grays (10YR 7/1–4/1), and some pieces are more grayish brown or brown. The surface is sometimes quite smooth with a metallic luster. The walls tend to be rather thick and the bases heavy, with one side higher than the other, hallmarks of vessels made by someone who is just learning to use the potter's wheel (See **13**). Most examples appear not to have been hard fired. Petrographic analysis of thin sections shows a composition of illitic clay (not well fired or fused) with diverse rock fragments, mostly metamorphic, other white and brown micas, and large quartz grains and composite quartz and quartzite.

Very similar to the gray ware at Stobi is a group of unpublished pieces from excavations at Nerezi and Studeničani near Skopje.[17] A selection of similar typical forms from Negotino has recently been published.[18] The closest dated parallel, however, for an assemblage of the kind at Stobi is to be found at Kale-Krševice near Vranje, a fortified Dardanian settlement dated to the late 4th, early 3rd centuries B.C. (on the basis of a coin of Cassander and Greek imports).[19] One bowl from Stobi (**11**) is similar in form to several bowls from Illyrian archaic graves dated to the 6th and 5th centuries B.C. near Štip.[20] Parallels with common forms of Hellenistic skyphoi and bowls suggest a date in the last half of the 4th and very early 3rd centuries B.C., although some of the material may be later.

The bulk of this gray pottery at Stobi comes from two very small areas below the Central Basilica, in the north and south aisles, respectively, and is associated with no architectural or cultural features of any kind. A few pieces were found in the fill of the 2nd-century B.C. graves in the Peristeria Court area and others from the 1st-century B.C. fill dumped over those graves.

Bowls, drinking cups, jars, and pitchers or large vessels for carrying water or wine (hydria) are the usual forms to be found both at Stobi and at Krševice. At Stobi, the most popular forms are

[11] Heurtley, *Prehistoric Macedonia*, 106–107.

[12] Ibid., and p. 232, nos. 468, 469, 471, and p. 235, no. 484.

[13] Mikulčić, *Pelagonia*, 53.

[14] Coja, 328, in reference to Histria. Wadsworth (1983) summarizes the process for bucchero.

[15] For Skopje, Nerezi, and Studeničani, see I. Mikulčić, "Das Vorgeschichtliche Stratum auf der Burg Kale in Skopje und Problem der Eisenzeit in Süddardanien," *Actes du VIII Congrès International des Sciences Préhistoriques et Protohistoriques vol. 2 (Belgrade, 1971); vol. 3 (Belgrade 1973)* 182, 184. Pelagonia: Mikulčić, *Pelagonia*, 29, 53; Paeonia (and Kumanovo): see Mikulčić, *Pelagonia*, 29, and by the same author, *Štip*, 197–209; Mikulčić and Jovanović, *Vranje*, 367–375, dated to the second half of the 4th century B.C. A more recent summary appears in Sokolovska (1986) 49, 80, 155, and Pl. 11.

[16] Mikulčić and Jovanović, *Vranje*, 371.

[17] This material is stored in the museum of the city of Skopje and comes from excavations carried out by the museum in 1953. I was able to look at this material thoroughly during a visit in April of 1975. For comments on the material, see Mikulčić, "Das vorgeschichtliche Stratum" (cited in note 15, above). Also see Sokolovska (1986) 35, 36.

[18] Sokolovska (1986) 46, 47.

[19] Mikulčić and Jovanović, *Vranje*, 363.

[20] Mikulčić, *Štip*, 206. E. Petrova, who has just completed a book on the Paeonians (forthcoming, Museum of Macedonia, Skopje), suggests (personal communication, November 1989) that Krševice was a Paeonian rather than a Dardanian stronghold.

the incurved rim bowl and the skyphos (Fig. 3.1). The only bowl with a complete profile preserved has a concave disk base. This base type was found exclusively among base fragments, and it is also the form common on incurved bowls at Krševice.

The rim profiles of these bowls vary considerably, and it is difficult to know (without other evidence for date) whether the variations are contemporary or a chronological indicator.[21]

Form 1. Kantharos

Kantharos shape with high-slung handles. Handles follow outward flare of the rim and return at point of widest diameter where the wall is curved (**1** and **2**) or sharply carinated. Slightly concave or flat disc base seems likely as seen in an example from Vranje (Mikulčić and Jovanović, *Vranje*, no. 382). All Stobi examples decorated with one or more grooves on the exterior at points of greatest diameter, the least diameter, or both. Estimated rim diameters range from 0.080 to 0.143.

Of the six examples of the kantharos at Stobi, two are from Lot 842, and four from Lot 843. Total: 6.

1. Lot 842, No. 7. Pl. 4.

P.H. 0.035. Est. D. rim 0.100. One fragment preserving rim, wall, and one handle. Very curvilinear profile with three grooves at point of greatest diameter. Broad, flattened strap handle. Hard fired, and both surfaces have a metallic luster, a result of the large amount of silver mica in the clay.

Cf. Mikulčić and Jovanović, *Vranje*, pl. 12, J.4-85.

2. Lot 843, No. 29. Pl. 4.

P.H. 0.042. Est. D. rim 0.140. One fragment preserving rim and part of wall. A taller rim and very round body with no handles remaining. Two widely spaced grooves at point of greatest curvature. Slight metallic luster on both surfaces.

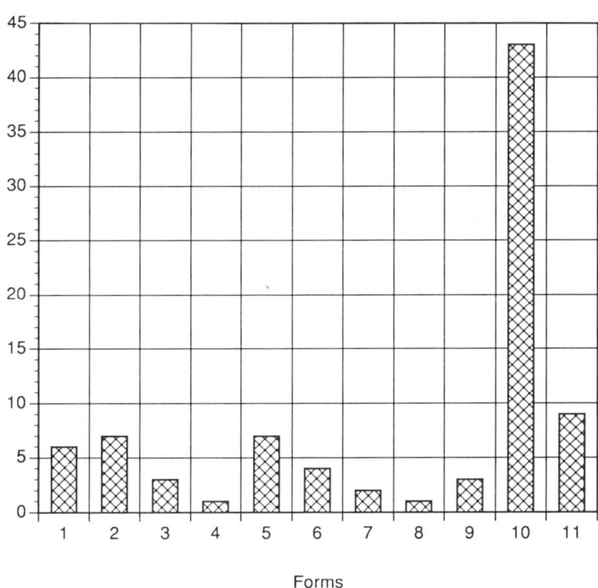

Figure 3.1. Hellenistic Gray Ware. Bar graph illustrating quantity of the various forms at Stobi

Form 1: Kantharos
Form 2: Skyphos
Form 3: Hydria
Forms 4, 5: Jars
Forms 6–9: Bowls
Form 10: Incurved rim Bowl
Form 11: Lid

[21] For example, note the variation on Pl. 2 of Edwards, *Corinth*. See also Taylor, "Cosa," with extensive bibliography on the incurved bowl, 85.

Form 2. Skyphos

No complete examples of the skyphos present at Stobi. All fragments have similar simple everted rim with beginning of rounded wall beneath. Handle placed at a slightly upward angle and flares outward in horseshoe shape. Diameters of all examples in a similar range. Of the seven examples of this shape, two are from Lot 842, and five from Lot 843. Total: 7.

3. Lot 842, No. 17. Pl. 4.

P.H. 0.036. Est. D. rim 0.110. One fragment preserving rim, wall, and one handle. Dull surfaces with some peeling of the self-slip at rim and on handle.

Cf. Edwards, *Corinth*, no. 341, dated 350 B.C.; no. 363, dated 325 B.C.; and no. 320, dated 300 B.C. Also see examples in Mikulčić and Jovanović, *Vranje*, pl. 12, but none is quite like this piece.

Form 3. Hydria

Only three rims, all rather different are probably from hydria. Nothing below neck has been preserved. Total: 3.

4. Lot 842, No. 8. Pl. 4.

P.H. 0.036. Est. D. rim 0.190. One fragment of rim and neck of hydria(?). Wide, flat rim with three grooves on upper surface.

Cf. Mikulčić and Jovanović, *Vranje*, pl. 17, J.4-95 and J.2-26.

5. Lot 843, No. 41. Pl. 4.

P.H. 0.035. Est. D. rim 0.170. Two fragments of rim and neck. Flaring rim slightly undercut. Single groove on neck. Smooth surfaces with slight metallic luster.

6. Lot 552, No. 527. Pl. 4.

P.H. 0.025. Est. D. rim 0.220. One fragment of rim and neck. Overhanging rim with sharp ridge at interior and single groove at exterior.

Cf. Mikulčić and Jovanović, *Vranje*, pls. 14, 17, J.4-112.

Form 4. Jar

Small jar with everted rim, straight wall. No bases remain. Only one example.

7. Lot 842, No. 9. Pl. 4.

P.H. 0.035. Est. D. rim 0.096. One fragment preserving single groove on wall. Very smooth surfaces with metallic luster.

Form 5. Jar

Wide-mouthed jar with flat, often grooved rim. No bases preserved. Estimated rim diameters range from 0.130 to 0.180. Four examples from Lot 843, three from Lot 842. Total: 7.

8. Lot 842, No. 11. Pl. 4.

P.H. 0.024. Est. D. rim 0.152. One rim fragment. Single groove on upper surface. Smooth surfaces without luster.

Cf. Mikulčić and Jovanović, *Vranje*, pl. 16, J.4-95.

Form 6. Bowl

Bowl with incurving wall and flat rim, often with grooves. Diameters range from 0.114 to 0.170. Concave or disc base probable. Two examples from Lot 843, one from Lot 842, and one from Lot 1532. Total: 4.

9. Lot 843, No. 46. Pl. 5.

P.H. 0.032. Est. D. rim 0.114. One fragment preserving rim and wall. Concave rim surface.

Cf. Mikulčić and Jovanović, *Vranje*, pl. 13, J.4-124.

Form 7. Bowl

Small bowl with rolled rim on incurved wall. No base preserved. Total: 2. Both examples are from the same Lot (843).

10. Lot 843, No. 35. Pl. 5.

P.H. 0.044. Est. D. rim 0.140. Single fragment of rim and wall. Sharp ridge along upper surface of rim.

Form 8. Bowl

Large bowl with incurved wall and deeply grooved rim. No base preserved. Only one example.

11. Lot 555, No. 26. Pl. 5.

P.H. 0.054. Est. D. rim 0.230. One fragment of rim and wall. Hard-fired, smooth surface without luster.

Cf. Mikulčić, *Štip*, p. 206, Pl. 33.

Form 9. Bowl

Bowl or dish with inturned rim. Only small rim fragments preserved. Estimated diameter ranges from approximately 0.140 to 0.220. Two fragments from Lot 843 and one from Lot 842. Total: 3.

12. Lot 843. No. 42. Pl. 5.

P.H. 0.020. Est. D. rim 0.110. One small rim fragment with slight overhang.

Form 10. Incurved Rim Bowl

Small to medium-sized bowls with a variety of incurved rim profiles, some very incurved, others almost vertical. Because almost all examples come from the same two deposits, it is impossible to assign any chronological significance to the profile changes. The one complete example has a concave disc base, and from the approximately twenty-five base fragments of this type found in the same deposit, we can suggest that the concave disc base was probably common to this rim. Diameters range from approximately 0.110 to 0.200m. Some examples have widely spaced grooves as decoration on the exterior. Dates for this shape at other sites range from the fifth to the first centuries B.C. Examples came from the following Lots: Lot 12: 1, Lot 22: 1, Lot 29: 1, Lot 88: 1, Lot 260: 1, Lot 545: 1, Lot 552: 2, Lot 563: 2, Lot 687: 2, Lot 689: 1, Lot 842: 7, Lot 843: 23. Total: 43.

13. Inv. No. C-70-126. Lot 842. Pls. 5, 152.
H. 0.054. Est. D. rim 0.105. D. base 0.055. Complete profile with base completely preserved but only a rather small portion of the rim. Shallow wheel-ridging visible on exterior. Both surfaces without luster. The vessel was not centered well during manufacture as the base circle bulges out slightly to one side and the carination on the base varies somewhat in height.

14. Lot 843, No. 38. Pl. 5.
P.H. 0.040. Est. D. rim 0.120. One fragment preserving rim and wall. Smooth surface but without luster and not completely fired as a darker core is visible.
Cf. Mikulčić and Jovanović, *Vranje*, pl. 11, B416; Edwards, *Corinth*, pls. 2, 26 (C-71-14) dated ca. 300 B.C.

15. Lot 563, No. 1. Pl. 5.
P.H. 0.033. Est. D. rim 0.140. One fragment with rim and wall. Two grooves at lip. Slight metallic luster on both surfaces. Cf. Coja, fig. 1:1, dated to the fifth century B.C.

16. Lot 552, No. 533. Pl. 6.
P.H. 0.033. Est. D. rim 0.140. One rim fragment. Two grooves where wall turns inward, lip slightly concave.

Form 11. Lid(?)

Small lid with flat knob and double convex profile. Most examples are not fired well and display a pinkish core. Diameter of most small fragmentary examples is approximately 0.120m. All but one example are from Lot 843. The exception is from Lot 842. Total: 9.

17. Lot 843, No. 68. Pl. 6.
P.H. 0.020. Est. D. rim 0.120. One fragment preserves complete profile. Smooth surface with metallic luster. Pink core.

Bases

18. Lot 843, No. 61. Pl. 6.
P.H. 0.045. Est. D. base 0.100. Large disc base with part of wall from hydria or other large vessel.

19. Inv. No. C-70-110. Lot 842. Pls. 6, 152.
P.H. 0.015. Est. D. 0.055. One fragment from small disc base with bucranion in relief centered on the underside of the half of the base section that has been preserved.

Black-Gloss Wares (20–54)

Very little black-gloss pottery was recovered in the excavations of the Stobi Project. The small amount is perhaps to be expected, in view of the small number of deposits dating to the 2nd century B.C. The greater part of the sample consists primarily of rims and bases. Furthermore it is impossible to assign these small pieces to any specific source. It should be mentioned, however, that a number of examples of black-gloss wares were apparently recovered in earlier excavations at Stobi, including a pyxis decorated in the West Slope technique.[22]

Aside from a single example of an Athenian Red Figure skyphos (**53**), only small scraps of Attic black-gloss have been identified at Stobi.[23]

Several examples of the Italian black-gloss

[22] Sokolovska, *Studies II*, 135.

[23] For a valuable overview of black-gloss wares, see J. W. Hayes, *Greek and Italian Black-Gloss Wares and Related Wares in the Royal Ontario Museum* (Toronto 1984).

wares, Campanian A or B, however, did find their way to Stobi.[24] The numbers are not large, however, and may represent personal possessions rather than established trade. The very thin-walled, broad-footed bowl (**20**) was found broken above the grave (Grave 313) of an adult male together with other sherds, including thin-walled and cooking wares also of probable Italian origin, as well as a lamp (L-75-1) of late 2nd-century B.C. type.[25]

Examples related to Campanian A and B

20. Broad-footed bowl. Inv. No. C-75-44. Lot 1636. Pl. 7.

H. 0.060. D. rim 0.160. Partially complete. The walls are very thin (.003), and the fabric fine and light red in color (2.5YR 6/8). Very metallic black gloss. Hemispherical bowl with broad foot and curved wall. Two grooves on exterior below rim. Dipping line for the gloss is visible at the midpoint of the vessel body.

Whereas the fabric seems to be related to Campanian A, the form is that of Lamboglia's Campanian B, Form 1, now classified by Morel in série 2323 (Morel, *Les Formes*, 164, pls. 47, 48). But the Stobi piece is extremely thin walled, the lip tapers inward, and the foot is almost vertical rather than flaring, features also not seen on the examples in Taylor's "bowl with broad foot and curved rim" (Taylor, "Cosa," Type II, 159, 160, Type IV, 182, 183). An example in Morel, *Palatin* (pl. 14:167) has a lip similar to ours. At Cosa the form was imported in the mid-2nd century B.C. and was popular during the second half of the 2nd century and early 1st century B.C. The examples cited in Morel's typology range in date from 120 to 50 B.C. The grave in which this vessel was found contained a Macedonian bronze coin of the late 2nd century B.C. (coin 75-10).

21. Broad-footed bowl. Inv. No. C-70-122. Lot 829. Pl. 7.

H. 0.058. D. rim 0.160. Partially complete. Fine, pink (7.5YR 7/4) fabric with smooth, matte, black gloss, fired brown in places on the exterior. Underside of foot reserved. Almost vertical walls and two deep grooves on exterior just below rim.

This piece is much closer to a true Lamboglia Campanian B, Form 1, in fabric and form, than the previous example, and to Taylor's Type II, "bowl with broad foot and curved wall." Taylor's Type II also has the underside of the foot reserved (Taylor, "Cosa," 71).

From the same group of deposits (Table 4.3), dated to the first half of the 1st century B.C., as the one in which this piece was found are two local imitations of this form, both with a wide band of rouletting on the floor and covered with a red, not black slip. See **743**.

Bowls of similar form occur at Florina (Keramopoullos, [1932] 61, fig. 10:1, 2, 3).

The influence of Campanian forms seems to have reached as far as Argos; see Bruneau, "Tombes d'Argos," figs. 101, 102, dated to the late 2nd, early 1st century B.C.

22. Ribbon-band bowl. Inv. No. C-71-286. Lot 252. Pl. 7.

H. 0.080. D. rim 0.176. Partially complete. Micaceous, medium-fine clay varies from light brown to pink (7.5YR 6/4–7/4). Exterior gloss varies from gray to brown (7.5YR N5/–5/2) and is metallic in spots as well as mottled so that the surface color changes slightly around the base. The resting surface of the ring is not slipped, nor is the underside except for a circular area in the center. Interior gloss is a very dark gray (N3/), extremely metallic, and worn on the floor.

The form is much like a black-gloss bowl from Sutri in Duncan, "Sutri," 141, 144, fig. 3, form 7. Morel has included it in his typology under 2534 (Morel, 179). The fabric described for the Sutri bowl is also similar, while the description for the surface quality and gloss match the Stobi bowl almost exactly. The material from Sutri dates to a period extending from the last half of the 2nd century B.C. and into the early 1st century B.C. Cf. also a bowl at Sovana in Orlanda Pancrazzi,

[24] The bibliography for Campanian wares is large. The preliminary classification was by N. Lamboglia, "Per una classificazione preliminare della ceramica campana," *Atti del Congresso Internazionale di Studi Liguri, I 1950* (Bordighera 1952). The most recent classification is by J. P. Morel, *Céramique campanienne. Les Formes* (Rome 1981). Other important earlier studies include Taylor, "Cosa" and Pasquinucci (1972). For a recent summary of the problems associated with black-gloss wares in the Mediterranean, see Kenrick, *Berenice 3*, 9–11, 31, 37, 39, 43.

[25] W-MZ (1976) 282.

"Sovana, localita Costone della Folonia," *NSc* 25 (1971) 148, 149, fig. 85, SF1/70, dated to the second half of the 2nd century B.C. For a local variant see **778**, **779**.

Date at Stobi: second half of 2nd century B.C.

23. Olpe. Inv. No. C-71-132. Lot 74. Pls. 7, 153.

H. 0.094. D. 0.050. Complete. Fine, pink (5YR 7/4) fabric with slightly metallic dark reddish brown gloss, worn away on body. Small, graceful pitcher or olpe with ovoid body on high ring base. One double handle extends from just above the body midpoint to the lip where there are two small petallike projections of clay, perhaps reflecting the influence of metalware. Just below the handle attachment two shallow grooves encircle the body.

The form is similar to a black-gloss olpe at Volterra, Pasquinucci (1972) 470, Form 1152, fig. 15, especially 477, although the piece from Stobi is much smaller and has a higher base. The brown coloring of the gloss is probably a result of the firing. The Volterra form, not common in Etruria nor commonly exported outside Volterra, is dated to the 3rd and 2nd centuries B.C. (470). Morel shows a similar form in his série 5212, 5213 (*Les Formes*, 339, 340, pl. 155) dated to the 4th and 3rd centuries B.C. The form is a common one in Hellenistic metal vases; for example, at Volterra, see Enrico Fiumi, "Gli scavi degli anni 1960–1965 nell'area della necropoli di Badia," *NSc* 26 (1972) 94, fig. 50.

This vase, together with **1125**, contained a hoard of Late Republican coins ranging in date from 211 to 125 B.C. It was deposited not long after 125, since the latest coins show little sign of wear. See W-MZ (1972) 410, 411; and Crawford, "Stobi Hoard," 7.

24. Olpe. Inv. No. C-71-78. Lot 132. Pl. 7.

P.H. 0.074. D. rim 0.060. Upper body and handle. Base not preserved. Fine, reddish yellow (5YR 6/6) fabric and black gloss with slight metallic luster with worn surfaces. Plump body with slight carination at point of greatest diameter. Single strap handle extends from shoulder to lip.

Cf. Form 58, no. 323 at Volterra, Pasquinucci (1972) 345, dated to the 3rd and 2nd centuries B.C. Also see Morel, *Les Formes*, espèce 5240 (346, pl. 160) dated to the 2nd centuries B.C. The Stobi example comes from a deposit of the first half of the 1st centuries B.C.

Other Black-Gloss wares

25. Large plate with wide rim. Lot 829, No. 10. Pl. 7.

P.H. 0.014. Est. D. rim 0.338. One rim fragment. Reddish yellow (5YR 6/6) clay with worn and dull black gloss.

This form is similar to the Campanian bowls with horizontal offset rim seen in Taylor, "Cosa," 154, Type II, and 174, Type IV, and Morel, *Les Formes*, série 1443 (114, 115, pl. 17) dated mid- to late second century B.C. The rim, however, on this example is not really offset or angular but rather more curved and may belong to those of 1st-century date (Taylor, "Cosa," 154). The form could also be Attic as well (Thompson, "TCHP," D1, E22).

26. Fish plate. Lot 547, No. 104. Pl. 8.

P.H. 0.040. Est. D. rim 0.240. Small rim fragment. Reddish yellow (5YR 6/6) clay with black gloss in interior; exterior unslipped.

27. Fish plate base. Inv. No. C-72-203. Lot 547. Pl. 8.

P.H. 0.018. Est. D. 0.070. Single base fragment. Reddish yellow (5YR 7/6) clay. Exterior unslipped with some gloss drippings from interior which has a mottled black to light brown (7.5YR 6/4) metallic gloss. The central depression and the surrounding groove are fired bright red.

28. Fish plate base. Inv. No. C-71-340. Lot 252. Pl. 8.

P.H. 0.028. Est. D. 0.068. One base fragment. Light red (2.5YR 6/6) clay with very metallic, mottled light reddish brown to black gloss on interior. Plain exterior, well smoothed.

29. Fish-plate base. Inv. No. C-72-202. Lot 564. Pl. 8.

P.H. 0.020. Est. D. 068. One base fragment. Shallow central depression. Light brownish gray (2.5YR 6/2) clay with plain exterior and black gloss on interior.

30. Large bowl. Lot 1085, No. 7. Pl. 8.

P.H. 0.026. Est. D. rim 0.300. Offset, flaring rim. Micaceous, light red (2.5YR 6/8) clay covered with black gloss, noticeably metallic on the interior.

31. Plate with upturned rim. Lot 14, No. 2. Pl. 8.

P.H. 0.021. Est. D. rim 0.260. Rim fragment.

Fine, light red (2.5YR 6/8–5/8) clay and metallic black gloss.

This form is related to Lamboglia's Campanian A, Form 5 (167, 168), with examples from the 2nd and 1st centuries B.C., Morel, *Les Formes*, série 2250. See also Taylor, "Cosa." "Plate with upturned rim," Type II, 156, 157, where it is common in the last quarter of the 2nd century B.C. and continues in use during the 1st c. B.C. See now the comments of Kenrick, *Berenice 3*, 117–20.

One other example of this form occurs in Lot 12.

32. Plate with upturned rim. Inv. No. C-74-4. Lot 1094. Pl. 8.

H. 0.042. D. rim 0.185. Complete. Black slip with red circle on floor center probably caused by stacking during firing. In the center of the floor are three stamped hearts joined by a single concentric circle. This plate was found with a small bowl, C-74-5 (**34**); a Thin-Walled beaker, C-74-13 (**147**); a small cooking pot, C-74-6 (**1124**); and three fusiform unguentaria, C-74-19, C-74-20 (**566**), and C-74-21.

33. Plate with upturned rim. Inv. No. C-72-66. Lot 545. Pl. 8.

P.H. 0.018. Est. D. rim 0.570. One rim fragment. Fine, pink (7.5YR 7/4) clay. Hard, very lustrous black gloss on both surfaces. Very similar in form to the preceding, but smaller and with sharper lip and no hint of angularity at the point where the side wall curves upward.

Similar form in Morel, *Palatin*, pls. I, 1 and 12, 131. The form is also similar to the popular Samaria Form 1 in Eastern Sigillata A (*Samaria*, fig. 73).

34. Small bowl with flaring wall. Inv. No. C-74-5. Lot 1094. Pls. 8, 153.

H. 0.044. D. rim 0.098. Mended and complete except for one small fragment from rim. Two grooves at mid body. Metallic slip variably fired red and black. Forms a set with C-74-4 (**32**) of the same fabric and surface treatment.

Lamboglia Form 2, Morel, *Les Formes*, espèce 1220, 1230 (93–96, pls. 7, 8), dated primarily late 2nd to mid-1st centuries B.C.

35. Bowl with upturned rim. Lot 687, No. 2. Pl. 9.

P.H. 0.022. Est. D. rim 0.140. One rim piece. Fine, light red (2.5YR 5/6–5/8) clay with exterior covered by black metallic gloss to mid-body. Below this point the surface is a dripped and mottled yellowish red (5YR 5/6) to metallic black. The interior is entirely covered with a metallic black gloss.

36. Small bowl. Lot 547, No. 58. Pl. 9.

P.H. 0.030. Est. D. rim 0.128. One fragment of bowl with flaring, outward-thickened rim. Fine micaceous, light red (2.5YR 6/6) clay with a black metallic gloss which is peeling away on both surfaces.

This form is similar to that of the small bowl, E-33 (late 2nd, early 1st centuries B.C.), pictured by Thompson, "TCHP," on p. 436, although our example has a groove under the exterior of the lip.

37. Incurved rim bowl. Inv. No. C-72-68. Lot 608. Pl. 9.

P.H. 0.040. Est. D. rim 0.287. Red (2.5YR 5/6) clay. The gloss on the interior and lower part of the exterior has been fired red while the upper part of the rim exterior was fired black. This is a result of stacking in the kiln where bowls were stacked not with the base touching the floor interior of the bowl below (as was the case with **39** below), but with the side walls touching so that only the upper exterior of the bowl was exposed to the reducing atmosphere and fired black.

For a discussion of the effects of stacking vessels in this way during the Hellenistic period, see Thompson, "TCHP," 430; *Antioch*, 10; *Samaria*, 249. Similar forms in Thompson, "TCHP," D9 (mid-2nd century B.C.), and *Samaria*, fig. 38 (mid- to late 2nd centuries B.C.).

38. Bowl with re-entrant rim. Inv. No. C-72-214. Lot 552. Pl. 9.

P.H. 0.020. Est. D. rim 0.150. Rim fragment. Fine, micaceous, reddish yellow (5YR 6/6) clay. The gloss on the exterior has been fired black at the rim and red on the body. The interior is unslipped. The variation in color on the exterior can be attributed to the practice of kiln stacking.

39. Plate-base ring. Inv. No. C-70-109. Lot 513. Pl. 9.

P.H. 0.027. D. 0.092. One fragment of base. Red (2.5YR 6/6) clay with metallic black gloss mottled red to reddish yellow (5YR) in spots and fired red in a circular area in center of floor. Underside of base is unslipped. The red area in the center was caused by stacking in the kiln. See above (**37**) for additional examples of this phenomenon.

40. Plate-base ring. Lot 263, No. 5. Pl. 9.
P.H. 0.022. D. 0.092. One base fragment. Medium fine, light red (2.5YR) micaceous clay with small white inclusions. A metallic black gloss covers the surface, with the exception of a small circle in center of the interior over the base ring that was fired red.

41. Plate-base ring. Lot 608, No. 21. Pl. 9.
P.H. 0.030. D. 0.092. Very high ring-base fragment. Light red (2.5YR) clay with black metallic gloss.

42. Plate-base ring. Inv. No. C-74-502. Lot 1442. Pl. 9.
P.H. 0.024. D. 0.076. One base fragment. Medium fine, soft and flaky, very micaceous clay, red (2.5YR) in color. Both interior and exterior are covered with a metallic blue-black gloss, except for an area left unslipped on the underside of the base. The gloss itself is peeling and very badly worn. Two shallow concentric grooves set off the plate interior within which are six stamped palmettes.

43. Plate-base ring. Inv. No. C-74-99. Lot 1538. Pls. 9, 153.
P.H. 0.030. D. 0.090. One fragment of tall base with moulded foot. Micaceous clay varies from reddish yellow (5YR 7/6) to light gray (5YR 6/1). Black gloss covers both surfaces, with the exception of part of the underside of the base. The floor is decorated with concentric rows of feather rouletting and stamped palmettes of which two are partly preserved.

44. Plate-base ring. Inv. No. C-70-111. Lot 842. Pls. 10, 153.
P.H. 0.022. D. 0.083. One fragment of base. Micaceous reddish yellow (5YR 7/6) clay. Semilustrous black gloss on both surfaces. The wide resting surface of the foot is unslipped but decorated with two concentric circles in black. The underside of the base is also reserved with a band of black near the foot and two small concentric circles in the center. On the floor are four palmettes or Isis crowns in relief. Each is surrounded by an oval frame and connected by a single circle that passes through the base of each.

The arrangement of the stamps so that all face outward is dated by Morel to the 3rd century B.C. ("Petites estampilles," fig. 3u, and for the stamp, cf. fig. 5, no. 22), a date which corresponds with the context of this piece.

45. Ring base. Inv. No. C-70-127. Lot 843. Pls. 10, 153.
P.H. 0.020. D. 0.062. One fragment of base. Micaceous and reddish yellow (5YR 7/6) clay similar to the example above, which comes from the same context. The black glossy slip is rather worn on both surfaces. Resting surface and underside of the foot are also unslipped. Three narrow black concentric circles spaced at equal intervals on underside. In center of floor are four unframed palmette stamps joined at their bases by a single circle. Same date as above.

46. Small ring base. Lot 610, No. 50. Pl. 10.
P.H. 016. D. 0.050. One fragment of base. Fine, hard-fired, micaceous reddish yellow (5YR 6/6) fabric with black metallic gloss.

47. Small base from closed vessel. Lot 687, No. 1. Pl. 10.
P.H. 0.018. D. 0.045. One fragment of concave disk base. Clay is reddish yellow (5YR 7/6) and exterior gloss is metallic black mottled with a mixture of reddish yellow and light red (2.5YR 6/6). Interior is unslipped. Both inside and underside carry incised circles.

48. Lekythos base. Lot 552, No. 196. Pl. 10.
P.H. 0.026. D. 0.092. One fragment of base. Light reddish brown (5YR 6/4) to reddish yellow clay. Metallic black gloss on interior and exterior.

49. Skyphos handle. Lot 843, No. 86. Pl. 10.
Max.P.Dim. 0.070. One horizontal strap handle. Reddish yellow (5YR 6/6) clay with small white inclusions. A black gloss with dull to metallic luster covers all surfaces.

Miscellaneous Black-Gloss with decoration

Corinthian(?)

50. Pyxis fragment. Inv. No. C-71-178. Lot 24. Pl. 153.
P.H. 0.031. One side wall fragment. Fine, light brown (7.5YR 6/4) clay with black gloss in several horizontal stripes.

51. Small bottle base. Inv. No. C-71-179. Lot 152. Pl. 153.

P.H. 0.050. D. base 0.015. One half of base and lower body of vessel. Very pale brown (10YR 7/4) clay with vertical stripes of black-brown gloss.

Others

52. Black-figure fragment. Inv. No. C-74-87. Lot 1090. Pl. 154.

M.P.Dim. 0.043. One small fragment of wall. Reddish yellow (5YR 6/6) clay with light red (2.5YR 6/8) surface and decoration in a very dark gray metallic (N3/) gloss on interior and exterior. The design consists of horizontal lines and part of a leaf pattern.

53. Red-figure skyphos. Inv. No. C-78-158. Lot 2302. Pls. 10, 154.

P.H. 0.134. Est. D. rim 0.194. Mended portion of rim and wall. Light red (2.5YR 6/8) fabric with black gloss on interior and exterior surfaces. Slightly inward-thickened rim on curving side wall. Traces of circular application of gloss at one point just below rim probably indicate the position of one handle. Partly preserved in red figure is the torso of a nude youth with head in profile and arm raised behind his head. The hair is indicated by solid black, while the facial features and body contours are represented by black relief lines. To the right of the figure are a series of foliage motifs and a large palmette. Wiseman (1978) 412.

The outward-turned lip is typical for later Attic Type A skyphoi. The date should be around 400 B.C., just at the time the lip starts to turn out but slightly before the body contracts below it; 400–390 B.C. at the latest (personal communication from John Oakely, 1/89). See B. A. Sparkes and L. Talcott, *Agora* 12. *Black and Plain Pottery of the 6th, 5th, and 4th Centuries* (Princeton 1970) 84, 85. Oakely dates the use of the single palmette to the beginning of the 4th century or later in a recent article, "Attic Red-figured Skyphoi of Corinthian Shape," *Hesperia* 57 (1988) 171, no. 71.

54. West Slope fragment. Inv. No. C-74-206. Lot 1301. Pl. 154.

P.H. 0.033. One rim fragment. Fine, pink (7.5YR 7/4) clay with dull black gloss on both surfaces. Preserves design of vines or ivy leaves applied in clay relief with incised tendrils.

Lagynoi (55, 56)

The lagynos, a pitcher with a long narrow neck and low carinated body with one handle, was a popular vessel for pouring wine during the Hellenistic period.[26] This vessel begins to appear in the 3rd century B.C., is most frequently found in contexts of the 2nd century, and continued to be used through the 1st century B.C. The surface of this type is covered with a thick, white, glossy, sometimes metallic slip, and the shoulder carination is emphasized with orange stripes painted on either side. Centers of manufacture seem to have been located at a number of Mediterranean sites, including North Africa, Cyprus, and Asia Minor.

At Stobi only two small fragments of lagynoi have been found, both with shoulder carination. Each is slightly different from the other in profile and painted decoration.

The first example comes from a later context, but the second comes from a deposit dated to the first half of the 1st century B.C.

55. Inv. No. C-71-5. Lot 373. Pl. 6.

M.P.Dim. 0.064. Th. 0.005. One fragment with ridged shoulder carination and part of body. Fine, hard, micaceous clay, reddish yellow (5YR 7/6–5/6) in color. Interior is plain. Exterior covered with a thick, weathered gloss and shoulder outlined with three reddish orange parallel lines.

56. Inv. No. C-72-25. Lot 608. Pl. 6.

M.P.Dim. 0.041. Th. 0.005. One fragment preserving shoulder carination and part of body. Fine clay and slip as above.

[26] For discussion and bibliography, see G. Leroux, *Lagynos* (Paris 1913); *Labraunda*, 17–19; *Pergamon* 2, 101–103; Thompson, "TCHP," 450–451, and most recently R. Pierobon, "Lagynos: funzione e forma," *RStLig* 45 (1979) 27–50.

Black-Gloss Wares with Gray Fabric (57–105)

Various black-gloss wares with gray fabric were very popular at Stobi during the 1st century B.C. This probably reflects a continuation of the earlier preference for gray wares in this area. There seem to be several traditions represented in the gray wares found at Stobi in this period, among them the Campanian of Italy, an East Greek or Asia Minor ware, and perhaps even the *terra nigra* of European tradition.

As explained above, gray wares have a long tradition in Macedonia and Asia Minor as well as in many areas of Europe.[27]

On the Italian peninsula, Etruscan bucchero and the later Campanian C of the Roman Republican period provide several examples of black-gloss wares that were products of an exclusively reducing atmosphere. These wares are unlike the Greek black glaze with red, pink, or buff clay body, the result of an elaborate reoxidizing process.[28]

Campanian C, characterized by light gray fabric and gloss of black, gray-black, or even olive, appears about the middle of the 2nd century B.C. and continued to be produced into the Augustan period, when the red-gloss wares became popular.[29] Much Campanian C has been found in Sicily as well as in southern Italy, where at Pizzica, near Metapontum, great quantities of gray ware were found.[30]

A series of large platters in a soft, grayish brown, micaceous fabric with a glossy surface of soapy quality not unlike Eastern Sigillata B have been found on a number of sites in the eastern Mediterranean. They occur in contexts of the 1st centuries B.C. and A.C. and are especially common in Asia Minor. Material has been published from Pergamon, Çandarli, Samos, and Lesbos that suggests an origin in southwest Asia Minor.[31]

Gray wares are also found in Europe and are the product of a complex combination of influences from La Tène and earlier gray pottery traditions together with the forms and gloss of late Campanian wares and terra sigillata.[32] These wares, sometimes called *terra nigra*, are primarily a product of the Augustan period and the 1st century A.C.[33] Gray wares with the forms of terra sigillata are not uncommon in many parts of the Roman world.

The gray wares with black gloss from Stobi included in this study have been arranged approximately chronologically in groups according to the tradition to which each belongs: Campanian C, Asia Minor, or terra sigillata. Other pieces that cannot be assigned to any of these are grouped together at the end of the section in a fourth group.

Campanian C

57. Plate with upturned rim. Inv. No. C-72-169. Lot 547. Pl. 11.

P.H. 0.037. Est. D. rim 0.286. Mended from three fragments preserving almost complete profile. Lip not preserved. Very high ring base. Slightly micaceous light gray to gray (10YR 6/1–5/1) fabric with metallic slip varying from dark gray to black. Exterior near and at foot was not entirely covered with slip. In the center of the

[27] For example, when the Phocaeans of Asia Minor founded Massalia and Emporion, they brought with them the "bucchero" or the gray ware technique of Asia Minor (Lamb, "Lesbos," 1; Moevs, "Cosa," 211), which combined with the local Hallstatt tradition to form various categories of gray wares. For a discussion of the problems, see Moevs, "Cosa," 211–227, and *Antioch*, 59–60.

[28] Moevs, "Cosa," 212, and note 12, and J. V. Noble, *The Technique of Painted Attic Pottery* (New York 1965).

[29] Lamboglia, 156–163; Taylor, "Cosa," 71, 164–166; Kenrick, *Berenice* 3, 49. Many of the early Arretine forms are those of the earlier black-gloss wares.

[30] J. C. Carter, "Preliminary Report on the Excavations at Pizzica Pantanello (1974–1976)," *NSc* 31 (series 8) 1977 (Rome 1983) 489; and L. Giardino, "Sulla ceramica a pasta grigia di Metaponto e sulla presenza in essa di alcuni bolli inscritti. Studi preliminari," *Studi di Antichita* 1980, 247–287. Also see A. M. Fallico, "Siracusa, saggi di scavo nell'area della Villa Maria," *NSc* (1971) 581–639; and P. Pelagatti, "Akrai (Siracusa). Ricerche nel territorio," *NSc* (1970) 470–476.

[31] Pergamon: *Pergamon* 2, 65; Thompson, "TCHP," 471; Candarli, Loeschcke, "Tschandarli," 398, 399. Samos: Techau, *Heraion*, 48. Lesbos: Lamb, "Lesbos." Kenrick, *Berenice* 3, 52, 53, sees a connection with the Ionian/Delian bowls.

[32] Discussion of this with bibliography in Moevs, "Cosa," 211–227.

[33] See M. Schindler, "Die schwarze Sigillata des Magdalensberges," *Archäologische Forschungen zu den Grabungen auf dem Magdalensberg* (Klagenfurt 1967).

floor a wide band of rouletting surrounds two palmette stamps and part of a third. One groove connects the palmettes and a third frames a six-petalled rosette in the center.

This form is closest to Lamboglia's Forms 5 and 7 (pp. 146, 148, 158). Also see Taylor, "Cosa," p. 167, 168. Gray-ware plates of this form appear at Cosa in the late 2nd century B.C. and are found in deposits dating to the mid-lst century B.C. there. Also see, "La Ceramica Campana della necropoli di S. Bernardo di Ornavasso," *RStLig* 35 (1969), figs. 1, 2, 4; F. Benoit, "L'Epave du Grand Congloue à Marseille," *Gallia* Supplement XIV (1961) pl. 14; and "Magdalensberg," Abb. 9:4 from Period 2 dated Late Republican to 30 B.C.

58. Plate with upturned rim. Lot 549, No. 35. Pl. 11.

P.H. 0.028. Est. D. rim 0.323. One fragment preserving rim and floor. Brown (7.5YR 5/2–5/4) clay with dark grayish brown (10YR 4/2–3/2) metallic slip.

A similar, almost concave rim is apparent on a piece from Sovana, in Orlanda Pancrazzi, "Sovana, localita costone della Folonia," *NSc* 25 (1971) 154, fig. 88, SP2/65.

There are ten additional examples of the plate with upturned rim form as seen in **57** and **58**: Lot 549: 3, Lot 550: 1, Lot 552: 6.

59. Plate with upturned rim. Inv. No. C-72-29. Lot 549. Pl. 11.

P.H. 0.035. Est. D. rim 0.170. One fragment preserving profile. Gray micaceous clay with slip varying from black to brownish gray (2.5Y 6/2) peeling on interior. A wide bank of very fine rouletting decorates the center of the plate.

Cf. Robinson, *Agora*, F27, for foot shape.

Seven additional examples of this smaller variety of the plate with upturned rim: Lot 554: 1, Lot 552: 3, Lot 549: 1, Lot 547: 1, Lot 231: 1.

60. Plate with upturned rim. Lot 230, No. 74. Pl. 11.

P.H. 0.035. Est. D. rim 0.310. One fragment preserving rim and floor. Gray micaceous clay with pinkish tinge. The slip varying in color from dark reddish brown (5YR) to metallic gray is badly chipped and peeling on both surfaces, perhaps a result of firing.

61. Bowl with upturned rim. Inv. No. C-71-349. Lot 12. Pl. 12.

P.H. 0.024. Est. D. rim 0.283. One fragment of rim and wall. Light brownish gray (10YR 6/2) micacous fabric with black to dark gray (10YR 4/1) gloss.

Cf. Taylor, "Cosa," pl. 26, B8, B9, and pl. 41, E5c1, p. 137, Type III; Benoit, "La Ceramica campana," under **57** (cite), fig. 11, second column from left, dated to 100 B.C.

A similar piece comes from Lot 22.

62. Bowl with upturned rim. Lot 1443, No. 14. Pl. 12.

P.H. 0.021. Est. D. rim 0.220. One fragment of rim and wall. Gray micaceous clay (10YR 5/1) with smooth, graphite-like gray (10YR 5/1–5/2) slip slightly darker on the interior.

Similar to Taylor, "Cosa," pl. 41, E5a, but the Stobi example has the indentation under the rim.

Three other examples of this form: Lot 552: 1, Lot 610: 1, Lot 1089: 1.

63. Bowl with incurving rim. Lot 22, No. 3. Pl. 12.

P.H. 0.023. Est. D. rim 0.205. One fragment of rim and wall. Grayish brown (10YR 5/2) clay with black gloss. Lamboglia's Campanian C, Form 5, p. 158.

Two other examples: Lot 1093: 1 and Lot 1417: 1.

64. Bowl with incurving rim. Inv. No. C-74-414. Lot 1471. Pl. 12.

P.H. 0.020. Est. D. rim 0.245. One rim fragment. Gray to light brownish gray (10YR 6/1–6/2) clay with black gloss.

Related to Campanian C, Form 5.

Other examples of this form are from Lots 608, 390, and 20 (1 each).

Asia Minor wares

The following pieces are all examples of what has been called black "Samian" or reduced "Samian," because its micaceous fabric and thick gloss are very similar to that of Eastern Sigillata B.[34] Large plates and very large flat-based platters are the most common forms on a number of sites. Both round and square cornered platters are found, some with simple incurved rim and others with more complex carinations and decora-

[34] See *Samaria*, 256; *Tarsus*, 186; Moevs, "Cosa," 212, note 14.

tion.[35] At Stobi, only the simple incurved rim is found.

All six platters at Stobi come from contexts dating to within the first three quarters of the 1st century B.C.

65. Large platter. Inv. No. C-72-204. Lot 549. Pl. 12.

P.H. 0.028. Est. D. rim 0.344. One fragment of rim and floor. Light brown (7.5YR 6/4) clay with mica. Very smooth and lustrous black slip.

Cf. a fragment in "Magdalensberg," 71, 74.

Three other examples of this form: 1 additional from Lot 549 and 2 from 547, C-72-103, one with lead repair.

66. Very large platter. Inv. No. C-72-206. Lot 552. Pl. 12.

P.H. 0.032. Est. D. rim 0.500. One fragment of rim and floor. Reddish yellow (5YR 6/6) clay with worn black gloss fired very dark grayish brown (10YR 3/2).

This form is found at Tarsus and called "reduced Samian," *Tarsus*, fig. 196, no. 556 and p. 253. See also *Ephesus I*, 175, no. 2. P16410, P16411, P6874, P2443, and P8465 from the American Excavations in the Athenian Agora come from contexts ranging in date from the 2nd century B.C. through the first half of the lst century B.C., with the exception of P8465 (from Q14:1, 7/KZ shaft) dated by John Hayes to post-30 B.C. on the basis of three coins; see also Kenrick, *Berenice 3*, 53–54.

67. Large platter. Lot 76, No. 9. Pl. 13.

P.H. 0.021. Est. D. rim 0.035. One fragment of rim and floor. Gray (10YR 5/1) clay with worn black lustrous gloss.

Terra sigillata derivatives

No attempt has been made to locate a particular center where these pieces might have originated. Examples of gray ware with black gloss that imitate the forms of terra sigillata are mentioned by Loeschke and Kenyon.[36] Perhaps it was produced at many places where red-slipped wares were produced (utilizing a reducing rather than oxidizing process), considering the spread of published pieces from Pergamon to Magdalensburg. At Stobi these terra sigillata derivatives are found in contexts dating to the 1st century A.C.

68. Bowl with carinated rim. Inv. No. C-71-79. Lot 258. Pl. 13.

P.H. 0.030. Est. D. rim 0.106. Single fragment of rim and wall. Gray (10YR 5/1) micaceous clay with dark grayish brown to very dark grayish brown (10YR 4/2–3/2) semi-lustrous slip. Rim and carination decorated with rouletting.

This is a standard sigillata form and is rather similar to Arretine forms, especially in Hayes, "Corinth," pl. 81, Form 16B, dated 5–30 A.C.

69. Plate with incurving wall. Inv. No. C-72-33. Lot 599. Pl. 13.

P.H. 0.035. Est. D. rim 0.140. Mended from four fragments preserving more than half of vessel. Gray (10YR) clay with very dark gray semi-lustrous slip. *Planta pedis* in center of floor.

Cf. Goudineau Form 30, in Arretine, and in Eastern Sigillata A, see Robinson, *Agora*, F3. A plate of similar form also with gray fabric and discolored surface is on display in the National Museum in Štip (no. 161) from the excavations of burial mounds at Tarinci Krst conducted by Dr. Milutin Garašanin of the University of Belgrade in 1960–62, *Arheološki Pregled* 3 (1961) 64–66, 5 (1963) 59, and *Zbornik na Štipskiot Naroden Musej*, II (1960–61) 65.

Four additional examples of this form: Lot 231: 1, Lot 258: 1, Lot 443: 1, Lot 1441: 1.

70. Bowl with double convex wall. Inv. No. C-71-122. Lot 29. Pl. 13.

P.H. 0.065. Est. D. rim 0.113. Mended from numerous fragments to give two-thirds of vessel. Grayish brown (10YR 5/2) clay with black, slightly glossy slip. *Planta pedis* preserved in center of floor.

There are two gray ware bowls, one slightly smaller than the other, in the Štip Museum, also from Tarinci Krst (nos. 290, 322).

71. Dish with wide rim. Inv. No. C-71-22. Lot 433. Pl. 13.

P.H. 0.022. Est. D. rim 0.160. Mended from several fragments giving one-third of vessel.

[35] Square-cornered platters and others with complex rims have been found in excavations of the American School of Classical Studies at Corinth: Wright (1980) 147 and 168, nos. 34, 31, and Slane (1986) 287, 289, nos. 64, 65.

[36] Loeschcke, "Tschandarli," 398, 399; and *Samaria*, 256.

Grayish brown (10YR 5/2) clay with some mica. Lustrous, very dark gray slip. Rim is rouletted and decorated with spiral-form floral sprays. Floor is slightly offset from side wall.

The applied decoration on the rim is similar to a flat-based dish of Eastern Sigillata B in Hayes, "Corinth," pl. 87, no. 153. The decoration is also seen on some Arretine rims (Hayes, "Corinth," no. 59, Form 17, p. 430; Goudineau (1970), p. 213, Zone C, couche 2B, 120, and Form 34). Two similar plates from Tarinci Krst can be seen in the Štip Museum (Nos. 289, 331). Both have *planta pedis* stamps; one (No. 289) has the Greek letters APIMO in the stamp, and because the floor of the other example (No. 331) is so badly worn, it is difficult to tell whether the *planta pedis* stamp is just illegible or never existed at all.

This form with similar decoration is common in Stobi local ware with light fabric and red slip.

72. Relief Ware fragment. Inv. No. C-75-64. Lot 1683. Pls. 13, 154.

P.H. 0.057. Th. 0.004. One fragment broken on all sides. Gray (10YR 5/1), slightly micaceous clay with black slip. Torso of male nude is rendered full front with head turned to the left, and left arm raised above his head. The hair is moulded into curls at the back of the head. Body musculature is outlined at front of torso, at chest, and along preserved left side. The arm is rather oversized for the proportion of the rest of the body. This figure is very similar to those youths in hunting and battle scenes on Arretine relief vessels of the M. Perennius workshops.

See Dragendorff-Watzinger (1948) pl. 9, no. 120, and p. 91. There this scene is classified as a hunting scene where the youth raises the stone over his head. See also George Chase, *The Loeb Collection of Arretine Pottery* (New York 1908), pl. 17:151, p. 91: a battle scene; and Christine Alexander, *CVA, USA. Metropolitan Museum*, fasc. 1, (Cambridge, MA. 1943) "Arretine Relief Ware," pl. XL:2, a fragment of a mould with a hunting scene where a hunter with an ax raised over his head is attacking a boar.

Other gray wares

This group contains a variety of wares and forms that cannot be closely related to any particular ware or form, and some may have been locally made. Many are similar to forms of late Campanian wares and to early Arretine. The sharply profiled overhanging rim of **76** and **77** is found on Campanian C, early Arretine, and Eastern Sigillata B1.

The small hemispherical bowls are common in black gloss as well as in the various red-gloss wares, especially Eastern Sigillata A.

No. **84** is the only gray-ware example of the practice of stamping decoration on the vessel side wall, a popular technique at Stobi in the 2nd and 3rd centuries. The form is reminiscent of the later MR Form 19, the three-ridged bowl. The date of **84**, however, is Augustan.

73. Large platter. Inv. No. C-71-328. Lot 259. Pl. 13.

P.H. 0.030. Est. D. rim 0.034. One fragment of rim and floor. Deep groove on the exterior separates the side wall from the floor. Pale brown (10YR 6/3) clay, fired gray at core with a yellowish brown (10YR 5/4–5/6) glossy slip.

74. Large plate. Inv. No. C-70-46. Lot 460. Pl. 14.

P.H. 0.045. Est. D. rim 0.314. One fragment, preserving rim and base. Shallow plate with thick, convex wall and grooved offset where wall meets base. Light gray (10YR 7/1) clay with black slip.

75. Dish with flaring rim. Inv. No. C-74-494. Lot 1419. Pl. 14.

P.H. 0.020. Est. D. rim 0.320. One fragment with rim and wall. Rounded upper surface on rim with wide groove near exterior. Dark grayish brown (10YR 4/2) clay with exterior unslipped and fired to a light gray (10YR 7/1), while interior has a dark gray gloss.

76. Dish with overhanging rim. Inv. No. C-72-207. Lot 552. Pl. 14.

P.H. 0.020. Est. D. rim 0.172. One fragment of rim and wall. Shallow groove at rim and sharp carination midway down wall. Light yellowish brown (10YR 6/4) clay with brown (7.5YR 5/4) worn slip, perhaps poorly fired.

77. Dish with overhanging rim. Lot 599, No. 57. Pl. 14.

P.H. 0.015. Est. D. rim 0.260. One fragment of rim. Gray (10YR 6/1) clay with black gloss on interior and exterior. Cf. "Magdalensberg," Abb.

12:5, in terra sigillata dated first half of the first century to 30 B.C.

Another example of overhanging rim without grooves comes from Lot 1093.

78. Jar. Lot 547, No. 126. Pl. 14.

P.H. 0.021. Est. D. rim 0.140. One fragment of rim. Light brownish gray (10YR 6/2) clay with black slip.

79. Deep bowl with flat rim. Lot 552, No. 541. Pl. 15.

P.H. 0.067. Est. D. rim 0.270. One fragment with rim and wall. Light brownish gray (2.5YR 6/2) clay with dark gray semilustrous slip. Shallow wheel-ridging on exterior.

80. Bowl with flat rim. Lot 547, No. 128. Pl. 14.

P.H. 0.041. Est. D. rim 0.195. One fragment of rim and wall. Single groove at rim exterior. Brown (10YR 5/3) clay with gray metallic slip.

A similar example comes from Lot 552.

81. Small bowl. Lot 552, No. 509. Pl. 15.

P.H. 0.033. Est. D. rim 0.100. Two fragments mended, giving rim and wall. Curved wall and pointed lip. Dark gray (10YR 4/1) clay with black gloss.

82. Small bowl. Lot 248, No. 8. Pl. 15.

P.H. 0.037. Est. D. rim 0.120. Five fragments mended, giving rim and wall. Dark grayish brown (10YR 4/2) micaceous clay with semilustrous black slip.

There are 27 other examples of small hemispherical bowls in gray ware: Lot 1443: 1, Lot 1420: 1, Lot 1418: 1, Lot 1094: 1, Lot 1089: 1, Lot 555: 1, Lot 554: 1, Lot 552: 7, Lot 549: 2, Lot 545: 2, Lot 390: 1, Lot 259: 1, Lot 252: 2, Lot 248: 1, Lot 231: 1, Lot 230: 1, Lot 75: 1, Lot 70: 1.

83. Small bowl. Inv. No. C-71-24. Lot 432. Pl. 15.

P.H. 0.040. Est. D. rim 0.135. One fragment of rim and wall. Grayish brown (10YR 5/2) with dark gray (4/1) gloss. Two grooves under rim, below which have been preserved five impressed circles. Fingerprints clearly visible on the convex circles on the interior.

84. Small bowl. Inv. No. C-72-47. Lot 545. Pl. 15.

P.H. 0.035. Est. D. rim 0.123. Three fragments mended, preserving rim and part of wall. Dark gray (10YR 4/1) clay with very dark gray (3/1) matte slip. Surface of vessel is decorated with stamped, circular rosettes.

85. Jar. Inv. No. C-71-364. Lot 452. Pl. 15.

P.H. 0.038. Est. D. rim 0.100. One fragment of rim and wall. Straight rim and globular body set off by two grooves. Gray to grayish brown (10YR 5/1–5/2) clay with black gloss on exterior only.

Cf. E. Ettlinger et al., *Römische Keramik aus dem Schutthügel von Vindonissa* (Basel 1952) Taf. 6:95 and 98 in *terra nigra* dated 50–70 A.C.

86. Large Jar. Inv. No. C-72-160. Lot 552. Pl. 15.

Est. H. 0.147. Est. D. rim 0.127. Mended from numerous fragments and almost complete. Deep bowl or jar with incurving walls on ring base. Fine light brownish gray (10YR 6/2) micaceous clay. Worn black slip with metallic luster on exterior. Matte slip on interior.

87. Baby feeder. Inv. No. C-74-310. Lot 1458. Pl. 16.

H. 0.053. D. opening 0.026. D. base 0.040. D. widest point 0.078. Intact. Gray (5YR 5/1) clay and black gloss.

Cf. *Apollonia*, fig. 84:520, a local form with buff clay and black gloss dated from the second half of the 4th century B.C. through the 2nd century B.C., found with a coin dated to 150 B.C. It is very close to our example, except that the body on the Stobi piece has a slight carination at the point of greatest diameter and the handle, more ring shaped, is placed higher and nearer the mouth.

88. Small bottle. Inv. No. C-74-335. Lot 1470. Pl. 16.

H. 0.081. D. rim 0.020. D. body 0.049. D. base 0.028. Intact. Dark gray (2.5YR N4/) fabric and very dark gray (N5/) metallic slip.

89. Lid. Lot 488, No. 13. Pl. 16.

P.H. 0.020. Max.P.D. 0.056. One fragment with knob and part of rim. Pointed central handle. Gray (10YR 5/1) fabric and black gloss.

90. Base fragment. Inv. No. C-72-126. Lot 552. Pl. 16.

M.P.Dim. 0.082. One fragment from plate floor. Three stamped palmettes framed by a wide band of rouletting preserved.

91. Base fragment. Inv. No. C-72-184. Lot 549. Pl. 16.

M.P.Dim. 0.045. One fragment preserving single stamped palmette.

92. Base fragment. Lot 545, No. 9. Pl. 16.

M.P.Dim. 0.070. Single fragment preserving

one large stamped palmette surrounded by a narrow band of rouletting.

93. Fragment of ring base. Inv. No. C-74-436. Lot 1358. Pls. 16, 154.

P.H. 0.027. D. base 0.057. M. P. Dim. 0.134. Four fragments mended. Micaceous light gray (5YR 7/1–6/1) with very dark gray (2.5YR N3/), thick gloss on both surfaces. A pair of double grooves enclose three stamped palmettes. In the center are three concentric circles.

94. Floor fragment. Inv. No. C-72-115. Lot 630. Pl. 16.

M.P.Dim. 0.044. One fragment broken on all sides. Gray (10YR 6/1) micaceous clay and brown to dark brown (10YR 4/2) lustrous slip on interior. Single palmette preserved.

95. Base fragment. Inv. No. C-72-170. Lot 545.

M.P.Dim. 0.036. Single fragment with only one surface preserved. Light brownish gray (10YR 6/2) fabric with black gloss. Single heart-shaped stamp preserved.

96. Base fragment. Inv. No. C-72-190. Lot 545. Pl. 16.

P.H. 0.020. D. base 0.050. Single fragment. Concave disc base. Light gray (10YR 7/1) clay with semilustrous black slip. Mouldmade decoration on exterior composed of vertical strips of short, horizontal lines.

Cf. the Aco vessel of the Augustan period in Pedrazzini (1987) 274, 275.

97. Base fragment. Inv. No. C-71-365. Lot 452. Pl. 16.

P.H. 0.025. D. base ring 0.060. Single fragment of tall ring base. Gray clay and slip.

98. Stamped base. Inv. No. C-71-282. Lot 231. Pl. 17.

M.P.Dim. 0.029. Fragment of base from small bowl. Gray (10YR) fabric and black gloss. Part of stamp preserved in rectangular frame.

99. Stamped base. Lot 231, No. 78. Pl. 17.

M.P.Dim. 0.032. Fragment of plate-base. Gray (10YR) fabric with black gloss. Only a very small part of one letter in a rectangular frame is preserved.

100. Stamped base. Inv. No. C-71-280. Lot 230. Pl. 17.

M.P.Dim. 0.033. Fragment of ring base. Light brownish gray (10YR 6/2) and black gloss with dull metallic luster. Partially preserved stamp in rectangular frame off-center with letters I(?) and M preserved.

101. Stamped base. Lot 249, No. 36. Pls. 17, 155.

M.P.Dim. 0.064. One fragment of ring base with gray (10YR) fabric and dark gray-black gloss. Rectangular frame with Greek letters: ΛΟΥΚ.

102. Stamped base. Inv. No. C-74-482. Lot 1420. Pls. 17, 155.

P.H. 0.108. D. 0.053. Ring base. Pale brown (10YR 6/3) fabric and black gloss with dull metallic luster. Greek stamp in rectangular frame: ΘΕΟΛ··ΟΥ.

103. Stamped base. Inv. No. C-72-23. Lot 536. Pls. 17, 155.

M.P.Dim. 0.022. One fragment of floor. Grayish brown (10YR 5/2) clay with lustrous dark brown (5YR 2.5.2) gloss. In rectangular frame are Greek letters: Ρ·ΥΙΤΑ.

104. Stamped base. Inv. No. C-70-100. Lot 1018. Pl. 17.

M.P.Dim. 0.026. Small fragments of ring base. Gray (10YR 6/1) clay with black gloss. The letters M O S are preserved in one end of a *planta pedis*.

105. Stamped base. Inv. No. C-71-281. Lot 440. Pl. 17.

M.P.Dim. 0.037. Ring-base fragment. Gray (10YR 5/1) clay and dark gray (4/1) gloss with slight luster. Part of *planta pedis* stamp with sandal preserved.

Hellenistic Moulded Relief Bowls (**106–146**)

During the course of the 3rd century B.C., the hemispherical bowl decorated with moulded relief decoration—the Megarian bowl—appeared in the Greek world.[37] Silver bowls with the same decorative style and motifs, originating in Alexandria, are thought to have provided the models for the ceramic examples.[38] Megarian bowls began to be manufactured in Athens in the years between 240 and 220 B.C., and recent scholarship indicates that it is likely they were invented there.[39] Quantities of these bowls including mould fragments have been also published from a number of major centers, such as Corinth, Delos, Antioch, Pergamon, Priene, and Ephesos.[40] Some cities like Athens were undoubtedly major producers of fine bowls for export. Most sites in the Mediterranean area, however, have some examples of these bowls, and it is probable that some were made locally in most cities, as they were at Stobi.

A total of fourteen fragmentary moulds have been found at Stobi. Most are too small to show much of the decoration in detail. Two pieces (C-71-73 and C-71-49, cat. nos. 8 and 9 in Chap. 2), however, recovered in the destruction debris of the Late Hellenistic potters' workshop below the narthex of the Central Basilica, were surely used for Megarian bowls. Two stamps that may have been used to decorate moulds or a vessel exterior have also been found at Stobi.[41]

The bases of Megarian bowls are usually flat and decorated with floral or vegetal medallions. Sometimes the bowls stood on three feet that were moulded in the form of lions' heads or comic masks.[42] Moulds for two lions' heads of this type were, in fact, found at Stobi (Chap. 2, cat. no. 7).

Relief bowls of this type continued to be produced down through the mid-1st century B.C. in the East and probably slightly later in Italy. As might be expected, there are a number of motifs common to the Italian relief wares that appear on Arretine pottery.[43]

Aside from the distinctive Delian/Ionian bowls, which come first in the catalogue, and the local series which appears last, the classification presented here is based on differences in decorative style and motif. The best known groups are the Figured, Foliage, and Long Petal bowls.[44] The majority of these, however, cannot be securely assigned to a production center.

For the most part the fragments are quite small, and many are too small to be included in the catalogue.

At Stobi, Megarian bowls occur in significant numbers in deposits that range in date from the

[37] Vases of metal and clay, decorated in relief, were produced earlier, but not in great quantity. The earliest and still the only major study of moulded relief ware in general is that of Courby, *Vases*. For the bowls that concern us here, see section 5 (277–437). Other most useful early discussions can be found in Thompson, "TCHP," 451–459; M. W. Schwabacher, "Hellenistische Reliefkeramik im Kerameikos," *AJA* 45 (1941) 182–228; L. Byvanck-Quarles van Ufford, "Les Bols Megariens," *BABesch* 28 (1953) 1–21, and "Variations sur le Thème des Bols Mégariens," 34 (1959) 58–67; Th. Kraus, *Megarische Becher im Römisch-Germanischen Zentralmuseum zu Mainz*, Katalog 14 (Mainz 1951); Edwards, *Pnyx*, 83–112; and *Labraunda*, 19–23.

[38] S. I. Rotroff, "Silver, Glass, and Clay, Evidence for the Dating of Hellenistic Luxury Tableware," *Hesperia* 51 (1982) 331.

[39] Rotroff, *Agora 22*, 9–13, also Rotroff, "Ceramic Workshops in Hellenistic Athens," in *Ancient Greek and Related Pottery. Proceedings of the International Vase Symposium*. Amsterdam 1984. *Allard Pierson Series*. vol. 5 (Amsterdam 1985) 173.

[40] Corinth: Edwards, *Corinth*, 151–187, and C. M. Edwards, "Corinthian Moldmade Bowls: The 1926 Reservoir," *Hesperia* 55 (1986) 389–419; Delos: Laumonier, *Délos 31*. Antioch: *Antioch*; Pergamon: Conze *Pergamon*, 274, figs. 1–21. Priene: *Priene*, 401–421.

[41] The technique for making these bowls is discussed by Rotroff in *Hesperia* 51 (1982) 332, and note 16, and *Agora 22*, 4, 5; see also G.M.A. Richter, "Ancient Plaster Casts of Greek Metalware," *AJA* 63 (1958) 369–377.

[42] Like those seen in J. Wiseman, "The Fountain of the Lamps," *Archaeology* 23 (1970) 135, upper right.

[43] For the Popilius and Lapius and the Italian series: Jones, "Popilius and Lapius"; H. Comfort, "A „Popilius Vase„ in the National Museum, Washington," *Studi Etruschi* 11 (1937) 407–410, with bibliography; see also M. S. Arena, "Ceramica Italo-Megarese nell'Antiquarium di Ostia," *RStLig* 35 (1969) 101–121; B. Adamsheck, "Hellenistic Relief Wares from Italy," *RCRFActa* 14–15 (1972–73) 5–11.

[44] According to Edwards, *Corinth*, 151–153, foliage-decorated bowls come first; Rotroff, *Agora 22*, Foliage (Floral) 17–18, figs. 19–20; Long Petal, 34–36; and now by the same author, "The Long-Petal Bowl from the Pithos Settling Basin," *Hesperia* 57 (1988) 89–93.

second half of the 2nd century B.C. into the third quarter of the 1st century B.C. Many also occur in later deposits as residual. It is to be expected that the Long Petal series occur in greatest numbers at Stobi inasmuch as this is its period of greatest popularity. The earlier types, Figured and Foliage, are found in much smaller numbers.

Two other decorative motifs occur on Megarian bowls at Stobi: the ivy leaf and the column. The ivy leaf covers the whole vessel surface, and in one example forms the termination of a series of radiating triple relief lines. These pieces date to the first half of the 1st century B.C. Widely spaced columns were used on three bowls to decorate the body. Since these examples are quite small, and the walls rather thick, it is not clear what shape is represented.

No examples of bowls with the concentric-semicircle and dot pattern have been found at Stobi. This motif is sometimes called the Macedonian shield pattern because of its similarity to the design on Macedonian bronze shields. As a result, some people have assigned these to Macedonian production. There is, however, no evidence for this assumption, and the conspicuous absence of this style at Stobi as well as in Upper Macedonia in general suggests either that the motif was never very popular there or that its production occurs too early for appearance in deposits of the late 2nd and 1st centuries B1.C.[45]

Delian/Ionian bowls

This group is characterized by a black gloss sometimes fired partially or entirely red. The rim is bent slightly inward. A horizontal arrangement of motifs is common. The stamps of potters or designers were often placed on the exterior wall of the vessel.

Although many of these bowls were found on Delos, they were probably not made there. There is, in fact, no source of clay on the island, and the sizeable quantities reflect instead the island's position as a commercial trade center. The particular type of bowl was, according to Alfred Laumonier, who has published the Delian material, most likely the product of Ionian factories, perhaps in Pergamon, Miletos, or Ephesos.[46] On the basis of the rather small number of bowls of this type published from well-dated contexts, the earliest examples appear in the second quarter of the 2nd century.[47]

Of the 19 fragments of the type at Stobi, 9 must be survival pieces. The remaining 10 come from deposits that range from the second half of the 2nd century B.C. to the mid-1st B.C. All appear to be products of the Square Monogram Workshop.[48]

106. Inv. No. C-75-65. Lot 1662. Pl. 155.

P.H. 0.066. Th. 0.004. Side wall fragment. Light red (2.5YR 6/6 clay. Most of the body is fired semilustrous red (2.5YR 4/6), but a small part below the rim is fired metallic black. Three zones of decoration are preserved.

Rim zone: Lesbian cymation; wall: garland of intertwining vine leaves, tendrils, and clusters of grapes; calyx: pointed petal flanked by bent acanthus. The lower is composed of alternating pointed petal and acanthus leaf bent in half, facing the petal.

Cf. Courby, *Vases*, p. 379, figs. 76:6, and 77:9; also *Labraunda*, pls. 9:108, 10:122. There are two bowls in Corinth, from the excavations of the American School of Classical Studies, C-47-792, and C-47-793, of the same general type with identical decoration in the lower zones. Clay and fabric are also similar. Although not in the catalogue of Edwards, *Corinth*, they are identified with Deposit 46, dated ca. 146 B.C. (p. 160, note 17); see also Laumonier, *Délos 31*, Pl. 46.2306, 1509, of the Square Monogram Workshop (as *Berenice 3*), the most important in the Aegean at the end of the 2nd century B.C. (Laumonier, *Délos 31*, 132); for the vine scroll and cymation, see pls. 30, 31, passim.

Two other fragments with Lesbian cymation only, from Lots 251, 252, both of late 2nd-century B.C. date.

45 Thompson, "TCHP," 456–457; P.V.C. Baur, "Megarian Bowls in Yale University," *AJA* 45 (1941) 241, but *Labraunda*, 22. Corinth has also been suggested as the source for these bowls by P. Callaghan, "Macedonian Shields, 'Shield bowls,' and Corinth: A Fixed Point in Hellenistic Ceramic Chronology?," *Athens Annals of Archaeology* 11 (1978) 53–60; note also the comments of Rotroff, *Agora 22*, 38.

46 Laumonier, *Délos 31*, 2–3. See Kenrick, *Berenice 3*, 105–107, for a recent discussion of the problems.

47 Kenrick, *Berenice 3*, 107.

48 The term Square Monogram Potter was adapted by Kenrick (p. 107), to refer to the workshop whose signature appears as a monogram . I follow Kenrick in using this term.

107. Lot 1441, No. 1.

Max.P.Dim. 0.040. Small fragment with decoration in the same style as the preceding, with similar clay and surface. Calyx: acanthus leaves.

Probably Square Monogram Workshop as part of the rosette is preserved from the base: Laumonier, *Délos* 31, p. 129.

108. Inv. No. C-70-5. Lot 1023. Pl. 156.

Max.P.Dim. 0.071. Small fragment with acanthus leaves in calyx.

109. Lot 608, No. 36. Pl. 155.

Max.P.Dim. 0.030. One small fragment from wall. Reddish yellow (5YR 6/6) fabric and red (2.5YR 4/6) slip. Bunches of ivy leaves and bayberries preserved on wall.

Cf. Courby, *Vases*, fig. 77:8 and Laumonier, *Délos* 31, pl. 46:2025. Date: mid-1st century B.C.

110. Inv. No. C-74-264. Lot 1441. Pls. 18, 155.

P.H. 0.038. Th. 0.005. One rim fragment. Reddish yellow (5YR 6/6) clay with black metallic gloss on exterior and reddish brown (2.5YR 5/4) on interior. Rim zone: rosettes.

Cf. Courby, *Vases*, p. 379, fig. 76:3; *Labraunda*, pl. 9: 100, 101; Vučković-Todorović (1961) pls. 99, 100, 101; "Fanagoria," p. 49, fig. 14b, far right, third from top; Laumonier, *Délos 31*, pl. 46.

One additional example from Lot 842.

111. Lot 140, No. 95. Pl. 155.

Max.P.Dim. 0.054. One rim fragment. Reddish yellow (5YR 6/6) clay with black metallic gloss. Rim zone: eight petalled rosettes.

Cf. Courby, *Vases*, fig. 76:3.

Date: first half of the 1st century B.C.

One additional example from Lot 26.

112. Inv. No. C-74-71. Lot 1093. Pl. 156.

Max.P.Dim. 0.050. One rim fragment. Light red (2.5YR) to pinkish gray (5YR 4/2) clay with a very dark gray metallic slip on both surfaces. Rim zone: wave pattern between ridges; wall: foliage with laurel leaves and berries.

Cf. Courby, *Vases*, figs. 76:8, 77:8; A. Laumonier, "Bols hellenistiques à reliefs," *BCH* Suppl. 1 (Paris 1973) 257, fig. 1; idem, *Délos* 31, pl. 32, center.

113. Inv. C-74-316. Lot 1599. Pls. 18, 156.

P.H. 0.050. Est. D. rim 0.128. Rim and wall. Light brown (7.5YR 6/4) clay with black metallic gloss. Rim zone: meandering swastika with X's inscribed in rectangles between meanders. Second zone: egg and dart. Wall: only the tips of long petals preserved.

Cf. Courby, *Vases*, figs. 76:4. 2, 80:3. The upper two zones are duplicated in the Corinth example noted in **106** above; cf. Laumonier, *Délos* 31, pl. 41.278.

One additional example from Lot 689.

114. Lot 252, No. 8. Pl. 156.

Max.P.Dim. 0.046. One small fragment. Reddish yellow (5YR 6/6) clay with lustrous red (2.5YR 4/6–4/8) slip on both surfaces, fired black on a small part of the exterior. Preserved are parts of two figures in a battle scene: a torso in a cuirass(?) on the left, and an arm wielding a sword on the right.

Cf. Courby, *Vases*, fig. 78:29; cf. Laumonier, *Délos*, 31, pls. 31, 32, passim. Date: second half of the 2nd century B.C.

115. Lot 1636, No. 61.

Max.P.Dim. 0.027. One small fragment from wall. Reddish yellow (5YR 6/6) clay and reddish brown (2.5YR 4/4) lustrous slip on both surfaces. Pointed imbricated leaves decorate the preserved surface.

Cf. Courby, *Vases*, fig. 80:8; Edwards, *Pnyx*, pl. 47.

Date: second half of the 2nd century B.C.

Other miscellaneous small fragments of Delian/Ionian bowls as follows: C-74-272 (Lot 1441), C-78-160 (Lot 2108), C-78-083 (Lot 2234), C-78-142 (Lot 2300).

Other bowls of uncertain provenience

Figured bowls

116. Inv. No. C-74-301. Lot 1442. Pl. 157.

Max.P.Dim. 0.027. Th. 0.004. One wall fragment. Light brown (7.5YR 6/6) clay with well-worn dark brown slip on both surfaces. Preserved are the head and shoulders of a male figure in profile to the right wearing a fringed, slightly peaked cap and a loose garmet or tunic clasped at his right shoulder. A spear stands behind his right arm and in front of his face are preserved the Greek letters: τω. The head is turned up slightly.

Homer Thompson (personal communication) has suggested that this scene may be a representation of Hippolytus in a scene from the play of Euripides. See Kurt Weitzmann, *Ancient Book Illumination* (Cambridge, MA 1959) 71, 73, 101, for a discussion of representations of the Hippolytus myth.

117. Inv. No. C-72-27. Lot 610. Pl. 156.

Max.P.Dim. 0.042. Wall fragment. Light brownish gray (10YR 6/2) clay with black metallic slip on both surfaces. Preserves only the hind part of a running animal, perhaps a griffin, probably part of a frieze of running animals. Four feet are preserved, a long doglike body, and wings.

Cf. Keramopoullos (1932) 69, Pl. 26, top; Edwards, *Corinth*, Pl. 73:843, dated to 146 B.C.; Courby, *Vases*, fig. 85:29 from Priene.

Date: mid-1st century B.C.

118. Lot 252, No. 9. Pl. 157.

Max. P. Dim. 0.048. One small fragment from wall. Reddish yellow (5YR 7/6) clay with light red to weak red (2.5YR) slip on both surfaces. Several very faint robed figures are visible.

Date: second half of the 2nd century B.C.

119. Lot 77, No. 1. Pl. 157.

Max.P.Dim. 0.049. One small fragment of wall. Pink (7.5YR 7/4) clay with dull red slip on exterior only. Parts of heads of three figures are preserved in very faint detail.

120. Inv. No. C-72-17. Lot 609. Pl. 157.

Max. P. Dim. 0.065. One wall fragment. Reddish yellow (5YR 7/6) clay with red (2.5YR 5/8) slip on exterior. Moulded decoration consists of a single row of small circles framed by a wide ridge. Below a series of large, flat, double circles are the faint traces of a figure with arms raised over its head.

Date: mid-1st century B.C.

121. Inv. No. C-72-93. Lot 783. Pl. 157.

M.P.Dim. 0.063. Fragment from side wall below rim. Gray (10YR 6/1) clay with black-brown slip on exterior. Interior is unslipped. From beneath rim is preserved what appears to be a row of moulded double circles. Beneath the moulding, the upper part of a female figure is preserved. Her hair is pulled back into a knot at the back of her head, and her right arm is extended forward and is holding an unidentified object. Other floral space fillers are located in front of the figure.

Foliage bowls

122. Inv. No. C-70-131. Lot 829. Pls. 18, 158.

P.H. 0.073. Est. D. rim 0.120. Two pieces from rim and body not joining. Rim form is the same as that in the Delian/Ionian group. Reddish yellow (5YR 6/6) clay with black slip almost entirely worn off. Rim zone decorated with a garland of leaves and berries. Wall zone: pointed leaves alternating with five-petalled rosette/tendril pattern.

Cf. Thompson, "TCHP," C17, pp. 351, 455; Keramopoullos (1932), eik. 31, from Florina; Vučković-Todorović (1961) T.76:211 from Level XI, dated to post-200 B.C.

Date: first half of the 1st century B.C.

Similar pieces: C-71-223 (Lot 140), three in Lot 552, and one in Lot 829.

123. Lot 552, No. 29. Pl. 158.

Max.P.Dim. 0.042. Two nonjoining wall fragments. Reddish yellow (5YR 6/6–7/6) clay with dark reddish brown (5YR 3/4) slip. Intertwining vines and heart-shaped leaves. There is a fragment with a similar decorative motif in the Archaeological Museum in Skopje, provenience unknown.

Date: second, third quarters of the 1st century B.C.

Two similar examples are one in Lot 545, one in Lot 547.

124. Inv. No. C-75-37. Lot 1637. Pl. 158.

Max.P.Dim. 0.043. Th. 0.003. One fragment of side wall. Dark gray to very dark gray (5Y 4/1–3/1) fabric. Black glossy slip on both surfaces. A series of closely placed, long, pointed leaves decorate the surface.

Cf. Vučković-Todorović (1961) 266, pl. 104; also U. Hausmann, *Hellenistische Reliefbecher aus attischen und bootischen Werkstatten* (Stuttgart 1959) pls. 1, 2; L. Byvanck-Quarles van Ufford, "Les bols megariens," *BABesch* 28 (1953) 14, fig. 10, in silver.

Date: late 2nd century B.C.

125. Inv. No. C-75-36. Lot 1672. Pl. 158.

Max.P.Dim. 0.047. Th. 0.007. Side wall preserving part of corolla. Gray to grayish brown (10YR 5/1–5/2) clay with brown to strong brown (7.5Y 5/2–5/4–5/3) slip on both surfaces. Alternating ferns and tendrils.

126. Lot 608, No. 35. Pl. 158.

Max.P.Dim. 0.036. One fragment of wall at corolla. Dark gray clay with dark gray surfaces (2.5Y N4/). Alternating fronds and pointed leaves. Date: mid-1st century B.C.

Small examples of foliage bowls (one each) exist in the following Lots: 130, 140, 257, 547, and 829.

Imbricated pine cones or nodules

127. Lot 551, No. 22. Pl. 158.

Max.P.Dim. 0.035. One wall fragment. Reddish yellow (5YR 7/6) clay with light red to reddish gray (2.5YR–5YR) slip.

Cf. Courby, *Vases*, fig. 80:6; Thompson, "TCHP," 362, fig. 47, C29; Edwards, *Pnyx*, pl. 48; *Labraunda*, pl. 11, 138–140.

Date: second, third quarters of the 1st century B.C.

Ivy-leaf bowls

128. Inv. No. C-71-83. Lot 127. Pls. 18, 159.

P.H. 0.066. Est. D. rim 0.100. One fragment of wall with everted rim. Light red (2.5YR 6/6) clay with thin, matt, weak red (2.5YR 6/8) slip. Below the undecorated zone under the rim, the body is covered with rows of small heart-shaped leaves larger at the top and diminishing in size toward the base.

Date: first half of the 1st century B.C.

129. Inv. No. C-72-64. Lot 552. Pl. 159.

Max.P.Dim. 0.038. Fragment of base and wall. Yellowish (10YR 7/6) clay with brownish gray slip worn away almost entirely. The base is encircled by small spirals and above the row of spirals the surface is covered with rows of heart-shaped leaves.

Date: second, third quarters of the 1st century B.C.

130. Inv. No. C-71-84. Lot 127. Pls. 18, 159.

P.H. 0.070. Est. D. rim 0.103. Almost complete bowl with everted rim. Light red (2.5YR 6/6) clay with matt red (2.5YR 5/6–4/6) slip. Alternating double tendrils and single hearts on long triple and double stems respectively. Base is covered with eight raised circles and four heart-shaped leaves.

Column bowls

131. Lot 547, No. 54. Pl. 159.

Max.P.Dim. 0.047. Two fragments of wall, mended. Reddish yellow (5YR 6/6) clay and slip. Decoration consists of a row of columns with circular capitals, each separated from the other by single ridge.

Date: second, third quarters of the 1st century B.C.

132. Inv. No. C-74-440. Lot 1510. Pl. 159.

Max.P.Dim. 0.056. One wall fragment. Reddish yellow (5YR 6/6) clay with light red (2.5YR 6/8) surfaces. Quite thick walled. Three individual Doric columns are preserved.

Long-petalled bowls

133. Lot 610, No. 49. Pl. 160.

Max.P.Dim. 0.030. Several fragments from base and wall. Light red (2.5YR 6/8) clay and slip that varies from reddish yellow to black in color.

Cf. *Labraunda*, pl. 11:144; Edwards, *Pnyx*, pl. 49:116.

Fragments from the lower side walls and bases of 16 other vessels of this style.

Date: mid-1st century B.C.

134. Lot 554, No. 1. Pl. 160.

Max.P.Dim. 0.038. One fragment of rim. Reddish yellow (5YR 6/6) clay with red slip. Widely spaced petals.

135. Inv. No. C-71-115. Lot 228. Pls. 18, 160.

Max.P.Dim. 0.075. Three fragments mended to give wall and part of base medallion. Very pale brown (10YR 7/4) fabric with brown slip. Body is decorated with long, narrow leaves separated from the ten-petalled rosette medallion by a single beaded circle.

Medallion-base fragments

136. Inv. No. C-71-98. Lot 262. Pls. 18, 160.

Max.P.Dim. 0.060. One fragment of base. Dark gray (7.5YR N6/N5) fabric with semilustrous black gloss. Part of a large double rosette medallion with overlapping petals.

Date: 1st century B.C.

137. Inv. No. C-72-15. Lot 552. Pl. 160.

Max.P.Dim. 0.046. One fragment of wall with part of base. Reddish yellow (5YR 7/6) clay with matt, red slip. Small, heart-shaped leaves preserved on the base. The central circle of the base is surrounded by a row of spirals from which narrow ridges continue onto the body.

Date: second, third quarters of the 1st century B.C.

138. Lot 441, No. 1. Pl. 161.

Max.P.Dim. 0.051. One fragment of base. Reddish brown to light reddish brown (5YR 5/4–6/4) clay with metallic dark reddish brown slip. A series of petals bounded by a very narrow band of crude egg and dart.

139. Lot 549, No. 9. Pl. 161.

Max.P.Dim. 0.044. One base fragment. Pale brown (10YR 6/3) clay with very worn gray to light gray slip. Rosette very badly worn.

Date: second, third quarters of the 1st century B.C.

140. Lot 551, No. 26. Pl. 161.

Max.P.Dim. 0.052. One fragment of wall and part of base. Light red (2.5YR) clay and thin, red (2.5YR 5/6) slip. Floral medallion with long ribs projecting upward.

Date: Second, third quarters of the 1st century B.C.

Inscribed fragments

141. Inv. No. C-72-20. Lot 552. Pl. 161.

Max.P.Dim. 0.040. One fragment of wall. Fine, black (10YR 3/1) clay and lustrous black slip. Below a single ridge, part of an inscription in raised letters: τοντ.

Date: second, third quarters of the 1st century B.C.

Local Series

Many moulded relief bowls were found in destruction-fill deposits associated with the Potter's Shop below the narthex of the later Central Basilica. (See Appendix 1.) Most interesting is a series of 25 fragments of bowls of unusual form and style. The fabric of all the examples is of local type. The slip varies from red to reddish brown to brown or black, and many were discolored by fire. The surface is typically dull, although some few examples display a metallic luster. The rim profile is paralleled elsewhere in Macedonia.[49]

All the bowls are of the same style and use the same repertoire of Dionysiac motifs that vary only slightly in detail.[50] The variation in motifs and their arrangement probably indicate the use of a number of different moulds. The design in relief consists of six isolated figures arranged at equal intervals around the bowl's circumference and separated by long petals, long pointed leaves, or vines. The arrangement of figures in panels divided by long leaves or petals is seen on bowls of the Italian workshop of Lapius.[51]

Figures preserved on all but two fragments are the same and consist of a dancing male(?), probably a satyr, with one foot raised and one arm over his head, carrying a bunch of grapes, and a standing figure, perhaps a maenad, shown in profile, wearing a long chiton and animal skin(?) on the shoulder, which hangs down in back. There seems to be a soft cap on the head.

The spaces above and below the figures are filled with rosettes, leaves, dots, squiggly lines, or all these motifs. The base is decorated only with several concentric circles in relief, from which the panel dividers originate. The rim above the relief zone is distinguished by several ridges, and the lip itself is slightly everted.

Most of the fragments are quite small or preserve only one or two panels, so that it is difficult to assign them securely to one mould group or another. Only on one vessel are the dancing figure and the draped figure preserved in alternation. On two fragments are represented the dancing Dionysiac figure and a partially draped Dionysos leaning on a support. It is not possible to know whether there were always only two different figures represented, so that on the pieces with the draped Dionysos there was only the additional figure of the dancer, or if there may have been all three figures represented on one vessel. Moreover, there may have been other figures that are not preserved.

Five different groups can be distinguished among the pieces preserved. The date for all should fall within the first half of the 1st century B.C.

[49] Maneva (1979) pl. 4.

[50] Dionysiac motifs are especially popular in the minor arts of Macedonia.

[51] Jones, "Popilius and Lapius," figs. 11, 12.

Group 1

142. Inv. No. C-70-124. Lot 829. Pl. 161.

P.H. 0.082. Th. 0.003. Best preserved of all the groups, but without a rim. Within the six panels divided by long petals are the dancing figure with grapes, alternating with the draped figure. The space around the figures is filled with zigzag lines, and below the rim, next to each divider, is a rosette and a half-sphere with incised decoration. In two cases, the bottom of the petal does not reach to the base circle.

Group 2

143. Inv. No. C-71-220. Lot 140. Pl. 162.

P.H. 0.048. Est. D. 0.111. Only one petal divider is preserved between the draped figure and the dancing figure. There is a rosette on each side of the petal top, and a bar running across the petal. No other space fillers such as the wavy lines in Group 1 are preserved. (C-70-92, Lot 829, is another example of this group.)

Group 3

144. Inv. No. C-71-181. Lot 829. Pls. 19, 162.

P.H. 0.073. Est. D. 0.060. One panel preserved. Long, pointed leaves of the *nymphaea caerulea* mark off the panel in which the dancing figure and draped figure are separated by a single vine with a large leaf at the top. Between the draped figure and the panel divider leaf are another vine and a leaf. To the right of the divider is a rosette followed by a tall frond reaching to the rim as does the divider. (Six additional examples: Lot 140: 2; Lot 829: C-70-93 and two other examples; Lot 831: 1.)

Group 4

145. Inv. No. C-70-132. Lot 829. Pls. 19, 162.

P.H. 0.054. Est. D. 0.140. In this group alone are two examples of the Dionysos figure standing with right hand over his head, one leg crossed over the other, and leaning on a curved support in the manner of the Lycian Apollo of Praxiteles. Other examples in this group show part or parts of the two other figures. Above and beneath the figures are single rows of punched dots; alongside are zigzag lines or vines in relief which end in single wide leaves. The panels are divided by long petals, and rosettes are preserved in some upper corners. (Eight additional examples: Lot 86: C-71-180; Lot 140: C-71-221; Lot 829: 4; Lot 831: C-70-13 and C-70-94.)

Group 5

146. Lot 829, No. 31. Pl. 162.

Max.P.Dim. 0.045. Small fragment preserving one dancing figure and the upper part of a long petal to one side. Above the figure's head is a row of half circles with dots inside, a motif very similar to one on a mould (Chap. 2, no. 8) found in these deposits.

Thin-Walled Wares (**147–224**)

A group of wares that served the Roman household as a tableware, along with the black-gloss Campanian wares, or the red-gloss Arretine and other sigillata wares, has become widely known as Thin-Walled Ware.[52] These wares, which are found in the greatest quantities in lands bordering on the western Mediterranean and in Italy and western Europe, are distinguished primarily by the thinness of their walls, but they share a variety of other attributes as well, such as form, decoration, and function. The very thin walls and the types of surface decoration probably reflect a desire to imitate metal vases.

Thin-Walled Wares begin to appear in the archaeological record at Cosa by the second quarter of the 2nd century B.C.[53] and continue to be made

[52] Comprehensive studies with extensive bibliography include: Moevs, "Cosa"; Mayet; and Vegas, *Cerámica común*. A recent summary appears in Kenrick, *Berenice* 3, 307–319 (Fabric A). Most comprehensive is the recently published study in *EAA* 2, "Ceramica a Pareti Sottili," by A. Ricci, 231–356.

[53] Moevs, "Cosa," 35.

with some variation throughout the 1st century A.C. at least, and perhaps later in some areas. During the Republican period, the walls are normally quite thin (2–2.5 mm.), but by the mid-1st century the generic term "thin-walled" is no longer quite accurate.

The surface of the earliest vessels is usually unslipped, but by the Augustan period the use of thin orange, pink, or purple slips, often with a metallic luster, becomes common. Unslipped vessels were often polished before firing in such a manner that a variegated striped surface was produced during firing. Shapes are limited to cups, bowls, jars, and some pitchers, although there is a great variety of forms within these broad categories. It has been suggested that the attribute shared by all members of this group is, in fact, their function primarily as drinking vessels rather than the thinness of the walls.[54]

The older forms are narrow, tall, and closed in shape. During the Augustan period, lower, shorter vessels and some large shapes became popular and frequently have handles. During the Tiberian period, small bowls and cups with round or carinated bodies are seen, while the number of other forms diminish.

The decoration is also a distinctive feature of this class of pottery, although it is not present on all vessels. Techniques used are several different types of barbotine, incision, thumb impression, and moulding.[55]

The various decorative techniques created a surface with a varied texture. As a result, the surface of these vessels is very different from the uniformly smooth and lustrous red gloss of the sigillata ware.

All the pieces at Stobi that belong to this tradition have been included here, even though some of them may be local or at least regional.[56] These might include some of the bowls decorated with sand decoration and many pieces of floral barbotine.

Most of the examples of Thin-Walled pottery at the site fall into six groups based on similar fabric, surface treatment, form, and decoration.

Group 1

The vessels in this group are the earliest examples of Thin-Walled Wares at Stobi and are probably all Italian imports. The fabric varies from light red (2.5YR 6/6) to reddish yellow (5YR 6/6–7/6) and is hard fired, and a few examples have a brown (7.5YR 5/2–5/4) core. No inclusions are visible to the naked eye. The surface is unslipped and in color varies from light red (2.5YR 6/8) to reddish brown (5YR 5/4). The ware is probably of central Italian origin.[57] The shapes represented are tall beakers and small jars.

Beaker with moulded lip

The form for **147** to **150** is Form 1 in both Moevs, "Cosa," 49–52, 261, 262, pls. 1:3, 2:11, and Mayet 24, 25, pl. 1; Vegas, *Cerámica común* 63, 65, 126, 127, type 23. It is the oldest form in the Thin-Walled category and is found in contexts ranging from the second quarter of the 2nd century B.C. to the third quarter of the 1st century B.C. The beaker with dot decoration may predate 54 B.C. (Moevs, "Cosa," 52), but it is also placed as late as 30 B.C. ("Magdalensberg," 8, Abb. 9). Two examples of similar shape with dot barbotine were found at Heraclea Lyncestis (Maneva [1979] pl. 12:317, 138). The fragmentary nature of both makes the dot configuration impossible to see.

The examples at Stobi belong to contexts ranging in date from late 2nd century to mid-1st centuries B.C.

147. Inv. No. C-74-13. Lot 1094. Pls. 19, 163.

H. 0.137. D. rim 0.078. Complete. Everted moulded lip on elongated, ovoid body with spreading concave base. Fine, micaceous, hard-fired, reddish yellow (5YR 7/6–6/6) clay with smoothed surface fired a variegated red (2.5YR 5/8). Small dots of applied clay encircle the body in a wavelike pattern under a single horizontal row encircling the vessel at the shoulder. I have found no examples from other sites that have the dots arranged in exactly the same design as ours.

Three additional fragments with similar dot decoration: Lot 547: 1; Lot 552: 2.

[54] Mayet, 3, but see J. U. Smit Nolen, review of Mayet, *Conimbriga* 15 (1976) 191.

[55] See the invaluable chart in Mayet, 8, with terms for types of decoration in French, Portuguese, Spanish, Italian, English, and German.

[56] Comment from J. W. Hayes.

[57] See Kenrick, *Berenice* 3, 307, 310; Moevs (personal communication).

148. Lot 262, No. 19. Pl. 19.
P.H. 0.030. Est. D. rim 0.102. One fragment of rim and body. Light red (2.5YR 6/8) fabric with brown (7.5YR 5/4) core. No decoration preserved.

149. Inv. No. C-75-84. Lot 1657. Pl. 19.
P.H. 0.023. Est. D. rim 0.070. One fragment of rim and wall. Light red (2.5YR 6/6) clay. Surface fired to reddish yellow (5YR 6/6). A horizontal line of small barbotine dots is preserved on the shoulder just above the break.

150. Lot 552, No. 1206. Pl. 19.
P.H. 0.017. Est. D. rim 0.084. Reddish yellow (5YR 6/6) clay. No decoration preserved.

Bases of tall beakers, Moevs Form 1 or 2

151. Lot 831, No. 71. Pl. 19.
P.H. 0.037. Est. D. 0.040. One fragment of wall and flat, spreading base. Light red (2.5YR 6/6) to reddish yellow (5YR 6/6) fabric with surface fired a somewhat mottled light red to reddish brown (5YR 6/4).

152. Inv. No. C-72-185. Lot 547. Pl. 19.
P.H. 0.046. Est. D. 0.040. One fragment of base and wall. Reddish yellow (5YR 6/6) clay. The vessel surface has alternating stripes of reddish yellow, reddish brown, and red (all 2.5YR), probably a result of the brush application of the self-slip.

153. Inv. No. C-71-342. Lot 130. Pl. 19.
P.H. 0.027. Est. D. 0.050. One fragment of base and wall. Reddish yellow (5YR 6/6) clay with light red (2.5YR 6/4–6/6) surface.

Beaker with plain rim

154. Lot 250, No. 5. Pl. 20.
P.H. 0.030. Est. D. rim 0.111. One rim fragment. Reddish yellow (5YR 5/6) clay.
Cf. Moevs, "Cosa," 264, Form 3, pl. 3:31 and 32, dated mid-2nd to mid-1st centuries B.C. One additional example from the same Lot.
Date at Stobi: late 2nd century B.C.

155. Inv. No. C-75-60. Lot 1636. Pl. 20.
P.H. 0.060. Est. D. rim 0.080. One rim fragment with very thin walls. Red (2.5YR 4/8) fabric with surfaces fired reddish brown (5YR 5/3).
Moevs Form 3, pl. 3:28, dated late 2nd, early 1st centuries B.C.
Date at Stobi: late 2nd century B.C.

Jars with vertical, swelling rim

A great many of these jars have been found at Stobi, all with thin walls and many with a striped surface, as **152** above, caused by the horizontal brush strokes made when the slip was applied. There is no other form of decoration. Since so many of the pieces consist of only rims and varying lengths of wall, it is difficult, except in a few cases, to determine the shape of the body—ovoid or globular. According to Mayet (pp. 5, 171) the taller the form, the older it is, so that the ovoid forms should be older than the globular ones. Moevs, "Cosa," 59–64, dates the three forms to which our group (i.e., **156–172**) belongs—(4, 5, and 6)—to the 1st century B.C.

156. Lot 551, No. 44. Pl. 20.
P.H. 0.045. Est. D. rim 0.090. One fragment with very tall rim.

157. Lot 552, No. 1100. Pl. 20.
P.H. 0.033. Est. D. rim 0.097. One rim fragment.

158. Lot 552, No. 1251. Pl. 20.
P.H. 0.041. Est. D. rim 0.118. One rim fragment.

159. Lot 134, No. 33. Pl. 20.
Est. H. 0.090. Est. D. rim 0.085. One rim and base fragment, not joining.

160. Lot 552, No. 1268. Pl. 20.
P.H. 0.038. Est. D. rim 0.090. One rim fragment.

161. Lot 134, No. 108. Pl. 20.
P.H. 0.080. Est. D. rim 0.110. One rim fragment.

162. Lot 134, No. 111. Pl. 20.
P.H. 0.075. Est. D. rim 0.097. One rim fragment.

163. Lot 140, No. 56. Pl. 21.
P.H. 0.060. Est. D. rim 0.078. One rim fragment.

164. Lot 829, No. 134. Pl. 21.
P.H. 0.035. Est. D. rim 0.110. One rim fragment.

165. Inv. No. C-74-356. Lot 1468. Pl. 21.
H. 0.060. D. rim 0.084. Almost complete.

166. Lot 552, No. 1254. Pl. 21.
P.H. 0.048. Est. D. rim 0.092. One rim fragment.

167. Lot 552, No. 1258. Pl. 21.
P.H. 0.050. Est. D. rim 0.082. One rim fragment.

168. Lot 1420, No. 4. Pl. 21.
P.H. 0.044. Est. D. rim 0.088. One rim fragment.

169. Lot 1089, No. 37. Pl. 21.
P.H. 0.030. Est. D. rim 0.090. One rim fragment.

170. Inv. No. C-72-53. Lot 552. Pl. 21.
H. 0.052. D. rim 0.140. Mended to give complete profile.
Additional rim fragments of this form: Lot 134: 3; Lot 140: 2; Lot 547: 3; Lot 549: 4; Lot 550: 1; Lot 551: 1; Lot 552: 16 (including C-72-180 to C-72-183); Lot 554: 1; Lot 829: 4.

171. Jar with ridged shoulder. Inv. No. C-72-163. Lot 552. Pl. 22.
P.H. 0.038. Est. D. rim 0.078. One rim fragment.

172. Jar base. Inv. No. C-72-164. Lot 552. Pl. 22.
P.H. 0.010. Est. D. 0.060. One base fragment.

Group II

These thin-walled, mouldmade vessels, chiefly beakers with small rolled lip and wide rim left plain and with moulded decoration below, were produced primarily during the Augustan period in a number of areas in northern Italy, southern Switzerland, Gaul, and Austria.[58] Most have signatures, the best known of which are those of the Aco workshops. The Aco-beaker group is essentially a mixture of the elements of the thin-walled class and the motifs and moulded techniques of Italian sigillata. This is a fragile ware, and most of the pieces recovered at Stobi are very small.[59]

173. Aco Beaker. Inv. No. C-71-46. Lot 221. Pl. 163.
Max.P.Dim. 0.027. Th. 0.002. One small fragment from side wall of an Aco beaker. Light red (2.5YR 6/8) clay with surfaces fired reddish yellow (5YR 6/6). Tiny moulded thorns preserved over entire surface.

Group III

A few beakers or jars with gray fabric and black slip have been found at Stobi. Their technique, shape, and decoration put them more comfortably in the class of Thin-Walled wares than with the Black-Gloss wares. Three pieces are decorated in an applied pinecone-scale pattern. The origin of this group is not known.

174. Inv. No. C-72-158. Lot 549. Pl. 22.
P.H. 0.015. D. 0.055. One base fragment, slightly concave. Gray (10YR 4/1) clay fired gray (5/1) on interior and covered with a dull black slip on the exterior. The exterior surface is covered with applied pinecone scales.
Cf. Moevs, "Cosa," 54–55, pl. 2: 14 in Form 1. These examples, however, dated within the period 150–75 B.C., are gray but without black slip. Other examples cited by Moevs are later and show the scales more widely spaced. Fragments with this treatment from the Athenian Agora suggest a date of mid-1st century A.C. (personal communication from John Hayes). Cf. Maneva (1979) pl. 12, no. 141.

175. Inv. No. C-72-48. Lot 552. Pls. 22, 163.
Max.P.Dim. 0.050. One fragment from side wall. Fabric and decoration as the preceding example.
One additional wall fragment, C-72-159, from Lot 549.

176. Inv. No. C-71-287. Lot 248. Pls. 22, 163.
P.H. 0.032. Est. D. rim 0.080. One rim fragment of globular jar. Dark gray (10YR 4/1) fabric and surface. A series of vertical ridges or long, pointed appliquéd leaves decorated the shoulder of the vessel.

[58] Recent discussions with bibliography appear in M. Lavizzari Pedrazzini, "Artigianato colto e di Tradizione ellenistica nella transpadana di età Augustea. La ceramica Tipo Aco," *RCRFActa* 25/26 (1987) 255–280, and L. Mazzeo Saracino in *EAA* 2, 175–230. See also M. Vegas, "Aco-Becher," *RCRFActa* 11/12 (1969–70) 107–124.

[59] **96** is perhaps another example of Aco ware.

177. Inv. No. C-75-34. Grave 304. Pl. 163.
Max.P.Dim. 0.023. Th. 0.003. One fragment of wall. Dark gray (10YR 4/1) fabric with dark gray to black lusterless thick slip on both surfaces. Dotlike pine-scale decoration covers surface.
Moevs, "Cosa," 93, 94, pls. 14, 63, no. 151, shows an example with this kind of decoration in the group of black-lacquered wares dated to the 1st century B.C.

Group IV

A series of small bowls and jars with incurving walls and everted or moulded rim occur at Stobi in deposits of the 1st century A.C. The fabric varies from light red to reddish yellow in color and is usually micaceous. All examples are slipped in red, orange, pink, or reddish brown tones, often with a metallic luster. Most are decorated with sand on one or both surfaces, usually with the area below the lip or shoulder carination on exterior reserved. According to Moevs, "Cosa," 127, 133–37, sand decoration derives from the La Tène tradition, appears at Cosa in the third quarter of the 1st century B.C., and continues to be produced through the Claudio-Neronian period, with greatest popularity in the second quarter of the 1st century A.C.[60] Most of the Stobi examples are probably of central Italian origin.[61] A few may be local.

Most of the bowls at Stobi belong either to the general Moevs, "Cosa," Form 36 (pl. 24:231, 232; pl. 25:238, 239) or Form 61.

Date of this group at Stobi: mid- to late 1st century A.C.

Bowls

178. Lot 249, No. 35. Pl. 22.
H. 0.050. Est. D. rim 0.070. Mended and complete. Dark grayish brown (10YR 4/2) clay with surface slip(?) brown to pale brown (10YR 5/3–6/3) and some dripping on exterior. Appears to have been discolored by fire.

179. Inv. No. C-71-289. Lot 231. Pl. 22.
P.H. 0.013. Est. D. rim 0.060. One rim with reddish yellow (5YR 6/6) fabric and reddish gray (5YR 5/2) metallic slip on exterior, reddish gray to brown (5/4) on interior. Irregularly spaced medium grains of applied sand cover surface below lip with medium heavy coverage.

180. Inv. No. C-74-444. Lot 1510. Pl. 22.
P.H. 0.020. Est. D. rim 0.090. One rim fragment. Light red (2.5YR 6/8) clay with red (2.5YR 5/6) lustrous slip on both surfaces. Sparse, irregular coating of fine sand on interior and exterior.
Moevs, "Cosa," Form 36.

181. Lot 231, No. 95. Pl. 22.
P.H. 0.013. Est. D. rim 0.080. One rim fragment. Reddish yellow (5YR 6/6) clay and light reddish brown (2.5YR) slip on exterior, light red to weak red on interior. Moderate irregular covering of find sand on exterior under lip groove.
Similar to Moevs, "Cosa," form 61.

182. Inv. No. C-71-41. Lot 30. Pls. 22, 163.
P.H. 0.038. Est. D. rim 0.070. One fragment of rim and wall. Reddish yellow (5YR 7/6) clay with weak metallic red to mottled reddish brown (2.5YR) in exterior and interior, respectively. Regular, heavy coating of fine sand on exterior under groove below rim.
Similar to Moevs, "Cosa," Form 61.

183. Lot 231, No. 7. Pl. 22.
P.H. 0.012. Est. D. rim 0.100. One small rim fragment. Reddish yellow (5YR 7/6) clay and red (2.5YR 5/6) slip alternating with gray on exterior, light red on interior fired gray at rim. Moderate, regular coating of fine sand on exterior under lip.
Similar to Moevs, "Cosa," Form 61.

184. Inv. No. C-71-291. Lot 248. Pl. 22.
P.H. 0.023. Est. D. rim 0.090. One fragment of rim and wall. Reddish yellow (5YR 6/6) clay with reddish gray to reddish brown (5YR 5/2–5/3) slip on exterior, yellowish red (5YR 5/6) on interior. Regular, sparse coating of find sand on exterior under groove at carination.

185. Inv. No. C-71-304. Lot 228. Pl. 22.
P.H. 0.027. Est. D. rim 0.120. One fragment of rim and wall. Pink (7.5YR 7/4) fabric and reddish brown slip with metallic luster on interior and ex-

[60] Nolen, Mayet review (cited in note 54, above) 195, suggests rather a range of Claudio-Neronian to Flavian, which fits the Stobi evidence better.

[61] M. M. Moevs (personal communication). See also Kenrick, *Berenice* 3, 315 (Fabric D).

terior. Heavy, regular coating of coarse sand on exterior below shoulder groove.
Moevs, "Cosa," form 36.

186. Inv. No. C-71-107. Lot 248. Pls. 22, 163.
P.H. 0.042. Est. D. rim 0.080. One fragment of rim and wall. Reddish yellow (5YR 6/6) clay with brown to dark brown (7.5YR) dull slip on interior and exterior. Moderate, irregular coating of coarse sand on exterior under shoulder groove in some areas and up to lip edge in others.
Moevs, "Cosa," Form 36.
One additional example from the same Lot.

187. Inv. No. C-71-305. Lot 249. Pl. 22.
P.H. 0.028. Est. D. rim 0.080. One fragment of rim and wall. Reddish yellow (5YR 6/6) clay and dark gray to yellowish red (5YR 5/6) slip on exterior, lustrous red (2.5YR) on interior. Irregular, moderate coverage of coarse sand on exterior under groove below lip.
Moevs, "Cosa," form 36.
One additional example from the same Lot.

188. Lot 1501, No. 11. Pl. 22.
P.H. 0.012. Est. D. rim 0.090. One rim fragment. Reddish yellow (5YR 5/6) clay with yellowish red to reddish yellow (5YR 4/6–6/6) mottled slip on exterior and reddish brown slip on interior. Very fine sand coating on exterior below rim ridge. Related to Mayet Forms 30, 37.

189. Lot 1495, No. 12. Pl. 22.
P.H. 0.018. Est. D. rim 0.070. One rim fragment. Light reddish brown (5YR 6/4) clay and dark brown (7.5YR 3/2) slip with very metallic luster on exterior and dull finish on interior. Fine sand coating on exterior below lip groove.
Related to Mayet Forms 30, 37 dated Tiberio-Claudian to Flavian (second and third quarters of the 1st century A.C.).

190. Lot 445, No. 9. Pl. 23.
P.H. 0.025. Est. D. rim 0.100. One fragment of rim and wall. Pinkish gray (7.5YR 7/2) clay and weak red to red (2.5YR 4/2–4/6) metallic slip on exterior, fired nonmetallic on interior. Regular, heavy coating of fine sand on exterior below lip.

Bowl with vertical rim

191. Inv. No. C-74-483. Lot 1089. Pl. 23.
P.H. 0.031. Est. D. rim 0.112. One rim fragment. Reddish yellow (5YR 6/6) clay and dull, thin reddish brown (5YR 5/4) slip on other surfaces. Regular, heavy coating of find sand on exterior below groove at lower edge of reserved space under rim.
Moevs, "Cosa," Form 48, pl. 69:242 in the group of Augustan Proto-Orange Glaze Ware. This form is not found among the metallic glazed or orange-glazed ware of the Tiberian period ("Cosa," 149). Related to Mayet Form 37.

Small jar with two handles

192. Inv. No. C-71-51. Lot 415. Grave 67. Pls. 23, 163.
H. 0.055. D. rim 0.040. Complete. Pink (7.5YR 7/4) clay and discolored yellowish red (5YR 5/6) to dull brown slip on exterior. Irregular, moderate coating of fine sand, badly worn on exterior.
Related to Moevs, "Cosa," Form 62.

193. Inv. No. C-71-130. Lot 43. Grave 80. Pl. 23.
H. 0.067. H. 0.040. Complete. Pink to light brown (7.5YR 7/4–6/4) clay with dull, well-worn brown slip on exterior. Traces of sand.
Related to Moevs "Cosa," Form 62.

194. Lot 248, No. 83. Pl. 23.
P.H. 0.190. Est. D. rim 0.050. One fragment of rim, shoulder, and handle. Reddish yellow (5YR 6/6) clay and red slip on both surfaces. Traces of sand.

195. Inv. No. C-71-295. Lot 248. Pl. 23.
P.H. 0.031. Est. D. rim 0.060. One fragment of rim and wall with traces of handles. Reddish yellow (5YR 7/6) fabric and dull red slip on interior and exterior. Regular, heavy coating of fine sand on exterior below shoulder.

Bases

196. Lot 249, No. 1. Pl. 23.
P.H. 0.020. D. 0.032. One base fragment. Reddish yellow (5YR 6/6) fabric and red (2.5YR 5/6–6/6) mottled with gray on exterior, metallic on interior. Irregular, moderate coating of coarse sand on exterior.

197. Inv. No. C-74-449. Lot 1510. Pl. 23.
P.H. 0.031. Est. D. 0.036. One base fragment. Red (2.5YR 5/6) fabric and slip of same color on exterior. Interior slip is lustrous reddish brown to red. Regular, heavy coating of fine white sand over exterior surface.

198. Lot 249, No. 103. Pl. 23.
P.H. 0.015. Est. D. 0.050. One base fragment. Yellowish brown (10YR) clay with yellowish brown to yellow (10YR 6/4–7/6) slip on exterior; interior is a metallic reddish yellow. Regular, medium heavy coating of coarse sand on interior.

199. Lot 249, No. 2. Pl. 23.
P.H. 0.020. Est. D. 0.050. One base fragment. Reddish yellow (5YR 6/6) clay with dull slip mottled red (2.5YR 5/6) to black (3/2) on exterior, weak red on interior. Regular, heavy coating of sand on the exterior.
Others: Lot 229: 1; Lot 230: 1; Lot 231: 3; Lot 249: 5; Lot 257: 1; Lot 443: 1; Lot 488: 1; Lot 1417: 1; Lot 1418: 1; Lot 1425: 1; Lot 1497: 1.

Group V

This group consists of small bowls with applied floral barbotine decoration. Light red (2.5YR 6/6) to reddish yellow fabric (5YR 7/6) with red, reddish yellow, pink, or reddish brown slip. Although the earliest examples of these bowls are probably imports from central or northern Italy or from provincial workshops in Noricum and Pannonia (Emona or Sirmium),[62] it is possible that some of the later examples are of local manufacture, based on the similarity of the fabric to that of local wares. The use of barbotine ornament extends into the mid-2nd century at Stobi and elsewhere until the late 2nd century.[63]

Bowls with straight wall, vertical rim

200. Inv. No. C-71-292. Lot 248. Pl. 23.
P.H. 0.083. Est. D. rim 0.070. One rim fragment. Light red (2.5YR 6/6) fabric with red to reddish yellow (2.5YR 5/6–5YR 5/6) lustrous slip on exterior; interior slip is dull and peeling at rim. Part of a floral barbotine design on wall.
Similar to Moevs, "Cosa," Form 62. The almost vertical wall is common to the Tiberian variation of this shape ("Cosa," 348, 349, 351, 353, pls. 38, 79). Imported.

201. Inv. No. C-71-230. Lot 248. Pl. 23.
P.H. 0.049. Est. D. rim 0.070. Two fragments of rim and wall. Light red (2.5YR 6/6) fabric with rather badly discolored surface. On interior lustrous reddish brown to dark reddish brown (5YR 4/3–3/3) slip. On the wall, within an area framed by two grooves, barbotine decoration consisting of small dots and a large flower petal or leaf.
Moevs, "Cosa," Form 62, Group 3 (pp. 180, 181) but without grooves. Imported.

202. Inv. No. C-74-430. Lot 1479. Pl. 23.
P.H. 0.036. Est. D. rim 0.072. One rim fragment. Reddish yellow (5YR 6/6) clay with dull red slip on exterior and weak red (2.5YR 4/2–3/2) to dusky red on interior. Plantlike barbotine decorates side wall.
Probably local.

Carinated bowl

203. Inv. No. C-74-236. Lot 1629. Pl. 24.
P.H. 0.060. Est. D. rim 0.120. Rim and wall fragment. Light brown (7.5YR 6/4) fabric with dull reddish yellow to reddish brown (5YR 6/6–5/4) slip on exterior and reddish brown on interior. Area above carination is decorated with a row of small dots and a large petal or leaf.
Probably local.

204. Lot 486, No. 25. Pl. 24.
P.H. 0.043. Est. D. rim 0.103. One fragment of rim and wall. Reddish yellow (5YR 6/6) fabric with red slip on interior and exterior (2.5YR 5/6). Floral barbotine above carination and groove below rim.
Probably local.
Additional examples of the carinated form: Lot 231: C-71-293; Lot 1415: C-74-241; Lot 1475: C-74-419; Lot 1478: C-74-427.

Group VI

These double-handled cups have a shape similar to those in Group V, but they are larger and taller with a pink, pinkish brown (7.5YR 7/4–6/4), to

[62] Brukner, *Rimska Keramika*, 36, 37.

[63] Brukner, *Rimska Keramika*, 37, and the technique occurs even later in Moesia Inferior, B. Soultov, *Centres antiques de poteries en Mésie inférieure* (Sofia 1976). A recent discovery of a kiln for Thin-Walled ware is discussed in L. Plešnicar-Gec, "Thin-Walled Pottery from Slovenia," *RCRFActa* 25/26 (1987) 451–464. For Thin-Walled production in Sirmium, see A. Premk, "Production of Early Roman Pottery in Sirmium," *RCRFActa* 25/26 (1987) 444–448.

pale brown (10YR 6/3) fabric and brown slip. Barbotine decoration is common. Moevs, "Cosa," Form 38.

205. Inv. No. C-74-2. Lot 1059. Grave 33. Pl. 24.
H. 0.100. D. rim 0.127. Mended and almost complete. Very pale brown (10YR 7/4) to pink (7.5YR 7/4) fabric with worn brown slip on both surfaces, fired gray in some areas.
Import.

206. Inv. No. C-75-79. Lot 1703. Pl. 24.
P.H. 0.050. Est. D. rim 0.173. One rim fragment. Fabric and slip as the preceding.
Additional examples of the same form: Lot 249: 1; Lot 1084: 1; Lot 1498: 1.

207. Inv. No. C-71-129. Lots 43, 488, Grave 80. Pl. 25.
H. 0.096. D. rim 0.133. Complete. Thickened rim and ring base. Light brown (7.5YR 6/4) clay with dull, uneven brown slip. On body the Greek inscription: ΜΑΚΕΔΟΝΙΚΟΥ.
W-MZ (1971) 415, pl. 87.

208. Inv. No. C-74-466. Lot 1418. Pl. 24.
P.H. 0.113. D. base 0.058. Mended from many fragments and preserving base and body of vessel. Pink (7.5YR 7/4) fabric with well-worn reddish brown (5YR 4/4) slip, metallic in spots. Very carelessly applied floral barbotine above and below double-ridged carination.

Miscellaneous

209. Jar with tall, curved rim. Inv. No. C-75-90. Grave 310. Pl. 25.
P.H. 0.042. Est. D. rim 0.100. Two fragments preserving rim. Light brown (7.5YR 6/4) micaceous clay. Surface fired varying tones of brown.
Import.

210. Small hemispherical cup. Inv. No. C-71-154. Lot 45. Pl. 25.
H. 0.050. D. rim 0.090. Complete. Two grooves at midpoint of body and two concentric grooves isolate the base. Light brown (7.5YR 6/4) clay with faint traces of red slip; surface, however, is discolored.
Cf. Moevs, "Cosa," form 36, 159, 160; and Mayet Form 33, dated to the first third of the 1st century A.C. but without the grooved base. Import.

211. Beaker. Inv. No. C-71-288. Lot 75. Pls. 25, 164.
Max.P.Dim. 0.070. Th. 0.003. Several fragments mended from side wall with overall rouletting. Single deep groove at point where side wall curves inward to met base. Reddish yellow (5YR 6/6) to light brown (7.5YR 6/4) fabric with very faint red slip visible only in groove and rouletting incisions now. Interior surface unslipped.
Import.

212. Small cup with handles. Inv. No. C-71-69. Lot 411, Grave 74. Pl. 25.
H. 0.059. D. rim 0.077. Complete. Very hard, gray (7.5YR N5/) fabric with dull, black slip. Burned from grave fire. Single, horizontal row of barotine dots.
Derivative of Moevs, "Cosa," Form 42, Mayet Form 37. The walls of this piece are rather thick. Tiberian.
Import.

213. Barbotine fragment. Inv. No. C-70-103. Lot 487.
Max.P.Dim. 0.027. Small fragment of wall decorated with pointed spines called "San Calocero" style by Moevs, "Cosa," (pls. 82:384 and 387, 41, 42). Micaceous light brown (7.5YR 6/4) fabric with reddish brown (5YR 5/4) metallic slip on interior.
One additional example from Lot 1418.

214. Small, narrow cup. Inv. No. C-70-58. Lot 487. Grave 21. Pls. 25, 164.
H. 0.067. D. rim 0.067. Complete. Dark gray (10YR 4/1) fabric and dark gray to black lusterless slip on both surfaces. Four deep oblong thumb impressions are placed evenly around circumference of body.
This kind of decoration reflects a similar decoration found on metal vases and on glass. Most examples of thumb-impressed decoration on metal and glass date to the second half of the 1st century A.C., but there are not many securely dated examples. Some of the pottery with this type of decoration at Cosa may date to the 1st century B.C. In Noricum, Raetia, and Pannonia, the form is produced in the 2nd century. For a discussion of the problem see Moevs, "Cosa," 86, 887, Mayet 37. For glass see Clasina Isings, *Roman Glass from Dated Finds* (Groningen 1957) 46, 47, Form 32, dated 30–70 A.C.
Import.

215. Small cup with handle. Inv. No. C-71-294. Lot 248. Pl. 25.

P.H. 0.038. Est. D. rim 0.090. One fragment of rim and curved wall. One handle preserved. Reddish yellow (5YR 6/6) fabric with light red (2.5YR 6/8) slip on both surfaces. One round thumb impression in the space between the rim groove and carination preserved.

Import.

216. Bowl. Inv. No. C-71-190. Lot 230. Pls. 25, 164.

P.H. 0.042. One fragment from wall and shoulder of a bowl with traces of handle attachment. Reddish yellow (5YR 6/6) clay with red, light red, weak red (2.5YR 5/6–6/6–5/2) metallic slip. Closely spaced diagonal bands of rouletting.

Perhaps Moevs, "Cosa," Form 61, pl. 21, nos. 206, 207, pl. 67, no. 207, dated to the Augustan period, but these examples have no slip. The slip color of the Stobi example would fit the metallic glaze-ware groups from Cosa, perhaps of the Tiberian period when orange and dark pink as well as the pink tone of the Augustan period were popular (Moevs, "Cosa," 173).

Import.

217. Large jar. Inv. No. C-74-451. Lot 1510. Pl. 26.

P.H. 0.093. Part of the lower portion of a large, closed vessel. Pink micaceous (5YR 8/4–7/4) fabric with light red (2.5YR 6/8) slip on exterior and splattered onto parts of interior. A single ridge is preserved at point of widest diameter and the surface below has double-petal floral barbotine decoration.

See Moevs, "Cosa," pl. 45:422, for similar decoration.

Jars and pitchers

It has not been possible to assign these pieces from the West Cemetery to a group because they have all been badly discolored from burning as a result of their presence in the grave fire. All have one sliced handle.

218. Small jar with one handle. Inv. No. C-74-253. Lot 1454. Grave 62. Pl. 26.

H. 0.093. D. rim 0.070. Complete. Pinkish white to pinkish gray (7.5YR 8/2–7/2) fabric with worn dark gray (5YR 4/1) slip on exterior dripped into interior.

Moevs, "Cosa," Form 51, pl. 26:249, pp. 154, 155, dated Late Augustan through Tiberian.

219. Tall jar with single handle. Inv. No. C-71-34. Lot 453. Grave 56. Pl. 26.

H. 0.130. D. rim 0.089. Complete. Discolored brownish yellow (10YR 6/4).

This is a popular shape in Aegean sites, and according to John Hayes (personal communication) it is probably an Aegean product. Cf. Robinson, *Agora*, G103, pl. 7, now Flavian with Hayes' revised dating. Inv. No. C-74-319 (Lot 1070) is a smaller example with very thin walls.

220. Tall plump jar with one handle. Inv. No. C-71-9. Lot 381. Grave 28. Pl. 26.

H. 0.137. D. rim 0.100. Complete. Pink (7.5YR 7/4) fabric with partial brown slip.

This form is of Italian origin and one of the most popular shapes in Roman pottery from the mid-1st century A.C. to the early 3rd century. Moevs, "Cosa," Form 68, pp. 237, 238, pl. 46, no. 433; Robinson, *Agora*, G117, G118, J10, J11, J20, J21; *Duklja*, no. 35, p. 204.

221. Small jar with one handle. Inv. No. C-71-37. Lot 19. Grave 58. Pl. 26.

H. 0.080. D. rim 0.073. Complete. Light red (2.5YR 6/8) clay with discolored gray surface.

222. Jar with one handle. Inv. No. C-71-40. Lot 412. Grave 51. Pl. 26.

H. 0.086. D. rim 0.070. Complete. Micaceous, light brown (7.5YR 6/4) fabric with dull, brown slip.

223. Jar with one handle. Inv. No. C-74-319. Lot 1070. Grave 252. Pl. 26.

P.H. 0.105. Est. D. 0.073. Th. 0.002. Mended from several fragments. Very thin and rather brittle and rough light gray (10YR 5/1–4/1) fabric with many white inclusions.

Cf. Hayes, "Paphos," fig. 7, no. 7, almost identical in form and dated to the first half of the 2nd century.

224. Inv. No. C-72-72. Lot 718. Pl. 26.

H. 0.087. D. rim. 0.075. D. base 0.042. Mended. Handle fragmentary. Fabric and slip discolored, but exterior shows metallic luster in areas extending over upper body and dripped down to flat base.

Terra Sigillata

During the early Roman period, fine tablewares covered with a red gloss were extremely popular and widely distributed throughout the Roman world. The term *terra sigillata* has come to be widely used for the various wares of this tradition.[64] Among these wares, the best known are Eastern Sigillata A, Eastern Sigillata B, Çandarli, Italian Sigillata (including products of Arezzo, Pozzuoli, and other Italian centers), Cypriot Sigillata, and Gaulish Sigillata. The term *terra sigillata* is not really an accurate descriptive term for all these wares since the Latin word *sigillata*, meaning "decorated with little figures," should not apply to those wares that are not decorated in relief. For lack of a better general category name, however, it continues to be used along with the term "red-gloss wares."

The arrangement of wares that follows is essentially chronological.

Eastern Sigillata A (225–234)

Eastern Sigillata A Ware, or Pergamene, as it used to be called, was the earliest of the red-gloss wares produced on a large scale.[65] Its center or centers of manufacture have not yet been securely identified, although it has been found in especially large quantities at Tarsus, Antioch, Samaria, and Tel Anafa. Possibilities, therefore, include southeastern Asia Minor, Syria, and Israel.

The clay of the ware is fine and light in color, primarily within the range 10YR 7/3, 7/4, 8/4, with some variations to reddish yellows (7.5YR, 5YR). The color is often referred to as buff with variations to cream, yellow, or pink. The combination of this light clay with its red to dark red (2.5YR 3/6, 4/6, 4/8), thick, smooth gloss is very distinctive.[66] The gloss is usually not very lustrous.

Eastern Sigillata A came into popularity during the mid-2nd century B.C. and was exported widely throughout the eastern Mediterranean during the second half of that century through the 1st century A.C.

Of the fourteen pieces of Eastern Sigillata A at Stobi that preserve enough of the profile to make the form clear, 10 are the Samaria Form 1 plates with upturned, incurved rim. All occur in deposits of the late 2nd century or the 1st century B.C. A number of large flat bases probably belong to plates of this shape also. It was one of the most popular shapes in the local ware.[67]

Two other forms of plates and one of a bowl occur at Stobi. Neither example of the shallow plate with small upturned lip (*Antioch*, Shape 137), which dates to the second half of the 2nd century, comes from a good context at Stobi.[68]

The small hemispherical bowl occurs at Stobi in a deposit dated to the Augustan period and provided a model for several local imitations. It was the plate with outrolled rim (Samaria Form 10), however, that proved to be extremely popular, and although only one example of the original import exists, a number of local imitations (ER Form 1) were produced in a variety of sizes. The greatest number of local imitations fall within the second half of the 1st century A.C.

225. Dish. Samaria Form 1. Inv. No. C-71-70. Lot 140. Pl. 27.

[64] See F. Krizek, "Vasa Arretina," *RCRFActa* 3 (1961) 35–44, and note 1. For comprehensive studies, see H. Comfort in *RE*, "Terra Sigillata," cols. 1291–1351, and in *EAA*, Supplement 1970, "Terra Sigillata." The meaning of the term *terra sigillata* or Samian ware is discussed in the following recent articles: A. King, "A Graffito from La Graufesenque and 'samia vasa,' " *Brittania* 11 (1980) 139–143; J. Bradley, "Medieval Samian Ware—A Medicinal Suggestion," *Ulster Journal of Archaeology* (3rd ser.) 44/45 (1981/82) 196, 197; with a response and discussion of the confusion of the Roman and Medieval definitions by A. King, "Medieval *terra sigillata*—A Source of Confusion?" *Ulster Journal of Archaeology* (3rd ser.) 47 (1984) 182, 183.

[65] The term Eastern Sigillata A was first proposed by K. Kenyon in the publication of the pottery from Samaria (*Samaria*, 282) and has been followed primarily by Hellstrom (*Labraunda*, 29, 30) and Hayes (in *Corinth*, 450–454, 468–470, and in *EAA* 2, 9–48). Note also J. Gunneweg, I. Perlman, J. Yellin, "The Provenience, Typology, and Chronology of Eastern Terra Sigillata," *Qedem* 17 (1983). The form numbers cited in the section of Eastern Sigillata A reflect the Samaria and Antioch typologies.

[66] See *Samaria*, 346, for Munsell colors of Eastern Sigillata A from Samaria and other sites.

[67] Stobi Hellenistic Form 3. In a recent article ("Presigillata from Morgantina," *AJA* 91 [1987] 85, 93), S. C. Stone III suggests that Eastern Sigillata A influenced the development of presigillata, especially the plate similar to Samaria Form 1.

[68] There is another example of this form from earlier excavations at Stobi in the Archaeological Museum in Skopje.

H. 0.024. D. rim 0.153. Partially preserved. Shall dish with flat floor and almost vertical wall. Low ring base with broad resting surface. Double-dipping streaks visible at center of interior, and on exterior at rim and underside of base where the red is darker (2.5YR 4/4). Parts of five palmette stamps are preserved within concentric circles of rouletting. Graffito has been scratched on underside of base.

The foot is similar to *Samaria*, fig. 73, nos. 3 and 4. For the palmette stamps, see fig. 74, no. 12. *Antioch*, Shape 126 has the diameter of the foot more than half the diameter of the rim (pl. IV:126K, similar to the Stobi example but for the foot profile). Antioch Shape 126k is dated to the first three quarters of the 1st century B.C. *Antioch*, Shape 124f has a foot more like ours, with indented exterior profile that is the earliest form for this shape. Cf. also Robinson, *Agora*, pl. 60, F2. A recent discussion of the shape may be found in Kenrick, *Berenice 3*, 225–227.

Context for this example dates to the first half of the 1st century B.C.

226. Dish. Samaria Form 1. Lot 841, No. 7. Pl. 27.

P.H. 0.018. Est. D. rim 0.325. One rim fragment.

Cf. *Samaria*, fig. 73, nos. 3 and 7 (dated pre-30 B.C. to Augustan); *Antioch*, pl. IV, Shape 126.

227. Dish. Samaria Form 1. Lot 549, No. 502. Pl. 27.

P.H. 0.025. Est. D. rim 0.260. One rim fragment. Double-dipping streaks visible on interior just below rim and on exterior wall.

Antioch, Shape 132k or possibly 124.

228. Dish. Samaria Form 1. Lot 610, No. 52. Pl. 27.

P.H. 0.025. Est. D. rim 0.166. Rim fragment.

Cf. *Samaria*, fig. 66, no. 3 (pre-30 B.C.).

229. Dish base. Samaria Form 1. Lot 549, No. 42. Pl. 28.

P.H. 0.017. D. 0.120. One fragment of ring base. Two concentric circles in center of floor surrounded by band of rouletting.

Seven additional rims and five bases of Samaria Form 1: Lot 609: 1r; Lot 552: 4r, 3b; Lot 549: 1r; Lot 547: 1r; Lot 594: 1b; Lot 48: 1b.

230. Plate. Inv. No. C-74-290. Lot 1327. Pl. 27.

P.H. 0.012. Max.P.Dim. 0.052. One rim fragment of shallow plate with small, upturned edge.

Cf. *Antioch*, Shape 137f or 137p, dated to the second half of the 2nd century B.C. One similar example from Lot 22.

231. Flat-based dish. Samaria Form 10. Inv. No. C-71-257. Lot 230. Pl. 28.

H. 0.024. Est. D. rim 0.150. One fragment of complete profile from dish with outrolled rim and flat, slightly concave base. Double line of narrow rouletting on floor at the point where side walls meet the floor.

Samaria, fig. 79, no. 2; *Antioch*, Shape 143, pl. 4, dated to the first three quarters of the 1st century B.C.; *EAA* 2, J.W. Hayes, "sigillate orientale A," 30, Form 12, no. 10 on fig. II, dated 40 B.C. to 10 A.C.; Kenrick, *Berenice 3*, 229 and fig. 41. This piece comes from a deposit dated approximately 40–60 A.D.

232. Hemispherical bowl. Samaria Form 16. Inv. No. C-71-315. Lot 259. Pl. 27.

H. 0.038. D. rim 0.090. Several fragments mended to give complete profile. Small bowl with moulded ring base.

Samaria, fig. 80:6 (last quarter of the 1st century B.C.); *Antioch*, Shape 164; Kenrick, *Berenice 3*, 230, 231.

233. Dish base. Lot 260, No. 4. Pl. 28.

P.H. 0.025. Est. D. 0.185. Part of ring base for large dish, probably Samaria Form 1. The foot profile is straight on the exterior, a characteristic dated to the late first century B.C.

Cf. Hayes, "Knossos," 264, fig. 114:1 and 2, dated 1st century B.C. or Augustan.

234. Small dish base. Lot 228, no. 25. Pl. 27.

P.H. 0.013. Est. D. 0.083. Part of small ring base, perhaps Samaria Form 1.

Italian Sigillata (235–296)

The finest of the Roman red-gloss tablewares were those produced in the workshops at Arezzo in north central Italy from ca. 30 B.C. until the third quarter of the 1st century A.C.[69] Following

[69] The bibliography for Italian sigillata is extensive. The recent volume of the *RCRFActa* (25/26, 1987) contains many articles concerned with the most recent work on Italian sigillata. Form numbers in the catalogue refer to the work of

the lead of the Arretine potters, other workshops in Italy at Pozzuoli, Pisa, Modena, Luna, the Po Valley, and at Lyon in France also produced wares that are virtually indistinguishable from Arretine of the same period, so fine was their technique and red-gloss surface. Only the potter's stamp can securely distinguish the products of the various workshops.[70]

Thus the term Italian sigillata is used to describe the class of wares with clay that is generally light red (2.5YR 6/6–6/8) in color but that may vary more toward red or reddish yellow (5YR 6/6 – 7/6) or even pink (7.5YR 7/4). The gloss is uniformly a 2.5YR 4/8 or 5/8, that is, a red that tends toward the darker and brownish tones and presents a very clear, lustrous finish.[71]

Italian workshops produced both plain or undecorated vessels made on the wheel and relief-decorated vessels made by a combination mould-wheel technique.[72]

Individual potters and workshops marked their products with stamps, usually on the exterior wall in the case of vessels decorated in relief, but on the plain wares or those decorated only with appliqués, the stamp was placed in the center of the vessel floor. Stamp frames are most often square or rectangular, but some frames are round, oblong, diamond-shaped, quatrefoil, lunate, or other unusual shapes.[73] During the Tiberian period, stamps in the form of a foot sole (*planta pedis*) became popular, and by ca. 30–40 A.C. they had become common.[74] Within the stamp frame, whatever its form, the potter's name is written in initials or is abbreviated in a variety of ways dependent upon the particular shop or branch, the vessel series, or the year.

At Stobi no fragments of the fine, early relief sigillata have been found. A black-gloss piece with gray fabric (**72**) does show part of a finely worked relief similar to scenes on vessels of the M. Perennius workshops in Arezzo. Several other pieces with relief decoration are, in fact, so small that it is impossible to identify the ware or motifs.

Almost all the Italian sigillata at Stobi belongs to the category of plain wares, some of which were decorated with appliquéd elements on the rim. Many do not occur in contemporary context and must be survival pieces. (Exceptions are **236**, **238**, **242**, **253**, **255**, **259**, **268**, **274**, **275**, **281** and stamps: **286**, **287**, **288** from Acropolis Lots 230, 231, 248, 249, 258, 259.)

Eleven examples of potters' stamps have been found at Stobi, five of which are in *planta pedis*.

Plate with overhanging rim

Haltern Type 1; Goudineau Types 15, 17; Kenrick, *Berenice 3*, 138, Group A.
Date: ca. 10 B.C. to 15 A.C.

235. Inv. No. C-71-102. Lot 228. Pl. 28.
P.H. 0.026. Est. D. rim 0.316. One fragment of rim and wall.

236. Lot 942, No. 29. Pl. 28.
P.H. 0.018. Est. D. rim 0.135. Rim and wall fragment.
Two other examples of this form: Lot 942: 1; Lot 400: 1.

Plate with moulded rim

Haltern Type 2; Hayes, "Corinth," Form 4B; Kenrick, *Berenice 3*, 141, Group B.
Date: ca. 10 B.C. to 35 A.C.

237. Inv. No. C-70-83. Lot 1016. Pl. 28.
P.H. 0.027. Est. D. rim 0.360. One rim fragment of large size.

238. Inv. No. C-71-336. Lot 231. Pl. 28.
P.H. 0.030. Est. D. rim 0.323. One fragment of rim and wall of large-size platter.

239. Inv. No. C-74-503. Lot 1453. Pl. 29.
P.H. 0.026. Est. D. rim 0.185. One rim fragment of standard size.

S. Loeschcke at Haltern, "Keramische Funde in Haltern," *Mitteilungen der Altertümskommission fur Westfalen* 5 (1909) 101–322; Goudineau at Bolsena, and Hayes, "Corinth." Recent detailed summaries with bibliography appear in Kenrick, *Berenice 3*, 125–135, and G. Pucci, "Terra Sigillata Italica," *EAA* 2, 359–404.

70 References to stamps follow Oxé-Comfort catalogue numbers. I am indebted to Howard Comfort for assistance in identifying many of the Stobi stamps.

71 For variations in fabric and discussion, see Kenrick, *Berenice 3*, 128–129.

72 A discussion of technique may be found in A. Stenico, *EAA*, 609–610, and *La ceramica arretina, II. Collezioni diverse; Funzoni, modelli, calchi, ecc.* (Milan 1966). Goudineau, deals with earlier plain wares, and Hayes, "Corinth," with the later ones.

73 Illustrations may be found in Oxé-Comfort, pls. VII–X, with discussion, and pp. 575–576.

74 Comfort, *RE*, 1312–1320; Oxé-Comfort, 575; Hayes, "Corinth," 442; Goudineau, 353, 354; Kenrick, *Berenice 3*, 133, 135.

240. Lot 249, No. 26. Pl. 29.
P.H. 0.030. Est. D. rim 0.153. One rim fragment with rouletting on lower moulding.

241. Inv. No. C-71-337. Lot 385. Pls. 29, 164.
P.H. 0.026. Est. D. rim 0.164. One rim fragment with rouletting on uppermost and lower moulding.

Plate with moulded rim and quarter-round moulding joining wall to floor

Haltern Type 3; Hayes, "Corinth," Form 11A; Kenrick, *Berenice* 3, 141, Group B, fig. 26, B206.
Date: ca. 1–30/35 A.C.

242. Inv. No. C-73-102. Lot 938. Pl. 29.
P.H. 0.021. Est. D. rim 0.151. One rim fragment with rouletting on upper moulding, carination, and below carination.
One similar example from Lot 1475.

243. Inv. No. C-74-484. Lot 1418. Pl. 29.
P.H. 0.022. Est. D. rim 0.122. One rim fragment.

Conical bowl with moulded rim

Haltern Type 8 or 9; Kenrick, *Berenice* 3, Group B or C.

244. Lot 231, No. 42. Pl. 29.
P.H. 0.014. Est. D. rim 0.132. One small rim fragment with rouletting on upper and lower mouldings.

245. Inv. No. C-71-310. Lot 230. Pl. 29.
P.H. 0.020. Est. D. rim 0.091. One small rim fragment.
One similar example from Lot 597.

Conical bowl with moulded rim

Goudineau Types 37a, 40; Hayes, "Corinth," Form 16c; Kenrick, *Berenice* 3, 145, Group C.
Date: ca. 5/10–45 A.C.

246. Lot 934, No. 3. Pl. 29.
P.H. 0.025. Est. D. rim 0.135. One rim fragment with rather thick walls and a wide band of rouletting on the exterior central moulding.
Rouletting on the central band is a characteristic of Kenrick's Group C.

247. Inv. No. C-74-509. Lot 1080. Pl. 30.
P.H. 0.025. Est. D. rim 0.163. One rim fragment.

248. Inv. No. C-71-21. Lot 389. Pl. 29.
P.H. 0.040. Est. D. rim 0.121. One fragment of rim and wall. Applied double spiral on central band and rouletting at upper moulding and carination.

249. Inv. No. C-71-311. Lot 445. Pls. 29, 164.
P.H. 0.030. Est. D. rim 0.124. One rim fragment. Rouletting on upper moulding and carination.
One similar piece in Lot 942.

Plate with vertical, moulded rim and flat floor

Goudineau Types 36, 39; Hayes, "Corinth," Form 8; Kenrick, *Berenice* 3, 145, Group C, fig. 27, B209.
Date: ca. 10/15–45 A.C.

250. Lot 483, No. 66. Pl. 30.
P.H. 0.016. Est. D. rim 0.240. One fragment of rim and floor from large plate. Wide band of rouletting on floor near side wall.

251. Lot 1475, No. 8. Pl. 29.
P.H. 0.016. Est. D. rim 0.140. One fragment of floor and wall. Band of rouletting in center of floor.

252. Lot 488, No. 55. Pl. 30.
P.H. 0.018. Est. D. rim 0.240. Two small rim fragments mended.

Plate with vertical, moulded rim

Goudineau Type 39c; Hayes, "Corinth," Form 12; Kenrick, *Berenice* 3, 150, Group D, fig. 288, B214.
Date: ca. 30–89/90 A.C.

253. Inv. No. C-71-52. Lot 245. Pls. 30, 164.
P.H. 0.028. Est. D. rim 0.178. Two fragments mended from rim and floor. Applied stars and rosettes on central band of rim. Band of rouletting in center of floor.

254. Inv. No. C-70-118. No Lot. Pls. 30, 165.
P.H. 0.022. Est. D. rim 0.178. One rim fragment. Groove at lip exterior and appliqué on exterior.

255. Inv. No. C-71-313. Lot 230. Pl. 30.
P.H. 0.024. Est. D. rim 0.153. One rim fragment. Pronounced upper and lower mouldings. Double spiral appliqué on central band.
Another similar example from the same Lot.

256. Inv. No. C-74-31. Lot 1319. Pls. 30, 165.
P.H. 0.038. Max.P.Dim. 0.062. One fragment of rim and wall, preserving garland and rooster in appliqué.

Plate with quarter-round moulding beneath rim

Hayes, "Corinth," Form 11D; Kenrick, *Berenice 3*, 150, Group D, fig. 28, B215.

257. Inv. No. C-71-350. Lot 258. Pl. 31.
P.H. 0.020. Est. D. rim 0.160. One rim fragment with rouletting at flange.

Conical bowl with moulded, vertical rim

Goudineau Type 40; Hayes, "Corinth," Form 23; Kenrick, *Berenice 3*, 150, Group D, fig. 29, B216.
Date: ca. 30–80/90 A.C.

258. Inv. No. C-73-107. Lot 934. Pl. 30.
P.H. 0.020. Est. D. rim 0.093. One rim fragment. Rouletting at top moulding and carination.

259. Inv. No. C-74-441. Lot 1510. Pl. 30.
P.H. 0.023. One rim fragment.
One additional example from Lot 248.

260. Inv. No. C-71-314. Lot 248. Pl. 30.
P.H. 0.045. Est. D. rim 0.112. One rim fragment.
A similar example from Lot 1418 has an appliqued rosette on the central band.

Dish with convex wall and rim moulding

Hayes, "Corinth," Form 6, pl. 86, nos. 17, 18.
Date: post-45 A.C.

261. Inv. No. C-70-97. Lot 1016. Pl. 31.
P.H. 0.020. Est. D. 0.138. One rim fragment. Spectacle spiral appliqué below rim.

Hemispherical flanged cup

Goudineau Type 38b; Hayes, "Corinth," Form 24; Kenrick, *Berenice 3*, 150, Group D, fig. 299, B217.
Date: ca. 35/40–89/90 A.C.

262. Inv. No. C-74-510. Lot 1510. Pl. 31.
P.H. 0.025. Est. D. rim 0.086. One rim fragment with rather thick walls.

263. Inv. No. C-74-424. Lot 1477. Pl. 31.
P.H. 0.020. Est. D. rim 0.111. One rim fragment.

264. Inv. No. C-75-31. Lot 1800. Pl. 31.
P.H. 0.023. Est. D. rim 0.130. One rim fragment. Rosette appliqué on rim.

265. Inv. No. C-74-155. Lot 1373. Pls. 31, 165.
P.H. 0.026. Est. D. rim 0.151. One rim fragment with star appliqué.

Miscellaneous forms

266. Krater. Inv. No. C-74-145. Lot 1474. Pl. 31.
P.H. 0.015. Est. D. rim 0.161. One small fragment of rim with rouletting.

267. Bowl. Lot 490, No. 16. Pl. 31.
P.H. 0.016. Est. D. rim 0.102. One fragment of rim.

268. Dish. Lot 934, No. 9. Pl. 31.
P.H. 0.023. Est. D. rim 0.235. One rim fragment.

269. Small bowl or beaker. Inv. No. C-71-106. Lot 258. Pl. 31.
P.H. 0.041. Est. D. rim 0.111. Two fragments from rim and wall mended. Rouletted band between grooves on side wall.
Cf. Hayes, "Corinth," Form 20A, pl. 84:62, dated 10–25 A.C.

270. Cup. Lot 230, No. 37. Pl. 31.
P.H. 0.035. Est. D. rim 0.067. One rim fragment with vertical wall.

271. Bowl with everted rim. Lot 942, No. 27. Pl. 32.
P.H. 0.016. Est. D. rim 0.090. One rim fragment.
Cf. Kenrick, *Berenice 3*, 165, Group H, fig. 30, B228.2, dated 15–60 A.C or later.

272. Bowl. Lot 26, No. 2. Pl. 32.
P.H. 0.036. Est. D. rim 0.103. One rim fragment.
Cf. Kenrick, *Berenice 3*, 163, Group G.

273. Beaker fragment. Inv. No. C-74-84. Lot 1434. Pl. 32.

P.H. 0.045. One fragment of side wall with incised diagonal lines.

274. Cylindrical beaker fragment. Inv. No. C-74-101. Lot 1358. Pl. 165.

P.H. 0.042. One fragment from side wall with diagonal rouletting.

Cf. Kenrick, *Berenice 3*, 173, fig. 31, B232.

275. Fragment of relief ware. Inv. No. C-74-420. Lot 1475. Pls. 32, 165.

Max.P.Dim. 0.055. One fragment from body of krater with floral decoration in relief.

Bases

276. Large plate base. Lot 259, No. 71. Pl. 32.

P.H. 0.022. Est. D. 0.278. One fragment of ring base. Double grooves on floor.

277. Large plate base. Lot 230, No. 3. Pl. 32.

P.H. 0.025. Est. D. 0.170. One fragment of ring base with double groove on floor.

Cf. Kenrick, *Berenice 3*, fig. 31, 233.2.

278. Large plate base. Lot 934, No. 1.

P.H. 0.026. Est. D. 0.205. One ring-base fragment with part of a band of rouletting preserved on floor.

279. Plate base. Lot 18, No. 3. Pl. 32.

P.H. 0.025. Est. D. 0.190. One ring-base fragment with wide band of rouletting on floor.

280. Small plate base. Inv. No. C-72-100. Lot 630. Pl. 32.

P.H. 0.018. Est. D. 0.063. Tall ring-base fragment.

281. Beaker base. Inv. No. C-71-351. Lot 441. Pl. 33.

P.H. 0.024. One small fragment.

282. Bowl base. Inv. No. C-74-160. Lot 1089. Pl. 33.

P.H. 0.022. Est. D. 0.061. One base fragment. Single groove on floor.

283. Bowl base. Lot 231, No. 1. Pl. 33.

P.H. 0.028. Est. D. 0.074. One ring-base fragment.

284. Bowl base. Lot 488, No. 53. Pl. 33.

P.H. 0.014. Est. D. 0.100. One ring-base fragment.

285. Bowl base. Inv. No. C-74-296. Lot 1569. Pl. 33.

P.H. 0.013. Est. D. 070. One ring-base fragment.

Stamps

286. Inv. No. C-71-120. Lot 259. Pls. 34, 166.

M.P.Dim. 0.023. Th. 0.005. Floor fragment preserving part of a two-line stamp in a rectangular frame: BLANDVS L. TITI, a workman of L. TITIVS at Rome; Oxé-Comfort 2074.

287. Inv. No. C-71-139. Lot 249. Pls. 34, 166.

M.P.Dim. 0.028. Floor fragment with two-line stamp in a rectangular frame: INVENTVS C. ANNI, workman of C. ANNIVS of Arezzo; Oxé-Comfort 83x.

288. Inv. No. C-71-116. Lot 248. Pls. 34, 166.

M.P.Dim. 0.019. Tiny ring base with horseshoe-shaped frame within which is the stamp of the potter GELLIVS QVADRATVS of Arezzo; Oxé-Comfort 737, 182 (cup bottom: Aquileia).

289. Inv. No. C-70-42. Lot 483. Pls. 34, 166.

M.P.Dim. 0.020. Ring base with rectangular frame preserving the stamp of the potter UMBRICIVS; Oxé-Comfort 2385, 54, or 39.

Cf. also S. v. Schnurbein, "Die römischen Militaranlagen bei Haltern," *Bodenaltentümer Westfalens* 14 (1974) no. 860, pl. 82.

290. Inv. No. C-73-44. Lot 940. Pls. 34, 166.

M.P.Dim. 0.035. Floor fragment with rectangular framed one-line stamp: illegible except for M.

291. Inv. No. C-74-76. Lot 1538. Pls. 34, 166.

M.P.Dim. 0.045. Floor fragment preserving part of a stamp (which may be in *planta pedis*) of the potter M. PERENNIVS of Arezzo by either SATURNINVS or CRESCENS; Oxé-Comfort 1281 or 1284.

292. Inv. No. C-74-224. Lot 1629. Pls. 34, 166.

M.P.Dim. 0.035. Floor fragment preserving part of stamp in *planta pedis* of the potter PESCENNIVS CLEMENS; Oxé-Comfort 1289.

293. Inv. No. C-72-99. Lot 620. Pls. 34, 166.

M.P.Dim. 0.065. Part of ring base with stamp of potter CAMVRIVS in *planta pedis*; Oxé-Comfort, pp. 132, 133.

294. Inv. No. C-74-67. Lot 1356. Pls. 34.
M.P.Dim. 0.031. Stamp of CAMVRIVS in *planta pedis.*

295. Inv. No. C-73-42. Lot 942. Pls. 34, 166.
M.P.Dim. 0.038. Floor fragment with stamp in *planta pedis* of the potter L. GELLIVS; Oxé-Comfort, p. 210, bottom left.

296. Inv. No. C-78-96. Lot 2094. Pl. 166.
M.P.Dim. 0.008. Th. 0.005. One fragment broken all around. Part of stamp in rectangular frame.

Other Western Sigillata (**297–302**)

As early as the first quarter of the 1st century A.C., potters in Gaul established factories producing red-gloss wares under the influence of Arretine. Others followed later in Pannonia, Spain, Britain, and elsewhere.[75] The fabric of the Gaulish and other provincial sigillata is darker than Arretine, and the surface finish has more the quality of a varnish than a gloss. Vessel walls are generally thicker than Arretine, and the range of vessel forms is not great. Moulded relief decoration is very common, and barbotine and appliquéd decoration less so.

At Stobi little provincial sigillata has been recognized, and all consists primarily of small, single fragments, all residual pieces in later contexts. Below are a few of the larger pieces.

297. Bowl. Inv. No. C-70-136. Lot 1049. Pl. 35.
M.P.Dim. 0.041. Est. D. .020. One fragment of deep bowl or krater with outward-rolled rim and groove above the point where moulded egg-and-dart decoration begins.
Perhaps Dragendorff 37. Red (2.5YR 5/6) clay and gloss. Pannonian(?), 2nd century A.C.(?).

298. Deep bowl. Inv. No. C-74-312. Pls. 35, 165.
P.H. 0.017. M.P.Dim. 0.051. Th. 0.008. Part of relief-decorated underside of vessel with ring base. Red (2.5YR 5/6) clay and red (2.5YR 4/8) gloss. Decoration is composed of a garland of leaves banded by a single row of interconnecting beads.

299. Bowl. Inv. No. C-75-30. Lot 1798. Pl. 167.
M.P.Dim. 0.038. Th. 0.005. Small fragment of relief-decorated underside of vessel. Red (10YR 4/6) clay and red (10R 5/8–4/8) gloss.

300. Bowl or dish. Inv. C-78-40. Lot 2208. Pl. 167.
P.H. 0.029. Th. 0.006. One fragment. Red (2.5YR 5/6) fabric with red (2.5YR 4/8) gloss.

301. Bowl. Inv. No. C-78-238. Lot 2236. Pl. 167.
M.P.Dim. 0.061. Th. 0.004–0.009. One fragment with leaves, petals, and a dog's paw(?). Red (2.5YR 5/6) fabric with red (2.5YR 4/8) gloss.
Perhaps Pannonian.

302. Bowl. Inv. No. C-78-88. Lot 2325. Pl. 167.
M.P.Dim. 0.038. Th. 0.006. One fragment with chevron decoration preserved. Red (2.5YR 5/6–5/8) fabric and gloss.

Eastern Sigillata B (**303–340**)

Eastern Sigillata B ware[76] is a red-gloss ware that is most frequently found in the Aegean and Black Sea areas from the turn of the era to the 2nd century A.C. The micaceous fabric varies in color from reddish brown or cinnamon to orange-red, and the gloss is a soapy or waxy lustrous red to orange-red.

Two varieties of this particular ware have been distinguished on the basis of differences in fabric, gloss, form, and potter's stamps.[77] The earliest of these, Eastern Sigillata B1 (Samian B of Robinson), has a generally harder fired and darker fabric than the later Eastern Sigillata B2 (Samian A of Robinson), which is rather soft and tends to flake off in layers. The gloss of the later series is usually a lighter, more orange-red, although still very lustrous. Perhaps as a result of poor firing and careless technique in general, the

[75] Comfort in *RE*, cols. 1324–1351, and *EAA*, 814–833; W. Glassbergen and S.M.E. van Lith in "Italische und frühe sudgallische Terra Sigillata aus Velsen (Provinz Nord-Holland)," *RCRFActa* 17–18 (1977) 5–21, for recent bibliography.

[76] A term first used by Kenyon, *Samaria*, 281–283; later by Hellstrom, *Labraunda*, 32, 33; and Hayes, *LRP*, 8, and "Corinth," 450.

[77] A brief description with a list of sites and bibliography was included by Kenyon in *Samaria*, 282, and by Hellstrom in *Labraunda*, 32, 33. Most recently, Hayes, "Corinth," 452–455, 467–470. A classification and chronology of the ware appears in Hayes, "Sigillata orientale B," *EAA* 2, 49–70. The classification into B1 and B2 and the form typology used here are derived from the Hayes *EAA* article.

thick surface finish (slip) was not well bonded with the fabric and thus tends to flake off easily.

The numerous forms of B1 are thin walled, and most forms have rather sharp profiles, many with complex mouldings. B2, on the other hand, tends to be thicker walled, and the range of forms is more limited and the shapes simpler. Stamps with the name of the potter, a motto, or convivial greeting are most often found on the earlier B1 series, while the B2 ware carries stamped floral motifs such as rosettes. Decoration on both is confined to rouletting on exterior mouldings with the addition of some appliquéd ornaments on the later B2 examples.

Most recent studies of deposits containing Eastern Sigillata B indicate that the period of production for the earlier ware should be placed within the first three quarters of the 1st century A.C., and for the later ware a beginning in the Flavian period or by the third quarter of the 1st century and continuing into the mid-2nd century A.C.[78]

At Stobi there is a good deal of Eastern Sigillata B, all of which, with the exception of one piece (303), belongs to the later group B2.[79] Most come from deposits connected with the construction of the Theater in the mid- 2nd century, the West Cemetery, and the residence below the later Large Bath (Table 4.7 and discussion in Chap. 4). As is the case with Italian sigillata, there are a number of examples of Eastern Sigillata B found in later context, especially in the fills below the north and south aisles of the Episcopal Basilica.[80]

Only one name stamp (**339**) occurs at Stobi, but there are several examples of rosettes or the star (one catalogued here: **340**), all characteristic of Eastern Sigillata B2.

B1

303. Deep bowl. Hayes Form 37. Lot 1468, No. 2. Pl. 35.

P.H. 0.042. Est. D. rim 0.090. One rim fragment with curved walls and pointed lip set off by groove on exterior. Dark grayish brown to very dark grayish brown (10YR 4/2–3/2) fabric with black gloss and red undertones on parts of exterior surface.

B2

304. Dish. Hayes Form 58. Inv. No. C-72-75. Lot 692. Pl. 35.

H. 0.040. D. rim 0.140. Mended and almost complete. Fabric and surface have been discolored by fire. Single band of rouletting on lower moulding.

Found with a bowl of the same design, **320**, and two other dishes (**310**, **309**) in a burned destruction level.

305. Dish. Hayes Form 58. Lot 392, No. 11. Pl. 35.

P.H. 0.024. Est. D. rim 0.140. One rim fragment. Grooves at upper and lower mouldings.

306. Dish. Hayes Form 58. Inv. No. C-74-228. Lot 1629. Pl. 35.

H. 0.033. Est. D. rim 0.140. One fragment, preserving complete profile. Rouletting at lower moulding.

307. Plate. Hayes Form 60, early. Inv. No. C-74-496. Lot 1417. Pl. 35.

H. 0.030. Est. D. rim 0.164. One fragment, preserving complete profile. Grooves on exterior and interior.

Cf. Hayes, "Corinth," pl. 87:152; also Robinson, *Agora*, M61, G25; Kenrick, *Berenice 3*, 249, 250, fig. 45, B352, Type A.

308. Plate. Hayes Form 60, early. Inv. No. C-74-428. Lot 1478.

P.H. 0.040. Est. D. rim 0.220. One rim fragment with grooves beneath exterior carination.

309. Plate. Hayes Form 60, late. Inv. No. C-72-78. Lot 692. Pl. 35.

H. 0.043. D. rim 0.180. Mended from many fragments and almost complete. Shallow groove at outer edge of base and several grooves on floor.

310. Plate. Hayes Form 60, late. Inv. No. C-72-76. Lot 692. Pl. 36.

H. 0.045. D. rim 0.188. Complete except for a few fragments from base. Shallow grooves at floor center.

311. Plate. Hayes Form 60, late. Lot 599, No. 1. Pl. 36.

[78] Hayes, "Corinth," 455.

[79] There are cases when it is difficult to clearly distinguish between B1 and B2. It is possible to have a B1 form with B2 clay, or the reverse, as in Robinson, *Agora*, G18, pl. 61, p. 24.

[80] Especially Context Storage Lots 1629, 1697.

P.H. 0.023. Est. D. rim 0.210. Rim fragment with rather sharp profile.

312. Large plate. Hayes Form 60, late. Inv. No. C-73-22. Lot 930. Pl. 36.

H. 0.061. Est. D. rim 0.270. One large fragment, preserving complete profile. Grooves offset rim from wall on interior. Concave base.

313. Large plate. Hayes Form 60, late. Inv. No. C-73-71. Lot 921. Pl. 36.

H. 0.042. Est. D. rim 0.228. One large fragment, preserving complete profile. Very open shape. Groove sets off wall from floor on interior. Concave base.

314. Plate. Hayes Form 60, late. Inv. No. C-75-26. Lot 1697. Pl. 36.

H. 0.034. Est. D. rim 0.350. One fragment with profile. Very rounded rim and slightly concave base. Three grooves on floor.

315. Plate. Hayes Form 60, late. Inv. No. C-74-297. Lot 1419. Pl. 37.

H. 0.033. Est. D. rim 0.300. One fragment giving complete profile. Short rim.

316. Plate base. Hayes Form 60. Lot 1478, No. 1. Pl. 37.

P.H. 0.018. D. 0.140. One fragment of slightly concave base. Grooves at center floor.

317. Plate base. Hayes Form 60. Lot 930, No. 51. Pl. 37.

P.H. 0.043. D. 0.208. One fragment of flat base with concave side wall. Three grooves on floor at a point midway between wall and center with an additional single groove preserved near center.

Additional examples of Hayes Form 60, early, as follows: Lot 18: 1r, Lot 932: 1.

Additional examples of Hayes Form 60, late, as follows: Lot 384: 1r; Lot 488: 1r; Lot 930: 1r; Lot 1417: 1r (C-74-495); Lot 1441: 1r (C-74-268); Lot 1475: 1r; Lot 1697: 1r (C-75-29); Lot 1933: 1r–b (C-77-65); Lot 2210: 1r (C-78-119).

318. Plate. Hayes Form 62A. Inv. No. C-73-54. Lot 955. Pl. 37.

H. 0.033. Est. D. rim 0.250. One fragment, preserving complete profile. Moulded rim with rouletting. Base appears to have been concave.

319. Hayes Form 63. Inv. No. C-78-197. Lot 2181. Pl. 37.

H. 0.033. Est. D. rim 0.030. Profile preserved.

320. Conical cup. Hayes Form 70. Inv. No. C-72-77. Lot 692. Pl. 38.

H. 0.035. D. rim 0.088. Almost complete. Rouletting on rim lower edge.

Counterpart of plate, C-77-75.

321. Conical cup. Hayes Form 70. Inv. No. C-74-245. Lot 1479. Pl. 38.

H. 0.048. Est. D. rim 0.084. Several fragments, giving complete profile. Grooves at upper edge and below carination.

322. Conical cup. Hayes Form 70. Inv. No. C-73-15. Lot 930. Pl. 38.

H. 0.051. Est. D. rim 0.115. Almost complete. Rouletting at lower moulding and single groove below carination.

323. Conical cup. Hayes Form 70. Lot 939, No. 66. Pl. 38.

P.H. 0.040. Est. D. rim 0.120. One fragment of rim and wall.

324. Conical cup base. Hayes Form 70. Inv. No. C-75-40. Lot 1799. Pl. 38.

P.H. 0.035. D. 0.040. One fragment, preserving base and walls of cup.

325. Conical cup base. Hayes Form 70. Inv. No. C-74-94. Lot 1538. Pl. 167.

P.H. 0.030. D. 0.054. One fragment of base. Single rosette stamp preserved in center.

A number of additional examples of the rim portions of either this form, Hayes Form 70, or Form 58, which are difficult to distinguish with only small fragments unreliable for diameter estimates, occur as follows: Lot 7: 1; Lot 249: 2; Lot 385: 1; Lot 392: 1; Lot 939: 1; Lot 1471: 1 (C-74-413); Lot 1474: 1 (C-74-415); Lot 1475: 1; Lot 1510: 1 (C-74-442); Lot 1537: 1 (C-74-446); Lot 1629: 1 (C-74-235); Lot 1799: 1 (C-75-40); Lot 2389: 1 (C-78-221) with rosette stamp on floor.

326. Small bowl. Hayes Form 71. Inv. No. C-73-21. Lot 929. Pl. 38.

H. 0.034. D. rim 0.096. One fragment with complete profile.

Cf. Hayes, "Corinth," pl. 87:155; Robinson, *Agora*, pl. 62:G29, G30.

327. Large bowl. Hayes Form 71. Inv. No. C-77-73. Lot 1957.

P.H. 0.042. Est. D. rim 0.217. One rim fragment.

Additional examples of Hayes Form 71 are as

follows: Lot 18: 1r; Lot 488: 1r; Lot 931: 1r; Lot 1511: 1r; Lot 1629: 1r; Lot 1800: 1r (C-75-25); Lot 1629: 1r (C-74-238).

328. Deep bowl. Hayes Form 74. Inv. No. C-75-88. Lot 1846. Pl. 39.
P.H. 0.040. Est. D. rim 0.125. One fragment of rim. Dark gray (2.5YR N4/) fabric and peeling black gloss.

329. Deep bowl. Hayes Form 74. Inv. No. C-74-289. Lot 1419. Pl. 39.
P.H. 0.045. Est. D. rim 0.150. One rim fragment with ribbon handle.
Additional rims of Hayes Form 74 are as follows: Lot 20: 1; Lot 929: 1; Lot 1475: 1 (C-74-285); Lot 1509: 1; Lot 1846: 1 (C-75-88).

330. Small bowl. Hayes Form 75. Inv. No. C-74-445. Lot 1510. Pl. 39.
P.H. 0.016. Est. D. rim 0.110. One rim fragment.

331. Small bowl. Hayes Form 75. Inv. No. C-74-89. Lot 1314. Pl. 39.
P.H. 0.040. Est. D. rim 0.120. One rim fragment.
One additional example of Form 75 in Lot 1629 (C-74-231).

332. Bowl with flat rim. Hayes Form 76. Inv. No. C-74-417. Lot 1474. Pl. 39.
P.H. 0.030. Est. D. rim 0.110. One rim fragment.

333. Bowl with flat rim. Hayes Form 76. Inv. No. C-74-287. Lot 1325.
P.H. 0.054. Est. D. rim 0.315. One rim fragment of a large example.

334. Open bowl. Hayes Form 80. Lot 929, No. 38. Pl. 39.
P.H. 0.027. Est. D. rim 0.170. One rim fragment with single groove at interior (base only: C-74-454, Lot 1511).

Miscellaneous examples without equivalent Hayes Forms

335. Dish with flat base. Lot 936, No. 76. Pl. 39.
H. 0.026. Est. D. rim 0.278. One fragment of complete profile from dish with outward thickened rim.

336. Bowl. Lot 1510, No. 3. Pl. 39.
P.H. 0.015. Est. D. rim 0.110. One fragment of bowl with flaring wall and squared rim.

337. Graffito. Inv. No. C-71-326. Lot 231.
M.P.Dim. 0.034. Th. 0.003.

338. Stamped rim. Inv. No. C-78-60. Lot 2360.
P.H. 0.025. Th. 0.005. Small fragment of rim with figure-8 stamp on interior just below rim.

339. Stamp. Inv. No. C-74-411. Lot 1475. Pl. 171.
M.P.Dim. 0.042. Th. 0.004. One floor fragment with Greek stamp ΕΡΜΗ.
See *EAA* 2, Hayes, "sigillate orientale B," 52. Because the fabric of this piece is unusual for Eastern Sigillata B, it has also been presented with "miscellaneous stamps" as item **488**.

340. Stamp. Inv. No. C-75-38. Lot 1697.
M.P.Dim. 0.061. Th. 0.004. Small ring base with stamped star on floor.

Çandarli Ware (**341–345**)

Çandarli Ware is another one of the branches of the terra sigillata tradition in the East and may be considered one of the Eastern Sigillata wares. Evidence for its production was discovered at Çandarli (ancient Pitane) near Pergamon by S. Loeschcke, who published the first typology for the ware.[81] An earlier series of the ware belongs to the 1st century A.C. and the later series of products to the 2nd and 3rd centuries.[82] Both series were exported, although the later one more widely throughout the Aegean and Mediterranean areas.

The fabric of Çandarli products varies from reddish brown to maroon (red or light red: 2.5YR 5/8 or 6/6) with a gloss of the same color (2.5YR 4/6 or 5/6), often better in quality on the interior of any given open vessel. The presence of gold mica, or biotite, is common in the fabric, while the slip or gloss sometimes displays silver or white mica.[83]

Shapes are few in number, and decoration is

[81] "Tschandarli," 350, fig. XXVIII.

[82] Hayes, *LRP*, 316–322, and now *Pergamon 6*.

[83] Hayes, *LRP*, 316.

limited to grooves. Çandarli ware may have been produced until the early 4th century; its market eventually taken over by Phocaean Red Slip Ware.[84]

Perhaps because of its geographical origin or because of other trading connections between Macedonia and Asia Minor, Çandarli Ware is virtually the only known import that occurs in any numbers at Stobi during the 2nd and 3rd centuries A.C., and that number is not very significant. Only a few examples of the earlier versions of the ware (Loeschcke ["Tschandarli"] typology) have been found at Stobi.

Forms 3 and 4 in the Hayes typology are most common among the approximately twenty-five examples whose forms can be ascertained. Most examples come from the destruction debris and overlying rubbish accumulation of an early imperial structure at the Inner City Wall of Stobi (Tables 4.8 and 4.9 and discussion in Chap. 4). The latest material in these deposits belongs to the second half of the 3rd and perhaps early 4th centuries A.C.

341. Flanged bowl. Loeschcke Form 19. Inv. No. C-72-303. Lot 594. Pl. 40.

P.H. 0.045. Th. 0.005. One fragment of flanged bowl rim. Red (2.5YR 5/6) fabric and red (2.5YR 4/6–4/8) gloss.

Pergamon 6, 107–109, N33c or N33d, figs. 13, 44, and 47, dated second quarter of the 1st century A.C. to first quarter of the 2nd century A.C.

342. Dish. Hayes Form 2. Inv. No. C-78-102. Lot 2355. Pl. 40.

P.H. 0.035. Est. D. rim. One rim fragment of dish. One fragment of a Form 2 dish, C-75-27 (Lot 1697). Both pieces residual.

343. Flanged bowl. Hayes Form 3. Lot 1295, No. 178. Pl. 40.

P.H. 0.030. Est. D. rim 0.183. One rim fragment of small flanged bowl.

Five other rim examples of this form are, C-78-204 (Lot 2234), a survival piece; one each from Lots 1295, 1296, 1302, and 1307.

344. Dish. Hayes Form 4. Inv. No. C-74-123. Lot 1295. Pl. 40.

P.H. 0.028. Est. D. rim 0.218. One fragment preserving rim and wall of medium-sized dish.

345. Dish. Hayes Form 4. Inv. No. C-74-59. Lot 1296. Pl. 40.

P.H. 0.027. Est. D. rim 0.220. One rim fragment of medium-sized dish.

Eight other fragments of Form 4: three from Lot 1296; four from Lot 1295; and one each from Lots 65 and 1404. Five base fragments: C-74-293 (Lot 1327), and one each from Lots 237, 298, 542, and 1295.

Cypriot Sigillata Ware (**346**)

Found commonly on Cyprus where it was most likely produced, Cypriot sigillata occurs in a variety of simple shapes, usually undecorated.[85] The fabric varies from brick-red to purplish red or dark brown, and the thin wash has a metallic luster with double-dipping streaks visible on dishes. Lime particles are common.

The shapes and limited decoration of this Cypriot red-gloss ware were probably influenced by Eastern Sigillata A. Cypriot sigillata was produced from the Augustan period to the 2nd century A.C. The example below, however, is residual.

346. Bowl. Hayes Form 25. Inv. No. C-78-237. Lot 2385. Pl. 40.

P.H. 0.037. Est. D. rim 0.245. Two fragments mended preserving rim and wall. Light red (2.5YR 5/6–6/6), with lime particles visible, fired gray at core. Slip or wash of same color with alternate bands of gray on interior. Faint wheel-ridging visible on vessel exterior.

Although the fabric appears to be Cypriot Sigillata, the form of this example is quite similar to Pontic Sigillata Hayes Form 1, *EAA* 2, fig. 22.

[84] The forms cited in this study are from the Hayes typology, "Ceramica di Çandarli, Produzione Pergamena," *EAA* 2, 71–78.

[85] J. W. Hayes, "Cypriot Sigillata," *RDAC*, 1967, 65–77, for the earliest discussion of the type. His revised typology appears in "Paphos," 96–108, and "sigillata cipriota" in *EAA* 2, 79–92. Note query by A. Negev, "Nabatean Sigillata," *Revue Biblique* 79 (1972) 381, and discussion in *Qedem* 17 (see note 65) 14, 15. Cypriot sigillata predominates at Anemurium; see Caroline Williams, *Anemurium. The Roman and Early Byzantine Pottery* (Toronto 1989) 1–8.

Red Slip Wares

Roman Red Slip Wares

Undecorated Red Slip Wares gained tremendous popularity during the Late Roman period. In areas formerly manufacturing Early Roman terra sigillata, such as Cyprus and Asia Minor, and even in places without a terra sigillata tradition, fine wares with red fabric and a smooth red slip or gloss, rather different from the characteristic laquerlike polish of terra sigillata, begin to appear in the archaeological record.

The most common of these wares, African Red Slip Ware, Phocaean Red Slip Ware, and Cypriot Red Slip Ware, were imported to Stobi in the Late Roman period.

Cypriot Red Slip Ware (**347**)

Often referred to as Late Roman D, this ware has been assigned a Cypriot origin because it is so common on that island. It is likely related to the earlier Cypriot Sigillata.[86]

The fabric, fully described by Hayes, varies from shades of red to brown in color and often contains visible particles of lime. The slip is matte and usually very similar to the fabric of the body. Dishes and bowls are the most common forms.

Only one example of this ware has been identified at Stobi and comes from a context of the late 5th, early 6th centuries A.C., together with African Red Slip Form 104 and Phocaean Red Slip Forms 3 and 5 (see classifications below).

347. Dish. Hayes Form 5. Inv. No. C-71-056. Lot 155. Pl. 40.

H. 0.045. Est. D. rim 0.187. Two fragments mended, preserving complete profile. Hard-fired, red (2.5YR 6/6) fabric with dull, red slip on both surfaces. Small dish with flat base and wheel-ridging on exterior.

Cf. Hayes Form 5.2, in *LRP*, 378, fig. 81.

African Red Slip Ware (**348–393**)

African Red Slip Ware, a fine ware known also as *terra sigillata chiara* and as Late Roman A and B wares, was initially competitor and then successor to the tradition and popularity of terra sigillata.[87] Produced in North Africa, probably in Tunisia, from the late 1st century until the 7th centuries A.C., this ware dominated much of the Mediterranean market for many centuries, especially during the Late Roman period.[88]

The fabric too of the African products differs from that of the various terra sigillata wares, being coarse and generally orange-red to brick-red (2.5YR 5/6 or 5/8, or 10R 5/8–4/8, all red) and with a smooth, often lustrous, but not very glossy surface of the same or somewhat lighter color (2.5YR 6/8).

Most African Red Slip products were not decorated except with grooves or rouletting. Anything more elaborate is either stamped, incised, or modeled in relief depending upon the form of the vessel.

At Stobi the earliest example of African Red Slip ware is one fragmentary example of Hayes Form 33 (**348**) dated to the early or mid-3rd century.[89] There are several other single examples of Form 44 (**349**) and Form 46 (**351**), but the earliest forms to be found in quantity at Stobi are Form 45 (**350**), a large bowl with flat rim, and Form 50 (**353**, **354**), a large dish with thin, straight wall and flat base, both popular forms from the mid-3rd to the early 4th centuries A.C. Thus Stobi follows the pattern of the Aegean where African Red Slip begins to be imported around the middle of the 3rd century.[90]

The latest examples of African Red Slip at Stobi were found in contexts of the late 6th century among the latest remains of occupations at the site, which was abandoned at some time after 570 A.C. One example each of Forms 107 and 108 were found in the Radial Corridor of the Theater

[86] Hayes, *LRP*, 371–386; and now see also Williams (1989) 27–37, cited in note 85.

[87] The full study of this ware can be found in Hayes, *LRP*. The term *terra sigillata chiara* was proposed by N. Lamboglia in "Terra sigillata chiara," *RstLig* 7 (1941) 7–22; Late Roman A and B wares derives from *Antioch* 43–47.

[88] LRP, 296.

[89] All form numbers cited derive from the Hayes typology in *LRP*.

[90] Hayes, *LRP*, 417.

together with a late spatheion amphora of small size (**706**).[91]

Sixty-six examples of twenty-five different forms of African Red Slip have been catalogued at Stobi. Most of the pieces at Stobi are undecorated, except for an example of Form 59 (**356**) with vertical gouged decoration and one of Form 82 (**374**) with feather rouletting. In addition there are ten examples of stamped decoration, most of which are floor fragments with palm branches and concentric circles of Hayes Style Aii, or Aiii, dated to the late 4th and 5th centuries A.C. There is one small fragment with the head and most of the body of a running lion modeled in relief (**383**).

The 4th and 5th centuries are clearly the period when African products were imported to Stobi in the largest numbers.

348. Plate. Hayes Form 33. Lot 998, no. 2. Pl. 41.

P.H. 0.020. Est. D. rim 0.140. One fragment with almost complete profile. Small, shallow plate with flat rim, sloping wall, and inset at junction of wall and floor.

Hayes date: ca. 200–250 or later. Residual at Stobi.

349. Small bowl. Hayes Form 44. Lot 1404, No. 378. Pl. 41.

P.H. 0.013. Est. D. rim 0.100. One rim fragment from small bowl with broad rim.

Hayes date: ca. 220/240 to late 3rd century.

350. Large bowl. Hayes Form 45A. Inv. No. C-77-63. Lot 1946. Pl. 41.

P.H. 0.007. Est. D. rim 0.220. One small fragment of broad, flat rim of large bowl. Single narrow band of rouletting toward exterior.

Four additional examples of this form, all rims: Inv. No. C-74-129 (Lot 1295); Inv. No. C-75-48 (Lot 1798); Inv. No. C-78-287 (Lot 2234); and one example from Lot 237.

Context indicates mid-3rd- to early 4th-century date for all but C-75-48 and C-78-287, which are residual. Hayes date: ca. 230/240–320.

351. Large bowl. Hayes Form 46. Lot 1404, No. 377. Pl. 41.

P.H. 0.016. Est. D. rim 0.189. One rim fragment of bowl with curved rim.

Context date: 4th century. Hayes date: last quarter of the 3rd, first quarter of the 4th centuries.

352. Plate. Hayes Form 48. Inv. No. C-71-58. Lot 236. Pl. 41.

P.H. 0.025. Est. D. rim 0.330. One fragment preserving profile.

Found in association with a coin of Justin II (569/70 A.C.). Hayes date: ca. 220–320.

353. Large dish. Hayes Form 50A. Inv. No. C-78-130. Lot 2213. Pl. 41.

P.H. 0.035. Est. D. rim 0.218. One fragment, preserving complete profile. Large dish with flat bottom and tall, straight wall.

Residual.

Five other examples of form 50A: Lot 238: 1; Lot 305: 1; Lot 1295: 1; Lot 1404: 2; all from contexts of the 4th century. Hayes date: ca. 230–325.

354. Large dish. Hayes Form 50B. Lot 946, No. 13. Pl. 41.

P.H. 0.040. Est. D. rim 0.258. One fragment of rim and wall.

Four other examples of Type B: Inv. No. C-78-280 (Lot 2407); C-79-67 (Lot 2581); one example from Lot 233; and one example from Lot 1282. All examples of 50B are from contexts of late 4th- to mid-5th-century date. Hayes date: 350–400 or later.

355. Bowl. Hayes Form 53. Inv. No. C-71-435. Lot 293. Pl. 41.

P.H. 0.035. Est. D. rim 0.150–0.170. Two fragments mended, preserving rim and wall of bowl with curved body and plain rim. Two grooves midway down the interior wall.

Context date: late 4th, early 5th centuries. Hayes date: ca. 350–430.

356. Dish. Hayes Form 59A. Inv. No. C-71-432. Lot 305. Pl. 41.

P.H. 0.030. Est. D. rim 0.250. Two fragments mended, preserving side wall, part of rim and base. Vertical gouging impressed with blunt implement on wall exterior creating slight ridges on interior.

Context date: late 4th, early 5th centuries. Hayes date: ca. 320–380/400.

357. Dish. Hayes Form 61A. Lot 1783, No. 4. Pl. 42.

P.H. 0.042. Est. D. rim 0.340. One fragment, preserving complete profile. Flat-based dish with slightly inturned rim.

[91] Context Storage Lot 875.

Four other examples of Form 61A, all single rim fragments: C-71-263 (Lot 302); C-72-304 (Lot 750); C-78-77 (Lot 2233); and one example from Lot 1285.

All from contexts ranging in date from mid-4th to mid- or third quarter of the 5th centuries. Hayes date: ca. 325–400/420.

358. Dish. Hayes Form 61B. Inv. No. C-75-47. Lot 1801. Pl. 42.

P.H. 0.034. Est. D. rim 0.298. One rim fragment. Short, vertical exterior and shallow groove or depression on interior.

359. Dish. Hayes Form 61B. Inv. No. C-78-172. Lot 2210. Pl. 42.

P.H. 0.033. Est. D. rim 0.360. One rim fragment. Short, curved exterior turned slightly inward with groove at interior.

This piece comes from the fill below the first floor of the Episcopal Basilica, dated to the third quarter of the 5th century and is the same deposit from which C-78-77 (Form 61A) comes.

Of the total of six examples of Form 61B, five are from the Episcopal Basilica: C-75-46 (Lot 1804); C-78-132 (Lot 2213); C-78-278 (Lot 2407) and **358** and **359** above. The sixth example is C-75-71 (Lot 1686).

Context dates range from late 4th to mid-5th for these five pieces. Hayes date: ca. 400–450.

360. Flat-based dish. Hayes Form 62B. Inv. No. C-79-86. Lot 2604.

No dimensions available. One rim fragment.

361. Dish. Hayes Form 64. Inv. No. C-78-283. Lot 2407. Pl. 42.

P.H. 0.042. Est. D. rim 0.320. One rim fragment with curved wall and plain rim.

Context date: approximately mid-5th century. Hayes date: early to mid-5th century.

One additional example, C-78-16, from Lot 2089.

362. Flat-based dish. Hayes Form 65? Inv. No. C-78-279. Lot 2407. Pl. 42.

P.H. 0.023. Est. D. rim 0.365. One rim fragment of large dish with very broad, flat rim.

Hayes date: uncertain.

363. Large bowl. Hayes Form 67. Inv. No. C-71-434. Lot 278. Pl. 42.

P.H. 0.034. Est. D. rim 0.320. One fragment of rim and wall. Large bowl with two-part angular rim. Smoothed and polished on interior, dull exterior.

Hayes date: late 4th to late 5th centuries.

364. Large bowl. Hayes Form 67. Lot 297, No. 72. Pl. 42.

P.H. 0.017. Est. D. rim 0.440. One small rim fragment. Rather thick walled, only slightly thickened at lip.

365. Large bowl. Hayes Form 67. Lot 298, No. 18. Pl. 42.

P.H. 0.027. Est. D. rim 0.370. One fragment preserving rim and wall. Slightly thickened lip, no groove.

Three additional examples of Form 67: C-78-276 (Lot 2407); C-79-68 (Lot 2604); and one example from Lot 293. Of the six pieces, four are from rubbish accumulation in the East Parodos of the Theater dating to the late 4th, early 5th centuries. The other two examples come from a context of the mid-5th century.

366. Large bowl. Hayes Form 68. Inv. No. C-71-244. Lot 169. Pl. 43.

P.H. 0.055. Est. D. rim 0.340. One fragment preserving rim and side wall.

Hayes date: 370–425.

367. Large bowl. Hayes Form 68. Inv. No. C-73-114. Lot 850. Pl. 43.

P.H. 0.032. Est. D. rim 0.300. One fragment of rim and side wall.

368. Large bowl. Hayes Form 68. Inv. No. C-78-90. Lot 2230. Pl. 43.

P.H. 0.028. Est. D. rim 0.275. One fragment of rim and side wall.

369. Large bowl. Hayes Form 68. Lot 514, No. 1. Pl. 43.

P.H. 0.043. Est. D. rim 0.358. One fragment of rim and side wall.

Contexts for these four examples of Form 68 range in date from late 4th (**366**) to the third quarter of the 5th century (**368**).

370. Small bowl. Hayes Form 72. Inv. No. C-79-8. Lot 2581. Pl. 44.

P.H. 0.023. Est. D. rim 0.166. One fragment of rim and wall. Small notches on rim exterior.

Hayes date: early 5th century.

371. Small bowl. Hayes Form 72. Inv. No. C-78-45. Lot 2210. Pl. 44.

P.H. 0.018. Est. D. rim 0.162. One rim fragment.

One additional small fragment, C-79-66 (Lot 2584) may be an example of Form 72 or of Form 73, both small bowls.

All these pieces belong to contexts of the mid-5th century.

372. Small bowl. Hayes Form 73. Inv. No. C-75-49. Lot 1798. Pl. 44.

P.H. 0.024. Est. D. rim 0.095. One fragment of rim and wall. Small bowl with plain rim and lip.

Hayes date: 420–475.

373. Small bowl. Hayes Form 73. Inv. No. C-79-3. Lot 2581. Pl. 44.

P.H. 0.027. Est. D. rim 0.180. One fragment, preserving rim and side wall.

This example also resembles Form 75. Two additional examples are of Form 73: C-79-65 (Lot 2583) and C-78-59 (Lot 2355). All three examples belong to contexts of the middle or third quarter of the 5th century.

374. Large plate. Hayes Form 82. Inv. No. C-71-2. Lot 514. Pls. 43, 168.

P.H. 0.030. Est. D. rim 0.302. One fragment of rim and side wall. Wide expanse of feather rouletting on wall exterior below rim.

Context: 5th century. Hayes date: 430–500.

375. Dish. Hayes Form 87. Inv. No. C-79-1. Lot 2455. Pl. 43.

P.H. 0.052. Est. D. rim 0.270. Five fragments mended from rim and wall. Widely spaced wheel marks on exterior.

Hayes date: second half of 5th to early 6th centuries.

376. Dish. Hayes Form 87. Inv. No. C-73-113. Lot 847. Pl. 43.

P.H. 0.028. Est. D. rim 0.280. One fragment of rim. Rather thin walled and with blurred angles.

377. Bowl. Hayes Form 99. Inv. No. C-74-525. Lot 1057. Pl. 43.

P.H. 0.027. One small rim fragment.

378. Large dish/bowl. Hayes Form 104. Inv. No. C-70-14. No Lot. Pl. 45.

P.H. 0.058. Est. D. rim 0.355. About one-quarter complete.

Hayes date: ca. 530–600.

379. Large dish/bowl. Hayes Form 104. Inv. No. C-71-429. Lot 166. Pl. 45.

P.H. 0.025. Est. D. rim 0.280. One small rim fragment.

380. Large plate. Hayes Form 105. Inv. No. C-71-126. Lot 235. Pl. 45.

H. 0.063. D. rim 0.394. Twenty-five pieces mended, preserving almost complete dish. Very rounded rim and high foot with marked offset where wall meets floor.

Context is third quarter of the 6th century. Hayes date: 580–660 or later.

381. Large bowl. Related to Hayes Form 107/93. Inv. No. C-73-51. Lot 875. Pl. 45.

H. 0.055. D. rim 0.308. Almost complete. Short, flat rim and very low, almost flat base. Three grooves at point where wall meets floor.

Style Eii (Hayes, *LRP*, fig. 57, no. 331, p. 222), stamped cross at center, dated 530–600. Found together with **382**.

382. Small bowl. Hayes Form 108. Inv. No. C-73-50. Lot 875. Pl. 45.

H. 0.051. D. rim 0.158. Almost complete. Restored.

Hayes date: early 7th century.

383. Decorated fragment. Inv. No. C-75-99. Lot 1922.

M.P.Dim. 0.049. Th. 0.003. One fragment broken on all sides, probably from rim of Form 52. Most of head and body of lion modeled in relief.

This type of decoration is dated second half of the 4th to early 5th centuries (Hayes, *LRP*, 211).

384. Stamped fragment from floor. Inv. No. C-71-195. Lot 297. Pl. 168.

M.P.Dim. 0.178. Th. 0.005. One fragment broken on all sides. Center contains palm branches (Hayes, *LRP*, fig. 38, nos. 1, 2) radiating from a single concentric circle with fringed concentric circles (fig. 40) at interstices. A second band of decoration consists of closely set square grille patterns (fig. 42, no. 67).

Style Aii (Hayes, *LRP*, pp. 218–219) dated 350–420. Context date: early 5th century.

385. Stamped fragment. Inv. No. C-71-431. Lot 236. Pl. 168.

P.H. 0.011. Est. D. base 0.100. Th. 0.005. One fragment, preserving part of base with low foot. Portion of stamped decoration preserving hind legs of an animal(?) on interior.

386. Stamped fragment from floor. Inv. No. C-75-83. Lot 1801. Pl. 168.

M.P.Dim. 0.030. Th. 0.007. One fragment broken on all sides. Glossy slip on interior, plain on exterior. Large circle surrounded by smaller circles, four of which are visible, within a rosette or circle in circle pattern surrounded by a dot fringe.

Cf. Hayes, *LRP*, fig. 41, nos. 60–66, and fig. 43, no. 88, and p. 224, dated ca. 410–470.

387. Stamped floor fragment. Inv. No. C-77-9. Lot 2076. Pl. 168.

M.P.Dim. 0.034. Th. 0.004. One fragment broken on all sides. Stamped palm branches and part of one concentric circle.

Cf. Hayes, *LRP*, fig. 40, no. 27, and fig. 38, nos. 2 or 4, Style Aii or Aiii, p. 219, probably 5th century.

388. Stamped fragment. Inv. No. C-78-73. Lot 2233. Pl. 168.

M.P.Dim. 0.033. Th. 0.005. One fragment broken on all sides. Stamped palm branch (Hayes, *LRP*, fig. 38, no. 1) and one concentric circle with four ridges (fig. 40, no. 27).

Probably Hayes Style Aii, or Aiii, of 5th-century date.

389. Stamped fragment. Inv. No. C-78-121. Lot 2213. Pl. 168.

M.P.Dim. 0.036. Th. 0.002. One fragment broken on all sides. Stamped concentric circle (Hayes, *LRP*, fig. 40) between two palm branches (fig. 38, no. 2), Style Aii or Aiii. Very worn.

390. Stamped fragment. Inv. No. C-78-224. Lot 2186. Pl. 168.

M.P.Dim. 0.053. Th. 0.006. One fragment broken on all sides probably from floor of plate. Stamped concentric circles with dot fringe (Hayes, *LRP*, fig. 40) and square grille with diagonal cross bars (fig. 42, no. 69), Style Aii or Aiii; 5th century.

391. Stamped fragment. Inv. No. C-78-273. Lot 2347. Pl. 169.

M.P.Dim. 0.046. Th. 0.005. One fragment broken on all sides. Two concentric grooves frame palm branch (Hayes, *LRP*, fig. 38, no. 1) and concentric circles; Style Aii or Aiii.

392. Stamped fragment. Inv. No. C-79-58. Lot 2581. Pl. 169.

M.P.Dim. 0.025. Th. 0.003. One very small fragment broken on all sides. Part of stamped palm motif(?) preserved.

393. Stamped fragment. Inv. No. C-74-148. Lot 1551. Pl. 169.

M.P.Dim. 0.045. Th. 0.005. One fragment of floor with two overlapping palm branches (Hayes, *LRP*, fig. 38, no. 3?).

Phocaean Red Slip Ware (**394–417**)

For whatever reason, Çandarli Ware was not exported after the 3rd century A.C., and another red ware from the east took its place in challenging the markets held by African Red Slip Ware.[92]

Originally known as Late Roman C, it is now called Phocaean Red Slip by Hayes as a result of the discovery of a major production center at Phocaea in western Turkey.[93] Phocaean Red Slip was most popular in the 5th to early 7th centuries A.C., when it is found in quantity at most Mediterranean centers. Hayes has divided the ware into ten shapes, primarily dishes and bowls. Decoration consists of various types of rouletting on the rim, or stamped motifs on the vessel floor.

The fabric is brownish red or purplish red (2.5YR 6/8 [light red], or 2.5YR 4/6, 4/8, 5/6, [red]) and hard fired with a large number of small white lime particles visible. The slip covering the surface is normally the same color as the fabric and is never glossy.

Most of the thirty-one examples of Phocaean Red Slip at Stobi that can be assigned to one of Hayes forms are either Form 2 or Form 3 and belong primarily to the 5th century A.C. There are no complete vessels preserved.

394. Dish. Hayes Form 1A. Inv. No. C-78-27. Lot 2111. Pl. 46.

P.H. 0.023. Est. D. rim 0.170. One rim fragment.

One other example of form 1A, C-78-236, comes from Lot 2201.

Hayes date: late 4th to early 5th centuries.

[92] Hayes, *LRP*, 317, 323.

[93] J.W. Hayes, *A Supplement to Late Roman Pottery* (London 1980), p. ix. Comments here derive from the Hayes works cited. For source, see F. Mayet and M. Picon, "Une sigillée phocéenne tardive ("Late Roman C Ware") et sa diffusion en Occident," *Figlina* 7 (1986) 129–142. Note also in the same journal J.-Y. Empereur and M. Picon, "A propos d'un nouvel atelier de 'Late Roman C,' " 143–146.

395. Dish. Hayes Form 1D. Inv. No. C-78-101. Lot 2223. Pl. 46.

P.H. 0.035. Est. D. rim 0.312. One fragment of rim and wall.

Hayes date: early to third quarter of the 5th century.

396. Dish. Hayes Form 1D. Inv. No. C-79-43. Lot 2579. Pl. 46.

P.H. 0.047. Est. D. rim 0.281. One fragment of rim and wall. Single groove on interior below rim.

Two additional examples of Form 1D, C-73-116 (Lot 955) and C-78-285 (Lot 2202).

397. Dish. Hayes Form 2A. Inv. No. C-75-50. Lot 1798. Pl. 46.

P.H. 0.045. Est. D. rim 0.366. One fragment of rim and wall.

Hayes date: late 4th to mid-5th centuries.

398. Dish. Hayes Form 2. Inv. No. C-78-6. Lot 2222. Pl. 46.

P.H. 0.028. Est. D. rim 0.308. One fragment of rim and wall.

399. Dish. Hayes Form 2. Inv. No. C-78-58. Lot 2354. Pl. 46.

P.H. 0.034. Est. D. rim 0.220. One fragment of rim and wall.

400. Dish. Hayes Form 2. Inv. No. C-78-118. Lot 2213. Pl. 46.

P.H. 0.017. Est. D. rim 0.172. Two fragments mended, giving rim and wall of small dish.

Five additional examples of Form 2: C-72-307 (surface); C-75-51 (Lot 1798); C-75-86 (Lot 1659); C-78-277 (Lot 2407); and one example from Lot 1733.

401. Bowl. Hayes Form 3. Inv. No. C-70-87. Lot 1016. Pl. 46.

P.H. 0.034. Est. D. rim 0.300. One fragment of rim and side wall.

Hayes date: second half of the 5th to first half of the 6th centuries.

402. Bowl. Hayes Form 3. Inv. No. C-79-42. Lot 2580. Pl. 46.

P.H. 0.035. Est. D. rim 0.268. One fragment of rim and side wall.

403. Bowl. Hayes Form 3. Inv. No. C-71-148. Lot 91. Pl. 47.

P.H. 0.044. Est. D. rim 0.170. One fragment of rim and wall.

404. Bowl. Hayes Form 3. Inv. No. C-78-138. Lot 2234. Pl. 47.

P.H. 0.030. Est. D. rim 0.370. One rim fragment.

405. Bowl. Hayes Form 3. Inv. No. C-73-115. Lot 850. Pl. 47.

P.H. 0.020. Est. D. rim 0.240. One rim fragment.

406. Bowl. Hayes Form 3. Inv. No. C-72-299. Lot 645. Pl. 47.

P.H. 0.023. Est. D. rim 0.260. One rim fragment.

407. Bowl. Hayes Form 3. Inv. No. C-71-430. Lot 166. Pl. 47.

P.H. 0.020. Est. D. rim 0.220. One rim fragment with rouletting on exterior face.

Four other examples of Form 3 as follows: C-71-148 (Lot 91); C-78-7 (Lot 2315); C-79-26 (Lot 2457); C-79-64 (no Lot).

408. Dish related to Hayes Form 3 or Form 4. Inv. No. C-78-123. Lot 2213. Pl. 47.

P.H. 0.032. Est. D. rim 0.295. Several fragments mended, giving rim and wall. Very small hole in vessel wall.

409. Dish. Hayes Form 4. Inv. No. C-78-261. Lot 2405.

P.H. 0.033. Est. D. rim 0.160. One rim fragment.

One additional example of Form 4, C-73-118.

Hayes date: second quarter of the 5th century.

410. Dish. Hayes Form 5A. Inv. No. C-71-245. Lot 148. Pl. 47.

P.H. 0.020. Est. D. rim 0.295. One rim fragment.

Hayes date: ca. 460–500.

411. Dish. Hayes Form 5B. Inv. No. C-71-433. Lot 165. Pl. 47.

P.H. 0.026. Est. D. rim 0.150. One rim fragment.

Hayes date: first half of the 6th century.

412. Dish. Hayes Form 10A. Inv. No. C-72-305. Lot 746. Pl. 47.

P.H. 0.035. Est. D. rim 0.260. One rim fragment.

Hayes date: late 6th, early 7th centuries.

413. Small bowl. Inv. No. C-77-71. Lot 1948. Pl. 47.

P.H. 0.020. Est. D. rim 0.092. One fragment of rim and wall from small bowl with rounded rim.

414. Small bowl. Inv. No. C-78-278. Lot 2407. Pl. 47.

P.H. 0.015. Est. D. rim 0.118. One fragment rim from small bowl with slightly thickened rim.

415. Decorated fragment. Inv. No. C-63-1. No Lot. Pl. 169.

M.P.Dim. 0.163. Th. 0.008. One fragment from floor of plate with carelessly executed bush or tree in center framed by alternating narrow and wide circles. Decoration appears to be a result of burnishing.

416. Stamped fragment. Inv. No. C-71-57. Lot 91. Pl. 47.

M.P.Dim. 0.066. Th. 0.008. One fragment from floor of plate with part of stamped rabbit(?) preserved.

Cf. Hayes, *LRP*, fig. 74, motif 35Y, from Group II, dated 440–490.

417. Stamped fragment. Inv. No. C-71-250. Lot 131. Pl. 169.

M.P.Dim. 0.054. Stamped horseshoes and circles.

Cf. Hayes, *LRP*, 355, Group IIA, early, motif 30, dated 440–490.

Macedonian Gray Ware (418–484)

The Late Roman Macedonian Gray Ware is surely a revival of the gray ware tradition at Stobi seen first in the earliest levels of the city.[94] Various gray wares were popular also in the late Hellenistic and early Roman periods, but disappear entirely during the 2nd and 3rd centuries. In the third quarter of the 4th century gray ware again appears at Stobi and is probably produced locally. It coincides with a period of prosperity in the late 4th century at Stobi when a number of large public buildings were constructed and at the time when the city was designated the capital of Macedonia Salutaris.[95]

A similar tradition of gray ware existed in Gaul and has been called Gaulish terre sigillée grise. It was the sucessor to the Iron Age and Archaic tradition of the northeastern Aegean taken west during the period of Greek colonization.[96] Despite the similarity of the two wares and although it may be a result of (as yet unknown) strong mercantile connections between the two areas, the Macedonian ware has fewer forms and a different and smaller range of decorative motifs than the Gaulish. This circumstance is not surprising, since Macedonia did not possess a sophisticated antecedent terra sigillata industry as did Gaul.

Decoration on Gaulish forms is confined almost entirely to the use of stamps and rouletting, whereas the Macedonian ware makes use of the scalloped and incised rim as well as a small number of stamps. No scalloped rim edges, with the exception of Rigoir's Form 3B, or incision, occur on the Gaulish ware, but predominate on Macedonian Gray Ware Forms 1 and 2.[97]

The fabric of the Macedonian Gray Ware at Stobi is composed of a fine, silver micaceous paste with few air spaces, small in size and with a percentage of nonplastics at less than 1 percent. The paste color varies from light to dark in the grays, brownish grays, and grayish browns (10YR 6/1, /5/1, 6/2, 5/2, 4/2 and 7.5YR N7/, N6/, N5/, 6/2). Approximately one-third of the total sherds studied contain a core, and most of these

[94] The ware was first identified by Hayes in *LRP*, 405–407 and called "Macedonian terre sigillée grise," based on material from Thessalonica and elsewhere in Macedonia, with a few pieces cited from Corinth, Athens, and Rumania.

[95] Wiseman, "City," 289–292, 295.

[96] A typology for Gaulish terra sigillée gríse appears in Rigoir (1960) and Rigoir (1968); see also G. Fouet, "Céramique estampée du IVe siècle dans la Villa du Montmaurin," *Ogam* 13 (1961) 271–285. Recent articles include M. Bonifay and J. P. Pelletier, "Elements d'évolution de céramiques del l'Antiquité tardive à Marseille d'apres les fouilles da la Bourse," *Revue Archeologique de Narbonnaise* 16 (1983), 285–346, and A. Bourgeois, "La diffusion de la céramique paleochretienne gríse et orangée dans les Grands Causses," *Revue Archeologique de Narbonnaise* 12 (1979) 201–251; and Y. and J. Rigoir, "Des dérivées des sigillées paleochretiennes," in P. Leveque and J. P. Morel, eds., *Céramique hellénistique et romains II. Centre de recherches d'histoire ancienne* vol. 70 (Besançon 1987) 329–338.

[97] Rigoir (1960) 90–93. For Form 3B, see Rigoir (1968) 218, Pl. 5.

are from bowls of Form 2. (See Type series below.) Petrographic analysis of thin sections of this ware reveal the presence of the mica minerals (illite, biotite, and muscovite), quartz/feldspar, and fine-grained igneous and metamorphic rock fragments.[98] Such a composition makes it very likely that the ware was produced at Stobi by potters utilizing clay from beds across the Crna at Stobi or from nearby Negotino in combination with sand from the Crna. (See Chapter 2.)

The smooth surface of the clay body is covered with a slip often similar in color or slightly darker than the fabric, less commonly almost black, which varies from dull to lustrous and is frequently metallic in appearance as might be expected from the very micaceous clay. A few examples have a burnished surface. The vessels appear to have been evenly fired since no mottling appears.

There was an oxidized version of the ware made only in Forms 1 and 2, the plate and flat-rimmed bowl (thirteen examples, 8 percent of the total number cataloged). A few fragments from the jug, Form 10, a tall base, and a skillet have also been found. The clay body varies from light red (2.5YR 6/6–6/8) to reddish yellow and yellowish red (5YR 7/6–6/6, 5/6–5/8) but is otherwise similar to the fabric of the gray version.

From the sample at Stobi I have distinguished a total of eleven forms presented in detail below, and examples of the ware from elsewhere do not give evidence of any additional shapes.[99] The most common forms are the flat-rimmed dish, Form 1, and the corresponding bowl, Form 2 (Fig. 3.2), both with stamped or incised decoration on the rim, which is most often scalloped around the edge. In addition to the decoration on the rim of Form 1, the floor of the dish may be decorated with rouletting or stamped motifs. These shapes are somewhat heavy, with vessel walls ranging from 5 to 7 mm. in thickness. Less popular was the dish with rolled rim, Form 3, and few examples of Form 4, the corresponding bowl, were found. Forms 8 and 9 are drinking cups or beakers with two or three handles, found in approximately the same numbers as Form 3, and Form 10 is a large screw-necked jug. Only two examples of Form 11, a trefoil-necked jug, have been found.

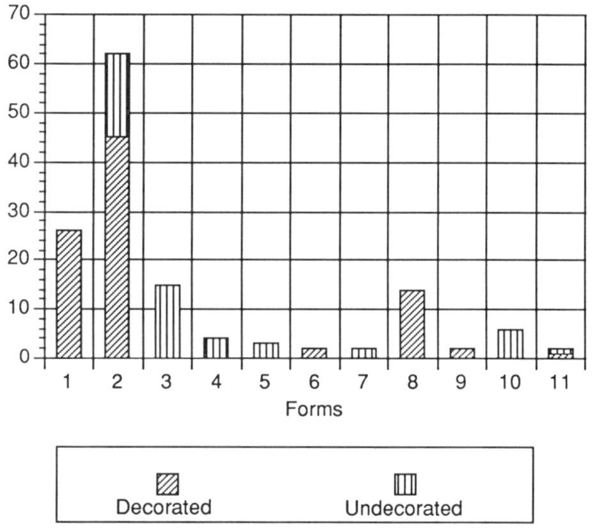

Figure 3.2. Macedonian Gray Ware. Bar graph illustrating quantity of the various forms at Stobi

Form 1: Dish with horizontal rim
Form 2: Bowl with horizontal rim
Form 3: Dish with rolled rim
Form 4: Bowl with rolled rim
Form 5: Plate with incurved wall
Form 6: Bowl with grooved rim
Form 7: Shallow dish with flanged rim
Form 8: Small jar
Form 9: Two-handled jar
Form 10: Screw-necked jug
Form 11: Trefoil-necked jug

A variety of impressed and incised motifs decorate the rims and walls of Macedonian Gray Ware. A running pattern of stamps in the form of circles, lozenges, or diamonds is frequently seen on the rims of Forms 1 and 2. The ridged rim of Form 2B may be modeled into a rope pattern. Others of these forms have their rims decorated with a series of grooves in the interior or along the line of scallops at the rim edge. The rim edge

[98] I am grateful to Dr. R. Wiebe of Franklin and Marshall College and to Dr. R. Folk of the University of Texas at Austin for their work with me in the preliminary identification of minerals in thin section. Dr. Georgeana Little of Boston University has written the results of her study, which appears in Appendix 2 of this volume.

Dr. Folk has noted that some of the samples of Macedonian Gray Ware were fired at a rather low temperature since the clay minerals were not fused, nor did the mica flakes show any signs of melting. Y. and J. Rigoir also suggest that the Gaulish ware was fired at a low temperature "Des dérivées" (cited in note 96 [above], p. 330 and note 23).

[99] A type series for the first ten forms was published in Anderson-Stojanović (1984).

is notched in some examples. The practice of decorating the rim begins on local buff fine wares in the late 3rd or early 4th centuries, but it was never very common. Instead, a wide variety of stamped motifs were regularly applied to the walls of bowls, beakers, and jugs (e.g., MR Form 19). Some motifs, such as the diamond, lozenge, rosette, and the grape cluster, seen on the walls of the Macedonian Gray Ware drinking cups (Forms 8 and 9) appear in the earlier period. Broad, irregularly shaped or scalloped and stamped rims are also not uncommon on various red-gloss wares in the Early and Late Roman periods. The incised patterns used on these wide rims, however, are reminiscent of those seen on rims of Iron Age gray ware from the Axios valley (e.g., **428**), suggesting the preservation of traditional pre-Roman motifs as well as the preference for gray ceramics.[100] The ware was also suggestive of metal vessels in shape and decoration. Broad, flat rims with notched edges and decorated upper surfaces were common on silver vessels and the ridges around the neck of Form 10, the screw-necked jug, are seen on metal vessels. The color of Macedonian Gray Ware is especially reminiscent of pewter.

The chronological evidence for a *terminus post quem* is not substantial, but the earliest examples at Stobi have been associated with coins of the last quarter of the 4th c. A.C.[101] The ware was not found in the deposit (Lot 1404, Table 4.11) dumped on the street near the east city wall after the paving slabs had themselves been covered over with mud-slide material in the late 3rd and 4th centuries. The absence of Macedonian Gray Ware in this deposit with large amounts of pottery (over 2,500 sherds, 638 RBH) is surprising in view of the coin (74-414) dated 383–392, a period when the ware is found elsewhere on the site. Lot 1404 contains primarily 3rd- and 4th-century material, with imports no later than the mid-4th. In deposits at a higher level in this area, Macedonian Gray Ware is more plentiful and in one case is found in association with a coin of the early 5th century (Lot 1390, with coin 74-248, dated 408–423).

The ware was well established by the early 5th century in Forms 1, 2, 3, 8, 9, and 10, since in the refuse deposits of the Theater Parodos (Table 4.12) it accounts for approximately 20 percent of the fine ware. These and the less common Forms 4, 5, 6, and 7 dominate the fine wares in both the destruction deposits of Building A and the fill beneath the first phase of the Episcopal Basilica, dated to the 3rd quarter of the 5th century (Fig. 3.3).[102] A full listing of forms and deposits may be found in Table 3.1.

In deposits below the floor of the large basilica beneath the present church of Haghia Sophia in Thessalonica, a number of examples of Macedonian Gray Ware occur in association with examples of Phocaean Red Slip, African Red Slip, and amphorae which taken together suggest a date after the third quarter of the 5th century for the deposit. Forms 1, 2, 8, and 10 predominate. Both the Macedonian Gray and the African Red Slip are almost equal in numbers (comprising approximately 11 percent of the significant RBH) but

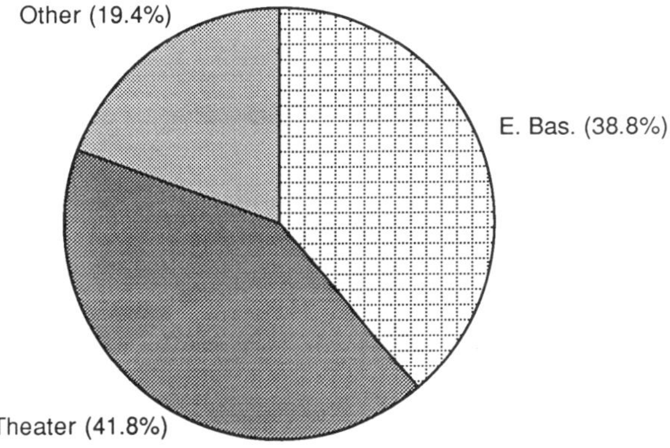

Figure 3.3. Proportion of Macedonian Gray Ware RBH found in 5th-century deposits at Stobi

[100] W. A. Heurtley, *Prehistoric Macedonia* (Cambridge 1939), 232, fig. 105.

[101] One example was found below the floor of Building A with coin 78–362, dated to the 360s or 370s; see Wiseman (1978) 405–406. **454** was found in association with coins 78–397 and 78–401 of Theodosius I, which date to 383–392 A.C; Wiseman (1978) 409–410. In the Fuller's House, Macedonian Gray Ware was found with coins of the late 4th, early 5th centuries. Additional examples were found below the floor of Synagogue II (Lot 1599) in association with coins dated post-324 (coin 70–211) and post-355–361 (coin 71–173). The fact that not one fragment of Macedonian Gray Ware has been found on the Acropolis suggests either that the deposits of the late 4th to late 5th centuries were removed or that there was no occupation during this period, since the ware is found in all deposits of this period elsewhere on the site.

[102] Wiseman, "Archaeology and History," 43.

Table 3.1. List of Macedonian Gray Ware forms and deposits

Form No.	Cat. No.	Inventory	Lot	Color
		C-71-044	127	gray
		C-74-081	none	gray
	474	C-78-079	2233	gray
	475	C-79-098	2605	gray
	476	C-78-075	2233	gray
	477	C-74-085	1507	red
	478	C-78-061	2319	gray
	479	C-73-028	none	gray
	480	C-77-001	1939	red
	481	C-71-050	178	gray
	482	C-67-001	none	gray
1		C-71-379	304	gray
1		C-78-026	2111	gray
1		C-78-129	2213	gray
1			274	red
1			277	gray
1			1298	gray
1	**421**	C-78-030	2111	gray
1	**425**	C-74-225	1625	gray
1	**426**	C-71-243	159	red
1	**427**	C-78-247	2307	red
1	**428**	C-75-020	1659	gray
1	**429**	C-74-131	1398	gray
1 or 2		C-75-072	1659	gray
1 or 2		C-79-072	2581	red
1 or 3		C-74-139	1390	gray
	483	C-78-120	2213	gray
	484	C-74-096	1552	gray
1A		C-75-013	1793	gray
1A		C-78-122	2213	gray
1A		C-78-124	2213	gray
1A	**418**	C-71-227	285	gray
1A	**419**	C-78-076	2233	gray
1A	**420**	C-79-041	2581	red
1B		C-67-001a	none	gray
1B		C-70-117	497	gray
1B		C-71-121	4	red
1B		C-79-071	2581	gray
1C		C-71-361	54	gray
1C	**422**	C-78-052	2111	gray
1C	**423**	C-79-099	2581	gray
1D	**424**	C-75-076	1770	gray
2			274	red
2			277	gray
2			277	gray
2			277	gray
2			277	gray
2			293	gray
2			293	gray
2			293	gray
2			299	gray
2			299	gray
2			299	gray
2			301	red
2			306	gray

Table 3.1. (*Cont.*)

Form No.	Cat. No.	Inventory	Lot	Color
2			306	gray
2			307	gray
2			274, 277	gray
2		C-71-264	306	gray
2		C-73-027	none	gray
2		C-73-082	883	gray
2		C-73-083	884	gray
2		C-74-315	1378	red
2		C-78-047	2211	gray
2		C-78-087	2194	gray
2		C-78-116	2212	gray
2		C-78-140	2263	gray
2		C-78-227	2212	gray
2		C-78-281	2407	gray
2		C-78-282	2406	gray
2		C-79-059	?	gray
2		C-79-081	2584, 2604	gray
2		C-79-083	?	gray
2		C-79-097	?	gray
2			293	gray
2A			299	gray
2A			307	gray
2A		C-78-035	2206	gray
2A		C-78-173	2213	gray
2A		C-79-076	2581	gray
2A	**430**	C-71-265	307	gray
2A	**431**	C-78-128	2213	gray
2A	**432**	C-73-041	917	gray
2A	**433**	C-72-071	789	gray
2A	**434**	C-71-218	274	gray
2A	**435**	C-71-219	293	gray
2A	**436**	C-72-046	612	gray
2A	**437**	C-71-226	282	gray
2A	**438**	C-73-057	902	gray
2A	**439**	C-75-011	1656	gray
2A	**440**	C-74-229	1398	gray
2A	**441**	C-73-007	917	gray
2A	**442**	C-70-116	509	gray
2A	**443**	C-78-032	2112	red
2A	**444**	C-79-012	2581	gray
2A	**445**	C-74-079	1370	gray
2A	**446**	C-77-070	1935	gray
2A	**447**	C-71-045	none	gray
2A	**448**	C-79-096	2581	gray
2A	**449**		299	gray
2B	**450**	C-74-142	1361	gray
2B	**451**	C-71-228	190	gray
2B	**452**	C-70-115	507	gray
2B	**453**	C-79-006	2581	gray
3			298	gray
3			298	gray
3			298	gray
3			298	gray
3			299	gray
3			301	gray

Table 3.1. (*Cont.*)

Form No.	Cat. No.	Inventory	Lot	Color
3		C-73-040	878	gray
3		C-74-100	1336	gray
3		C-75-014	1806	gray
3		C-78-080	2233	gray
3		C-79-024	2604	gray
3		C-79-074	2581	gray
3	**454**	C-78-155	2263	gray
3	**455**		998	gray
3	**456**		2393	gray
4		C-79-087	2581	gray
4		C-79-089	2581	gray
4	**457**	C-79-100	2581	gray
5	**458**	C-74-035	1551	gray
5	**459**	C-74-144	1362	gray
5	**460**	C-78-270	2218	gray
6		C-72-243	773	gray
6	**461**	C-74-063	1319	gray
7		C-78-074	2233	gray
7	**462**	C-78-091	2234	gray
8			297	gray
8			297	gray
8			943	gray
8		C-71-043	179	gray
8		C-78-115	2212	gray
8		C-78-274	2403	gray
8		C-79-088	2581	gray
8	**463**	C-71-238	307	gray
8	**464**	C-72-012	762, 763	gray
8	**465**	C-71-417	171	gray
8	**466**	C-78-062	2355	gray
8	**467**	C-78-050	2211	gray
8	**468**	C-72-241	523	gray
8	**469**	C-79-077	2588	gray
9	**470**	C-79-095	2604	gray
9	**471**		294	gray
10			295	gray
10			304	red
10			306	gray
10		C-78-028	2111	gray
10		C-78-049	2111	gray
10	**472**	C-74-508	1349	gray
11		C-78-057	2323	gray
11	**473**		**303**	**gray**

outnumbered by twice as many examples of Phocaean Red Slip.[103]

Production of Macedonian Gray Ware ended at Stobi by the mid-6th century, since there are no examples of the ware in the deposits of the third quarter of the 6th century on the Acropolis (Table 4.6), or in the contemporary Lot 875 in the Radial Corridor of the Theater. The range of production corresponds roughly to that for African Red Slip, Hayes Forms 61A and B, 67, 68, and 75, and Phocaean Red Slip, Hayes Forms 1, 2, and 3C.

Aside from the many examples of the ware at Stobi and those published by Hayes from Thessalonica, Athens, and Corinth, it has also been found at Prilep, Heraclea, Marvinci, and Scupi in Yugoslav Macedonia, and at Philippi and Torone in Greece.[104] In Bulgaria (ancient Thrace) there is a long tradition of gray wares, and numerous examples of "Thracian Gray Ware" plates and bowls of Forms 1 and 2 have been published from Plovdiv and more recently Sandanski.[105] A

[103] I would like to express my thanks to Mr. Sotiris Kissas of the Byzantine Ephoria of Thessalonica for the opportunity to examine and study this unpublished material.

[104] I have seen unpublished examples in the City Museum of Skopje from Scupi, at Štip, and in the museum at Philippi (A476, Form 2 bowl with scalloped rim). Several examples of Forms 1 and 2 appear in K. Kepeski, "Villa Rustica in Pesterica," *Macedoniae Acta Archaeologica* 2 (1976) 154, pl. Va. See Sokolovska (1986) 122, pls. 81–83, where some examples are said to have come from graves. At Heraclea I have seen several examples of Macedonian Gray Ware dishes and bowls. In the publication of material from below the Great Basilica, the construction of which has been dated to post-425 A.C. (Maneva [1979] 63), only one fragment that may be Macedonian Gray Ware was found (198, Pl. 17). Mr. John Papadopoulos, who has completed a study of the Roman pottery at Torone, tells me that a few examples of Macedonian Gray Ware bowls with scalloped rims were found at Torone. Just as at the coastal center of Thessalonica, however, at Torone, Phocaean Red Slip outnumbers African Red Slip by far—just the reverse of the situation at Stobi.

[105] D. Tsontchev, "Sivata Trakiista Keramika v Bulgaria," *Godišnik na Narodni Arheološki Musej*, Plovdiv. III. 1959, 104–106, and T. Ivanov, D. Serafimova, and N. Nikolov, "Raskopi v Sandanski prez 1960," *Izvestia na Arheologičeskia Institut* 31 (1969) 179–183, figs. 62–64. After seeing P67/N39 and N37, both Form 2A, and a plate of Form 5 in the museum at Sandanski, I would say that the ware is identical to that at Stobi.

As well as reviving an earlier tradition, the gray fabric and typical dinner-ware service of Macedonian Gray Ware may have appealed to a new clientele of immigrant Visigothic aristocracy settled in Thrace and the surrounding areas after 382, who were eager to emulate the customs of Roman society. The appearance of burnished gray wares in Dacia, Moesia, and Pannonia has been attributed by various scholars to the arrival and subsequent settlement of the Visigoths; see G. Bockisch and B. Bottger, "Spätrömische und fruhbyzantische Keramik," in "Das Limeskastell Iatrus in Moesia Inferior," *Klio* 47 (1966) 209–256. The same cause has been adduced for the popularity of gray ware in southern Gaul, the final homeland of the Visigothic tribes, in Rigoir (1960) 9, and Y. and J. Rigoir, "Des dérivées des sigillées paleochretiennes," in P. Leveque and J. P. Morel, eds., *Céramique hellénistique et romains II. Centre de recherches d'histoire ancienne*, vol. 70 (Besançon 1987) 178.

few pieces have also been found on Rumanian sites.[106] A similar gray ware occurs in Pannonia, and one example has even been reported to me from England.[107]

Because only a few pieces have been published from other sites, and no quantitative information has been published, it is impossible to know whether this Late Roman gray ware occurs elsewhere in the quantities that it does at Stobi.

Form 1

Form 1 is a flat-based dish with wide, horizontal rim. Variant A is large and deep, Variant B often smaller and more shallow. Variant C is deep like A, but the rim has a beveled surface sloping to the interior. Variant D has a straighter wall with an offset where the wall meets the floor. The upper surface of the rim of all variants is sometimes set off from the body by a groove or a series of grooves and often embellished with impressed, stamped, or incised decoration. The rim itself may also be finger-impressed or scalloped at the edge on Variants A or B. The floor on some examples has stamped decoration or rouletting, but only a few examples of complete plates or floor fragments have been preserved.

The most commonly found decoration on Variants A or B is a finger-impressed rim edge with a stamped double crescent following the curve of the finger impressions and circles in between.

Several examples of Form 1 were made in a curious fashion. As evident in the drawing of the rim sherd (**425**), the decoration was not stamped onto the wheelmade rim, but rather, a thick layer of additional clay was added to the relatively thin wheelmade form both above and below the rim; then the decorative stamps were impressed onto this surface. Such a practice may have added greater stability to the rim, which was to be decorated with a variety of stamped motifs rather than the usual incised lines or small stamped circles. Several examples of this particular technique (**425, 426**) have been preserved.

Diameter of Variant A: 0.250 to 0.320 m.; Variant B: 0.200 to 0.300 m.; Variant C: 0.300 to 0.350 m.

Anderson-Stojanović (1984) 103.

Corresponds to Rigoir Form 1 in the Gaulish series. Variant A is similar to Hayes, African Red Slip Forms 58 and 59.

Variant A

418. Inv. No. C-71-227. Lot 285. Pl. 48.

H. 0.044. Est. D. rim 0.280. Three fragments mended, preserving rim to floor. Four single lines have been burnished on rim and appear darker than the surface.

419. Inv. No. C-78-76. Lot 2233. Pl. 48.

H. 0.050. Est. D. rim 0.320. Five fragments mended, preserving rim to floor. Two grooves at rim interior and two at exterior with small, stamped, closed crescent between.

420. Inv. No. C-79-41. Lot 2581. Pl. 48.

P.H. 0.042. Est. D. rim 0.300. Single fragment of rim and part of side wall. Yellowish red (5YR 5/6) fabric with light reddish brown (5YR 6/4) core. The once red-slipped surface is now discolored to a light reddish brown (5YR 6/4) or a metallic pinkish white (5YR 8/2). Two grooves at rim exterior. At exterior rim edge are finger impressions bounded by a row of alternating double crescents and small circles.

Variant B

421. Inv. No. C-78-30. Lot 2111. Pl. 48.

P.H. 0.028. Est. D. rim 0.275. One fragment, giving rim to floor. Finger-impressed rim edge with double groove in scalloped pattern toward exterior. Four additional grooves at center and interior edge of rim. On floor two widely spaced grooves with angular rouletting between. Lustrous black slip.

Variant C

422. Inv. No. C-78-52. Lot 2211. Pl. 48.

P.H. 0.037. Est. D. rim 0.318. One fragment of

[106] *Sucidava IV. Materiale si cercetari arheologice* 1 (1953) 711, 712, fig. 13: h, i.

[107] For examples in Pannonia, see Bojović, *Singidunum*, nos. 131, 132, t.XI, 107. Several examples of this gray ware from Sirmium seen in Brukner, *Rimska Keramika*, t.66, nos. 23 and 26, must surely belong to Macedonian Gray Ware of the Late Roman period, and not to the first and second centuries as dated on p. 86. Malcolm Lyne (personal communication, October, 1989) reports a rim of Form 2A at the Saxon shore fort at Pevensey in Sussex in 5th-century A.C. context.

rim and side wall. Lustrous metallic slip. Incised zigzag groove along center of rim.

423. Inv. No. C-79-99. Lot 2581. Pl. 48.
P.H. 0.032. Est. D. rim 0.032. One fragment of rim and side wall. Black, lustrous slip. Rim edge decorated with tiny notches and on interior a row of irregularly shaped, gouged tear drops. Single groove on interior toward floor and on exterior wall just above break.

Variant D

424. Inv. No. C-75-76. Lot 1770. Pl. 48.
H. 0.043. Est. D. 0.254. One fragment preserves complete profile. Lustrous, metallic slip.

Rim fragments of Variants A or B

425. Inv. No. C-74-225. Lot 1625. Pls. 49, 169.
P.H. 0.044. Est. D. rim 0.230. One fragment of rim and side wall. Lustrous, metallic slip. This piece and two others (**426** below, and one other from Lot 277) were made in several steps. First the flat-rimmed dish seems to have been made on the wheel with a relatively thin rim and a single groove incised at the exterior. Over this rim a thick application of more clay was made and smoothed into roughly the same profile. The result is a rim surface irregular in thickness and shape, with no wheel marks. Onto this extra layer of clay a series of motifs was impressed with stamps: A cluster of raised dots surrounded by a circle framed first by a palm frond on each side and then by a motif consisting of a rod on either side of a row of raised dots.

426. Inv. No. C-71-243. Lot 159. Pl. 170.
M.P.Dim. 0.067. Th. at rim 0.015. One rim fragment made in two steps as described for **425** above. Reddish yellow (5YR 6/6) clay with lustrous red (2.5YR 5/8) slip. Stamped decoration on rim consisting of three motifs: one wheellike circle with three dots between each spoke and one in the center; a palm frond or rod and segmented line; a stamp composed of three concentric circles.

427. Inv. No. C-78-247. Lot 2307. Pl. 170.
M.P.Dim. 0.044. Th. 0.008–0.020. One rim fragment. Light red (2.5YR 6/6) clay with lustrous red (2.5YR 4/8) slip. Irregularly shaped rim, or perhaps part of a handle. Upper surface decorated with a large sunburst stamped motif flanked by five small diamond shapes. Irregular decorated surface may be a result of manufacture like that for **425**, **426**.

428. Inv. No. C-75-20. Lot 1659. Pl. 170.
M.P.Dim. 0.056. Th. 0.008. Small rim fragment. Lustrous slip. Scalloped rim edge with single groove. A continuous band of impressed decoration on upper rim surface consisting of figure 8's with a groove on either side.

429. Inv. No. C-74-131. Lot 1398. Pls. 49, 170.
P.H. 0.024. Est. D. rim 0.284. One fragment of rim and small part of side wall. Metallic, lustrous slip. Incised design of nicks and curved slashes.

Form 2

Form 2 is a hemispherical bowl with wide, horizontal rim and small, ring base. Variant A has a flat rim and is usually between 0.04 and 0.05 m. in height, although some larger versions exist. Variant B is of similar size but has a sharp ridge at the center of the rim. This form is the counterpart to the Form 1 plate. Decoration is of the same sort as is found on the larger dish. Since twice as many examples of the Form 2 bowl have been preserved, a greater variety of motifs are evident.

Because Forms 1 and 2 are so similar in shape and decoration, it may be difficult to assign a fragment to one form or the other when only a small portion of the rim circumference has been preserved, since the difference in diameter determines what the form is.

Diameter of Variant A: 0.110 to 0.165 m. (most). Some others as large as 0.180 to 0.200 m.

Diameter of Variant B: 0.180 to 0.240 m.

Anderson-Stojanović (1984) 105.

Similar to Rigoir Form 2 in the Gaulish series.

Variant A

430. Inv. No. C-71-265. Lot 307. Pl. 49.
H. 0.046. Est. D. rim 0.138. One fragment, preserving complete profile. Lustrous slip. Single groove on upper face of rim toward exterior.

Twelve additional examples (all gray): Lot 293: 3; Lot 299: 2; Lot 306: 2; Lot 883: C-73-82; Lot 884: C-73-83; Lot 2212: C-78-227; Lot 2406: C-78-282; Lot C-79-59.

431. Inv. No. C-78-128. Lot 2213. Pl. 49.

P.H. 0.033. Est. D. rim 0.137. One fragment of rim and side wall. Lustrous slip. On upper rim surface alternating stamped, perforated circle and linear motif. Two grooves at rim interior.

432. Inv. No. C-73-41. Lot 917. Pl. 49.

P.H. 0.018. Th. 0.004. One rim fragment. Stamped decoration on rim and single groove at rim interior.

433. Inv. No. C-72-71. Lot 789. Pl. 49.

P.H. 0.030. Th. 0.005. Three pieces mended, giving rim and side wall. Lustrous slip. Stamped lentoid motif on rim. Double groove at rim interior.

434. Inv. No. C-71-218. Lot 274. Pl. 170.

P.H. 0.020. Est. D. rim 0.140. One fragment with rim and side wall. Lustrous, metallic slip. Double groove at interior and exterior edge of rim and in center a row of stamped diamonds with dots in the center.

435. Inv. No. C-71-219. Lot 293. Pl. 49.

P.H. 0.030. Th. 0.005. One fragment with rim and side wall. Black lustrous slip. At rim exterior a row of small stamped drops, then two grooves, then a series of stamped rectangles alternating with double blades running perpendicular to the groove lines, and two grooves at rim interior.

436. Inv. No. C-72-46. Lot 612. Pl. 49.

P.H. 0.029. Th. 0.004. One fragment of rim and side wall. Lustrous slip. Small notches removed all along rim edge. At rim center a row of stamped double crescents framing circles, bounded by double grooves toward exterior of rim and at rim interior.

437. Inv. No. C-71-226. Lot 282. Pl. 49.

P.H. 0.042. Est. D. rim 0.140. One fragment with rim and side wall. Double row of tiny, stamped rectangles on rim surface.

438. Inv. No. C-73-57. Lot 902. Pl. 49.

P.H. 0.042. Est. D. rim 0.140. One fragment with rim and side wall. Lustrous slip. Single groove at rim exterior. Stamped half-wheels with triangular cut-out pattern on rim surface.

439. Inv. No. C-75-11. Lot 1656.

M.P.Dim. 0.034. Th. 0.007. One rim fragment. Single groove at rim edge and upper surface decorated with a row of barbotine dots.

440. Inv. No. C-74-229. Lot 1398.

P.H. 0.019. One rim fragment. Single groove at rim interior and exterior with a row of small notches in between.

441. Inv. No. C-73-7. Lot 917. Pl. 50.

H. 0.043. D. 0.120. Two fragments mended, giving complete profile. Black lustrous slip. Two grooves at rim interior, and at rim edge finger impressions framed by stamped double crescent in a continuous pattern.

442. Inv. No. C-70-116. Lot 509. Pl. 50.

P.H. 0.050. Est. D. rim 0.200. Four fragments mended, giving rim and side wall. Metallic slip. Two grooves at rim interior, and at rim edge a continuous pattern of finger impressions framed by stamped double crescent with stamped circles where the crescents meet.

Five additional examples of bowls with this same design as follows: Lot 306: C-71-264, C-73-27; Lot 2211: C-78-47; Lot 2407: C-78-281; and 1 in Lot 277.

443. Inv. No. C-78-32. Lot 2112. Pl. 50.

P.H. 0.050. Est. D. rim 0.198. One fragment of rim and side wall. Light red (2.5YR 6/8) fabric with lustrous red (2.5YR 4/6) slip. Rather than the stamped crescents as in preceding examples, this piece and others (listed below) have a double groove following the outline of the finger-impressed decoration at rim edge. Stamped circles at each point.

The following are additional examples: Lot 277: 2; Lot 2407: C-78-281; Lot 2581: C-79-72.

One example each in Lots 277, 293, and 2194: C-78-87) have similar decorative motifs but rim edge as 444 and following.

444. Inv. No. C-79-12. Lot 2581. Pl. 50.

P.H. 0.028. Est. D. rim 0.165. One fragment of rim and side wall. Metallic and lustrous slip. Broadly scalloped rim edge with single groove along outline and two grooves at rim interior.

445. Inv. No. C-74-79. Lot 1370. Pl. 50.

P.H. 0.031. Est. D. rim 0.100. One fragment with rim and side wall. Glossy slip. Scalloped rim with small stamped circles at scallop points. Interior half of rim's upper surface is decorated with a continuous row of angular S-shapes. Two grooves at interior rim edge.

446. Inv. No. C-77-70. Lot 1935. Pl. 50.

P.H. 0.015. Th. 0.004. One small rim fragment. Scalloped rim edge defined on upper surface by a continuous row of dots and a large stamped circle at the point of each scallop. Double groove toward rim interior. (The vessel illustrated in Pl. 50 is C-67-2, and shows how C-77-70 would appear if better preserved.)

447. Inv. No. C-71-45. Pl. 50.
M.P.Dim. 0.045. Th. 0.004. Two rim fragments mended. Lustrous slip. The flat, upper surface of the rim is divided in half by a single groove. The rim edge has finger-impressed decoration framed by segmented arcs. Toward rim interior a pattern of alternating triangles and circles.

448. Inv. No. C-79-96. Lot 2581. Pl. 51.
P.H. 0.063. Est. D. rim 0.260. One fragment with rim and side wall. Black, metallic slip. Scalloped rim edge and horizontal burnishing marks on exterior.

449. Lot 299, No. 51. Pl. 51.
P.H. 0.025. Est. D. rim 0.164. Two fragments mended, preserving rim and side wall. Scalloped rim edge. Two widely spaced incised wavy lines generally follow the line of the rim edge. At rim interior stamped circles at regular intervals.

Variant B

450. Inv. No. C-74-142. Lot 1361. Pl. 51.
P.H. 0.032. Est. D. rim 0.194. One fragment with rim and side wall. Lustrous, metallic slip. Upper surface of rim is decorated with a series of four grooves.

451. Inv. No. C-71-228. Lot 190. Pl. 51.
P.H. 0.033. Est. D. rim 0.240. One fragment with rim and side wall. Modeled rope decoration along center of upper rim face.

452. Inv. No. C-70-115. Lot 507. Pl. 51.
P.H. 0.045. Est. D. rim 0.220. One fragment with rim and side wall. Lustrous, metallic slip. Modeled rope decoration on rim.

453. Inv. No. C-79-6. Lot 2581.
P.H. 0.033. Est. D. rim 0.188. One rim fragment. Lustrous, metallic slip. Raised rim at exterior edge and diagonal slashes decorate upper rim surface.

Form 3

Form 3 is a flat-based dish with rolled rim. Two grooves set off the bottom of the vessel from the side wall. The floor is frequently decorated with stamped decoration or rouletting.

Rim diameter ranges from 0.210 to 0.330 m. with most falling between 0.210 to 0.260 m.

Anderson-Stojanović (1984) 105.

Resembles Rigoir Form 4 in the Gaulish series (see note 96 above).

454. Inv. No. C-78-155. Lot 2263. Pls. 51, 170.
H. 0.049. D. rim 0.218. Almost complete vessel mended from many fragments. Metallic slip. At center of floor a circular band of rouletting with concentric grooves on either side. Double groove on exterior where side wall meets bottom of dish.
Found with coin dating 383–392; see Wiseman (1978) 410.

455. Lot 998, No. 1. Pl. 52.
P.H. 0.037. Est. D. rim 0.330. One rim fragment of large dish. Wall somewhat more flaring than most examples of Form 3. Double groove on interior, midway down the wall, and fine, narrow rouletting on exterior.

456. Lot 2393, No. 10. Pl. 52.
P.H. 0.028. Est. D. rim 0.245. One fragment of side wall. Tear-shaped rouletting on interior.

Form 4

The Form 4 bowl corresponds to the dish of Form 3 with rolled rim and small ring base. The shape was apparently not decorated, but only three examples have been found at Stobi. All come from the same context.

Anderson-Stojanović (1984) 105.

457. Inv. No. C-79-100. Lot 2581. Pl. 52.
P.H. 0.065. Est. D. rim 0.134. Two fragments, not joining, from rim and part of side wall and base. Lustrous, metallic slip.
Two additional examples, C-79-87 and C-79-89, are also from Lot 2581.

Form 5

Form 5 is a plate with incurved wall and flat base. Both small and large examples occur. No decoration has been preserved on the three examples of this form.

Anderson-Stojanović (1984) 105.

458. Inv. No. C-74-35. Lot 1551. Pl. 52.
H. 0.033. Est. D. rim 0.160. One fragment, preserving complete profile. Offset just above floor on interior wall. Lustrous, metallic slip.

459. Inv. No. C-74-144. Lot 1362. Pl. 52.
H. 0.040. Est. D. rim 0.310. One fragment, preserving complete profile. Black, lustrous slip. Double groove on exterior at point where side wall meets bottom.

460. Inv. No. C-78-270. Lot 2218. Pl. 52.
P.H. 0.032. Est. D. rim 0.320. One fragment preserving rim and side wall. Single, deep groove toward rim interior and single groove below rim on exterior.

Form 6

Form 6 is a small bowl with slightly incurved wall and grooved rim. As only rim sections of this form have been preserved, the form of the base is not known although a ring base seems likely. The side wall is usually decorated with stamped motifs or rouletting.
Anderson-Stojanović (1984) 105.

461. Inv. No. C-74-63. Lot 1319. Pl. 52.
P.H. 0.043. Est. D. rim 0.150. One fragment of rim and wall. Black, lustrous slip. Double ridge at rim and on exterior wall part of stamped ornament preserving one motif of three concentric circles and part of two segmented rods or arcs with a circle in each segment.

Form 7

Form 7 is a small shallow dish with flanged rim. Base shape unknown. Not decorated.
Anderson-Stojanović (1984) 105.

462. Inv. No. C-78-91. Lot 2234. Pl. 53.
P.H. 0.036. Est. D. rim 0.155. One fragment of rim and side wall. Lustrous, metallic slip.

Form 8

Form 8 is a small jar or beaker with two handles. Variant A has a straight, vertical rim with slight waist and plump body below. Variant B has an everted, moulded rim with a marked groove or indentation at the waist. The upper body is usually decorated with one or more stamped motifs. Since no complete examples have been preserved, the base form is not known. Rim diameters range from 0.073 to 0.110 m.
Anderson-Stojanović (1984) 105.

Variant A

463. Inv. No. C-71-238. Lot 307. Pl. 53.
P.H. 0.063. Est. D. rim 0.080. One fragment preserving rim, side wall, and part of handle. One complete stamped grape cluster and part of another preserved between rim and shoulder.

Variant B

464. Inv. No. C-72-12. Lots 762, 763. Pl. 53.
P.H. 0.058. Est. D. rim 0.110. Six fragments mended, preserving rim, part of side wall, and one handle. Lustrous, metallic slip. Double groove beneath lip and single groove marks off neck from shoulder. Two lozenge-shaped stamps preserved on neck.

465. Inv. No. C-71-417. Lot 171. Pl. 53.
P.H. 0.049. Est. D. rim 0.082. Two fragments joined to form rim, side wall, and part of handle. Fire-blackened surface. One complete and part of another segmented V-shape stamped on neck.

466. Inv. No. C-78-62. Lot 2355. Pl. 53.
P.H. 0.060. Est. D. rim 0.073. One fragment preserving rim, side wall, and one complete handle. Two examples of the same stamp consisting of a line and a rod preserved on neck.

467. Inv. No. C-78-50. Lot 2211. Pl. 53.
P.H. 0.039. Est. D. rim 0.090. One fragment of rim and wall. Lustrous, black slip. Side wall preserves one diamond-shaped stamp and one composed of three concentric circles.

No variant ascertainable

468. Inv. No. C-72-241. Lot 523. Pl. 53.
P.H. 0.034. Est. D. rim 0.15. One fragment of rim and wall. Lustrous slip. Rouletting in rope pattern under rim and two grooves below. Stamped design of circles and segmented lines partially preserved.

469. Inv. No. C-79-77. Lot 2588.
P.H. 0.035. Th. 0.003. One fragment of rim and wall. Lustrous slip. One *planta pedis* stamp preserved on wall.

Form 9

Form 9 is a two-handled jar with wide, open body, and a carination at the point of greatest diameter. Stamped decoration is common between rim and carination. No bases remain on the two examples preserved.

Anderson-Stojanović (1984) 106.

470. Inv. No. C-79-95. Lot 2604. Pl. 54.

P.H. 0.070. Est. D. rim 0.145. One fragment with rim, side wall, and one handle. Lustrous, metallic slip. Part of a segmented rod-and-line motif stamp preserved on wall.

471. Lot 294, No. 1. Pl. 54.

P.H. 0.045. Est. D. rim 0.140. One fragment of wall. Lustrous, metallic slip. Modeled rope design at carination and part of a stamped motif consisting of a diamond flanked by rods on the wall.

Form 10

Form 10 is a large screw-necked jug with round, plump body and small ring foot. A series of grooves below the neck and at mid-body are the only decoration. No handles are preserved on any examples.

Anderson-Stojanović (1984) 106.

472. Inv. No. C-74-508. Lot 1349. Pl. 54.

P.H. 0.282. Est. D. neck 0.048. Max. D. body 0.234. Ten fragments, not all joined, forming profile of vessel. Rim is missing. Three grooves around body at point of greatest diameter.

Form 11

Form 11 is a trefoil pitcher. Short neck and plump body are clear, but since only rim and neck fragments have survived it is difficult to reconstruct the rest of the shape.

473. Lot 303, No. 16. Pl. 54.

P.H. 0.045. Est. D. rim 0.102. Two fragments mended, giving rim and neck. Metallic slip.

Miscellaneous

474. Dish. Inv. No. C-78-79. Lot 2233. Pl. 54

P.H. 0.032. Est. D. rim 0.235. One fragment with rim and wall. Lustrous, metallic black slip.

475. Jar. Inv. No. C-79-98. Lot 2605. Pl. 55.

P.H. 0.046. Est. D. rim 0.149. One fragment of rim and wall. Lustrous slip. Vertical rouletted lines on rim exterior and part of stamped grape cluster on side wall.

476. Base. Inv. No. C-78-75. Lot 2233. Pl. 55.

P.H. 0.053. D. 0.082. One fragment of pedestal foot. Lustrous slip. Bead rouletting on first moulding, vertical rouletting on next three mouldings, and two stamped ovals preserved in center.

477. Base. Inv. No. C-74-85. Lot 1507. Pl. 55.

P.H. 0.030. D. 0.112. One fragment of foot. Yellowish red (5YR 5/8) clay and lustrous red (2.5YR 5/8) slip. Feather rouletting on top moulding. Finger-impressed edge on foot. Each impression framed by a double stamped arc with circles at the point where they join.

478. Handle. Inv. No. C-78-61. Lot 2319. Pl. 170.

P.L. 0.056. W. 0.025. Th. 0.006. One handle broken at the point where it met the vessel wall. Flat, rectangular in shape. Lustrous slip. Two widely spaced grooves at end.

479. Handle. Inv. No. C-73-28. Basilica Cemetery. Pl. 171.

M.P.Dim. 0.082. One fragment of irregularly shaped handle. Part of grooved decoration preserved at handle edge.

480. Handle. Inv. No. C-77-1. Lot 1939. Pls. 55, 170.

P.L. 0.035. W. 0.042. Th. 0.006–0.010. One flat handle fragment of triangular shape and notched end. Light red (2.5YR 6/8) clay with pale brown (10YR 6/3) core and red (2.5YR 5/8) lustrous slip. Decoration on upper surface includes three stamped concentric circles surrounding a segmented rod. The edges of the fragment are pinched on all sides.

481. Rim. Inv. No. C-71-50. Lot 178. Pls. 55, 171.

P.L. 0.037. P.W. 0.095. Th. 0.025. One fragment of rim and space for handle attachment. Metallic slip. Rim portion is thickened to accommodate handle which would have fitted into the opening in the side of the thick rim. Rouletting at outer edge of rim, and on upper surface rouletting follows scalloped outline of rim. Stamped motifs include two dotted wheellike shapes, one dotted horseshoe, and two dotted lozenges.

482. Figurine(?) or Handle(?). Inv. No. C-67-1. Pl. 171.

M.P.Dim. 0.034. One fragment preserving head of a catlike animal with long pointed ears and round eyes formed by stamped concentric circles. Lustrous slip.

483. Floor fragment. Inv. No. C-78-120. Lot 2213. Pl. 55.

M.P.Dim. 0.077. Th. 0.004. One fragment. Lustrous slip. On upper surface single groove and two different stamped motifs: a palm branch(?) and a patterned square.

484. Floor fragment. Inv. No. C-74-96. Lot 1552. Pl. 55.

M.P.Dim. 0.056. Th. 0.006. One fragment. Lustrous slip. Double groove at center and a variety of stamped motifs: circles, diamonds, leaves(?).

Miscellaneous Stamps (**485–510**)

A total of nineteen name, three device, and five anepigraphic *planta pedis* stamps are included in the catalogue.[108] Both Latin and Greek signatures are found, as well as Latin names written with Greek letters. Most of the stamps presented here are from contexts of the second half of the 1st century (Acropolis, Table 4.5) and the first half of the 2nd century A.C. (Large Bath, Table 4.7) Among the name stamps are three of ΕΠΙΓΟΝΟΣ and four of AFRI.

Only a selection of the many anepigraphic stamps in *planta pedis* have been included. Most of these occur in fills used for buildings of the 4th and 5th centuries on the site.

485. Inv. No. C-71-80. Lot 258. Pls. 56, 171.

M.P.Dim. 0.092. Th. 0.008. Single base fragment. Pink (7.5YR 7/4) clay with red to reddish brown (2.5YR–5YR) glossy slip on interior; underside is plain. The surface of the interior is scored with engraved lines. In a rectangular stamp are the Greek letters ΕΠΙΓΟΝΟΣ.

Cf. Iliffe, 33, also found in Athens in both Greek and Latin letters. There was an EPIGONVS of Pozzuoli (Oxé-Comfort 634) and workmen by that name: EPIGONVS C. TELLI (Oxé-Comfort 1917), EPIGONVS P. CORNELII of the factory of P. CORNELIVS (Oxé-Comfort 498), and EPIGONVS L. ANNI of the L. ANNIVS workshops of Arezzo (Oxé-Comfort 86h). All three stamps at Stobi with this name (**485–487**) vary, and all are in Greek letters.

Date: post-40 A.C.

486. Inv. No. C-71-141. Lot 230. Pls. 56, 171.

M.P.Dim. 0.043. Reddish yellow (5YR 6/6) clay, red slip. In a rectangular stamp are the well-worn Greek letters ΕΠΙΓΟΝΟΣ.

Date: second half of the 1st century A.C.

487. Inv. No. C-71-347. Lot 230. Pls. 56, 171.

M.P.Dim. 0.040. Reddish-yellow (5YR 6/6) clay with worn red slip. Soft-fired clay body. Part of a stamp in Greek which is probably ΕΠΙΓΟΝΟΣ. Preserved are the Ε, Π and the tops of Γ and Ο on the next line.

Date: second half of the 1st century A.C.

488. Inv. No. C-74-411. Lot 1475. Pl. 171.

M.P.Dim. 0.042. Reddish-yellow (5YR 6/6) clay with red to light red (2.5YR) slip. Rectangular stamp in Greek: ΕΡΜΗ.

Cf. Iliffe, 31, dated to the Augustan period, and *EAA*, 2, Hayes, "sigillate orientale B" 52. This piece may, in fact, be Eastern Sigillata B. See **339**.

489. Inv. No. C-73-106. Lot 938. Pls. 56, 171.

M.P.Dim. 0.045. Pink (7.5YR 7/4) clay with red slip. In *planta pedis* are preserved the letters ΜΟΙ—probably the ending of a Greek name.

Date: first half of the 2nd century A.C.

490. Inv. No. C-71-104. Lot 249. Pl. 56.

M.P.Dim. 0.072. Reddish yellow (5YR 6/6) clay with lustrous red slip on both surfaces. Within a circle surrounded by a band of rouletting is a stamp in *planta pedis* with what appear to be the Greek letters ΟΙΥΛΟΝ.

Date: post-75 A.C.

491. Inv. No. C-71-118. Lot 248. Pls. 57, 171.

M.P.Dim. 0.081. Reddish yellow (5YR 7/6) clay with red slip on both surfaces. Within a *planta pedis* stamp are Greek letters, all but illegible.

Date: post-75 A.C.

[108] Additional stamps that may be local are included in the section on Black-Gloss Wares with Gray Fabric. References to stamps follow Oxé-Comfort serial numbers.

492. Inv. No. C-75-28. Lot 1645. Pls. 56, 171.
M.P.Dim. 0.050. Pink (7.5YR 7/4) clay with red slip. In a rectangular stamp are what appear to be the Greek letters ΜΡΛΥ.

493. Inv. No. C-71-137. Lot 249. Pls. 57, 172.
M.P.Dim. 0.062. Reddish yellow (5YR 6/6) clay and red slip. Stamp in *planta pedis* appears to be ΛΥΣΥΣ, perhaps for LVCIVS.
Date: post-75 A.C.

494. Inv. No. C-71-214. Lot 433. Pl. 57.
M.P.Dim. 0.036. Pink (7.5YR 7/4) clay with red slip. The letters in a rectangular frame are only partially preserved, ICIVS, perhaps the end of a name.

495. Inv. No. C-74-75. Lot 1324. Pls. 57, 172.
M.P.Dim. 0.042. Reddish gray to reddish brown (5YR 5/2–5/3) clay with red slip. In a rectangular frame are the Greek letters ΤΕΡΤ.
Cf. Oxé-Comfort 1942–1947.

496. Inv. No. C-73-103. Lot 934. Pls. 57, 172.
H. 0.016. D. base 0.075. Pink (7.5YR 7/4) clay with worn red slip. Soft-fired clay. In a depressed circular area of a small plate in a rectangular frame, ΓΑΙΟΣ retrograde, the Latin name GAIVS in Greek letters.
Date: first half of the 2nd century A.C.

497. Inv. No. C-74-426. Lot 1478. Pl. 57.
P.H. 0.019. D. base 0.058. Reddish yellow (5YR 6/6) clay with red slip. In a rectangular frame are the letters: VIT.

498. Inv. No. C-71-348. Lot 228. Pls. 58, 172.
M.P.Dim. 0.032. Pink (7.5YR 7/4) clay with red slip. Rectangular frame with the stamp: *AFRI*.
Perhaps related to the workshop of SEXTVS ANNIVS AFER of Arezzo. His stamps never occur in *planta pedis*. Our stamp may be from one of the workshops established outside of Italy. See Oxé-Comfort 87–92, p. 28. There are four stamps of AFRI at Stobi. See below (**499–501**).
Date: post-75 A.C.

499. Inv. No. C-74-298. Lot 1493. Pl. 58.
M.P.Dim. 0.040. Reddish yellow (5YR) clay with red slip. In a rectangular frame: AFRI.

500. Inv. No. C-74-313. Lot 1420. Pls. 58, 172.
P.H. 0.017. D. base. 0.046. Pink (7.5YR 7/4) clay with red slip. In a rectangular frame: AFRI.

501. Inv. No. C-74-58. Lot 1057. Pl. 58.
M.P.Dim. 0.024. Reddish yellow (5YR) clay with red slip. The last three letters of *AFRI* in a rectangular frame.

502. Inv. No. C-74-501. Lot 1416. Pls. 58, 172.
M.P.Dim. 0.032. Reddish yellow (5YR) clay with red slip. In a rectangular frame a stamp of the potter C. VIBIENVS is preserved with the letters *C. VIB*.
Cf. Oxé-Comfort 521, 522; Iliffe, p. 49.

503. Inv. No. C-74-65. Lot 1090. Pls. 58, 172.
M.P.Dim. 0.066. Reddish yellow (5YR) clay with light red (2.5YR) metallic lustrous slip. *Planta pedis* stamp with faint letters or sandal markings.

504. Lot 30, No. 4. Pl. 58.
M.P.Dim. 0.065. Reddish yellow (5YR) clay with red slip. *Planta pedis* stamp with sandal.

505. Inv. No. C-74-223. Lot 1479. Pl. 59.
P.H. 0.023. D. base. 0.050. Reddish yellow (5YR) clay with red slip. *Planta pedis* stamp with sandal.

506. Inv. No. C-74-433. Lot 1358. Pl. 59.
P.H. 0.018. D. base 0.038. Reddish yellow (5YR) clay and red slip. *Planta pedis* stamp very faint.

507. Inv. No. C-74-221. Lot 1538. Pl. 59.
P.H. 0.035. D. base. 0.053. Reddish yellow (5YR) clay with red slip. *Planta pedis* stamp with sandal bounded by carelessly rendered circular groove.

508. Inv. No. C-72-96. Lot 552. Pls. 59, 173.
M.P.Dim. 0.063. Reddish yellow (5YR) clay with plain exterior, dark reddish brown (5YR) slip on interior. The stamp consists of three hearts joined by a circle and surrounded by a band of rouletting. The stamp is similar to that on a Campanian plate (**32**).
Date: second and third quarters 1st century B.C.

509. Inv. No. C-71-117. Lot 248. Pl. 59.
M.P.Dim. 0.065. Reddish yellow (5YR) clay with red slip. A rectangular frame with an X circumscribed by a square.
Cf. Oxé-Comfort, Pl. VIII:3.
Date: post-75 A.C.

510. Inv. No. C-74-265. Lot 1441. Pl. 173.
M.P.Dim. 0.080. Reddish yellow (5YR) with metallic lustrous slip, light red to red (2.5YR 6/6–5/6). A heart-shaped central stamp.

Italian Mugs (511–516)

Imported mugs or pitchers of small size, gray or reddish brown in color, or frequently fired red on the upper body and gray below occur at Stobi in deposits of the 2nd and 3rd centuries A.C. They may originate in Italy—the "urnette a collarino," or alternatively in the Aegean where they are common.[109] The examples at Stobi, wherever they originate, seem a homogenous group.

The fabric of the Stobi pieces is almost uniformly red, rather hard fired, and thin walled. Sometimes there is a reddish brown or gray core. The gray surface often has a very shiny, sometimes vitreous glaze, perhaps owing to a high firing temperature. Some examples have ribbing on the body, a few others are decorated with sand as in the earlier Thin-Walled tradition. On several of the pieces a third type of decoration consisting of white painted dots or vegetal patterns is found (Pl. 60).

With so few examples of this ware, it is difficult to assign a precise date. None occurs in the late 1st-century deposits of the Acropolis, but some do appear in later Acropolis Lots from the same Room 2 area, which have little evidence for date but which must be at least 3rd or 4th century (**511**, **512**). A number of examples come from the Large Bath, primarily from Lot 931. The Large Bath deposits (Table 4.7) contain considerable amounts of Eastern Sigillata B, almost all of which belong to the later B2 variety, which dates to the first half of the 2nd century, but no Çandarli ware, which on this site appears during the second half of the 2nd century. The other significant amounts of Italian mugs (**514**, **515**) come from destruction debris and dumped fill in the Inner City Wall West area. Those deposits belong to the second half of the 3rd century (Tables 4.8 and 4.9).

Only rim, base, and body fragments have been found. There are no complete profiles.

511. Rim. Lot 238, No. 15. Pl. 60.

P.H. 0.039. Est. D. rim 0.086. One fragment from rim. Slight ridge at neck. Thin red (2.5YR 5/8) fabric with reddish brown (2.5YR 5/4) core and pinkish gray (7.5YR 6/2) surface decorated with sand.

512. Rim. Lot 239, No. 33. Pl. 60.

P.H. 0.062. Est. D. rim 0.066. One fragment with rim, wall, and one handle. Slight ridge at neck. Thin red (2.5YR 5/6) fabric with gray core and dark gray surface decorated with fine sand.

513. Base. Inv. No. C-73-112. Lot 992.

P.H. 0.051. Th. 0.003. One fragment preserving portion of lower body and flat, disc base. Red (2.5YR 5/8) fabric and surface of upper body section. Base and lower body fired gray.

514. Base. Lot 1295, No. 181. Pl. 60.

P.H. 0.040. P.D. body 0.085. D. base 0.031. One fragment preserving flat base and part of body. Slight offset at base exterior. Red (2.5YR 5/6) fabric with reddish brown mottled surface. A row of painted white dots encircles the lower body.

Date: second half of the 3rd century A.C.

515. Base. Lot 1296, No. 111. Pl. 60.

P.H. 0.026. D. base 0.038. One fragment of flat base with groove toward exterior. Red (2.5YR 5/8) fabric with reddish brown (5/4) core and surface.

Date: second half of the 3rd century A.C.

516. Base. Lot 1417, No. 19. Pl. 60.

P.H. 0.018. D. base 0.036. One fragment of plain, flat base. Reddish yellow (5YR 6/6) fabric with red core. Lower part of base exterior fired gray.

There are 16 additional fragments of rims and bases, and 53 body fragments as follows: Lot 237: 9 (3r, 6); Lot 238: 14 (1r, 13); Lot 239: 1; Lot 433: C-71-377; Lot 448: 1; Lot 476: C-70-28; Lot 924: 1b; Lot 931: 12; Lot 936: 1b; Lot 938: 1; Lot 1295: 6 (2b, 4); Lot 1296: 10 (2b, 8); Lot 1298: 1b; Lot 1300: 3; Lot 1302: 2 (1r, 1b); Lot 1308: 1b; Lot 1404: 2; Lot 1407: 1.

109 Hayes, "Villa Dionysus," 107–121, fig. 4, no. 48; 124, fig. 6, nos. 72–74, with other bibliography.

Marbeled Slip (517–519)

Marbeled slip, in colors of reds, oranges, and yellows, rare in the Eastern Mediterranean, appears on only a few examples at Stobi. The technique itself is common from the Claudian period until the 4th century and occurs on different wares at various sites in western and central Europe.[110] Marbeled slip is apparently an imitation of the swirling pattern of colored marble and marbelized glass vessels.

Imitations occur in Pannonia during the second and third centuries.[111] The three examples at Stobi could represent experiments by a local potter, since the fabric and shapes of two, at least, are those of the local ware. Furthermore, the decoration on these three pieces is not so much marbelized as striped.[112]

517. Flat-based dish with horizontal rim. Inv. No. C-70-017. Lot 462. Pl. 61.

H. 0.055. Est. D. rim 0.325. One fragment preserving complete profile. Red (2.5YR 5/8) fabric. Marbeled slip applied in stripes varies from red to pale yellowish brown. Stobi MR Form 1.

518. Flat-based dish with curved wall. Lot 239, No. 57. Pl. 60.

H. 0.034. Est. D. rim 0.220. One fragment preserving complete profile. Brown (10YR 5/3) fabric with yellowish red (5YR) and red slip applied in stripes.

Stobi MR Form 6.

Date: 3rd/4th centuries A.C.(?).

519. Shallow plate or platter. Inv. No. C-70-043. Lot 460. Pls. 61, 173.

H. 0.020. Est. D. rim 0.340. One fragment preserving profile. Red (5YR 6/6) fabric. Two grooves encircle floor near wall. Interior and exterior covered with alternating stripes of red and reddish yellow (5YR 7/6).

Lead-Glazed Wares (520–531)

The few examples of Lead-Glazed Wares found at Stobi consist primarily of fragments from mortaria along with a few examples of bowls and pitchers.[113] Their origin is most likely Pannonia where Lead-Glazed wares are common in the 4th century A.C.

The earliest examples of lead-glazed pottery are found in Asia Minor at Tarsus, dated to the 1st century B.C., and they appear somewhat later in Italy in contexts of the 1st century A.C.[114] The most popular shape in this early period is the small cup, often decorated in relief. These were not common, however, and must be considered luxury items. The production of lead glaze continued during the 2nd and 3rd centuries in central and eastern Europe—that is, in Germany, Pannonia, Moesia, and Dacia—gradually being used for a wider range of forms and without relief decoration.[115]

By the 4th century, lead-glazed wares are distributed widely through North Italy, where a kiln site has been found at Carlino, Switzerland, and the Roman provinces in present-day Austria, Hungary, Rumania, and Yugoslavia.[116] Current

[110] Greene (1977) 114.

[111] Brukner, *Rimska Keramika*, 33.

[112] Ibid., T.75, no. 84.

[113] W-MZ (1971) 418, 419, discuss the significance of the discovery of lead-glazed wares at Stobi. See Peacock, *PRW*, 63–65, for general comments.

[114] A. Hochuli-Gysel, *Kleinasiatische Glasierte Reliefkeramik und ihre öberitalischen Nachahmungen* (Bern 1977); Blake, "Ceramica Paleo-italiana," 22, 23.

[115] The continuity between early Imperial lead-glazed wares and the later Roman products has not been firmly established. For a discussion of the evidence, see Blake, "Ceramica paleo-italiana," 37–39; also Brukner, *Rimska Keramika*, 34, and N. Gudea, "Pannonian Glazed Pottery, A View from the East," *RCRFActa* 25/26 (1987) 419–421. Glazed wares are also common at Carnuntum, see M. Grunewald, *Die Gefässkeramik des Legionslagers von Carnuntum. Der Römische Limes in Osterreich. Vol. 29* (Vienna 1979) 67–74, and figs. 63–69. Note also M. Picon and A. Desbat, "Note sur l'origine des céramiques à glacure plombifère géneralement bicolore des IIeme et IIeme siècles, de Vienne et St. Romain-en-Gaul," *Figlina* 7 (1986) 125–127.

[116] Blake, "Ceramica Paleo-Italiana," 23, 24.

evidence suggests Roman Pannonia as the greatest producer of the 4th-century lead-glazed wares.[117] The commonest forms are mortaria, bowls, and jugs with glaze that varies in color from olive green to brownish yellow. Mortaria are normally glazed only on the interior.

Although the majority of examples of lead-glazed ware at Stobi occur in late 4th- to early 5th-century contexts, a few pieces were found in 3rd-century deposits (**528**, **529**).

520. Mortarium. Inv. No. C-71-200. Lot 295. Pl. 61.

P.H. 0.057. Est. D. rim 0.358. Single rim fragment. Reddish yellow (5YR 6/8), highly porous fabric with gritty inclusions and at interior, sharply defined wide, gray core. Greenish brown glaze visible in spots but thin enough over vessel surface so that the red fabric is visible. On rim double grooves at interior and exterior with an incised wavy line running between.

Context date: late 4th, early 5th centuries A.C.

521. Mortarium. Inv. No. C-71-30. Lot 127. Pl. 61.

P.H. 0.069. Single rim fragment, perhaps portion of spout. Dark gray (7.5YR N4/) gritty, micaceous fabric with light gray (5YR 7/1) multiple core. On interior and part of exterior, dark reddish brown (5YR 3/3) lustrous glaze with some greenish spots. Single groove at rim exterior.

Context date: 4th century A.C.

522. Mortarium. Inv. No. C-71-262. Lot 305. Pl. 61.

P.H. 0.060. Est. D. rim 0.340. Two fragments of rim mended. Red (5YR 4/8) highly porous fabric with reddish brown (5YR 4/3) core toward interior and gray at interior edge. Many inclusions. Rim and interior originally covered with greenish brown glaze now white in places as a result of accidental contact with hydrochloric acid. The rim preserves part of the spout. Closely spaced zigzag line incised on rim surface.

Context date: late 4th, early 5th centuries A.C.

Seven other similar fragmentary mortaria: Lot 169: C-71-142, C-71-143; Lot 305: C-71-266; Lot 1430: C-71-334; Lot 529: C-72-81; one example from Lot 299, and one from Lot 304. The majority of glazed mortaria (six out of ten) were found among the rubbish deposits that accumulated in the East Parodos during the early 5th century A.C. after the theater was no longer in use. They are of roughly the same size and have a green to greenish brown glaze on rim and interior.

523. Dish with flaring rim. Inv. No. C-73-33. Lot 881. Pl. 62.

P.H. 0.030. Est. D. rim 0.260. Rim and wall mended from five fragments. Hard-fired, reddish yellow to light red (5YR 7/6–2.5YR 6/6), highly porous clay with a small amount of sand or grit visible. Brown (7.5YR 5/6) glaze on interior and exterior. A single groove extends along the face of the rim exterior decorated with small teardrop appliqué, glazed olive (2.5Y 6/6 olive yellow).

Context date: late 4th century A.C.

524. Bowl. Inv. No. C-74-62. Lot 1316. Pl. 62.

P.H. 0.039. Est. D. rim 0.144. One rim fragment. Light brownish gray (2.5Y 6/2) with light gray (7.5YR N7/) core. Good, thick, greenish brown (10YR 4/4 dark yellow-brown) glaze on both interior and exterior. Straight wall with rolled rim.

525. Jug. Inv. No. C-78-144. Lot 2367. Pl. 62.

P.H. 0.036. Est. D. rim 0.065. Two fragments of rim mended. Red (2.5YR 5/6) gritty fabric with multiple gray core. Yellowish green glaze on exterior and part of interior.

526. Jug. Lot 300, No. 3. Pl. 62

P.H. 0.044. Est. D. neck 0.048. One fragment of neck and handle from small jug. Yellowish red (5YR 5/8) fabric and on exterior only, yellowish red (5YR 4/6) glaze.

527. Closed vessel. Lot 297, No. 1. Pl. 62.

P.H. 0.033. Est. D. body 0.084. One fragment of wall carination. Gray to light gray fabric and olive brown (2.5Y 4/4) glaze on exterior.

528. Base from Jug(?). Inv. No. C-71-62. Pl. 62.

P.H. 0.058. D. base 0.070. Four pieces mended from base. Gritty and micaceous red clay with gray core near exterior edge. Greenish brown glaze on exterior only.

529. Small base. Inv. No. C-74-294. Lot 1306. Pl. 62.

P.H. 0.010. D. base 0.023. One small base frag-

[117] Gudea ("Pannonian Glazed Pottery," [cited in note 115]) 409–436; P. Arthur and D. Williams, "Pannonische Glasierte Keramik: An Assessment," in Anderson and Anderson (1981) 481–510.

ment. Hard-fired, fine white (10YR 8/2) clay. Olive brown (2.5Y 4/4) glaze on exterior only.

530. Small base. Inv. No. C-78-288. Lot 2382. Pl. 62.

P.H. 0.012. Est. D. base 0.050. Three fragments mended. Gray (10YR 5/1) fabric with light brownish gray (10R 6/2) core. Dark yellowish brown (10YR 6/4) glaze on interior and exterior.

531. Fragment with portrait in relief. Inv. No. C-74-60. Lot 1629. Pl. 173.

M.P.Dim. 0.035. Th. 0.004. One fragment broken on all sides. Reddish yellow (5YR 7/8) fabric. Olive yellow (2.5Y 6/8) glaze on face and yellowish red (5YR 4/6) glaze on wall exterior. Interior without glaze. Head and neck of woman in profile looking left. Hair pulled back to nape of neck.

Miscellaneous Imports (532–541)

The following are very unlike the local products, but they cannot be assigned to any known wares at this time. Each is rather distinctive in its combination of fabric and surface treatment.

532. Plate with flaring rim. Inv. No. C-70-135. Lot 799. Pl. 63.

H. 0.042. Est. D. rim 0.268. Mended from three fragments, giving complete profile. Light reddish brown (5YR 6/4) clay and slip (5YR 5/4). Plate has very curved wall and flaring rim with grooves on interior. On the resting surface are two shallow grooves beyond which the bottom of the vessel is concave.

Date: 4th century A.C.

533. Plate with flaring rim. Inv. No. C-74-308. Lots 799, 1599. Pl. 63.

H. 0.035. Est. D. rim 0.264. Mended from many fragments, giving about one-fifth of vessel. Reddish yellow (5YR 6/6) clay with lustrous reddish brown slip on interior with traces on exterior. Part of a rosette stamp preserved on floor. The shape is the same as that of the preceding example (**532**) and from the same context. This example, however, has somewhat thinner walls.

Date: 4th century A.C.

534. Bowl with flat rim. Inv. No. C-75-15. Lot 1659. Pl. 63.

P.H. 0.037. Est. D. rim 0.172. One fragment of rim and wall. Hard-fired, pink (5YR 7/4) clay and lustrous pink to reddish yellow (5YR 7/4–6/6) slip. Shallow bowl with carinated wall and flat rim. Upper surface of rim is decorated with grooves toward interior and around exterior edge with a stamped tear-drop motif.

Date: 4th/5th centuries A.C.

535. Small jar. Inv. No. C-74-72. Lot 1315. Pls. 63, 173.

P.H. 0.049. Est. D. rim 0.072. One fragment of rim, wall, and single handle attachment. Light reddish brown (5YR 6/4) clay with very lustrous light red (2.5YR 6/8) gloss on rim and exterior. Thin-walled vessel with moulded rim, plump body, and one handle. Stamped curvilinear shapes preserved on side wall.

536. Large bowl. Inv. No. C-74-73. Lot 1300. Pls. 63, 174.

P.H. 0.078. Est. D. rim 0.285. One fragment of rim and wall. Reddish yellow (5YR 7/8) clay and red (2.5YR 5/8) gloss. Large bowl with curved body and rolled rim. Three stamped rosettes preserved on wall just below rim.

Date: 3rd century A.C.

537. Large bowl. Inv. No. C-78-33. Lots 2228, 2229, 2207. Pls. 64, 174.

P.H. 0.070. Est. D. rim 0.230. Four fragments mended, preserving rim and wall. Reddish yellow (5YR 7/6) fabric with red slip on exterior. Ridged rim bowl with curved, almost carinated body. Rouletting on rim ridges, at and below carination. A pattern of stamped grape clusters decorated the exterior, of which four are preserved.

Date: 4th century A.C.

538. Mushroom flask. Lot 1302, No. 15. Pl. 64.

P.H. 0.032. Est. D. 0.230. One fragment of wall. Fabric is white (10YR 8/1), and surface is smooth but dull and of same color as fabric.

Cf. Hayes, "Villa Dionysus," fig. 4, no. 35, African Red Slip Form 147, pilgrim flask, which seems to approximate the shape of this example as well as of **539** and **541**.

Date: 3rd century A.C.

539. Mushroom flask. Lot 240, No. 11. Pl. 64.

P.H. 0.032. Est. D. 0.255. One fragment of side wall with traces of horizontal handle. Fine, reddish yellow (7.5YR 7/6) fabric with light red (2.5YR 6/8) multiple cores. Slip is smooth, lustrous red (2.5YR 5/6) on both surfaces.

540. Mushroom flask. Lot 810, No. 348. Pl. 64.

P.H. 0.019. Est. D. 0.240. One fragment of wall. Reddish yellow (5YR 6/6) fabric with red (2.5YR 5/6) slip. For the shape, see Slane (1986) 287, no. 58, in fig. 10.

541. Mushroom flask. Lot 2121, No. 11. Pl. 64.

P.H. 0.036. D. 0.270. One fragment of wall. Light red (2.5YR 6/8) fabric with red (2.5YR 5/6) slip.

Miscellaneous Vessels with Relief Decoration (**542–557**)

The following pieces have been grouped together as distinct from Hellenistic mouldmade bowls either because they are later in date—probably Roman—or were produced by a different technique. Several have been identified as Corinthian or Cnidian, but the rest are of unknown origin.

542. Corinthian relief bowl. Body sherd. Inv. No. C-78-1. Lot 2111. Pl. 174.

M.P.Dim. 0.032. Th. 0.004. One fragment of lower body and carination. Light reddish brown (5YR 6/3) fabric with brown (7.5YR 5/2) slip. Preserved above carination is Heracles, whose legs are shown moving to the left through the grass. The lower part of his club appears on the right.

The standard study of Corinthian Relief bowls is D. Spitzer, "Roman Relief Bowls from Corinth," *Hesperia* 11 (1942) 162–192. Cf. Kenrick, *Berenice 3*, B509, with the same scene.

543. Cnidian Head Cup. Inv. No. MF-74-147. Lot 1482. Pls. 65, 174.

P.H. 0.055. P.W. 0.060. Front half of a moulded cup; broad nose, large mouth turned down at the corners in a grimace, heavy lips with some teeth indicated in the space between the lips. The one preserved eye is small and wide open. None of the features is exaggerated, and the only expression comes from the shape of the mouth. A small portion of the neck serves as the base. Fabric is 5YR 7/4 (pink) with 5YR 4/2 (dark reddish gray) slip on the surface. Some of the slip has worn away from the projecting features.

The face is carefully modeled, and although it is unlike any published examples, Donald Bailey would classify it as Cnidian (personal communication); see also D. M. Bailey, "Cnidian Relief Ware Vases and Fragments in the British Museum I: Lagynoi and Head Cups," *RCRFActa* 14–15 (1972–1973) 11–25, note pl. 4, p. 24. For the type, see J. W. Salomonson, "Kleinasiatische Tonschalen mit Reliefverzierung," *BABesch* 54 (1979) 117–137; and J. W. Salomonson, "Der Trunkenbold und die Trunkene Alte," *BABesch* 55:1 (1980) 65–135.

Date: 2nd century A.C.

544. Base medallion. Inv. No. C-71-196. Lot 260. Pls. 65, 174.

P.H. 0.020. Est. D. base 0.054. One fragment from center of floor. Brown (10YR) clay with gloss of the same color. Moulded portrait medallion of young boy in right profile with thick, short hair and folds of drapery around the shoulders. The medallion is raised from the vessel floor so that it looks like a boss when seen in section.

For other such medallions in clay, see *Samaria*, pl. xxii, I, 345–346, a relief head of a man in red-gloss ware. It is dated to the 1st century B.C. and, according to Henry Robinson (personal communication), belongs to a group of early Roman medallion plates found at Athens (note E. B. Harrison, *Ancient Portraits from the Athenian Agora* [Excavations of the Athenian Agora, Picture Book 5] [Princeton 1960] figs. 3–6), Corinth, in Asia Minor, Olbia, and Alexandria, probably Augustan in date. See also R. Colonia, "Mytilini-Leipsana Ellenistikis Ochuroseos," *Athens Annals of Archaeology* 7 (1974) 203, 204, pl. 4 from Lesbos; and Kenrick, *Berenice 3*, "Cnidian Gray Ware," fig. 10 and p. 62. Susan Rotroff discusses relief busts on West Slope Ware in "A Ptolemaic Portrait in Athens," *Proceedings of the 3rd Symposium on Greek and Related Pottery. Copenhagen. Aug. 31–*

Sept. 14, 1987, J. Christiansen and T. Melander, eds. (Copenhagen 1988), 516–521.

Date: late 1st century B.C.

545. Base with medallion. Inv. No. C-72-8. Lot 552. Pl. 175.

M.P.Dim. 0.059. Th. 0.008. One fragment of bottom of a plate, tray, or plaque with broad, flat floor and apparently rectangular or square in shape. Part of one edge or wall is preserved. The fabric is light red (2.5YR 6/6) with some mica visible. The surfaces are plain. Medallion bounded by three grooves within which is preserved the head in profile and frontal nude upper torso of Dionysus with a large bunch of grapes partly preserved at the far left. He wears a cloak, the folds visible on his right shoulder, and he carries the thyrsus. The head has been partly scraped away by a comblike instrument while the clay was still wet to create the impression of hair. Long ringlets of hair curl over the figure's shoulder.

Date: second, third quarters of the 1st century B.C.

546. Base with medallion. Inv. No. C-72-50. Lot 783. Pl. 175.

M.P.Dim. 0.081. Th. 0.008. Several fragments mended, preserving the bottom of a tray like the one above (**545**) with part of one lower wall preserved. The fabric is light red (2.5YR 6/6) and slightly micaceous, as the example above. The partly raised medallion is bounded by two grooves, and beyond the grooves, to right and left, are partially preserved rosettes. Above is a moulding with cable pattern. Within the medallion the upper torso of a standing winged figure (Nike) is seen frontally with the head in left profile. The left arm with hand on hip holds a palm branch. A Greek inscription to the left of the head preserves the letters M E.

The overall design is reminiscent of a coin.

547. Fragment with medallion. Inv. No. C-78-86. Lot 2211. Pls. 65, 175.

M.P.Dim. 0.073. Th. 0.007. One fragment with moulded figural decoration similar to example above (**547**). Micaceous pink (5YR 7/3) fabric with pink to reddish yellow (5YR 7/3–7/4–7/6) slip on exterior and part of interior. Lower part of winged victory figure within medallion. Part of rosette preserved just to the left. Fragmentary letters left of feet appear to be N E M, perhaps the beginning of the name of the goddess Nemesis, seen here and in **546** as a Victory.

Nemesis presided over the gladiatorial combats in the theater at Stobi, and in the scene building there was a sanctuary of this same goddess. See E. Gebhard, "The Theater at Stobi: A Summary," *Studies II*, 18. **546** and **547** were found not far from the theater and may have been plaques dedicated to Nemesis as Nike.

A medallion of similar design, but with an erotic scene, is published in Bogdan Soultov, *Centres Antiques de poteries en Mésie Inférieure* (Sofia 1970) 62 (from Pavlikeni).

548. Fragment with gladiatorial scene. Inv. No. C-74-304. Lot 1328. Pl. 175.

M.P.Dim. 0.049. Th. 0.004. One fragment with relief decoration on interior. Micaceous pink (7.5YR 7/4) fabric with light red (2.5YR 6/6) slip. The scene is of two figures facing one another. Both wear armor and stand or stride with legs wide apart. The figure on the left wears a helmet with a knob on the top and carries a trident in his left hand and a dagger in his right, clearly the retiarius (although no net is visible). The other figure wears a helmet with a crest and carries a shield in his left hand. His dagger or sword has fallen and is seen just below the ground line.

549. Fragment from body. Inv. No. C-79-10. Lot 2537. Pl. 176.

M.P.Dim. 0.033. Th. 0.001. One fragment of wall with relief decoration. Reddish yellow (5YR) fabric and red slip (10R 4/8). The lower part of a rectangular field preserves a battle scene. A figure in boots who carries a sword in his right hand is either seated with bent knees or, more likely, has just fallen backward. Traces of another figure to the right.

550. Fragment from body. Inv. No. C-74-161. Lot 1398. Pl. 175.

M.P.Dim. 0.050. Th. 0.018. One fragment with relief decoration. Light red (2.5YR 6/6) to reddish brown (2.5YR 5/4) with weak red (2.5YR 5/2) slip. Exterior surface preserves part of a face, probably male, with curls around the face in high relief. Left side of the head, part of nose, chin, and mouth broken away.

551. Base medallion. Inv. No. C-78-170. Lot 2129. Pl. 176.

Est. D. 0.046. Th. 0.006. One fragment of what appears to be burned red-gloss sigillata. Part of portrait preserves the figure's hair and part of the cheek. The swirling style of hair, the horns, and what may be part of a diadem suggest Alexander the Great as Heracles or Zeus Ammon.

552. Fragment from body. Inv. No. C-75-69. Lot 1662.

M.P.Dim. 0.045. Th. 0.006. One fragment. Micaceous reddish yellow (5YR–7.5YR) clay with red slip. Part of winged cupid(?) visible.

553. Floor fragment with medallion. Inv. No. C-71-59. Lot 169. Pl. 176.

M.P.Dim 0.065. Th. 0.014. One fragment of base preserving in relief part of a pastoral scene: a man's leg next to a lamb or sheep(?).

Erotic Scenes

554. Rim and wall. Inv. No. C-72-56. Lot 686. Pl. 176.

M.P.Dim. 0.068. One fragment. Light gray (10YR 6/1) clay with gray (10YR 5/1) slip. Slightly everted rim with guilloche framed by grooves. Just at the bottom of the piece is a nude woman with hair pulled back into a knot, seated and bending to the left.

555. Fragment from body. Inv. No. C-71-133. Lot 11. Pl. 177.

M.P.Dim. 0.053. Th. 0.004. Mended from two pieces. Light yellowish brown (2.5YR 6/4) fabric with grayish black slip. A female figure and the head/face of another figure just to the right, apparently in an embrace. The chest and left arm of another figure preserved to the left of the female.

556. Medallion base. Inv. No. C-71-20. Lot 433. Pls. 65, 176.

Est. D. base 0.100. Th. 0.008. One fragment from ring base with medallion in center. Micaceous reddish yellow (5YR) clay with red gloss, somewhat worn, on interior. In the center of the floor, framed by two concentric grooves, is the upper portion of two figures in an erotic pose.

557. Base. Inv. No. C-74-286. Lot 1414. Pl. 177.

Est. D. base. 0.080. Th. 0.008. One fragment of high ring base. Reddish yellow (5YR 7/6) with red slip. Preserved on center of floor is an erotic scene.

Imitation Çandarli (558, 559)

Several examples of an unknown ware, with gloss similar in color and character to Çandarli and Phocaean Red Slip but quite different in fabric, have been discovered in contexts of late 3rd- and 4th-century date. Only one shape has been identified: a flat-based dish with inturned rim, not unlike the Middle Roman dish forms (local MR Form 8) derived from Eastern Sigillata B2 Hayes Form 60, but with no overhang. The dusty, dark reddish brown color of the gloss, often peeling or pitted and usually worn away on the exterior, retains its smoothness and finish on the interior. One example (**559**) has extremely mottled surfaces. The fabric is light red (2.5YR 6/6) with a light grayish brown core; common are gold and silver micas with white particles and voids.

558. Inv. No. C-78-112. Lot 2126. Pl. 65.

P.H. 0.030. One fragment of rim and wall.

559. Lot 1328. No. 3. Pl. 65.

H. 0.050. Several fragments mended, giving profile.

Unguentaria (560–610)

Small ceramic bottles or unguentaria are familiar artifacts on Hellenistic and Early Roman sites and are especially common in cemeteries throughout the Mediterranean.[118] The unguentarium was

[118] Because this topic was treated in a recent article, my comments here will be brief. See Anderson-Stojanović (1987) 105–122, for a summary and bibliography. Also note Riley, *Berenice* 2, 299–303. Marshall Joseph Becker recently pre-

produced in two basic shapes: (1) the fusiform or spindle shape and (2) the bulbous shape with long neck, rounded body, and flat base. Both shapes occur at Stobi, although the bulbous outnumber the fusiform. Most come from graves, but a series of nine fusiform was found in the Potters' Shop area below the Central Basilica.[119]

A variety of fusiform shapes were found at Stobi and they have been classified into Types A–G based on distinctions of fabric and shape. The closest parallels for types found at Stobi are seen elsewhere in Macedonia and in Asia Minor.[120] The very slender profile seen on gray unguentaria with horizontal, white-striped decoration, common in Athens and elsewhere in Greece during the 2nd and 1st centuries B.C., does not occur at Stobi.[121]

The bulbous unguentarium appeared during the 1st century B.C. and remained popular during the 1st century A.C., until it was gradually replaced by blown-glass unguentaria.[122] This sequence is clear from the study of grave goods in the Stobi West Cemetery. Since a great variety of bulbous unguentaria was found in the graves, the number of forms is greater. Bulbous unguentaria have been classified into Types A–P.

Out of a total of 313 graves excavated by the Stobi Project, only 29 had unguentaria. It is not unusual, however, to find several in one grave (see Table 3.2). Almost all funerary unguentaria at Stobi were found in cremation burials. Since the majority of ceramic unguentaria have a burned or discolored surface, and many glass examples have been distorted or melted by heat, Wesolowsky has suggested that both were placed in a secondary grave fire which served the purpose of consecrating the site and offerings.[123]

The contents may have been perfumed oil, wine, or incense. Many unguentaria were certainly mass-produced, simple grave offerings and may have had a symbolic use only. Two examples from the West Cemetery, one fusiform (**572**) and one bulbous (**600**) could not have held any substance since the neck was closed off through careless manufacture.

The problems with looking to other sites for chronology based on form alone are clear from the variety of dates one finds for comparable or similar shapes. Any chronology will be valid only for a single ware or fabric. Even then, one may expect to find a wide variation within an apparently contemporary group, such as Stobi Type F.

Fusiform unguentaria

Type A

Large, pear-shaped body with faint carination at point of widest diameter. Body is completely hollow down to a spreading, concave base. Rather short, narrow neck flaring outward to overhanging rim.

560. Inv. No. C-72-44. Grave 102. Pls. 66, 177.

H. 0.135. Max. D. 0.056. Intact. Light red (2.5YR 6/6) clay with metallic black to strong brown slip worn over large areas of surface.

Anderson-Stojanović (1987), fig. 1. There is an unguentarium (unpublished) with similar shape and fabric in the National Museum in Budva, Yugoslavia.

Type B

Large, very plump body on solid stemmed foot and spreading concave base. Cylindrical neck with wide, outward-thickened rim.

561. Inv. No. C-74-343. Grave 295. Pls. 66, 177.

H. 0.159. Max. D. 0.061. Intact. Reddish yellow (5YR 6/6) clay discolored gray to dark gray on the surface. This form is very similar to the giants in Type C below.

---

sented a paper in which he summarized the evidence for the use of small funerary vessels, such as unguentaria, as containers for the *os exceptum* or the *os resectum*, "The Contents of Funerary Vessels as Clues to Mortuary Customs: Identifying the *Os Exceptum*." *Proceedings from the 3rd Symposium on Ancient Greek and Related Pottery. Aug. 31–Sept. 14, 1987*, J. Christiansen and T. Melander, eds. (Copenhagen 1988) 25–32. See also F. T. Bertocchi, *Le necropoli daunie di Ascoli Satriano e Arpi* (Genoa 1985). Small vessels for medicinal ointment are discussed by M. Hershkovitz, "Miniature Ointment Vases from the Second Temple Period," *Israel Exploration Journal* 36 (1986) 45–51.

[119] On the Potter's Shop below the Central Basilica narthex, see Appendix 1.

[120] Anderson-Stojanović (1987) 109, note 21.

[121] Ibid., 106–110.

[122] Ibid., 110–114.

[123] Ibid., 121; A. B. Wesolowsky, "Burial Customs in the West Cemetery," *Studies I*, 108, 135.

Table 3.2. List of Unguentaria types in Stobi graves

	FUSIFORM										BULBOUS																			
	A	B	C	D	E	F	G1	G2	Fus. Ft.	Prob. Fus. Neck	A	B1	B2	C	D	E	F	G	H	I	J	K	L	M	N	O	P		Bulb. Body	Prob. Bulb. Neck
Grave 14																										1				
18																	10	7					1							
21																										8	4			
76																	4	2					1							2
84				3																										
88																1														
94																	6									1			1	
95																		1							7	2				
102	1																													
107																							3						1	
259																	3													
260																1														
262													5		2			5	1											
264													2	2			1							1						
265							2				2																			
271													3			1													9	4
273							4	4												3										
277											6	7	6																	
281			2						1																					
282																	1													
283																					1									
285																								6		2	1			
288				3					3	5																				
291																						1							1	
295		1	3	3					3	6																				
298					1					2																				
303							3			2																				
309											1																			
311																									1					
Lot 1098					3																									
Potter's Shop						9																								

Type C

Tall vessel with very large, plump body, thin walls on solid stemmed foot with high, flaring, concave base. Cylindrical neck with flaring rim.

562. Inv. No. C-74-355. Grave 281. Pl. 66.

H. 0.276. Max. D. 0.105. Mended and almost complete. Very brownish yellow to very pale brown (10YR 8/3 to 6/6) clay. Rim and neck dipped in dark reddish brown (5YR 3/3) slip. Entire body well smoothed.

W-MZ (1976) 280, 281, fig. 11.

563. Inv. No. C-74-354. Grave 281. Pls. 66, 178.

H. 0.228. D. 0.079. Slightly smaller than C-74-355 (**562**) and with moulded foot. Light red fabric (2.5YR 6/6), and reddish yellow (5YR 6/6), well-smoothed exterior. Interior and neck covered with metallic, dark reddish brown (5YR 3/3) to black slip.

This giant form is similar to Forti Type IV or V, dated from the last quarter of the 3rd century B.C. to the 2nd century B.C. The fabric also suggests a South Italian origin. As pointed out to me by Homer Thompson, there are several giant examples in the Athenian Agora, including P14400 (from a cistern dated to the last quarter of the 2nd century B.C.). The Agora example has a gray, gritty clay, however, and white bands on the neck and body, unlike the color and surface of the Stobi examples.

Type D

Very plump body on narrow, solid, cylindrical foot with small flaring base, flat on underside. Narrow neck spreads upward to wide mouth with everted rim.

564. Inv. No. C-74-374. Grave 295. Pl. 67.
H. 0.160. Max. D. 0.053. Complete except for small piece from body. Dark gray (2.5YR N4/) clay with light gray, white, and yellow discolorations on body.
Anderson-Stojanović (1987), fig. 1.

565. Inv. No. C-74-380. Graves 295, 288. Pl. 67.
H. 0.173. Max. D. 0.049. Complete. Light gray to gray (10YR 6/1) surface, discolored, which varies within the gray shades.

566. Inv. No. C-74-20. Grave 84. Lot 1094. Pls. 67, 178.
H. 0.170. Max. D. 0.046. Fired dark gray (2.5YR N4/). Traces of white-painted decoration of long leaves or petals arranged diagonally on the body.

567. Inv. No. C-74-349. Grave 288. Pl. 67.
H. 0.154. Max. D. 0.042. Intact. Reddish gray (5YR 5/2) at surface, red (2.5YR 5/6) at core.
Cf. Bruneau, *Tombes d' Argos*, 512, no. 188.49, fig. 211, from a tomb dated to the second half of the 2nd century B.C. or the beginning of the 1st century.

Type E

Narrow body with wide mouth and overhanging rim. Tall, solid, stemmed foot on flat, untrimmed base.

568. Inv. No. C-74-106. Lot 1098. Pl. 67.
H. 0.185. Max. D. 0.045. Almost complete. Fired dark gray (2.5YR N4/) to light red at base (2.5YR 6/8).
Cf. *Tarsus*, fig. 187, no. 233.

569. Inv. No. C-74-342. Grave 298. Lot 1468. Pl. 67.
P.H. 0.145. Max. D. 0.057. Neck and rim missing. Discolored.
Cf. Bruneau, "Tombes d'Argos," 466, No. 58.8, fig. 210, from a tomb dated to the second half of the 2nd century B.C.

Type F

Small, short vessel on tall, solid, stemmed foot with offset, flaring base, slightly concave underneath. Profile of body is plumper on some examples. Local Fabric 1. Unslipped, rather carelessly finished surface. From Potter's Shop below narthex of Central Basilica, W-MZ (1971) 409. Appendix 1. Each is slightly different in profile.

570. Inv. No. C-71-85. Lot 132. Pl. 68.
H. 0.134. Max. D. 0.039. Complete.

571. Inv. No. C-71-87. Lot 132. Pl. 68.
H. 0.110. Max. D. 0.038. Complete.

572. Inv. No. C-71-88. Lot 132. Pl. 68.
H. 0.114. Max. D. 0.035. Intact. Section of clay on neck interior blocks body opening.
W-MZ (1971) 409, pl. 86, fig. 2.

573. Inv. No. C-71-89. Lot 132. Pl. 68.
H. 0.131. Max. D. 0.039. Several small fragments missing.

574. Inv. No. C-71-91. Lot 132. Pls. 68, 178.
H. 0.140. Max. D. 0.040. Complete.

575. Inv. No. C-71-92. Lot 132. Pl. 68.
H. 0.134. Max. D. 0.040. Complete.

576. Inv. No. C-71-93. Lot 132. Pl. 68.
H. 0.128. Max. D. 0.035. Complete.

C-71-86 and C-71-90, also from this context, are not illustrated.

Type G

Tall form with solid foot and correspondingly long neck.

This appears to be a rather late form of the fusiform shape as it was found together with examples of bulbous Form A. There is much discoloration on the body surface and variation in the color of clay, although on the whole it varies from reddish yellow (5YR 7/6) to pink (7.5YR 7/4) and appears to be local fabric.

Variant 1 has a short, rounded body. Variant 2 has a short, almost biconical body.

Variant 1

577. Inv. No. C-74-104. Grave 265. Lot 1421. Pl. 67.
H. 0.197. D. body 0.057. Intact.

578. Inv. No. C-74-102. Grave 265. Lot 1421. Pl. 69.
H. 0.185. D. body 0.054. Intact.
Anderson-Stojanović (1987), figs. 1, 6.

579. Inv. No. C-74-219. Grave 273. Lot 1452. Pls. 69, 178.
H. 0.185. D. body 0.050. Complete.

Variant 2

580. Inv. No. C-74-112. Grave 273. Lot 1452. Pl. 69.
H. 0.210. D. body 0.056. Intact.

581. Inv. No. C-74-189. Grave 273. Lot 1452. Pl. 69.
H. 0.200. D. body 0.055. Complete.

582. Inv. No. C-74-109. Grave 273. Lot 1452. Pl. 69.
H. 0.210. D. body 0.055. Intact.
Anderson-Stojanović (1987), figs. 1, 4. Cf. *Tarsus*, fig. 135, nos. 247, 249; fig. 187, nos. 247, 250.

Bulbous unguentaria

All the bulbous unguentaria, with the exception of types A, C, J, and K, which are probably imports, have a very similar clay texture, color, and surface finish and are probably local products in Fabric 1. Many pieces are discolored as a result of the funeral fire. Rim and neck were normally dipped in a red or reddish brown slip.

Type A

Very thin-walled, tall vessel with bulbous body, everted rim, flat or slightly concave base. Fabric is very pale brown (10YR 8/3–8/4). The surface is extremely smooth with an almost burnished appearance.

Anderson-Stojanović (1987), fig. 7. Found at Tarsus; see *Tarsus*, fig. 159:735. Hayes (*ROM Pottery*) suggests a Campanian origin for this type; see his no. 157.

583. Inv. No. C-74-105. Grave 265. Lot 1421. Pls. 70, 179.
H. 0.164. D. body 0.067. Complete.
Anderson-Stojanović (1987), figs. 1, 7.

584. Inv. No. C-74-103. Grave 265. Lot 1421. Pl. 70.
H. 0.162. D. body 0.068. Complete.

585. Inv. No. C-75-59. Grave 309. Pls. 70, 179.
H. 0.145. D. body 0.070. Intact.

Type B

Form is similar to Type A but has lower point of maximum diameter. Fabric not so fine or thin walled and is probably a local product.

586. Inv. No. C-74-166. Grave 277. Lot 1456. Pl. 70.
H. 0.144. D. body 0.063. Complete.

587. Inv. No. C-74-183. Grave 277. Lot 1456. Pl. 70.
H. 0.136. D. body 0.056. Intact.

Type C

Same ware as Type A but smaller form.

588. Inv. No. C-74-22. Grave 264. Pl. 70.
H. 0.119. D. body 0.051. Intact.

Type D

Similar to Type B in shape but body is taller and neck shorter.

589. Inv. No. C-74-37. Grave 262. Pl. 70.
H. 0.145. D. body 0.053. Complete.

Type E

Similar to Type D but with continuous profile.

590. Inv. No. C-74-18. Grave 260. Lot 1092. Pl. 70.
H. 0.120. D. body 0.042. Almost complete.

Type F

Small size with rounded body.

591. Inv. No. C-70-68. Grave 18. Lot 197. Pl. 71.
H. 0.125. D. body 0.046. Intact.

592. Inv. No. C-70-67. Grave 18. Lot 197. Pl. 71.
H. 0.120. D. body 0.045. Intact.

Type G

Short, broad neck, bulbous body.

593. Inv. No. C-70-71. Grave 18. Lot 197. Pl. 71.
H. 0.107. D. body 0.044. Complete.
Anderson-Stojanović (1987), fig. 1.

Type H

Small size, long neck.

594. Inv. No. C-74-45. Grave 262. Pl. 71.
H. 0.100. D. body 0.037. Intact.

Type I

Small with slender neck and broad body.

595. Inv. No. C-74-114. Grave 273. Lot 1452. Pl. 71.
H. 0.076. D. body 0.039. Complete.
W-MZ (1974) 137, fig. 18; Anderson-Stojanović (1987), figs. 1, 5.

Type J

Small, short neck and very rounded body.

596. Inv. No. C-74-128. Grave 283. Pl. 71.
H. 0.088. D. body 0.049. Intact. Red (2.5YR 5/6) fabric with light red (2.5YR 6/6) surface upon which faint wheel marks are visible.
Unique.
Anderson-Stojanović (1987), fig. 1.

Type K

Broad, short neck, pyramidal-shaped body.

597. Inv. No. C-74-371. Grave 271. Pl. 71.
H. 0.071. D. body 0.044. Intact. Pink (7.5YR 7/4) to very pale brown (10YR 8/3) fabric and body. Brown slip on neck.
Unique.

Type L

Similar to Type K but with longer neck.

598. Inv. No. C-72-84. Grave 107. Lot 708. Pl. 71.
H. 0.077. D. body 0.039. Intact.

Type M

Small with very plump body and flaring neck.

599. Inv. No. C-74-370. Grave 285. Lot 1462. Pl. 71.
H. 0.069. D. body 0.045. Intact.

600. Inv. No. C-74-363. Grave 285. Lot 1462. Pl. 71.
H. 0.074. D. body 0.045. Intact. Body cavity blocked by clay projecting from inner wall.
Anderson-Stojanović (1987), fig. 1.

Type N

Very small with low point of maximum diameter.

601. Inv. No. C-71-168. Grave 95. Pl. 71.
H. 0.067. D. body 0.038. Intact.
Anderson-Stojanović (1987), fig. 8.

Type O

Plump body with low point of maximum diameter and very thick walls.

602. Inv. No. C-70-49. Grave 21. Lot 487. Pl. 72.
H. 0.078. D. body 0.046. Intact.

603. Inv. No. C-70-57. Grave 21. Lot 487. Pl. 72.
H. 0.076. D. body 0.041. Complete.

604. Inv. No. C-70-53. Grave 21. Lot 487. Pl. 72.
H. 0.079. D. body 0.046. Intact.

605. Inv. No. C-70-55. Grave 21. Lot 487. Pl. 72.
H. 0.083. D. body 0.052. Mended.

Type P

Short neck with almost biconical body.

606. Inv. No. C-70-48. Grave 21. Lot 487. Pl. 72.
H. 0.077. D. body 0.058. Complete.

607. Inv. No. C-70-59. Grave 21. Lot 487. Pls. 72, 179.
H. 0.072. D. body 0.055. Intact.

608. Inv. No. C-70-52. Grave 21. Lot 487. Pl. 72.
H. 0.079. D. body 0.058. Intact.

Type Q

Large form.

609. Inv. No. C-74-27a, b. Lot 1080. Pl. 72.
P.H. 0.170. Max. D. 0.100. Base missing.

610. Lot 1099, No. 2. Pl. 72.
P.H. 0.040. Max. D. 0.093. Fragmentary. Red slip on exterior.

Mortaria (611–614)

Mortaria in light buff or pink fabric with flanged rim and either rounded or squared-off lip occur at Stobi only in deposits of the Late Hellenistic and Early Roman periods.[124] The rim exterior is frequently decorated with appliqué, or the simple flange may be pinched in pie-crust fashion. A raised, flat base is typical. Some examples are partially slipped, others plain. Diameters range from 0.200 to 0.300m. None of the Stobi mortaria is stamped.

The examples below do not seem to have been made from local clay, and petrographic analysis of a mortarium sample from Lot 1809 showed a primarily volcanic composition (perhaps andesite), one quite different from the metamorphic minerals present in local clays. It is likely, therefore, that most of these mortaria were imported.

The first two examples (**611** and **612**) are a rather standard Late Hellenistic type, but the third, **613**, is unusual.[125] The other example (**614**) in the catalogue belongs to the Early Roman period.

Ceramic mortaria do not reoccur at the site until the Late Roman period, when they were produced with a greenish brown lead glaze and probably imported from Pannonia (see **520–522**).

611. Inv. No. C-71-19. Lot 131. Pl. 73.
P.H. 0.042. Est. D. rim 0.280. One fragment of rim with beginnings of spout. Micaceous pink (5YR 8/4 to 7.5YR 7/4) clay with gray and white grits. Single knob at rim exterior beside spout. Unslipped.

612. Inv. No. C-71-346. Lot 140. Pl. 73.
P.H. 0.034. Est. D. rim 0.202. Two fragments of rim, spout, and wall mended. Micaceous pink (5YR 7/4) to very pale brown (10YR 8/3) fabric. Unslipped with wheel marks visible on exterior.

613. Inv. No. C-72-3. Lot 549. Pl. 73.
H. 0.070. Est. D. rim 0.265. Single fragment preserving complete profile and about one-fourth of vessel. Pale brown (10YR 6/4) fabric. Central rim flange has been pinched as decoration, a more common technique on incense burners. Unslipped. Four sharp stone fragments in floor center.
Cf. Vegas, *Cerámica común*, fig. 8, no. 5; fig. 58.

614. Inv. No. C-73-25. Lot 881. Pl. 177.
H. 0.130. Est. D. rim 0.400. D. base. 0.028. Mended from numerous pieces. The fabric is reddish yellow (5YR 6/8) with gray and reddish brown inclusions. The surface is covered with a white (2.5Y 8/2) slip. Large mortarium with broad, down-curved rim and flat base.

This is an Early Roman type and probably dates to the 2nd or perhaps the 3rd century. Later examples seem to have straighter rims. Cf. Hayes, "Paphos," fig. 6, no. 10, dated to the 2nd century, and Riley, *Berenice 2*, 295, 296, and fig. 112, no. 669; Brukner, *Rimska Keramika*, T.60, nos. 1, 4.

[124] A recent discussion of mortaria may be found in Riley, *Berenice 2*, 292–298.

[125] Cf. Riley, *Berenice 2*, nos. 663, 664; Vegas, *Cerámica común*, fig. 8, Type 7. nos. 3 and 4, dated to the Late Republican period.

Tan Micaceous Ware (615–627)

In deposits of the 4th century A.C. at Stobi a tan, hard-fired, highly micaceous ware makes its appearance. The vessel surfaces are normally smooth and have a gold metallic luster from the presence of significant gold-colored mica. Petrographic analysis of samples of this ware showed primarily fine inclusions with some medium and coarse grains present. The inclusions consisted of a large percentage of "rose" mica with lesser amounts of quartz/feldspar and some biotite. The "rose" mica could not be more accurately identified using petrography, but its optical properties differed markedly from the muscovite and biotite micas seen in most other samples.[126]

This fabric is quite similar to cooking ware (Fabric 3) of the same period, although it has finer inclusions and a higher percentage of "rose" mica than does the cooking ware; furthermore, it was not used for cooking, as is clear from the absence of burning. These two wares are the only ones with "rose" mica in any measurable amount. The consistent presence of "rose" mica in this ware may be an indication that it was not a local product.

The vessel forms are confined to those appropriate for the table: dishes, small bowls, and jugs. Most shapes have sharp, carinated profiles and thin walls. These features, together with the golden, micaceous surface, are suggestive of metal—bronze or even gold.

615. Bowl. Inv. No. C-74-11. Lot 1074. Pl. 180.

H. 0.063. D. rim 0.160. Almost complete, mended from many fragments. Bowl with broad, flat rim, notched edge, and plump body with marked carination at point of greatest diameter. Concave base with pointed foot.

616. Dish. Inv. No. C-70-140. Lot 799. Pl. 74.

H. 0.063. D. rim 0.150. Mended and preserving about half of vessel. Small dish with curved, carinated wall and flaring rim thickened toward exterior at lip. Flat bottom with short foot.

617. Dish. Inv. No. C-72-300. Lot 763. Pl. 74.

P.H. 0.040. Est. D. rim 0.135. One fragment of rim and wall.

Similar to **616**.

618. Dish. Inv. No. C-72-4. Lot 763. Pl. 74.

H. 0.053. D. rim 0.145. Mended, about four-fifths complete.

This dish belongs to the same form group as **616** and **617**.

There are two additional examples of this form: one from Lot 1599 and one from Lot 277.

619. Dish. Inv. No. C-74-210. Lot 1345. Pl. 74.

H. 0.062. D. rim 0.106. Mended, two-thirds complete.

616–620 are similar in shape, but this example has a narrower opening, more like a jar, and has a rather globular body. For the context, see W-MZ (1974) 139, and **1225**, **1233**, **1267**, **1276–1278**, found in the same deposit.

Date: early 6th century A.C.

620. Dish. Inv. No. C-70-141. Lot 799. Pl. 74.

H. 0.056. D. rim 0.125. Mended from five fragments, preserving complete profile.

Similar to **616–619** but with a very sharp and somewhat straighter profile.

621. Jar. Inv. No. C-70-88. Lot 1016. Pl. 74.

P.H. 0.035. Est. D. rim 0.197. One rim fragment. Jar with sharp, angular profile.

622. Dish. Inv. No. C-78-48. Lot 2211. Pl. 75.

P.H. 0.035. Est. D. rim 0.180. One fragment of rim and wall. Shallow dish with curved body and flaring rim. No base preserved.

623. Jar. Inv. No. C-75-102. Lot 1657. Pl. 75.

P.H. 0.078. Est. D. rim 0.069. One fragment of rim, wall, and one handle. Small jar with one handle, perhaps two, vertical rim, and globular body. Shallow wheel-ridging on exterior.

624. Jug. Inv. No. C-78-154. Lot 2145. Pl. 75.

P.H. 0.053. Est. D. rim 0.083. Nine fragments mended, preserving rim, neck, and part of handle. Faint wheel-ridging on neck.

625. Jug. Lot 302, No. 5. Pl. 75.

P.H. 0.035. Est. D. rim 0.060. One fragment from rim and neck of jug.

Similar to **624** but smaller and with no trace of a handle.

One additional example from Lot 306.

[126] These are the components of the Crna river sand which was probably used as tempering material. I am grateful to Georgeana Little for help with the vocabulary of this section as well as the analysis that appears in Appendix 2.

626. Jar. Lot 293, No. 79. Pl. 75.
P.H. 0.033. Est. D. rim 0.096. One fragment of flaring rim and side wall.

627. Base. Lot 293, No. 80. Pl. 74.
P.H. 0.018. D. base 0.065. One base fragment, probably from the common dish shape as seen in **616–620**.

Red Micaceous Ware (628–631)

A few examples of a reddish orange (2.5YR 6/6–6/8 or 5YR 7/3–6/3), coarse fabric with lime(?) or shell(?) particles and mica (gold and silver) and with a red-slipped surface occur in several large vessel types of late 3rd-, early 4th-century date. Most examples are of the large bowl with ribbon or horizontal handle as local MR Color-Slipped and Plain Form 23, with either a flat or grooved rim. Diameters range from 0.290 to 0.450 m.

There is no evidence at present to suggest where the ware was produced.

628. Inv. No. C-72-222. Lot 677. Pl. 73.
P.H. 0.075. Est. D. rim 0.340. Two nonjoining pieces, each mended from several fragments, preserving rim, wall, and handle.

629. Lot 1616, No. 2. Pl. 73.
P.H. 0.050. Est. D. rim 0.450. One fragment of rim and wall. Flat rim with groove at exterior and incised wavy lines on upper surface.

630. Lot 1697, No. 2. Pl. 73.
P.H. 0.055. Est. D. 0.300. Single fragment of simple grooved rim and horizontal handle.

631. Inv. No. C-78-234. Lot 2281. Pl. 73.
P.H. 0.059. Est. D. rim 0.302. One fragment of rim and wall. Grooved rim with edge pinched away at regular intervals to give a scalloped effect.

Mica-Dusted Ware (632–638)

A few pieces of an unusual red coarse ware covered with a thick, light tan/cream micaceous and metallic slip belong to this group. Hayes has identified a similar ware he terms *mica-dusted ware* at Saraçhane in Istanbul.[127] It seems the closest parallel to the five pieces at Stobi. Our surface covering, however seems thicker than is implied by the term *dusting*.

Unfortunately, no complete vessels exist at Stobi, and from the odd base or rim it is impossible to suggest shapes.

The fabric of the Stobi examples varies from light red to light orange-red and contains large flakes of silver and gold mica. Approximately half show a gray core.

All examples come from the latest deposits on the Acropolis, the flood plain of the lower city, or the Fuller's House.

[127] Hayes, *DOP* 22 (1968) 212.

632. Base. Lot 943, No. 5. Pl. 75.
P.H. 0.017. D. 0.046. One fragment of flat base with concave moulding at base of wall. Reddish yellow (5YR 6/6) fabric with light brown (5YR 6/4) core and large inclusions. Lustrous, mottled slip, light tan/pink (7.5YR 7/4) in color.

633. Base. Lot 1285, No. 10. Pl. 75.
P.H. 0.022. D. 0.054. One fragment of concave base. Light red (2.5YR 6/8) fabric with dark gray core and reddish yellow lustrous covering.

634. Handle. Inv. No. C-72-301. Lot 728. Pl. 179.
P.L. 0.064. Th. 0.022. Fragment of pinched handle. Light red (2.5YR 6/8) fabric with very pale brown (10YR 7/4) thick, very metallic/micaceous slip.

635. Jug. Inv. No. C-70-8. Lot 514. Pl. 75.
P.H. 0.120. Max. D. body 0.090. D. base 0.048. Mended and restored. Very micaceous light

brown (7.5YR 6/4) fabric with smooth and very micaceous surface. Pear-shaped body, concave bottom, and single strap handle.

636. Jug. Inv. No. C-71-421. Lot 514. Pl. 179.
P.H. 0.029. Est. D. base 0.156. One fragment of flat base. Reddish yellow (7.5YR 7/6) fabric, very micaceous with white grits. Metallic surface of same color. Lower portion of diagonal gouged decoration is preserved.

637. Handle. Inv. No. C-70-4. Pls. 75, 178.
P.L. 0.094. One fragment of handle. Reddish yellow (5YR 6/6–5YR 7/6) fabric with very micaceous surface. Two stamped wheels on upper surface.

638. Rim. Inv. No. C-78-34. Lot 2206.
P.H. 0.026. One fragment of rim. Micaceous reddish brown (2.5YR 5/4–5/6) to red fabric. Gold micaceous wash on exterior.

Additional fragments are in Lot 1285 (1 rim), Lot 234 (1 handle, 1 body sherd), and Lot 58 (1 body sherd).

Amphorae (**639–715**)

Transport amphorae as actual containers of commodities (primarily liquid) are among the most sensitive indicators of trade over long distances.[128]

Despite the presence of a variety of amphorae at Stobi, the numbers are small overall, indicating that few amphorae reached Stobi and that commodities normally transported in amphoras throughout the Mediterranean came to Stobi in containers of other, perishable material, such as wooden barrels or skins, for example. Because Stobi was inland and not a center of river-borne commerce, we ought not to expect the great quantities of amphorae found at seaport towns like Athens, Ostia, Carthage, or Berenice.[129]

The amphora types identified at Stobi come from all over the Mediterranean.[130] Quantitative studies have been limited, however, because of a lack of complete vessels. When possible, I have referred to the most common and recently used typologies.

The majority of identifiable amphorae in contexts of the 2nd and 1st centuries B.C. at Stobi are Italian and Western types. These include some varieties of the Greco-Italic group, Dressel 1A and 1B, several Adriatic types, including the stamped pieces *SONVS* and *ANTIO*, others of Brindisi type, and many examples of Roman Coan.[131]

Given that P. Sestius went to Macedonia in 62 B.C. as proquaestor and that the younger L. Sestius also served as proquaestor there in 43–42 B.C., we might expect to find some evidence of Sestius amphorae in Macedonia.[132] From a com-

[128] Peacock and Williams, *Amphorae*. This work contains a comprehensive typology and bibliography of Roman amphorae. For the late Hellenistic/Republican types, see now the survey articles in Leveque and J. P. Morel, eds., *Céramiques hellénistiques et romaines* II (Bensançon 1987) including U.-Y. Empereur, Al. Hesnard, "Les amphores hellénistiques," 25–30, for Greco-Italic; 30–33, for Dressel 1; 36, for Dressel 2–4; 33–34, for Lamboglia 2; 34–36, for Brindisi. Not included in Peacock and Williams are Josine M. Schuring, "Studies on Roman Amphorae," *BABesch* 59 (1984) 137–195, and Marie Brigitte Carre, "Les amphores de la Cisalpine et de l'Adriatique au début de l'Empire," *MEFRA* 97 (1985) 207–245.

[129] Amphorae discovered elsewhere in Macedonia are discussed in Sokolovska (1986) 83, pls. 30, 75, where most are Rhodian or Thasian jars of 4th to 1st centuries B.C. date; Mila Surbanoska, "A Contribution to the Research of the Hellenistic Amphoras in Macedonia" (in Macedonian with English summary), *Macedoniae Acta Archaeologica* 7–8 (1981–82) 65–70; Maneva (1979) pl. 18.

[130] Although recently publications of amphorae attempt to give very full fabric descriptions, it remains very difficult to utilize such data to identify type or origin. Furthermore, many typologies exist, with new publications introducing new numbering systems. The cross-referencing, concordances, and multiple references to form, such as seen in Riley, *Berenice 2*, are of great assistance. Thanks are owed to the scholars who were of assistance in identifying amphorae types at Stobi, including John Hayes, Barbara Johnson, Kathleen Slane, and Elizabeth Lyding Will.

A full description of the amphora types in this catalog may be found in Peacock and Williams, *Amphorae*, and in Riley, *Berenice* 2.

[131] Elizabeth Will has identified these types. The type numbers in the catalogue refer to her typology of Roman amphorae in the forthcoming book, *Stamped Roman Amphoras in the Eastern Mediterranean*, a volume in the Athenian Agora series.

[132] E. Will, "The Sestius Amphoras: a Reappraisal," *JFA* 6 (1979) 347, note 27.

parison of a sample of Cosan clay used for the Sestius jars, and the various fabric groups of a similar nature identified at Stobi, no Sestius amphorae or at least Cosan jars are apparent.

Most of these western Hellenistic and Early Roman amphorae carried oil or wine to the east. The recovery of a number of these at Stobi suggests that the central plain of Macedonia did not supply Stobi with all the oil or wine necessary for its inhabitants and that the products of Italy and the coast of Dalmatia, known for its vines and olive trees, were imported.[133]

Although it has been difficult to recognize Greek amphoras at Stobi, all but two of the stamped amphora handles are of Greek origin, including several from Cnidos and examples from Cos and Rhodes, almost all in residual context.[134]

Most of the fragments of amphorae from the early period at Stobi come from the areas later occupied by the Civil and Central Basilicas (Tables 4.2 and 4.3) near the Late Hellenistic potter's workshop (Appendix 1). A number of others derive from a Late Hellenistic–Early Roman fill (Table 4.4), which contained quantities of imported fine wares and cooking vessels.

Amphorae from later periods at the site (i.e., from the 2nd to the 6th centuries) derive from North Africa and the eastern Mediterranean or Aegean areas, mirroring the pattern observed in imported fine wares. Many come from the various residences of the late antique city, but a significant number also were recovered in deposits associated with the Episcopal Basilica, not surprising in view of the necessity for wine in the church sacraments.

Hellenistic and Early Roman Amphorae

Eight different fabric groups have been identified within a rather limited number of Hellenistic and Early Roman amphora types at Stobi. These groups do not always correspond to particular forms, an indication that individual types were produced in a variety of centers, each using different raw materials. Among the examples of Greco-Italic amphoras at Stobi, for example, Fabric groups 1, 6, and 8 were common. Dressel 1A, however, occurs primarily in group 4. A description of the fabric groups identified at Stobi follows.

Fabric group 1. Color varies from light brown (7.5YR 6/4) to reddish yellow (5YR 7/6). Texture is fine, with much grog visible. Surface salts produce a white surface.

Fabric group 2. Color is light yellowish brown (10YR 6/4) to light brown (7.5YR 6/4). Fabric contains grayish brown and large white inclusions as well as many voids.

Fabric group 3. Color is light reddish brown to reddish brown (2.5YR 6/4–5/4) and contains light gray, gray, and white grits with lime.

Fabric group 4. Light brown fabric (7.5YR 6/4), fine and compact with only a few voids, micaceous, containing grog and very small and sparse grits.

Fabric group 5. Very pale brown (10YR 7/4) to light yellowish brown (10YR 6/4). Texture is fine and dense, containing mica and very small inclusions. Rather similar to group 2.

Fabric group 6. Pink to light brown (7.5YR 8/4–7/4–6/4) fabric, micaceous, with small red, white, and gray grits.

Fabric group 7. Reddish yellow (5YR 6/6–7/6) to reddish brown (5YR 5/4), dense, micaceous fabric with varying amounts of lime and other very small inclusions.

Fabric group 8. Reddish gray (5YR 5/2) to reddish brown (5YR 5/4) with variations to reddish yellow (5YR 7/6) or light red (2.5YR 6/8), containing much black/gray sand or grit. White surface salts or slip.

Greco-Italic Amphorae

Will Type 1 (see below). Riley, *Berenice 2*, Hellenistic Amphora 7. Peacock and Williams Class 2.

This group has been studied by E. Will ("Greco

[133] N.G.L. Hammond, *A History of Macedonia*, vol. I (Oxford 1972) 204–205, suggests that Macedonia could not provide enough oil for its population.

[134] Readings for the Greek stamps were done by Carolyn Koehler from the files of Virginia Grace in the Athenian Agora. Dates are those of V. R. Grace. I am grateful to Carolyn Koehler for help with references. VG R with a number refers to Miss Grace's list of Rhodian fabricants, VG RE to a Rhodian Eponym, and VG KT to a Knidian Type.

Italic Amphoras," *Hesperia* 52 [1982] 338–356). Five forms of the type exist, a–e, each probably in a different place: a, perhaps in Sicily, b, c, and d in Italy (c from Cosa, d from Cosa and Pompei), and e in Spain. Greco-Italic amphorae range in date from the 4th century B.C. to ca. 130 B.C. All the examples below occur in residual deposits, most of the 1st century B.C.

639. Rim, Will Type a. Lot 12, No. 9. Pl. 76.

P.H. 0.080. Est. D. rim 0.160. Est. D. mouth 0.114. One fragment of rim, neck, and part of one oval handle.

Fabric group 6.

640. Rim, Will Type d. Inv. No. C-72-279. Lot 545. Pl. 76.

P.H. 0.053. Est. D. rim 0.153. Est. D. mouth 0.120. One fragment of rim.

Fabric group 8.

Other rims in the same fabric group as follows: Lot 552: 2; Lot 82: 1; Lot 88: 1; Lot 1498: 1; Lot 1580: 1. One handle in the same fabric from Lot 552.

641. Toe, Will Type b. Lot 249, No. 152. Pl. 76.

P.H. 0.105. Max. D. 0.170. One large toe fragment.

Fabric group 1.

Two other examples in the same fabric in Lots 552 and 547.

642. Toe. Lot 610, No. 19. Pl. 76.

P.H. 0.103. Max. P.D. 0.094. One fragment.

Fabric group 6.

One similar toe from Lot 552.

643. Toe. Lot 610, No. 20. Pl. 76.

P.H. 0.065. Max. D. 0.041. One fragment.

Fabric group 1.

Other Amphorae

644. Rim. Dressel 1A. Lot 134, No. 17. Pl. 76.

P.H. 0.055. Est. D. rim 0.016. Est. D. mouth 0.014. One rim fragment.

Fabric group 4. Peacock and Williams Class 3, dated ca. 130 B.C. to mid-1st century B.C. One additional rim in same fabric from Lot 130.

645. Rim. Dressel 1A. Inv. No. C-71-323. Lot 130. Pl. 76.

P.H. 0.125. Est. D. rim 0.170. Est. D. mouth 0.134. One fragment of rim, neck, and handle stub.

Fabric group 4. One additional rim of the same fabric from Lot 448. One similar rim with pale brown (10YR 8/4) fabric from Lot 130. (Cf. V. von Gonzenbach, "Pottery from Closed Deposits," in *Excavations at Salona, Yugoslavia*, by C. W. Clairmont [Park Ridge, N.J. 1975] 206, Clay A, cited for Dressel 1A). Peacock and Williams Class 3.

646. Rim. Dressel 6. Will Type 8 (North Adriatic). Inv. No. C-72-200. Lot 552. Pl. 76.

P.H. 0.157. Est. D. rim 0.195. Est. D. mouth 0.150. Several fragments of rim and neck mended. White (2.5Y 8/2) powdery fabric with grog and many voids.

Cf. *Salona* [cited under **645**], 206, fabric A. Peacock and Williams Class 8.

647. Toe. Will Type 10 (Apulian). Lot 1441, No. 28. Pl. 77.

P.H. 0.150. Max.D. 0.120. Min. D. 0.041. One toe fragment. Pink (5YR 8/4–7.5YR 7/4) fabric with grog. Very pale brown (10YR 8/3) surface.

648. Toe. Will Type 11a (Brindisi). Inv. No. C-72-287. Lot 552. Pl. 77.

P.H. 0.072. Max.D. 0.087. D. at knob 0.046. One toe fragment. Light red to reddish yellow fabric with sand, grits, and white particles. Pink surface.

Several other similar toes in the same fabric: Lot 552: 1; Lot 1443: 1; Lot 1098: 1. Peacock and Williams Class 1.

649. Stamped rim. Will Type 13 (North Adriatic). Inv. No. C-72-60. Lot 552. Pls. 77, 180.

P.H. 0.064. Est. D. rim 0.137. Est. D. mouth 0.110. One fragment of rim. Light red (2.5YR 6/6–6/8) fabric with grit and white inclusions. Surface is pink to reddish yellow (7.5YR 7/4–7/8). On rim exterior is the stamp: A N T I O.

Context date: 75–25 B.C.

One additional example of the same rim form but in Fabric group 7 comes from Lot 134.

650. Neck and body. Dressel 6. Will Type 14 (North Adriatic). Inv. No. C-72-109. Lot 552. Pl. 77.

P.H. 0.280 (without handle). D. neck 0.130. Max. D. 0.280. Preserved are the neck, shoulder, which is slightly offset, and portions of both handles. Fabric is white (10YR 8/2) with patches of brown discoloration.

Peacock and Williams Class 8.

Context: 75–25 B.C.

651. Almost complete amphora. Lamboglia Form 2. Lot 1636, No. 100. Pl. 78.

P.H. 0.388. Max.P.D. 0.330. D. neck 0.120. Rim, neck, and handles missing. Buff (7.5YR 7/4) fabric with few inclusions.

Cf. Riley, *Berenice* 2, ER 5, and Peacock and Williams Class 8.

Context: 2nd century B.C.

652. Shoulder and handle. Lamboglia Form 2. Lot 552, No. 668. Pl. 78.

P.H. 0.144 (with handle). Est. Max. D. 0.280. Two fragments mended from shoulder with handle. Fabric is pink (7.5YR 7/4) with grog and large white inclusions. Surface is very pale brown (10YR 8/4).

Peacock and Williams Class 8.

653. Greek type. Inv. No. C-72-110. Lot 563. Pl. 78.

P.H. 0.186. Est. D. rim 0.118. Est. D. mouth 0.098. Four fragments mended, preserving rim, neck, shoulder, and strap handles. Very hard-fired fabric varies from reddish brown (2.5YR 5/4) to reddish yellow (2.5YR) with mica and small white inclusions. Surface is very pale brown (10YR 8/4). Finger indentations at shoulder. On handle:

654. Rim. Roman Coan. Dressel 3. Will Type 12. Inv. No. C-71-324. Lot 456. Pl. 77.

P.H. 0.085. Est. D. rim 0.120. Est. D. mouth 0.096. One fragment of rim and upper part of one double rolled handle. Reddish yellow (5YR 6/6–7/6) fabric with grit and white inclusions. Very pale brown (10YR 8/3) surface.

Two additional examples of this type in Fabric 2 as follows: Lot 13 (1); Lot 88 (1). Peacock and Williams Class 10.

Twenty-one additional examples of this type as follows: Lot 12: 1; Lot 18: 1; Lot 260: 1; Lot 261: 1; Lot 486: 1; Lot 489: 1; Lot 547: 2; Lot 549: 1; Lot 551: 1; Lot 552: 2; Lot 554: 1; Lot 608: 1; Lot 831: 1; Lot 1093: 2; Lot 1418: 1; Lot 1442: 1; Lot 1538: 1; Lot 1636: 1.

655. Toe. Roman Coan. Dressel 3. Will Type 12. Inv. No. C-72-281. Lot 549. Pl. 77.

P.H. 0.070. Max.P.Dim. 0.089. One fragment of toe. Reddish yellow (5YR 6/6–7/6) fabric with white inclusions. Very pale brown surface (10YR 8/3).

Two additional fragments: Lot 552: 1; Lot 1580: 1.

656. Rim. Berenice ER Amphora 7. Lot 18, No. 19. Pl. 78.

P.H. 0.035. Est. D. 0.220. One rim fragment. Fabric group 7.

Other similar rims with similar fabric in Lot 608 (1) and Lot 1501 (1). One other similar rim in Lot 82 has very pale brown (10YR 8/3) fabric.

657. Rim. Spanish(?). Lot 1501, No. 19. Pl. 78.

P.H. 0.070. Est. D. rim 0.140. One fragment. Reddish yellow (5YR 7/6) fabric with grog and white inclusions. Red core (2.5YR 5/6) and pink surface (7.5YR 7/4) not unlike fabric of the ANTIO amphora above (**649**).

658. Rim. Spanish(?). Lot 134, No. 8. Pl. 78.

P.H. 0.067. Est. D. rim 0.148. One rim fragment. Red (2.5YR 6/6) fabric with light brown (7.5YR 6/4) surface.

659. Rim. Spanish(?). Lot 547, No. 254. Pl. 78.

P.H. 0.064. Est. D. rim 0.170. One rim fragment. Reddish yellow (5YR 6/6) fabric with light red (2.5YR 6/8) core. Very pale brown (10YR 8/3) surface.

660. Rim. Spanish(?). Lot 1442, No. 15. Pl. 78.

P.H. 0.590. Est. D. rim 0.160. One rim fragment. Light red (2.5YR 6/8) fabric with small white inclusions. White (10YR 8/2) surface.

661. Rim. Spanish(?). Lot 608, No. 22. Pl. 78.

P.H. 0.047. Est. D. rim 0.170. One rim fragment.

Fabric group 7.

662. Handle. Lot 552, No. 671.

P.H. wall 0.064. D. 0.050. One handle fragment of Fabric group 3.

Two additional handles of same type and fabric in Lots 1636 and 1441.

663. Rim. Inv. No. C-72-201. Lot 552. Pl. 79.

P.H. 0.090. Est. D. rim 0.136. Several fragments of rim and wall mended. Reddish yellow (5YR 7/6) fabric with sand, grog, and white inclusions. Pink (7.5YR 7/4) surface.

Similar rims as follows: Lot 22 (1); Lot 140 (1); Lot 486 (1); Lot 547 (1); Lot 550 (1); Lot 552 (1); Lot 555 (1).

664. Rim. Lot 610, No. 10. Pl. 79.
P.H. 0.050. Est. D. rim 0.168. One rim.
Fabric group 1.

665. Rim. Lot 1493, No. 19. Pl. 79.
P.H. 0.090. Est. D. rim 0.144. One fragment of rim and wall.
Fabric group 3.
One other rim with the same fabric in Lot 248.

666. Rim. Lot 1580, No. 3. Pl. 79.
P.H. 0.055. Est. D rim. 0.152. One rim fragment. Medium fine yellow (10YR 8/6–7/6) to brownish yellow fabric.

667. Rim. Lot 1581, No. 1. Pl. 79.
P.H. 0.094. Est. D. rim 0.130. One fragment of rim.

668. Toe. Lot 610, No. 22. Pl. 79.
P.H. 0.090. Max. D. 0.100. One fragment with knob. Reddish yellow (5YR 7/6) fabric with sand and white inclusions.

669. Toe. Lot 547, No. 605. Pl. 79.
P.H. 0.080. Max. D. 0.095. One toe fragment of Fabric group 1.

670. Toe. Lot 249, No. 153. Pl. 79.
P.H. 0.054. Max. D. 0.070. One toe fragment with weak red (2.5YR 5/2) fabric, light red core and reddish brown (2.5YR 5/2) surface.

671. Toe. Inv. No. C-74-491. Lot 1090. Pl. 79.
P.H. 0.090. Max. D. 0.132. Several fragments of toe mended. Light red (2.5YR 6/8–5YR 7/8) to reddish yellow fabric with much coarse dark sand. Surface is pale brown (10YR 8/3).

672. Toe. Lot 1094, No. 2. Pl. 79.
P.H. 0.110. Max. D. 0.120. Two toe fragments. Reddish yellow (5YR 7/8) with grit, grog, and black sand. Surface is very pale brown (10YR 8/3).

673. Toe. Lot 1416, No. 67. Pl. 79.
P.H. 0.107. Max. D. 0.126. One toe fragment with light red (2.5YR 6/8) fabric with much sand.

Stamps: Greek

674. Rhodian stamp. Inv. No. C-71-177. Lot 24. Pl. 181.
L. 0.094. One fragment preserving upper portion of round handle. Pink (7.5YR 7/4) fabric. Circular stamp is Rhodian rose with fabricant Τιμό[ξενος]. Secondary stamp is E.

Handles of the productive fabricant ΤΙΜΟΞΕΝΟΣ (VG R 513) have been found from Italy to Israel, and from Egypt to the Black Sea shores, and in quantity in Alexandria. Many of his handles have secondary stamps. The date should fall within the early part of Period V, that is, the third quarter of the 2nd century B.C. V. R. Grace, "The Middle Stoa Dated by Amphora Stamps," *Hesperia* 54 (1985) 10, 42; see Y. Calvet, *Salamine de Chypre III, Les Timbres Amphoriques* (Paris 1972) 36, no. 71 (with secondary stamp); *Syria* 55 (1978) 65, no. 72/0012.

675. Rhodian stamp. Inv. No. C-74-36. Lot 1298. Pl. 181.
Max.P.Dim. 0.070. One oval handle fragment. Reddish yellow (5YR 7/6) fabric. Circular stamp is a rose surrounded by letters: [Ἐπὶ Ἀρχε]μ̣βρότο̣[υ Δαλίου] ? VG RE 065.
See V. R. Grace, *Amphoras and the Ancient Wine Trade*, Excavations of the Athenian Agora, Picture Book 6, rev. ed. (Princeton 1979), fig. 62; V. R. Grace and M. Savvatianou-Petropoulakou, "Les timbres amphoriques grecs," in *Exploration archeologique de Délos, 27, L'iLot de la Maison des Comediens*, P. Bruneau, ed. (Paris 1970), no. E40, pl. 55. Date should fall in Period V or VI, that is, between 146 and 88 B.C. See chart of V. Grace in *Hesperia* 54 [cited under **674**], 42.

676. Angular handle with stamp. Rhodian. Inv. No. C-74-387. Lot 1442. Pl. 182.
Max.P.Dim. 0.133. One rim fragment with horned handle. Pink (5YR 8/3) fabric with light reddish pink (2.5YR 6/6–5YR 7/4) core. Rectangular stamp on handle:

Δρακο̣ν̣[τίδα]
anchor point left

VG R 186A. The name ΔΡΑΚΟΝΤΙΔΑΣ is noted in a filling of ca. 150 B.C. at Samaria. See J. W. Crowfoot et al., *Samaria-Sebaste I. The Buildings at Samaria* (London 1942) 119–120. Period V, or the second half of the second century B.C.

677. Handle fragment. Unidentified. Inv. No. C-72-2. Lot 795. Pl. 182.
Max.P.Dim. 0.050. One fragment with rather fine, micaceous, buff clay (7.5YR 6/4). Stamp: Φιλ̣[---] (retr.).
The same reading, but not retrograde, is found on Late Cnidian amphoras (V. R. Grace, "Timbres amphoriques trouves à Délos," *BCH* 76

[1952] 535, fig. 12 on pl. 20), but the clay of this piece does not seem to be Cnidian.

678. Handle fragment. Cnidian. Inv. No. C-72-94. Lot 672. Pl. 182.

Max.P.Dim. 0.084. One fragment of pink (5YR 7/4–6/4) to light reddish brown sandy fabric. A worn stamp:

['Επὶ Φιλίπ]
[που] Κ̣λε(υ)πὀ̣
λ̣ι̣ο̣ς Κνίδ̣ι
ον double axe left

VG KT 0909. Date is Phrourarchy, Period IVAa (188–183 B.C.) or V (early in 146–108 B.C.). Cf. R. Etienne and J.-P. Broun, *Tenos I: Le Sanctuaire de Poseidon et d'Amphitrite* (Ecole française d'Athenes 1986) 245, no. 109.

679. Stamped fragment. Cnidian. Inv. No. C-78-284. Lot 2408. Pl. 182.

Max.P.Dim. 0.061. One fragment with reddish yellow (5YR 6/6) fabric and surface.

['Επὶ Εὐφρα]γ̣όρα
[K]νίδιον double
[K]λευ̣πόλ̣ι̣ο̣ς axe r.

Lunate sigma, broken-barred alpha

VG KT 0900.

Period IVB or 167–146 B.C. See list of dates and names in V. Grace, cited under **674** above, 31, 33. Cf. *Tenos* I [cited in **678** above], 242, No. 69.

680. Stamped double-rolled handle. Coan. Inv. No. C-74-150. Lot 1434. Pl. 183.

Max.P.Dim. 0.089. One rim fragment with handles. Micaceous fabric varies in color from pink (7.5YR 7/4) to reddish yellow (5YR 6/4) to reddish brown. Light slip on surface. Stamp: Ἱππί[ας].

Stamps: Latin

681. Small oval handle. Will Type 8. Inv. No. C-72-1. Lot 610. Pl. 183.

Max.P.Dim. 0.071. One small fragment. Fine, pink (7.5YR 7/4) fabric with white (10YR 8/3) surface. Stamp: S O N V S.

Middle Roman Amphorae

"Big Red." Berenice MR Amphora 5.

This amphora has a broad mouth with flat rim and several deeply cut grooves beneath. Because the fabric of this amphora is similar to a number of contemporary types (such as "Aegean Red" or Berenice MR Amphora 7 below), it is difficult to identify the type without the rim. According to Riley, it occurs in deposits of the late 2nd and 3rd centuries at Istanbul, Athens, and Ostia (Riley, *Berenice 2*, 188).

682. Rim and wall. Lot 1296, No. 93. Pl. 80.

P.H. 0.052. Est. D. rim 0.186. Very rough fabric with lime, a little mica. Reddish yellow (5YR 7/6) with definite gray core. Very messy cut rim with groove squashed together on one side.

683. Rim and wall. Lot 1296, No. 92. Pl. 80.

P.H. 0.105. Est. D. rim 0.166. Very rough fabric with lime, white mica, and white grits, probably quartz as described by Riley (*Berenice 2*, 188). Orange-red (5YR 6/6–6/8) in color with traces of gray core in some areas. Surface varies from dark reddish brown to light reddish brown (5YR).

Additional rims of this type come from Lots 1285, 1297, and 1308, all contexts of the 3rd century except Lot 1285, where the piece is probably residual.

"Aegean Red." Berenice MR Amphora 7. Peacock and Williams Class 47.

Of similar fabric as the preceding type but smaller and with different shape. The rim/neck is conical with a sharp ridge at exterior or interior, as in the two examples illustrated here. The type is most common in the Mediterranean during the 3rd and 4th centuries, according to Riley (*Berenice 2*, 190).

684. Rim, neck, and one handle. Inv. No. C-74-216. Lot 1298. Pl. 80.

P.H. 0.220. D. rim 0.080. Very coarse fabric with mixed grit inclusions. Reddish yellow to yellowish red (5YR) fabric with gray core. Widely spaced wheel-ridging.

685. Rim. Lot 1404, No. 21. Pl. 80.

P.H. 0.075. Est. D. rim. 0.085. One rim fragment. Same fabric as C-74-216, but surfaces are fired more reddish brown (5YR 5/4). Wheel-ridging.

Additional examples of rims as follows: Inv. No. C-71-427 from Lot 65; 1 rim each from Lots 1008, 1404.

686. Toe(?) Lot 302, No. 17. Pl. 80.

P.H. 0.115. D. Base 0.068. One fragment of base hollow all the way to the bottom where the underside is recessed with large nipple in center. Fabric is red (2.5YR 6/6–5YR 6/6) with traces of lime and mica. Wheel-ridging at base.

The type occurs at Stobi in contexts ranging in date from the mid-3rd to the mid-4th centuries. Handles of this type are fairly common.

"Africano grande."
Berenice MR Amphora 16/17.

This Tunisian amphora, thought to have carried oil, is common in the Mediterranean area during the 3rd and 4th centuries, extending into the late 4th century when it is common at Ostia (Riley, *Berenice* 2, 200–204). Distinctive is the cream wash on the exterior, usually with shallow vertical scraping or brush strokes.

687. Incomplete profile. Inv. No. C-74-469. Lot 1349. Pl. 81.

(a) Rim. P.H. 0.200. D. rim 0.114. (b) Toe. P.H. 0.228. Max.P.Dim. 0.114. Several fragments not joining, giving almost complete profile. Burned and discolored, but fabric appears to be pink/reddish yellow (5YR 7/4–6/6). White slip with vertical scraping.

Most closely resembles Riley, *Berenice* 2, MR Amphora 17a, no. D280, a 4th-century type.

688. Incomplete profile. Inv. No. C-74-505. Lot 1349. Pl. 183.

P.H. 0.480. Th. 0.010. Mended and partially complete. Rim and toe missing. Hard, red (2.5YR 5/6) fabric, gritty with sand and white inclusions. Thin grayish brown to brownish gray (2.5Y 7/2–6/2) wash covers surface. Scraped or smoothed in vertical strips.

Many body fragments and part of a toe of this type, burned after being broken, and certainly representing several vessels, were found in Lot 1307.

Other examples of the type occur in Lots 299 and 304, both contexts of the late 4th, early 5th centuries, and in Lots 1404, 2120, and 2121.

Globular Amphora.
Berenice MR Amphora 9. Dressel 20.
Peacock and Williams Class 25.

This Spanish amphora from the southern province of Baetica carried olive oil. It occurs from the late 1st century B.C. through the 3rd and perhaps 4th centuries A.C., especially in the West, although some examples are known from the East as well (Riley, *Berenice* 2, 162; and Will [1983]).

689. Body, base, and toe. Inv. No. C-75-7. Lot 1642. Pl. 184.

P.H. 0.630. D. body 0.445. D. toe 0.035. Mended from many well-worn fragments. Rim, neck, and handles missing. Micaceous fabric tending to foliate. Color varies from reddish yellow (5YR 7/6–6/6) to pink (5YR 8/4–7/4). Greatest diameter at shoulder. Small spike with moulded bottom.

An additional base and toe, Inv. No. C-75-6, comes from the same Lot and another was inventoried as C-72-192.

Miscellaneous Middle Roman Amphorae

690. Outward-thickened rim. Lot 1610, No. 1.

P.H. 0.068. Est. D. rim. 0.140. One fragment with groove at rim exterior and one below. Light red (2.5YR), gritty and micaceous fabric, not unlike **682**, **683**. Surface fired red with traces of pink/white slip.

691. Convex rim. Lot 1298, No. 54. Pl. 80.

P.H. 0.095. Est. D. rim 0.142. Pink (7.5YR 7/4) fabric with mica, gray, and white grits. White (10YR 8/3–8/4) slip.

692. Rim. Lot 1599, No. 74. Pl. 81.

P.H. 0.065 D. rim. 0.130. Fabric pink (7.5YR 7/4–7/6) to buff in color has much grog and white slip on surface.

693. Neck and handles. Lot 2121, No. 106. Pl. 81.

P.H. 0.230. Est. D. upper neck 0.140. Very micaceous and discolored from burning, but a light red fabric.

The toe described below (**694**) is probably from this vessel. The context for both seems to be late 1st or 2nd century A.C.

694. Toe. Lot 2120, No. 41. Pl. 81.

P.H. 0.145. D. base. 0.050. One fragment discolored from burning but with the same fabric as the piece directly above (**693**).

695. Neck and toe. Inv. No. C-78-94. Lot 2090. Pl. 183.

(a) Rim with neck, handles. P.H. 0.238. D. rim 0.157. D. neck 0.108. Th. 0.012. (b) Toe. P.H. 077. Two pieces not joining. Fine, micaceous fabric light red (2.5YR 6/8) to reddish yellow (5YR 6/6), fired pink (7.5YR 7/4) on surface. Smoothed finish.

Cf. Riley, *Berenice 2*, D301.

696. Rim with overhang. Lot 1328, No. 8. Pl. 81.

P.H. 0.060. Est. D. rim 0.145. One fragment. Very pale brown (10YR 8/4) fabric with large fragments of grog and many air pockets. White exterior.

697. Inturned rim. Lot 1599, No. 27. Pl. 81.

P.H. 0.075. Est. D. rim. 0.170. One fragment. Very sandy pink (5YR 7/4) fabric.

698. Rim, neck, and handles. Inv. No. C-74-215. Lot 1509. Pl. 82.

P.H. 0.163. D. rim. 0.065. One fragment. Reddish yellow (5YR 7/6) to pink (7.5YR 7/4) sandy fabric.

Surface is pale yellow (2.5YR 8/4), worn over much of surface.

Late Roman Amphorae

Carthage LR Amphora 1.

Common from the late 4th to late 6th and 7th centuries A.C. and apparently produced in Cilicia (J.W. Hayes, op. cit., Chapter 1, note 9; (Riley, *Berenice 2*, 212–215).

699. Rim and wall. Lot 514, No. 50. Pl. 82.

P.H. 0.085. Est. D. rim 0.080.

Other fragments of this type in Lots 1599, 2323, and 2325.

Carthage LR Amphora 2.

Common in the Mediterranean from late 5th to late 6th or early 7th centuries A.C. (Riley, *Berenice 2*, 217–219).

700. Profile. Inv. No. C-74-357. Lot 1349. Pl. 82.

P.H. 0.650. D. shoulder 0.420. Th. 0.011. D. mouth 0.120. Mended and restored. Very pale brown (10YR 7/4–6/4) to light yellowish brown varying to pink (7.5YR 7/4) fabric with grog, white inclusions, and traces of lime explosions on surface that is fired very pale brown (10YR 7/3).

From a context of the late 4th, early 5th centuries A.C.; see W-MZ (1974) 139 for a description of Room 32 of the Fuller's House.

Another example, C-71-359 (Lot 254), with combed decoration on the shoulder, is illustrated on Pl. 184. The fabric of this example, however, is a gritty red (10R 5/6–2.5YR 5/6) fabric with small white inclusions. Surface is reddish yellow (5YR 6/6).

701. Inv. No. C-70-26. Lot 1015. Pl. 82.

P. H. 0.073. Est. D. rim 0.110. Pinkish orange clay.

Other examples in Lot 1828.

Context at Stobi: early to mid-5th century.

Carthage LR Amphora 3.
Berenice LR Amphora 10.
(Micaceous Water jar).

702. Inv. No. C-79-39. Lot 2581. Pl. 82.

P.H. 0.059. Est. D. rim 0.034. Two pieces mended preserving rim, neck, and two handles. Fine, hard, micaceous red (2.5YR 4/5–5/6) fabric.

The presence of two handles indicates a date after the mid- or late 4th century. Cf. *Berenice 2*, 229.

Other examples date to the end of the 4th, early 5th centuries A.C. One other rim from Lot 298. Rare at Stobi.

Carthage LR Amphora 4.
Berenice LR Amphora 3.
Gaza Amphora.

Common in the Mediterranean from ca. 400–600 A.C.

703. Inv. No. C-78-93. Lot 2434. Pls. 82, 184.

P.H. 0.174. D. rim 0.099. Max. D. 0.230. Mended from many fragments and preserving rim, two handles, and upper body. Gritty, reddish yellow (5YR 6/6) fabric with applied clay at rim and handles. Messy ridging of varying width begins at shoulder.

704. Inv. No. C-79-23. Lot 2604.

P.H. 0.042. Est. D. 0.080. One rim fragment. Very coarse, light reddish brown (5YR 6/4) fabric. Short, vertical rim.

Other examples of Gaza amphoras: C-71-422 in Lot 514; one each in Lots 298, 2323, and 2325.

Berenice LR Amphora 8. Spatheion or ampulla.

Long, narrow body in small or large size. Characteristic is white or light green wash on exterior.

705. Rim and body. Inv. No. C-70-104. Lot 514. Pl. 83.

P.H. 0.590. D. mouth 0.128. Lower body and toe missing. Coarse red (2.5YR 5/8–4/8) fabric with many large chunks of lime. Exterior has white slip with vertical scraping on body.

706. Incomplete profile. Inv. No. C-73-76. Lot 875. Pl. 83.

(a) Rim. P.H. 0.045. Est. D. rim 0.080. (b) Base. P.H. 0.072. D. base 0.020. (c) Body. P.H. 0.35. Max. Dim. 0.114. Three sections not joining and perhaps not from the same vessel. Gritty, light red (2.5YR 6/6) clay with lime and thin white slip or salts on surface.

707. Rim and neck. Inv. No. C-74-506. Lot 1349. Pl. 185.

(a) Rim and neck. P.H. 0.085. D. mouth 0.105. Th. 0.050. (b) Neck, handles. P.H. 0.120. D. neck 0.070. Two pieces not joining. Red, sandy, gritty fabric, light red (2.5YR 6/8) in color with light brown (97.5YR 6/4), thin wash, now peeling.

See ref. under **700** for context and date.

708. Toe. Inv. No. C-74-507. Lot 1349. Pl. 185.

P.H. 0.180. Max. D. 0.050. One fragment of solid toe. Micaceous, gritty red (2.5YR 6/4–5/4) fabric, with core and surface fired deeper red (2.5YR 6/6–5/6).

709. Toe. Inv. No. C-74-309. Lot 1599. Pl. 185.

P.H. 0.115. Th. 0.007. One fragment. Gritty reddish yellow (7.5YR 8/6) fabric.

Miscellaneous Late Roman Amphorae

710. Convex rim. Lot 297, No. 14. Pl. 83.

P.H. 0.047. D. rim 0.108. Two fragments joining. Rather fine pink to reddish yellow (7.5YR 7/4–7/6) fabric.

711. Grooved rim. Lot 1809, No. 1. Pl. 83.

P.H. 0.044. D. rim 0.015. One fragment. Red (2.5YR 6/6) to reddish brown (5YR 5/3) at core with lime and gold mica. Surface is pink (5YR 7/4–8/4).

Amphora lids or operculae

712. Disk lid. Inv. No. C-72-63. Lot 552. Pl. 83.

H. 0.040. D. 0.107. Complete except for one portion of a side. White (10YR), gritty fabric. Handle consisting of five fingerprints pinched into clay and pulled up to a point.

See comments of Peacock and Williams, *Amphorae*, p. 51, on lids and stoppers; also Slane (1986) nos. 30, 31, pl. 63, and p. 306.

713. Disk lid. Lot 545, No. 162. Pl. 83.

H. 0.034. D. 0.100. One fragment two-thirds complete. Reddish brown to pink (7.5YR 6/4–7/4) fabric with white inclusions, grit, and sand. Pinched handle, hollow underneath.

714. Disk lid. Inv. No. C-72-7. Lot 110.

H. 0.021. D. 0.023. One small fragment of profile. Fabric is reddish brown (2.5YR 5/4).

715. Disk lid. Inv. No. C-71-253. Lot 250. Pl. 184.

H. 0.029. D. 0.110. Complete. Pink (5YR 8/3–7/3) fabric. Finger-pinched handle.

One additional example with the same fabric from the same Lot (C-71-252).

Other amphora lids as follows: Lot 13: C-71-325; Lot 608 (1); Lot 552 (2); Lot 547 (1); Lot 545 (1); Lot 456 (1); Lot 1082 (1); Lot 40 (1).

Pompeian Red Ware (716–721)

Pompeian Red Ware is the name given to a group of dishes with very coarse, gritty fabric and a thick, glossy slip, much like the red of Pompeian wall paintings, covering the interior and rim exterior of the vessel. The vessels are unslipped on the bottom and on the exterior walls, where they are frequently burned as if used over a fire for cooking or baking.[135] In fact, it has been sug-

[135] Recent studies with full bibliography include D.P.S. Peacock, "Pompeian Red Ware," in Peacock (1977) 147–162, and Goudineau (1970) 159–186. See also comments of Hayes, "Corinth," 458–459.

gested that these large plates were used for baking dough of some sort or making the equivalent of pancakes and that the smooth, glossy surface would prevent sticking—the ancient Teflon, as it were.[136] This category of pottery has been found widely throughout the Roman world in contexts ranging in general from the early 1st century B.C. into the 2nd century A.C.[137] The origin of this ware is at present unknown, and the variety of fabrics seen within the catalogue suggests that Pompeian Red Ware was manufactured in a number of different centers.

David Peacock has distinguished seven different fabric groups based on differences in appearance and composition.[138] The most common and distinctive of the Pompeian Red Ware fabrics is Peacock's Fabric 1, reddish brown in color and containing much black sand, whose origin may be in the region of Pompei and Herculaneum.[139] Of the six other fabrics described by Peacock, Fabric 2 is similar to that of a number of pieces found at Stobi. This is not surprising, since an origin in the Aegean or Anatolia is suggested for this type.[140]

Pompeian Red Ware is not plentiful at Stobi, and the forms and fabrics do not, for the most part, readily correspond to the published typologies of the ware. In fact, only the dish with rolled rim is readily paralleled at other sites. It is present in the greatest numbers at Stobi in deposits of 1st-century B.C. date. Aside from a few examples of Augustan date, the other examples are of rather unusual form and come from contexts of late 1st- to mid-2nd-century date.

Pompeian Red Ware is not common in the 2nd century, and examples found in 2nd-century deposits may be survival pieces. There is accumulating evidence, however, that some of the ware may still have been produced at this late date.[141]

716. Dish with rolled rim. Lot 127, No. 25. Pl. 84.

H. 0.044. Est. D. rim 0.350. One fragment giving almost complete profile. Dark brown (10YR 3/3) fabric with coarse black sand and gold (biotite-brown) and silver (muscovite-white) mica visible. The exterior is unslipped, the interior covered with a red slip (2.5YR 4/5–4/6) with dull metallic luster. The bottom is rough and burned black.

A base fragment with grooved floor was found in the same context (Lot 134, No. 99, Pl. 84).

This is the earliest form cited by Goudineau (1970) pl. I:1, dated 123–60 B.C., and pl. VII:7, dated 90–30 B.C.; Vegas, *Cerámica común*, Type 15, fig. 16:2, p. 49, dated 80–70 B.C.; Auguste Bruckner, "Kuchengeschirr aus der casa del Fauno in Pompeji," *RCRFActa* 7 (1965) 7–14; "Magdalensburg," 76, 122, dated late Republican to 30 B.C.

717. Dish with rolled rim. Lot 554, No. 47. Pl. 84.

P.H. 0.038. Est. D. rim 0.362. One fragment of rim and wall. Yellowish red (5YR 5/6) fabric with sand or grit, biotite (brown) and muscovite (white), and white inclusions. Perhaps Peacock Fabric 2. Red (10R 4/6) gloss on interior.

Other examples of this form: Lot 127: 1r, with fabric as No. 1; Lot 554: 1r, with fabric (5YR 4/6), sand, both micas; Lot 550: 1r, with fabric having white inclusions Lot 554: 1r, Peacock Fabric 2(?) as No. 2.

718. Dish with incurved rim. Inv. No. C-74-435. Lot 1358. Pl. 84.

P.H. 0.031. Est. D. rim 0.348. One rim fragment from dish with groove setting off rim on exterior. Yellowish red (5YR 5/6) fabric with inclusions as Peacock Fabric 2. Red (2.5YR 6/6–5/6) interior gloss.

Cf. Dyson, *Cosa*, fig. 30, PD16, dated to the last quarter of the 1st century B.C.

Another example, badly discolored from burning in Lot 259.

719. Dish with flaring rim. Lot 1538, No. 22. Pl. 84.

P.H. 0.038. Est. D. rim 0.315. One rim fragment. Deeply cut groove sets off rim on exterior. Single groove at rim interior. Reddish yellow (5YR 6/6) fabric with inclusions as Peacock Fabric 2. Red (2.5YR 4/6–5/6) gloss on interior.

[136] Goudineau (1970), 165.

[137] Hayes, "Corinth," 459.

[138] Peacock (1977) 149–156.

[139] Ibid., 153.

[140] Ibid., 154.

[141] Hayes, "Paphos," fig. 1:1–3, pp. 96–97, 100, and note 7; also Hayes, "Villa Dionysus," p. 108, note 29; Peacock, "Pompeian Red Ware," 59; Kenrick, *Berenice 3*, 320–321, and B481, p. 325; but see Slane (1986) 312, note 75, where only single fragments of Pompeian Red Ware appear in the cellar fill of the third quarter of the 1st century A.C.

720. Dish with flat rim. Lot 1538, No. 23. Pl. 84.
P.H. 0.021. Est. D. rim 0.246. One rim fragment. Yellowish red (5YR 4/6) fabric with coarse sand. Peacock Fabric 1? Red (2.5YR 5/6) interior gloss.
Cf. Dyson, *Cosa*, fig. 30, PD22, dated to the last quarter of the 1st century B.C.

721. Dish with flat rim. Lot 1501, No. 8. Pl. 84.
P.H. 0.027. Est. D. rim 0.264. One rim fragment. Brown (7.5YR 4/4) fabric with inclusions as Peacock Fabric 2. Red (2.5YR 4/6–5/6) interior gloss.
Cf. Goudineau (1970) 175, pl. VI:40, dated 120–90 B.C., and 178, pl. VIII:14, dated 90–30 B.C.; Vegas, *Cerámica común*, 46, fig. 16:4, dated to the Augustan period; Dyson, *Cosa*, fig. 19, VD14, dated to ca. 70 B.C.; Kenrick, *Berenice 3*, fig. 60, B481.

Campanian Cooking Ware (722)

Only a few examples of this distinctive Italian fabric, similar to that of Pompeian Red Ware, have been found at Stobi. It is characterized by an orange fabric with black grits.

722. Lid. Inv. No. C-72-55. Lot 552. Pl. 84.
H. 0.044. Est. D. 0.358. Several fragments mended giving complete profile. Reddish orange (2.5YR 6/8–5/8: light red to red) fabric, with black sand particles common. Convex profile and plain, thickened rim with concave, ring knob.
See Riley, *Berenice 2*, Imported Cooking Ware B239, B324.
One other tiny rim fragment from another similar lid was found in Lot 1442.

Aegean Cooking Ware (723, 724)

Some examples of cooking ware imported from the Aegean occur in contexts of the 2nd and 3rd centuries at Stobi.[142] The trefoil-mouth jug and a small cooking pot are the shapes represented. The fabric is a light red or red (2.5YR 6/6, 6/8) and the walls rather thin (0.002 to 0.004 m.) with no core. The surface is fired gray.

723. Small pot. Inv. No. C-77-6. Lot 1959. Pl. 85.
P.H. 0.035. Est. D. rim. 0.100. One fragment of rim with wall and handle. Short, everted rim and small sliced handle with shallow groove down one side.
Cf. Hayes, "Villa Dionysus," 124, fig. 6, no. 70 on p. 167, dated mid-2nd century or later.

724. Trefoil-mouthed jug. Lot 929, No. 9. Pl. 85.
P.H. 0.042. Max. D. opening 0.063. D. neck 0.034. Three fragments mended, preserving rim and part of body. Small example with very thin walls.
Cf. Hayes, "Villa Dionysus," 124, fig. 6, no. 76 on p. 167.
Three other examples of this form: Lot 543: C-72-126, Lot 1404: C-74-281, and one from Lot 1296.

Local/Regional Color-Slipped and Plain Wares

At Stobi it is the local Color-Slipped and Plain wares of Fabric 1 (Table 2.1) that dominate the fine table wares, amounting to between 70 percent and 95 percent of the fine ware RBH (Table

[142] Hayes, "Villa Dionysus," 105–107.

5.1) depending on the chronological period.[143] The forms of these tablewares tend to imitate the shapes of popular contemporary imports. Although the shapes change over the centuries, with the least change in the Middle Roman period, the most common forms are always the plate or dish and bowls of varying sizes. Larger shapes include mixing bowls and large jugs or pitchers. The popularity of the various shapes may be seen in Figures 3.4, 3.5, and 3.6.[144] Kantharoi, jars, or cups for drinking are also common, but such shapes were probably augmented by drinking vessels in other materials such as metal, glass, and wood, depending on the wealth of the family.

In this portion of the catalogue, the pottery of each major chronological period (Hellenistic, Early Roman, Middle Roman) has been subdivided into two groups, with the exception of Late Roman. The first group is comprised of examples of forms and variants of forms that constitute the formal typology of local ceramics at Stobi. The

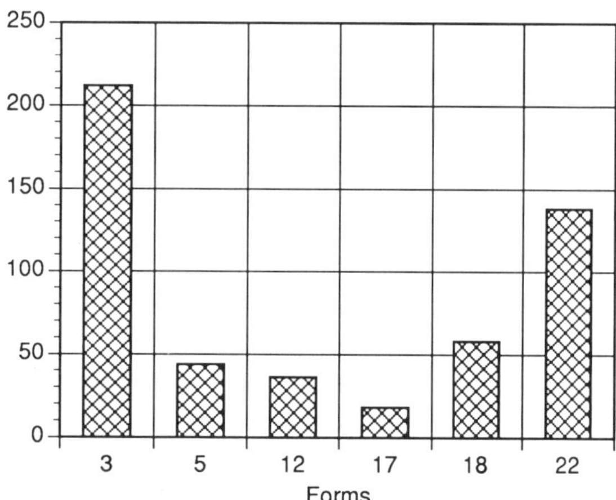

Figure 3.4. Bar graph illustrating quantity of the most popular Hellenistic Color-Slipped and Plain forms at Stobi

Form 3: Shallow Plate with incurved wall
Form 5: Lekanis
Form 12: Shallow Bowl with incurved wall
Form 17: Trefoil-mouthed pitcher
Form 18: Hydria
Form 22: Stamnos

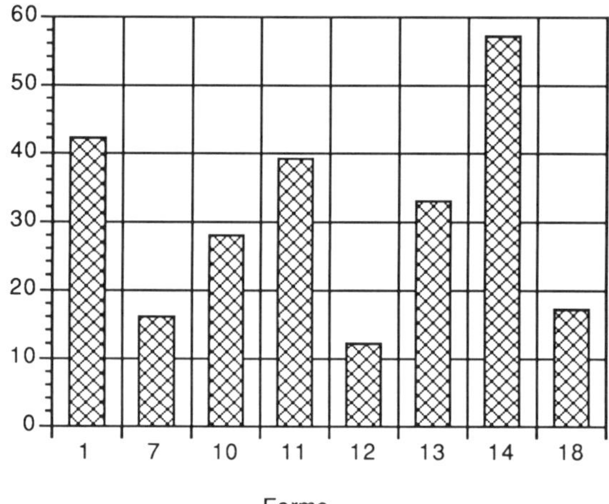

Figure 3.5. Bar graph illustrating quantity of the most popular Early Roman Color-Slipped and Plain forms at Stobi

Form 1: Flat-based Dish
Form 7: Bowl
Form 10: Carinated Bowl
Form 11: Flanged-rim Bowl
Form 12: One-handled Cup
Form 13: Tall Jar
Form 14: Jar with folded rim
Form 18: Stamnos

forms for each period are numbered consecutively, beginning with Form 1. Twenty-three Hellenistic forms have been distinguished, eighteen Early Roman forms, and thirty-four Middle Roman forms. Since the forms for each period are different, yet each sequence begins with 1, the prefix indicating to which period the form belongs is an integral part of the form designation, e.g., ER Form 7 is not the same form as MR Form 7.

In the Late Roman period at Stobi there seem to have been no *new* forms produced in Fabric 1, and therefore no typology has been proposed for Late Roman Color-Slipped and Plain wares. It is possible that the forms common in the Middle Roman period continued to be produced or used. Tableware shapes were instead produced in Fabric 2 (Macedonian Gray Ware) and Fabric 3 (Tan Micaceous Ware and Cooking Ware).

The variation in the number of forms for each

143 The local fabric groups are described above in Chapter 2 and discussed in Appendix 2.

144 The representation of certain forms in any context is also a function of vessel form and the degree to which a complete profile tends to be preserved and is recognizable from any given fragment. Note comments under "Local/Regional Cooking Wares" and under "MR Form 19." The number of types in a given chronological period is also a function of the quantity of deposits on the site dating to that period; see Chapter 4 and Table 4.14.

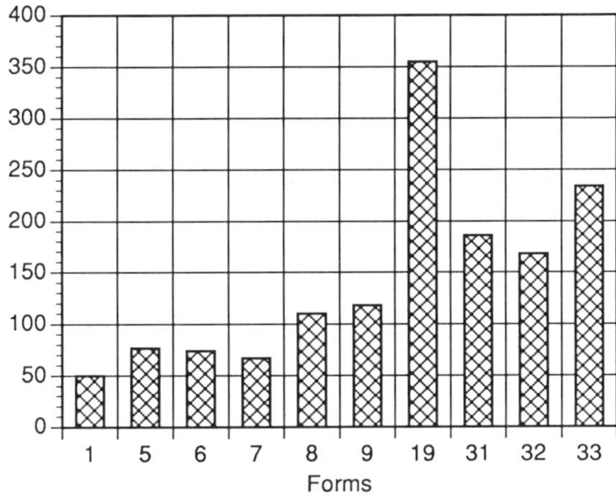

Figure 3.6. Bar graph illustrating quantity of the most popular Middle Roman Color-Slipped and Plain forms at Stobi

Form 1: Flat-based Dish with horizontal rim
Form 5: Flat-based Dish with straight rim
Form 6: Flat-based Dish with curved wall
Form 7: Shallow Dish
Form 8: Flat-based Dish with inturned rim
Form 9: Small Bowl with horizontal rim
Form 19: Three-ridged Bowl
Form 31: Large Jug
Form 32: Large Basin
Form 33: Stamnos

period is in large part a function of the size and number of deposits from each period that were excavated by the Stobi Project.

Because not all pieces could be assigned to forms in the typology, either because they are too fragmentary or because they display a unique or unusual shape or other feature, a second group comprising these miscellaneous examples follows the typology of each chronological period, e.g., "Hellenistic wares: Other." These pieces are classified according to generic subheadings (such as Dishes or Bowls).

Although this chapter is devoted to Local/Regional Color-Slipped and Plain wares, it is possible that there are some unidentified imports concealed in both groups.

Hellenistic wares: Forms 1–23 (**725–767**)

Form 1

Fish plate with overhanging rim and circular depression in the center of the floor, usually the diameter of the base ring. Unfortunately only one rim can be assigned to this form, but several bases, easily identified, have been found. Some are slipped, some plain.

The fish plate got its name from the large fish that, in early black-gloss examples, was usually painted in red figure on the plate interior. The "fish plate" begins to appear in the Mediterranean world in the late 5th and early 4th centuries B.C. and continues to be found throughout the 2nd and into the 1st centuries in some areas. For additional comments, see *Tarsus*, p. 155 and note 13; *Samaria*, p. 220, fig. 37; pp. 260, 262, fig. 54; and Lamboglia Form 23, p. 172. Total: 5 bases, 1 rim.

725. Lot 555, No. 22. Pl. 85.

P.H. 0.014. Est. D. rim 0.198. One fragment of rim and wall. Dull black slip on interior while exterior is slipped under rim only, with drips of slip on lower wall.

Cf. *Samaria*, fig. 54:10, p. 161, dated to 2nd/1st centuries B.C.

Date: second and third quarters of the 1st century B.C.

726. Inv. No. C-75-107. Lot 1636. Pl. 85.

P.H. 0.043. Est. D. base 0.110. One fragment of base. Large, thick-walled base with very pale brown (10YR) surfaces.

Date: second half of the 2nd century B.C.

727. Inv. No. C-72-178. Lot 563. Pl. 85.

P.H. 0.015. Est. D. base 0.065. One fragment of base.

Preserved section appears to be unslipped.

Date: 2nd century B.C.

Form 2

Small dish with offset rim. No bases preserved. Diameters range from 0.170 to 0.200 m.

Cf. Taylor, "Cosa," "plate with horizontal offset rim," D1a, pl. 33, dated 130/20 to 70/60 B.C.; C22d, pl. 33, dated 167 to 140 B.C. Total: 4.

728. Lot 552, No. 339. Pl. 85.

P.H. 0.012. Est. D. rim 0.170. One fragment of rim and small part of wall. Red slip on both surfaces.

Date: second and third quarters of the 1st century B.C.

Form 3

Shallow plate on high ring base with curved or slightly flaring wall. The join between wall and floor may be curved (Variant A) or angular (Variant B) and the lip rounded or pointed. Variant A resembles a common Eastern Sigillata A plate form, Samaria Form 1. In fact, **729** and **730** were found in the same context as **225**, an example of the Samaria form. Variant B belongs to the groups of forms common in Campanian wares, Lamboglia Forms 5 and 7. Diameters range from 0.18 to 0.22 m. The form is the most common one in the 1st century B.C. at Stobi. Total: 212.

Variant A

729. Inv. No. C-71-208. Lot 140. Pl. 86.

P.H. 0.039. Est. D. rim 0.199. Several fragments mended, preserving profile and about one-quarter of plate. Red slip. Two bands of rouletting on floor, and in center a pattern of very blurred, stamped palmettes.

730. Inv. No. C-70-123. Lot 831. Pl. 86.

P.H. 0.038. Est. D. rim 0.189. Several fragments mended, preserving about one-half of plate. Metallic black slip fired red near center and off to one side. Wide band of rouletting on floor and stamped oval shapes (meant to be palmettes?) in center.

Variant B

731. Inv. No. C-70-119. Lot 831. Pl. 86.

P.H. 0.038. Est. D. rim 0.223. One large fragment preserving profile and about one-quarter of vessel. Yellowish red/brown (10YR 5/6) slip. Wide band of rouletting on floor.

732. Inv. No. C-70-120. Lot 829. Pl. 86.

P.H. 0.035. Est. D. rim 0.203. Mended from many fragments, preserving about one-third of vessel. Red slip. Wide band of rouletting on floor.

Form 4

Bowl with flaring wall and probable ring base. On some examples the wall continues into a flat rim. A carination at mid-body is also seen on some examples. Diameters range from 0.155 to 0.200 m. This shape is related to Lamboglia form 28.

Date: first half of the 1st century B.C. Total: 10.

733. Lot 829, No. 83. Pl. 87.

P.H. 0.038. Est. D. rim 0.169. Mended from several fragments, giving rim and wall. Single groove on rim and on lower wall. Red metallic slip on interior and upper half of exterior, while lower part of exterior is unslipped.

734. Lot 610, No. 25. Pl. 87.

P.H. 0.042. Est. D. rim 0.154. Single fragment of rim and wall. Offset on interior wall at point where the body curves outward. Black slip with some areas fired red.

Form 5

Large, deep bowl with horizontal rim or lekanis. Ring base is probable, although no complete profiles have been recovered. This shape also occurs in gray ware. Diameters range from 0.200 to 0.300 m.

Cf. Drougou and Touratsoglou, *Veroia,* 159, fig. 44. Total: 44.

735. Lot 552, No. 327. Pl. 87.

P.H. 0.072. Est. D. rim 0.200. One fragment of rim and wall. Single groove at rim edge. Red slip.

Date: second and third quarters of the 1st century B.C.

Form 6

Small, deep bowl with flaring wall and overhanging rim. No bases have been preserved. Diameters range from approximately 0.10 to 0.20 m. Total: 11.

736. Lot 552, No. 361. Pl. 87.

P.H. 0.044. Est. D. rim 0.100. One fragment of rim and wall. Slight offset on wall where body begins to curve inward. Red slip.

Date: second and third quarters of the 1st century B.C.

Form 7

Small, shallow bowl with flaring wall, moulded rim and grooved base. Several examples of this form exist in gray ware. Total: 6.

737. Inv. No. C-71-332. Lot 26. Pl. 87.

H. 0.031. Est. D. rim 0.119. Four fragments mended, giving complete profile. Very glossy, lustrous strong brown (7.5YR) to brown slip.

Form 8

Bowl with incurving rim and ring base. The degree of rim curvature varies considerably in this form, with some examples curved slightly inward and others re-entrant. Most examples were slipped completely on the interior but only partially on the exterior—to about mid-body. Diameters range from 0.130 to 0.200 m.

The incurved rim bowl is perhaps the most popular shape in the fineware category during the Hellenistic period and occurs in a variety of profiles in contemporary contexts. For additional examples from Stobi, see the Gray Ware and Black-Gloss categories. See Taylor, "Cosa," p. 85, for an extensive bibliography. More recent comments in Drougou and Touratsoglou, *Veroia*, 129–133, fig. 21. Total: 13.

738. Lot 1636, No. 64. Pl. 87.

P.H. 0.025. Est. D. rim 0.195. One fragment of rim and wall. Red slip.

Date: second half of the 2nd century B.C.

739. Inv. No. C-71-136. Lot 14. Pl. 87.

H. 0.061. D. rim 0.150. Mended from several fragments, about two-thirds preserved. Reddish brown slip.

Date: second and third quarters of the 1st century B.C.

740. Inv. No. C-71-357. Lot 259. Pl. 87.

P.H. 0.065. Est. D. rim 0.175. Two fragments mended to give rim and wall. Red slip with metallic luster.

Form 9

Deep hemispherical bowl on grooved base. Grooves are common at rim interior or exterior. Diameters range from 0.095 to 0.125.

Cf. Pasquinucci (1972) 283, Form 122, fig. 1, note 69, and p. 392, for a hemispherical bowl with concave grooves on base in black gloss, fired brown-olive. See also, *Pergamon 6*, fig. 9:64.B6, with grooves on inside of lip, dated (p. 79) to the first quarter of the 1st century B.C. Total: 4.

741. Inv. No. C-71-283. Lots 131, 134. Pl. 88.

H. 0.064. D. rim 0.098. Mended from numerous fragments, giving complete profile. Mottled yellowish red (5YR 5/6) slip.

Date: first half of the 1st century B.C.

742. Inv. No. C-72-58. Lot 552. Pl. 88.

H. 0.063. D. rim 0.112. Mended from several fragments, preserving complete profile. Yellowish red to brown (5YR 5/6) slip.

Date: second and third quarters of the 1st century B.C.

Form 10

Bowl with incurving walls on broad foot. Single groove just below lip on exterior.

The form is that of Lamboglia's Campanian B, Form 1. Cf. the example of Campanian (21) from the same context as the example described below (**743**). Total: 2.

743. Inv. No. C-71-303. Lot 134. Pl. 88.

H. 0.051. D. rim. 0.135. Mended from several fragments, giving profile and about one-third of vessel. Broad band of rouletting on floor. Red slip.

Form 11

Shallow bowl with carinated wall, ring base. Diameters range from 0.100 to 0.140.

Similar to Taylor, "Cosa," D12, pl. 25, p. 127: "Small bowl with vertical rim," and p. 181: "Rimless bowl with vertical wall," both dated 130/20–70/60 B.C. Total: 4.

744. Inv. No. C-72-31. Lot 552. Pl. 88.

H. 0.054. Est. D. rim 0.135. Mended from several fragments, giving complete profile. About half the vessel preserved. Red slip.

Date: second and third quarters of the 1st century B.C.

Form 12

Shallow bowl with incurved wall and ring base. Single groove at lip exterior is common as well as on interior or exterior wall. Diameters range from 0.130 to 0.145 m.

This form may be related to Moevs, "Cosa," Form 19, dated to the third quarter of the 1st century B.C.; and Taylor, "Cosa," D12. Total: 36.

745. Lot 552, No. 176. Pl. 88.

P.H. 0.041. Est. D. rim 0.139. Two fragments of rim and wall. Reddish brown slip.

746. Lot 552, No. 173. Pl. 88.

P.H. 0.040. Est. D. rim 0.144. Three fragments of rim and wall. Red slip.

747. Lot 552, No. 174. Pl. 88.

P.H. 0.030. Est. D. rim 0.137. Two fragments mended, giving rim and wall. Slip varies from dark brown to black and has a slightly metallic luster.

Date for **745–747**: second and third quarters of the 1st century B.C.

Form 13

Kantharos. Only rims and handles have been preserved to give an idea of the shape, which may have curved or vertical walls. Total: 8.

748. Inv. No. C-72-67. Lot 552. Pl. 89.

P.H. 0.053. Est. D. rim 0.103. Two fragments mended, giving some idea of upper profile with straight rim and bolster handle. Red slip.

Date: second and third quarters of the 1st century B.C.

749. Inv. No. C-71-341. Lot 76. Pl. 89.

P.H. 0.046. Est. D. rim 0.133. Single fragment with rim, wall, and bolster handle. Slip varies from reddish brown to black.

Form 14

Small jar with one handle, or olpe. Simple flaring rim and gently curving wall with three grooves. Base not preserved. Total: 6.

750. Lot 829, No. 4. Pl. 89.

P.H. 0.062. Est. D. rim 0.081. Mended from several fragments. Red slip on exterior.

Date: first half of the 1st century B.C.

Form 15

Jar with curved, offset rim, plump body, and ring base. Some examples have handles preserved. Diameters range from 0.080 to 0.100 m. Total: 6.

751. Lot 552, No. 67. Pl. 89.

P.H. 0.035. Est. D. rim 0.089. Mended from two fragments, giving rim, wall, and handle. Exterior slip is mottled black, red, and brown.

752. Lot 20, No. 4. Pl. 89

P.H. 0.090. Est. D. rim 0.085. Five nonjoining pieces from rim and base, giving almost complete profile. Red slip.

This example is similar to a Campanian form. Cf. Orlanda Pancrazzi, "Sovana, localita Costone della Folonia," *NSc* 25 (1971), fig. 84, p. 147, SF4/31.

Date: second and third quarters of the 1st century B.C.

Form 16

Small, globular jar with everted rim. Base not preserved. Total: 3.

753. Inv. No. C-71-301. Lot 252. Pl. 89.

P.H. 0.041. Est. D. rim 0.093. One fragment of rim and wall. Black slip.

Date: second half of the 2nd century B.C.

Form 17

Trefoil-mouth (squashed-rim) pitcher with one handle. No base preserved.

Cf. *EAA* 2, J.W. Hayes, "sigillata orientale A," 44, Form 105, fig. 9, no. 6, dated to the 1st century B.C. Total: 18.

754. Inv. No. C-70-121. Lot 829. Pl. 89.

P.H. 0.100. D. rim 0.052. Mended from numerous fragments, preserving rim, neck, handle, and shoulder. Convex collared rim. Single, strap handle. Red slip.

Date: first half of the 1st century B.C.

Form 18

Hydria or large pitcher with flaring wall and overhanging rim. Only rim and neck fragments preserved, making secure identification difficult in many cases. Some examples are unslipped while others are decorated with splashes of red or brown slip at rim and on exterior. Diameters at rim vary from 0.140 to 0.200 m., depending on overall size. Total: 58.

755. Lot 552, No. 681. Pl. 90.

P.H. 0.079. Est. D. rim 0.197. Several fragments of rim, neck, and handle mended. Unslipped.

Date: second and third quarters of the 1st century B.C.

756. Lot 610, No. 11. Pl. 90.

P.H. 0.041. Est. D. rim 0.140. One fragment of rim and wall. Unslipped.

Form 19

Two-handled jug with offset, grooved rim and ring base. Most examples are rim fragments only, but one complete example can be seen in the Early Roman section (**843**). Rim diameters range from 0.110 to 0.114 m. Total: 16.

757. Lot 134, No. 107. Pl. 90.
P.H. 0.050. Est. D. rim 0. 113. One fragment of rim, neck, and handle. Unslipped.

Form 20

Very large jar with narrow mouth. Only portions of rim and wall preserved. Total: 5.

758. Inv. No. C-72-306. Lot 547. Pl. 90.
P.H. 0.106. Est. D. rim 0.128. One fragment of rim and wall. Brown slip. Three grooves at shoulder.
Date: second and third quarters of the 1st century B.C.

Form 21

Large, close-mouthed jar. Rim may be straight, everted, or concave. No bases preserved. Diameters range from 0.150 to 0.300 m. depending on overall size. Total: 4.

759. Lot 140, No. 34. Pl. 90.
P.H. 0.040. Est. D. rim 0.148. One fragment of rim and wall. Unslipped.

760. Lot 547, No. 550. Pl. 90.
P.H. 0.032. Est. D. rim 0.220. One fragment of rim and wall. Red slip on exterior.

761. Lot 547, No. 549. Pl. 90.
P.H. 0.032. Est. D. rim 0.300. One fragment of rim and wall. Unslipped.

Form 22

Stamnos or water jar. Neatly finished complex profile of rim and neck. Two strap handles and moulded concave base ring. Base diameters range from 0.080 to 0.135 m., depending on size and height of vessel. These vessels are always unslipped.
Cf. Drougou and Touratsoglou, *Veroia*, 117–120, especially the moulded concave base of no. 1321, fig. 14. Total: 51 rims, 87 bases.

762. Inv. No. C-72-91. Lot 552. Pl. 90.
P.H. 0.124. D. rim 0.060. One fragment preserving most of rim and one handle.

763. Lot 75, No. 91. Pl. 90.
P.H. 0.024. Est. D. base 0.114. One fragment of base.

764. Lot 552, No. 1131. Pl. 90.
P.H. 0.053. Est. D. base 0.107. Three fragments of base mended.

765. Lot 552, No. 1142. Pl. 90.
P.H. 0.015. Est. D. base 0.120. One fragment of base.

Form 23

Incense burner with wide body and flanged rim. No bases preserved.
For the general form, see E. Ettlinger, *Römische Keramik aus dem Schutthügel von Vindonissa* (Basel 1952) taf. 8:143, but it is later. Cf. also Vegas, *Cerámica común*, fig. 58, Type 64:1. Total: 4.

766. Inv. No. C-72-285. Lot 552. Pl. 91.
P.H. 0.035. Est. D. rim 0.153. Two fragments mended, giving rim and small part of wall. Projecting flange has been pinched to form ruffle. Traces of reddish brown slip on exterior.

767. Inv. No. C-72-286. Lot 552. Pl. 91.
P.H. 0.027. Est. D. rim 0.151. One fragment of rim and wall. Twisted rope pattern decorates space between lip and flange. Unslipped.
Date for both examples: second and third quarters of the 1st century B.C.

Hellenistic wares: Other (**768–813**)

Dishes

768. Flat-based dish with overhanging rim. Inv. No. C-71-77. Lot 140. Pl. 91.
H. 0.024. Est. D. rim 0.195. Three pieces mended, giving complete profile. Fine, soft, micaceous pink (7.5YR 7/4) fabric. Thin red gloss worn away entirely on exterior and peeling on interior. Single circle of rouletting on floor.

769. Flat-based dish with overhanging rim. Inv. No. C-72-111. Lot 552. Pl. 91.
H. 0.029. Est. D. rim 0.320. Several pieces mended, giving profile and about one-fifth of

vessel. Fine, hard-fired, red (2.5YR 5/6) clay. Red slip.

770. Flat-based dish with overhanging rim. Inv. No. C-72-69. Lot 552. Pl. 91.

H. 0.040. Est. D. rim 0.360. One fragment giving complete profile. Micaceous reddish yellow (5YR 6/6) fabric with soapy red gloss on interior and rim exterior. Remainder of exterior and base very smooth but unslipped.

All three dishes above (**768–770**) are reminiscent of Pompeian Red Ware forms and slip. The fabric, however, is not the coarse cooking fabric associated with Pompeian Red Ware. All come from contexts dated to the first half of the 1st century B.C.

771. Flat-based dish with curving wall. Lot 555, No. 40. Pl. 91.

P.H. 0.026. Est. D. rim 0.320. Two fragments mended, giving profile. Unslipped.

Date: second and third quarters of the 1st century B.C.

Bowls / jars

772. Jar or beaker. Lot 1636, No. 43. Pl. 91.

P.H. 0.028. Est. D. rim 0.130. One fragment of rim and wall. Single groove on body. Unslipped.

Date: second half of the 2nd century B.C.

773. Jar or beaker. Inv. No. C-72-191. Lot 547. Pl. 91.

P.H. 0.055. Est. D. rim 0.110. Two fragments mended, giving rim and wall. Red slip. Incised wavy lines flanked by grooves on exterior.

Date: second and third quarters of the 1st century B.C.

774. Jar or bowl. Lot 550, No. 28. Pl. 91.

P.H. 0.030. Est. D. rim 0.132. One fragment of rim and wall. Unslipped.

Date: second and third quarters of the 1st century B.C.

775. Hemispherical bowl. Lot 547, No. 4. Pl. 91.

P.H. 0.048. Est. D. rim 0.100. One fragment of rim and wall. Interior moulding below pointed lip. Reddish brown to brown slip.

Cf. the series of Eastern Sigillata A bowls with interior mouldings in *Samaria*, fig. 80:15, Form 18, dated to pre-30 B.C.; *Tarsus*, fig. 188:295, unstratified; Thompson, "TCHP," fig. 118:D28, p. 437, dated to the mid-2nd century B.C.; Lamboglia Form 9, p. 149. See also Form 10 in the Hellenistic form typology. A similar form exists in glass: see J. W. Hayes, *Roman and Pre-Roman Glass in the Royal Ontario Museum* (Toronto 1975), fig. 1, no. 41, p. 18, dated to the lst century B.C.

Date: second and third quarters of the 1st century B.C.

776. Hemispherical bowl. Inv. No. C-71-256. Lot 251. Pl. 91.

H. 0.070. Est. D. rim 0.162. Mended from many fragments, giving complete profile and about half of vessel. Very thin walls with slightly incurving lip. High ring base. Red slip on interior and exterior with drips to the foot. Slip appears to have been applied with a brush.

777. Hemispherical bowl. Inv. No. C-71-284. Lot 75. Pl. 91.

H. 0.048. D. rim 0.093. Mended from several fragments, giving complete profile and approximately two-thirds of vessel. Moulding at lip exterior. High, flaring ring base. Red slip.

This appears to be an imitation of the Eastern Sigillata A bowl, *Samaria*, Form 16. This bowl and **776** come from contexts of the 2nd century B.C.

778. Bowl with ribbon band rim. Lot 549, No. 121. Pl. 92.

P.H. 0.027. Est. D. rim 0.242. One fragment of rim and wall. Discolored red to black slip.

This form is related to the Campanian ribbon band bowl. See Lamboglia, p. 195, Form 51; Taylor, "Cosa," B43A, pl. 38:A28, A29, pl. 24; Goudineau (1970), fig. 6, 69-187-4, 69-190-1, 69-190-24, dated to the second quarter of the 2nd century B.C. The form disappears by the 1st century B.C.

779. Carinated bowl. Lot 549, No. 80. Pl. 92.

P.H. 0.032. Est. D. rim 0.160. One fragment of rim and wall. Brown slip.

Date: second and third quarters of the 1st century B.C.

Jars

780. Small jar. Lot 829, No. 110. Pl. 92.

P.H. 0.025. Est. D. rim 0.113. One fragment of rim and wall. Unslipped.

Date: first half of the 1st century B.C.

781. Small jar. Lot 548, No. 12. Pl. 92.
P.H. 0.023. Est. D. rim 0.100. One fragment of rim and wall. Unslipped.
Date: second and third quarters of the 1st century B.C.

Pitchers

782. Small pitcher with spout. Lot 546, No. 1. Pl. 92.
P.H. 0.018. Est. D. rim 0.070. Three fragments of rim and neck. Unslipped.

783. Pitcher with moulded rim. Lot 831, No. 58. Pl. 92.
P.H. 0.044. Est. D. rim 0.040. Three fragments of rim, neck, and handle. Unslipped.
Date: first half of the 1st century B.C.

784. Small pitcher with moulded rim. Lot 547, No. 62. Pl. 92.
P.H. 0.038. Est. D. rim 0.025. Single fragment of rim, neck, and handle. Brown metallic slip.
Date: second and third quarters of the 1st century B.C.

785. Pitcher with carinated rim. Lot 831, No. 88. Pl. 92.
P.H. 0.070. Est. D. rim 0.040. One fragment of rim, neck, and handle.
Date: first half of the 1st century B.C.

786. Lagynos. Inv. No. C-74-262. Lot 1458. Grave 278. Pl. 93.
H. 0.162. D. rim 0.030. D. body 0.134. Mended from many fragments. Almost complete. Red slip on rim, neck, and shoulder with drips onto lower part of body, which is unslipped and very smooth.

787. Pitcher with straight, vertical rim. Lot 829, No. 199. Pl. 93.
P.H. 0.055. Est. D. rim 0.040. Two fragments mended to give rim, neck, and handle. Red slip.
Date: first half of the 1st century B.C.

788. Pitcher with wide mouth, narrow neck. Lot 262, No. 13. Pl. 93.
P.H. 0.077. Est. D. rim 0.088. Six fragments mended, giving rim, neck, and remains of one handle. Reddish brown metallic slip on exterior only.
Date: 1st century B.C.

789. Pitcher with wheel-ridged exterior. Inv. No. C-71-339. Lot 262. Pl. 93.
P.H. 0.090. Est. D. rim 0.136. Many fragments mended from rim and neck. Reddish brown slip on exterior. Entire preserved exterior of neck is covered with narrow wheel-ridging except for a space just below rim.
Date: 1st century B.C.

790. Jug with two handles. Inv. No. C-70-2. Lot 1025. Pl. 93.
H. 0.020. D. body 0.118. D. neck 0.046. Complete except for fragments missing at rim and neck. Unslipped. Concave base with long, narrow cutting for depositing coins. Cf. Drougou and Touratsoglou, *Veroia*, 117–120, figs. 13, 14.

Miscellaneous large vessels

791. Pitcher fragment. Lot 550, No. 75.
P.H. 0.026. Est. D. rim. 0.053. One fragment of rim, neck, and handle. Perhaps part of stamnos. Unslipped.

792. Large dish. Lot 74, No. 65.
P.H. 0.117. Est. D. 0240. One fragment of rim and wall. Outward-turned rim over plump body. Unslipped.

793. Basin. Lot 134, No. 12. Pl. 93
P.H. 0.057. Est. D. rim 0.270. One fragment of rim and wall. Unslipped.
Date: first half of the 1st century B.C.

794. Lid. Inv. No. C-72-289. Lot 552. Pl. 186.
P.H. 0.052. Th. 0.010. One large fragment. Knob and wide band on body painted reddish brown (5YR 5/4). Incised wavy line on exterior.
Date: second and third quarters of the 1st century B.C.

795. Stamped pithos rim. Inv. No. C-72-43. Lot 551. Pl. 186.
P.H. 0.077. Est. D. rim. 0.030. One fragment of flat rim with stamp.
Date: second and third quarters of the 1st century B.C.

796. Stand. Inv. No. C-72-26. Lot 547. Pl. 186.
H. 0.095. M.P.Dim. 0.072. Mended from two fragments. Unslipped. Four-sided pedestal on hollow square base.
Date: second and third quarters of the 1st century B.C.

Miscellaneous other shapes

797. Decorated sherd. Inv. No. C-72-14. Lot 609. Pl. 186.

M.P.Dim. 0.067. One fragment with red slip on interior and exterior. Globular body with incised wavy lines on shoulder. Small row of gouged depressions at carination.

798. Painted sherd. Inv. No. C-72-36. Lot 547. Pl. 186.

M.P.Dim. 0.059. One fragment of wall. Burnished on both surfaces. Design painted in dark red (2.5YR 3/6) on exterior and consists of spiral and diagonal lines.

799. Painted sherd. Inv. No. C-75-12. Lot 1637. Pl. 186.

M.P.Dim. 0.036. One fragment of wall. Linear decoration on exterior in red (10YR 4/8).

800. Krater. Lot 829, No. 103. Pl. 94.

P.H. 0.093. Est. D. rim 0.190. One fragment of rim, handle, and neck. Wide, horizontal rim with grooves, flaring neck, and high-rising, round handles placed horizontally. Unslipped.

Date: first half of the 1st century B.C.

801. Krater. Lot 552, No. 48. Pl. 94.

P.H. 0.057. Est. D. rim 0.240. One fragment of rim, wall, and handle. Unslipped except for diagonal strips of red slip below rim on exterior.

Date: second and third quarters of the 1st century B.C.

802. Large jar. Lot 547, No. 250. Pl. 94.

P.H. 0.073. Est. D. rim 0.340. One fragment of rim and wall. Unslipped except for traces of brown slip dripped over exterior surface.

Date: second and third quarters of the 1st century B.C.

803. Amphoriskos. Inv. No. C-71-207. Lot 250. Pl. 94.

H. 0.128. D. rim 0.044. Mended from many fragments, giving complete profile. About two-thirds preserved. Small vessel with plain rim curving out to pronounced shoulder. Small, flat base. Unslipped but very smooth surface with fine, shallow wheelmarks on body.

804. Amphoriskos. Inv. No. C-71-206. Lot 250. Pl. 94.

P.H. 0.105. Max. D. body 0.074. Mended from several fragments, preserving body and base. Brown metallic slip on exterior.

Date for **803**, **804**: second half of the 2nd century B.C.

805. Baby feeder/lamp filler. Inv. No. C-75-4. Grave 308. Pl. 94.

H. 0.063. D. body 0.075. D. base 0.039. Intact except for end of spout which was mended. Red slip on interior and exterior. Same form as **87** in black gloss but without as clear a profile.

806. Strainer fragment. Inv. No. C-72-179. Lot 552. Pl. 94.

P.H. 0.040. D. rim 0.080. D. body 0.090. D. base 0.065. Two fragments mended, giving upper profile. Brown slip.

807. Incense burner. Inv. No. C-74-212. Lot 1452, Grave 273. Pl. 94.

H. 0.093. D. rim 0.090. D. base 0.076. Intact except for two small fragments from rim. Unslipped and blackened on interior.

808. Incense burner. Inv. No. C-74-213. Lot 1453, Grave 273. Pl. 94.

H. 0.090. Est. D. rim 0.130. D. base 0.120. Mended from two pieces, giving about two-thirds of vessel. Unslipped.

809. Incense burner. Inv. No. C-74-282. Grave 288. Pl. 94.

H. 0.042. D. rim 0.130. D. base 0.120. Mended from several fragments and complete except for part of base, which has several chips missing. Diagonal slashes of white slip on foot. Black deposit on upper surface. A small hole (0.004 m. in diameter) was pierced through the floor from above.

Lids

810. Lid. Lot 250, No. 7. Pl. 95.

H. 0.058. Est. D. 0.150. Mended from several fragments, giving complete profile. Unslipped.

Date: second half of the 2nd century B.C.

811. Lid. Lot 552, No. 1239. Pl. 95.

H. 0.310. Est. D. 0.096. One fragment, giving complete profile. Two grooves on upper part of wall. Unslipped.

812. Lid. Lot 552, No. 1242. Pl. 95.

H. 0.037. Est. D. rim 0.120. Mended from several fragments, giving complete profile. Unslipped.

813. Lid. Lot 552, No. 1209. Pl. 95.
H. 0.063. Est. D. 0.154. Several fragments, giving profile. Unslipped.
Date for **811–813**: second and third quarters of the 1st century B.C.

Early Roman wares: Forms 1–18 (814–855)

Form 1

Flat-based dish with curved wall and outward-thickened rim. In some cases the rim is quite rounded and overhanging. The wall is frequently offset from the base, either at exterior or interior. Red slip is normal. Diameters range from 0.220 to 0.300 m. with some small examples measuring between 0.110 and 0.120 m.

This form is an imitation of an earlier Eastern Sigillata A form, *Samaria*, Form 10, fig. 79, pp. 329–331, dated to the 1st century B.C.; *Antioch*, Shapes 143, 144, dating to within the first three quarters of the 1st century B.C. Our examples date to the 1st century A.C. and also find parallels at Vindonissa. See E. Ettlinger, C. Simonett, and L. Ohlenroth, *Römische Keramik aus dem Schutthügel Vindonissa* (Basel 1952) taf. 16:375, dated to 33–101 A.C. Total: 42.

814. Lot 248, No. 115. Pl. 95.
H. 0.038. Est. D. rim 0.240. One fragment preserving complete profile. The wall of this example has an especially pronounced curve.

Form 2

Dish with curved wall and thickened rim with flat surface. No bases preserved. Red slip is normal. Diameters range from 0.310 to 0.338 m. Total: 6.

815. Lot 230. No. 60. Pl. 95.
P.H. 0.024. Est. D. rim 0.336. One fragment of rim.
Date: second half of the 1st century A.C.

Form 3

Small hemispherical bowl on ring base. Diameters range from 0.075 to 0.120 m. Slip colors vary from red to reddish yellow (5YR 7/6), reddish brown (5YR 5/4, 5/4), and black. Many examples have a metallic luster. Frequently the base is reserved. Total: 6.

816. Inv. No. C-71-285. Lot 260. Pl. 95.
H. 0.045. D. rim 0.096. D. base 0.047. Two fragments mended, giving complete profile. Red metallic slip mottled black in places. Base and area just above are reserved. Cf. *Samaria*, 295, Form 16, fig. 67, no. 10, dated late 1st century B.C.

817. Lot 1085, No. 201. Pl. 95.
H. 0.034. Est. D. rim 0.075. One fragment preserving complete profile. Red slip.

818. Lot 248, No. 81. Pl. 95.
P.H. 0.040. Est. D. rim 0.090. One fragment of rim and wall. Red slip.

Form 4

Large bowl with straight, thick wall. No base preserved. Diameters range from 0.240 to 0.310 m. Total: 10.

819. Lot 1419. No. 9. Pl. 96.
P.H. 0.040. Est. D. rim 0.311. One fragment of rim and wall with groove on interior. Red slip.

820. Lot 228, No. 68. Pl. 96.
P.H. 0.042. Est. D. rim 0.310. One fragment of rim and wall. Lip is concave at exterior. Single groove on interior. Red metallic slip.
Date: post-75 A.C.

821. Lot 230, No. 82. Pl. 96.
P.H. 0.028. Est. D. rim 0.306. One fragment of rim and wall. Single groove at exterior. Upper surface of rim is grooved. Red slip.

Form 5

Small bowl with grooved rim. No bases preserved. Total: 2.

822. Lot 231, No. 61. Pl. 96.
P.H. 0.031. Est. D. rim 0.100. Two fragments mended, giving rim and wall. Red slip.

Form 6

Small bowl with grooved rim. Ring base probable (on the analogy of the related Form 7), but none preserved. Upper surface of rim commonly has one or more grooves and is decorated with either applique floral decoration or rouletting. Variably fired red to black. Diameters range from 0.110 to 0.140 m. Total: 13.

823. Lot 248, No. 61. Pl. 96.
P.H. 0.022. Est. D. rim 0.130. One fragment of rim and wall. Fragments of petals preserved on rim. Red slip.

824. Lot 486, No. 11. Pl. 96.
P.H. 0.019. Est. D. rim 0.140. One fragment of rim and wall. Rouletting and barbotine floral decoration on rim. Red slip.

Form 7

Bowl with outward-thickened rim and ring or flat disc base. Walls tend to be rather thick. Diameters range from 0.090 to 0.160 m. for all except the very large example, **827**. Slip is usually red, but some have been fired brown or black and have metallic luster. Total: 16.

825. Inv. No. C-74-17. Lot 1092. Grave 260. Pl. 96.
H. 0.038. D. rim 0.090. Mended and almost complete. Badly peeling red slip with sections fired or burned black.

826. Inv. No. C-71-11. Lot 381, Grave 28. Pl. 96.
H. 0.053. D. rim 0.135. About two-thirds preserved of profile. Worn brown slip. A single hole was made through the center of the base at some time after its manufacture.

827. Inv. No. C-71-17. Lot 386, Grave 38. Pl. 96.
H. 0.120. D. rim 0.310. Mended and almost complete. Unusually large variant. Interior and upper part of exterior slipped reddish brown (5YR 5/4). Faint wheel-ridging visible on exterior.

828. Inv. No. C-71-38. Lot 391, Grave 39. Pl. 96.
H. 0.050. D. rim 0.130. Mended and almost complete. Worn red slip. Single groove on floor.

Form 8

Bowl with rolled rim. No bases preserved. Diameters range from approximately 0.145 to 0.220 m. All examples have red slip.

Cf. Robinson, *Agora*, G174, pl. 67, dated to the late 1st, early 2nd century A.C. For the date of Deposit G, see Hayes, "Corinth," 425. See also Hayes, "Paphos," fig. 4, no. 10, dated to the late 1st century A.C. Total: 13.

829. Lot 1418, No. 22. Pl. 96.
P.H. 0.042. Est. D. rim 0.146. One fragment of rim and wall. Red slip.

Form 9

Bowl or dish with overhanging rim, triangular in section. No bases preserved. Red slip is normal. Diameters range from 0.145 m. for small, thinner-walled examples to 0.245 m. for larger examples.

This form is related to Eastern Sigillata B2, *EAA* 2, J.W. Hayes, "sigillata orientale B," Forms 60 and 76, dated late 1st to mid-2nd centuries A.C. Total: 4.

830. Lot 384, No. 1. Pl. 96.
P.H. 0.033. Est. D. rim 0.244. One fragment of rim and wall with two grooves on interior. Red slip.

831. Lot 1417, No. 14. Pl. 96.
P.H. 0.028. Est. D. rim 0.155. One fragment of rim and wall. Single groove below rim on interior and exterior. Red slip.

Form 10

Imitation terra sigillata small carinated bowl or bell cup with ring base. All have carinated rim, some with grooves, others plain. Red slip is normal. Diameters range from 0.075 to 0.160 m. Total: 29.

832. Lot 230, No. 70. Pl. 97.
P.H. 0.023. Est. D. rim 0.110. One fragment of rim and wall. Red slip.
Date: second half of the 1st century A.C.

833. Inv. No. C-71-302. Lot 248. Pl. 97.
H. 0.066. Est. D. rim 0.144. Three fragments mended, giving complete profile. Badly chipped and discolored over most of surface but had red slip originally. Two grooves on rim exterior. Part of roughly made *planta pedis* preserved on floor.
Cf. the Arretine Form 23 seen in Hayes, "Corinth," pl. 84, nos. 71, 72.
Date: post-75 A.C.

834. Lot 488, No. 5. Pl. 97.
P.H. 0.038. Est. D. rim 0.075. One fragment of rim and wall. Red slip.
Cf. the Çandarli Form A6b in *EAA* 2, J.W. Hayes, "ceramica di Çandarli," fig. 16, no. 8; also

Hayes, "Paphos," fig. 3:25, dated to the first half of the first century A.C. See also Schäfer (1962), Abb. 2:22; and most recently, *Pergamon 6*, 114, Taf. 6, no. 40, dated second half of the 1st century B.C. to first half of the 1st century A.D.

835. Lot 258, No. 20. Pl. 97.

P.H. 0.036. Est. D. rim 0.081. One fragment of rim and wall. Well-worn red slip.

Cf. Hayes, "Corinth," pl. 85, 119 in Arretine; also see *Antioch*, pp. 34, 38, Shape 453, in Eastern Sigillata A, dated 25 B.C. to 25 A.C.

Form 11

Bowl with flanged rim and ring base. All have red or brown slip. Diameters range from very small examples at 0.085 m. to very large bowls with diameters ranging from 0.210 to 0.275 m.

The flanged bowl is found in most of the terra sigillata wares such as Arretine, Çandarli, and Eastern Sigillata A and B, and the local bowls imitate one or another of these depending upon rim shape and details. For the Arretine form, see Goudineau, pp. 39–43, Type 38b (post-20 A.C.), 183, 184, 227, C-2A-63 through C-26-67, p. 215, C-2B-129 through C-2B-131; Hayes, "Corinth," form 27, dated to 45 A.C. and later. For the Çandarli form, see *EAA* 2, J.W. Hayes, "Ceramica di Çandarli," L19, fig. 17, nos. 5, 6, and 7. For Eastern Sigillata A, see Robinson, *Agora*, G74, pl. 66, and G13, 14, pl. 61, dated to the first half of the 1st century A.C.; also Hayes, "Paphos," figs. 7:5, 4:27. Total: 39.

836. Lot 545, No. 89. Pl. 97.

P.H. 0.028. Est. D. rim 0.130. One fragment of rim and wall. Single groove at lip interior. Red slip.

837. Inv. No. C-71-155. Lot 43, Grave 80. Pl. 97.

P.H. 0.040. Est. D. rim 0.086. Almost complete. Traces of reddish brown (2.5YR 5/4) slip, but most of surface is discolored, probably from burning.

838. Inv. No. C-74-460. Lot 1501. Pl. 97.

P.H. 0.044. Est. D. rim 0.160. One fragment of rim and wall. Very small flange and rounded lip. Red slip.

839. Inv. No. C-74-252. Lot 1453, Grave 62. Pl. 98.

H. 0.085. D. rim 0.210. Mended and almost complete. Well-worn, reddish brown (5YR 5/4) slip discolored on much of surface. Rounded lip with single groove on exterior and very prominent flange.

840. Inv. No. C-74-251. Lot 1453, Grave 62. Pls. 98, 187.

H. 0.107. D. rim 0.275. Almost complete. Originally covered with red slip on interior and upper part of exterior, now discolored gray to reddish brown. Flat lip with groove and prominent flange.

Form 12

Cup with one handle and either carinated or globular body. Base not preserved, but on analogy with Thin-Walled cups of similar shape, a flat base is likely. Diameters range from 0.080 to 0.130 m. Total: 12.

841. Inv. No. C-71-343. Lot 75. Pl. 97.

P.H. 0.055. Est. D. rim 0.080. Five fragments mended, giving rim, side wall, and one handle. Single groove on rim exterior just below lip. Weak red (10R 4/2 to 4/3 to 5/4 mixed) and black mottled, metallic slip.

842. Inv. No. C-71-344. Lot 249. Pl. 97.

P.H. 0.050. Est. D. rim 0.120. Two fragments mended, giving rim, wall, and handle. Red slip.

Date: post-75 A.C.

Form 13

Tall jar with everted rim, double handles, and ring base. Only one complete example preserved (below: **843**). Some examples have red or reddish brown slip on the lip and exterior, others are unslipped. Diameters range from 0.110 to 0.160 m. Total: 33.

843. Inv. No. C-74-455. Lot 1099. Grave 266. Pl. 98.

H. 0.190. D. rim 0.130. Mended from many pieces and now two-thirds complete and restored. Unslipped. Found in the same grave context was the lid (C-74-456), not described in the catalogue, but visible in Pl. 98, suggesting the vessel's function as an urn.

Form 14

Jar with folded rim. The rim may be squared off or overhanging. No bases preserved. The rim is usually slipped and the body plain except for one or more horizontal stripes just below the rim. Slip varies in color from red to brown. Diameters range from 0.100 to 0.160 m. Total: 57.

844. Lot 248, No. 40. Pl. 98.
P.H. 0.038. Est. D. rim 0.100. One fragment of rim and wall. Two grooves on exterior just below rim. Metallic red slip on lower half of rim exterior.
Date: post-85 A.C.

845. Lot 1089, No. 30. Pl. 98.
P.H. 0.024. Est. D. rim 0.160. One fragment of rim and wall. Brown slip on lower half of rim exterior.

Form 15

Large basin with wide, flat rim and oval body. The base is usually flat except for the center, which is concave. This form becomes especially popular in the 2nd and 3rd centuries A.C. (MR Form 32). Total: 7.

846. Inv. No. C-71-31. Lot 386. Pls. 99, 187.
H. 0.182. Max. D. rim 0.362. Min. D. rim 0.200. D. base 0.178. Almost complete. Unslipped.

Form 16

Large jar with globular body and folded rim. One example preserves ring base. Partially slipped or with several stripes of colored slip below rim. Rim form is similar to that of Form 14. Diameters range from 0.140 to 0.200 m. It is frequently difficult to distinguish between examples of Form 14 and this form if part of the side wall is not preserved along with the rim to show the wall angle. Total: 3.

847. Inv. No. C-74-516. Lot 1417. Pl. 98.
P.H. 0.213. Est. D. rim 0.160. D. base 0.098. Two large pieces each mended from several fragments, preserving almost complete profile. Unslipped except for brown stripes just below rim.

848. Lot 1418, No. 15. Pl. 99.
P.H. 0.050. Est. D. rim 0.160. One fragment of rim and wall. Single groove on exterior. Broad stripe of red slip under rim.

Form 17

Very large, close-mouthed jar. No bases preserved. Unslipped or partial red or brown slip. Diameters range from 0.200 to 0.230 m. Total: 9.

849. Lot 259, No. 84. Pl. 99.
P.H. 0.025. Est. D. rim 0.202. One fragment of rim. Unslipped.
Date: early 1st century A.C.

850. Lot 1538, No. 9. Pl. 99.
P.H. 0.033. Est. D. rim 0.223. One fragment of rim and wall. Unslipped.

Form 18

Stamnos or small water jar with double-ridged strap handles and concave, moulded base with central boss. Unslipped. Wheel-ridging visible on interior and exterior of vessel. Diameters of mouth range from approxiately 0.045 to 0.065 m. The two complete examples suggest a height between 0.400 and 0.500 m. Total: 17 rims, 73 bases.

851. Inv. No. C-74-270. Lot 1095. Pl. 101.
P.H. 0.115. D. rim 0.050. One fragment of neck with one complete and one fragmentary handle.

852. Inv. No. C-71-127. Grave 60. Pl. 100.
H. 0.430. D. rim 0.054. D. body 0.220. D. base 0.103. Almost complete except for several fragments from body.

853. Inv. No. C-71-201. Grave 45. Pl. 100.
H. 0.500. D. rim 0.060. D. body 0.260. D. base 0.120. Mended from many fragments, preserving complete profile and about three-fourths of vessel.

854. Lot 486, No. 43. Pl. 100.
P.H. 0.020. Est. D. base 0.120. One fragment of base with small foot and deep, concave underside.

855. Lot 1098, No. 17. Pl. 100.
P.H. 0.017. Est. D. base 0.098. One fragment of flat base with concave center.

Early Roman wares: Other (**856–910**)

Dishes / plates

856. Plate with offset rim. Lot 1098, No. 3. Pl. 101.

P.H. 0.023. Est. D. rim 0.310. One fragment of rim and wall. This piece has a rather sharp profile but is similar to an Eastern Sigillata A plate with wide, offset rim and angular side in *Samaria* (Form 3, fig. 77:1, dated to pre-30 B.C.). See also *EAA* 2, J.W. Hayes, "sigillata orientale A" Form 6.

857. Plate with flaring rim. Inv. No. C-72-11. Lot 546. Pl. 101.

H. 0.048. Est. D. rim 0.320. Three fragments mended, giving complete profile. Hard fired with sharp-edged profile. Red slip. Curved body on short ring base. The border of the rim is decorated with dot and comma-shaped appliqués while the exterior edge carries rouletting.

Imitation Eastern Sigillata B2, *EAA* 2, J.W. Hayes, "sigillata orientale B," Form 78; Robinson, *Agora*, pl. 65:G50, dated to the first half of the 1st century A.C. For the date of Deposit G, see Hayes, "Corinth," 42.

858. Plate with flaring rim. Inv. No. C-70-18. Lot 465. Pl. 101.

H. 0.037. Est. D. rim 0.284. One fragment giving complete profile. Same shape as **857** above but with sharp division between rim and body. Discolored from probable exposure to fire. Feather rouletting at floor center.

859. Shallow dish with flaring rim. Lot 1093, No. 2. Pl. 101.

P.H. 0.027. Est. D. rim 0.340. One fragment of rim and wall. Very thick walls and hard fired. Red slip.

This form is similar to an Arretine form at Magdalensberg; cf. Goudineau, p. 53, Type 14, but the Stobi form has a shorter rim and grooves on the exterior. The Magdalensberg form is dated to the third quarter of the 1st century B.C.

860. Dish with flat rim. Lot 1497, No. 4. Pl. 101.

H. 0.028. Est. D. rim 0.240. One fragment giving complete profile. Red slip. Similar to *Samaria*, Form 5, plate with short rim, flat on top, fig. 77:3. Also see *Antioch*, Shape 105, pl. 3.

861. Plate with straight wall on flat base. Lot 259, No. 62. Pl. 101.

H. 0.030. Est. D. rim 0.313. One fragment giving complete profile. Red slip. Perhaps imitation terra sigillata.

See Goudineau Form 1, p. 371, B-3-29, p. 111, and B-2C-21, p. 125. Also "Magdalensberg," Abb. 2, p. 69, 1, period 4, dated late Augustan to ca. 10 A.D.

862. Plate with straight wall on flat base. Lot 1416, No. 21. Pl. 101.

H. 0.025. Est. D. rim 0.215. One fragment giving complete profile. Red slip. Shape as **861** above.

863. Plate with moulded rim. Lot 392, No. 12. Pl. 103.

P.H. 0.020. Est. D. rim 0.200. One fragment of rim and wall. Red slip.

Imitation terra sigillata related to Arretine plate Form 8 in Hayes, "Corinth," pl. 82:24, dated 20–45 A.C.

864. Plate with flaring, moulded wall. Lot 231, No. 23. Pl. 102.

P.H. 0.018. Est. D. rim 0.161. One fragment of rim and wall. Red slip. Imitation terra sigillata.

See Çandarli plate in Schäfer (1962) 777–802, Abb. 1:11 and 12. Also see the Arretine Form 8 in Hayes, "Corinth."

865. Plate with flaring, moulded wall. Lot 231, No. 21. Pl. 102.

P.H. 0.028. Est. D. rim 0.340. One fragment of rim and wall. Red slip. Large example of the same form as **864** above.

866. Large platter with moulded wall. Lot 257, No. 66. Pl. 102.

P.H. 0.033. Est. D. rim 0.360. One fragment of rim and wall. Red slip.

Cf. Çandarli rims in Schäfer (1962) 783, Abb. 1:14 and 12. Our example has much thicker walls than the original Çandarli form it copies.

867. Plate with moulded rim. Lot 1418, No. 89. Pl. 103.

P.H. 0.020. Est. D. rim 0.130. One fragment of rim and wall. Red slip.

Perhaps related to Hayes, "Corinth," Form 12, dated to 40 A.C. and after.

868. Plate with double convex wall. Lot 1441, No. 4. Pl. 103.

P.H. 0.027. Est. D. rim 0.260. Two fragments of rim and wall. Red slip. This is probably another terra sigillata imitation. Upper rim section decorated with faint rouletting.

Cf. Hayes, "Corinth," Form 11, pl. 83, nos. 31 and 32, dated to 40 A.C. and after.

869. Plate with double curved rim. Inv. No. C-74-33. Lot 1511. Pl. 103.

P.H. 0.022. Est. D. rim 0.178. One fragment of rim and wall. Red slip. Wide band of rouletting on upper part of rim, narrow strip of rouletting at carination.

Terra sigillata imitation. See Arretine, Goudineau Form 23, and Hayes, "Corinth," Form 4. For Eastern Sigillata A, see *Samaria*, fig. 79, Form 13, dated Augustan, and *Antioch*, Shape 412.

870. Large plate with overhanging rim. Lot 44, No. 2. Pl. 102.

H. 0.025. Est. D. rim 0.395. One fragment, giving complete profile. Red slip.

871. Flat-based dish with curved wall. Inv. No. C-71-504. Lot 231. Pl. 102.

H. 0.045. Est. D. rim 0.365. One fragment, giving complete profile. Red slip.

872. Large dish with incurved wall. Inv. No. C-71-330. Lot 257. Pl. 102.

H. 0.045. Est. D. rim 0.340. One fragment of rim and wall. Small groove on rim surface. Red, glossy slip.

873. Dish with incurving wall. Inv. No. C-71-331. Lot 248. Fig. 102.

P.H. 0.035. Est. D. rim 0.234. One fragment of rim and wall. Slight inset on interior where wall meets floor. Reddish brown to red metallic slip.

Cf. Goudineau Form 30b; Hayes, "Corinth," Form 6, pl. 82, dated 15–65 A.C.

Bowls

874. Tall bowl with vertical wall. Lot 811, No. 35. Pl. 103.

H. 0.073. Est. D. rim 0.080. Vessel is more than half complete. Red slip. Double grooves below rim and at carination.

Related to Moevs, "Cosa," Forms 43 and 48.

875. Tall bowl with vertical wall. Lot 248, No. 2. Pl. 103.

P.H. 0.029. Est. D. rim 0.100. One fragment of rim and wall. Red slip. Single groove below rim and on wall. Fine rouletting covers space between the two grooves.

Date: post-75 A.C.

876. Bowl with incurved wall. Lot 1417, No. 23. Pl. 104.

P.H. 0.027. Est. D. rim 0.100. One fragment of rim and wall. Red slip. Rim is flattened on top with deep groove on exterior.

877. Bowl with incurved wall. Inv. No. C-71-35. Lot 451. Pl. 104.

H. 0.061. D. rim 0.163. Several pieces mended, about three-fourths complete. Dull brown slip on interior and upper part of exterior. Very thick, curving walls on low ring base. Rim is flattened on upper surface. Wheel-ridging visible on both surfaces.

878. Deep bowl with incurved wall. Lot 1078, No. 1. Pl. 104.

P.H. 0.053. Est. D. rim 0.170. One fragment of rim and wall. Red slip. Deep groove below rim.

879. Carinated dish. Lot 1419, No. 5. Pl. 104.

P.H. 0.045. Est. D. rim 0.210. One fragment of rim and wall. Red slip.

880. Krater on pedestal foot. Inv. No. C-75-1. Grave 310. Pls. 104, 187.

H. 0.164. D. rim 0.130. Mended and two-thirds complete, giving full profile. Dark reddish brown (5YR 3/4) slip. Fine dot rouletting encircles the vessel at the shoulder. Deep, globular bowl with sharply undercut rim and hollow two-tiered foot.

Imitation of Arretine or green lead-glazed krater form.

881. Krater rim. Lot 259, No. 73. Pl. 104.

P.H. 0.051. Est. D. rim 0.132. One fragment of rim and wall. Red slip.

Date: early 1st century A.C.

882. Bowl with double convex profile. Lot 1080, No. 1. Pl. 105.

P.H. 0.044. Est. D. rim 0.127. One fragment of rim and wall. Glossy yellowish red (5YR 5/6) slip.

See *Antioch*, 38, pl. 5, Shape 450, Roman Pergamene, dated the first quarter of the 1st century B.C. to first quarter of the lst century A.C.; for the Arretine, see Goudineau Form 32, dated 5–10 A.C.

883. Large bowl. Lot 259, No. 89. Pl. 102.

P.H. 0.070. Est. D. rim 0.300. One large fragment of rim and wall. Unslipped. Slight carination below rim.

Date: early 1st century A.C.

884. Large bowl. Lot 230, No. 90. Pl. 102.

P.H. 0.082. Est. D. rim 0.190. One fragment of rim and wall with sharp carination. Unslipped.

Date: second half of the 1st century A.C.

885. Large lekanis. Lot 384, No. 12. Pl. 102.
P.H. 0.045. Est. D. rim 0.320. One fragment of rim, wall, and horizontal handle. Red slip. Flat grooved rim with handles just below.

Jars

886. Small jar. Lot 248, No. 74. Pl. 104.
P.H. 0.038. Est. D. rim 0.080. One fragment of rim and wall. Unslipped. Simple everted rim and wide, flat ridge on shoulder.
Date: post-75 A.C.

887. Short jar with sharply carinated body. Lot 39, No. 3. Pl. 104.
P.H. 0.040. Est. D. rim 0.102. Several fragments mended. Unslipped except for traces of white paint.

888. Pitcher. Lot 399, No. 1. Pl. 105.
P.H. 0.036. Est. D. rim 0.032. One fragment of rim, neck and traces of two handles. Unslipped.

889. Small pitcher with one handle. Lot 1418, No. 134. Pl. 105.
P.H. 0.036. Est. D. rim 0.035. One fragment of rim, neck, and handle. Black slip.

890. Pitcher with one handle. Inv. No. C-74-318. Lot 1465. Pl. 105.
H. 0.180. D. rim 0.047. Several fragments mended, giving complete vessel except base. Light red (2.5YR 6/6) slip on rim and shoulder, unslipped below.
Cf. *Tarsus*, fig. 170:D; 280, Inc. Bonjoan, no. 1, dated to the Tiberio-Claudian period.

891. Jar. Lot 486, No. 83. Pl. 105.
P.H. 0.042. Est. D. rim 0.063. Several fragments mended. Unslipped.

892. Pitcher with one handle. Lot 389, No. 1. Pl. 105.
P.H. 0.117. Est. D. rim 0.100. Several fragments mended, giving rim, neck, handle, and part of globular body. Reddish brown (5YR 5/4) slip on rim, neck, and upper part of body.

893. Pitcher with one handle. Lot 401, No. 5. Pl. 105.
P.H. 0.077. Est. D. rim 0.066. Several fragments mended, giving rim, neck, part of body, and handle attachments. Smaller version of **892** above with rounded instead of everted rim. Brown slip.

894. Pitcher. Lot 391, No. 3. Pl. 106.
P.H. 0.214. Est. D. rim 0.099. Est. D. body 0.165. Mended from several fragments. Rim, neck, and body in one section, base in another, not joining. Discolored very dark gray.

895. Jar. Lot 391, No. 4. Pl. 106.
H. 0.165. Est. D. rim 0.093. Est. D. body 0.150. Mended from several fragments, giving complete profile. One groove below rim and two widely spaced grooves on body. Red slip on rim, neck, and upper part of body.

896. Jar. Lot 248, No. 27. Pl. 105.
P.H. 0.075. Est. D. rim 0.096. One fragment with rim, neck, and handle attachment. Dark gray slip.

897. Squat jar. Inv. No. C-75-2. Grave 310. Pl. 106.
H. 0.143. D. rim 0.076. Mended and three-fourths complete. Unslipped except for a wide strip of mottled brown slip on the shoulder. Very squat, globular body on ring base. Two strap handles extend from flaring rim to shoulder.

898. Large pot. Inv. No. C-70-62. Grave 13. Pl. 106.
H. 0.230. D. rim 0.165. Mended from several fragments. Part of body, one handle, and rim missing. Unslipped.
W-MZ (1971) 404–405.
Several glass unguentaria and one mould-blown Sidonian glass bottle, G-70-18, published by D. Stojanović, "Zwei Reliefglaser von Sidon aus Stobi," *Macedoniae Acta Archaeologica* 3 (1977) 117–123, were found in this vessel.

899. Large jar. Lot 1098, No. 4. Pl. 107.
P.H. 0.030. Est. D. rim 0.190. One fragment of rim and neck. Wide lid seating or groove on rim. Unslipped.

900. Jar with convex grooved rim. Lot 1087, No. 3. Pl. 107.
P.H. 0.047. Est. D. rim 0.175. Several fragments mended, giving rim, wall, and one handle attachment. Red to reddish brown slip.

901. Jar with double handles. Lot 229, No. 5. Pl. 107.
P.H. 0.047. Est. D. rim 0.170. Several fragments mended, giving rim, body and handles. Unslipped.
Date: second half of the 1st century A.C.

902. Jar with double handles. Lot 486, No. 10. Pl. 106.

P.H. 0.088. Est. D. rim 0.100. Several fragments of rim, body, and handles mended. Dark brown slip with metallic luster.

903. Large jar with overhanging rim. Lot 230, No. 15. Pl. 107.

P.H. 0.035. Est. D. rim 0.290. One fragment of rim and wall. Unslipped.

Date: second half of the 1st century A.C.

904. Large jar. Lot 1454, No. 4. Pl. 107.

P.H. 0.065. Est. D. rim 0.202. One large fragment of rim and wall. Unslipped. Rope appliqué at shoulder carination.

905. Large jar. Lot 231, No. 135. Pl. 107.

P.H. 0.060. Est. D. rim 0.182. One fragment of rim and wall. Unslipped.

Date: second half of the 1st century A.C.

906. Large jar. Lot 488, No. 11. Pl. 107.

P.H. 0.035. Est. D. rim 0.206. One fragment of rim and wall. Unslipped.

907. Large jar. Lot 18, No. 12. Pl. 107.

P.H. 0.037. Est. D. rim 0.221. One fragment of rim and wall. Unslipped.

Lids

908. Lid. Lot 249, No. 155. Pl. 107.

P.H. 0.030. Est. D. top 0.040. One fragment. Unslipped.

Date: post-75 A.C.

909. Lid. Lot 1416, No. 1. Pl. 107.

H. 0.020. D. 0.090. Single fragment, two-thirds complete with profile. Unslipped.

910. Lid. Inv. No. C-74-317. Lot 1469. Pl. 107.

P.H. 0.027. Est. D. 0.082. Several fragments with complete profile preserved.

Middle Roman wares: Forms 1–34 (**911–1016**)

Form 1

Dish with broad, flat rim and usually one or more grooves, normally at interior or exterior of rim. Rim surface may be curved, at an upward angle, or both. The base is flat or slightly concave on some examples. On interior, the floor is frequently inset from side wall and marked by a groove. Diameters range primarily from 0.170 to 0.280 m., although there are some examples as large as 0.330 m.

The earliest examples come from deposits belonging to the 3rd century. The latest examples found in any quantity (there are individual examples that are probably survival pieces in deposits of the late 4th century A.C. or later) belong to deposits of the mid-4th century A.C. Cf. African Red Slip Hayes Forms 32, 58, and 59, dated 3rd century to ca. 400 A.C. Also Brukner, *Rimska Keramika* T.94/173, dated 4th century A.C.

Date: 200–350 A.C. Total: 50.

911. Lot 1310, No. 1. Pl. 108.

H. 0.044. Est. D. rim 0.240. One fragment preserving almost complete profile. Rim almost convex, and bottom is concave. Red-slipped surface.

912. Inv. No. C-74-261. Lot 1307. Pl. 108.

H. 0.034. Est. D. rim 0.196. One fragment giving profile. Horizontal rim surface with groove at both interior and exterior. Red-slipped surface.

913. Inv. No. C-74-55. Lot 1298. Pl. 108.

H. 0.039. Est. D. rim 0.200. Three fragments mended, giving profile. Rim has slight upward angle with groove at exterior. Groove separates wall from floor, and base is slightly concave. Red-slipped surface.

914. Inv. No. C-71-72. Lot 237. Pl. 108.

H. 0.038. Est. D. rim 0.236. One fragment giving profile. Horizontal rim surface with wide, shallow groove at interior. Interior wall thickens near join with floor, producing inset. Flat base. Red-slipped surface.

915. Inv. No. C-70-40. Lot 482. Pl. 108.

H. 0.043. Est. D. rim 0.230. One fragment of rim, wall, and base, giving most of profile. Short, horizontal rim with shallow groove on surface. This example apparently has a short ring base, otherwise unknown for this shape. Red-slipped surface.

Form 2

Dish with short, flat rim, frequently grooved on top, perhaps versions of Form 1, or a deeper vessel. Base not preserved. Diameters range from 0.230 to 0.270 m.

Date: late 2nd to early 4th centuries A.C. Total: 23.

916. Inv. No. C-78-100. Lot 2173. Pl. 108.
P.H. 0.040. Est. D. rim 0.260.

917. Lot 1296, No. 197. Pl. 108.
P.H. 0.043. Est. D. rim 0.260. One fragment of rim and wall. Reddish brown (2.5YR 4/4) slip.

Form 3

Dish with broad, flat rim, cut so that parts of the rim are very wide and generally scalloped in outline. Concave moulding below rim. No bases preserved. Diameters range from 0.275 to 0.410 m.

Date: 3rd and 4th centuries A.C. Total: 5.

918. Lot 238, No. 39. Pl. 108.
P.H. 0.035. Est. D. rim 0.275. One fragment of rim and wall. Red-slipped surface.

Form 4

Shallow dish with wide, flaring rim, curved body. No base preserved. Diameters are usually 0.270 or 0.280 m.

Date: 3rd to 4th centuries A.C. Total: 8.

919. Lot 1407, No. 58. Pl. 109.
P.H. 0.034. Est. D. rim 0.280. One fragment of rim and wall. Reddish yellow (7.5YR 6/6) slip.

Form 5

Flat-based dish with straight or slightly flaring wall rising to plain rim with tapering lip. Flat, grooved, or sometimes concave bottom. On some examples the lip is thickened or grooved on interior wall. Rim diameters range from 0.174 to 0.330 m.

Cf. African Red Slip Hayes Form 50.

Date: late 2nd to mid-4th centuries A.C. Total: 77.

920. Inv. No. C-70-156. Lot 800. Pl. 109.
H. 0.045. Est. D. rim 0.222. One fragment of profile. This example has very thin walls and most closely resembles the African Red Slip form. Red-slipped surfaces.

921. Inv. No. C-74-273. Lot 1328.
H. 0.040. Est. D. rim 0.279. One fragment preserving profile. This example has a rather pointed rim, and the vessel wall varies in thickness. Light red (2.5YR 6/8) slip.

922. Inv. No. C-74-198. Lot 1302. Pl. 109.
H. 0.045. Est. D. rim 0.285. One fragment of profile. The lip on this example is almost flat, and the side walls are rather thick. Light red (2.5YR 6/8) slip.

923. Lot 1295, No. 100.
H. 0.032. Est. D. rim 0.174. One fragment. Wall offset from floor. Red-slipped surfaces.

924. Inv. No. C-74-208. Lot 1297. Pl. 109.
H. 0.039. Est. D. rim 0.177. One fragment preserving profile. Single groove on interior just below thickened rim. Reddish brown (2.5YR 5/4) slip.

925. Lot 238, No. 31. Pl. 109.
H. 0.040. Est. D. rim 0.180. One fragment of complete profile. Rim slightly inturned with a series of three grooves on upper part of interior wall.

926. Lot 929, No. 103. Pl. 109.
H. 0.044. Est. D. rim 0.187. One fragment preserving complete profile. Single groove just at interior rim edge.

927. Inv. No. C-74-52. Lot 1296. Pl. 109.
H. 0.034. Est. D. rim 0.220. One fragment of profile. Pointed lip acceptable for form but rather more curved wall, so that this example might almost belong in Form 6. Double-grooved base has become almost a foot. Red-slipped.

Form 6

Flat-based dish with curved wall and slightly incurved plain rim. Base is either flat or grooved and sometimes concave. On some examples the interior wall is offset from the floor. Diameters range from 0.185 to 0.330 m.

Date: late 2nd to early or mid-4th century A.C. Total: 74.

928. Inv. No. C-71-71. Lot 238. Pl. 109.
H. 0.051. Est. D. rim 0.290. Three fragments mended, giving profile. Dull red slip.

929. Inv. No. C-74-320. Lot 1307. Pl. 109.
H. 0.050. Est. D. rim 0.265. Two fragments mended, giving profile. Red slip.

930. Inv. No. C-74-201. Lot 1301. Pl. 110.
H. 0.040. Est. D. rim 0.194. One fragment preserving profile. Two grooves on exterior, below rim. Red slip.

931. Inv. No. C-73-35. Lot 881. Pl. 110.
H. 0.033. Est. D. rim 0.229. Mended from twelve fragments, giving profile. Grooved base with short foot and offset between wall and floor on interior. Two grooves just below rim on exterior. Red slip.

932. Inv. No. C-74-77. Lot 1296. Pl. 110.
H. 0.035. Est. D. rim 0.187. One fragment of profile. Interior wall offset from floor. Slightly concave base. Red slip.

933. Inv. No. C-72-13. Lot 762. Pl. 110.
H. 0.043. Est. D. rim 0.220. Mended. Metallic red slip. Wheel-ridging on exterior.

Form 7

Shallow dish with straight wall, often curved inward at lip; probably a low ring base. Diameters range from 0.145 to 0.275 m.

Cf. Çandarli Hayes Form 4.

Date: late 2nd to late 4th centuries A.C.(?). Total: 71.

934. Lot 1296, No. 363. Pl. 110.
P.H. 0.028. Est. D. rim 0.213. One fragment of rim and wall. Two shallow grooves on wall interior. Red slip.

935. Lot 239, No. 27. Pl. 110.
P.H. 0.036. Est. D. rim 0.260. One fragment of rim and wall. Red slip.

Form 8

Flat-based dish with straight or concave flaring wall and tall, vertical or inturned rim, frequently with overhang and/or groove on interior. Diameters range from 0.150 to 0.390 m.

The form was ultimately derived from Eastern Sigillata B2 Form 60 but is common at Stobi and elsewhere from the mid-2nd to early 4th centuries A.C. See Hayes, "Villa Dionysus," 128, 129, nos. 122, 123, and Robinson, *Agora*, G176, pl. 67, and K13, pl. 68, mid-2nd to mid-3rd centuries A.C.

Date: 2nd to 4th centuries A.C. Total: 110.

936. Lot 1310, No. 6. Pl. 111.
H. 0.040. Est. D. rim 0.152. One profile fragment. Very slight overhang on curved rim. Single groove on bottom. Red slip.

937. Lot 1307, No. 31. Pl. 111.
P.H. 0.044. Est. D. rim 0.215. One fragment of rim and wall. Rounded rim edge with clear overhang and inset at interior. No base preserved. Red slip.

938. Inv. No. C-73-36. Lot 881. Pl. 111.
H. 0.053. Est. D. rim 0.223. One fragment of profile. Pointed lip and rim overhang with groove at interior. Reddish brown (2.5YR 5/4) slip.

939. Inv. No. C-74-322. Lot 1307. Pl. 111.
H. 0.040. Est. D. rim 0.184. Three fragments mended, giving profile. Rim is almost vertical with no overhang or interior groove. Red slip.

940. Lot 238, No. 13. Pl. 111.
P.H. 0.060. Est. D. rim 0.280. One fragment of rim and wall. Tall, curved rim with overhang and concave moulding beneath. Red slip.

941. Inv. No. C-73-52. Lot 890. Pl. 111.
H. 0.062. Est. D. rim 0.317. One fragment of profile. Concave bottom. Red slip.

Form 9

Small bowl with flat or curved horizontal rim and ring base. There may be grooves on rim or on interior and exterior wall. Diameters range from 0.130 to 0.185 m. Most fall within the 0.130 to 0.160 m. range.

Date: 3rd to 4th centuries A.C. Total: 118.

942. Lot 1404, No. 225. Pl. 111.
H. 0.043. Est. D. rim 0.147. One fragment giving complete profile. Shallow groove at rim edge. Red slip.

943. Lot 1306, No. 3. Pl. 111.
P.H. 0.039. Est. D. rim 0.132. One fragment of rim and wall. Red slip.

944. Lot 239, No. 19. Pl. 111.
P.H. 0.037. Est. D. rim 0.151. One fragment of rim and wall. Very curved rim with carination on wall exterior below. Red slip.

Form 10

Shallow bowl with flaring walls, rounded lip. No base preserved. Diameters range from 0.140 to 0.160 m.

Date: 3rd century A.C. Total: 3.

945. Lot 1407, No. 60. Pl. 112.

P.H. 0.030. Est. D. rim 0.146. One fragment of rim and wall. Red slip.

Form 11

Small bowl with curved wall, straight vertical or slightly inturned rim. Slight carination on some examples where wall turns inward or up. No base preserved. Diameters range from 0.085 to 0.120 m.

Date: 2nd and 3rd centuries A.C. Total: 20.

946. Lot 237, No. 19.

P.H. 0.035. Est. D. rim 0.086. One fragment of rim and wall. Shallow grooves below lip on interior and exterior. Strong brown (7.5YR 6/6) slip.

947. Lot 1296, No. 330. Pl. 112.

P.H. 0.025. Est. D. rim 0.101. One fragment of rim and wall. Light red (2.5YR 6/8) slip.

948. Lot 1407, No. 28. Pl. 112.

P.H. 0.033. Est. D. rim 0.113. One fragment of rim and wall. Reddish yellow (5YR 6/6) slip.

Form 12

Cup or narrow bowl with straight, flaring walls and flat or concave base. Grooves below rim on exterior are common. Diameters range from 0.115 to 0.125 m.

Date: 2nd and 3rd centuries A.C. Total: 11.

949. Inv. No. C-70-19. Lot 801. Pl. 112.

H. 0.067. Est. D. rim 0.119. Three fragments mended, giving complete profile. Two grooves below rim exterior. Reddish brown (5YR 5/4) metallic slip.

950. Inv. No. C-70-39. Lot 483. Pl. 112.

H. 0.052. Est. D. rim 0.120. Two fragments mended, giving complete profile. Reddish brown (5YR 5/4) metallic slip.

951. Inv. No. C-74-194. Lot 1296. Pl. 112.

H. 0.050. Est. D. rim 0.124. One fragment, giving profile. Very thin walls on this example. Lustrous red slip.

Form 13

Deep bowl with curved wall, straight rim, and ring base. Diameters range from 0.165 to 0.220 m.

Date: 2nd to 4th centuries A.C. Total: 28.

952. Lot 1404, No. 223. Pl. 112.

H. 0.089. Est. D. rim 0.188. One fragment giving complete profile. Red slip.

Form 14

Dish with outward-thickened rim. No base preserved. There may be grooves below rim on exterior. Diameters range from 0.250 to 0.330 m.

Date: second half of the 2nd century A.C. Total: 11.

953. Lot 937, No. 11. Pl. 113.

P.H. 0.040. Est. D. rim 0.250. One fragment of rim and wall. A series of grooves on wall exterior. Red slip.

954. Lot 930, No. 126. Pl. 113.

P.H. 0.048. Est. D. rim 0.320. One fragment of rim and wall. Red slip.

Form 15

Jar with moulded and carinated rim. Exterior wall normally carries stamped decoration. No base preserved. Total: 3.

955. Inv. No. C-77-78. Lot 1959. Pl. 113.

P.H. 0.058. Est. D. rim 0.196. One fragment of rim and wall. Light red (2.5YR 6/8) slip on exterior only.

Form 16

Large bowl with curved wall and folded rim. Stamped ornament below rim. No base preserved. Diameters range from 0.260 to 0.295 m. Total: 21.

956. Inv. No. C-74-118. Lot 1295. Pl. 113.

P.H. 0.045. Est. D. rim 0.285. One fragment of rim and wall. A group of three stamped diamonds preserved just below rim. Brown (7.5YR 4/4) slip.

Date: second half of the 3rd to early 4th centuries A.C.

Form 17

Large bowl with curved, often very plump body and ring base. Tall rim with flat or curved surface set off from body by groove or grooves. Exterior wall surface normally carries stamped decoration. Diameters range from 0.225 to 0.335 m., with most falling between 0.250 and 0.270 m.

Date: late 3rd to mid-4th centuries A.C. Total: 13.

957. Lot 1307, No. 50. Pl. 113.

P.H. 0.055. Est. D. rim 0.262. One fragment of rim and wall. Red slip.

958. Inv. No. C-73-87. Lot 890. Pl. 114.

P.H. 0.099. Est. D. rim 0.270. Six fragments mended, giving rim and wall. A group of three stamped diamonds preserved on wall. Red slip.

959. Lot 1404, No. 354. Pl. 113.

P.H. 0.040. Est. D. rim 0.225. One fragment of rim and wall. Two grooves on rim surface. Stamped ovals on wall. Reddish brown (5YR 3/4) slip.

960. Inv. No. C-74-266. Lot 1328. Pl. 113.

P.H. 0.063. Est. D. rim 0.240. One fragment of rim and wall. Red slip. Stamped arcs above rosettes.

Form 18

Bowl with carinated body, rounded rim, and a series of grooves below rim, on body, or both. Small ring base is probable. This would appear to be related to and perhaps the predecessor of the most popular form, the "three-ridged" bowl. There is, however, no stamped decoration on this form. Diameters average about 0.220 m., with one large one at 0.280 m. Total: 5.

961. Inv. No. C-70-142. Lot 1652. Pl. 114.

P.H. 0.070. Est. D. rim 0.211. One fragment of rim and wall. A series of shallow grooves, or wheel-ridges that extend between rim and the point where the wall turns downward to the base. Reddish brown (5YR 5/4) metallic slip.

Form 19

Deep bowl with three-ridged or grooved rim with rounded, often plump body on ring base. The ridged rim is clearly marked off from the body by a deep groove. Small examples often do not have the full three ridges. The point of greatest diameter is usually decorated with stamped ornament. This is the most common form from the late 2nd into the early 4th centuries at Stobi and occurs in a variety of sizes and slip colors and with a varied series of stamped and impressed motifs. Unlike many of the other popular forms that cannot be securely identified without their base, this rim can be recognized from even a small fragment. Diameters range from 0.108 to 0.160 m. for small examples, and from 0.240 to 0.290 m. for larger examples. A few pieces fall between these groups, and several are larger.

Date: late 2nd to 4th centuries A.C. Total: 355.

Small

962. Inv. No. C-74-53. Lot 1509. Pl. 114.

P.H. 0.048. Est. D. rim 0.128. One fragment of rim and wall. Two grooves just below point of greatest diameter. The band between these grooves and rim is filled with a continuous series of stamped bats of varying height. Lustrous, metallic red slip.

963. Inv. No. C-73-37. Lot 881. Pls. 114, 188.

P.H. 0.047. Est. D. rim 0.133. Two fragments mended, giving rim and wall. Stamped bat motif on wall as in **962**. Yellowish red/reddish brown (5YR) metallic slip.

964. Inv. No. C-78-127. Lot 2213. Pl. 114.

P.H. 0.044. Est. D. rim 0.108. One fragment of rim and wall. Stamped leaf design partially preserved on wall. Red slip.

Large

965. Inv. No. C-71-204. Lot 87. Pls. 114, 188.

P.H. 0.105. Est. D. rim 0.277. Two fragments mended, giving rim and wall. A grouping of three double *planta pedis* stamps preserved on wall below rim. Red slip.

966. Inv. No. C-74-489. Lot 1310. Pl. 115.

H. 0.110. Est. D. rim 0.231. Six fragments mended, giving complete profile and about one-third of vessel. Single band of rouletting at point of greatest diameter. Light red (2.5YR 6/8) slip on interior and upper third of exterior wall.

967. Inv. No. C-74-12. Lot 1356. Pl. 115.

H. 0.142. Est. D. rim 0. 252. Mended from numerous fragments, giving complete profile. About two-thirds complete. Clusters of three diamond motifs stamped on wall. Red slip.

968. Inv. No. C-74-32. Lot 1298. Pl. 114.
P.H. 0.072. Est. D. rim 0.262. Seven fragments mended, giving rim and wall. Very thick walls. Stamped arcs joined by diamond shapes on wall. Reddish brown (2.5YR 5/4) slip.

Form 20

Small cup with vertical or slightly incurving wall, flat base, and one sliced handle. The wall may be decorated with barbotine dot or floral decoration. Diameters range from 0.063 to 0.075 m.
Date: primarily 2nd century A.C. Total: 7.

969. Inv. No. C-73-60. Lot 940. Pl. 115.
H. 0.056. Est. D. rim 0.075. Six fragments mended, giving complete profile. Red mottled to brown and black slip.

970. Inv. No. C-73-16. Lot 927. Pl. 115.
P.H. 0.058. Est. D. rim 0.063. One fragment of rim, wall, and handle. Red slip.

Form 21

Small cup with double handles, plump body, and tall rim. No base preserved. A series of grooves is often seen on exterior. Diameters of small examples range from 0.080 to 0.095 m., and larger examples average about 0.130 m.
Date: 2nd century A.C. Total: 6.

971. Inv. No. C-78-200. Lot 2152. Pl. 115.
P.H. 0.053. Est. D. rim 0.085. Eight fragments mended, giving, rim, wall, and handle. Red slip.

972. Lot 242, No.9. Pl. 115.
P.H. 0.070. Est. D. rim 0.125. Five fragments mended, giving rim, wall and handle. Mottled red slip.

Form 22

Small, one-handled jar with everted rim and usually globular body. No base preserved. This form is similar to that of the Italian pitcher/mug (**511–516**). Diameters for most examples range from 0.060 to 0.090 m., with a few larger examples at 0.100 m.
Date: late 2nd and 3rd centuries A.C. Total: 39.

973. Inv. No. C-72-74. Lot 692. Pl. 115.
H. 0.072. D. rim 0.068. D. base 0.035. Mended and restored. Discolored by fire. Exterior now has brown slip. Flat base.

974. Lot 1307, No. 24. Pl. 115.
P.H. 0.067. Est. D. rim 0.060. Two fragments mended, giving rim, wall, and handle. Mottled reddish yellow (7.5YR 6/6) slip.

975. Lot 1332, No. 2. Pl. 115.
P.H. 0.055. Est. D. rim 0.072. One fragment of rim, wall, and handle. Red slip.

976. Inv. No. C-70-113. Lot 799. Pl. 115.
P.H. 0.086. Est. D. rim 0.060. Mended from numerous fragments, giving rim, wall, and handle. Light red (2.5YR 6/6) slip.

977. Lot 1310, No. 7. Pl. 116.
P.H. 0.061. Est. D. rim 0.100. One fragment of rim and wall. Reddish brown (2.5YR 5/4) slip.

978. Inv. No. C-72-40. Lot 763. Pl. 116.
H. 0.103. Est. D. rim 0.080. D. base 0.039. Mended and partly complete. Handle missing. Mottled red-brown slip extending from rim to just above base. Ring base.

Form 23

Large dish with flat, grooved rim, and twisted or plain, horizontal (ribbon) handle at rim level or below. Diameters range from 0.295 to 0.350 m.
Date: late 2nd to early 4th centuries A.C. Total: 13.

979. Lot 1302, No. 40. Pl. 116.
P.H. 0.052. Est. D. rim 0.325. One fragment of rim, wall, and twisted handle. Three wide grooves on rim surface. Red slip.

Form 24

Small strainer with plain rim, straight wall, and ring base. Diameters range from 0.100 to 0.170 m. Total: 37.

980. Lot 1407, No. 743. Pl. 116.
H. 0.083. Est. D. rim 0.108. Ten fragments mended, giving complete profile. Red slip.

981. Lot 1404, No. 363. Pl. 116.
P.H. 0.059. Est. D. rim 0.145. Two fragments mended, giving rim and wall. Rim is slightly outward thickened with hollow beneath. Red slip.

982. Inv. No. C-74-28. Lot 1057. Pl. 116.
P.H. 0.085. Est. D. rim 0.168. Mended from numerous fragments, giving approximately one-third vessel. Red slip.

Form 25

Deep bowl with rim flattened on top, slightly concave or rounded. High ring base. Diameters range from 0.190 to 0.270 m. These bowls are always unslipped.

Date: 3rd to mid-4th centuries A.C. Total: 15.

983. Inv. No. C-72-38. Lot 763. Pl. 116.
H. 0.120. D. rim 0.193. Mended and three-fifths complete.

984. Inv. No. C-71-231. Lot 110. Pl. 116.
H. 0.123. D. rim 0.230. Two-thirds complete.

985. Inv. No. C-71-395. Lot 163. Pl. 117.
P.H. 0.057. Est. D. rim 0.262. One rim fragment.

986. Inv. No. C-78-149. Lot 2377. Pl. 117.
P.H. 0.083. Est. D. rim 0.239. Two fragments mended, giving rim and wall.

Form 26

Double-handled pot with convex, grooved rim. No base preserved. The body is also often decorated with grooves, particularly just above the lower handle attachment. Diameters range from 0.110 to 0.170 m.

Date: late 2nd to mid- 4th centuries A.C. Total: 19.

987. Lot 1308, No. 6. Pl. 117.
P.H. 0.082. Est. D. rim 0.140. Three fragments mended, giving rim, handles, and wall. Reddish brown (5YR 4/4) slip.

988. Inv. No. C-71-225. Lot 110. Pl. 117.
P.H. 0.084. Est. D. rim 0.140. Mended from five fragments, giving rim, handles, and wall. Partially slipped light red to brown around rim area. Graffito on shoulder.

989. Inv. No. C-71-28. Lot 223. Pl. 117.
P.H. 0.089. Est. D. rim 0.161. Mended from eight fragments, giving rim, handle, and wall. Red slip on rim and partially on exterior.

Form 27

Jar with everted, grooved rim, with or without handles. None with bases preserved. Diameters range from 0.160 to 0.220 m. Total: 14.

990. Inv. No. C-72-262. Lot 729. Pl. 117.
P.H. 0.059. Est. D. rim 0.201. One fragment of rim and wall.

Form 28

Globular jar with short, everted, or collared rim, ring base, and double handles. Diameters range from 0.100 to 0.160 m. Total: 19.

991. Inv. No. C-71-232. Grave 91. Pl. 118.
H. 0.154. D. rim 0.100. Mended and almost complete. Discolored from burning but was probably slipped red or brown originally.

992. Lot 1295, No. 33. Pl. 118.
P.H. 0.037. Est. D. rim 0.110. One fragment of rim, handle, and wall.

993. Inv. No. C-77-19. Lot 1941. Pl. 118.
P.H. 0.040. Est. D. rim 0.115. One fragment of rim and wall.

994. Inv. No. C-73-29. Lot 974.
H. 0.150. D rim 0.092. D. base 0.059. Mended. Three-fourths complete. Discolored. Light brown wash on upper portion.

Form 29

Closed-mouth jar with flat, grooved rim and two horizontally placed handles, sometimes rising above rim level. The handles may be round in section or of the grooved strap type. There are frequently grooves on the shoulder, and the surface may be partially slipped or painted. Diameters range from 0.090 to 0.140 m.

Date: 3rd century A.C. Total: 18.

995. Lot 1407, No. 913. Pl. 117.
P.H. 0.095. Est. D. rim 0.092. Mended from numerous fragments, giving about two-thirds of vessel without base. Rim and upper half of exterior covered with red to reddish brown slip.

996. Inv. No. C-72-257. Lot 672. Pl. 117.
P.H. 0.047. Est. D. rim 0.135. One fragment of rim, wall, and handle. Brown (7.5YR 4/4) slip.

Form 30

Large jug with two handles similar to Form 31, but with flanged or moulded rim. Only rims preserved. Partially color slipped. Diameters range from 0.145 to 0.180 m. Total: 7.

997. Lot 1295, No. 55. Pl. 118.
P.H. 0.062. Est. D. rim 0.136. One fragment of rim, neck, and handle stub. Plain with traces of red painted below rim.

Form 31

Large jug with long neck, globular body, and one or two handles. Most are decorated with splashes or bands of red, pink or brown slip at rim, neck, and body. Base shape is uncertain. Rim forms vary from simple, flat, and horizontal to inturned and overhanging. An additional round handle seems to have been placed horizontally at the point of greatest diameter. Diameter of mouth ranges from 0.135 to 0.180 m.
Date: 2nd to 4th centuries A.C. Total: 186.

998. Inv. No. C-75-74. Lot 1676. Pl. 118.
P.H. 0.120. Est. D. rim 0.135. Fifteen fragments mended, giving rim, neck, and handle. Two wide grooves on neck. A wide band of red slip occurs just below the rim and at the point where the neck turns outward to form the body.

999. Lot 1300, No. 24. Pl. 118.
P.H. 0.065. Est. D. rim 0.154. One fragment of rim and neck. Two grooves below rim.

1000. Inv. No. C-71-394. Lot 164. Pl. 118.
P.H. 0.062. Est. D. rim 0.160. One fragment of rim and neck. Wide band of brown slip at rim and extending halfway down preserved neck piece.

1001. Lot 939, No. 109. Pl. 118.
P.H. 0.188. Est. D. neck 0.105. Est. D. body 0.247. Six fragments mended, giving neck, two handles, and part of body. Light red slip in bands at neck at body midpoint with other randomly placed bands connecting these.

1002. Lot 237, No. 74. Pl. 119.
P.H. 0.145. Est. D. neck 0.120. Nine fragments mended, giving neck, shoulder, and two handles. Band of dark red slip at point where neck turns outward to body, and red slip splashed upward onto neck.

Form 32

Large basin or casserole with broad horizontal rim, sometimes grooved, and flat or concave base. On many pieces, the walls have been pushed together before firing to form an oval rather than a round mouth. (Note the early version of this form, ER Form 15.) Some examples had double round handles placed horizontally. The interior and the rim are usually slipped, while the exterior may be plain or decorated with bands and splashes of red or brown slip. Diameters range from 0.300 to 0.460 m.
Date: 2nd to early or mid-4th century A.C. Total: 168.

1003. Inv. No. C-72-42. Lot 8. Pl. 187.
H. 0.208. Est. D. base 0.197. About half complete. Reddish brown slip on interior.

1004. Lot 1307, No. 200. Pl. 120.
H. 0.187. Est. D. rim 0.456. Six fragments mended, giving complete profile. Red slip on interior and at rim.

1005. Lot 1307, No. 92. Pl. 120.
P.H. 0.080. Est. D. rim 0.335. Four fragments mended, giving rim, wall, and handle. Two grooves around body at handle height. Brown slip on interior and in the wavy lines on rim surface.

1006. Lot 2126, No. 12. Pl. 120.
P.H. 0.080. Est. D. rim 0.320. One fragment of rim, wall, and handle. Red slip on interior, at rim, and in wavy lines on rim surface.

Form 33

Stamnos or amphora with double handle and concave base. Unslipped. Diameter of rim ranges from 0.055 to 0.080, and base diameter from 0.080 to 0.125 m. Unlike examples from the Early Roman period, ER Form 18, no complete examples survive. Total: 68 rims, 166 bases.

1007. Lot 929, No. 109. Pl. 119.
P.H. 0.150. Est. D. rim 0.062. Two fragments mended, giving rim and handle.

1008. Lot 1298, No. 38. Pl. 119.
P.H. 0.131. Est. D. rim 0.068. Two fragments mended, giving rim, neck, and two handles. Two grooves on neck.

1009. Lot 1309, No. 63. Pl. 119.
P.H. 0.025. Est. D. base 0.085. One fragment of base.

1010. Lot 1298, No. 200. Pl. 119.

P.H. 0.103. Est. D. base 0.100. Two fragments of base mended.

1011. Lot 1404, No. 154. Pl. 119.

P.H. 0.028. Est. D. base 0.080. One fragment of base.

Form 34

These small bottles with squat, solid base have been considered by some to be amphora stoppers: see Vegas, *Cerámica común*, fig. 56, Type 61; Brukner, *Rimska Keramika*, T.169. It has been pointed out, however, that no examples of such stoppers in place in the necks of amphorae have been published, and therefore, there is doubt that such flasks were used in that way. See Peacock and Williams, *Amphorae*, 51.

Since all but one of our examples appear to be made of local fabric, they would tend to be poor candidates for stoppers. This assumes that the stoppers would be manufactured with the amphora. Ours could possibly be substitutes for the originals.

A variety of profiles are presented, but the fabric is the same and most seem rather poorly made and fired at a low temperature. All are unslipped.

Local

1012. Inv. No. C-74-3. Lot 1098. Pl. 121.

P.H. 0.105. Max. D. 0.062. Est. D. base 0.047. Rim missing and part of base chipped away. Wheel-ridging on neck and upper body.

Date: 3rd and 4th centuries A.C. Total: 17.

1013. Inv. No. C-74-149. Lot 1296. Pl. 121.

P.H. 0.063. Max. D. 0.043. D. base 0.024. Rim missing.

Other examples of this shape as follows: from Lot 943: 2; Lot 1296: 2; Lot 1404: 2; Lot 1407: 3; Lot 2211: 1; Lot 2216: 1; Lot 2178: 1; Lot 2234: 1.

1014. Inv. No. C-71-192. Lot 163. Pl. 121.

H. 0.079. Max. D. 0.038. Intact. String-cut base.

A similar example, C-71-193, from Lot 110.

1015. Lot 1330, No. 12. Pl. 121.

P.H. 0.045. Max. D. 0.040. D. base 0.018. One fragment of lower body and base.

Imported

1016. Lot 1697, No. 1. Pl. 121.

P.H. 0.060. Max. D. 0.060. D. base 0.025. One fragment of lower body and base. Light reddish brown (2.5YR 6/4) fabric with white (10YR 8/3) slip.

This example is similar to the fabric of many amphoras: see Hellenistic and Roman Amphoras, Fabric group 1.

Middle Roman wares: Other (**1017–1074**)

N.B. Slip is red unless otherwise indicated.

Dishes / plates

1017. Platter. Lot 1302, No. 37. Pl. 121.

H. 0.020 Est. D. 0.380. One fragment of profile. Flat-based platter with rounded edge and groove marking off base.

Date: 3rd century A.C.

1018. Platter. Lot 278, No. 18. Pl. 121.

H. 0.022. D. 0.330. One fragment with profile. Fine fabric with lustrous and mottled smooth interior and exterior. Shape similar to preceding with small foot preserved.

Date: first half of the 4th century A.C.

1019. Dish with flaring wall. Lot 1300, No. 49. Pl. 121.

P.H. 0.040. Est. D. rim 0.280. One fragment of rim and wall. Slightly outward-turned, rounded rim. Shallow grooves on interior. Reddish brown (2.5YR 5/4) slip.

Date: 3rd century A.C.

1020. Dish with wide, scalloped rim. Inv. No. C-74-030. Lot 1296. Pl. 121.

P.H. 0.032. Est. D. rim 0.318. One fragment of rim and wall. Incised circles flank an "H" shape punched out of the rim surface.

Date: mid-3rd to mid-4th centuries A.C.

1021. Dish with flaring wall. Lot 1298, No. 92. Pl. 121.

P.H. 0.042. Est. D. rim 0.270. One fragment of rim. Single groove just inside rim on interior.

Date: mid-3rd to mid-4th centuries A.C.

1022. Shallow dish with broad rim. Lot 1308, No. 22. Pl. 121.

P.H. 0.029. Est. D. rim 0.188. One fragment of

rim and wall. Wide rim with upturned edge is decorated with a broad band of rouletting.
Date: 3rd century A.C.

1023. Shallow dish with moulded rim. Lot 1302, No. 76. Pl. 121.
P.H. 0.024. Est. D. rim 0.205. Single fragment of rim and wall. Moulded and grooved rim with single band of incised wavy lines toward interior.
Date: 3rd century A.C.

1024. Dish with grooved rim. Lot 1285, No. 28. Pl. 122.
P.H. 0.027. Est. D. rim 0.220. One fragment of rim. Rim interior has wide ledge.

1025. Dish. Inv. No. C-78-212. Lot 2236. Pls. 122, 188.
P.H. 0.036. Est. D. rim 0.300. One fragment. Rim is notched on interior ledge; upper surface of rim toward exterior has stamped rods with a row of dots on inside.
Imitation *EAA*, 2, Hayes, "sigillata orientale B," Form 62.

1026. Dish. Inv. No. C-74-279. Lot 1307. Pl. 122.
P.H. 0.013. Est. D. 0.025. One small fragment of rim with triangular lip on offset rim and applied ribbon handle.
Cf. *EAA* 2, Hayes, "sigillata orientale B," Form 62B or 79.

1027. Imitation Çandarli base. Inv. No. C-75-27. Lot 1697. Pl. 122.
P.H. 0.032. Est. D. base 0.144. One fragment.
Hayes, *LRP*, Form 1.

Bowls

1028. Small bowl. Inv. No. C-74-323. Lot 1308. Pl. 122.
H. 0.052. Est. D. rim 0.135. Two fragments mended, giving complete profile. Flat disc base with wire marks visible on the bottom.
Date: 3rd century A.C.

1029. Small bowl. Lot 1301, No. 26. Pl. 122.
P.H. 0.025. Est. D. rim 0.115. One fragment of rim and wall.
Date: 3rd century A.C.

1030. Small bowl. Lot 1303, No. 26. Pl. 122.
P.H. 0.035. Est. D. rim 0.110. One fragment of rim and wall of bowl with flaring rim.
Date: 3rd century A.C.

1031. Small, one-handled cup. Inv. No. C-78-9. Lot 2350. Pl. 122.
H. 0.032. Est. D. rim 0.090. One fragment with profile. Unslipped.

1032. Bowl. Lot 1295, No. 57. Pl. 122.
P.H. 0.047. Est. D. rim 0.192. One fragment of thick-walled bowl with offset grooved rim and internal ledge. Single groove on exterior.
Date: mid-3rd to mid-4th centuries A.C.

1033. Tiny bowl or saltcellar. Lot 934, No. 26. Pl. 122.
H. 0.025. D. rim 0.060. One fragment with complete profile. Flaring rim, curved wall and low ring base.
Date: second half of the 2nd century A.C.

1034. Bowl. Inv. No. C-74-193. Lot 1297. Pl. 122.
P.H. 0.040. Est. D. rim 0.140. One fragment of rim. Brown (7.5YR 5/2) slip. Entire surface of preserved fragment is covered with feather rouletting.
Date: mid-3rd to mid-4th centuries A.C.

1035. Small bowl with everted rim. Lot 1308, No. 24. Pl. 122.
P.H. 0.038. Est. D. rim 0.092. One fragment of rim and wall. Single groove at mid-body.
Date: 3rd century A.C.

1036. Small bowl. Lot 1296, No. 296. Pl. 123.
P.H. 0.050. Est. D. rim 0.130. One fragment of rim and wall. Grooves below rim and at mid-body.
Date: mid-3rd to mid-4th centuries A.C.

1037. Small carinated bowl. Lot 801, No. 329. Pl. 123.
P.H. 0.053. Est. D. rim 0.115. One fragment of rim and wall. Two grooves below rim and at carination.

Jars and deep bowl

1038. Small carinated jar. Lot 239, No. 56. Pl. 123.
P.H. 0.057. Est. D. rim 0.100. One fragment of rim and wall. Single groove just above carination.

1039. Small jar. Lot 1404, No. 353. Pl. 123.
P.H. 0.054. Est. D. rim 0.100. One fragment of rim and wall. Exterior is decorated with irregularly spaced rouletting.

1040. Jar. Lot 274, No. 141. Pl. 123.
P.H. 0.065. Est. D. rim 0.120. One fragment of rim and wall. Grooves below rim and above carination.

1041. Small jar. Lot 1404, No. 299. Pl. 123.
P.H. 0.047. Est. D. rim 0.080. One fragment of rim and wall. Everted, grooved rim with raised ridges on shoulder.

1042. Small jar. Lot 1300, No. 45. Pl. 123.
P.H. 0.033. Est. D. rim 0.088. One fragment of rim and wall.
Date: 3rd century A.C.

1043. Small cup with handles. Lot 242, No. 10. Pl. 123.
P.H. 0.057. Est. D. rim 0.145. One fragment of rim, wall, and handle. Everted rim with ledge on interior. Wide groove at mid-body. Reddish brown (5YR 5/4) slip.

1044. Small cup with handles. Inv. No. C-71-150. Lot 448. Pl. 123.
H. 0.084. Est. D. rim 0.070. Almost complete vessel, but not joining fragments, give complete profile. Wheel ridging on exterior.

1045. Small jar. Lot 1295, No. 54. Pl. 123.
P.H. 0.033. Est. D. rim 0.080. One fragment of rim and wall. Two grooves on shoulder.
Date: mid-3rd to mid-4th centuries A.C.

1046. Jar. Lot 932, No. 20. Pl. 123.
P.H. 0.037. Est. D. rim 0.147. One fragment of rim and wall. Irregular band of red slip on shoulder.
Date: second half of the 2nd century A.C.

1047. Jar. Inv. No. C-75-57. Lot 1697. Pl. 124.
P.H. 0.110. Est. D. rim 0.195. Five fragments mended from rim and wall. Everted grooved rim with two grooves on shoulder. Gray (2.5YR N5/) metallic slip.

1048. Jar. Lot 1697, No. 100. Pl. 124.
P.H. 0.057. Est. D. rim 0.215. One fragment of rim and wall of vessel very similar to the previous one.

1049. Jar. Lot 245, No. 5. Pl. 124.
P.H. 0.070. Est. D. rim 0.172. One fragment of rim and wall. The exterior has a number of sharp curves and carinations.

1050. Jar. Inv. No. C-74-283. Lot 1325. Pl. 124.
P.H. 0.055. Est. D. rim 0.238. One fragment of rim and wall. Grooves at shoulder and below are preserved part of two circular stamped motifs.

1051. Jar. Inv. No. C-75-21. Lot 1697. Pl. 124.
P.H. 0.045. Est. D. rim 0.297. One fragment of rim and wall. On exterior remains of three stamped motifs, one consisting of a twelve-pointed star framed by a circle.

1052. Deep bowl. Inv. No. C-75-5. Lot 1663. Pl. 124.
H. 0.095. Est D. 0.0220. Three-fourths complete. Mended. Small, punched dots on shoulder below carination.

1053. Large jar. Lot 1697, No. 6. Pl. 125.
P.H. 0.076. Est. D. rim 0.266. One fragment of rim, wall and handle. Wide, shallow groove on shoulder.

1054. Deep bowl with three handles. Inv. No. C-73-13. Lot 929. Pl. 125.
H. 0.159. D. rim 0.219. D. base 0.078. D. body. 0.207. Mended. Upper third and handles have red slip. Squat body on concave base. Three grooves on rim. Poor workmanship.
Cf. Bojović, *Singidunum*, T.36, 37, for other examples of such typically northern types. See also **1202**.
Date: late 2nd, early 3rd centuries A.C.

Jugs or pitchers

1055. Small jug. Lot 930, No. 37. Pl. 124.
P.H. 0.047. Est. D. rim 0.042. Single fragment of rim and neck with evidence of handles.
Date: second half of the 2nd century A.C.

1056. Small jug. Lot 237, No. 59. Pl. 124.
P.H. 0.033. Est. D. rim 0.063. Single fragment of rim and neck with remains of handles.

1057. Jug. Lot 240, No. 9. Pl. 124.
P.H. 0.040. Est. D. rim 0.061. One fragment of rim, neck and handles. Brown (7.5YR 4/2) slip.

1058. Jug. Lot 1296, No. 174. Pl. 125.
P.H. 0.050. Est. D. rim 0.072. One fragment of rim and neck. Brown (7.5YR 5/4) slip.
Date: mid-3rd to mid-4th centuries A.C.

1059. Jug. Lot 1407, No. 19. Pl. 125.
P.H. 0.032. Est. D. rim 0.095. One fragment of rim and neck.
Date: late 3rd century A.C.

1060. Jug. C-72-294. Lot 1052. Pl. 125.
P.H. 0.038. Est. D. rim 0.125. One fragment of rim and neck.

1061. Jug. Lot 1296, No. 177. Pl. 125.
P.H. 0.035. Est. D. rim 0.095. One fragment of rim and neck. Reddish brown (7.5YR 4/4) slip.
Date: mid-3rd to mid-4th centuries A.C.

1062. Jug. Lot 1404, No. 315. Pl. 125.
P.H. 0.040. Est. D. rim 0.100. One fragment of rim and neck. Reddish brown (7.5YR 5/4) slip.

1063. Jug. Lot 1296, No. 171. Pl. 125.
P.H. 0.070. Est. D. rim 0.103. One fragment of rim and neck. Reddish brown (5YR 5/4) slip.
Date: mid-3rd to mid-4th centuries A.C.

1064. Jug. Lot 1404, No. 323. Pl. 125.
P.H. 0.066. Est. D. 0.128. One fragment of rim and neck. Brown (7.5YR 5/2) slip.

1065. Large Jug. Lot 1310, No. 5. Pl. 125.
P.H. 0.130. Est. D. rim 0.118. One fragment of rim and neck. Three grooves at neck.
Date: 3rd century A.C.

1066. Jug. Inv. No. C-70-24. Lot 799. Pl. 126.
P.H. 0.094. Est. D. rim 0.095. Several fragments mended to give rim, neck, and remains of handle. Reddish brown (5YR 5/4) metallic slip. Graffito on shoulder: XNEΓ̣Ρ̣.
Date: first half of the 4th century A.C.

1067. Jug. Lot 1296, No. 98.
P.H. 0.091. Est. D. rim 0.096. One fragment of rim and neck. Two widely spaced grooves below rim.

1068. Small jug with one handle. Inv. No. C-71-236. Grave 46. Pl. 126.
H. 0.100. D. rim 0.097. Mended. Almost complete. A series of grooves on neck and at mid-body. A row of roughly diamond-shaped stamped motifs on shoulder.

Miscellaneous bases

1069. Moulded base. Lot 940, No. 30. Pl. 126.
P.H. 0.032. Est. D. base 0.096. One fragment of base. Reddish yellow (5YR–7.5YR) to pink fabric with red gloss.
Date: second half of the 2nd century A.C.

1070. Base from large pitcher. Lot 1295, No. 84. Pl. 126.
P.H. 0.064. Est. D. base 0.046. Several fragments mended. Red slip dripped on exterior surface.
Date: mid-3rd to mid-4th centuries A.C.

1071. Base from pitcher. Lot 1332, No. 3. Pl. 126.
P.H. 0.055. Est. D. base. 0.032. Two fragments. Red slip on exterior only.
Date: 3rd century A.C.

1072. Pitcher base. Lot 237, No. 66. Pl. 126.
P.H. 0.070. Est. D. base 0.036. One fragment of base. Partial red slip.

1073. Pitcher base. Inv. No. C-78-168. Lot 2128. Pl. 126.
P.H. 0.043. Est. D. base. 0.035. One fragment of base with traces of two handles on lower wall. Red slip on exterior.

1074. Pitcher base. Lot 1295, No. 77. Pl. 126.
P.H. 0.024. Est. D. base 0.035. One fragment. Brown slip.
Date: mid-3rd to mid-4th centuries A.C.

Late Roman wares: Other (**1075–1081**)

1075. Bowl. Lot 305, No. 67. Fig. Pl. 126.
P.H. 0.033. Est. D. rim 0.150. One fragment of rim and wall. Unslipped. Exterior of everted rim has appliqué beaded ornament.

1076. Dish with outward-thickened rim. Inv. No. C-78-044. Lot 2209. Pl. 126.
H. 0.050. Est. D. rim 0.288. One fragment, preserving complete profile. Rolled or outward-thickened rim and flat base. Red slip. Double-dipped on exterior and bands of light and dark slip visible on interior. Perhaps an imitation of North African Red Slip, Hayes Form 99.

1077. Dish with overhanging rim. Inv. No. C-78-135. Lot 2234. Pl. 126.
P.H. 0.032. Est. D. rim 0.370. One fragment of rim and wall. Red slip.
Imitation of African Red Slip, Hayes Form 61B, dated 400–450 A.C., which agrees with the context of this piece.

1078. Small jar. Lot 274, No. 57. Pl. 127.
P.H. 0.042. Est. D. rim 0.085. One fragment of rim and neck. Red slip.

1079. Small jar. Lot 277, No. 22. Pl. 127.

P.H. 0.043. Est. D. rim 0.102. One fragment of rim and wall. Shallow grooves on shoulder. Red slip.

1080. Small jar. Lot 277, No. 60. Pl. 127.

P.H. 0.054. Est. D. rim 0.110. One fragment of rim and neck. Unslipped.

1081. One-handled jug. Inv. No. C-71-53. Lot 94. Pl. 127.

H. 0.118. D. mouth 0.077. D. body 0.122. Mended and complete. Dark brown slip on exterior. Vertical gouged decoration from shoulder to mid-body.

Cf. Robinson, *Agora*, L38, pl. 16, dated to the late 4th century A.C.

Local/Regional Cooking Wares

The form typology for the cooking wares (Fabric 3) may seem rather limited in comparison with the tablewares of Fabric group 1 (see Chapter 2). The fewer types are not a reflection of the numbers of cooking ware overall but of the smaller number of shapes we were able to reconstruct from fragments, given the brittle nature of the ware and frequency of tall profiles. With the exception of pie pans or casseroles, which are not very tall, complete profiles for cooking wares were rarely found or able to be reconstructed. Furthermore, very few examples of cooking wares were found in burials, the best source for whole vessels at Stobi.

Many of the shapes common in the 1st century B.C. and 1st century A.C. are those common in Italy also, so it is possible, given the number of Italian fine-ware imports, that many of these are imports. During the 2nd and 3rd centuries, cooking-ware shapes were similar over a broad area of the Mediterranean, and since imported fine wares were less common in this period than in the Early Roman period, it is tempting to suggest that these examples are a local variation and not imported.

It has been traditional to think of coarse cooking wares as a local product, since it has seemed unlikely that such unattractive pottery would be carried very far. This is, perhaps, an uninformed view, since the value of any cooking ware probably depended more on its price, durability, and heat-retaining qualities than on its appearance.

Aside from some examples of Pompeian Red Ware, Campanian Ware, and Aegean Cooking Ware, which have a rather distinctive fabric, surface treatment, or both, it has not been possible to identify imported cooking wares at Stobi because the fabric of most of the cooking wares is very similar and because a broad range of color is often found on the same vessel, either a result of firing or of later use in cooking.[145]

Cooking-ware shapes in all periods include stewpots and jars with narrow necks, pans, and casseroles. Jars and stewpots are found in the largest numbers in all periods but the Middle Roman when the pan is the most popular form, while such open forms (pan, casserole, bowl) take second place in other periods. (Figs. 3.7–3.10). Furthermore, whereas in the earlier centuries at Stobi tableware shapes like pitchers, jugs, and bowls were made in local Fabric 1, in the Late Roman period one sees a whole range of these shapes in Fabric 3, that is, Forms 9–13 (Fig. 3.10).

Each chronological division has its own set of form numbers, so that Hellenistic Form 1 is not the same as Early Roman Form 1.

Hellenistic cooking wares: Forms 1–13 (**1082–1109**)

Form 1

Flat-based pan with straight wall and grooved or "orlo-bifido" rim. Angle and thickness of wall vary. Rim diameters vary from 0.220 to 0.380, depending on vessel size.

Cf. Thompson, "TCHP," E145, fig. 121, p. 467, dated to the late 2nd, early 1st centuries B.C.; Dyson, "Cosa." VD5, fig. 18. Total: 10.

[145] Petrographic analysis has been useful for identifying the mineral composition of the cooking wares at Stobi (see Appendix 2), but it is clearly impossible to subject every sherd to petrographic analysis in order to ascertain its type or origin; note comments in Anderson-Stojanović (1982) 336–337 and note 14.

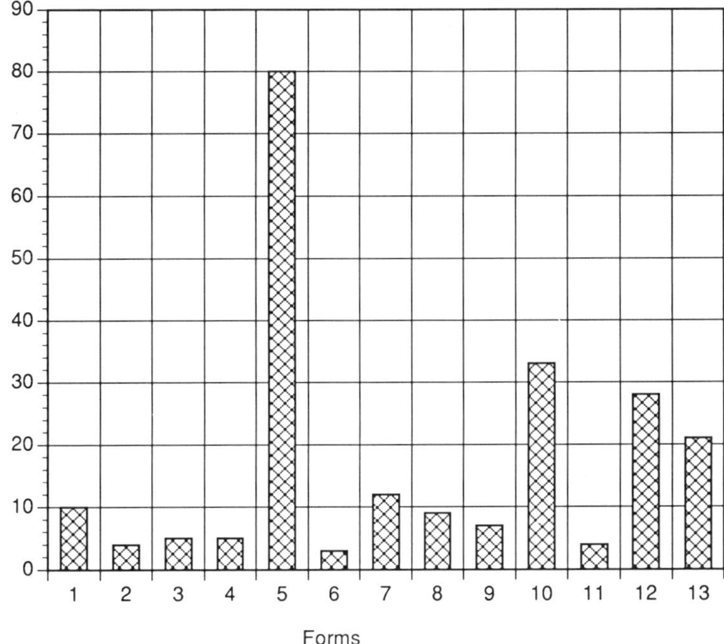

Figure 3.7. Bar graph illustrating quantity of Hellenistic Cooking Ware forms at Stobi

Form 1: Pan
Form 2: Pan
Form 3: Pan
Form 4: Casserole
Form 5: Jar
Form 6: Jar
Form 7: Stewpot
Form 8: Jar
Form 9: Stewpot
Form 10: Stewpot
Form 11: Jar
Form 12: Stewpot
Form 13: Jar

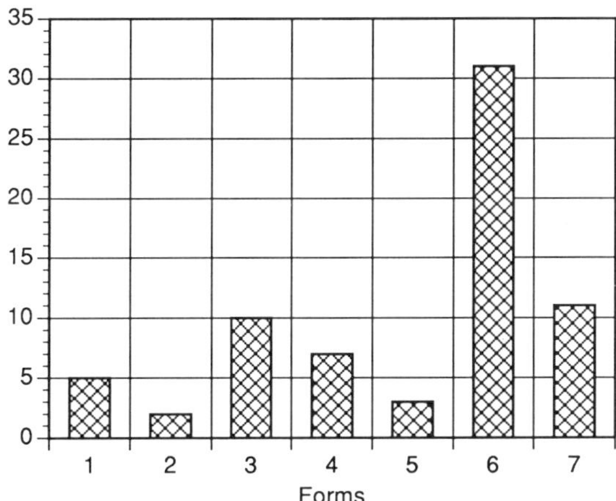

Figure 3.8. Bar graph illustrating quantity of Early Roman Cooking Ware forms at Stobi

Form 1: Pan
Form 2: Pan
Form 3: Pan
Form 4: Small Jar
Form 5: Small Jar
Form 6: Stewpot
Form 7: Stewpot

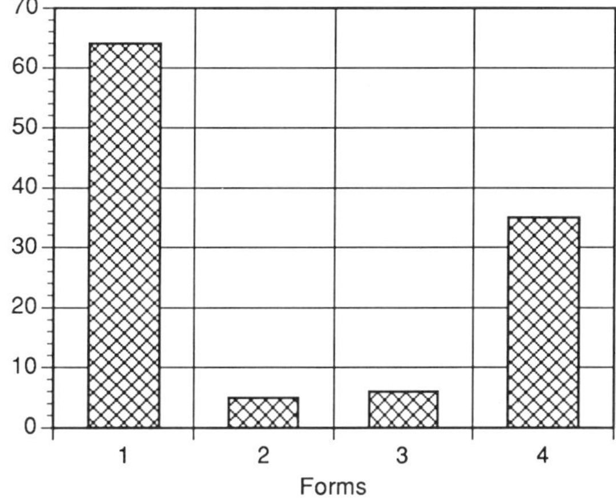

Figure 3.9. Bar graph illustrating quantity of Middle Roman Cooking Ware forms at Stobi

Form 1: Pan
Form 2: Pan
Form 3: Stewpot
Form 4: Two-handled Stewpot

1082. Lot 1636, No. 7. Pl. 127.

P.H. 0.040. Est. D. rim 0.280. One fragment of rim and wall.

1083. Inv. No. C-71-254. Lots 250, 252. Pl. 127.

H. 0.049. Est. D. rim 0.278. Three fragments mended, giving complete profile and about one-fourth of vessel.

1084. Inv. No. C-71-373. Lot 12. Pl. 127.

H. 0.057. Est. D. rim 0.380. Five fragments mended, giving profile.

This example copies the classic shape rather closely.

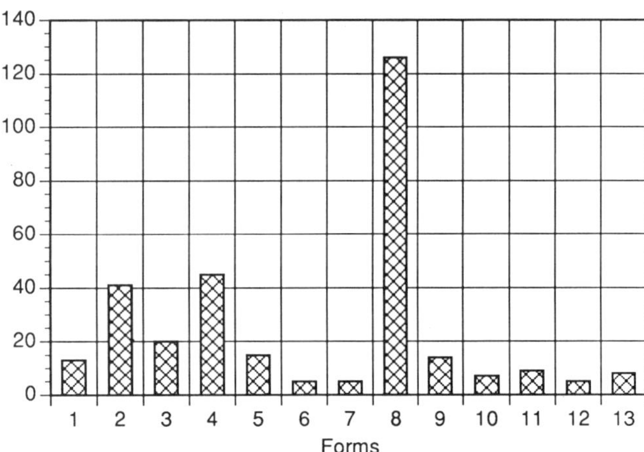

Figure 3.10. Bar graph illustrating quantity of Late Roman Cooking Ware forms at Stobi

Form 1: Bowl with flat rim
Form 2: Casserole
Form 3: Deep Bowl
Form 4: Deep Bowl
Form 5: Small Jar
Form 6: Jar with folded rim
Form 7: Jar
Form 8: Two-handled Stewpot
Form 9: Jug
Form 10: Pitcher
Form 11: Trefoil Pitcher
Form 12: Stamnos
Form 13: Jug

Form 2

Flat-bottomed pan with curved wall and grooved rim. Total: 4.

1085. Lot 550, No. 5. Pl. 127.
P.H. 0.032. Est. D. rim 0.173. One fragment of rim and wall.
Date: second and third quarters of the 1st century B.C.

Form 3

Flat-bottomed pan with straight wall and rounded rim. Angle of wall varies.
Date: first half of the 1st century B.C. Total: 5.

1086. Inv. No. C-71-277. Lots 14, 552. Pl. 127.
H. 0.050. Est. D. rim 0.304. Mended from three fragments (1 from Lot 552 and two from Lot 14).

1087. Lot 552, No. 753. Pl. 127.
H. 0.025. Est. D. rim 0.320. One fragment of rim and wall.

Form 4

Casserole with double horizontal handles and convex rim. Base not preserved but was probably rounded. Similar to **1146** of later date (ER). Diameters range from approximately 0.160 to 0.240 m.
Cf. Robinson, *Agora*, F77, pl. 72.
Date: first half of the 1st century B.C. Total: 5.

1088. Inv. No. C-71-371. Lot 140. Pl. 127.
P.H. 0.039. Est. D. rim 0.162. One fragment of rim, wall and handle.

1089. Lot 552, No. 842. Pl. 127.
P.H. 0.032. Est. D. rim 0.244. One fragment of rim and wall.

Form 5

Jar with convex rim, flat base. Most examples are tall. Rim diameters for the large size range from 0.090 to 0.155 m., but smaller examples such as **1090** are also found. This shape is like that common in the various Thin-Walled wares of Italy and the Western Mediterranean; e.g., Moevs, "Cosa," Forms 4, 6.
Date: first half of the 1st century B.C. Total: 80.

1090. Inv. No. C-71-39. Lot 134. Pl. 128.
H. 0.077. D. rim 0.074. Fragmentary and mended, with only small pieces missing from body and base. Concave bottom.

1091. Lot 831, No. 82. Pl. 128.
P.H. 0.160. Est. D. rim 0.095. Several fragments mended, giving rim and wall section and base and wall section, not joining.

1092. Lot 140, No. 42. Pl. 128.
P.H. 0.060. Est. D. rim 0.125. Two fragments of rim and wall mended.

Form 6

Jar with convex, grooved rim. No base preserved. Total: 3.

1093. Lot 552, No. 781. Pl. 128.
P.H. 0.030. Est. D. rim 0.108. One fragment of rim and wall.

1094. Lot 552, No. 798. Pl. 128.
P.H. 0.032. Est. D. rim 0.132. One fragment of rim and wall.

Form 7

Pot with short, flaring neck and overhanging rim. Base not preserved. Rim diameters range from 0.160 to 0.190 m.

Cf. Dyson, "Cosa," fig. 8, FG, fig. 9, FG31, dated ca. 200 B.C.; fig. 29:21, VD25, dated to late 2nd, early 1st centuries B.C.; also U. Wintermeyer, "Bemerkungen zur Typologie und Chronologie der hellenistisch-kaiserzeitlichen Gebrauchskeramik," *IstMitt* 34 (1984) 245, and fig. 2, no. 1, p. 150. Total: 12.

1095. Inv. No. C-75-23. Lot 1636. Pl. 128.
P.H. 0.092. Est. D. rim 0.188. Three fragments of rim and wall.

1096. Lot 610, No. 24. Pl. 128.
P.H. 0.044. Est. D. rim 0.183. One fragment of rim and wall.

Form 8

Jar with simple, flaring rim. Only bases preserved. Total: 9.

1097. Lot 552, No. 774. Pl. 128.
P.H. 0.037. Est. D. rim 0.123. One fragment of rim and wall.

Form 9

Pot with vertical, offset rim. Very thin walls. Total: 7.

1098. Inv. No. C-72-230. Lot 552, No. 787. Pl. 128.
P.H. 0.035. Est. D. rim 0.134. One fragment of rim and wall.
Date: second and third quarters of the 1st century B.C.

Form 10

Large pot with short, offset rim, frequently grooved on exterior and with lid seating groove on interior. Two strap handles extend from rim to a point just above maximum diameter. No bases preserved. Rim diameters range from 0.130 to 0.180 m. Total: 33.

1099. Inv. No. C-75-22. Lot 1636. Pl. 128.
P.H. 0.108. Est. D. rim 0.135. Six fragments mended to give rim, handle, and wall.

1100. Lot 554, No. 73. Pl. 128.
P.H. 0.042. Est. D. rim 0.135. Several fragments of rim, neck, and handle. Two grooves on rim exterior.

1101. Inv. No. C-72-108. Lot 552. Pl. 128.
P.H. 0.122. Est. D. rim 0.130. Many fragments mended to give rim, wall, and handles.

1102. Lot 551, No. 41. Pl. 129.
P.H. 0.063. Est. D. rim 0.160. One fragment of rim and neck. Single groove on neck.

1103. Lot 552, No. 861. Pl. 129.
P.H. 0.045. Est. D. rim 0.180. Two fragments of rim and wall.

1104. Lot 1538, No. 36. Pl. 129.
P.H. 0.040. Est. D. rim 0.160. One fragment of rim and neck.

Form 11

Large jar with flaring rim, wide lid seating on interior. Total: 4.

1105. Lot 552, No. 51. Pl. 129.
P.H. 0.032. Est. D. rim 0.225. One fragment of rim and wall.

Form 12

Pot with convex rim, plump body, and two strap handles extending from rim to just above point of maximum diameter. Rim diameters range from 0.095 to ca. 0.150 m. Total: 28.

1106. Lot 134, No. 109. Pl. 129.
P.H. 0.138. Est. D. rim 0.150. One fragment of rim and wall.

1107. Inv. No. C-71-276. Lot 134. Pl. 129.
P.H. 0.120. Est. D. rim 0.095. One fragment of rim and wall.

Form 13

Globular, close-mouthed jar with high-rising double horizontal handles. Vertical, frequently convex rim. Shoulder decorated with grooves. Diameters range from 0.150 to 0.205 m. Total: 21.

1108. Inv. No. C-72-216. Lot 552. Pl. 129.
P.H. 0.054. Est. D. rim 0.180. Two fragments of rim, wall, and handle mended.

1109. Inv. No. C-72-215. Lot 551. Pl. 129.

P.H. 0.043. Est. D. rim 0.205. Four fragments mended, preserving about one-half of rim, shoulder, and one handle.

Hellenistic cooking wares: Other (1110–1131)

Casseroles

1110. Round-bottomed pan. Inv. No. C-72-157. Lot 547. Pl. 130.

P.H. 0.063. Est. D. rim 0.245. Mended from many fragments, giving rim and body. About one-half preserved. Rounded rim with pronounced groove on interior suitable for lid. Two grooves just below point of maximum diameter which are neither concentric nor parallel to each other.

Date: second and third quarters of the 1st century B.C.

1111. Casserole with wide rim. Inv. No. C-72-193. Lot 547. Pl. 130.

P.H. 0. 032. Est. D. rim 0.280. One fragment of rim and wall. Rim interior preserves flange for lid.

Cf. Thompson, "TCHP," E141, fig. 121, p. 467, dated to the late 2nd, early 1st centuries B.C.

Date: second and third quarters of the 1st century B.C.

1112. Large casserole. Inv. No. C-72-231. Lot 552. Pl. 130.

P.H. 0.064. Est. D. rim 0.308. One fragment preserving rim, wall, and handle. Flat, outward-turned rim and double, rolled handles attached just below rim, rising in an arc about rim level.

Date: second and third quarters of the 1st century B.C.

Jars or bowls

1113. Bowl. Lot 608, No. 23. Pl. 130

P.H. 0.038. Est. D. rim 0.192. Single fragment of rim and wall. Two grooves below rim.

Date: first half of the 1st century B.C.

1114. Jar with convex rim. Lot 131, No. 28. Pl. 130.

P.H. 0.036. Est. D. rim 0.151. One fragment of rim and wall.

1115. Jar with convex rim. Lot 552, No. 862. Pl. 130.

P.H. 0.030. Est. D. rim 0.192. One fragment of rim and wall.

1116. Jar with everted rim. Lot 552, No. 788. Pl. 130.

P.H. 0.042. Est. D. rim 0.124. One fragment of rim and wall. Two grooves below rim.

1117. Jar with carinated rim. Lot 140, No. 47. Pl. 130.

P.H. 0.040. Est. D. rim 0.128. Two fragments of rim and wall.

1118. Jar with everted rim. Lot 610, No. 31. Pl. 130.

P.H. 0.024. Est. D. rim 0.120. Two fragments of rim and wall. Single ridge around neck.

1119. Jar. Lot 547, No. 500. Pl. 130.

P.H. 0.025. Est. D. rim 0.130. One fragment of rim.

1120. Jar with horizontal rim. Lot 552, No. 808. Pl. 130.

P.H. 0.028. Est. D. rim 0.109. One fragment of rim, wall, and horizontal handle.

Jar or stewpots

1121. Large jar with outward-turned rim. Lot 547, No. 32. Pl. 130.

P.H. 0.056. Est. D. rim 0.168. One fragment of rim and wall. Two wide grooves just above shoulder.

1122. Large jar with rounded rim. Lot 546, No. 5. Pl. 130.

P.H. 0.057. Est. D. rim 0.123. One fragment of rim and wall.

1123. Large, double-handled stewpot. Inv. No. C-72-188. Lot 552. Pl. 131.

P.H. 0.078. Est. D. rim 0.179. Several fragments mended, giving rim, body, and handles. Sharply angled and grooved rim with wide lid seating on interior. Grooves at shoulder. Double, horizontally placed handles.

1124. Small, two-handled stewpot. Inv. No. C-74-6. Lot 1094. Grave 84. Pl. 131.

H. 0.110. D. rim 0.080. Complete. One handle broken and mended. Small, globular pot with

convex rim on flat base. Two oval handles extend from rim to point of greatest diameter.
Found together with **32**, **34**, **147**, and **566**.
Date: early 1st century B.C.

1125. Small jug. Inv. No. C-71-131. Lot 74. Pl. 131.
H. 0.123. D. rim 0.078. Part of rim and small fragment from body missing. Round-bottomed jug with simple, everted rim and one strap handle. Bottom and lower body covered with narrow wheel-ridging.
This jug was found with an olpe (**23**) and the two vessels contained a hoard of silver denarii (W-MZ [1971] fig. 10). See the discussion in the entry for **23**.
Date: last quarter of the 2nd century B.C.

1126. Stewpot with one handle. Inv. No. C-71-278. Lot 12. Pl. 131.
P.H. 0.114. Est. D. rim 0.137. Mended from several fragments, preserving rim, wall, and remains of one handle.

1127. Large stewpot. Inv. No. C-71-125. Lot 442. Pl. 131.
H. 0.225. D. rim 0.153. D. body 0.253. Several large pieces missing but otherwise complete. Wide, flat rim, very plump body, and rounded bottom with concave button base. Single twisted handle rises up from rim to be attached just above point of maximum diameter.
Cf. Drougou and Touratsoglou, *Veroia*, 120–122, fig. 16.
Date: probably late 1st century B.C./early 1st century A.C.

1128. Small stewpot. Lot 552, No. 811. Pl. 131.
P.H. 0.037. Est. D. rim 0.114. One fragment of rim and wall.

Lids

1129. Lid fragment. Lot 12, No. 11. Pl. 131.
H. 0.046. D. top 0.034. Conical lid with flat knob.

1130. Lid. Lot 134, No. 105. Pl. 131.
H. 0.055. Est. D. 0.132. One fragment with complete profile.

1131. Lid. Lot 550, No. 15. Pl. 131.
H. 0.045. Est. D. 0.116. Complete profile.

Early Roman cooking wares: Forms 1–7 (**1132–1145**)

Form 1

Flat-based pan with straight wall and grooved or "orlo-bifido" rim. Angle and thickness of wall may vary. Same form as Hellenistic Cooking Ware Form 1, which occurs in much greater numbers. These Early Roman examples may, in fact, be residual. The rim groove is, however, uniformly large. Diameters range from 0.180 to 0.300 m. Total: 5.

1132. Lot 257, No. 71. Pl. 132.
H. 0.048. Est. D. rim 0.180. One fragment, giving complete profile.
Date: post-75 A.C.

1133. Inv. No. C-74-481. Lot 1416. Pl. 132.
H. 0.053. Est. D. rim 0.304. One fragment of complete profile with horizontal handle.

Form 2

Flat-bottomed pan with straight wall and rounded lip. Similar to Hellenistic Cooking Ware Form 3. Total: 3.

1134. Lot 488, No. 1. Pl. 132.
H. 0.036. Est. D. rim 0.240. One fragment of rim and wall.

1135. Lot 1416, No. 2. Pl. 132.
P.H. 0.040. Est. D. rim 0.193. One fragment of rim, wall, and ribbon handle.

Form 3

Pan with flat, horizontal rim, carinated body and round bottom. This shape is an early variant of the later MR Form 1, which has a flat bottom. Diameters range from 0.190 to 0.260 m. Total: 10.

1136. Inv. No. C-71-370. Lot 75. Pl. 132.
P.H. 0.033. Est. D. rim 0.190. One fragment of rim and wall.
Date: late 1st century B.C./early 1st century A.C.

Form 4

Small jar with convex rim. No bases preserved. Cf. Hellenistic Cooking Form 6. Rim diameters range from 0.070 to 0.100 m. Total: 7.

1137. Lot 488, No. 11. Pl. 132.
P.H. 0.031. Est. D. rim 0.090. One fragment of rim and wall.

1138. Lot 443, No. 2. Pl. 132.
P.H. 0.042. Est. D. rim 0.070. One fragment of rim and wall.

Form 5

Very small jar with narrow mouth. No bases preserved. Diameters range from 0.040 to 0.075 m. Total: 3.

1139. Lot 391, No. 1. Pl. 132.
P.H. 0.048. Est. D. rim 0.063. One fragment of rim and wall. Single groove on wall exterior.

1140. Lot 386, No. 9. Pl. 132.
P.H. 0.032. Est. D. rim 0.040. One fragment of rim and wall.

Form 6

Pot with grooved rim, wide lid seating, and two strap handles. Rim diameters range from 0.130 to 0.230 m. Cf. Maneva (1979) pl. 21, nos. 212, 213. Total: 31.

1141. Lot 258, No. 36. Pl. 132.
P.H. 0.045. Est. D. rim 0.198. One fragment of rim and neck. Single groove on neck.
Date: post-40 A.C.

1142. Lot 1441, No. 17. Pl. 132.
P.H. 0.044. Est. D. rim 0.150. One fragment of rim, wall, and handle.

1143. Lot 1098, No. 6. Pl. 132.
P.H. 0.040. Est. D. rim 0.160. One fragment of rim and wall.

Form 7

Large, globular, close-mouthed pot with double, horizontal, strap handles. Base not preserved. Diameters range from 0.180 to 0.200 m. Total: 11.

1144. Lot 260, No. 6. Pl. 133.
P.H. 0.050. Est. D. rim 0.196. One fragment of rim and wall.
Date: late 1st century B.C.

1145. Inv. No. C-74-331. Lot 1418. Pl. 133.
P.H. 0.207. Est. D. rim 0.185. Est. D. body 0.185. About one-half complete. Two shallow grooves on body, between handles only. Ridged strap handles rise above rim level.

Early Roman cooking wares: Other (**1146–1161**)

Open pans or casseroles

1146. Casserole with grooved rim. Inv. No. C-74-453. Lot 1511. Pl. 133.
P.H. 0.048. Est. D. rim 0.255. One fragment of rim, wall, and single handle. Grooved rim, sharply carinated wall, and probable round bottom. Round handles, placed horizontally, rise above rim level.
Date: mid-2nd century A.C.

1147. Casserole. Inv. No. C-75-87. Lot 1673. Pl. 133.
P.H. 0.103. Est. D. rim 0.156. Several fragments mended, giving separate sections of rim and body with handle. Very pointed lip with lid seating at interior. Carinated body with vertical strap handles.
For similar rim treatment, see Hayes, "Paphos," 99, 108, fig. 7:8, dated to the first half of the 2nd century A.C.; and Hayes, "Villa Dionysus," 105, 122, fig. 7, no. 79, dated early 2nd century A.C. The latter was apparently round-based, unlike the Stobi profile.

1148. Casserole or bowl with flaring rim. Lot 1538, No. 30. Pl. 133.
P.H. 0.041. Est. D. rim 0.210. One fragment of rim and wall.

1149. Casserole or bowl with grooved rim. Lot 456, No. 6. Pl. 133.
P.H. 0.050. Est. D. rim 0.200. One fragment of rim and wall.

Jars and pots

1150. Jar with folded rim. Lot 249, No. 32. Pl. 133.
P.H. 0.074. Est. D. rim 0.149. One fragment of rim and wall.
Date: post 75 A.C.

1151. Jar with folded rim. Lot 1418, No. 109. Pl. 133.
P.H. 0.029. Est. D. rim 0.154. One fragment of rim and wall.

1152. Jar with convex rim. Lot 1441, No. 19. Pl. 134.
P.H. 0.048. Est. D. rim 0.120. One fragment of rim and wall.

1153. Jar with grooved rim. Lot 231, No. 167. Pl. 134.
P.H. 0.034. Est. D. rim 0.140. One fragment of rim and wall.
Date: second half of the 1st century A.C.

1154. Jar with everted rim. Lot 259, No. 150. Pl. 134.
P.H. 0.045. Est. D. rim 0.100. One fragment of rim and wall.
Date: early 1st century A.C.

1155. Wide-mouthed jar. Lot 1420, No. 10. Pl. 134.
P.H. 0.025. Est. D. rim 0.162. One fragment of rim and wall.

1156. Jar. Lot 1094, No. 1. Pl. 134.
P.H. 0.055. Est. D. rim 0.130. One fragment of rim and wall.

1157. Jar. Lot 1441, No. 16. Pl. 134.
P.H. 0.037. Est. D. rim 0.094. One fragment of rim and wall.

1158. Large stewpot with double handles. Inv. No. C-71-32. Lot 391, Grave 39. Pl. 134.
H. 0.155. D. rim 0.125. Intact. Rounded, concave base. Two vertical handles, strap in section. W-MZ (1972) fig. 20.
Date: late 1st, early 2nd centuries A.C.(?).

1159. Large stewpot with double handles. Inv. No. C-74-7. Lot 1066, Grave 254. Pl. 134.
H. 0.167. D. rim 0.130. Complete. Two splayed handles. Fingerprints visible at base of handle where attached to body. This vessel is similar in profile to **1058** but is very roughly made and distinctly off-center.

1160. Large stewpot. Lot 1420, No. 11. Pl. 134.
P.H. 0.038. Est. D. rim 0.163. One fragment of rim and wall.

1161. Large stewpot. Lot 395, No. 1. Pl. 134.
P.H. 0.034. Est. D. rim 0.200. One fragment of rim and wall.

Middle Roman cooking wares: Forms 1–4 (1162–1175)

Form 1

Flat-based pie pan with wide, flat rim placed horizontally or at an angle. Bottom may be concave in center. A red or orange slip is common on the interior. Unless otherwise indicated, all are fire blackened on the exterior. Diameters range from 0.220 to 0.295 m. for smaller examples, and from 0.320 to 0.370 m. for the larger ones.
Date: mid-2nd and 3rd centuries A.C. Total: 64.

1162. Lot 1300, No. 4. Pl. 135.
H. 0.053. Est. D. rim 0.345. Six fragments mended, giving complete profile. Horizontally placed rim.

1163. Inv. No. C-74-162. Lot 1298. Pl. 135.
H. 0.041. Est. D. rim 0.260. Two fragments mended, giving complete profile. Short rim at an angle.

1164. Inv. No. C-73-72. Lot 890. Pl. 135.
H. 0.054. Est. D. rim 0.320. One fragment, giving complete profile. Orange (reddish yellow, 5YR 6/6) slip on rim and interior. Exterior is rough and fire blackened, but bottom is quite smooth, almost as if burnished. No burnishing lines, however, are visible.
Cf. Hayes, "Villa Dionysos," 126, 127, nos. 103, 104, 107, 108, dated mid-2nd to mid-3rd centuries A.C.

1165. Inv. No. C-74-140. Lot 1298. Pl. 135.
H. 0.055. Est. D. rim 0.240. One fragment of profile. Slightly concave rim place at an angle.

1166. Lot 1302, No. 2. Pl. 135.
H. 0.032. Est. D. rim 0.220. One fragment of profile. Rim at an angle. Slight projection of wall at bottom.

1167. Lot 1300, No. 3. Pl. 135.
H. 0.058. Est. D. rim 0.230. Five fragments mended, giving profile. Short rim at an angle and inset on interior where wall meets floor.

1168. Lot 1308, No. 550. Pl. 135.
H. 0.042. Est. D. rim 0.243. Three fragments mended, giving profile. Rim has a curved surface, and bottom is quite concave.

Form 2

Flat-based pan with tall, concave rim and small offset at base of wall. Diameters range from 0.23 to 0.30 m.

Date: late 3rd, first half of the 4th centuries A.C. Total: 5.

1169. Inv. No. C-77-60. Lot 1958. Pl. 136.
H. 0.060. Est. D. rim 0.268. One fragment, giving complete profile.

1170. Lot 1599, No. 42. Pl. 136.
H. 0.065. Est. D. rim 0.257. One fragment of complete profile. Red slip on rim and interior.

Form 3

Pot with tall, concave rim and plump body. No base preserved. Rim diameters range from 0.110 to 0.175 m. Total: 6.

1171. Lot 237, No. 111. Pl. 136.
P.H. 0.038. Est. D. rim 0.166. One fragment of rim and wall.
Date: early 4th century A.C.(?).

1172. Lot 2121, No. 11. Pl. 136.
P.H. 0.038. Est. D. rim 0.110. One fragment of rim and wall.

Form 4

Two-handled pot with broad rim usually placed at right angles to the side wall, although some examples have a more horizontally placed rim. Small handles extend from just below rim to the point of greatest diameter on the body or just above. Wall is straight or curves gently in to base. No base preserved but was probably concave or flat. Rim diameters range from 0.145 to 0.215 m.

See Hayes, "Villa Dionysus," Cooking pots, Type 2, fig. 5, dated to the 2nd and 3rd centuries A.C. Total: 35.

1173. Lot 1296, No. 24. Pl. 136.
P.H. 0.075. Est. D. rim 0.163. One fragment of rim, handle, and wall.

1174. Lot 924, No. 8. Pl. 136.
P.H. 0.070. Est. D. rim 0.165. One fragment of rim, handle, and wall.

1175. Lot 1404, No. 39. Pl. 136.
P.H. 0.080. Est. D. rim 0.135. One fragment of rim, handle, and wall.

Middle Roman cooking wares: Other (**1176–1209**)

Pans or dishes

1176. Dish. Lot 1298, No. 10. Pl. 137.
P.H. 0.035. Est. D. rim 0.235. One fragment of rim.
Date: mid-3rd to mid-4th centuries A.C.

1177. Dish with flanged rim. Lot 1599, No. 33. Pl. 137.
P.H. 0.053. Est. D. rim 0.259. One fragment of rim and wall.
Date: 4th century A.C.

1178. Dish with flanged rim. Lot 1300, No. 11.
P.H. 0.023. Est. D. rim 0.280. One fragment of rim.
Date: 3rd century A.C.

Small jars

1179. Jar. Lot 932, No. 76. Pl. 137.
P.H. 0.082. Est. D. rim 0.133. One fragment of rim and wall.
Date: first half of the 2nd century A.C.

1180. Small jar. Inv. No. C-71-211. Lot 164. Pl. 137.
H. 0.104. Est. D. rim 0.080. Mended from eight fragments, giving profile. Small pot with two sliced handles and flat base. Wheel-ridging on exterior from neck to base.
Cf. Hayes, "Villa Dionysus," 124, fig. 6, no. 70.

1181. Narrow-mouthed jar. Lot 932, No. 25. Pl. 137.
P.H. 0.050. Est. D. rim 0.084. One fragment of rim and wall. Two grooves at neck.
Date: first half of the 2nd century A.C.

1182. Small jar. Lot 931, No. 8. Pl. 137.
P.H. 0.040. Est. D. rim 0.093. One fragment of rim and wall.

1183. Jar. Inv. No. C-77-012. Lot 1957. Pl. 137.
P.H. 0.034. Est. D. rim 0.113. One fragment of rim and wall.

1184. Small jar. Lot 1302, No. 5. Pl. 137.
P.H. 0.037. Est. D. rim 0.117. One fragment of rim and wall.
Date: 3rd century A.C.

1185. Two-handled jar. Lot 1296, No. 8. Pl. 137.
P.H. 0.035. Est. D. rim 0.106. One fragment of rim and wall, with remains of two handles.
Date: mid-3rd to mid-4th centuries A.C.

Stewpots or large jars

1186. Stewpot. Lot 1296, No. 45. Pl. 138.
P.H. 0.065. Est. D. rim 0.160. Two fragments mended, giving rim and wall.
Date: mid-3rd to mid-4th centuries A.C.

1187. Stewpot. Lot 930, No. 136. Pl. 138.
P.H. 0.033. Est. D. rim 0.124. One fragment of rim and wall.
Date: first half of the 2nd century A.C.

1188. Large jar. Lot 1302. No. 4. Pl. 138.
P.H. 0.038. Est. D. rim 0.160. One fragment of rim and wall.
Date: 3rd century A.C.

1189. Stewpot. Lot 78, No. 57. Pl. 138.
P.H. 0.045. Est. D. rim 0.160. One fragment of rim and wall.

1190. Stewpot. Lot 1297, No. 17. Pl. 138.
P.H. 0.050. Est. D. rim 0.160. One fragment of rim and wall. Grooves just below neck.
Date: mid-3rd to mid-4th centuries A.C.

1191. Stewpot. Lot 937, No. 27. Pl. 138.
P.H. 0.042. Est. D. rim 0.184. One fragment of rim and wall.

1192. Double-handled pot. Lot 1298, No. 4. Pl. 138.
P.H. 0.060. Est. D. rim 0.134. One fragment of rim, wall, and handles. Thin-walled pot with double handles.
Date: mid-3rd to mid-4th centuries A.C.

1193. Double-handled pot. Lot 924, No. 6. Pl. 138.
P.H. 0.092. Est. D. rim 0.170. One fragment of rim, wall, and handle.
Similar to **1192** above.

1194. Large pot. Lot 1296, No. 38. Pl. 138.
P.H. 0.075. Est. D. rim 0.140. One fragment of rim and wall. Exterior decorated with a series of grooves at regular intervals.

1195. Large pot with handles. Lot 68, No. 141. Pl. 139.
P.H. 0.083. Est. D. rim 0.200. One fragment of rim, wall, and handle. Large pot with concave rim and double strap handles.

1196. Large pot with handles. Lot 1302, No. 8. Pl. 139.
P.H. 0.057. Est. D. rim 0.254. One fragment of rim, wall, and handle. Flat rim with wide body and high-rising handle.
Date: 3rd century A.C.

1197. Large pot with handles. Lot 1310, No. 13. Pl. 139.
P.H. 0.079. Est. D. rim 0.229. Mended from two fragments, giving rim, wall, and handle. Wide-mouthed pot with shoulder carination and double handles.
Date: 3rd century A.C.

1198. Large jar. Lot 1299, No. 3. Pl. 139.
P.H. 0.103. Est. D. rim 0.230. One fragment of rim and wall.
Date: mid-3rd to mid-4th centuries A.C.

Jugs / Pitchers

1199. Jug neck. Lot 1302, No. 6. Pl. 139.
P.H. 0.035. Est. D. rim 0.111. One fragment of rim and wall from collared jar.

1200. Pitcher neck. Lot 1302, No. 3. Pl. 139.
P.H. 0.040. Est. D. rim 0.081. One fragment of rim, neck, and one handle.

1201. Large pitcher neck. Inv. No. C-70-133. Lot 810. Pl. 139.
P.H. 0.096. Est. D. rim 0.094. One fragment of rim, neck, and two handles. Red slip on exterior and bitumin on interior and at rim.

1202. Three-handled pot. Inv. No. C-72-54. Lot 762. Pl. 140.
P.H. 0.166. D. Rim 0.199. Base missing. Incised decoration on neck and shoulder: wavy lines alternating with dots and teardrops.
Vessels with three handles for suspension (cf. **1054**) are seen more commonly in the northern provinces of Moesia, Dacia, and Pannonia; see Brukner, *Rimska Keramika*, 183, T.105, dated 3rd and 4th centuries A.C.

Miscellaneous bases

1203. Small base. Lot 242, No. 1. Pl. 140.
P.H. 0.012. Est. D. base 0.052. One fragment of

base with concave bottom and offset near bottom at interior and exterior.

1204. Small base. Lot 1407, No. 11. Pl. 140.
P.H. 0.013. Est. D. base 0.080. One fragment of base with concave bottom.
Date: second half of the 3rd century A.C.

1205. Concave base. Lot 1296, No. 114. Pl. 140.
P.H. 0.015. Est. D. base 0.050. One fragment of base with concave bottom.
Date: mid-3rd to mid-4th centuries A.C.

1206. Rounded base. Lot 929, No. 14. Pl. 140.
P.H. 0.040. Est. D. base 0.060. One fragment of rounded base.

Lids

1207. Small lid. Inv. No. C-73-26. Lot 929. Pl. 140.
H. 0.022. Est. D. 0.093. Complete profile.

1208. Broad, flat lid. Lot 1300, No. 2. Pl. 140.
H. 0.018. Est. D. 0.170. Lower portion of short lid.
Date: 3rd century A.C.

1209. Pithos lid. Inv. No. C-71-242. Lot 237. Pl. 140.
P.H. 0.019. D. 0.250. Central part missing.

Late Roman cooking wares: Forms 1–13 (**1210–1242**)

Form 1

Bowl with broad, flat rim and curved body. Sometimes there is a slight carination on the wall below the rim or at mid-point. Rim surface may be grooved or decorated with wavy lines, and edge may be notched. No base preserved. Because this shape is so similar to the casserole shape of Form 2, some of these may actually belong to that group, but without handles it is difficult to tell. Diameters range from 0.155 to 0.222 m.
Date: 4th and 5th centuries A.C. Total: 13.

1210. Lot 1285, No. 2. Pl. 140.
P.H. 0.033. Est. D. rim 0.176. One fragment of rim and wall. Notched rim edge.

1211. Lot 277, No. 78. Pl. 140.
P.H. 0.060. Est. D. rim 0.164. One fragment of rim and wall.

1212. Inv. No. C-70-89. Lot 514. Pl. 140.
P.H. 0.060. Est. D. rim 0.180. One fragment of rim and wall.

1213. Lot 304, No. 31. Pl. 140.
P.H. 0.044. Est. D. rim 0.185. One fragment of rim and wall.

Form 2

Casserole with two handles, broad, flat rim, and carination on body at point of maximum diameter which is rather high. Concave, button base. Diameters range from 0.140 to 0.260 m.
Date: 4th and 5th centuries A.C. Total: 41.

1214. Lot 1296, No. 36. Pl. 141.
P.H. 0.047. Est. D. rim 0.143. One fragment of rim, handle, and wall. A rather small version.
Only two other examples have handles beginning under the rim. Most are an extension of the rim itself. This may be the earliest example of the shape and the only example from a Middle Roman context of approximately the mid-3rd century. See Hayes, "Villa Dionysus," 106, and fig. 7 on p. 125.

1215. Inv. No. C-74-164. Lot 1352. Pl. 141.
H. 0.092. Est. D. rim 0.190. Three fragments mended, giving complete profile.

1216. Lot 297, No. 40. Pl. 141.
P.H. 0.058. Est. D. rim 0.250. One fragment of rim, handle, and wall.

1217. Inv. No. C-71-360. Lot 54. Pl. 141.
H. 0.075. Est. D. rim 0.180. Mended from nine fragments, preserving about one-third of vessel. Two wide grooves on body above point of maximum diameter.

1218. Inv. No. C-78-18. Lot 2089. Pl. 141.
P.H. 0.068. Est. D. rim 0.183. Two fragments mended, giving rim, handle, and wall. Very thick rim. Handles extend from below rim to point of maximum diameter.

Form 3

Deep bowl with straight or slightly curved wall and plain or thickened rim, flat or concave on top. Base not preserved. Diameters range from 0.200 to 0.285 m. with small examples at about 0.165 m.
Date: 4th century A.C. Total: 20.

1219. Lot 243, No. 1. Pl. 141.
P.H. 0.042. Est. D. rim 0.166. One fragment of rim and wall.

1220. Lot 295, No. 9. Pl. 141.
P.H. 0.080. Est. D. rim 0.280. One fragment of rim and wall. Single groove preserved on wall just above the break.

Form 4

Deep bowl with straight wall and rounded or thickened lip. No base preserved. Some examples show a groove below rim or on the side wall. Diameters range from 0.210 to 0.240 m.

Date: 3rd and 4th centuries A.C. Total: 45.

1221. Lot 278, No. 63. Pl. 142.
P.H. 0.070. Est. D. rim 0.215. One fragment of rim and wall.

1222. Lot 305, No. 17. Pl. 142.
P.H. 0.060. Est. D. rim 0.224. One fragment of rim and wall.

Form 5

Small jar/cup with flaring rim or slightly concave rim with globular body and concave bottom. A single handle is found on the cup examples. Rim diameters range from 0.075 to 0.090 m.

Date: late 4th to 6th centuries A.C. Total: 15.

1223. Lot 278, No. 58. Pl. 141.
P.H. 0.049. Est. D. rim 0.092. One fragment of rim and wall.

1224. Inv. No. C-71-3. Lot 157. Pl. 142.
P.H. 0.065. Est. D. rim 0.085. Two fragments mended, giving rim, handle, and wall.

1225. Inv. No. C-74-257. Lot 1345. Pl. 142.
H. 0.090. D. rim 0.092. Mended from several fragments, giving almost complete vessel. One strap handle from below rim to point of maximum diameter on body.

1226. Inv. No. C-74-258. Lot 1345. Pl. 142.
H. 0.083. D. rim 0.092. Mended from several fragments to give almost complete vessel.

Same shape as **1225**. This example and **1225** are from a deposit of household debris (including **619**, **1233**, **1267**, **1276–1278**) left on the floor of Room 32 of the Fuller's House when it was destroyed, perhaps by an earthquake, in the early 6th century A.C.; see W-MZ (1974) 139–140.

1227. Inv. No. C-74-332. Lot 1334. Pl. 142.
H. 0.093. Est. D. rim 0.100. Mended from many fragments, giving complete profile. Small hole just below rim.

Form 6

Jar with folded rim, either vertical or inturned. Only rims preserved. Diameters range from 0.135 to 0.170 m.

Date: 4th and 5th centuries A.C. Total: 5.

1228. Lot 302, No. 9. Pl. 142.
P.H. 0.050. Est. D. rim 0.158. One rim fragment.

1229. Lot 277, No. 92. Pl. 142.
P.H. 0.050. Est. D. rim 0.138. One rim fragment.

Form 7

Jar or pot with everted rim and curved wall. Wavy line decoration is often incised on shoulder. Rim diameters vary from 0.115 to 0.180 m.

Date: 6th century and later. Total: 5.

1230. Inv. No. C-73-73. Lot 849. Pl. 142.
P.H. 0.130. Est. D. rim 0.158. Three fragments mended, giving rim and wall. Simple, everted rim and plump body.

Form 8

Two-handled pot with everted rim. Upper rim surface may be flat or grooved to hold lid. Strap handles extend from rim to just above point of maximum diameter. Concave base. Many examples have wheel-ridging on shoulder. The latest examples (**1233**) have a simple everted or vertical rim and very thin walls. Rim diameters range from 0.100 to 0.180 m.

Date: early 5th to mid-6th centuries A.C. Total: 126.

1231. Lot 300, No. 1. Pl. 143.
P.H. 0.057. Est. D. rim 0.108. One fragment of rim, handle, and wall. Wheel-ridging on shoulder.

Date: early 5th century A.C.

1232. Inv. No. C-78-29. Lot 2111. Pl. 143.
P.H. 0.040. Est. D. rim 0.110. One fragment of rim, handle, and wall. Wide groove on shoulder.

1233. Inv. No. C-74-330. Lot 1345. Pl. 143.
P.H. 0.150. D. rim 0.170. Many fragments mended, giving profile and part of one handle. Very thin fabric.
Date: early 6th century A.C. See **1226** for discussion of context.

1234. Inv. No. C-73-30. Lot 853. Pl. 143.
H. 0.189. D. rim 0.137. Mended from numerous fragments, giving about seven-eighths of vessel. Wheel-ridging on shoulder.

1235. Lot 1338, No. 1. Pl. 143.
H. 0.180. D. rim 0.153. Complete profile preserved.
Another example (C-74-211) comes from the same deposit; see W-MZ (1974) 139.
Date: early to mid-5th century A.C.

1236. Inv. No. C-71-128. Lot 168. Pl. 143.
P.H. 0.170. Est. D. rim 0.130. Fragmentary and mended, preserving rim, wall, and handle.

Form 9

Jug with collared rim and one handle. Only rim and neck preserved. Rim diameters range from 0.085 to 0.140 m. Both of the examples below date to the early 5th century A.C. Total: 14.

1237. Lot 305, No. 42. Pl. 144.
P.H. 0.045. Est. D. rim 0.075. One fragment of rim and neck with stub of a handle.

1238. Lot 299, No. 3. Pl. 144.
P.H. 0.048. Est. D. rim 0.131. One fragment of rim and neck.

Form 10

Pitcher with one handle and simple everted rim. Total: 7.

1239. Lot 307, No. 32. Pl. 144.
P.H. 0.059. Est. D. rim 0.060. One fragment of rim, neck, and trace of handle attachment.

Form 11

Pitcher with trefoil mouth. Total: 9.

1240. Inv. No. C-75-100. Lot 1657. Pl. 144.
P.H. 0.075. Est. D. rim 0.074. Four fragments mended, giving rim and neck.

Form 12

Stamnos or tall table amphora with two handles. Total: 5.

1241. Lot 307, No. 29. Pl. 144.
P.H. 0.067. Est. D. rim 0.105. One fragment of rim, neck, and remains of two handles.

Form 13

Large jug with everted rim and wide neck with curved profile. Total: 8.

1242. Inv. No. C-71-399. Lot 150. Pl. 144.
P.H. 0.098. Est. D. rim 0.143. One fragment of rim and neck.

Late Roman cooking wares: Other (**1243–1292**)

Bowls and dishes

1243. Dish with flanged rim. Inv. No. C-71-424. Lot 150. Pl. 144.
P.H. 0.048. Est. D. rim 0.233. One fragment of rim and wall. Gray fabric. Faint wheel-ridging on exterior.
Cf. Phocaean Red Slip, Hayes Form 8.

1244. Dish with flanged rim. Inv. No. C-77-62. Lot 2033. Pl. 144.
P.H. 0.044. Est. D. rim 0.212. One fragment of rim and wall. Red fabric blackened on rim and interior.

1245. Small bowl. Lot 277, No. 57. Pl. 145.
P.H. 0.035. Est. D. rim 0.124. One fragment of rim and wall. Flat, slightly concave rim and thin walls.

1246. Small bowl. Lot 298, No. 601. Pl. 145.
P.H. 0.028. Est. D. rim 0.185. One fragment of rim and wall. Flat, slightly concave rim has incised band of wavy lines.

1247. Bowl. Lot 293, No. 46. Pl. 145.
P.H. 0.040. Est. D. rim 0.230. Two fragments mended, giving rim and wall. Wide, flaring rim has groove at interior.
Cf. David E. Johnston in W.H.C. Frend, "The Byzantine Basilica Church at Knossos," *BSA* 57 (1962) 227, fig. 19, nos. 88, 90.

1248. Small bowl or jar neck. Lot 306, No. 27. Pl. 145.

P.H. 0.045. Est. D. rim 0.093. One fragment of rim and wall. Rolled rim and wheel-ridging on exterior.

Date: early 5th century A.C.

1249. Small bowl. Inv. No. C-78-156. Lot 2263. Pl. 145.

H. 0.054. Est. D. rim 0.135. Mended from five fragments, giving about one-half of vessel. Flat, slightly concave rim, plump body, and concave base.

1250. Incurved bowl. Inv. No. C-72-252. Lot 645. Pl. 145.

P.H. 0.035. Est. D. rim 0.215. One fragment of rim and wall. Red fabric with gray core. Two grooves on exterior.

Casseroles or jars

1251. Casserole. Inv. No. C-78-125. Lot 2213. Pl. 145.

P.H. 0.048. Est. D. rim 0.332. One fragment of rim and wall. Red fabric with gray core.

1252. Casserole. Inv. No. C-70-105. Lot 1017. Pl. 145.

H. 0.105. Est. D. rim 0.320. Several pieces mended, preserving profile and about one-half of vessel. Very gritty, micaceous gray fabric. Wide, flaring rim over carinated body with slight offset at base. Flat bottom. Remains of one horizontally placed handle directly below rim. The rim edge is decorated with irregularly spaced notches, and the body carination has been pinched rather haphazardly in pie-crust fashion.

Cf. Frend, *BSA* 57 (1962) [cited under **1247**] 225, fig. 18, for similar broad and deep shapes, and Brukner, *Rimska Keramika*, T.96, no. 195 for similar rim treatment.

1253. Jar. Lot 304, No. 26. Pl. 146.

P.H. 0.046. Est. D. rim 0.095. Single fragment of rim and wall.

1254. Jar. Inv. No. C-73-111. Lot 878. Pl. 146.

P.H. 0.045. Est. D. rim 0.111. One fragment of rim and wall. Red fabric.

1255. Jar. Lot 274, No. 107. Pl. 146.

P.H. 0.038. Est. D. rim 0.135. One fragment of rim and wall.

1256. Jar. Lot 299, No. 16. Pl. 146.

P.H. 0.045. Est. D. rim 0.102. Two fragments of rim and wall, mended.

1257. Jar. Lot 277, No. 73. Pl. 146.

P.H. 0.043. Est. D. rim 0.085. One fragment of rim and neck.

Stewpots or large jars

1258. Stewpot. Inv. No. C-71-423. Lot 165. Pl. 146.

P.H. 0.060. Est. D. rim 0.126. One fragment of rim and wall. Rounded rim concave on interior. Grooves on shoulder.

1259. Stewpot. Lot 1404, No. 46. Pl. 146.

P.H. 0.050. Est. D. rim 0.125. One fragment of rim and wall.

1260. Pot. Inv. No. C-71-8. Lot 146. Pl. 146.

P.H. 0.050. Est. D. rim 0.115. One fragment of rim and wall. Everted rim curving in to form sharply carinated shoulder. Incised wavy lines on shoulder.

1261. Stewpot. Inv. No. C-75-58. Lot 1810. Pl. 146.

P.H. 0.043. Est. D. rim 0.145. One fragment of rim and wall. Tall rim with incised wavy band on shoulder.

1262. Stewpot. Lot 1404, No. 36. PL. 146.

P.H. 0.042. Est. D. rim 0.140. One fragment of rim and wall.

1263. Stewpot. Inv. No. C-71-401. Lot 159. Pl. 146.

P.H. 0.050. Est. D. rim 0.160. One fragment of rim, neck, and wall. Grooves on shoulder.

1264. Stewpot. Inv. No. C-71-400. Lot 147. Pl. 147.

P.H. 0.047. Est. D. rim 0.172. One fragment of rim and wall. Sharp ridge at shoulder.

1265. Stewpot. Lot 307, No. 108. Pl. 147.

P.H. 0.034. Est. D. rim 0.220. One fragment of rim.

1266. Pot with two handles. Lot 277, No. 105. Pl. 147.

P.H. 0.054. Est. D. rim 0.223. One fragment of rim and remains of handle.

1267. Large jar. Inv. No. C-74-333. Lot 1345. Pl. 147.

P.H. 0.174. Est. D. rim 0.115. Mended from many fragments, giving nonjoining profile. Straight, everted rim offset from body by wide groove. Flat base.

Date: early 6th century A.C. For context, see comments under **1226**.

1268. Large jar. Inv. No. C-72-70. Lot 523. Pl. 148.

P.H. 0.115. Est. D. rim 0.172. One fragment of rim and wall. Light red clay and reddish brown slip. Everted rim and globular body with slight carination at point of maximum diameter. Exterior is decorated with small squares impressed upon the wall while the clay was still damp.

Both the shape and decoration of this piece are unusual, and perhaps missing handles would place it in the category of three-handled jars. Note the shape of no. 315, T.34, in Bojović, *Singidunum* as well as of T.95 of Brukner, *Rimska Keramika,* dated 4th century there.

Date: late 4th, early 5th centuries A.C.

1269. Two-handled pot. Lot 1819, No. 5. Pl. 147.

H. 0.145. D. rim 0.130. Mended and almost complete.

Similar to LR Form 8.

1270. Pot with double handles. Lot 304, No. 21. Pl. 147.

P.H. 0.107. Est. D. rim 0.164. One fragment of rim, wall, and handle.

Date: early 5th century A.C.

1271. Pot with double handles. Lot 274, No. 71. Pl. 148.

P.H. 0.079. Est. D. rim 0.140. One fragment of rim, wall, and handle. Wheel-ridging on exterior.

1272. Jar. Lot 297, No. 27. Pl. 148.

P.H. 0.049. Est. D. rim 0.113. One fragment of rim and neck.

1273. Jar. Lot 277, No. 71. Pl. 148.

P.H. 0.055. Est. D. rim 0.146. One fragment of rim, neck, and handle.

Pitchers and jugs

1274. Pitcher. Lot 299, No. 6. Pl. 148.

P.H. 0.037. Est. D. rim 0.060. One fragment of rim and neck.

1275. Trefoil-mouth pitcher. Inv. No. C-71-203. Lot 169. Pl. 148.

H. 0.151. D. rim 0.065. Several fragments mended, giving two-thirds of vessel and complete profile. Single strap handle extends from neck to point of maximum diameter.

Date: late 4th, early 5th centuries A.C.

1276. Jug. Inv. No. C-74-255. Lot 1345. Pl. 148.

P.H. 0.140. Est. D. neck 0.026. Est. D. base 0.067. Neck and body of jug mended from several fragments. Reddish brown fabric. Body is decorated with a double row of incised wavy lines flanked by triple grooves.

Date: early 6th century A.C. For context, see **1226**.

1277. Double-handled jug. Inv. No. C-74-467. Lot 1346. Pl. 148.

P.H. neck 0.075. Est. D. neck 0.024. P.H. bottom 0.045. Est. D. base 0.067. In two pieces, each mended from several fragments. Two handles attached to neck flange. Flat base. Red fabric.

Date: early 6th century A.C. For context, see **1226**.

1278. Pot. Inv. No. C-74-259. Lot 1345. Pl. 149.

P.H. 0.074. Est. D. neck 0.045. Max. D. body 0.096. Rim and handle missing from piriform-shaped pot. Reddish brown fabric.

Date: early 6th century A.C. For context, see **1226**.

Miscellaneous bases

1279. Base. Lot 297, No. 44. Pl. 149.

P.H. 0.025. Est. D. base 0.040. One fragment of flat base with offset on interior.

1280. Base. Lot 277, No. 112. Pl. 149.

P.H. 0.040. Est. D. base 0.042. Portion of vessel bottom.

1281. Small base. Lot 299, No. 37. Pl. 149.

P.H. 0.018. Est. D. base 0.043. Concave base, small moulding at exterior of base.

1282. Large base. Lot 277, No. 113. Pl. 149.

P.H. 0.040. Est. D. base 0.080. Concave base.

1283. Large base. Lot 301, No. 7. Pl. 149.

P.H. 0.033. Est. D. base 0.090. Concave base with two widely spaced grooves on exterior.

1284. Large base. Lot 297, No. 46. Pl. 149.
P.H. 0.050. Est. D. base 0.090. Lower portion of large vessel with offset at base exterior.

1285. Large base. Lot 297, No. 47. Pl. 149.
P.H. 0.056. One fragment of flat base with straight wall.

Lids

1286. Very small lid. Lot 297, No. 51. Pl. 149.
P.H. 0.009 Est. D. 0.043. One fragment giving complete profile of lid with concave top and upturned rim.

1287. Lid. Inv. No. C-71-64. Lot 239. Pl. 149.
H. 0.026. Est. D. 0.091. Single piece with flat top and wheel-ridged surface.

1288. Lid. Inv. No. C-73-74. Lot 853. Pl. 149.
H. 0.080. Est. D. 0.093. Almost complete. Flat top with beveled rim edge.

1289. Lid. Inv. No. C-75-18. Lot 1656. Pl. 149.
H. 0.048. Est. D. 0.060. One fragment giving complete profile. Tall profile with beveled rim edge.

1290. Lid. Lot 305, No. 7. Pl. 149.
P.H. 0.040. One fragment of curved knob and part of wall.

1291. Lid. Lot 296, No. 7. Pl. 149.
P.H. 0.034. One fragment of flat top and wall.

1292. Thick-walled lid. Lot 274, No. 114. Pl. 149.
P.H. 0.043. Est. D. 0.145. Sizeable portion of wall preserved.

4

CHRONOLOGY AND DEPOSITS

•

Introduction

To establish the pottery chronology presented here, a selection of dated deposits ranging from the period of earliest documented occupation at the site in the 3rd century B.C. to the abandonment of the city in the 6th century A.C. were chosen for study. In addition to selecting those deposits with reliable stratigraphy and with relatively well established date, as much as possible we chose deposits with large amounts of pottery. All the pottery in these deposits was studied and quantified with the aid of computer analysis.[1] Descriptions of the core deposits follow these introductory comments.

In addition to the pottery from the core deposits, catalogued (inventoried) pieces from elsewhere on the site have been included in order to present as comprehensive a picture of the ceramic assemblage as possible. Some of these items are unique, for example, imports or complete vessels from the cemeteries; others provide better illustrations of types found in core deposits.

Unfortunately, no wells or cisterns have been located or excavated by the Stobi Project. Whole vessels or shapes, therefore, are rare except in the cemeteries.

Vertical sequences spanning a long period of time are also rare. A long trench on the Acropolis provides a stratified sequence of habitation from the 2nd century B.C. to the 6th century A.C.—that is, representing the entire life of the city. The area excavated was not large, however, and the overall quantities of pottery are not great.

The destruction levels in public buildings and large residential complexes of the 2nd through the 5th centuries contained substantial quantities of pottery, in some cases sealed beneath mosaic floors of the Central Basilica, the Early Roman building west of the Inner Wall, and the Episcopal Basilica.

The great amount of pottery from the later 2nd and 3rd centuries comes in large part from fills used in the considerable construction and remodelling that took place in the 4th and 5th centuries at Stobi. Material is also plentiful in the areas where refuse was allowed to accumulate after structures had been abandoned: the East Parodos of the Theater and the street along the East City Wall are good examples.

Dates given for the deposits are based on the latest material found therein. In some cases the coin evidence may be the only indication of a later date in a deposit with much earlier material used as fill.[2] Because of the lack of an established chronology for Macedonia, it was necessary to rely in large part on dated imports.[3] Carbon-14 analyses of charcoal have been carried out on samples from graves in the West Cemetery, but this information is of limited use because the range of dates is so great and the amount of pottery associated with the samples is quite small. In some cases the dates obtained from analysis

[1] A comprehensive account of the procedures used for the computer analysis by the author appears in Anderson-Stojanović (1982).

[2] Stobi staff numismatists have been Michael Crawford and Alan Walker.

[3] Initial identification of many imports was generously made by John W. Hayes. Identification and dating of the glass have been undertaken by Dragan Stojanović.

are much earlier than well-established pottery dates.[4]

Not all the deposits on the site could, of course, be studied completely, and those in the Deposit Lists fall into two groups: (1) those core deposits used to establish the pottery chronology (Tables 4.13–4.15) and (2) other deposits from which the additional material presented in this volume originates (Tables 4.16 and 4.17).[5] The core deposits that have provided the basis for the organization of the local pottery typology into Hellenistic, Early Roman, Middle Roman, and Late Roman periods are shown grouped by periods in Table 4.1. A full account of other significant deposits will appear in the forthcoming publications of the various buildings and monuments at the site.

The descriptions of context are based on information recorded by the excavators in the field notebooks and reports and on published preliminary reports.

The deposits have been grouped according to the formal subdivisions (areas) of the site in which they occurred.[6] These areas are the site divisions set up by the Stobi Project for the purpose of organizing records. In some cases, the name given to the area refers to a building that is later than the actual deposit. A narrative description of the main groups of core deposits together with the evidence for dating precedes the complete tabulated list (Tables 4.16 and 4.17) organized according to Lot number.[7] Tables follow the descriptions and set forth the contents of each deposit including quantities of wares and the catalogue numbers of items published in this volume. Form numbers of relevant published typologies are also included. The discussion of deposits follows an approximate chronological order. Locations of major buildings and roads are shown on the site plan (Pl. 2).

Table 4.1. Summary of Core Deposits divided into chronological periods

Hellenistic Lots (2nd, 1st centuries B.C.)
Total RBH: 2349 40 Lots

12, 13, 14, 74, 75, 76, 87, 88, 89, 130, 131, 132, 134, 135, 140, 250, 251, 252, 262, 263, 547, 548, 549, 550, 551, 552, 554, 555, 557, 558, 563, 564, 608, 610, 687, 689, 829, 831, 1636, 1637

Early Roman Lots (1st century A.C.)
Total RBH: 658 13 Lots

228, 229, 230, 231, 248, 249, 257, 258, 259, 260, 261, 545, 546

Middle Roman Lots (2nd, 3rd, 1st half of the 4th century A.C.)
Total RBH: 3425 46 Lots

237–247, 924, 929, 930, 931, 932, 933, 934, 936, 937, 938, 939, 940, 941, 942, 1295, 1296, 1297, 1298, 1299, 1300, 1301, 1302, 1303, 1304, 1306, 1307, 1308, 1309, 1310, 1332, 1333, 1407, 1408, 1409, 1410

Late Roman Lots (2nd half of 4th–6th centuries A.C.)
Total RBH: 2873 33 Lots

234 235, 236, 274, 277, 278, 293, 294, 295, 297, 298, 299, 300, 301, 302, 303, 304, 305, 306, 307, 308, 943, 944, 945, 946, 1278, 1279, 1280, 1281, 1282, 1284, 1285, 1404

[4] See Anderson-Stojanović (1987) 113, note 41.

[5] Material from the West Cemetery is identified by Grave Number and may not always be associated with a Lot.

[6] See "Introductory Notes for Catalogue," Chapter 1, for list of abbreviations.

[7] For the typologies used in the descriptions of the Core Deposits, see the List of Abbreviations and the Explanatory Notes at the end of Chapter 1. Although the Handmade wares referred to on pages 14, 184, 194, and 199 are not published in this volume, a category entitled "Handmade" indicates this type on Table 4.3. The category is also included in the numbers presented on Table 4.13.

Descriptions of Core Deposits

Civil Basilica

Hellenistic buildings. Lots 12–14, 608, 610. Date: second and third quarters of the 1st century B.C. Table 4.2.

Publication: W-MZ (1972) 412; W-MZ (1973) 392; Dj. Mano-Zissi, "Stratigraphic Problems and the Urban Development of Stobi," *Studies I*, 187–199. Stobi Field NB 36 and reports of the excavator, Nada Proeva, for 1972.

Excavations in the area of the later Roman Civil Basilica (Pl. 2, no. 4) uncovered the remains of several earlier buildings, perhaps small houses or shops. The earth in the pits, floor levels, and water channels of these structures contained lamps and ceramics of the second and perhaps third quarters of the 1st century B.C. One complete Hellenistic wheelmade lamp, C-71-24, Broneer Type XII, Howland Types 22, 34A, dating to the late 2nd or early 1st century B.C., and two other Late Hellenistic lamps, C-71-27, and C-72-3, were found in association with fragments of Black-Gloss Wares, Eastern Sigillata A, and Campanian C. A complete listing of the contents of these deposits appears in Table 4.2.

Table 4.2. Quantity of RBH for pottery types in Lots 12–14, 608, 610. Civil Basilica

Ware	Form	Cat. Nos.	RBH
Black-Gloss		**31, 37, 41**	6
Campanian C		**46,61**	3
Eastern Sigillata A		**228**	4
Lagynos		**56**	1
Hellenistic Relief Bowls		**109, 117, 120, 126, 133**	0
Amphorae			
Greco-Italic		**639, 642, 643**	3
Dressel 3			3
Misc.		**661, 664, 668**	26
Color-Slipped and Plain			
Hellenistic	Form 4	**734**	1
	Form 8	**739**	1
	Form 18	**756**	2
	Form 23		1
	Misc.		39
Cooking			
Hellenistic	Form 1	**1084**	2
	Form 3		1
	Form 7	**1096**	3
	Form 8		1
	Misc.	**1113, 1118, 1126**	29
	Total		126
Imports RBH			14
Amphorae RBH			32
Color-Slipped and Plain RBH			44
Cooking RBH			36

Central Basilica

Potter's Shop, Lots 87–89, 130–132, 134, 135, 140, 829, 831. Date: first half of the 1st century B.C. Table 4.3.

Publication: W-MZ (1972) 408–411. Stobi Field NBs 6, 23, 28, and 40, and reports of the excavators, Phyllis Della Croce, Harriet Blitzer, and John Cherry, for 1970 and 1971.

During excavations below the narthex and the southwest corner of the nave of the Central Basilica (Pl. 2, no. 6) in 1970 and 1971, a series of destruction deposits associated with a potter's shop were excavated. The structure (see Appendix 1) consists of mud-brick walls and a mortar floor resting upon sterile river gravels. The soils in these deposits were mixed with some clay, burned tiles, bricks, and much pottery (Pl. 191).

Among the datable finds were lamps, including L-71-7, and L-71-25, Howland Type 29A or 39, late 2nd to 1st centuries B.C. (Howland, *Agora 4*, 124, no. 515, pls. 19, 45, and nos. 409, 410, pl. 14), and a rim fragment of plain olive-colored glass bowl in Lot 134, perhaps Syro-Palestinian. Cf. J. W. Hayes, *Roman and Pre-Roman Glass in the Royal Ontario Museum* (Toronto 1975) 18, nos. 40, 41; fig. 1, p. 166. Imported pottery suggests a date within the first half of the 1st century B.C. for these deposits. The uppermost levels of debris were covered by deposits of the 4th century A.C., suggesting that the area was leveled off at the time the basilica was constructed. A complete listing of the ceramics found in these deposits can be seen in Table 4.3.

Table 4.3. Quantity of RBH for pottery types in Lots 87–89, 130–132, 134, 140, 829, 831. Central Basilica. Potter's Shop

Ware	Form	Cat. Nos.	RBH
Black-Gloss		**25**	1
Campanian A,B	Lamboglia Form 1	**21**	1
	Misc.	**24**	1
Campanian C			1
Hellenistic Relief Bowls		**111, 122, 142–146**	22
Thin-Walled	Moevs Form 1 or 2	**151, 153**	2
	Moevs Forms 4,5,6	**159, 161–164**	14
	Misc.		1
Eastern Sigillata A	Samaria Form 1	**225**	1
Unguentaria		**570–576**	9
Pompeian Red Ware			1
Amphorae			
Greco-Italic			1
Dressel 1A		**644, 645**	4
miscellaneous		**658**	9
Color-Slipped and Plain			
Hellenistic	Form 1		1
	Form 3	**729**	57
	Form 4		1
	Form 8		1
	Form 9		2
	Form 10	**743**	2
	Form 13		1
	Form 14		6
	Form 15		2
	Form 17		20
	Form 18		1
	Form 19		1
	Form 20	**758**	1
	Form 21	**759**	1
	Form 22		2
	Misc.	**768, 780, 783, 785 787, 793, 800**	141
Handmade coarse			1
Cooking Ware			
Hellenistic	Form 4	**1088**	1
	Form 5	**1090, 1092**	28
	Form 7		1
	Form 10		8
	Form 12	**1106, 1107**	3
	Misc.	**1114, 1117, 1130**	42
	Total		393
Imports RBH			23
Amphorae RBH			14
Color-Slipped and Plain RBH			272
Cooking RBH			84

Peristeria Court

Late Hellenistic dump over 2nd-century B.C. cemetery. Lots 547–552, 554, 555, 557, 558. Date: second and third quarters of the 1st century B.C. Table 4.4.

Publication: Sokolovska, *Studies II*, 123–138; W-MZ, (1973), 401–402. Stobi Field NB 47 and reports of the excavator, Al B. Wesolowsky, for 1972.

Excavations in the courtyard of the House of Peristeria (Pl. 2, no. 11) revealed that the area had been a cemetery in the 2nd century B.C. When the city began to expand in the early Augustan period, early in the last quarter of the 1st century B.C., the cemetery was covered over with fill and buildings were constructed above. The

Table 4.4. Quantity of RBH for pottery types in Lots 547–552, 554, 555, 557, 558. Peristeria Court

Ware	Form	Cat. Nos.	RBH
Hellenistic Gray	Form 3	**6**	1
	Form 8	**11**	1
	Form 10	**16**	3
	Misc.		8
Black-Gloss		**26, 27, 36, 38, 48**	6
Campanian C		**57, 58, 59**	45
Asia Minor Gray		**65, 66**	4
Black-Gloss with Gray Fabric		**76, 78–81, 86, 90, 91**	55
Thin-Walled	Moevs Form 1	**150, 152, 174**	6
	Moevs Forms 4, 5, 6	**156–158, 160, 166 167, 170, 171, 172, 175**	34
	Misc.		5
Eastern Sigillata A	Samaria Form 1	**227, 229**	11
	Misc.		8
Hellenistic Relief Bowls		**123, 127, 129, 131, 134, 137, 139, 140, 141**	42

Table 4.4. *continued on p. 148*

Table 4.4. (*Cont.*)

Ware	Form	Cat. Nos.	RBH
Pompeian Red		**717**	14
Amphorae			
Greco-Italic			6
North Adriatic		**649**	1
Dressel 6		**646, 650**	2
Lamboglia Form 2		**652**	1
Brindisi		**648**	1
Misc.			43
Color-Slipped and Plain			
Hellenistic	Form 1	**725**	2
	Form 2	**728**	4
	Form 3		91
	Form 4		6
	Form 5	**735**	16
	Form 6	**736**	6
	Form 7		3
	Form 9	**742**	4
	Form 11	**744**	2
	Form 12	**745–747**	34
	Form 13	**748**	2
	Form 15	**751**	2
	Form 17		3
	Form 18	**755**	27
	Form 19		14
	Form 20	**758**	2
	Form 21	**760, 761**	2
	Form 22	**762, 764, 765**	50
	Form 23	**766, 767**	3
	Misc.	**769–771, 773–775, 778–779, 781, 784, 801, 802, 806**	700
Cooking Ware			
Hellenistic	Form 1		4
	Form 2	**1085**	4
	Form 3	**1086, 1087**	4
	Form 4		2
	Form 5		47
	Form 6	**1093, 1094**	3
	Form 7		3
	Form 8	**1097**	5
	Form 9	**1098**	7
	Form 10	**1100–1103**	22
	Form 11	**1105**	3
	Form 12		20
	Form 13	**1108, 1109**	20
	Misc.	**1110–1112, 1115, 1116, 1119–1121, 1123, 1128, 1131**	228
	Total		1655
Imports RBH			128
Amphorae RBH			54
Color-Slipped and Plain RBH			1082
Cooking RBH			391

dumped fill, about one meter in depth, contained great quantities of pottery, animal bones, scattered ash, and carbonized vegetal material.

This dumped material appears to have been deposited over a relatively short period of time, and in the case of the lower deposits where many joins occur between layers, probably represents a single deposition. Aside from the uppermost layers, Lots 545 and 546, which contain some material of the 1st century A.C., the pottery is homogeneous throughout the dump. A detailed list setting forth the quantities of wares and forms appears in Table 4.4.

One illegible Greek coin (71-123) of pre-Augustan date was found in the deposit, and lamps, including L-72-12, Broneer Type XVIII, second half of the 2nd century to 50 B.C. (Broneer, *Corinth* 4); L-72-13, Ephesus type; L-72-15, Ephesus type, no volutes; L-72-16, Howland Type 37a, 2nd, early 1st B.C. (Howland, *Agora* 4); L-72-19, Broneer Type XVIII, or Howland Type 52, late 2nd century to ca. 25 B.C.; a glass base (G-72-27) of 2nd century B.C. (G. A. Eisen, *Glass*, vol. 1 [New York 1927] 25, fig. 23, and imported pottery suggest a date within the second and third quarters of the 1st century B.C.

Acropolis

Early Roman houses or shops. Rooms 2, 5, and south of wall 5. Lots 228–231, 248, 249, 257–261. Date: Lots 259–262—late 1st century B.C. early 1st century A.C.; Lots 229–231, 258—mid-1st century A.C.; Lots 228, 248, 249, 257—post 75 A.C. Table 4.5.

Publication: W-MZ (1972) 411–412. Stobi Field NBs 25 and 38, and reports of the excavator, Carolyn Snively, for 1971.

A long trench on the highest part of the site designated the Acropolis (Pl. 2, upper left) revealed evidence of small houses or shops beginning in the 2nd century B.C. and continuing to the 6th century A.C., with a possible hiatus in the second half of the 1st century B.C. and in the 5th century A.C.

Deposits of the 1st century A.C. were excavated in three areas of the trench, Room 2, Room 5, and south of Wall 5, separated from one another by fieldstone walls. These deposits constitute the major source for significant quantities of late 1st-century B.C. and 1st-century A.C. pottery at Stobi. Table 4.5 illustrates the quantity of wares and forms in these deposits.

Lots 259, 260, and 261 appear to date to the late 1st century B.C./early 1st century A.C. on the basis of ceramics, an Augustan volute lamp fragment, and an Arretine stamp of BLANDVS L. TITIVS (**286**; Oxé-Comfort 2074).

Dating to the mid-1st century or slightly later are Lots 229, 230, 231, and 258, all of which contained quantities of Arretine and Thin-Walled ware with sanded decoration, but only a few small pieces of Eastern Sigillata B. An Augustan coin (71–531) and several lamps (L-71-28, an Ephesus type, and L-71-29, Howland Type 35D, Broneer Type XVI, group 3) provide further indications of a mid-1st-century date.

Table 4.5. Quantity of RBH for pottery types in Lots 228–231, 248, 249, 257–261. Acropolis

Ware	Form	Cat. Nos.	RBH
Hellenistic Gray			1
Thin-Walled	Moevs Forms 36, 61	**178, 179, 181, 183–187**	10
	Mayet Form 37		11
	Moevs Form 62	**194, 195, 200, 201**	4
	Moevs Form 38		1
	Bases	**196, 198, 199**	3
	Misc.	**176**	1
Black-Gloss Gray		**60, 68, 73, 82, 98–100**	15
	stamp	**101**	1
Hellenistic Relief Bowls		**135**	0
Eastern Sigillata A	Samaria Form 1	**233, 234**	2
	Samaria Form 10	**231**	1
	Samaria Form 16	**232**	1
Arretine	Haltern Type 1	**235**	1
	Haltern Type 2	**238, 240**	2
	Haltern Types 8, 9	**244, 245**	2
	Hayes, Corinth Form 12; Goudineau 39	**255**	1
	Hayes, Corinth Form 11D	**257**	1
	Hayes, Corinth Form 23; Goudineau 40	**260**	1
	Stamps	**286–288**	0
	Misc.	**269, 270, 276, 277, 283**	23
Eastern Sigillata B	Hayes, *EAA*, 58, 70		2
	Misc.	**337**	2
Pompeian Red Ware			2
Amphorae			
Greco-Italic		**641**	1
Misc.		**670**	6
Color-Slipped and Plain			
Hellenistic	Form 8	**740**	1
Early Roman	Form 1	**814**	10
	Form 2	**815**	2
	Form 3	**816, 818**	3
	Form 4	**820, 821**	3
	Form 5	**822**	2
	Form 6	**823**	3
	Form 7		4
	Form 8		1
	Form 10	**832, 833, 835**	19
	Form 11		6
	Form 12	**842**	10
	Form 13		13
	Form 14	**844**	23
	Form 17	**849**	3
	Form 18		11
	Misc.	**861, 865, 866, 871–873, 875, 881, 883, 884, 886, 896, 901, 903, 905, 908**	314
Cooking Ware			
Early Roman	Form 1	**1132**	1
	Form 3		3
	Form 4		2
	Form 6	**1141**	13
	Form 7	**1144**	3
	Misc.	**1153, 1154**	26
	Total		574
Imports RBH			74
Amphorae RBH			7
Color-Slipped and Plain RBH			445
Cooking RBH			48

Lots 228, 248, 249, and 257 must be dated post-75 A.C., as they all contain Eastern Sigillata B2, especially the conical cup (*EAA* 2, Form 70), as well as quantities of Thin-Walled ware with sanded decoration. Stamps of the Arretine potters INVENTVS C. ANNI and L. GELLIVS QUADRATVS (**287**, **288**) also suggest a date after the third quarter of the 1st century (Slane [1987] 191). Lamp fragments and one with a shield handle are of mid- to late 1st-century date (L-71-23, Broneer Type XXI; Perlzweig, *Agora*, no. 30, p. 74).

Acropolis

Late Roman houses or shops. Room 2. Lots 234–236. Date: late 6th century A.C. Table 4.6.

Publication: W-MZ (1972) 411–412. Stobi Field NBs 25 and 38 and reports of the excavator, Carolyn Snively, for 1971.

The latest period of occupation on the Acropolis came to an end by the late 6th century A.C. with the destruction of the buildings in the Acropolis trench. Destruction debris in these Lots included many fallen roof tiles and burned wood. In addition to a coin (71–135, Justin II, 570 A.C.), the late 6th-century date is supported by an almost complete dish of African Red Slip, Hayes Form 105, dated 580–660 A.C. or later (**380**). For other ceramics in the Lots see Table 4.6.

Large Bath

Peristyle building. Lots 924, 929–934, 936–942. Date: first half of the 2nd century A.C. Table 4.7.

Publication: W-MZ (1974) 148. Stobi Field NB 67 and reports of the excavator, Saržo Saržoski, for 1973.

South and east of the Large Bath at Stobi a building with a partly preserved peristyle of the Early Roman period, or perhaps earlier, was excavated. Coins (73–64 and 73–72, 1st, 2nd centuries A.C.), and imported pottery types including Eastern Sigillata B suggest that the building was destroyed by the mid-2nd century A.C., since no fragments of Çandarli ware were found. Table 4.7 lists the pottery contents of these Lots.

Table 4.6. Quantity of RBH for pottery types in Lots 234–236. Acropolis

Ware	Form	Cat. Nos.	RBH
Arretine			2
Eastern Sigillata B			1
African Red Slip	Hayes Form 48	**352**	1
	Hayes Form 105	**380**	1
	Misc.	**385**	9
Mica dusted			1
Aegean Cooking			1
Color-Slipped and Plain Middle Roman	Form 1		1
	Form 5		1
	Form 6		1
	Form 8		1
	Form 9		1
	Form 13		2
	Form 16		2
	Form 19		1
	Form 22		1
	Form 25		1
	Form 31		3
	Form 32		1
	Form 33		1
	Misc.		73
Cooking Late Roman	Form 1		1
	Form 2		1
	Form 6		1
	Form 8		2
	Form 10		1
	Misc.		38
	Total		151
Imports RBH			16
Amphorae RBH			1
Color-Slipped and Plain RBH			90
Cooking RBH			44

Inner Wall West

Room 2, Public building, Second Phase. Lots 1306–1310, 1332, 1333. Date: second half of the 3rd century A.C. Table 4.8.

Publication: W-MZ, (1974), 121–126; Sanev and Saržoski, *Studies III*, 232–234. Stobi Field NBs 61 and 87 and reports of the excavators, Voislav Sanev and Saržo Saržoski, for 1973 and 1974.

In Room 2 of the large public building over which the Inner City Wall (Pl. 2, no. 27) was built, there were a series of fills (ca. 3 m. in depth) dumped onto the destruction debris of an earlier phase of the building. A mosaic floor was then laid over this fill. Coins below the mosaic, one Antonine to mid-3rd century (74–442) and the other of Marcus Aurelius (161–180); lamps, including L-74-31, Broneer Type XXVIII, dated mid-3rd century or later, and L-74-36, Broneer Type XXIX, dated to the 3rd and 4th centuries A.C.; and imports such as Çandarli, Pannonian Lead-Glazed, and amphorae including the Africano Grande (Berenice MR 16/17) and Big Red (Berenice MR 5), suggest the second half of the 3rd century as the date for the fills. The pottery is quite homogeneous, with virtually no residual material as can be seen from Table 4.8. The material probably represents a primary deposition of contemporary material.

Table 4.7. Quantity of RBH for pottery types in Lots 924, 929–934, 936–942. Large Bath

Ware	Form	Cat. Nos.	RBH
Thin-Walled			17
Arretine	Haltern Type 1	**236**	2
	Haltern Type 3	**242**	1
	Hayes, Corinth Form 12		1
	Hayes, Corinth Form 16c	**246**	1
	Hayes, Corinth Form 23	**258**	1
	Stamps	**290, 295**	0
	Misc.	**271, 278**	1
Eastern Sigillata B	Hayes, EAA Form 60	**312, 317**	4
	Hayes, EAA Form 70	**322, 323**	6
	Hayes, EAA Form 71	**326**	2
	Hayes, EAA Form 74		1
	Hayes, EAA Form 80	**334**	1
	Misc.	**335**	4

Table 4.7. (*Cont.*)

Ware	Form	Cat. Nos.	RBH
Italian Mugs			4
Aegean Cooking		**724**	1
Color-Slipped and Plain			
Early Roman	Form 11		8
Middle Roman	Form 5	**926**	3
	Form 7		4
	Form 8		5
	Form 11		5
	Form 14	**953, 954**	3
	Form 15		1
	Form 16		9
	Form 17		8
	Form 18		2
	Form 20	**969**	3
	Form 22		3
	Form 23		2
	Form 27		2
	Form 28		6
	Form 29		6
	Form 30		3
	Form 31	**1001**	13
	Form 32		5
	Form 33	**1007**	36
	Misc.		447
Cooking			
Middle Roman	Form 3		1
	Form 4	**1174**	2
Late Roman	Form 4		1
	Misc.	**1179, 1181, 1182, 1187, 1191, 1193, 1206, 1207**	102
	Total		729
Imports RBH			48
Amphorae RBH			
Color-Slipped and Plain RBH			575
Cooking RBH			106

Table 4.8. Quantity of RBH for pottery types in Lots 1306–1310, 1332, 1333. Inner Wall West

Ware	Form	Cat. Nos.	RBH
Çandarli	Hayes Form 3		2
Pannonian Lead-Glaze		**529**	1
Italian mug			1

Table 4.8. *continued on p. 152*

Table 4.8. (*Cont.*)

Ware	Form	Cat. Nos.	RBH
Amphorae			
Africano Grande			1
Berenice MR 5			1
Misc.			11
Color-Slipped and Plain			
Middle Roman	Form 1	**911, 912**	5
	Form 2		2
	Form 5		2
	Form 6	**929**	19
	Form 7		6
	Form 8	**936, 937, 939**	8
	Form 9	**943**	12
	Form 11		1
	Form 13		1
	Form 17	**957**	1
	Form 19	**966**	49
	Form 20		1
	Form 22	**974, 975, 977**	8
	Form 24		4
	Form 26	**987**	2
	Form 27		4
	Form 28		1
	Form 29		1
	Form 31		31
	Form 32	**1004, 1005**	65
	Form 33	**1009**	49
	Misc.	**1022, 1026, 1028, 1035, 1065, 1071**	226
Cooking ware	MR Form 1	**1168**	3
	MR Form 4		1
	LR Form 8		2
	Misc.	**1197**	28
	Total		549
Imports RBH			4
Amphorae RBH			13
Color-Slipped and Plain RBH			498
Cooking Local RBH			34

Inner Wall West

Room 3, Public building, Second Phase. Lots 1295–1304. Date: mid-3rd to mid-4th centuries A.C. Table 4.9.

Publication: W-MZ (1974) 121–126; Sanev and Saržoski, *Studies III*, 232–234. Stobi Field NBs 61 and 87 and reports of the excavators, Voislav Sanev and Saržo Saržoski, for 1973 and 1974.

The area to the west of Room 2 was also filled up with debris (three and one-half m. in depth), beginning at the same time as the filling in Room 2, and continuing after it had been covered with mosaic, since these deposits contain examples of Çandarli Hayes Form 4, not present in the fills below the mosaic. A coin (74-229) of Claudius II Gothicus (268–270 A.C.) was found in Lot 1296, one of the uppermost of the rubbish deposits, and in Lot 1295, comparable to 1296 in elevation, were two examples of African Red Slip Ware (Hayes Forms 45, 50) dated mid-3rd to early 4th centuries. See Table 4.9 for a complete listing of the contents of these Lots.

Table 4.9. Quantity of RBH for pottery types in Lots 1295–1304. Inner Wall West

Ware	Form	Cat. Nos.	RBH
Çandarli	Hayes Form 3	**343**	4
	Hayes Form 4	**344, 345**	9
African	Hayes Form 45		1
Red Slip	Hayes Form 50		1
Italian mug		**514, 515**	10
Aegean Cooking			1
Amphorae			
Berenice MR 5		**682, 683**	3
Berenice MR 7		**684**	1
Rhodian stamp			1
Misc.		**691**	5
Color-Slipped and Plain			
Early Roman	Form 11		2
Middle Roman	Form 1		10
	Form 2	**917**	9
	Form 3		1
	Form 5	**922–924, 927**	12
	Form 6	**930, 932**	22
	Form 7	**934**	28
	Form 8		24
	Form 9		60
	Form 11	**947**	8
	Form 12	**951**	6
	Form 13		12
	Form 16		3
	Form 17		11
	Form 19	**968**	172
	Form 21		3
	Form 22		4
	Form 23		5
	Form 24		19
	Form 27		2

Table 4.9. (*Cont.*)

Ware	Form	Cat. Nos.	RBH
	Form 28	**992**	7
	Form 29		3
	Form 30	**997**	2
	Form 31	**999**	73
	Form 32		47
	Form 33	**1008, 1009, 1010**	47
	Form 34	**1013**	1
	Misc.	**1017, 1019–1021, 1029, 1030, 1032, 1034, 1036, 1042, 1045, 1058, 1061, 1063, 1067, 1070, 1074**	507
Cooking ware			
Middle Roman	Form 1	**1162, 1163, 1165–1167**	30
	Form 3		1
	Form 4		12
	Misc.	**1173, 1176, 1178, 1184, 1185, 1186, 1188, 1190, 1192, 1194–1196, 1198–1200**	15
Late Roman	Form 2	**1214**	4
	Form 4		1
	Form 5		1
	Form 8		6
	Form 11		2
	Form 12		1
	Misc.		94
	Total		1290
Imports RBH			26
Amphorae RBH			10
Color-Slipped and Plain RBH			1100
Cooking RBH			154

East City Wall

Street with stone paving. Lots 1404, 1407–1410. Date: third quarter of 3rd century through 4th century A.C. Tables 4.10, 4.11.

Publication: W-MZ (1974) 121–123, 127–128. Stobi Field NBs 79 and 89 and reports of the excavator, Carolyn S. Snively, for 1974. See discussions by R. Folk, "Geologic Urban Hindplanning: an Example from a Hellenistic-Byzantine City, Stobi in Yugoslavian Macedonia," *Environmental Geology* 1 (1975) 15–17, and by Snively in the chapter, "The Casa Romana and Other Structures near the East City Wall," in Hemans et al., *Stobi 4* (forthcoming).

Alongside the East City Wall of Stobi was a paved street (Pl. 2, no. 29) constructed during the early Imperial period. The paving of this street began to be covered first with a deposit of clay mixed with earth and cultural material, perhaps part of a landslide deposit (Lots 1407–1410, Table 4.10) sometime after the mid-3rd century, as suggested by coin of Gallus, 251–253 A.C. (coin 74-444), and imports such as Çandarli and African Red Slip (Hayes Forms 44, 46, 50A), and then with a hard deposit, used for a time as a surface (Lot 1405, not in our deposit list). Finally the area was used as a rubbish dump (Lot 1404, Table 4.11) throughout the 4th century, but not into the 5th, as indicated by the absence of Macedonian Gray Ware, a ubiquitous 5th-century type. Lot 1404 contained a coin (74-414) dated 383–392 A.C.

Table 4.10. Quantity of RBH for pottery types in Lots 1407–1410. East City Wall. Paved street

Ware	Form	Cat. Nos.	RBH
Color-Slipped and Plain			
Middle Roman	Form 4	**919**	1
	Form 8		10
	Form 9		1
	Form 10	**945**	3
	Form 11	**948**	3
	Form 24	**980**	1
	Form 29	**995**	1
	Form 33		10
	Misc.		141
Cooking			
Middle Roman	Form 1		1
	Form 4		2
Late Roman	Form 8		1
	Misc.	**1204**	23
	Total		198
Imports RBH			
Amphorae RBH			
Color-Slipped and Plain RBH			171
Cooking RBH			27

Table 4.11. Quantity of RBH for pottery types in Lot 1404. East City Wall. Paved street

Ware	Form	Cat. Nos.	RBH
African	Hayes Form 44	**349**	1
Red Slip	Hayes Form 46	**351**	1
	Hayes Form 50A		2
Aegean			
Cooking			1
Amphorae			
Berenice MR 16/17			1
Berenice MR 7		**685**	2
Misc.			6
Color-Slipped and Plain			
Middle Roman	Form 1		8
	Form 2		5
	Form 5		18
	Form 6		5
	Form 7		8
	Form 8		2
	Form 9		16
	Form 13	**952**	3
	Form 16		1
	Form 17	**959**	2
	Form 22		1
	Form 23		4
	Form 24	**981**	1
	Form 26		5
	Form 27		1
	Form 33	**1011**	1
	Misc.	**1062**	478
Cooking			
Middle Roman	Form 1		7
	Form 4	**1175**	3
Late Roman	Form 2		2
	Form 8		2
	Misc.	**1259, 1262**	50
	Total		638
Imports RBH			6
Amphorae RBH			9
Color-Slipped and Plain RBH			559
Cooking RBH			64

Theater

East Parodos Dump. Lots 274, 277, 278, 293–295, 297–308. Date: first quarter of the 5th century A.C. Table 4.12.

Publication: W-MZ (1972) 417–419, Ill. 2; W-MZ (1973) 400–401, Ill. 9. Stobi Field NBs 26 and 41 and reports of the excavator, John Cherry, for 1971.

After the theater was no longer in use, the east parodos was filled with rubbish for a period of perhaps 25 years, after which small houses were built above. The homogeneity of the ceramic material indicates that a relatvely short period is probably represented by the fill. A series of sloping layers contained much ash, charcoal, slag, a human skeleton, and great quantities of animal bones and pottery. The several hundred coins found in these deposits range in date from the late 4th century to the first quarter of the 5th century. The lamps, L-71-41, and L-71-43, Broneer Type XXVII, date to the 3rd/4th centuries A.C., and a green-glass base fragment (G-71-68) dates to the late 4th, early 5th A.C. Imports include approximately equal numbers of Pannonian Lead-Glazed Wares and African Red Slip (Hayes Forms 53, 59, 61, and 67) and one fragment of a Gaza amphora. See Table 4.12 for a list of the contents of these deposits. Phocaean Red Slip Ware, which occurs at Stobi in the mid-5th century, was not present in the east parodos dump. The date, therefore, for the accumulation of refuse ought to fall somewhere within the first quarter of the 5th century A.C.

Table 4.12. Quantity of RBH for pottery types in Lots 274, 277, 278, 293–295, 297–308. Theater. East Parodos

Ware	Form	Cat. Nos.	RBH
Arretine			1
Eastern Sigillata B			5
Çandarli	Hayes Form 4		1
African	Hayes Form 50A		1
Red Slip	Hayes Form 53	**355**	1
	Hayes Form 59A	**356**	1
	Hayes Form 61A		1
	Hayes Form 67	**363–365**	4
	Misc.	**384**	2
Lead-Glazed	Mortaria	**520, 522**	5
	Pitcher	**526, 527**	3
Phocaean Red Slip			1
Tan Micaceous		**625–627**	34
Amphorae			
Gaza			1
Aegean Red		**686**	1
Berenice MR 16/17			1
Carthage LR 3			1
Misc.			5
Macedonian	Form 1	**418**	3
Gray Ware	Form 2	**430, 434, 435, 437**	24

Table 4.12. (*Cont.*)

Ware	Form	Cat. Nos.	RBH
	Form 3		6
	Form 8	**463**	3
	Form 9	**471**	1
	Form 10		3
	Form 11	**473**	1
	Misc.		15
Color-Slipped and Plain			
Middle Roman	Form 1		2
	Form 2		2
	Form 5		1
	Form 6		2
	Form 7		7
	Form 8		10
	Form 9		4
	Form 13		2
	Form 14		1
	Form 16		1
	Form 17		3
	Form 19		21
	Form 24		4
	Form 25		3
	Form 27		2
	Form 28		1
	Form 29		3
	Form 30		2
	Form 31		20
	Form 32		20
	Form 33		5
	Misc.	**1078, 1079, 1080**	219

Table 4.12. (*Cont.*)

Ware	Form	Cat. Nos.	RBH
Cooking Ware			
Middle Roman	Form 1		5
	Form 4		10
Late Roman	Form 1	**1211, 1213**	6
	Form 2	**1216**	24
	Form 3	**1220**	6
	Form 4	**1221, 1222**	43
	Form 5	**1223**	13
	Form 8	**1231**	101
	Form 9	**1237, 1238**	2
	Form 10	**1239**	6
	Form 11		4
	Form 12	**1241**	3
	Form 13		7
	Misc.	**1245, 1248, 1253, 1255–1257, 1265, 1266, 1270–1274, 1279–1286, 1290–1292**	966
	Total		1613
Imports RBH			26
Amphorae RBH			9
Local Color-Slipped and Plain RBH			335
Local Cooking RBH			1243

Quantification of Pottery at Stobi

The quantitative data on pottery types for the core deposits at Stobi is presented in Table 4.13 along with the date for each lot. Despite the higher numerical representation of sherds of some periods (the Middle or Late Roman, for example) in the core deposits, as seen in Table 4.14 and Figure 5.12, percentages of the major types based on the total population of RBH for all pe-

Table 4.13. Quantified list of RBH from Core Deposits with date

Lot	Area / Date	CS	Imp	Amp	Plain	Cook	RBH Tot.	Tot. Sherds
12*	Civ.Bas. 75–25 B.C.	4	2	2	3	10	21	161
13*	Civ.Bas. 75–25 B.C.	2		2	1	4	9	109
14*	Civ.Bas. 75–25 B.C.	3	1			2	6	33
74	Cent.Bas. late 2nd c. B.C.		1			1	2	7
75	Cent.Bas. 25 B.C.–25 A.C.	19	2		6	2	29	163
76	Cent.Bas. 1st B.C./1st A.C.	7	1		1	2	11	107
87*	Cent.Bas. 1st B.C.–2nd A.C.	2			3		5	65
88*	Cent.Bas. 1st 1/2 1st B.C.	7		3	1		11	236
89*	Cent.Bas. Hell.	1				2	3	22
130*	Cent.Bas. 1st 1/2 1st B.C.	8	1	3	6	5	23	118

Table 4.13. *continued on p. 156*

Table 4.13. (*Cont.*)

Lot	Area / Date	CS	Imp	Amp	Plain	Cook	RBH Tot.	Tot. Sherds
131*	Cent.Bas. 1st 1/2 1st B.C.	13			5	8	26	172
132*	Cent.Bas. 1st 1/2 1st B.C.	2	1		10		13	97
134*	Cent.Bas. 1st 1/2 1st B.C.	20	7	6	19	20	72	361
135*	Cent.Bas. 1st 1/2 1st B.C.	2			3	8	13	149
140*	Cent.Bas. 1st 1/2 1st B.C.	32	3	1	13	14	63	585
228*	Acro. post-75 A.C.	44	4	1		8	57	437
229*	Acro. 2nd 1/2 1st	30	3			2	35	311
230*	Acro. 2nd 1/2 1st	32	10		28	4	74	1320
231*	Acro. 2nd 1/2 1st	26	18		41	3	88	
234*	Acro. late 6th	2	2		1	6	11	44
235*	Acro. late 6th	17	8		13	18	56	154
236*	Acro. late 6th	33	6	1	24	20	84	473
237	Acro. 3rd–mid-4th	79	8		57	26	170	677
238	Acro. 3rd–mid-4th	62	4	1	37	17	121	580
239	Acro. 3rd/4th(?)	117	1	13	38	15	184	933
240	Acro. 3rd/4th(?)	33	3		18	7	61	530
241	Acro.	10	1		7	2	20	162
242	Acro.	19	2		19	6	46	264
243	Acro.	3			3	2	8	70
244	Acro.	1			1		2	50
245	Acro.	12	1	1	13		27	314
246	Acro.	1			4	1	6	29
247	Acro.	4	2	1	5	2	14	68
248*	Acro. post-75 A.C.	33	12	1	26	6	78	595
249*	Acro. post-75 A.C.	24	14	3	21	4	66	843
250	Acro. 2nd 1/2 2nd B.C.	3	2	2	1	1	9	60
251	Acro. 2nd 1/2 2nd B.C.	4				3	7	106
252	Acro. 2nd 1/2 2nd B.C.	13	2	1		2	18	78
257*	Acro. post-75 A.C.	18	3		25	7	53	520
258*	Acro. post-40 A.C.	15	2		11		28	161
259*	Acro. early 1st	17	7		49	13	86	1259
260*	Acro. late 1st B.C.(?)	3	1	1		1	6	35
261*	Acro. 1st B.C.	2		1			3	24
262	Acro. 1st B.C.	7	1	1	3	3	15	140
263	Acro. 2nd, 1st B.C.	2	1				3	11
274*	Theater early 5th	79	1	1	55	195	331	2163
277*	Theater early 5th	37	1		23	142	203	963
278*	Theater early 5th	28	1		14	99	142	996
293*	Theater early 5th	20	3	1	12	85	121	688
294*	Theater early 5th				2	26	28	116
295*	Theater early 5th	7	1		5	31	44	229
297*	Theater early 5th	20	2	1	12	93	128	595
298*	Theater early 5th	16	4	1	17	80	118	628
299*	Theater early 5th	26	2	1	14	90	133	549
300*	Theater early 5th	2	1			9	12	41
301*	Theater early 5th	12	1		13	54	80	345
302*	Theater early 5th	4	1	1	1	24	31	180
303*	Theater early 5th	6	1		5	28	40	200

Table 4.13. (*Cont.*)

Lot	Area / Date	CS	Imp	Amp	Plain	Cook	RBH Tot.	Tot. Sherds
304*	Theater early 5th	13	2	1	4	38	58	232
305*	Theater post-378 A.C.	19	4		23	82	128	602
306*	Theater late 4th	15			18	81	114	511
307*	Theater late 4th	16			17	48	81	493
308*	Theater late 4th	15		2	13	38	68	356
545	P.C. 25 B.C.–25 A.C.	37				43	80	949
546	P.C. early 1st	3				1	4	74
547*	P.C. 75–25 B.C.	82	14	16	118	52	282	1691
548*	P.C. 75–25 B.C.	192	1	1	1		22	111
549*	P.C. 75–25 B.C.	61	32	2	58	49	202	1279
550*	P.C. 75–25 B.C.	28	3	1	10	15	57	248
551*	P.C. 75–25 B.C.	26	2	2	9	15	54	272
552*	P.C. 75–25 B.C.	408	65	31	222	243	969	6618
554*	P.C. 75–25 B.C.	19	10	1	9	14	53	327
555*	P.C. 75–25 B.C.	4			6	1	11	217
557*	P.C. 75–25 B.C.	1	1				2	28
558*	P.C. 75–25 B.C.				1	2	3	3
563	P.C. 2nd B.C.	12		1	2	1	16	89
564	P.C. 2nd B.C.	2	1			2	5	44
608*	Civ.Bas. mid-1st B.C.	7	5	13	9	3	37	455
610*	Civ.Bas. mid-1st B.C.	6	6	15	9	17	53	679
687	Cent.Bas. mid–late 2nd B.C.	5	2		2		9	91
689	Cent.Bas. 2nd B.C.?	4		1	5	1	11	75
829*	Cent.Bas. 1st 1/2 1st B.C.	84	10		21	18	133	536
831*	Cent.Bas. 1st 1/2 1st B.C.	15	1	1	5	9	31	237
924*	L.B. 2nd c.	10	2		5	4	21	150
929*	L.B. 2nd c.	20	4		35	7	66	417
930*	L.B. 1st 1/2 2nd	49	4		28	12	93	536
931*	L.B. 2nd c.	12	9		11	5	37	210
932*	L.B. 2nd c.	24	11		25	14	74	442
933*	L.B. 2nd c.	8	1		7	8	24	282
934*	L.B. 1st 1/2 2nd	54	3		65	20	142	1161
936*	L.B. 1st 1/2 2nd	34	1		37	10	82	564
937*	L.B. 1st 1/2 2nd	15	3		15	4	37	260
938*	L.B. 1st 1/2 2nd	10	3		12	3	28	227
939*	L.B. 1st 1/2 2nd	12			10	7	29	187
940*	L.B. 1st 1/2 2nd	11	1		13	6	31	225
941*	L.B. 2nd c.	21	1		10	2	34	214
942*	L.B. 2nd c.	15	5		7	4	31	259
943	I.W.W. 5th c.				2	5	7	36
944	I.W.W. 4th/5th	6	1		1	14	22	155
945	I.W.W. 4th/5th	4			2	2	8	79
946	I.W.W. post-mid-4th	20			3	10	33	132
1278	I.W.W. 4th					4	4	19
1279	I.W.W. 4th/5th	1	1		3	6	11	150
1280	I.W.W. post-mid-4th	1				2	3	31
1281	I.W.W. mid-4th				2		2	3

Table 4.13. *continued on p. 158*

Table 4.13. (*Cont.*)

Lot	Area / Date	CS	Imp	Amp	Plain	Cook	RBH Tot.	Tot. Sherds
1282	I.W.W. post-mid-4th	10	1		3	17	31	137
1284	I.W.W. 4th/5th	5				10	15	43
1285	I.W.W. late 4th, early 5th	30	4	1	17	36	88	596
1295*	I.W.W. mid-3rd to early 4th	138	13	1	79	25	256	1668
1296*	I.W.W. 3rd to early 4th	200	9	3	146	42	400	2627
1297*	I.W.W. 3rd	53			24	7	84	364
1298*	I.W.W. 3rd	120	1	3	52	35	211	1086
1299*	I.W.W. 3rd	12			9	5	26	161
1300*	I.W.W. 3rd	48		1	26	14	89	526
1301*	I.W.W. 3rd	43			24	6	73	424
1302*	I.W.W. 3rd	75	3	1	42	20	141	845
1303*	I.W.W. 3rd	6			1		7	15
1304*	I.W.W. 3rd	2		1			3	25
1306*	I.W.W. late 2nd–mid-3rd	33	1		20	4	58	303
1307*	I.W.W. late 2nd–mid-3rd	150	2	3	129	15	299	1949
1308*	I.W.W. late 2nd–mid-3rd	32	1	2	35	2	72	425
1309*	I.W.W. late 2nd–mid-3rd	25		1	23	2	51	269
1310*	I.W.W. late 2nd–mid-3rd	13		6	12	9	40	187
1332*	I.W.W. late 2nd–mid-3rd	12		1	6	1	20	90
1333*	I.W.W. late 2nd–mid-3rd	6			2	1	9	45
1404*	C.W.E. mid- to late 4th	328	6	9	231	64	638	2522
1407*	C.W.E. post-mid-3rd	63			14	10	87	586
1408*	C.W.E. mid-3rd	10				3	13	65
1409*	C.W.E. mid-3rd	11			5	3	19	104
1410*	C.W.E. mid-3rd	48			20	11	79	422
1636	F.H. late 2nd B.C.	9	4	4	1	16	34	182
1637	F.H. late 2nd B.C.	1				5	6	16
Total		3756	410	176	2465	2498	9305	57964

riods illustrated on pie charts (Figs. 4.1–4.4) give us the best indication of the importance of various types through time. Note, for instance, that even though there are large numbers of imported fine wares on Table 4.14 for the Hellenistic (182) and the Middle Roman (100) periods, the percentage of these imports is actually greatest in the Early Roman period, comprising 11.2 percent of all pottery RBH (Table 4.14 and Fig. 4.2).

The grouping of the core deposits into broad chronological periods was a necessity for presenting the nature of the local typology. The Middle Roman period, however, includes the 2nd century, and fine ware imports continued to be high (Fig. 5.9) in the early part of that century but drop off markedly for the remainder of the period. That the percentage of imports is greater in the Middle Roman (Fig. 4.3) than the Late Roman period (Fig. 4.4) results from the inclusion of the early 2nd-century material. A comparison of deposits of the 3rd and early 4th centuries with those of Late Roman date shows a considerable increase in numbers for the later period. Furthermore, the Late Roman Core deposits include more material of the early 5th and 6th centuries than of the second half of the 5th century, when the greatest number of imported wares reached Stobi. The fills below the Episcopal Basilica were not included in the core deposits because excavation was not completed in that area when this quantification study was undertaken. As a result, although a great deal of material

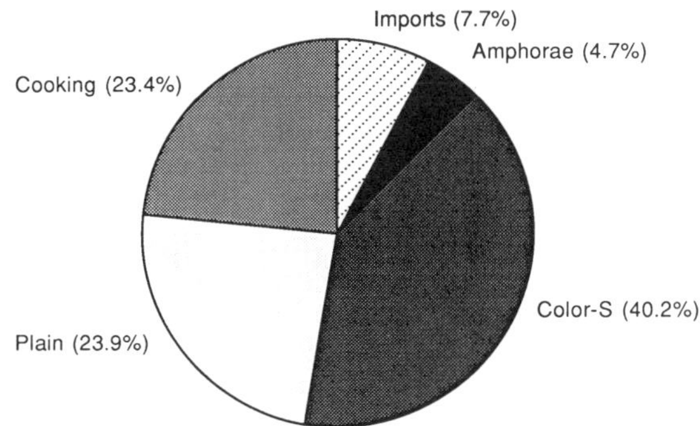

Figure 4.1. Proportions of pottery types expressed as percentage of total RBH in Hellenistic core deposits

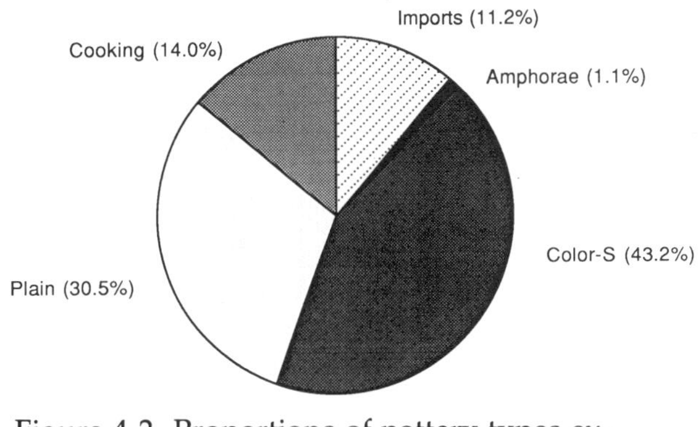

Figure 4.2. Proportions of pottery types expressed as percentage of total RBH in Early Roman core deposits

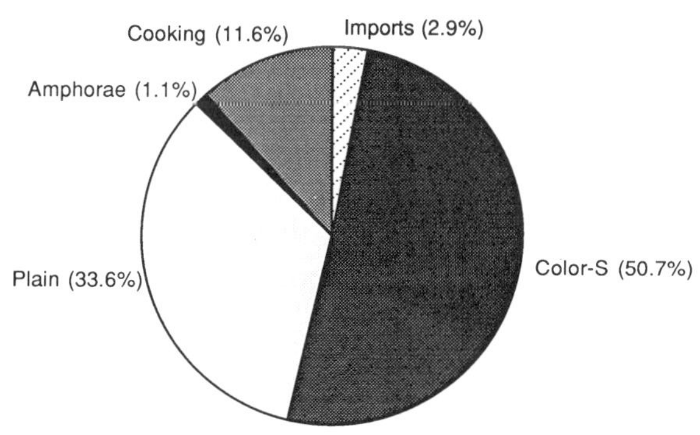

Figure 4.3. Proportions of pottery types expressed as percentage of total RBH in Middle Roman core deposits

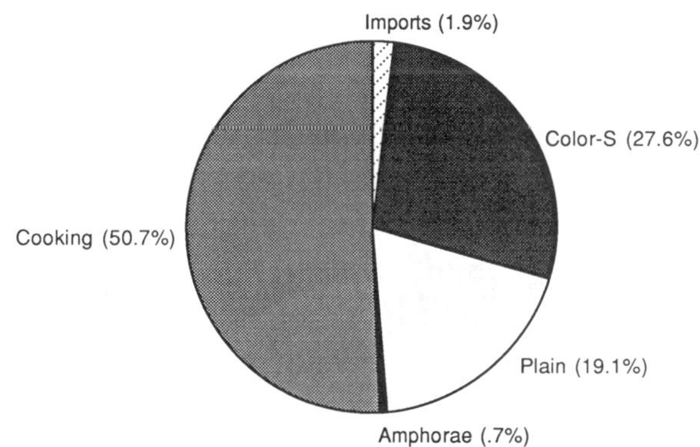

Figure 4.4. Proportions of pottery types expressed as percentage of total RBH in Late Roman core deposits

from the Episcopal Basilica appears in this volume, the pie charts for the Late Roman period, with the exception of Figure 3.3, reflect the results of excavation in the Episcopal Basilica before 1978.

Explanatory notes for Tables 4.13–4.17

- The category *Imports* (Imp) contains only known and clearly identifiable imported wares, *including* Pompeian Red Ware and Aegean Cooking Ware.
- Amphorae (Amp) are an entirely separate category.
- Color-Slipped (CS) and Plain wares include Early Hellenistic Gray Ware, Miscellaneous Gray Ware, Megarian bowls, Macedonian Gray Ware, and local Color-Slipped and Plain wares. Even though this places some gray-ware imports and Ionian relief bowls in a non-imported category, the numbers of those cases are rather small. Furthermore, relief bowls were manufactured locally, and in many cases (including the gray wares), it has been impossible to distinguish local from import.
- Cooking Ware includes Handmade wares (see p. 14) and Tan Micaceous Ware.
- Residual material has been included in all cases.
- The RBH columns add up to the total RBH.
- Blank spaces on the tables indicate that (1) no examples exist for that category in the Lot, or

Table 4.14. Counts of RBH for all types of pottery in Core Deposits combined in broad chronological periods

Type	Hell.	ER	MR	LR	Total
Imports	182	74	100	54	410
Amphorae	110	7	39	20	176
Color-Slipped	944	284	1736	792	3756
Plain	563	201	1151	550	2465
Cooking	550	92	399	1457	2498
Total	2349	658	3425	2873	9305

(2) in the case of the column for total sherd count, not all ceramics were retained, or (3) no information was available.

- An * beside the Lot number indicates that a deposit description is given in Chapter 4.
- All dates are A.C., unless otherwise indicated, and refer to centuries.

For abbreviations used in the tables, consult the list of abbreviations at the end of Chapter 1.

Table 4.15. Core Deposit List. Description of Lots

Lot No.	Area	Location	Nature of Deposit	Area function
12*	Civ.Bas.	Nave, below Bldg. D	Destruction	
13*	Civ.Bas.	Nave, below Bldg. D	Living surface	
14*	Civ.Bas.	Nave, below Bldg. D	Fill of clay pit	
74	Cent.Bas.	Nave 5	Pit 1, 1A	Courtyard
75	Cent.Bas.	Nave 5	Pit 2	Courtyard
76	Cent.Bas.	Nave 5	Pit 5 w/equus	Courtyard
87*	Cent.Bas.	Nave 6	Floor w/ threshold	
88*	Cent.Bas.	Nave 6	Destruction	Potter's shop
89*	Cent.Bas.	Nave 6		Potter's shop
130*	Cent.Bas.	Narthex	Destruction	Potter's shop
131*	Cent.Bas.	Narthex	Destruction	Potter's shop
132*	Cent.Bas.	Narthex	Destruction	Potter's shop
134*	Cent.Bas.	Narthex	Destruction	Potter's shop
135*	Cent.Bas.	Narthex	Destruction	Potter's shop
140*	Cent.Bas.	SW Room	Destruction	Potter's shop
228*	Acro.	S. of wall 5		Residential
229*	Acro.	S. of wall 5		Residential
230*	Acro.	S. of wall 5	Use level, road(?)	Residential
231*	Acro.	S. of wall 5	Floor(?)	Residential
234*	Acro.	Room 2	Destruction	Residential
235*	Acro.	Room 2	Destruction	Residential
236*	Acro.	Room 2	Destruction	Residential
237	Acro.	Room 2	Destruction	Residential
238	Acro.	Room 2	Use level	Residential
239	Acro.	Room 2	Destruction	Residential
240	Acro.	Room 2	Destruction	Residential
241	Acro.	Room 2	Use level	Residential
242	Acro.	Room 2	Use level	Residential
243	Acro.	Room 2	Use accumulation	Residential
244	Acro.	Room 2	Sand	Residential
245	Acro.	Room 2	Use accumulation	Residential
246	Acro.	Room 2	Sand	Residential

Table 4.15. (*Cont.*)

Lot No.	Area	Location	Nature of Deposit	Area function
247	Acro.	Room 2	Destruction	Residential
248*	Acro.	Room 2	Destruction, floor(?)	Residential
249*	Acro.	Room 2	Destruction, debris(?)	Residential
250	Acro.	Room 2		
251	Acro.	Room 2	Fill of small pit	
252	Acro.	Room 2		
257*	Acro.	Room 5	Floor?	Residential
258*	Acro.	Room 5		Residential
259*	Acro.	Room 5		Residential
260*	Acro.	Room 5		Residential
261*	Acro.	Room 5	Living surface	Residential
262	Acro.	Room 5		Residential
263	Acro.	Room 5	Living surface w/ drain	Residential
274*	Theater	E. Parodos	Rubbish accumulation	Dump
277*	Theater	E. Parodos	Rubbish accumulation	Dump
278*	Theater	E. Parodos	Rubbish accumulation	Dump
293*	Theater	E. Parodos	Rubbish accumulation	Dump
294*	Theater	E. Parodos	Rubbish accumulation	Dump
295*	Theater	E. Parodos	Rubbish accumulation	Dump
297*	Theater	E. Parodos	Rubbish accumulation	Dump
298*	Theater	E. Parodos	Rubbish accumulation	Dump
299*	Theater	E. Parodos	Rubbish accumulation	Dump
300*	Theater	E. Parodos	Bonding of Wall 11	Dump
301*	Theater	E. Parodos	Rubbish accumulation	Dump
302*	Theater	E. Parodos	Test Trench #1, Grave 97	Dump
303*	Theater	E. Parodos	Rubbish accumulation	Dump
304*	Theater	E. Parodos	Rubbish(?)/floor(?)	Dump
305*	Theater	E. Parodos	Rubbish above floor	Dump
306*	Theater	E. Parodos	Rubbish accumulation	Dump
307*	Theater	E. Parodos	Rubbish accumulation	Dump
308*	Theater	E. Parodos	Rubbish accumulation	Dump
545	P.C.	Courtyard	1st deposit	Dump
546	P.C.	Courtyard	Pit	Dump
547*	P.C.	Courtyard		Dump
548*	P.C.	Courtyard	Around Wall 1	Dump
549*	P.C.	Courtyard	Between Wall 1, 3	Dump
550*	P.C.	Courtyard	Surface w/ Wall 1(?)	Dump
551*	P.C.	Courtyard	Surface w/ Wall 1	Dump
552*	P.C.	Courtyard	SW half of trench	Dump
554*	P.C.	Courtyard	Living surface	Dump
555*	P.C.	Courtyard	Above surface 1	Dump
557*	P.C.	Courtyard	Small pit	Dump
558*	P.C.	Courtyard	Small pit	Dump
563	P.C.	SE part of trench	Burial, Grave 99	Cemetery
564	P.C.	W. end pit	Burial, Grave 99	Cemetery
608*	Civ.Bas.	Rooms outside S. wall	W. of Wall 5	

Table 4.15. *continued on p. 162*

Table 4.15. (*Cont.*)

Lot No.	Area	Location	Nature of Deposit	Area function
610*	Civ.Bas.	Rooms outside S. wall	E. of Wall 5	
687	Cent.Bas.	Atrium, S. of drain		
689	Cent.Bas.	Atrium, S. of drain		
829*	Cent.Bas.	Nave 6	Destruction	Potter's Shop
831*	Cent.Bas.	Nave 6	Destruction	Potter's Shop
924*	L.B.	S. of Wall 2, E. Wall 7	Destruction	Residential
929*	L.B.	S. of Wall 2, E. Wall 7	Destruction	Residential
930*	L.B.	S. of Wall 2, E. Wall 7	Destruction	Residential
931*	L.B.	S. of Wall 2, E. Wall 7	Destruction	Residential
932*	L.B.	S. of Wall 2, E. Wall 7	Use level	Residential
933*	L.B.	S. of Wall 2, E. Wall 7	Use level	Residential
934*	L.B.	S. of Wall 2, W. Wall 7	Use accumulation	Residential
936*	L.B.	S. of Wall 2, W. Wall 7	Destruction	Residential
937*	L.B.	N. of Wall 2, W. Wall 7	Destruction	Residential
938*	L.B.	N. of Wall 2, W. Wall 7	Destruction	Residential
939*	L.B.	S. of Wall 2, E. Wall 7	Terre pisé wall	Residential
940*	L.B.	S. of Wall 2, W. Wall 7	Destruction	Residential
941*	L.B.	On Wall 7	Destruction	Residential
942*	L.B.	S. of Wall 2, W. Wall 7	Use accumulation	Residential
943	I.W.W.	Room 2, above mosaic	Sand	Public structure
944	I.W.W.	Room 2, above mosaic	Sand	Public structure
945	I.W.W.	Room 2, above mosaic	Destruction	Public structure
946	I.W.W.	Room 2, on mosaic	Destruction	Public structure
1278	I.W.W.	Room 2, above mosaic	Use level	Public structure
1279	I.W.W.	Room 2, above mosaic	Sand	Public structure
1280	I.W.W.	Room 2, above mosaic	Construction	Public structure
1281	I.W.W.	Room 2, above mosaic	Destruction	Public structure
1282	I.W.W.	Room 2, above mosaic	Destruction	Public structure
1284	I.W.W.	Room 3, Tr. I–III	Destruction	Public structure
1285	I.W.W.	Room 3, Tr. I–III	Rubbish accumulation	Dump
1295*	I.W.W.	Room 3, Tr. I–IV	Rubbish accumulation	Dump
1296*	I.W.W.	Room 3, Tr. I–III	Rubbish accumulation	Dump
1297*	I.W.W.	Room 3, Tr. I–III	Rubbish accumulation	Dump
1298*	I.W.W.	Room 3, Tr. I–III	Rubbish accumulation	Dump
1299*	I.W.W.	Room 3, Tr. I–III	Rubbish accumulation	Dump
1300*	I.W.W.	Room 3, Tr. I–III	Rubbish accumulation	Dump
1301*	I.W.W.	Room 3, Tr. I–III	Rubbish accumulation	Dump
1302	I.W.W.	Room 3, Tr. I–III	Rubbish accumulation	Dump
1303*	I.W.W.	Room 3, Tr. I–III	Destruction	Public Structure
1304*	I.W.W.	Room 3, Tr. I–III	Destruction	Public Structure
1306*	I.W.W.	Room 2, below mosaic	Dumped fill	Public Structure
1307*	I.W.W.	Room 2, below mosaic	Dumped fill	Public Structure
1308*	I.W.W.	Room 2, below mosaic	Dumped fill	Public Structure
1309*	I.W.W.	Room 2, below mosaic	Dumped fill	Public Structure
1310*	I.W.W.	Room 2, below mosaic	Dumped fill	Public Structure
1332*	I.W.W.	Room 2, below mosaic	Dumped fill	Public Structure
1333*	I.W.W.	Room 2, below mosaic	Destruction	Public Structure

Table 4.15. (*Cont.*)

Lot No.	Area	Location	Nature of Deposit	Area function
1404*	C.W.E.	Street	Rubbish accumulation	Dump
1407*	C.W.E.	Street	River clay, silt	Public Street
1408*	C.W.E.	Street	River clay, silt	Public Street
1409*	C.W.E.	Street	River clay, silt	Public Street
1410*	C.W.E.	Street	River clay, silt	Public Street
1636	F.H.	Room 29	Burial, sacr.meal	
1637	F.H.	Room 29	Burial, Grave 313	

Table 4.16. List of other deposits arranged by Lot number

Lot	Area	Location	Nature Deposit	Area Function	Period
	W.C.	Grave 13	Cremation pit	Cemetery	1st
	W.C.	Grave 45	Cremation pit	Cemetery	1st/2nd
	W.C.	Grave 46	Cremation	Cemetery	
	W.C.	Grave 60	Cremation pit	Cemetery	1st
	W.C.	Grave 84	Cremation pit	Cemetery	Early 1st B.C.
	W.C.	Grave 91	Cremation pit	Cemetery	
	W.C.	Grave 95	Cremation	Cemetery	Late 1st
	W.C.	Grave 262	Cremation	Cemetery	Late 1st–to 2nd
	W.C.	Grave 264	Cremation	Cemetery	1st
	W.C.	Grave 271	Cremation	Cemetery	1st
	W.C.	Grave 283	Cremation	Cemetery	1st B.C.
	W.C.	Grave 288	Cremation pit	Cemetery	1st B.C.
	W.C.	Grave 308	Inhumation infant	Cemetery	2nd/1st B.C.
	W.C.	Grave 310	Cremation pit	Cemetery	25 B.C.–25 A.C.
3	Theater	Radial Corridor	Destruction debris	Public	4th–5th
4	Theater	Radial Corridor	Destruction debris	Public	4th–5th
7	Cent.Bas.	Tr. 2	Destruction debris		Late 1st
8	Cent.Bas.	Tr. 2	Destruction debris		2nd/3rd
11	Civ.Bas.	Nave/Bldg. D	Use		1st B.C./1st A.C.
18	W.C.	South	General	Cemetery	Late 1st to early 2nd
19	W.C.	South	General		1st
20	W.C.	South	General	Cemetery	Late 1st to early 2nd
22	W.C.	South	General	Cemetery	2nd half lst
24	W.C.	Overall	General		1st
25	W.C.	Overall	General		lst
26	W.C.	Graves 80,88	Burials	Cemetery	Late 1st B.C. to early 1st A.C.
29	W.C.	Grave 79	Horse burial	Cemetery	Late 1st to early 2nd

Table 4.16. *continued on p. 164*

Table 4.16. (*Cont.*)

Lot	Area	Location	Nature Deposit	Area Function	Period
30	W.C.	Grave 55	Burial	Cemetery	1st/2nd (post-2nd qtr. 1st)
39	W.C.	Grave 72	Burial	Cemetery	1st B.C. 1 to early 1st A.C.
43	W.C.	Grave 80	Burial	Cemetery	Mid-1st
44	W.C.	Grave 88	Burial		1st
45	W.C.	Grave 88	Burial	Cemetery	1st third 1st
48	Cent.Bas.	Room 1	Fill of pit		4th
54	Cent.Bas.	Room 1	Use level		Second half 5th–6th
57	Cent.Bas.	Room 1	Mixed		1st–2nd
58	F.H.	Room 21	Use level	Residential	5th
65	Cent.Bas.	Nave	Destruction debris	Public	2nd/3rd, maybe early 4th
68	Cent.Bas.	Nave	Ash layer, Floor 10		3rd–4th
70	Cent.Bas.	Nave	Floor		Post-1st
77	Cent.Bas.	Nave	Mixed Earth		1st B.C.–1st A.C.
78	Cent.Bas.	Nave	Brick-wall debris		1st
83	Cent.Bas.	Nave	Near pillaging trench		1st B.C.–1st A.C.
90	F.H.	Room 21	Destruction debris	Residential	Late 4th
91	F.H.	Room 21	Use level	Residential	5th
94	F.H.	Room 21	Floor	Residential	Late 4th
110	F.H.	Room 24	Use level	Residential	4th
127	Cent.Bas.	Narthex	Destruction debris		4th
141	F.H.	Room 22	Rubbish		4th
145	F.H.	Sectors A and B	Rubbish		5th–6th
146	F.H.	Sectors A and B	Rubbish		2nd 1/2 5th
147	F.H.	Sectors A and B	Rubbish		2nd 1/2 5th
148	F.H.	Along Wall 13	Rubbish	Residential	2nd 1/2 5th
150	F.H.	Sectors A and B	Destruction debris	Residential	2nd 1/2 5th
152	F.H.	Corridor Sector A	Use level		Late 4th, early 5th
155	F.H.	Sector B, pit 1	Rubbish		2nd 1/2 5th
157	F.H.	Rooms 23 and 25	Use level	Residential	Mid-5th
159	F.H.	Rooms 23 and 29	Use level	Residential	1st 1/2 5th
162	F.H.	Room 25	Use level	Residential	4th
163	F.H.	Room 25	Dumped fill	Residential	3rd/4th
164	F.H.	Room 25	Dumped fill	Residential	3rd/4th
165	F.H.	Room 22	Destruction debris	Residential	Late 5th
166	F.H.	Room 22	Destruction debris	Residential	Late 5th, early 6th
168	F.H.	Room 22	Roof collapse		Early 5th
169	F.H.	Room 22	Use accumulation	Residential	Late 4th
171	F.H.	Room 23	Use accumulation	Residential	4th/5th
172	F.H.	Room 23	Use accumulation	Residential	4th
178	Bridge Access	Tr. IV, VI	Clay/silt		4th–5th
179	Bridge Access	Tr. IV, VI	Clay/silt		4th
181	Bridge Access	Tr. IV	Clay/silt		4th

Table 4.16. (*Cont.*)

Lot	Area	Location	Nature Deposit	Area Function	Period
184	Bridge Access	Tr. IV	Clay/silt		4th
190	Bridge Access	Tr. IV	Sand		3rd
197	Bridge Access	Tr. XII	Silt		3rd/4th
221	Acropolis	Room 4	Use level		5th/6th
223	Acropolis	Room 3	Destruction debris	Residential	4th–6th
267	Acropolis	Room 1	Destruction debris	Residential	6th
282	Theater	East Parodos	Rubbish accumulation	Dump	Late 4th
285	Theater	East Parodos	Gray, ashy	Habitation	4th
313	Acropolis	Between Rooms 1/2	Use level	Habitation	3rd
373	W.C.	Grave 8	Burial	Cemetery	3rd/4th
381	W.C.	Grave 28	Burial	Cemetery	3rd
384	W.C.	Grave 37	Burial	Cemetery	Mid- to late 1st/ into early 2nd
385	W.C.	Over Grave 38 et al.	Green gravel	Cemetery	Late 1st, early 2nd
386	W.C.	Grave 38	Fill over tops of stones in pit	Cemetery	Mid-1st and later
388	W.C.	Grave 38	Fill in pit, but outside stones	Cemetery	1st
389	W.C.	Grave 38	Fill under tiles	Cemetery	1st
390	W.C.	Grave 39	Fill within Grave 39 but over tiles	Cemetery	2nd half 1st
391	W.C.	Grave 39	Loose fill under grave tiles	Cemetery	1st, maybe early 2nd
392	W.C.	Graves 40, 44	Burial	Cemetery	Late 1st, early 2nd
395	W.C.	Grave 47	Burial	Cemetery	ER
399	W.C.	Grave 81	Burial	Cemetery	Early 1st
400	W.C.	Grave 77	Burial	Cemetery	1st
401	W.C.	Grave 77	Burial	Cemetery	1st
406	W.C.	Grave 94	Burial	Cemetery	1st
411	W.C.	Grave 74	Burial	Cemetery	1st
412	W.C.	Grave 51	Burial	Cemetery	1st
415	W.C.	Grave 67	Burial	Cemetery	1st/2nd
416	W.C.	Grave 70	Burial	Cemetery	1st
432	W.C.	Over Graves 32, 33, 34	Red/ashy	Cemetery	3rd
433	W.C.	Graves 36, 37	Above Graves 36, 37	Cemetery	3rd
435	W.C.	Over Graves 43,45	Land fill	Cemetery	1st
440	W.C.	Over Grave 48	Land fill	Cemetery	1st
441	W.C.	Over Grave 50	Land fill	Cemetery	2nd/3rd
442	W.C.	Over Graves 52, 53	Land fill	Cemetery	1st/2nd
443	W.C.	General	Over Grave 57	Cemetery	1st
445	W.C.	General	Over Grave 61	Cemetery	Mid-1st or later
446	W.C.	Grave 61	Grave pit	Cemetery	1st

Table 4.16. *continued on p. 166*

Table 4.16. (*Cont.*)

Lot	Area	Location	Nature Deposit	Area Function	Period
448	W.C.	Above Graves 67, 68, 70, 77, 95	Above graves	Cemetery	Mid-1st or later
449	W.C.	Graves 67, 68, 76, 77, 95	Above graves(?)	Cemetery	1st
451	W.C.	Grave 30	Ash-fill grave	Cemetery	1st
452	W.C.	West of pit for Grave 37	Compact deposit	Cemetery	Mid- to late 1st
453	W.C.	Grave 56	Burial	Cemetery	1st/2nd
456	W.C.	Perimeter of Grave 95	Hard, tan soil overlying bedrock	Cemetery	Mixed 1st B.C. to late 1st A.C.
460	W.C.	Entire trench	Humus		5th–6th
462	W.C.	Exposing wall 2	Humus		5th
465	W.C.	Walls 1, 3, hearth 1	Surface fill		3rd/4th
476	W.C.	Over Grave 6	Landfill	Cemetery	3rd
482	W.C.	Exposed Grave 8	Dumped fill	Dump	3rd
483	W.C.	Exposed Grave 10	Dumped fill	Dump	3rd
486	W.C.	Exposing Graves 11, 12, 13, 14	Landfill soil exposing graves	Cemetery	mid- to 3rd qtr. 1st
487	W.C.	Grave 21	Soil near small pot (C-71-60)	Cemetery	2nd or 3rd qtr 1st
488	W.C.	Graves 11, 12, 13, 14, 21	Hard, tan soil among graves	Cemetery	2nd to 3rd qtr. 1st
490	W.C.	Exposing Grave 18	Exposing Grave 18	Cemetery	Very late 1st B.C. to mid-1st A.C.
497	Museum Trench	Sectors A, B	Destruction debris		4th
505	Theater	Orchestra	2nd Construction	Public	Late 2nd/Early 3rd
507	Theater	West Parados	Rubbish accumulation		4th
509	Theater	West Parodos	Destruction debris		3rd–4th
513	Theater	Orchestra	Construction	Public	Late 1st, e. 2nd
514	F.H.	Room 2	Destruction debris	Residential	Early 5th
515	Theater	East Parodos	Rubbish accumulation	Dump	4th
517	Theater	East Parodos, Tr. VIII	Rubbish accumulation	Dump	3rd
523	Theater	East Parodos	Rubbish accumulation	Dump	2nd half 4th
529	Theater	East Parodos	Rubbish accumulation	Dump	4th
536	Theater	East Parodos	2nd construction	Public	late 2nd/e. 3rd
542	Theater	East Parodos	2nd construction	Public	late 2nd/e. 3rd
543	Theater	East Parodos	2nd construction	Public	late 2nd/e. 3rd
566	I.W.W.	Surface	Humus		8th
586	I.W.W.	Room 1	Gray silt/sand		2nd/3rd
594	Civ.Bas.	Tr. 2, Room 1	Burnt destruction debris		1st

Table 4.16. (*Cont.*)

Lot	Area	Location	Nature Deposit	Area Function	Period
599	Civ.Bas.	Tr. 2, Room 1	Burnt destruction debris		1st
612	Theater	Tr. 9	Destruction debris		4th–5th
620	Theater	Tr. 9	Use level		Late 4th
630	Theater	Tr. 9	Construction	Public	
645	E.Bas.	Sector 2, Room 3	Humus		5th–6th
650	E.Bas.	Sector 2, Room 3	Use level		5th
672	Cent.Bas.	Atrium	Drain		2nd/3rd
675	Cent.Bas.	Atrium	Drain		2nd/3rd
677	Cent.Bas.	Atrium	Drain		2nd or later
686	Cent.Bas.	Atrium	Fill under floor		1st
692	Cent.Bas.	North Corridor	Earth on slabs		1st half 2nd
700	Bas.Cem.	Grave 103	Burial	Cemetery	1st
708	Bas.Cem.	Grave 107	Fill under tiles		1st B.C.–1st A.C.
712	C.W.E.	Tr. 1–4	Riverine deposit		4th
718	C.W.E.	Room 2	Mortar, fresco, carbon, clay		Late 4th
728	C.W.E.	Tr. 4, E. Ext.	Soft, dark, sandy earth		4th
729	C.W.E.	Tr. 4, E. Ext, e. Wall 15	Soft, dark, sandy		4th
730	C.W.E.	Tr. 4, E. Ext, e. Wall 15	Clayey soil		3rd–4th
746	E.Bas.	South	Destruction/abandonment debris		6th
750	E.Bas.	Room 3	Destruction debris		5th
759	F.H.	Room 25	Use level	Residential	4th
762	F.H.	Room 24	Use accumulation	Residential	3rd to 4th
763	F.H.	Room 24	Use accumulation	Residential	3rd
764	F.H.	Room 24	Use accumulation	Residential	3rd
765	F.H.	Room 24	Use accumulation	Residential	3rd
767	F.H.	Room 24	Construction	Residential	4th
773	F.H.	Corridor	Use accumulation	Residential	5th
783	S.C.W.	Grave 98	Content of grave		2nd
789	S.C.W.	Tr. 3	Use accumulation		ER
791	E.Bas.	Apse/Ambulatory	Dumped fill	Dump	2nd half 4th
795	E.Bas.	Apse/Crypt	Fill	Public	3rd
797	Cent.Bas.	Nave, fill Synagogue 1	Destruction debris	Public	Early 4th
799	Cent.Bas.	Nave, fill of Synagogue 1	Destruction debris	Public	Late 3rd–early 4th
800	Cent.Bas.	Nave, fill of Synagogue 1	Destruction debris	Public	Early 4th
801	Cent.Bas.	Tr. 1, below Synagogue 1	Destruction debris	Public	Mid-3rd or later

Table 4.16. *continued on p. 168*

Table 4.16. (*Cont.*)

Lot	Area	Location	Nature Deposit	Area Function	Period
802	Cent.Bas.	Nave, floor, Synagogue 1	Destruction debris	Public	3rd
810	Cent.Bas.	Nave, Tr. II, above floor	Destruction debris	Public	3rd
811	Cent.Bas.	Nave, Tr. 2	Destruction debris	Public	
841	Cent.Bas.	N. Stylobate	Destruction debris	Public	4th
842	Cent.Bas.	N. Aisle	Contaminated		Late 4th, early 3rd B.C.
843	Cent.Bas.	N. Aisle	Destruction debris		Late 4th, early 3rd B.C.
847	F.H.	Rooms 28, 29, 30	Use level	Residential	5th
849	F.H.	Rooms 29, 30	Roof collapse		5th
850	F.H.	Room 29	Use accumulation	Residential	5th
853	F.H.	Room 27	Destruction debris	Residential	Late 4th to early 5th
875	Theater	Radial Corridor	Destruction level	Squatters	6th
878	Theater	Skene, Room 2	Surface		4th
881	Theater	Skene	Wind-blown silt over floor	Public	?
882	Theater	Skene	Destruction debris	Public	4th
883	Theater	Skene	Destruction debris	Public	4th
884	Theater	Skene	Destruction debris	Public	4th
885	Theater	Skene	Floor	Public	5th
890	Theater	Skene	Construction	Public	3rd
892	Theater	Skene	Construction	Public	3rd
902	Theater	Skene	Surface	Public	4th
917	L.B.	General	Destruction debris	Residential	4th, 5th
921	L.B.	General	Destruction debris	Residential	2nd
953	E.Bas.	South	T.T. 2	Public	6th
954	E.Bas.	S. Stairway	Material from wall, channel	Public	5th/6th
955	E.Bas.	S. Aisle	Fill/destruction debris		Mid-5th
974	Bas. Cem.	Pit 3	Fill		4th
985	C.W.E.	Room 2	Destruction debris		3rd/4th
992	Perist. Apse	I, near Wall 1	Fill		ER
998	E.Bas.	East	Silt		5th
1001	E.Bas.	East	Destruction debris		Mid-5th
1015	F.H.	Room 2	Destruction debris	Residential	Early 5th
1016	F.H.	Room 11	Destruction debris	Residential	Early 5th
1017	F.H.	Room 1, apse	Destruction debris	Residential	Mid-5th
1018	F.H.	Room 1, apse	Destruction debris	Residential	Mid-5th
1023	F.H.	Rooms 1, 9	Fill for floor	Residential	Late 4th
1025	F.H.	Room 9	Destruction debris?	Residential	1st
1047	E.Bas.	Presbyterium	Fill	Public	5th
1049	E.Bas.	Presbyterium	Fill	Public	Early 5th
1052	I.W.W.	Room 1	Earth and mortar		3rd

Table 4.16. (*Cont.*)

Lot	Area	Location	Nature Deposit	Area Function	Period
1057	W.C.	Sector X2	Use accumulation	Cemetery	4th/5th
1059	W.C.	Grave 33	Fill inside grave	Cemetery	1st
1066	W.C.	Grave 32	Fill inside grave	Cemetery	2nd/3rd
1070	W.C.	Grave 252	Fill over tiles	Cemetery	LR
1074	W.C.	Graves 42, 257, 258, 259, 260	Dark, sandy soil, rocks above graves	Cemetery	2nd/3rd
1078	W.C.	Over Grave 260's cairn	same as 1074	Cemetery	ER
1080	W.C.	Graves 42, 257, 258, 259, 260	Compact, ashy soil	Cemetery	Mid-1st A.C.
1084	W.C.	Grave 257	Fill under tiles	Cemetery	1st
1085	W.C.	Wall 31B	Dismantling wall		1st/2nd
1086	W.C.	Grave 259	Cairn and fill over tiles	Cemetery	Mid-1st
1087	W.C.	Grave 258	Fill in pit	Cemetery	ER
1089	W.C.	General deposit over sector X2	Ashy, gray soil	Cemetery	Mid-1st
1090	W.C.	General	Graves 84, 254, 262, 263, 264,	Cemetery	Mid-1st
1092	W.C.	Grave 200	Fill in pit	Cemetery	ER
1093	W.C.	General deposit over Sector X2	Light ashy soil over Graves 261, 265, 266	Cemetery	Mid-1st
1094	W.C.	Grave 84	Fill of cairn and within outer pit	Cemetery	Early 1st B.C.
1095	W.C.	Grave 262	Fill over tiles of Grave 262	Cemetery	Early 1st B.C.
1098	W.C.	Exposed Grave 266	Compact soil above bedrock gravel	Cemetery	Mid- to late 1st
1099	W.C.	Grave 266	Fill in pit of Grave 266	Cemetery	25 B.C.–25 A.C.
1314	E.Bas.	N. Aisle	Dumped fill	Public	2nd half 4th
1315	E.Bas.	N. Aisle	Use level		4th
1316	E.Bas.	N. Aisle	Dumped fill		Post-2nd qtr. 4th
1317	E.Bas.	N. Aisle	Dumped fill	Public	4th
1319	E.Bas.	N. Aisle	Dumped fill		3rd–4th
1324	E.Bas.	N. Aisle	Dumped fill	Public	MR
1325	E.Bas.	N. Aisle	Dumped fill	Public	MR
1327	E.Bas.	N. Aisle	Dumped fill		3rd to mid-4th
1328	E.Bas.	N. Aisle	Dumped fill	Public	3rd to mid-4th
1330	E.Bas.	S. Aisle	Fill	Public	3rd
1334	F.H.	Room 28	Use accumulation	Residential	Early 6th
1336	F.H.	Room 28	Destruction debris	Residential	4th/5th
1338	F.H.	Room 29	Destruction debris	Residential	Mid-5th
1344	F.H.	Room 32	Wall collapse	Residential	Early 6th

Table 4.16. *continued on p. 170*

Table 4.16. (*Cont.*)

Lot	Area	Location	Nature Deposit	Area Function	Period
1345	F.H.	Room 32	Use accumulation	Residential	6th
1346	F.H.	Room 32	Use level	Residential	5th/6th
1347	F.H.	Room 32	Floor 1	Residential	Early 6th
1349	F.H.	Room 32	Destruction debris	Residential	4th/5th
1352	Theater	Radial Corridor	Dumped fill	Public	4th/5th
1356	Theater	Radial Corridor	Use accumulation	Public	3rd/4th
1358	Theater	Radial Corridor	Fill 2nd construction	Public	2nd/3rd
1361	Theater	Skene	Use accumulation	Public	LR
1362	Theater	Skene	Use accumulation	Public	4th/5th
1370	C.W.E.	Tr. EXC 74-18	Mud slide		Late 4th, early 5th
1373	C.W.E.	Tr. EXC 74-9	Destruction debris		3rd/4th
1378	C.W.E.	Tr. EXC 74-18	Above mud-slide debris		4th/5th
1382	C.W.E.	Tr. EXC 74-6	Sand, mortar, debris		5th
1388	C.W.E.	Tr. EXC 74-6	Construction	Public	5th
1390	C.W.E.	Tr. EXC 74-6	Destruction debris		1st qtr. 5th
1398	C.W.E.	Tr. EXC 74-6	Rubbish accumulation		4th
1401	C.W.E.	Tr. EXC 74-6	Rubbish accumulation		4th
1413	C.W.E.	Rooms 3, 5	Soft, black earth with mortar		4th/5th
1414	W.C.	Sector X4	Surface		Early 5th
1415	W.C.	Sector X4	Use accumulation	Habitation	4th/5th
1416	W.C.	General deposit over X4	Grayish tan soil over Graves 272, 274, 275	Cemetery	Mid- to late 1st
1417	W.C.	General deposit over X4	Over Graves 274, 286, 283, 281	Cemetery	Mid- to late 1st
1418	W.C.	General deposit over X4	Over Graves 282, 287, 288, 295	Cemetery	2nd 1/2 1st
1419	W.C.	General deposit over X4	Over Graves 291, 292, 293	Cemetery	2nd and 3rd qtrs. 1st
1420	W.C.	General Sector X4	Lowest deposit	Cemetery	Mid- to late 1st
1421	W.C.	Grave 265	Fill in pit	Cemetery	1st B.C.
1423	W.C.	Over tiles Grave 272	Soft grave fill over tiles	Cemetery	1st
1425	W.C.	Grave 286	Fill over tiles	Cemetery	1st
1426	W.C.	Grave 282	Fill in pit	Cemetery	1st
1430	W.C.	General	Surface		5th
1431	W.C.	Sector X3	Gravel		LR
1433	W.C.	Sector X3	Fills		3rd–5th
1434	W.C.	Sector X3	Fills		2nd–3rd
1441	W.C.	Sector X3	Over Graves 277, 278, 279, 285	Cemetery	Mixed 1st B.C. to late 1st A.C.
1442	W.C.	Sector X3	Over Graves 285, 294, 298, 299, 300	Cemetery	2nd and 3rd qtrs. 1st

Table 4.16. (*Cont.*)

Lot	Area	Location	Nature Deposit	Area Function	Period
1443	W.C.	Sector X3	Pit of Graves 285 and over Grave 297	Cemetery	Late 1st B.C. to mid-1st A.C.
1452	W.C.	Grave 273	Grave construction	Cemetery	1st B.C.
1453	W.C.	Sector X3	Grave 62 pit	Cemetery	Post mid-1st
1454	W.C.	Grave 62	Grave construction	Cemetery	1st
1456	W.C.	Grave 277	Grave pit	Cemetery	1st
1458	W.C.	Grave 278	Grave pit	Cemetery	2nd B.C.–1st A.C.
1462	W.C.	Grave 285	Grave construction	Cemetery	1st
1465	W.C.	Grave 294	Grave pit	Cemetery	1st B.C.
1467	W.C.	Grave 297	Grave construction	Cemetery	2nd
1468	W.C.	Grave 298	Grave construction	Cemetery	1st B.C.–1st A.C.
1469	W.C.	Grave 299	Burial pit	Cemetery	1st
1470	W.C.	Grave 300	Grave construction	Cemetery	1st B.C.–1st A.C.
1471	Theater	Skene	Construction	Public	Mid-2nd
1474	Theater	Skene	Construction	Public	Mid-2nd
1475	Theater	Skene	Construction	Public	2nd
1477	Theater	Skene	Construction	Public	Mid-2nd
1478	Theater	Skene	Construction	Public	Mid-2nd
1479	Theater	Skene	Construction	Public	Mid-2nd
1482	Theater	Skene			1st
1493	Theater	Skene	Pre-Theater silt		1st/2nd
1495	Theater	Skene	Pre-Theater silt		Late 1st
1497	Theater	Skene	Destruction	Public	Late 1st
1498	Theater	Skene	Destruction	Public	Late 1st
1501	Theater	Skene	Destruction	Public	Late 1st
1507	Theater	Skene	Use accumulation	Public	5th
1509	Theater	Terrace	Use accumulation	Public	2nd/3rd
1510	Theater	Terrace	Construction	Public	1st/2nd
1511	Theater	Skene/Terrace	Construction	Public	Mid-2nd
1532	Theater	Orchestra	Post hole fill	Public	1st
1537	Theater	Skene	Construction	Public	Mid-2nd
1538	Theater	Skene	Pre-Theater silt		Late 1st
1551	Theater	Barrier-wall passage	Rubbish accumulation	Public	4th
1552	Theater	Skene	Destruction debris	Public	4th
1569	Theater	Refuge, center	Water-deposited silt	Public	4th
1580	Theater	Tr. 14	Fill	Public	1st B.C./1st A.C.
1581	Theater	Tr. 14	Fill		1st B.C.
1599	Cent.Bas.	S. Aisle	Below Synagogue II floor		4th
1610	E.Bas.	East	Destruction debris	Public	4th
1616	E.Bas.	East	Theater dismantling debris	Public	4th
1625	E.Bas.	East	Dumped fill	Public	5th

Table 4.16. *continued on p. 172*

Table 4.16. (*Cont.*)

Lot	Area	Location	Nature Deposit	Area Function	Period
1629	E.Bas.	S. Aisle	Dumped fill	Public	Late 4th
1642	F.H.	Room 27	Floor 2	Residential	Mid-4th
1645	F.H.	Room 32	Fill below floor IV	Residential	Late 4th
1652	Theater	Trench I	Use accumulation	Public	2nd/3rd
1656	Peristerias H.	Room 10	Rubbish accumulation	Residential	4th/5th
1657	Peristerias H.	Room 12, 13	Rubbish accumulation	Residential	4th
1658	Peristerias H.	Room 17	Destruction debris	Residential	4th
1659	Theater	Skene	Rubbish accumulation		5th
1662	Theater	Skene	Construction	Public	Late 1st/early 2nd
1672	Theater	Skene	Construction	Public	1st/early 2nd
1673	Theater	Skene	Construction	Public	1st/early 2nd
1676	Theater	East Parodos	Use level	Residential	2nd
1683	Theater	Tr. 16	Fill	Public	1st/2nd A.C.
1686	Theater	Cavea	Fill		LR
1689	Theater	Cavea	Theater destruction	Public	Late 4th
1696	E.Bas.	N. Aisle	Destruction debris	Public	MR
1697	E.Bas.	N. Aisle	Dumped fill	Public	2nd/3rd
1703	E.Bas.	Presbyterium	Fill	Public	MR
1770	Cent.Bas.	S. Aisle W.	Dumped fill for Cent.Bas.	Public	4th/5th
1783	Cent.Bas.	S. Aisle W.	Post-Synagogue/pre-Bas.	Public	Late 4th
1793	E.Bas.	S. Aisle	Dumped fill	Public	4th/5th
1798	E.Bas.	S. Aisle	Fill	Public	3rd qtr. 5th
1799	E.Bas.	S. Aisle	Fill	Public	3rd qtr. 5th
1800	E.Bas.	S. Aisle	Fill	Public	3rd qtr. 5th
1801	E.Bas.	S. Aisle	Fill	Public	3rd qtr. 5th
1804	E.Bas.	S. Aisle	Dumped fill	Public	4th/5th
1806	E.Bas.	S. Aisle	Dumped fill	Public	4th/5th
1809	E.Bas.	S. Aisle	Destruction debris	Public	Late 4th
1810	E.Bas.	S. Aisle	Water deposited clay	Public	ER
1819	E.Bas.	S. Aisle	Construction S. Stylobate	Public	5th
1846	Theater	Cavea	2nd construction	Public	Late 2nd/early 3rd
1922	Cent.Bas.	Apse	Reliquary		5th
1933	Cent.Bas.	Nave	Stratum D	Public	2nd
1934	Cent.Bas.	Nave	Fill or collapsed terre pisé		ER
1935	Cent.Bas.	General	Topsoil		4th–5th
1939	Cent.Bas.	S. Aisle E.	Detritus of terre pisé		4th
1941	Cent.Bas.	S. Aisle E.	Stratum B		3rd, 4th
1946	Cent.Bas.	S. Aisle E.	Use level		3rd/4th
1948	Cent.Bas.	S. Aisle E.	Use level	Public	4th

Table 4.16. (*Cont.*)

Lot	Area	Location	Nature Deposit	Area Function	Period
1955	Cent.Bas.	Nave	Stratum D		ER
1957	Cent.Bas.	S. Aisle E.	Destruction debris		Late 1st
1958	Cent.Bas.	Nave VIII	Riverine gravel		
1959	Cent.Bas.	S. Aisle E.	Destruction debris		Late 1st
2033	E.Bas.	Atrium	Construction	Public	LR
2062	E.Bas.	West, Room 1	Destruction debris	Public	LR
2076	E.Bas.	S. Aisle	Fill over crypt	Public	425–475
2084	E.Res.	E. Wall, Room 9	Wall cleaning		MR
2089	A.G.S.	Small bath north	Destruction debris		5th
2090	A.G.S.	Small Bath north	Fill		1st
2094	Theater	Tr. 16	Fill	Public	LR
2111	E.Bas.	S. Aisle	Dumped fill	Public	LR
2112	E.Bas.	S. Aisle	Dumped fill	Public	LR
2120	Cent.Bas.	S. Aisle	Dumped fill	Public	1st
2121	Cent.Bas.	S. Aisle E.	Destruction 1st-c. bldg. (D)	Public	Early 2nd
2126	Cent.Bas.	S. Aisle E.	Stratum B.	Public	4th/5th
2128	Cent.Bas.	S. Aisle E.	Stratum C/D	Public	2nd/3rd
2129	Cent.Bas.	S. Aisle E.	Destruction debris	Public	1st/2nd
2137	Cent.Bas.	S. Aisle E.	Stratum D/E	Public	1st
2143	Cent.Bas.	S. Aisle W.	Construction (B)	Public	Early 5th
2144	Cent.Bas.	S. Aisle W.	Construction (B)	Public	Early 5th
2145	Cent.Bas.	S. Aisle W.	Construction (B)	Public	Early 5th
2147	Cent.Bas.	S. Aisle W.	Construction (B)	Public	Early 5th
2148	Cent.Bas.	S. Aisle W.	Stratum C	Public	3rd
2152	Cent.Bas.	S. Aisle W.	Dark brown silt/ sand, gravel		1st
2173	Cent.Bas.	Apse	Pre-Basilica		3rd/4th
2181	Cent.Bas.	Apse	Pre-Basilica		3rd
2186	Cent.Bas.	Apse	Destruction debris		4th/5th
2194	E.Bas.	South, Room 2	Destruction debris		4th/5th
2201	E.Bas.	South, Sector II, Tr. 10			5th
2201	E.Bas.	South, Sector II, Tr. 10			5th
2206	E.Bas.	Nave	Dumped fill	Public	3rd qtr. 5th
2208	E.Bas.	Nave			
2209	E.Bas.	Nave	Mortar, phase 1 floor	Public	Mid-5th
2210	E.Bas.	Nave	Dumped fill		3rd qtr. 5th
2211	E.Bas.	Nave	Dumped fill	Public	3rd qtr. 5th
2212	E.Bas.	Nave	Destruction Bldg. A	Public	Mid-5th
2213	E.Bas.	Nave	Destruction debris	Public	Mid- to 3rd qtr. 5th
2218	E.Bas.	Nave	Destruction Bldg. A	Public	Mid-5th
2222	E.Bas.	Nave	Surface		Mixed

Table 4.16. *continued on p. 174*

Table 4.16. (*Cont.*)

Lot	Area	Location	Nature Deposit	Area Function	Period
2223	E.Bas.	Nave	Contents of recent pit	Dump	Mixed
2228	E.Bas.	Nave	Floor E.Bas. II	Public	5th
2230	E.Bas.	Nave	Construction Phase I	Public	Mid- to 3rd qtr. 5th
2233	E.Bas.	Nave	Dumped fill	Public	3rd qtr. 5th
2234	E.Bas.	Nave	Destruction of Bldg. A	Public	Mid-5th
2236	E.Bas.	Nave			
2262	E.Bas.	South, Room 2	Mixed soils		3rd/4th
2263	E.Bas.	South, Room 2	Fill over piscina pipe	Public	Late 4th, early 5th
2265	E.Bas.	South, Room 2	Debris		4th
2275	E.Bas.	South, Room 2			4th/5th
2281	E.Bas.	South, Room 6			4th
2302	E.Bas.	Baptistry	Below floor	Public	1st
2306	E.Bas.	South, Tr. II			5th
2307	E.Bas.	South, Tr. I		Public	
2315	E.Bas.	Atrium	Use level	Public	Late 5th
2319	E.Bas.	Atrium	Drains		5th
2323	E.Bas.	Atrium	Construction		Late 5th
2325	E.Bas.	Atrium	Dumped fill		6th
2347	E.Bas.	Atrium	Pre-Basilica fills		5th
2350	E.Bas.	Atrium	Fill		LR
2354	E.Bas.	Atrium	Fill	Public	LR
2355	E.Bas.	Atrium	Use accumulation		5th
2360	E.Bas.	Atrium	Test Trench NW	Public	5th
2367	E.Bas.	Atrium	Pre-Basilica fills		4th
2377	E.Bas.	Atrium	Use accumulation		4th
2380	E.Bas.	Atrium	Destruction debris		4th
2382	E.Bas.	Atrium	Early fills		2nd/3rd
2385	E.Bas.	Atrium	Early levels		2nd
2389	E.Bas.	Atrium	Early levels		2nd
2393	E.Bas.	S. Aisle	Below Bldg. A	Public	Late 4th
2403	E.Bas.	Nave	Dumped fill		3rd qtr. 5th
2405	E.Bas.	Nave	Destruction Bldg. A		Mid-5th
2406	E.Bas.	Nave	Destruction Bldg. A		Mid-5th
2407	E.Bas.	Nave	Destruction Bldg. A		Mid-5th
2408	E.Bas.	Nave	Fill	Public	LR
2429	E.Res.	Room 29	Below floor 2		Mid-4th
2434	E.Bas.	Nave			
2455	E.Bas.	South, Sector II, Tr. 10	Mixed		Early 6th
2457	E.Bas.	South, Sector II, Tr. 10	Mixed		
2580	E.Bas.	Nave	Dumped fill	Public	5th
2581	E.Bas.	Nave	Dumped fill	Public	3rd qtr. 5th

Table 4.16. (*Cont.*)

Lot	Area	Location	Nature Deposit	Area Function	Period
2583	E.Bas.	Nave	Dumped fill	Public	3rd qtr. 5th
2584	E.Bas.	Nave	Destruction Bldg. A	Public	3rd qtr. 5th
2586	E.Bas.	Nave	Destruction Bldg. A	Public	Mid-5th
2588	E.Bas.	Nave	Destruction Bldg. A	Public	3rd qtr. 5th
2604	E.Bas.	Nave	Construction Phase I	Public	Mid-5th
2605	E.Bas.	Nave	Construction Phase I	Public	Mid-5th

Table 4.17. List of other deposits arranged by date

Century	Lot	Area	Location
Late 4th, early 3rd B.C.	842	Cent.Bas.	N. Aisle
Late 4th, early 3rd B.C.	843	Cent.Bas.	N. Aisle
2nd B.C./1st A.C.	1458	W.C.	Grave 278
2nd/1st B.C.		W.C.	Grave 308
2nd B.C. to 2nd A.C.	1441	W.C.	Sector X3
1st B.C., early		W.C.	Grave 84
1st B.C.	1452	W.C.	Grave 273
1st B.C.		W.C.	Grave 288
1st B.C.	1421	W.C.	Grave 265
1st B.C.	1465	W.C.	Grave 294
1st B.C./1st A.C.	456	W.C.	S. of Wall 9 (Grave 95).
1st B.C., late to early 1st A.C.		W.C.	Grave 310
1st B.C., late to mid-1st A.C.	490	W.C.	Exposing Grave 18
1st B.C., late/early 1st A.C.	1099	W.C.	Grave 266
1st B.C., late/early 1st A.C.	26	W.C.	Around Graves 80, 88
1st B.C., late/early 1st A.C.	1443	W.C.	Sector X3
1st B.C./1st A.C.	1468	W.C.	Grave 298
1st B.C./1st A.C.	1470	W.C.	Grave 300
1st B.C./1st A.C.	708	Bas.Cem.	Grave 107
1st B.C./1st A.C.	77	Cent.Bas.	Nave
1st B.C./1st A.C.	83	Cent.Bas.	Nave
1st B.C./1st A.C.	11	Civ.Bas.	Nave/Bldg. D
1st, early	399	W.C.	Grave 81
1st, 1st 1/3	45	W.C.	Grave 88
1st		W.C.	Grave 13
1st		W.C.	Grave 60
1st	19	W.C.	South
1st	24	W.C.	Overall
1st	25	W.C.	Overall
1st	44	W.C.	Grave 88
1st	700	Bas.Cem.	Grave 103

Table 4.17. *continued on p. 176*

Table 4.17. (*Cont.*)

Century	Lot	Area	Location
1st	400	W.C.	Grave 77
1st	401	W.C.	Grave 77
1st	406	W.C.	Grave 94
1st	2137	Cent.Bas.	S. Aisle E.
1st	2152	Cent.Bas.	S. Aisle W.
1st	78	Cent.Bas.	Nave
1st	70	Cent.Bas.	Nave
1st	412	W.C.	Grave 51
1st	435	W.C.	Over Graves 43, 45
1st	440	W.C.	Over Grave 48
1st	446	W.C.	Grave 61
1st	448	W.C.	Graves 67, 68, 76, 77, 95
1st	451	W.C.	Grave 30
1st	1059	W.C.	Grave 33
1st	1084	W.C.	Grave 257
1st	594	Civ.Bas.	Tr. 2, Room 1
1st	411	W.C.	Grave 74
1st	388	W.C.	Grave 38
1st	389	W.C.	Grave 38
1st	443	W.C.	General
1st	1094	W.C.	Grave 84
1st	1095	W.C.	Grave 262
1st	1426	W.C.	Grave 282
1st	1423	W.C.	Over arched tiles of Grave 272
1st	1425	W.C.	Grave 286
1st	2302	E.Bas.	Baptistry
1st	1025	F.H.	Room 9
1st	1532	Theater	Orchestra
1st	1454	W.C.	Grave 62
1st	1456	W.C.	Grave 277
1st	1462	W.C.	Grave 285
1st	1469	W.C.	Grave 299
1st	1453	W.C.	Sector X3
1st, mid	43	W.C.	Grave 80
1st, mid	1080	W.C.	Near Graves 42, 257, 258, 259, 260
1st, mid	1089	W.C.	General deposit over Sector X2
1st, mid	1090	W.C.	General
1st, mid	448	W.C.	Above Graves 67, 68, 70, 77, 95
1st, mid	1086	W.C.	Grave 259
1st, mid	1093	W.C.	General deposit over Sector X2
1st, mid	445	W.C.	General
1st, post mid	386	W.C.	Grave 38
1st, 2nd 1/2	22	W.C.	South
1st, 2nd 1/2	384	W.C.	Grave 37
1st, 2nd 1/2	390	W.C.	Grave 39
1st, 2nd 1/2	1418	W.C.	General deposit over Sector X4
1st, 2nd 1/2	1419	W.C.	General deposit over Sector X4

Table 4.17. (*Cont.*)

Century	Lot	Area	Location
1st, 2nd 1/2	1442	W.C.	Sector X3
1st, 2nd 1/2	488	W.C.	Among Graves 11, 12, 13, 14, 21
1st, 3rd qtr	487	W.C.	Grave 21
1st, late	452	W.C.	West of pit for Grave 37
1st, late	7	Cent.Bas.	Tr. 2
1st, late	1959	Cent.Bas.	S. Aisle E.
1st, late	384	W.C.	Grave 37
1st, late	1416	W.C.	General deposit over Sector X4
1st, late	1417	W.C.	General deposit over Sector X4
1st, late	1957	Cent.Bas.	S. Aisle E.
1st, late	1420	W.C.	General Sector X4
1st, late	1495	Theater	Skene
1st, late	1497	Theater	Skene
1st, late	1498	Theater	Skene
1st, late	1538	Theater	Skene
1st, late	1501	Theater	Skene
1st, late	1098	W.C.	Grave 266, unguentarium feature
1st/2nd		W.C.	Grave 45
1st/2nd	415	W.C.	Grave 67
1st/2nd	442	W.C.	Over Graves 52, 53
1st/2nd	1510	Theater	Terrace
1st/2nd	57	Cent.Bas.	Room 1
1st/2nd	1085	W.C.	Wall 31B
1st/2nd	2129	Cent.Bas.	S. Aisle E.
1st/2nd	30	W.C.	Grave 55
1st/early 2nd	391	W.C.	Grave 39
1st/early 2nd	385	W.C.	Over Graves 38, 39, 40, 44, 47, 48
1st/early 2nd	513	Theater	Orchestra
1st/early 2nd	1672	Theater	Skene
1st/early 2nd	1673	Theater	Skene
1st/early 2nd	1662	Theater	Skene
1st/early 2nd	18	W.C.	South
1st/early 2nd	20	W.C.	South
1st/early 2nd	29	W.C.	Grave 79
1st/early 2nd	392	W.C.	Graves 40 and 44
2nd early	2121	Cent.Bas.	S. Aisle E.
2nd	1467	W.C.	Grave 297
2nd	921	L.B.	General
2nd	783	S.C.W.	Grave 98
2nd	1475	Theater	Skene
2nd	1676	Theater	East Parodos
2nd	2385	E.Bas.	Atrium
2nd	2389	E.Bas.	Atrium
2nd	1933	Cent.Bas.	Nave
2nd, mid	1471	Theater	Skene

Table 4.17. *continued on p. 178*

Table 4.17. (*Cont.*)

Century	Lot	Area	Location
2nd, mid	1474	Theater	Skene
2nd, mid	1477	Theater	Skene
2nd, mid	1478	Theater	Skene
2nd, mid	1479	Theater	Skene
2nd, mid	1511	Theater	Skene/Terrace
2nd, mid	1537	Theater	Skene
2nd or later	677	Cent.Bas.	Atrium
2nd, 1st 1/2	692	Cent.Bas.	North Corridor
2nd/3rd	672	Cent.Bas.	Atrium
2nd/3rd	675	Cent.Bas.	Atrium
2nd/3rd maybe early 4th	65	Cent.Bas.	Nave
2nd/3rd	2128	Cent.Bas.	S. Aisle E.
2nd/3rd	1697	E.Bas.	N. Aisle
2nd/3rd	2382	E.Bas.	Atrium
2nd/3rd	586	I.W.W.	Room 1
2nd/3rd	1358	Theater	Radial Corridor
2nd/3rd	1509	Theater	Terrace
2nd/3rd	441	W.C.	Over Grave 50
2nd/3rd	1066	W.C.	Grave 32
2nd/3rd	1074	W.C.	Exposed Graves 42, 257, 258, 259, 260
2nd/3rd	1434	W.C.	X3
2nd/3rd	1652	Theater	Trench I
2nd/early 3rd	1846	Theater	Cavea
2nd/early 3rd	542	Theater	East Parodos
2nd/early 3rd	536	Theater	East Parodos
2nd/early 3rd	543	Theater	East Parodos
2nd/early 3rd	505	Theater	Orchestra
3rd	763	F.H.	Room 24
3rd	764	F.H.	Room 24
3rd	1052	I.W.W.	Room 1
3rd	517	Theater	East Parodos, Tr. VIII
3rd	890	Theater	Skene
3rd	381	W.C.	Grave 28
3rd	432	W.C.	Over 32, 33, 34
3rd	433	W.C.	Graves 36, 37
3rd	476	W.C.	Over Grave 6
3rd	482	W.C.	Exposed Grave 8
3rd	483	W.C.	Exposed Grave 10
3rd	486	W.C.	Exposed Graves 11, 12, 13, 14
3rd	892	Theater	Skene
3rd	765	F.H.	Room 24
3rd	313	Acropolis	Between Rooms 1, 2
3rd	190	Bridge Access	Tr. IV
3rd	802	Cent.Bas.	Nave, floor, Synagogue I
3rd	2148	Cent.Bias.	S. Aisle W.
3rd	2181	Cent.Bas.	Apse
3rd	810	Cent.Bas.	Nave, Tr. II, above floor

Table 4.17. (*Cont.*)

Century	Lot	Area	Location
3rd/mid 4th	1327	E.Bas.	N. Aisle
3rd/mid 4th	1328	E.Bas.	N. Aisle
3rd, mid or late	801	Cent.Bas.	Tr. 1, below Synagogue 1
3rd late/early 4th	799	Cent.Bas.	Nave, fill of Synagogue 1
3rd/4th	68	Cent.Bas.	Nave
3rd/4th	197	Bridge Access	Tr. XII
3rd/4th	1941	Cent.Bas.	S. Aisle E.
3rd/4th	1946	Cent.Bas.	S. Aisle E.
3rd/4th	2173	Cent.Bas.	Apse
3rd/4th	730	C.W.E.	Tr. 4, E. Ex., Wall 15
3rd/4th	985	C.W.E.	Room 2
3rd/4th	1373	C.W.E.	EXC 74-9
3rd/4th	1319	E.Bas.	N. Aisle
3rd/4th	2262	E.Bas.	South, Room 2
3rd/4th	163	F.H.	Room 25
3rd/4th	164	F.H.	Room 25
3rd/4th	762	F.H.	Room 24
3rd/4th	509	Theater	West Parodos
3rd/4th	1356	Theater	Radial Corridor
3rd/4th	465	W.C.	Walls 1, 3, hearth 1
3rd/5th	1433	W.C.	Sector X3
4th	179	Bridge Access	Tr. IV, VI
4th	181	Bridge Access	Tr. IV
4th	184	Bridge Access	Tr. IV
4th	48	Cent.Bas	Room 1
4th	127	Cent.Bas.	Narthex
4th	1315	E.Bas.	N. Aisle
4th	1317	E.Bas.	N. Aisle
4th	1616	E.Bas.	East
4th	2265	E.Bas.	South, Room 2
4th	2281	E.Bas.	South, Room 6
4th	162	F.H.	Room 25
4th	172	F.H.	Room 23
4th	759	F.H.	Room 25
4th	767	F.H.	Room 24
4th	2367	E.Bas.	Atrium
4th	285	Theater	East Parodos
4th	507	Theater	West Parodos
4th	515	Theater	East Parodos
4th	529	Theater	East Parodos
4th	878	Theater	Skene, Room 2
4th	882	Theater	Skene
4th	883	Theater	Skene
4th	884	Theater	Skene
4th	902	Theater	Skene

Table 4.17. *continued on p. 180*

Table 4.17. (*Cont.*)

Century	Lot	Area	Location
4th	1551	Theater	Barrier-wall passage
4th	1552	Theater	Skene
4th	1569	Theater	Refuge, center
4th	2377	E.Bas.	Atrium
4th	1657	Peristerias	Rooms 12, 13
4th	1658	Peristerias	Room 17
4th	2380	E.Bas.	Atrium
4th	1939	Cent.Bas.	S. Aisle E.
4th	712	C.W.E.	Tr. 1–4
4th	729	C.W.E.	Tr. 4, E. Ext., Wall 15
4th	1398	C.W.E.	EXC 74–6
4th	1948	Cent.Bas.	S. Aisle E.
4th, early	797	Cent.Bas.	Nave, fill Synagogue 1
4th, early	800	Cent.Bas.	Nave, fill Synagogue 1
4th, mid/late?	1599	Cent.Bas.	S. Aisle
4th, mid	1316	E.Bas.	N. Aisle
4th, mid	1642	F.H.	Room 27
4th, mid	157	F.H.	Rooms 23, 25
4th, mid	2429	E.Res.	Room 29
4th, 2nd 1/2	791	E.Bas.	Apse/Ambulatory
4th, 2nd 1/2	1314	E.Bas.	N. Aisle
4th, 2nd 1/2	523	Theater	East Parodos
4th, late	282	Theater	East Parodos
4th, late	1689	Theater	Cavea
4th, late	1783	Cent.Bas.	S. Aisle W.
4th, late	1023	F.H.	Rooms 1, 9
4th, late	169	F.H.	Room 22
4th, late	1645	F.H.	Room 32
4th, late	718	C.W.E.	Room 2
4th, late	1629	E.Bas.	S. Aisle
4th, late	2393	E.Bas.	S. Aisle
4th/early 5th	853	F.H.	Room 27
4th/early 5th	1370	C.W.E.	EXC 74-18
4th/early 5th	152	F.H.	Corridor Sector A
4th/early 5th	2263	E.Bas.	South, Room 2
4th/5th	1770	Cent.Bas.	S. Aisle W.
4th/5th	178	Bridge Access	Tr. IV, VI
4th/5th	1935	Cent.Bas.	General
4th/5th	2126	Cent.Bas.	S. Aisle E.
4th/5th	2186	Cent.Bas.	Apse
4th/5th	1378	C.W.E.	EXC 74-18
4th/5th	1413	C.W.E.	Rooms 3 and 5
4th/5th	1793	E.Bas.	S. Aisle
4th/5th	1804	E.Bas.	S. Aisle
4th/5th	1806	E.Bas.	S. Aisle
4th/5th	2194	E.Bas.	South, Room 2
4th/5th	2275	E.Bas.	South, Room 2
4th/5th	171	F.H.	Room 23

Table 4.17. (*Cont.*)

Century	Lot	Area	Location
4th/5th	1336	F.H.	Room 28
4th/5th	1349	F.H.	Room 32
4th/5th	917	L.B.	General
4th/5th	1656	Peristerias	Room 10
4th/5th	3	Theater	Radial Corridor
4th/5th	4	Theater	Radial Corridor
4th/5th	612	Theater	Tr. 9
4th/5th	1352	Theater	Radial Corridor
4th/5th	1362	Theater	Skene
4th/5th	1057	W.C.	Sector X2
4th/5th	1415	W.C.	Sector X2
4th/5th	223	Acropolis	Room 3
5th, early	2143	Cent.Bas.	S. Aisle W.
5th, early	2144	Cent.Bas.	S. Aisle W.
5th, early	2147	Cent.Bas.	S. Aisle W.
5th, early	2145	Cent.Bas.	S. Aisle W.
5th, early	168	F.H.	Room 22
5th, early	514	F.H.	Room 2
5th, early	1016	F.H.	Room 11
5th, 1st qtr.	1390	C.W.E.	EXC 74-6
5th, 1st 1/2	159	F.H.	Rooms 23, 29
5th	58	F.H.	Room 21
5th	91	F.H.	Room 21
5th	773	F.H.	Corridor
5th	847	F.H.	Rooms 28, 29, 30
5th	849	F.H.	Rooms 29, 30
5th	850	F.H.	Room 29
5th	750	E.Bas.	Room 3
5th	998	E.Bas.	East
5th	2089	A.G.S.	Small bath north
5th	1382	C.W.E.	EXC 74-6
5th	1388	C.W.E.	EXC 74-6
5th	1992	Cent.Bas.	Apse
5th	650	E.Bas.	Sector 2, Room 3
5th	1625	E.Bas.	East
5th	1819	E.Bas.	S. Aisle
5th	2201	E.Bas.	South, Sector II, Tr. 10
5th	566	IWW	Surface
5th	885	Theater	Skene
5th	1659	Theater	Skene
5th	462	W.C.	Exposing Wall 2
5th	1430	W.C.	General
5th	2201	E.Bas.	South, Sector II, Tr. 10
5th	2228	E.Bas.	Nave
5th	2306	E.Bas.	South, Tr. II
5th	2319	E.Bas.	Atrium

Table 4.17. *continued on p. 182*

Table 4.17. (*Cont.*)

Century	Lot	Area	Location
5th	2347	E.Bas.	Atrium
5th	2355	E.Bas.	Atrium
5th	2580	E.Bas.	Nave
5th	2360	E.Bas.	Atrium
5th, 2nd to 3rd qtr.	2076	E.Bas.	S. Aisle
5th, mid	955	E.Bas.	S. Aisle
5th, mid	1001	E.Bas.	East
5th, mid	2209	E.Bas.	Nave
5th, mid	2212	E.Bas.	Nave
5th, mid	2218	E.Bas.	Nave
5th, mid	2234	E.Bas.	Nave
5th, mid	2405	E.Bas.	Nave
5th, mid	2406	E.Bas.	Nave
5th, mid	2407	E.Bas.	Nave
5th, mid	2604	E.Bas.	Nave
5th, mid	2605	E.Bas.	Nave
5th, mid	1017	F.H.	Room 1, apse
5th, mid	1018	F.H.	Room 1, apse
5th, mid	1338	F.H.	Room 29
5th, mid to 3rd qtr.	2213	E.Bas.	Nave
5th, mid to 3rd qtr.	2230	E.Bas.	Nave
5th, 3rd qtr.	1798	E.Bas.	S. Aisle
5th, 3rd qtr.	1799	E.Bas.	S. Aisle
5th, 3rd qtr.	1800	E.Bas.	S. Aisle
5th, 3rd qtr.	1801	E.Bas.	S. Aisle
5th, 3rd qtr.		E.Bas.	Nave
5th, 3rd qtr.	2210	E.Bas.	Nave
5th, 3rd qtr.	2211	E.Bas.	Nave
5th, 3rd qtr.	2233	E.Bas.	Nave
5th, 3rd qtr.	2403	E.Bas.	Nave
5th, 3rd qtr.	2581	E.Bas.	Nave
5th, 3rd qtr.	2583	E.Bas.	Nave
5th, 3rd qtr.	2584	E.Bas.	Nave
5th, 3rd qtr.	2588	E.Bas.	Nave
5th, 2nd 1/2	146	F.H.	Sectors A and B
5th, 2nd 1/2	147	F.H.	Sectors A and B
5th, 2nd 1/2	148	F.H.	Along Wall 13
5th, 2nd 1/2	150	F.H.	Sector A and B
5th, 2nd 1/2	155	F.H.	Sector B, pit 1
5th, late	2315	E.Bas.	Atrium
5th, late	2323	E.Bas.	Atrium
5th, late	165	F.H.	Room 22
5th/6th	54	Cent.Bas.	Room 1
5th/6th	954	E.Bas.	S. Stairway
5th/6th	221	Acropolis	Room 4
5th/6th	645	E.Bas.	Sector 2, Room 3
5th/6th	145	F.H.	Sectors A and B, Room 32
5th/6th	1346	F.H.	Room 32

Table 4.17. (*Cont.*)

Century	Lot	Area	Location
5th/6th	460	W.C.	Entire trench
5th/early 6th	166	F.H.	Room 22
6th, early	2455	E.Bas.	South, Sector II, Tr. 10
6th, early	1344	F.H.	Room 32
6th, early	1347	F.H.	Room 32
6th, early	1334	F.H.	Room 28
6th	1345	F.H.	Room 32
6th	267	Acropolis	Room 1
6th	746	E.Bas.	South
6th	953	E.Bas.	South
6th	875	Theater	Radial corridor
ER	1934	Cent.Bas.	Nave VIII
ER	1955	Cent.Bas.	Nave
ER	1810	E.Bas.	S. Aisle
ER	992	Perist. Apse I	Near Wall 1
ER	789	S.C.W.	Tr. 3
ER	395	W.C.	Grave 47
ER	1078	W.C.	Over Grave 260's cairn
ER	1087	W.C.	Grave 258
ER	1092	W.C.	Grave 200
MR	1324	E.Bas.	N. Aisle
MR	1325	E.Bas.	N. Aisle
MR	1696	E.Bas.	N. Aisle
MR	1703	E.Bas.	Presbyterium
MR	2084	E.Res.	E. Wall, Room 9
LR	2111	E.Bas.	S. Aisle
LR	2112	E.Bas.	S. Aisle
LR	2033	E.Bas.	Atrium
LR	2062	E.Bas.	West, Room 1
LR	1361	Theater	Skene
LR	1686	Theater	Cavea
LR	1431	W.C.	Sector X3
LR	1070	W.C.	Grave 252
Mixed	2222	E.Bas.	Nave
Mixed	2223	E.Bas.	Nave

5

SUMMARY AND CONCLUSIONS

•

The aim of this study has been to establish a preliminary typology and chronology of the Hellenistic and Roman pottery at Stobi. It should not be considered the final word, and, as more material is published from chronologically secure deposits, it will need refinement.[1]

The location of the ancient city of Stobi at a major crossroads is clearly reflected in the diversity of ceramic imports throughout the city's history. The more heavily traveled road between Thessalonica and Sirmium through Naissus, which connected the east with central Europe, crossed the Erigon at Stobi; the other road ran between Serdica in Thrace and the Via Egnatia at Heraclea Lyncestis.[2]

The earliest pottery recovered in any measurable quantities belongs to the early Hellenistic period, perhaps the late 4th or early 3rd century B.C. This material, however, cannot be associated with any structures and comes from several isolated deposits, primarily in the area of the later Central Basilica.[3] A few pieces of black-gloss dishes, including bases with palmette stamps, are Greek imports, but the primary wares are of two types. The first and oldest is a coarse, thick-walled, handmade ware of Bronze and Iron Age tradition made in large, open forms with handles of horseshoe shape and decorated with finger-impressed designs.[4] The second type is a wheelmade, burnished gray ware that imitates some of the forms of Greek black-gloss pottery, including the kantharos, skyphos, incurved bowl (echinus bowl), and hydria. Both of these types are common in the broader area of ancient Paeonia as well as among the Dardani and Thracian tribes, so that we are not able to say whether these wares are regional imports or were made at Stobi.

The handmade and wheelmade gray wares are present at Stobi in the Late Hellenistic and Early Roman periods as well, although quantities are small, and it is impossible to tell whether these pieces are residual or represent contemporary manufacture.[5]

Gray wares have a long tradition in Macedonia and adjoining areas, culminating in the Late Roman period with the production of Macedonian Gray Ware.[6] Gray wares are common in the Early

[1] In Macedonia the study of regional production has not yet begun. Study of clays, fabric, kilns, all remain to be done at other sites in Macedonia. At Stobi itself such studies could profitably be pursued to a larger extent than was possible during the Stobi Project.

[2] Strabo VIII.C389; Tabula Peutingeriana, G. A. Škrivanić, *Monumenta Cartographica Jugoslaviae*. Historical Institute Monograph 17 (Beograd 1974) 54, 55 (in Serbo-Croatian with English summary); Charlesworth, *Trade Routes*, 119.

[3] Primarily Lots 842 and 843, but similar material was recovered elsewhere in the lowest deposits of the Central Basilica in the south aisle in Lots 2133 and 2135.

The general discussion and observations relating to the history of the site that follow derive from many years of work at the site with the documents and the pottery and from discussions with other participants of the project. The influence and ideas of many people, then, especially the syntheses of the director, James Wiseman, presented in the preliminary reports and other articles, have clearly influenced my own thinking. A brief history of the site was presented recently by Wiseman in "Archaeology and History at Stobi, Macedonia," with relevant bibliography; he treats the history in detail in Vol. 7 of this series. An earlier summary of the pottery at Stobi was presented by the author in *Studies III*.

[4] The handmade pottery, much of which is prehistoric, has not been included in this study and will be published by Mr. Voislav Sanev. For illustrations of the type, see Sokolovska (1986) 160, figs. 9, 10, 62, 79, and 80. See also Appendix 2 of this volume, where the composition of the ware is discussed.

[5] Peacock, *PRW*, 89, suggests that handmade wares found elsewhere in the Roman period, primarily as a continuation of the La Tène tradition (as at Stobi), may be evidence for household industry. With the amount of handmade pottery in Macedonia, this possibility certainly merits further study.

[6] In Britain, wheelmade gray wares are common in the Roman period and "are commonly associated with the small iso-

and Middle Imperial periods as well, but most were probably imported from Italy and Asia Minor.

During the late Hellenistic period most of the fine wares in Macedonia proper appear to be part of the Greek tradition, as one might expect. At Stobi, many of the graves dated to the 2nd and 1st centuries B.C. contain fusiform unguentaria, some imported and others probably produced locally, as the most common grave offering. Most of the other complete vessels from the graves are simple cups and bowls or pitchers.

Elsewhere on the site, small amounts of black-gloss wares are found, and it is probable that most are Greek imports. Several amphora handles carry Greek (Cnidian and Rhodian) stamps and indicate trade with the Aegean.[7] Aegean trade is further documented by the presence of Asia Minor Gray Ware and Ionian moulded relief bowls, both with a probable origin in southwest Asia Minor, as has been suggested recently by the analyses of P. M. Kenrick.[8]

The presence of Eastern Sigillata A from the Syro-Palestinian area, even in small numbers (and most of these Samaria Form 10), is of interest for an inland city like Stobi and should, perhaps, be associated with other, as yet unidentified and perhaps perishable, commodities imported from the same area.

But the quantities of the pottery types from several small deposits of the late 2nd century and others of a more substantial nature dating to the first three quarters of the 1st century B.C. indicate that although Italian pottery constitutes a very small part of the total ceramic assemblage at Stobi the majority of *imports* from any single source are those from Italy.[9] Figures 5.1 through 5.4 illustrate the situation for the Late Hellenistic *and* Early Roman periods. During the Hellenistic period, Italian imports make up 37.5% of the fine wares (Fig. 5.5), a greater percentage than that of any other group. These Italian imports include the black-gloss Campanian wares, Thin-Walled vessels, Pompeian Red Ware, and probably cooking pots as well (Tables 5.1, 5.2, Fig. 5.5). It is likely that Stobi Hellenistic Cooking Ware Form 1, the "orlo bifido" pan, and Form 7, a stewpot (Fig. 3.7), as well as Early Roman Form 1 (Fig. 3.8), also an "orlo bifido" pan, are either imports or derived from Italian prototypes.[10] Transport amphoras of Greco-Italic, Dressel 1, and Adriatic types (Fig. 5.6) provide further indications of the city's early connections with the west and its need for imported oil and wine. Considerable numbers of amphora fragments were found in association with early structures below the Civil Basilica.[11]

Many of the Italian imports were found in the destruction debris of a potter's shop beneath the narthex of the Central Basilica in a part of the city that was perhaps devoted to commerce and crafts.[12] Several of the Italian pieces were used as models for imitations made in local ware (e.g., **21** and **743**).

Following the conquest of Macedonia by the Romans in 168 B.C. and the creation of the province of Macedonia in 146 B.C., there are certain factors that would account for the appearance of Italian pottery in the later 2nd century and its increase in popularity during the following century.

Since Stobi was on the northern frontier of Macedonia and as such held a strategic position, it must have come under Roman military control shortly after the victory over Perseus.[13] In fact, Roman soldiers engaged in many battles with the northern and eastern neighbors of Macedon from the second half of the 2nd century to the Augustan period.[14] The aim and result of all these campaigns was the stabilization of the border regions through the pacification of these neighboring peoples. Eventually, under the rule of the Em-

lated workshop" (Peacock, *PRW*, 90–91). Note the comments of Georgeana Little in Appendix 2 of this volume regarding the implications of variability in mineral composition of Macedonian Gray Ware. Also see Chapter 2, note 9.

[7] But no Cnidian Gray Ware has yet been identified at Stobi. Note recent comments of Kenrick, *Berenice* 3, 58.

[8] Ibid., 53.

[9] This topic was explored by the author in Anderson-Stojanović (1987).

[10] It has been impossible to distinguish imported from local cooking fabric except in a few instances, and therefore, the comparison has been made on the basis of form.

[11] Lots 12–14, 608, 610. Table 4.2.

[12] W-MZ (1971) 408–411; Lots 130–140, 829, 831. The destruction probably took place around the mid-1st century B.C. See the descriptions of these deposits in Chapter 4, Table 4.3, and Appendix 1.

[13] Livy xxxiii. 19; W-MZ (1971) 411, note 20; Papazoglu (1986) 227, would put the creation of the *oppidum Stobi civium Romanorum* in the period of Julius Caesar. Also see Papazoglu, "Province," 312–318; Mocsy, *Pannonia*, 12–17, 23–27, 30.

[14] The nonrecovery of a coin hoard found at Stobi may be associated with a raid of the Scordisci (Crawford, "Stobi Hoard," 8).

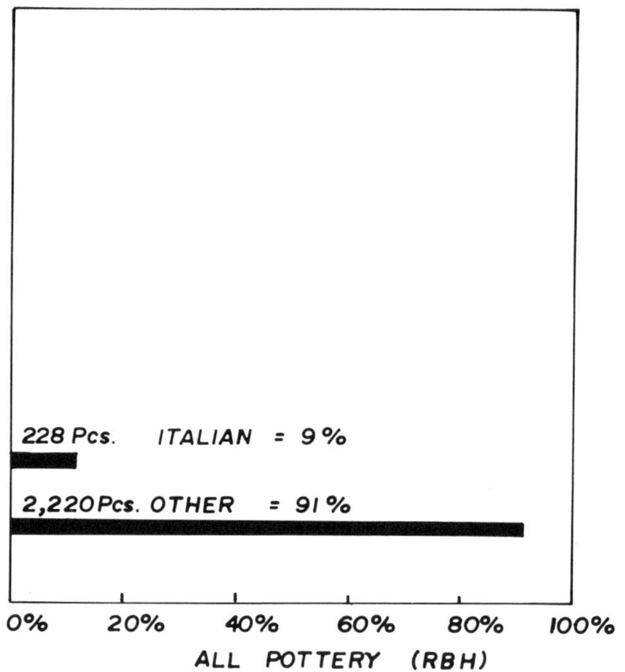

Figure 5.1. Quantity of Italian pottery in total RBH of Hellenistic and Early Roman deposits at Stobi

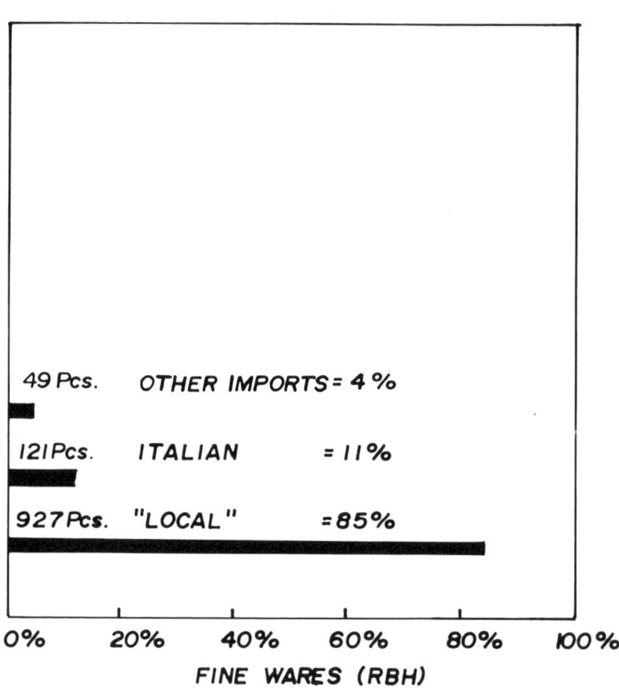

Figure 5.2. Quantity of Fine Ware RBH at Stobi divided according to origin

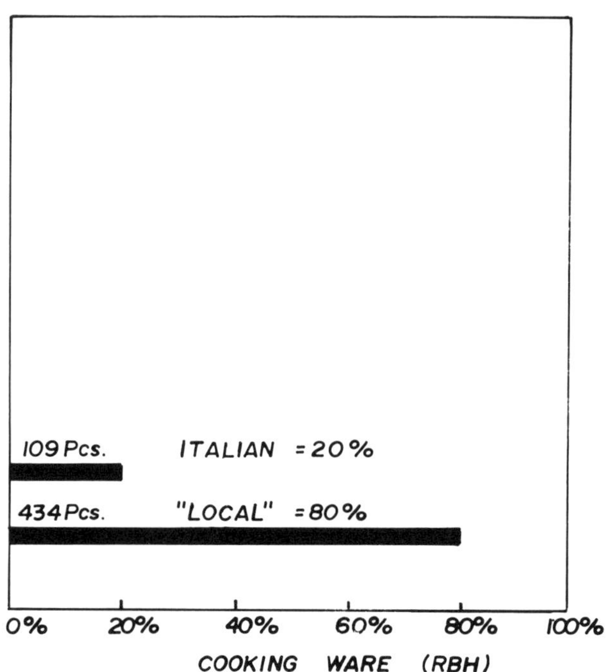

Figure 5.3. Quantity of Cooking Ware RBH at Stobi divided according to origin

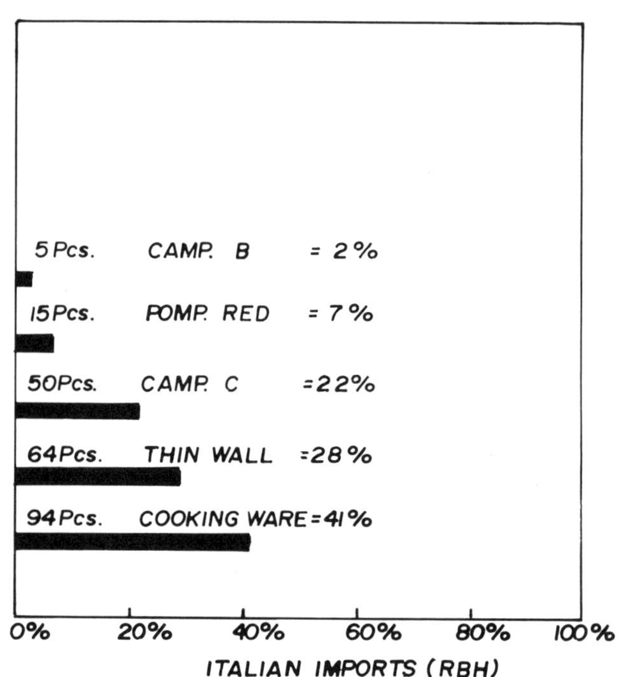

Figure 5.4. Breakdown of various types among Italian imports at Stobi

Table 5.1. Quantity of Fine-Ware RBH in Core Deposits for each chronological period

	Hell.	ER	MR	LR	Total
Hellenistic Gray	23	3			26
Black-Gloss	15	1			16
Campanian A, B	5				5
Campanian C	50				50
Thin-walled	68	28	19		115
Asia Minor Gray	5				5
Black-Gloss Gray	65	22			87
Mouldmade Bowl	73				73
Eastern Sigillata A	24	4			28
Western Sigillata		34	9	3	46
Eastern Sigillata B		4	27	6	37
Candarli			16	2	18
Italian Mugs			20		20
African Red Slipped			5	28	33
Phocaean Red Slipped				2	2
Pannonian Lead-Glazed Marbled			1	9	10
Macedonian Gray				42	42
Color-Slipped	783	260	1736	753	3532
Total	1111	356	1833	845	4145

Table 5.2. Quantity of Coarse-Ware RBH in Core Deposits for each chronological period

	Hell.	ER	MR	LR	Total
Amphorae	110	7	39	20	176
Handmade	17				17
Pompeian Red Ware	15	2			17
Aegean Cooking Ware			3	1	4
Cooking Ware	533	92	399	1457	2481
Total	675	101	441	1478	2695

peror Tiberius, Moesia was established as a province, and by the mid-1st century Thrace had also become a part of the empire.[15] With the creation of these new provinces on the northern and eastern borders of Macedonia, the frontier moved away from Stobi.

While it is true that conditions were somewhat unsettled for major commercial enterprise, such as is possible in more peaceful times, the number of Italian imports suggests a strong Roman presence throughout the 1st century B.C. and first half of the 1st century A.C. Furthermore, we must rely upon the archaeological evidence in the absence of direct literary and epigraphical documentation.

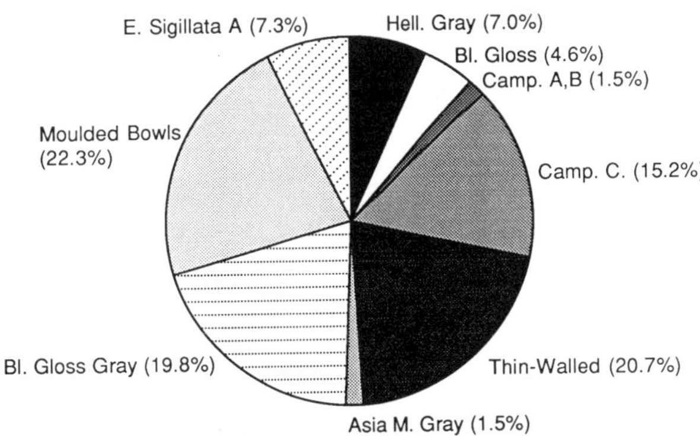

Figure 5.5. Proportion of fine wares (excluding local color-slipped) expressed as percentage of total RBH of these wares in Hellenistic core deposits

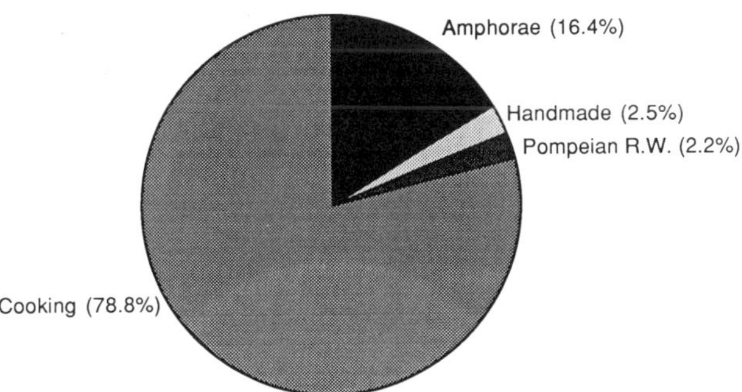

Figure 5.6. Proportion of coarse wares expressed as percentage of total RBH of these wares in the Hellenistic core deposits

The laying of the Via Egnatia (in the late 2nd or early 1st century B.C.), the highway between Rome and the East which ran through Macedonia from Dyrrachium to Thessalonica and on to Byzantium, facilitated the movement of troops through Macedonia and to the border regions, thus also to Stobi.[16] There probably was already

[15] Papazoglu, "Province," 329; Mocsy, *Pannonia*, 116; S. Velkov, "Thrace and Lower Moesia," *Klio* 63 (1981) 474–475.

[16] Papazoglu, "Province," 328, and note 116; N.G.L. Hammond, *A History of Macedonia*, vol. 1 (Oxford 1972) 19–58, 66, 67, and N.G.L. Hammond, *Migrations and Invasions in Greece and Adjacent Areas* (Park Ridge, NJ, 1976), 29–33; Charlesworth, *Trade Routes*, 118.

at this time a road between Heraclea and Stobi. The choice of Stobi as a center for the distribution of salt for the third region of Macedonia in the 2nd century B.C. reflects its strategic location, and it is likely that Stobi served as a general market for various commodities.[17]

The influx of Roman officials who were connected with the governing of the new province, the military command and ex-soldiers settled in Macedonia, along with the usual *negotiatores*, bankers, and others who are found in frontier areas all had their effect in Romanizing the city and creating a demand for Italian goods.[18] Slaves, wool, textiles, cattle, skins, and even cheese, are possible commodities acquired by Roman traders in exchange for salt, oil, wine, and other Mediterranean products.[19]

Craftsmen, including several potters from Italy, appear to have settled at Stobi to supply the needs of the soldiers and other foreigners living there. A potter who used the signature AFRI (in rectangular frame) may have been affiliated with the workshop of SEXTVS ANNIVS AFER of Arezzo.[20] Other examples of potters' stamps include several with the Latin names LVCIVS, GAIVS, and TERT in Greek letters.[21] Burial goods from what may be graves of Italians buried at Stobi provide further evidence of Italian pottery at the site in these early years.[22]

That Stobi had significant numbers of Italian imports should not be surprising. This was also true at Corinth within forty years after the Roman colony was established.[23] The new evidence from Stobi, however, has altered earlier ideas about when Roman influence can be documented in the material culture of Macedonia. Earlier studies suggested Romanization only in the Augustan period, since Roman colonies had been founded in Macedonia after the period of the civil wars, as well as following the battle of Actium (48 B.C., 42 B.C., and 31 B.C.).[24]

Could Stobi's position on the northern frontier, which necessitated military personnel, and the considerable number of Romans residing at Stobi have brought more Italian goods there than elsewhere in Macedonia?

Recent research indicates that some Italian pottery of the 1st century B.C. reached other Macedonian cities besides Stobi. Excavations at Florina, Heraclea, and Styberra have produced a few examples of Thin-Walled beakers of a type common in the first three quarters of the 1st century B.C.[25] Until more Italian wares have been identified elsewhere in Macedonia and published with quantitative information on types, we will not know if Stobi was unusual in the quantity of Italian imports recorded.

Throughout the 1st century A.C. the number of

[17] Livy XLV. 29:13.

[18] Papazoglu (1986) 229–231, discusses the number of Roman citizens at Stobi with Italic, nonimperial *cognomina*. The prosopography of Stobi is now much larger, as a result of Wiseman's study of the seat inscriptions from the theater in *Stobi 3*. Also see Papazoglu, "Province," 356; Greene (1986) 166–167; Mocsy, *Pannonia*, 71. Crawford ("Stobi Hoard," 7) suggests that the Stobi coin hoard may have belonged to a mercenary or pirate rather than a trader. Greene ("Invasion and Response: Pottery and the Roman Army," in Burnham and Johnson [1979], 99–106) suggests that when a garrison fort was established (as opposed to a temporary marching camp), the quartermaster would turn his attention to the supply of pottery (p. 99) and proposes (p. 102) several models to explain the effects of Roman influence on local potters.

[19] Mocsy, *Pannonia*, 26, 32. Among the products of Macedonia mentioned by Pliny (*Nat.Hist.*) are pitch (xvi.22), timber (xvi.76), figs (xvi.40), and iris root (xxi.19).

[20] Oxé-Comfort, 87–92, p. 28; F. Papazoglu "Oppidum Stobi civium Romanorum et municipium Stobensium," *Chiron* 16 (1986) 213–237, cites an occurrence of the Annii. See **498**, **499**, **500**, **501**.

[21] The signature *TERT* may be related to the Terentii cited by Papazoglu (1986) 235 (cited in note 20), but more probably stands for the common name "Tertius," see **495**.

[22] A number of graves from cemeteries at Stobi contain Italian pottery. Grave 313, an inhumation of the mid- to late 2nd century B.C., contained fragments of a Campanian black-gloss bowl (**20**) and a fine, Thin-Walled beaker. Grave 84, a cremation burial of the early 1st century B.C., contained three fusiform unguentaria and four vessels, at least three of which are of Italian origin: a Thin-Walled beaker (**147**), and a plate and small bowl (**32**, **34**), probably Campanian. Other isolated examples occur in various graves, most belonging to the Thin-Walled category of the 1st century A.C.

[23] Hayes, "Corinth," 470; Wright (1980) 174; and Slane (1986) 317–318.

[24] Mikulčić, *Pelagonia*, 85, 86; Papazoglu, "Province," 356; but Papazoglu gives several examples of Italian immigrants to the territory of Stobi during the late Republic in "Notes epigraphiques de Macédoine," *Živa Antika* 32 (1982) 39–52, and now considers an earlier date more likely: Papazoglu (1986) (cited in note 20) 227.

[25] Florina: Keramopoullos (1932) 61, no. 123, a Thin-Walled beaker (Moevs, "Cosa," Form 1), p. 62, no. 148, a Campanian black-gloss bowl (Lamboglia Form 1) of late 2nd-century B.C. date. I saw both of these in the museum at Florina as well as an example of an Aco beaker of the Augustan period (inv. no. 190). I was not able to see the other examples of Thin-Walled vessels illustrated in Keramopoullos (1932) 61–62. Heraclea: Maneva (1979), fig. 12, Nos. 137–139, 141, all Thin-Walled beakers of Moevs, "Cosa," Form 1. Styberra (modern Čepigovo), Mikulčić, *Pelagonia*, fig. 38b, an example of Moevs, "Cosa," Form 1, with overlapping pine-scale decoration.

western imports at Stobi remains very high in comparison with other imported wares (Fig. 5.2). Because the Augustan period, however, and the 1st century A.C. are not well represented in the deposits excavated at Stobi, it is not surprising that no examples of fine Arretine relief ware have been discovered, although two stamps of the early workshops of M. PERENNIVS and BLANDVS L. TITIVS have been found (**291**, **286**). All the Italian sigillata at Stobi belongs to the Plain Ware class, although some have appliqué decoration. The remaining stamps, some in *planta pedis*, belong to the second and third quarters of the 1st century A.C. (L. GELLIVS, UMBRICIVS, CAMVRIVS, **288**, **289**, **293**).

During the 1st century, although the undecorated Italian sigillata is the popular import, the number of Thin-Walled pieces with sanded decoration, barbotine floral patterns, or both, is high (Table 5.1, Fig. 5.7). The techniques of barbotine and rough-casting or sanding were popular and widely produced throughout most of the Roman empire in Europe, so that it is virtually impossible to ascertain the origin of such imports.

The decline in numbers of amphorae in the 1st century (Fig. 5.8) may be a function of the domestic nature of those deposits. Numbers of Pompeian Red Ware remain the same as in the Hellenistic period (Fig. 5.6).

Imports from the Aegean and eastern Mediterranean are rarely found at Stobi during the Augustan period or, in fact, for most of the 1st century. Some of the various gray wares of unidentified origin, however, which occur during this period, may be from Asia Minor. No examples of Eastern Sigillata B1 or Çandarli ware, another Asia Minor product, found their way to Stobi in the first part of the 1st century A.C. Perhaps for some reason, trade that brought fine wares from Asia Minor was not taking place, or it is possible that these wares could not compete with the well-established and traditional Italian products.

By the last quarter of the 1st century A.C., the picture began to change, and we find eastern or Aegean influence increasing. Among imports, Eastern Sigillata B2 now appears, and there are a few Çandarli flanged bowls, which, along with

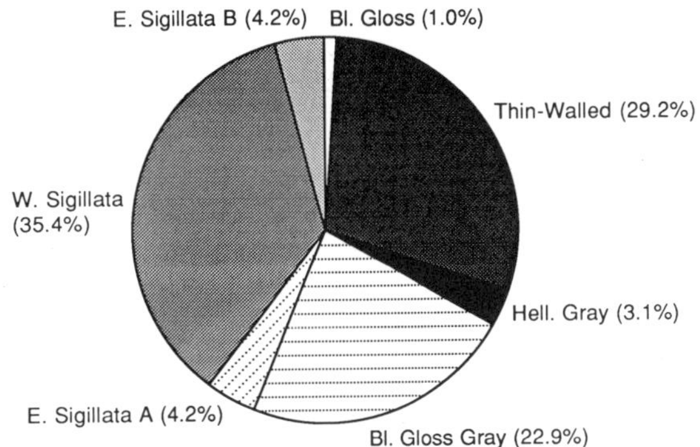

Figure 5.7. Proportion of fine wares (excluding local Color-Slipped) expressed as percentage of total RBH of these wares in Early Roman core deposits

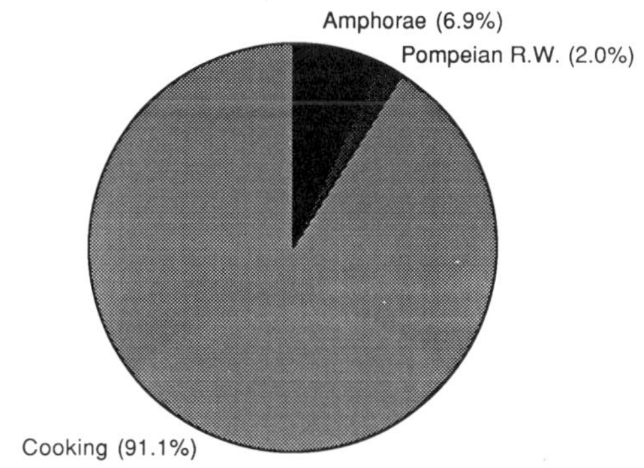

Figure 5.8. Proportion of coarse wares expressed as percentage of total RBH of these wares in the Early Roman core deposits

Arretine forms, were widely imitated in the local wares of the late 1st century and even into the 2nd and 3rd centuries.[26]

There are several factors that may be associated with this increased role of the eastern wares. By the second half of the 1st century, more and more pottery was being produced in the provinces that was good enough to rival Arretine. Eastern Sigillata B and Çandarli had been produced since about the turn of the era. Local imitations were common and, of course, cheaper. In Italy there was anarchy in the years 68–69 A.C. Normal business and trade may have been affected, and for this reason, eastern customers

[26] Early Roman Forms 6, 9, 10, 11. Greene suggests that imitations of imports may have been produced as a result of the scarcity of the original, or, alternatively, the presence of plentiful amounts of the import may have stimulated the production of imitations; see his "Terra Sigillata: Imitations and Alternatives," *RCRFActa* 21/22 (1982) 71–78.

may have been forced into trying the Asia Minor products or producing their own.[27]

The latter part of the 1st and the early 2nd centuries saw the wide-scale immigration of settlers to the provinces of Moesia and Thrace where many new towns were founded.[28] Roads connecting these areas to the east and to the west were built. The minting of local coinage suggests that economic prosperity and growth as well as increased commerce took place over a broad area. Stobi began minting coins in the reign of Vespasian (69 A.C.).[29]

It was in this period that a number of public buildings were constructed in the city, including the theater and the Synagogue of Polycharmos.[30] Inscriptions dated to the 2nd century testify to the status and wealth of many prominent citizens at this time.[31]

In the first half of the 2nd century, Eastern Sigillata B2 predominates as the most common import (Fig. 5.9). Thin-Walled wares with barbotine and sand decoration continue to be popular, and bi-color Italian mugs appear (Table 5.1, Fig. 5.10). These small mugs, or pitchers, are the only shapes known in this ware that is similar to Thin-Walled ware.

From the later 2nd century through the 3rd and into the 4th, the number of standard Mediterranean imports declines markedly and the local/regional products dominate to a much greater degree than ever before (Fig. 5.11).[32] It is apparent that by this time, Stobi shares in what Andras Mocsy has called the "standardization of local culture in the third century" in Upper Moesia and Pannonia.[33] Similar vessel forms and decorative techniques are seen over a broad area of the Balkans, and the ceramic assemblage at Stobi shows a new influence from the northern provinces.

The decorative technique most characteristic of the local Color-Slipped wares in this period is that of stamping the vessel exterior or rim with a variety of motifs derived both from terra sigillata and from earlier local traditional designs.[34] At Stobi the technique is seen almost exclusively on Middle Roman Form 19, the three-ridged bowl. It is not clear to what extent this technique was common in Macedonia—that is, how far south its use extended. Although it is seen at Demir Kapija and Marvinci, south of Stobi along the Vardar, it does not seem to be found at Heraclea. The technique is not at all common in the other Greek provinces.

Additional evidence for the Moesian/Pannonian connection is provided by a few examples of Lead-Glazed wares in 3rd-century deposits.

[27] C. R. Whittaker, "Trade and the Aristocracy in the Roman Empire," *Opus* 3 (1984) 68, comments that oriental senators formed a substantial proportion of the senators with known origins, rising from 3 percent in the Flavian period to ca. 20 percent in the Antonine. He also notes that Aegean wine rises from a negligible quantity to about 5 percent, and other wines of unidentified origin rise from less than 5 percent to 15 percent of the total imports during the same period.

[28] Velkov, "Thrace and Lower Moesia," *Klio* 63 (1981) 476–478; Mocsy, *Pannonia*, 115, 119.

[29] The coins carried the legend *MUN(icipium)STOB(ensium)*. See S. Dušanić, "A Foundation Type on the Coinage of the Municipium Stobi," *Revue Belgique de Numismatique* 113 (1967) 11–29.

[30] Wiseman, "Archaeology and History," 39, 40. For the Synagogue of Polycharmus, see W. Poehlman, "The Polycharmos Inscription and Synagogue I at Stobi," *Studies III*, 243. For the Theater, see E. Gebhard, *Stobi 2*, and "The Theater at Stobi: A Summary," *Studies III*, 13–19. The large public buildings (the Casa Romana, the bath) in the lower city, or the flood plain of the Crna river, may also have been built in this period, but no construction deposits have been excavated for these buildings (Wiseman, "Archaeology and History," 39).

[31] Wiseman, "Gods," 143–183, and "Family," 567–582.

[32] At Carthage, imports begin declining by the end of the 1st century; see M. Fulford, "Pottery and the Economy of Carthage and its Hinterland," *Opus* 2 (1983) 8. Fulford sees the absence of ceramic imports as a "reflection of self-sufficiency in these goods and commodities" (p. 10) and concludes that depression in the local economy may be indicated by greater quantities of imported pottery, as seen at Carthage and elsewhere in the Mediterranean in the 1st century (p. 11) and at Carthage also in the 5th and 6th centuries (p. 12).

While it is true that a lack of imported wares makes the local industry dominant, this does not necessarily imply prosperity, but, in fact, may imply the reverse. It seems unlikely that a depressed local economy could afford imports. The absence of imports can also be a result of geographical location, economic or political situation, and conditions of transport, which make imports difficult to acquire or unavailable in certain areas.

[33] Mocsy, *Pannonia*, 246, 247; Velkov, *Klio* 63 (cited in note 28, above) 477.

[34] Mocsy, *Pannonia*, 176, 177; Brukner, *Rimska Keramika*, 178; V. Sokolovska, "A Contribution to the Study of the Pottery with Sealed Ornaments from Macedonia," *Macedoniae Acta Archaeologica* 2 (1976) 157–167 (in Macedonian with English summary); Anderson-Stojanović (1981) 51, and note 24 with references. Note also E. Bonis, "Origin of the Potter's Craft and Early Pottery," in A. Lengyel and G.T.B. Radan, eds., *The Archaeology of Roman Pannonia* (Lexington, Kentucky and Budapest 1980) 358, 359.

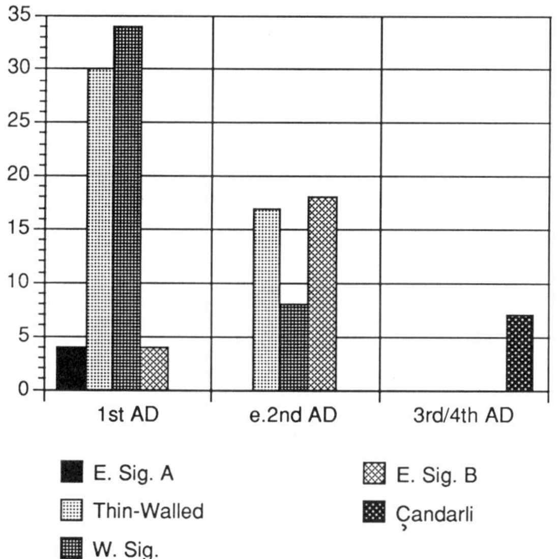

Figure 5.9. Quantity of imported fine ware RBH in Early and Middle Roman core deposits

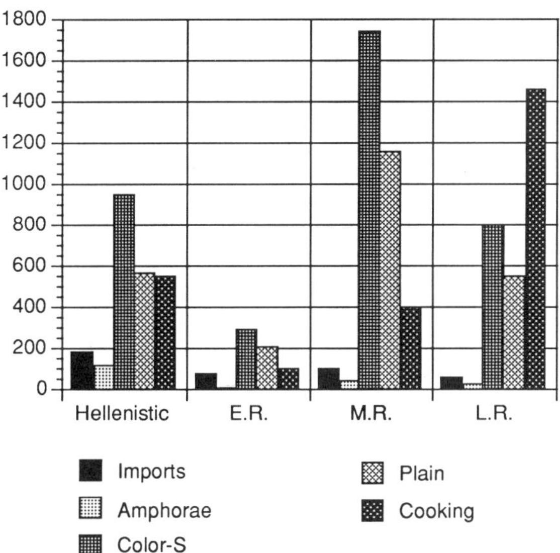

Figure 5.11. Quantity of pottery types in each chronological period

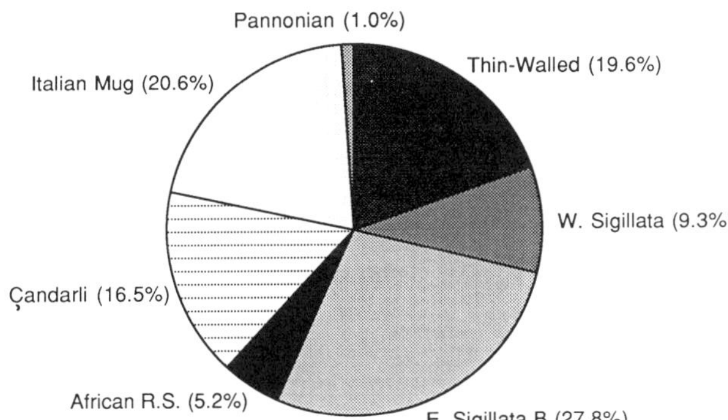

Figure 5.10. Proportion of fine wares (excluding local Color-Slipped) expressed as percentage of total RBH of these wares in Middle Roman core deposits

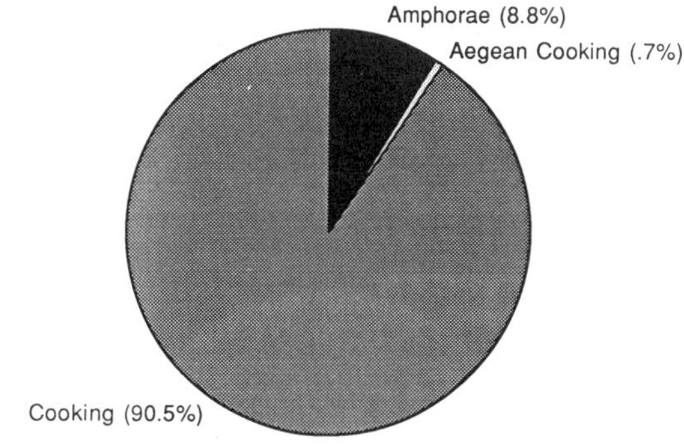

Figure 5.12. Proportion of coarse wares expressed as percentage of total RBH of these wares in the Middle Roman core deposits

Despite the predominance of the local industry, some Çandarli Ware appears in the late 2nd- and 3rd-century deposits, and early examples of African Red Slip reached Stobi in the mid-3rd and early 4th centuries. The dish with flat base and high wall (Hayes Form 50) was the inspiration for the local Middle Roman Form 5. A few examples of imported Aegean Cooking Ware appear during this period (Fig. 5.12). Cooking pans (MR Form 1) with red-slipped interior and pots with double handles (MR Form 4) may also be Aegean imports. Amphorae, probably from an Aegean source (Berenice MR 5 and Berenice MR 7), as well as the Africano Grande (Berenice MR 16/17) of Tunisian origin, are found in deposits of the 3rd and 4th centuries.

The 3rd and 4th centuries were difficult times for the city of Stobi and for the Balkans in general. Earthquakes appear to have caused destruction in several areas of the site, and the city may have suffered at the hands of the Goths on their way through this area.[35] Imported pottery is extremely rare in these destruction deposits. Local Color-Slipped wares continue in the same tradi-

[35] Wiseman, "Archaeology and History," 41.

tional forms as seen in the mid-2nd and 3rd centuries.

Repeated flooding of the Crna river made habitation impossible in the lower city, and the buildings of the early Christian city of Stobi were built on the higher ground to the west. The last quarter of the 4th century saw a revival for the city, and many public buildings and private residences were constructed.[36] The synagogue was rebuilt following the destruction of the earlier structure of Polycharmus and furnished with mosaic floors. A Christian basilica (Building A) was constructed just behind the theater, which may have already gone out of use by this time.

During the same period a new ceramic type, Macedonian Gray Ware, appears at Stobi. Gray wares had been popular in the Hellenistic and Early Roman periods, but they disappear from the archaeological record during the 2nd and 3rd centuries. Macedonian Gray Ware revived the native preference for gray pottery. Traditional types of decoration that may have been preserved on metal or wooden vessels reappear on the wide rims of Macedonian plates and bowls.

The local, light-bodied Color-Slipped and Plain wares of the city's earlier ceramic production are no longer seen in quantity, supplanted by the new gray ware and by a variety of rather coarse, micaceous, hard-fired wares of local or regional manufacture. Most of the earlier local shapes have disappeared, and some that were formerly made in the light clay are now seen in gray ware or in the other cooking fabrics.[37] It is possible that the Crna floods required potters to use another clay source or different types of fuel, or in some other way caused the disruption and consequent change in the earlier manufacturing process.

The renewed prosperity of the later 4th century brought increased contact with the rest of the Roman empire, illustrated by the rise in the numbers of imported fine wares that reached Stobi: dishes of African Red Slip from North Africa and some Phocaean Red Slip from Asia Minor (Table 5.1, Fig. 5.13).

Not all of Stobi's imports came from the Mediterranean or Aegean areas. Interaction and exchange with Moesia and Pannonia continued as in the Middle Roman period. Lead-Glazed vessels came from Pannonia, a well-known production center, and occur primarily in 4th-century deposits at Stobi. The most common form is the mortarium, a shape commonly traded in the Roman empire and not seen at Stobi since the Early Roman period. Examples of Macedonian Gray Ware are also found in small numbers in Moesia and Pannonia.

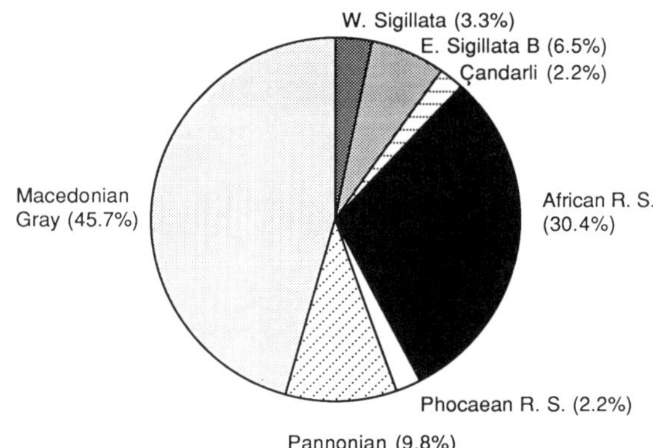

Figure 5.13. Proportion of fine wares (excluding local Color-Slipped Wares) expressed as percentage of total RBH of these wares in Late Roman core deposits

The evidence for the importation of coarse wares to Stobi is not so clear as that for fine tablewares. Aside from the early Italian and Aegean cooking wares, amphorae form the best documented group of imports whose origin is known (Table 5.2). Fragments from the Late Antique period indicate that the city received products from North Africa, Palestine, Asia Minor, and the Aegean. Wine, oil, olives, fish sauce, salted fish, honey, or other products were imported in these jars. Oil was probably not readily available in the areas near Stobi; the olive-growing areas today are much farther south in Macedonia and on the Adriatic.[38] The one grape seed recovered from botanical analysis at Stobi is hardly enough evidence to suggest viticulture in the area.[39] The growing of grapes has been made possible in the

[36] Wiseman, "Archaeology and History," 42, and "City," 295–306; and the dissertation of Frederick P. Hemans, "Late Antique Residences at Stobi" (Boston University, January 1986). An expanded version of this study forms the basis of Hemans, *Stobi 4*.

[37] See Chapter 2 and note 8.

[38] Hammond, *Macedonia* (cited in note 16 above), 204–205, and map on p. 11 of Greene (1986).

[39] E. M. Davis, "Paleoecological Studies at Stobi," *Studies III*, 91. We know very little about the agricultural production of Macedonia in the Roman period.

There is some evidence, however, for the production of textiles at Stobi. A small lens of pure bentonite, a substance used in the fulling of wood or the removal of grease from cloth,

Vardar valley in modern times only through the use of irrigation.

The presence of both amphorae and fine ware from North Africa makes it likely that the two traveled together, since fine pottery did not normally constitute a shipment on its own.[40] In comparison with port cities, however, very few complete amphorae were found at Stobi, not surprising in view of Stobi's location so far from the sea (cf. Figs 5.6, 5.8, 5.11, 5.12). It is likely that other lightweight containers were used for the transport of wine and other products and have left no trace in the archaeological record.[41] The small number of amphorae at Stobi may even represent re-used containers rather than direct imports.[42]

Throughout the 5th and 6th centuries African Red Slip and Phocaean Red Slip continue as primary competitors of the local Macedonian Gray Ware, although the African red slip is found in greater quantities than the Phocaean Red Slip (Fig. 5.13). These two wares are the latest dated imports on the site, continuing into the late 6th century.

So far as the archaeological evidence indicates, the site of Stobi was abandoned in the second half of the 6th century for a variety of reasons, including the repeated flooding of the Crna river, drier climatic conditions, earthquakes, and the invasion of the Slavs.[43]

Despite the relatively small quantities of imported pottery, it is of some interest to consider how imported products reached Stobi. Before the creation of the provinces of Moesia and Pannonia two routes were possible from the sea: from the Adriatic across the Via Egnatia to Heraclea and then up to Stobi, a distance of appoximately 325 km., or from the Aegean up the Vardar valley from Thessalonica, a distance of 160 km. (Pl. 1). Considering the cost of land transport, the route from Thessalonica, with its distance about half that of the other, seems preferable. This route would be even more logical if the Vardar were navigable upstream. There is, however, no evidence of its use for transport in antiquity. The Vardar (ancient Axius) is now extremely shallow, navigable for flat-bottomed boats or barges only from Djevdjelija to the sea. Furthermore, even if barges could be pulled upstream (somewhat unlikely given the course of the river and the rough terrain in some areas), goods would have to be removed and transported by land at the gorges of Djevdjelija and Demir Kapija.[44] The Crna (ancient Erigon) is a small river, and it is unlikely that it was used for any kind of regular transport of goods.

For goods from Italy, the former route along the Via Egnatia from the Adriatic may have been used. That is the longer route by land, and transport by land is thought to have been the more expensive. But if the Italian products were part of official government or army baggage, the cost may not have been a factor. The transport of Italian sigillata north of the Alps to the Roman military camps on the German frontier provides a parallel for such an uneconomical practice.[45]

After the Romanization of the areas to the north, the provinces of Moesia and Pannonia, it

---

was found at the site (Robert L. Folk, "The Geologic Framework of Stobi," *Studies I*, 51). A quantity of murex shells was found in the Fuller's House (W-MZ [1972] 420), but it is impossible to say if these were a result of a dyeing establishment. The processing of murex shells for purple dye is most commonly associated with coastal areas. If sheep were as common in the area as they are now, woolen cloth may have been exported. The study of faunal remains now in progress may substantiate this hypothesis.

Textiles were easy to transport, especially overland, being lightweight and flexible, and apparently always in demand. E. Badian (*Publicans and Sinners* [Oxford 1972] 28, 29) cites a contract for military garments consisting of 6,000 togas and 30,000 tunics to be shipped to Macedonia in 167 B.C. Note the amount of space taken up with the category of clothing in the Edict of Diocletian, discussed in T. Frank, *An Economic Survey of Ancient Rome, Vol. 5. Rome and Italy of the Empire* (Baltimore 1940) 369–413, Appendix by E. R. Graser.

[40] Peacock, *PRW*, 158; Greene (1986) 167; Kenrick, *Berenice 3*, 495.

[41] See the chapter entitled "Transport in the Roman Empire," and p. 157 in Greene (1986); Y. Garlan, "Greek Amphoras and Trade," in P. Garnsey, K. Hopkins, C. R. Whittaker, eds., *Trade in the Roman Economy* (London 1983) 30; Fulford, *Opus* 2 (1983) 6. See also A.K.B. Evans, "Pottery and History," in Anderson and Anderson (1981) 517–535. It is probably logical to assume that the local inhabitants found alternatives to olive oil in other plant oils and animal fats. Or, as is common in modern Greece, individuals may have traveled to olive-producing areas to work during the harvest season and have taken home their own share of the oil as payment.

[42] Garlan, "Greek Amphoras and Trade" [cited in note 41] 31–32. Evans, "Pottery and History" [cited in note 41] 526, cites reuse of amphoras for functions as varied as burials and urinals.

[43] Wiseman, "City," 309–313.

[44] It is possible that with flat-bottomed boats, rafts, or barges, the Vardar could have been utilized for transport over short distances. Furthermore, the nature of the river and its course may have changed since antiquity.

[45] Peacock, *PRW*, 119, comments on the rather remote location of many major terra sigillata producers.

is logical to assume that some goods came to Stobi by land from the north. The pottery suggests northern influence perhaps in the 2nd century A.C. and certainly by the 3rd.

It is clear that any imported wares would have been relatively expensive, given the cost of land transport, and thus purchased only by the wealthier inhabitants of the city.[46] Thus, there was always a need for a local ceramic industry to provide for local consumption.

Among the consumers of luxury items, the Christian church must be included, both as an institution and as a group with wealthy patrons. Most of the Gaza wine amphoras at Stobi were found in the atrium of the Episcopal Basilica. The prevalence of the large imported dishes in deposits associated with the bishop's church reflects the wealth of the church and the need for tableware and serving plates. The large amount of glassware found in the area of the Episcopal Basilica reinforces this role of the church as consumer of luxury goods.

Throughout the history of the city as we know it, the numbers of imported wares are small in comparison to the locally manufactured vessels (Fig. 5.11). For most of the city's history the local fine wares tended to imitate the more expensive imported wares like those from Italy, Asia Minor, or North Africa. In some cases the models themselves have survived, as in the Potter's Shop; other examples are seen only in their local form.

The larger study of Macedonian regional ceramic production in the Hellenistic and Roman periods outside of Stobi has not yet begun.[47] The limited amount of pottery that has been published from the Greek and Roman periods in Macedonia has been primarily imported; little has been written about local wares. It is unlikely, however, that more than a few of the local wares ever gained regional distribution. Local potters probably brought their products to the closest market to be purchased by individuals.[48] Larger workshops might be able to send a man from market to market, but such a practice would have been expensive (transport overland, living expenses), necessitating a corresponding increase in the price of the product. To sell regionally, a workshop would have to be producing a ware far superior to the others available in order to make a profit. It is possible, of course, that some workshop products might travel with other shipments, as was done by sea, but this is rather unlikely, given the conditions of transport on land where weight is a disadvantage.

Several distinct local wares have been identified at Stobi, and it is worth considering whether or not we have found any trace of these elsewhere in Macedonia. The Hellenistic and Late Roman Gray wares are certainly found throughout the region of Upper Macedonia, including Scupi in Moesia Superior, and less commmonly farther afield, toward the Aegean coast, and north in Pannonia. Because of the quantity of the Macedonian Gray Ware found at Stobi in contrast to other centers, it is suggested here that the ware was produced at Stobi.

Hellenistic moulded relief bowls with a profile like that seen on the local Dionysiac series at Stobi (**142–146**) are seen also within Upper Macedonia, but no examples of other bowls made from the same moulds as those at Stobi. The Stobi three-ridged bowl (MR Form 19), although seen at Marvinci, is not very common elsewhere in Macedonia. It is, however, found at Sirmium, so that there may be a connection between the two distant cities we are unaware of now. The apparent unimportance of the shape elsewhere in Macedonia, however, may be a function of the shortage of published material from the Roman period.

The two Late Roman wares identified at Stobi, Tan Micaceous and Mica-Dusted Ware, are, so far as I know, not found elsewhere. It is possible that cooking wares were traded within the region, but no evidence exists yet for this hypothesis beyond a general similarity of shapes.

The publication of the pottery from other settlements located along major land routes in Macedonia and currently under excavation is eagerly awaited. Such research offers the potential for greater understanding of regional ceramic production and of the nature and direction of trade in the area, but only if quantitative information is presented.

It is hoped that this volume will provide a foundation for future systematic studies of pottery in Macedonia.

[46] Greene (1986) 39, 40.

[47] See Chapter 2. Some time ago a large, ancient kiln for firing pottery was discovered at Ohrid below the modern town. I have seen another smaller kiln (presumably ancient) just outside the city. So far as I know, neither one has been published.

[48] Note comments of Peacock, *PRW*, 156–158.

APPENDIX 1
THE POTTER'S SHOP

•

Part of a structure (Pl. 189a) sunken into riverine sand and gravels was uncovered during excavation in the narthex and southwest room of the Central Basilica (Pl. 2, no. 6) during 1970 and 1971.[1] Although destroyed by fire and then damaged and disturbed by later leveling and building activities connected with the synagogues and Central Basilica, it is possible to gain some idea of the structure and its contents.

Two parallel brick walls (Walls 6 and 7), 1.25 m. apart, run on an east-west axis through the area below the narthex. There are traces of a third wall in the south scarp of the southwest corner of the nave, which is perpendicular to Walls 6 and 7. The walls are built of poorly fired bricks, and the north face of Wall 6 (0.82 m. in width, Pl. 189a) and both faces of Wall 7 (0.50 m. in width) are coated with lime mortar (Pl. 189b). Wall 7 has a curved, finished end at the north and was perhaps an interior partition (Pl. 190a). The floor between the walls was coated with very coarse, white mortar.

Since the third wall is preserved only in the south scarp of the southwest room, and the part of the south aisle where the wall might be found has not been excavated, it is difficult to gain a clear idea of the structure's eastern extent. To the west, both Walls 6 and 7 enter the scarp, and the area where the walls might be expected to continue has not been excavated to this level so that the overall size of the structure is not known. The whole feature is sunk into the prehistoric bed of the Crna river (Pl. 190b).

Below a section of the nave, at roughly the same level as the remains of the potter's shop, several pits were excavated in what may have been the gravel courtyard for the shop (Lots 74 and 75). One of the pits contained two small ceramic vessels filled with silver coins of the late 3rd and 2nd centuries B.C.[2] A series of contemporary layers of destruction debris filled the area between Walls 6 and 7 as well as to the north of Wall 7 (Pl. 191). The soils in these deposits were mixed with some clay and varying amounts of burned material. The destruction deposit extended to the east into the southwest corner of the nave, where the badly preserved wall was found, and still further east of that room. Similar pottery types were represented in both areas, and numerous joins were made within these deposits indicating contemporary deposition. Within the debris were found a number of items appropriate for a potter's establishment.

Comparison of the form of this structure with kilns in Italy, which consist of a simple two-room combustion chamber separated by a central wall rounded at one end, suggests that the Stobi structure may have been part of what was once the combustion chamber of a simple kiln.[3] The remains under the narthex most closely resemble Class IIa (Fig. 5.2 in Caprio) with a central wall running from the back wall of the combustion chamber. The author states that this type is not common and has not been recorded in southern Italy.

The only other kiln in the region is the large one at Ohrid (unpublished), discovered during the construction of a supermarket in the center of town and very different from this structure at Stobi. It corresponds to Caprio's Class IID (Fig. 5.2 there). The only signs of burning in the Stobi structure, however, seem to reflect the destruction of the establishment rather than any indication of kiln use. No wasters were found in the immediate area, although wasters have been found elsewhere on the site. The use of sun-

[1] W-MZ (1971) 408–411. See also Chapter 4, Deposit descriptions for Central Basilica Lots.

[2] Crawford, "Stobi Hoard," 2–3; the latest coins date to 125 B.C.

[3] See N. Cuomo di Caprio, "Pottery and Tile Kilns in South Italy and Sicily," in A. McWhirr, ed., *Roman Brick and Tile. BAR Int. Series* 59 (Oxford 1979) 75.

dried bricks is not common and primarily characteristic of specialist kilns or workshops of military tradition.[4] Because of the complexity of overlying structures, further excavation was not carried out in this area, and it has since been covered over with earth fill.

Found in the excavations were three fragmentary moulds for relief bowls and two for small lions' heads, the latter probably used as feet or supports for the bowls (see Chapter 2, nos. 7–9). A series of 9 fusiform unguentaria of identical fabric (of which seven, **570–576**, are described in Chapter 3) were probably newly made products of the shop. Other clay objects (Chapter 2, nos. 3, 4) also found here may be kiln furniture. These include small discs with flat areas on one surface, and curved, handmade fragments of rings (supports) and square bricks.[5] For a full listing of the pottery found in the area of the Potter's Shop, see Table 4.3.

[4] See Swan (1984) 32, but note also E. Bonis, "Origin of the Potter's Craft and Early Pottery," in A. Lengyel and G.T.B. Radan, eds., *The Archaeology of Roman Pannonia* (Univ. Press of Kentucky: Lexington and Budapest 1980) 362–365.

[5] Swan (1984) pl. 23, p. 66.

APPENDIX 2

PETROGRAPHIC ANALYSIS OF SELECTED CERAMIC SAMPLES

by Georgeana Little

•

In the fall of 1988 petrographic analyses were undertaken for a small number of ceramic samples from excavations at the site of Stobi. The ceramics had previously undergone other technical analyses, that is, neutron activation analysis and x-ray diffraction, but the results proved to be ambiguous and inconclusive. In addition, a qualitative analysis of the thin-sections had been conducted by Dr. Robert Folk of the University of Texas at Austin. The results of this last analysis were useful for general statements concerning the pottery, but quantitative data were deemed necessary for comparative purposes.

Twenty ceramic samples, spanning the Hellenistic through Late Roman periods, were selected by Virginia Anderson-Stojanović for petrographic analysis. In addition, three clay samples (one from Negotino and two from Stobi), sand from the banks of the Crna river, and sandstone from Stobi were available for comparison with the pottery. The pottery was analyzed in the Boston University Archaeology Laboratories by means of a standard point-counting technique.[1] To maximize the number of nonplastic inclusions counted, the points were located at 0.5 mm. intervals along the thin-section. Voids and matrix were also counted, but all percentages presented below reflect inclusions only. The geological samples, the clays, sand, and sandstone were not analyzed quantitatively. The clays were unfired, and any quantitative data collected would not have been comparable to those collected from the ceramic samples.

[1] Georgeana M. Little, "The Technology of Pottery Production in Northwestern Portugal during the Iron Age," Ph.D. diss., Boston University, 1989, 98–99.

The major question to be addressed was which of the pottery samples were likely to be locally produced and which, if any, might have been imports. Unfortunately, the small number of samples available for analysis and the variable geology of the Stobi region precluded any final answer to the questions posed. It is possible, however, to see some general trends and to suggest areas in which future research would be useful.

Each of the ceramic samples was assigned to one of the three local fabric groups outlined by Anderson-Stojanović (App. Table 2.1). Fabric

App. Table 2.1 Ceramic samples by fabric group and period

Fabric group 1	Unguentarium	Early Roman
	Early Roman Plain Ware	Early Roman
	Sanded Ware	Early Roman
	Loomweight Fragment	Middle Roman
	Local Fine Ware	Middle Roman
Fabric group 2	Hellenistic Gray Ware	Hellenistic
	Hellenistic Gray Ware	Hellenistic
	Early Roman Gray Ware	Early Roman
	Macedonian Gray Ware	Late Roman
	Macedonian Gray Ware	Late Roman
Fabric group 3	Hellenistic Cooking Ware	Hellenistic
	Early Coarse Handmade	Hellenistic
	Early Roman Cooking Ware	Early Roman
	Middle Roman Cooking Ware	Middle Roman
	Tile Fragment	Middle Roman
	Pithos Fragment	Middle Roman
	Late Roman Cooking Ware	Late Roman
	Late Roman Cooking Ware	Late Roman
	Late Roman Cooking Ware	Late Roman
	Tan Micaceous Ware	Late Roman

group 1 is a fine, light ware, group 2 represents the gray wares, and group 3 consists of coarse wares. For ease of presentation, only the major mineral inclusions are presented in the graphs below. Quartz and feldspar are grouped together, since these two minerals are very similar petrographically, and the small size of most of the inclusions made differentiating between them impossible. The micas, muscovite, and biotite are present in nearly all samples in varying proportions and offer a useful comparative guide. The lithic fragments are primarily metamorphic in origin, schists and gneisses, but some sedimentary rocks, that is, sandstone, as well as rocks of igneous origin were also present. The mineral identified as "rose" mica was present in only three samples but is so unique in its properties that it warranted a separate classification. The mineral appears as gold-colored plates on the surface of the pottery, as opposed to biotite, which is black or very dark brown, and muscovite, which is transparent. In thin-section it possessed optical properties different from those associated with the two other, common, micas. The category of "other minerals" included inclusions too small to be accurately identified, but most probably belong to the amphibole or pyroxene families. The small size and limited occurrence of these minerals make them of little use for this study.

Particle-size distributions are also presented below for each of the samples. These distributions follow the Wentworth Scale.[2]

Silt	<0.065 mm.
Very Fine Sand	0.07–0.12 mm.
Fine Sand	0.13–0.25 mm.
Medium Sand	0.26–0.50 mm.
Coarse Sand	0.51–1.00 mm.
Very Coarse Sand	>1.00 mm.

All measurements were taken using a calibrated micrometer ocular.

Local Fabric group 1 consists of five samples from the Early and Middle Roman periods. The mineralogy of these samples is presented in Appendix Figure 2.1a, while the particle-size distributions appear in Appendix Figure 2.1b. The unguentarium and loomweight fragments are similar, consisting primarily of quartz/feldspar sand. The Early Roman plain ware and the local fine ware are similar in containing quartz/feldspar as well as both common types of mica, with biotite more prevalent than muscovite. The fact that each of these sub-groups contains one sample from each time period represented, suggests a tradition, probably local, that spanned at least the Early and Middle Roman periods. The particle-size distributions, however, show a slight change in manufacturing technique, with the Early Roman samples containing finer inclusions than those from the later period.

The Sanded Ware differs from the other samples in containing more muscovite than biotite and in having lithic fragments present in measurable amounts. This last ware differs also from the others in ways not easily quantified. It contains primarily silt through very fine, sand-sized inclusions, but larger inclusions are present near the surfaces. These larger inclusions were added after the piece had been formed and were deliberately left protruding from the surface, giving the sherd a rough appearance.

The gray wares, presented in Appendix Figure 2.2, span the Hellenistic through Late Roman periods, and suggest some interesting questions. The two gray wares from the Hellenistic period are similar both mineralogically and in their particle-size distributions. They differ from the later gray wares in containing far less mica. This fact adds some weight to Anderson-Stojanović's suggestion that the gray wares may not, at first, have represented a local tradition. There is also a slight diminution in the particle sizes present in the pottery, with the finest inclusions occurring in the Early Roman period, as was observed above in Fabric group 1. Of interest in this group also is that the two samples of Macedonian Gray Ware differ dramatically in the percentages of the three major minerals present. One contains nearly equal amounts of quartz/feldspar, muscovite, and biotite, while the other contains very little biotite and only half as much muscovite as quartz/feldspar. Their particle-size distributions, however, are similar. The implication is that either more than one workshop, utilizing slightly different resources, were producing this ware in the Late Roman period or that production was no

[2] A. O. Shepard, *Ceramics for the Archaeologist* (Carnegie Institution Publication 609: Washington, D.C., 1980) 118.

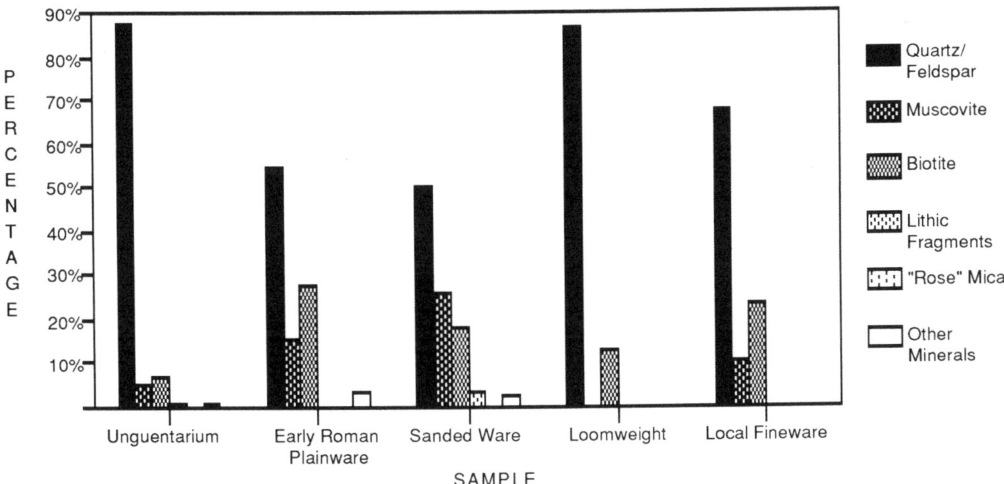

Appendix Figure 2.1a. Major mineral constituents of Fabric group 1, fine wares

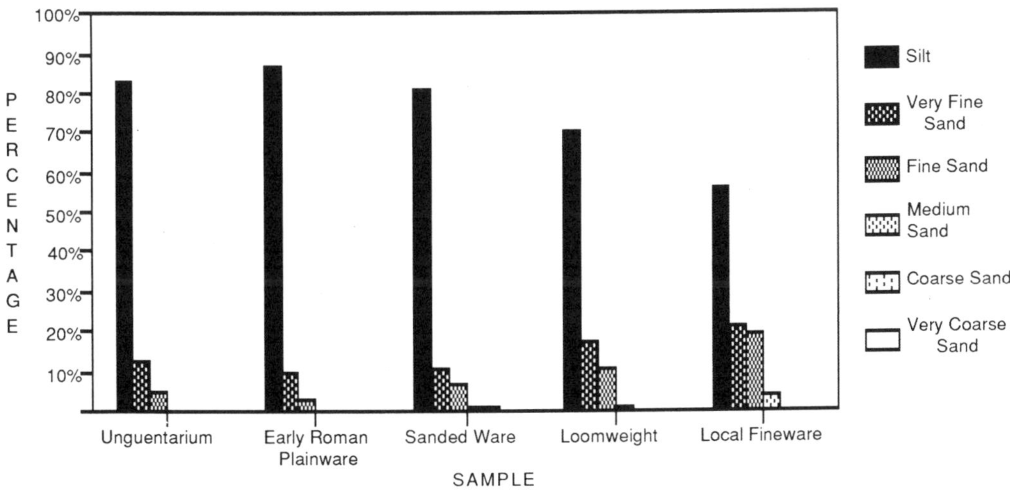

Appendix Figure 2.1b. Particle-size distributions for Fabric group 1, fine wares

longer on the workshop level, so that there was a drip-off in standardization that such a production change implies.

Fabric group 3 (App. Figs. 2.3 and 2.4) contains samples from all periods, Hellenistic through Late Roman. The most obvious trend, as noted by Anderson-Stojanović, is an increase in mica from the earlier through the later periods. The two samples from the Hellenistic period differ from one another in both mineralogy and particle-size distribution. The Early Coarse Handmade contains a large percentage of lithic fragments, and the particle-size distribution shows the distinct bimodality indicative of tempering. The Early and Middle Roman Cooking Wares are similar to the Hellenistic Cooking Wares and indicate a continuing tradition in this functional class. The tile and pithos fragments, both dated to the Middle Roman period, appear to have been tempered with crushed rock, as the elevated amount of lithic fragments and the bimodal particle-size distributions indicate. Functional

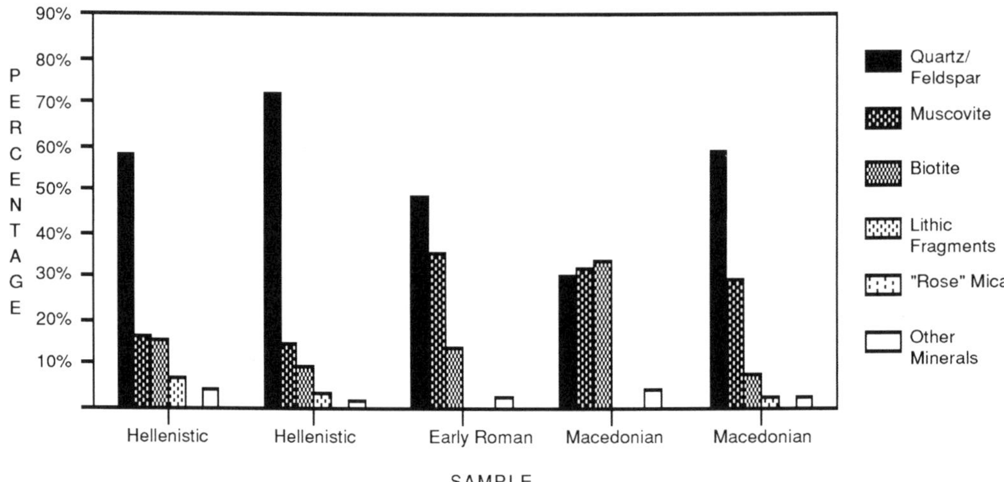

Appendix Figure 2.2a. Major mineral constituents of Fabric group 2, gray wares

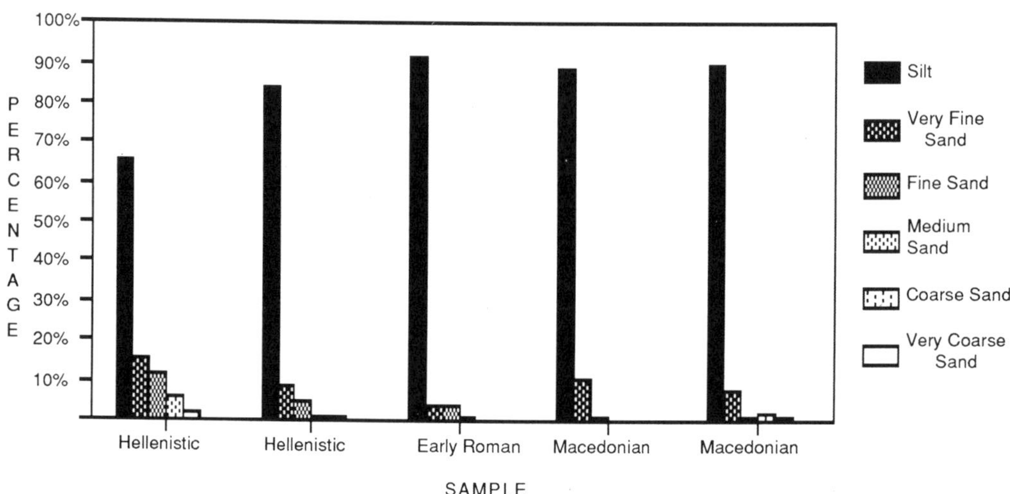

Appendix Figure 2.2b. Particle-size distributions for Fabric group 2, gray wares

differences, rather than differing manufacturing centers, would most likely account for the differences observed between these samples and the cooking ware of the same period.

The first two samples of Late Roman Cooking Ware are very similar, although one contains fewer, very coarse, sand-sized inclusions than does the other. The third sample of Late Roman Cooking Ware contains "rose" mica in significant amounts and is more similar to the Tan Micaceous Ware than to the other samples of cooking ware from this period. The appearance of this unusual type of mica in the Late Roman period is puzzling. To further confuse the matter, the third sample that contained "rose" mica, although not in measurable amounts, is the Sanded Ware dating to the Early Roman period. The geological samples, the clays, sand, and sandstone, do not contain "rose" mica, so the origin of this particular mineral cannot be resolved. It is tempting to suggest a non-local origin for the samples in which "rose" mica is present, but such a suggestion would be premature. The appearance of this particular mica in both the Early and Late Roman periods, but in no others, rather suggests a raw material source little utilized in the earlier peri-

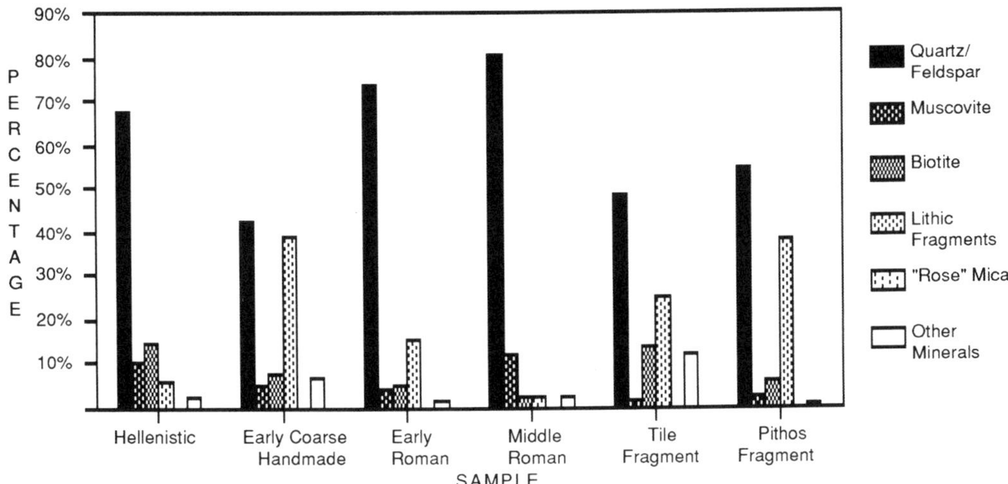

Appendix Figure 2.3a. Major mineral constituents for Fabric group 3, Coarse Wares, Hellenistic to Middle Roman periods

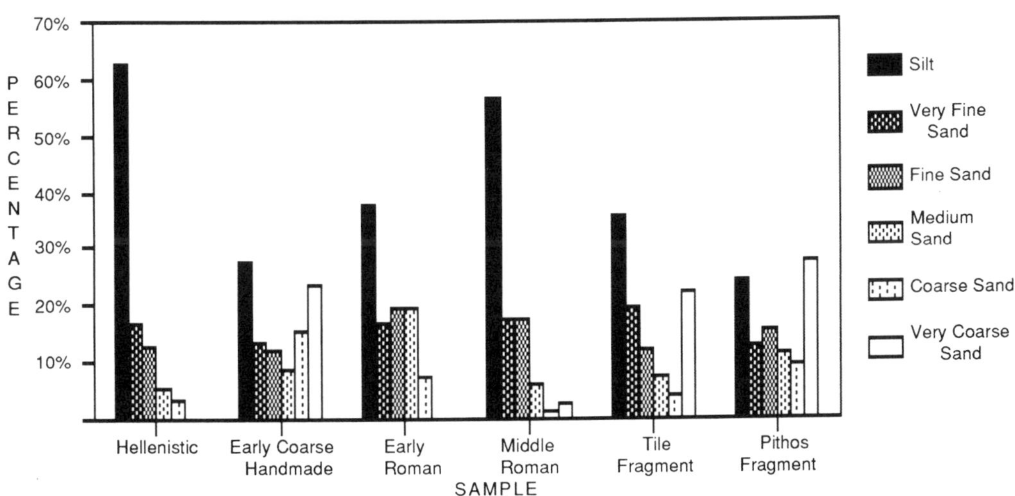

Appendix Figure 2.3b. Particle-size distributions for Fabric group 3, Coarse Wares, Hellenistic to Middle Roman periods

ods. Until more samples are studied, and a more thorough geological survey is conducted in the region, conclusions concerning the significance of the appearance of "rose" mica cannot be drawn.

A petrographic analysis of twenty samples chosen non-randomly cannot be used to draw any broad conclusions concerning manufacturing centers represented or production techniques employed. This analysis, however, does suggest that most of the ceramics analyzed were locally produced, since the general mineralogy of all the samples, with the exception of those containing "rose" mica, is similar, the differences being in the proportion of one mineral to another.

Fabric group 1 appears to represent at least two traditions spanning the Early and Middle Roman periods, with the differences in mineralogy probably indicative of function. The Sanded Ware, because of its differing mineralogy and unusual ap-

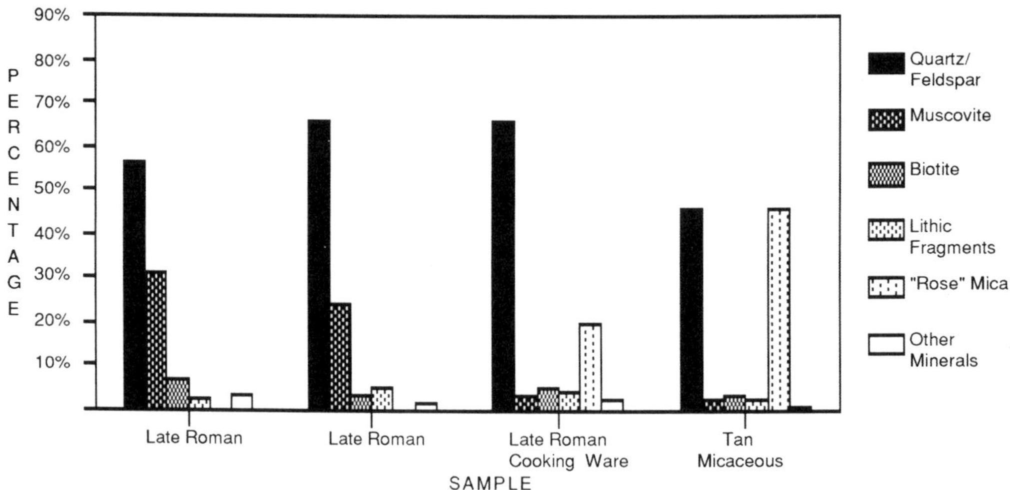

Appendix Figure 2.4a. Major mineral constituents for Fabric group 3, Coarse Wares, Late Roman period

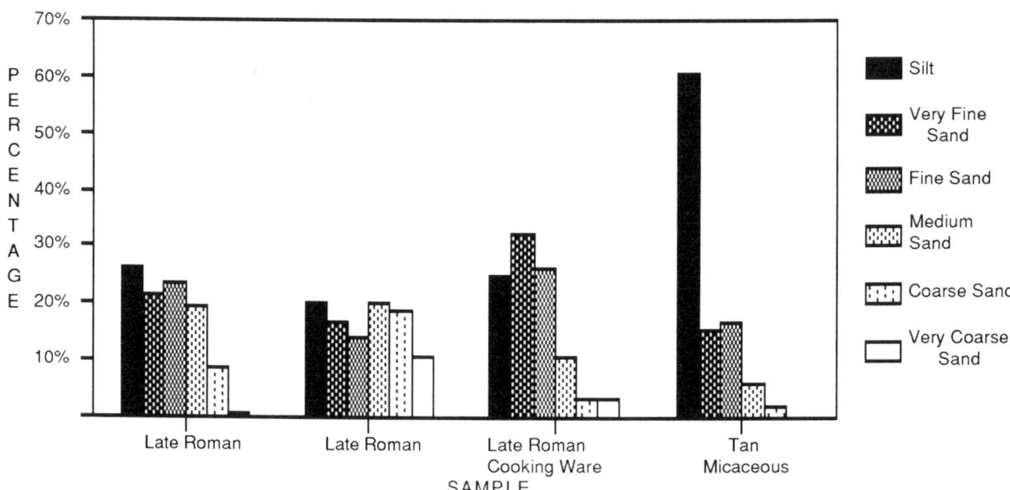

Appendix Figure 2.4b. Particle-size distributions for Fabric group 3, Coarse Wares, Late Roman period

pearance, deserves to be studied in more detail to determine both its method of manufacture and the possible functional role of its roughened surfaces. The differences between the Hellenistic Gray Wares and the later Gray Wares in Fabric group 2 could indicate a non-local source for the former. It could also, however, indicate an adopted tradition not yet fully adapted to local conditions. The mineralogic differences between the two Macedonian Gray Ware samples deserve further attention, to determine if more than one workshop were producing this pottery, or if production had shifted from the workshop to the household level. Among the samples from Fabric group 3, the two Late Roman wares containing "rose" mica offer the most interesting problems. If no local source for this type of mica can be located, then a foreign origin would be likely.

CONCORDANCE

•

This concordance contains items in Chapter 3 only. In cases where an item was not given an Inventory Number, the Lot and sherd number in the Lot serve as the primary means of identification. Those items appear first in this concordance in order of Lot number. See Explanatory Notes on the catalogue at the end of Chapter 1 for an explanation of the two systems. When an item originates from more than one Lot, only the lowest numbered Lot appears in this list. For graves with Lot numbers, only the Lot number appears in this list.

Inv. No.	Cat. No.	Lot	Sherd No.
	639	12	9
	1129	12	11
	31	14	2
	279	18	3
	656	18	19
	907	18	12
	752	20	4
	63	22	3
	272	26	2
	504	30	4
	887	39	3
	870	44	2
	1195	68	141
	792	74	65
	763	75	91
	67	76	9
	119	77	1
	1189	78	57
	716	127	25
	1114	131	28
	159	134	33
	161	134	108
	162	134	111
	644	134	17
	658	134	8
	757	134	107
	793	134	12
	1106	134	109
	1130	134	105
	111	140	95
	163	140	56
	759	140	34
	1092	140	42
	1117	140	47
	234	228	25
	820	228	68
	901	229	5
	60	230	74
	270	230	37

Inv. No.	Cat. No.	Lot	Sherd No.
	277	230	3
	815	230	60
	821	230	82
	832	230	70
	884	230	90
	903	230	15
	99	231	78
	181	231	95
	183	231	7
	244	231	42
	283	231	1
	822	231	61
	864	231	23
	865	231	21
	905	231	135
	1153	231	167
	946	237	19
	1002	237	74
	1056	237	59
	1072	237	66
	1171	237	111
	511	238	15
	918	238	39
	925	238	31
	940	238	13
	512	239	33
	518	239	57
	935	239	27
	944	239	19
	1038	239	56
	539	240	11
	1057	240	9
	972	242	9
	1043	242	10
	1203	242	1
	1219	243	1
	1049	245	5
	82	248	8
	194	248	83

Inv. No.	Cat. No.	Lot	Sherd No.
	814	248	115
	818	248	81
	823	248	61
	844	248	40
	875	248	2
	886	248	74
	896	248	27
	101	249	36
	178	249	35
	196	249	⟨1⟩
	198	249	103
	199	249	⟨2⟩
	240	249	26
	641	249	152
	670	249	153
	908	249	155
	1150	249	32
	154	250	5
	810	250	7
	114	252	8
	118	252	9
	866	257	66
	1132	257	71
	835	258	20
	1141	258	36
	276	259	71
	849	259	84
	861	259	62
	881	259	73
	883	259	89
	1154	259	150
	233	260	4
	1144	260	6
	148	262	19
	788	262	13
	40	263	5
	1040	274	141
	1078	274	57
	1255	274	107
	1271	274	71
	1292	274	114
	1079	277	22
	1080	277	60
	1211	277	78
	1229	277	92
	1245	277	57
	1257	277	73
	1266	277	105
	1273	277	71
	1280	277	112
	1282	277	113
	1018	278	18
	1221	278	63
	1223	278	58
	626	293	79

Inv. No.	Cat. No.	Lot	Sherd No.
	627	293	80
	1247	293	46
	471	294	1
	1220	295	9
	1291	296	7
	364	297	72
	527	297	1
	710	297	14
	1216	297	40
	1272	297	27
	1279	297	44
	1284	297	46
	1285	297	47
	1286	297	51
	365	298	18
	1246	298	601
	449	299	51
	1238	299	3
	1256	299	16
	1274	299	6
	1281	299	37
	526	300	3
	1231	300	1
	1283	301	7
	625	302	5
	686	302	17
	1228	302	9
	473	303	16
	1213	304	31
	1253	304	26
	1270	304	21
	1075	305	67
	1222	305	17
	1237	305	42
	1290	305	7
	1248	306	27
	1239	307	32
	1241	307	29
	1265	307	108
	830	384	1
	885	384	12
	1140	386	9
	892	389	1
	894	391	3
	895	391	4
	1139	391	1
	305	392	11
	863	392	12
	1161	395	1
	888	399	1
	893	401	5
	138	441	1
	1138	443	2
	190	445	9
	1149	456	6

Inv. No.	Cat. No.	Lot	Sherd No.
	250	483	66
	204	486	25
	824	486	11
	854	486	43
	891	486	83
	902	486	10
	89	488	13
	252	488	55
	284	488	53
	834	488	5
	906	488	11
	1134	488	1
	1137	488	11
	267	490	16
	369	514	1
	699	514	50
	92	545	9
	713	545	162
	836	545	89
	782	546	1
	1122	546	5
	26	547	104
	36	547	58
	78	547	126
	80	547	128
	131	547	54
	659	547	254
	669	547	605
	760	547	550
	761	547	549
	775	547	4
	784	547	62
	802	547	250
	1119	547	500
	1121	547	32
	781	548	12
	58	549	35
	139	549	9
	227	549	502
	229	549	42
	778	549	121
	779	549	80
	774	550	28
	791	550	75
	1085	550	5
	1131	550	15
	127	551	22
	140	551	26
	156	551	44
	1102	551	41
	6	552	527
	16	552	533
	48	552	196
	79	552	541
	81	552	509
	123	552	29
	150	552	1206
	157	552	1100
	158	552	1251
	160	552	1268
	166	552	1254
	167	552	1258
	652	552	668
	662	552	671
	728	552	339
	735	552	327
	736	552	361
	745	552	176
	746	552	173
	747	552	174
	751	552	67
	755	552	681
	764	552	1131
	765	552	1142
	801	552	48
	811	552	1239
	812	552	1242
	813	552	1209
	1087	552	753
	1089	552	842
	1093	552	781
	1094	552	798
	1097	552	774
	1103	552	861
	1105	552	51
	1115	552	862
	1116	552	788
	1120	552	808
	1128	552	811
	134	554	1
	717	554	47
	1100	554	73
	11	555	26
	725	555	22
	771	555	40
	15	563	1
	77	599	57
	311	599	1
	41	608	21
	109	608	36
	126	608	35
	661	608	22
	1113	608	23
	46	610	50
	133	610	49
	228	610	52
	642	610	19
	643	610	20
	664	610	10
	668	610	22

Inv. No.	Cat. No.	Lot	Sherd No.
	734	610	25
	756	610	11
	1096	610	24
	1118	610	31
	35	687	2
	47	687	1
	1037	801	329
	540	810	348
	874	811	35
	25	829	10
	146	829	31
	164	829	134
	733	829	83
	750	829	4
	780	829	110
	787	829	199
	800	829	103
	151	831	71
	783	831	58
	785	831	88
	1091	831	82
	226	841	7
	1	842	7
	3	842	17
	4	842	8
	7	842	9
	8	842	11
	2	843	29
	5	843	41
	9	843	46
	10	843	35
	12	843	42
	14	843	38
	17	843	68
	18	843	61
	49	843	86
	1174	924	8
	1193	924	6
	334	929	38
	724	929	9
	926	929	103
	1007	929	109
	1206	929	14
	317	930	51
	954	930	126
	1055	930	37
	1187	930	136
	1182	931	8
	1046	932	20
	1179	932	76
	1181	932	25
	246	934	3
	268	934	9
	278	934	1
	1033	934	26
	335	936	76
	953	937	11
	1191	937	27
	323	939	66
	1001	939	109
	1069	940	30
	236	942	29
	271	942	27
	632	943	5
	354	946	13
	348	998	2
	455	998	1
	878	1078	1
	882	1080	1
	30	1085	7
	817	1085	201
	900	1087	3
	169	1089	37
	845	1089	30
	859	1093	2
	672	1094	2
	1156	1094	1
	855	1098	17
	856	1098	3
	899	1098	4
	1143	1098	6
	610	1099	2
	633	1285	10
	1024	1285	28
	1210	1285	2
	343	1295	178
	514	1295	181
	923	1295	100
	992	1295	33
	997	1295	55
	1032	1295	57
	1045	1295	54
	1070	1295	84
	1074	1295	77
	515	1296	111
	682	1296	93
	683	1296	92
	917	1296	197
	934	1296	363
	947	1296	330
	1036	1296	296
	1058	1296	174
	1061	1296	177
	1063	1296	171
	1067	1296	98
	1173	1296	24
	1185	1296	8
	1186	1296	45
	1194	1296	38
	1205	1296	114

Inv. No.	Cat. No.	Lot	Sherd No.
	1214	1296	36
	1190	1297	17
	691	1298	54
	1008	1298	38
	1010	1298	200
	1021	1298	92
	1176	1298	10
	1192	1298	4
	1198	1299	3
	999	1300	24
	1019	1300	49
	1042	1300	45
	1162	1300	4
	1167	1300	3
	1178	1300	11
	1208	1300	2
	1029	1301	26
	538	1302	15
	979	1302	40
	1017	1302	37
	1023	1302	76
	1166	1302	2
	1184	1302	5
	1188	1302	4
	1196	1302	8
	1199	1302	6
	1200	1302	3
	1030	1303	26
	943	1306	3
	937	1307	31
	957	1307	50
	974	1307	24
	1004	1307	200
	1005	1307	92
	987	1308	6
	1022	1308	22
	1035	1308	24
	1168	1308	550
	1009	1309	63
	911	1310	1
	936	1310	6
	977	1310	7
	1065	1310	5
	1197	1310	13
	559	1328	3
	696	1328	8
	1015	1330	12
	975	1332	2
	1071	1332	3
	1235	1338	1
	942	1404	225
	349	1404	378
	351	1404	377
	685	1404	21
	952	1404	223

Inv. No.	Cat. No.	Lot	Sherd No.
	959	1404	354
	981	1404	363
	1011	1404	154
	1039	1404	353
	1041	1404	299
	1062	1404	315
	1064	1404	323
	1175	1404	39
	1259	1404	46
	1262	1404	36
	919	1407	58
	945	1407	60
	948	1407	28
	980	1407	743
	995	1407	913
	1059	1407	19
	1204	1407	11
	673	1416	67
	862	1416	21
	909	1416	1
	1135	1416	2
	516	1417	19
	831	1417	14
	876	1417	23
	829	1418	22
	848	1418	15
	867	1418	89
	889	1418	134
	1151	1418	109
	819	1419	9
	879	1419	5
	168	1420	4
	1155	1420	10
	1160	1420	11
	107	1441	1
	647	1441	28
	868	1441	4
	1142	1441	17
	1152	1441	19
	1157	1441	16
	660	1442	15
	62	1443	14
	904	1454	4
	303	1468	2
	251	1475	8
	316	1478	1
	665	1493	19
	189	1495	12
	860	1497	4
	188	1501	11
	657	1501	19
	721	1501	8
	336	1510	3
	719	1538	22
	720	1538	23

Inv. No.	Cat. No.	Lot	Sherd No.
	850	1538	9
	1104	1538	36
	1148	1538	30
	666	1580	3
	667	1581	1
	692	1599	74
	697	1599	27
	1170	1599	42
	1177	1599	33
	690	1610	1
	629	1616	2
	115	1636	61
	651	1636	100
	738	1636	64
	772	1636	43
	1082	1636	7
	630	1697	2
	1016	1697	1
	1048	1697	100
	1053	1697	6
	357	1783	4
	711	1809	1
	1269	1819	5
	694	2120	41
	541	2121	11
	693	2121	106
	1172	2121	11
	1006	2126	12
	456	2393	10
C-63-001	**415**		
C-67-001	**482**		
C-70-002	**790**	1025	
C-70-004	**637**		
C-70-005	**108**	1023	
C-70-008	**635**	514	
C-70-014	**378**		
C-70-017	**517**	462	
C-70-018	**858**	465	
C-70-019	**949**	801	
C-70-024	**1066**	799	
C-70-026	**701**	1015	
C-70-039	**950**	483	
C-70-040	**915**	482	
C-70-042	**289**	483	
C-70-043	**519**	460	
C-70-046	**74**	460	
C-70-048	**606**	487	
C-70-049	**602**	487	
C-70-052	**608**	487	
C-70-053	**604**	487	
C-70-055	**605**	487	
C-70-057	**603**	487	
C-70-058	**214**	487	
C-70-059	**607**	487	
C-70-062	**898**	Grave 13	
C-70-067	**592**	197	
C-70-068	**591**	197	
C-70-071	**593**	197	
C-70-083	**237**	1016	
C-70-087	**401**	1016	
C-70-088	**621**	1016	
C-70-089	**1212**	514	
C-70-097	**261**	1016	
C-70-100	**104**	1018	
C-70-103	**213**	487	
C-70-104	**705**	514	
C-70-105	**1252**	1017	
C-70-109	**39**	513	
C-70-110	**19**	842	
C-70-111	**44**	842	
C-70-113	**976**	799	
C-70-115	**452**	507	
C-70-116	**442**	509	
C-70-118	**254**		
C-70-119	**731**	831	
C-70-120	**732**	829	
C-70-121	**754**	829	
C-70-122	**21**	829	
C-70-123	**730**	831	
C-70-124	**142**	829	
C-70-126	**13**	842	
C-70-127	**45**	843	
C-70-131	**122**	829	
C-70-132	**145**	829	
C-70-133	**1201**	810	
C-70-135	**532**	799	
C-70-136	**297**	1049	
C-70-140	**616**	799	
C-70-141	**620**	799	
C-70-142	**961**	1652	
C-70-156	**920**	800	
C-71-002	**374**	514	
C-71-003	**1224**	157	
C-71-005	**55**	373	
C-71-008	**1260**	146	
C-71-009	**220**	381	
C-71-011	**826**	381	
C-71-017	**827**	386	
C-71-019	**611**	131	
C-71-020	**556**	433	
C-71-021	**248**	389	
C-71-022	**71**	433	
C-71-024	**83**	432	
C-71-028	**989**	223	
C-71-030	**521**	127	
C-71-031	**846**	386	
C-71-032	**1158**	391	
C-71-034	**219**	453	
C-71-035	**877**	451	
C-71-037	**221**	19	

Inv. No.	Cat. No.	Lot	Sherd No.
C-71-038	**828**	391	
C-71-039	**1090**	134	
C-71-040	**222**	412	
C-71-041	**182**	30	
C-71-045	**447**		
C-71-046	**173**	221	
C-71-050	**481**	178	
C-71-051	**192**	415	
C-71-052	**253**	245	
C-71-053	**1081**	94	
C-71-056	**347**	155	
C-71-057	**416**	91	
C-71-058	**352**	236	
C-71-059	**553**	169	
C-71-062	**528**		
C-71-064	**1287**	239	
C-71-069	**212**	411	
C-71-070	**225**	140	
C-71-071	**928**	238	
C-71-072	**914**	237	
C-71-077	**768**	140	
C-71-078	**24**	132	
C-71-079	**68**	258	
C-71-080	**485**	258	
C-71-083	**128**	127	
C-71-084	**130**	127	
C-71-085	**570**	132	
C-71-087	**571**	132	
C-71-088	**572**	132	
C-71-089	**573**	132	
C-71-091	**574**	132	
C-71-092	**575**	132	
C-71-093	**576**	132	
C-71-098	**136**	262	
C-71-102	**235**	228	
C-71-104	**490**	249	
C-71-106	**269**	258	
C-71-107	**186**	248	
C-71-115	**135**	228	
C-71-116	**288**	248	
C-71-117	**509**	248	
C-71-118	**491**	248	
C-71-120	**286**	259	
C-71-122	**70**	29	
C-71-125	**1127**	442	
C-71-126	**380**	235	
C-71-127	**852**	Grave 60	
C-71-128	**1236**	168	
C-71-129	**207**	488	
C-71-130	**193**	43	
C-71-131	**1125**	74	
C-71-132	**23**	74	
C-71-133	**555**	11	
C-71-136	**739**	14	
C-71-137	**493**	249	
C-71-139	**287**	249	
C-71-141	**486**	230	
C-71-148	**403**	91	
C-71-150	**1044**	448	
C-71-154	**210**	45	
C-71-155	**837**	43	
C-71-168	**601**	Grave 95	
C-71-177	**674**	24	
C-71-178	**50**	24	
C-71-179	**51**	152	
C-71-181	**144**	829	
C-71-190	**216**	230	
C-71-192	**1014**	163	
C-71-195	**384**	297	
C-71-196	**544**	260	
C-71-200	**520**	295	
C-71-201	**853**	Grave 45	
C-71-203	**1275**	169	
C-71-204	**965**	87	
C-71-206	**804**	250	
C-71-207	**803**	250	
C-71-208	**729**	140	
C-71-211	**1180**	164	
C-71-214	**494**	433	
C-71-218	**434**	274	
C-71-219	**435**	293	
C-71-220	**143**	140	
C-71-225	**988**	110	
C-71-226	**437**	282	
C-71-227	**418**	285	
C-71-228	**451**	190	
C-71-230	**201**	248	
C-71-231	**984**	110	
C-71-232	**991**	Grave 91	
C-71-236	**1068**	Grave 46	
C-71-238	**463**	307	
C-71-242	**1209**	237	
C-71-243	**426**	159	
C-71-244	**366**	169	
C-71-245	**410**	148	
C-71-250	**417**	131	
C-71-253	**715**	250	
C-71-254	**1083**	250	
C-71-256	**776**	251	
C-71-257	**231**	230	
C-71-262	**522**	305	
C-71-265	**430**	307	
C-71-276	**1107**	134	
C-71-277	**1086**	14	
C-71-278	**1126**	12	
C-71-280	**100**	230	
C-71-281	**105**	440	
C-71-282	**98**	231	
C-71-283	**741**	131	
C-71-284	**777**	75	

Inv. No.	Cat. No.	Lot	Sherd No.
C-71-285	**816**	260	
C-71-286	**22**	252	
C-71-287	**176**	248	
C-71-288	**211**	75	
C-71-289	**179**	231	
C-71-291	**184**	248	
C-71-292	**200**	248	
C-71-294	**215**	248	
C-71-295	**195**	248	
C-71-301	**753**	252	
C-71-302	**833**	248	
C-71-303	**743**	134	
C-71-304	**185**	228	
C-71-305	**187**	249	
C-71-310	**245**	230	
C-71-311	**249**	445	
C-71-313	**255**	230	
C-71-314	**260**	248	
C-71-315	**232**	259	
C-71-323	**645**	130	
C-71-324	**654**	456	
C-71-326	**337**	231	
C-71-328	**73**	259	
C-71-330	**872**	257	
C-71-331	**873**	248	
C-71-332	**737**	26	
C-71-336	**238**	231	
C-71-337	**241**	385	
C-71-339	**789**	262	
C-71-340	**28**	252	
C-71-341	**749**	76	
C-71-342	**153**	130	
C-71-343	**841**	75	
C-71-344	**842**	249	
C-71-346	**612**	140	
C-71-347	**487**	230	
C-71-348	**498**	228	
C-71-349	**61**	12	
C-71-350	**257**	258	
C-71-351	**281**	441	
C-71-357	**740**	259	
C-71-360	**1217**	54	
C-71-364	**85**	452	
C-71-365	**97**	452	
C-71-370	**1136**	75	
C-71-371	**1088**	140	
C-71-373	**1084**	12	
C-71-394	**1000**	164	
C-71-395	**985**	163	
C-71-399	**1242**	150	
C-71-400	**1264**	147	
C-71-401	**1263**	159	
C-71-417	**465**	171	
C-71-421	**636**	514	
C-71-423	**1258**	165	
C-71-424	**1243**	150	
C-71-429	**379**	166	
C-71-430	**407**	166	
C-71-431	**385**	236	
C-71-432	**356**	305	
C-71-433	**411**	165	
C-71-434	**363**	278	
C-71-435	**355**	293	
C-71-504	**871**	231	
C-72-001	**681**	610	
C-72-002	**677**	795	
C-72-003	**613**	549	
C-72-004	**618**	763	
C-72-007	**714**	110	
C-72-008	**545**	552	
C-72-011	**857**	546	
C-72-012	**464**	762	
C-72-013	**933**	762	
C-72-014	**797**	609	
C-72-015	**137**	552	
C-72-017	**120**	609	
C-72-020	**141**	552	
C-72-023	**103**	536	
C-72-025	**56**	608	
C-72-026	**796**	547	
C-72-027	**117**	610	
C-72-029	**59**	549	
C-72-031	**744**	552	
C-72-033	**69**	599	
C-72-036	**798**	547	
C-72-038	**983**	763	
C-72-040	**978**	763	
C-72-042	**1003**	8	
C-72-043	**795**	551	
C-72-044	**560**	Grave 102	
C-72-046	**436**	612	
C-72-047	**84**	545	
C-72-048	**175**	552	
C-72-050	**546**	783	
C-72-053	**170**	552	
C-72-054	**1202**	762	
C-72-055	**722**	552	
C-72-056	**554**	686	
C-72-058	**742**	552	
C-72-060	**649**	552	
C-72-063	**712**	552	
C-72-064	**129**	552	
C-72-066	**33**	545	
C-72-067	**748**	552	
C-72-068	**37**	608	
C-72-069	**770**	552	
C-72-070	**1268**	523	
C-72-071	**433**	789	
C-72-072	**224**	718	
C-72-074	**973**	692	

Inv. No.	Cat. No.	Lot	Sherd No.
C-72-075	**304**	692	
C-72-076	**310**	692	
C-72-077	**320**	692	
C-72-078	**309**	692	
C-72-084	**598**	708	
C-72-091	**762**	552	
C-72-093	**121**	783	
C-72-094	**678**	672	
C-72-096	**508**	552	
C-72-099	**293**	620	
C-72-100	**280**	630	
C-72-108	**1101**	552	
C-72-109	**650**	552	
C-72-110	**653**	563	
C-72-111	**769**	552	
C-72-115	**94**	630	
C-72-126	**90**	552	
C-72-157	**1110**	547	
C-72-158	**174**	549	
C-72-160	**86**	552	
C-72-163	**171**	552	
C-72-164	**172**	552	
C-72-169	**57**	547	
C-72-170	**95**	545	
C-72-178	**727**	563	
C-72-179	**806**	552	
C-72-184	**91**	549	
C-72-185	**152**	547	
C-72-188	**1123**	552	
C-72-190	**96**	545	
C-72-191	**773**	547	
C-72-193	**1111**	547	
C-72-200	**646**	552	
C-72-201	**663**	552	
C-72-202	**29**	564	
C-72-203	**27**	547	
C-72-204	**65**	549	
C-72-206	**66**	552	
C-72-207	**76**	552	
C-72-214	**38**	552	
C-72-215	**1109**	551	
C-72-216	**1108**	552	
C-72-222	**628**	677	
C-72-230	**1098**	552	
C-72-231	**1112**	552	
C-72-241	**468**	523	
C-72-252	**1250**	645	
C-72-257	**996**	672	
C-72-262	**990**	729	
C-72-279	**640**	545	
C-72-281	**655**	549	
C-72-285	**766**	552	
C-72-286	**767**	552	
C-72-287	**648**	552	
C-72-289	**794**	552	

Inv. No.	Cat. No.	Lot	Sherd No.
C-72-294	**1060**	1052	
C-72-299	**406**	645	
C-72-300	**617**	763	
C-72-301	**634**	728	
C-72-303	**341**	594	
C-72-305	**412**	746	
C-72-306	**758**	547	
C-73-007	**441**	917	
C-73-013	**1054**	929	
C-73-015	**322**	930	
C-73-016	**970**	927	
C-73-021	**326**	929	
C-73-022	**312**	930	
C-73-025	**614**	881	
C-73-026	**1207**	929	
C-73-028	**479**		
C-73-029	**994**	974	
C-73-030	**1234**	853	
C-73-033	**523**	881	
C-73-035	**931**	881	
C-73-036	**938**	881	
C-73-037	**963**	881	
C-73-041	**432**	917	
C-73-042	**295**	942	
C-73-044	**290**	940	
C-73-050	**382**	875	
C-73-051	**381**	875	
C-73-052	**941**	890	
C-73-054	**318**	955	
C-73-057	**438**	902	
C-73-060	**969**	940	
C-73-071	**313**	921	
C-73-072	**1164**	890	
C-73-073	**1230**	849	
C-73-074	**1288**	853	
C-73-076	**706**	875	
C-73-087	**958**	890	
C-73-102	**242**	938	
C-73-103	**496**	934	
C-73-106	**489**	938	
C-73-107	**258**	934	
C-73-111	**1254**	878	
C-73-112	**513**	992	
C-73-113	**376**	847	
C-73-114	**367**	850	
C-73-115	**405**	850	
C-74-002	**205**	1059	
C-74-003	**1012**	1098	
C-74-004	**32**	1094	
C-74-005	**34**	1094	
C-74-006	**1124**	1094	
C-74-007	**1159**	1066	
C-74-011	**615**	1074	
C-74-012	**967**	1356	
C-74-013	**147**	1094	

Inv. No.	Cat. No.	Lot	Sherd No.
C-74-017	**825**	1092	
C-74-018	**590**	1092	
C-74-020	**566**	1094	
C-74-022	**588**	Grave 264	
		1080	
C-74-028	**982**	1057	
C-74-030	**1020**	1296	
C-74-031	**256**	1319	
C-74-032	**968**	1298	
C-74-033	**869**	1511	
C-74-035	**458**	1551	
C-74-036	**675**	1298	
C-74-037	**589**	Grave 262	
C-74-045	**594**	Grave 262	
C-74-052	**927**	1296	
C-74-053	**962**	1509	
C-74-055	**913**	1298	
C-74-058	**501**	1057	
C-74-059	**345**	1296	
C-74-060	**531**	1629	
C-74-062	**524**	1316	
C-74-063	**461**	1319	
C-74-065	**503**	1090	
C-74-067	**294**	1356	
C-74-071	**112**	1093	
C-74-072	**535**	1315	
C-74-073	**536**	1300	
C-74-075	**495**	1324	
C-74-076	**291**	1538	
C-74-077	**932**	1296	
C-74-079	**445**	1370	
C-74-084	**273**	1434	
C-74-085	**477**	1507	
C-74-087	**52**	1090	
C-74-089	**331**	1314	
C-74-094	**325**	1538	
C-74-096	**484**	1552	
C-74-099	**43**	1538	
C-74-101	**274**	1358	
C-74-102	**578**	1421	
C-74-103	**584**	1421	
C-74-104	**577**	1421	
C-74-105	**583**	1421	
C-74-106	**568**	1098	
C-74-109	**582**	1452	
C-74-112	**580**	1452	
C-74-114	**595**	1452	
C-74-118	**956**	1295	
C-74-123	**344**	1295	
C-74-128	**596**	Grave 283	
C-74-131	**429**	1398	
C-74-140	**1165**	1298	
C-74-142	**450**	1361	
C-74-144	**459**	1362	
C-74-145	**266**	1474	
C-74-148	**393**	1551	

Inv. No.	Cat. No.	Lot	Sherd No.
C-74-149	**1013**	1296	
C-74-150	**680**	1434	
C-74-155	**265**	1373	
C-74-160	**282**	1089	
C-74-161	**550**	1398	
C-74-162	**1163**	1298	
C-74-164	**1215**	1352	
C-74-166	**586**	1456	
C-74-183	**587**	1456	
C-74-189	**581**	1452	
C-74-193	**1034**	1297	
C-74-194	**951**	1296	
C-74-198	**922**	1302	
C-74-201	**930**	1301	
C-74-206	**54**	1301	
C-74-208	**924**	1297	
C-74-210	**619**	1345	
C-74-212	**807**	1452	
C-74-213	**808**	1453	
C-74-215	**698**	1509	
C-74-216	**684**	1298	
C-74-219	**579**	1452	
C-74-221	**507**	1538	
C-74-223	**505**	1479	
C-74-224	**292**	1629	
C-74-225	**425**	1625	
C-74-228	**306**	1629	
C-74-229	**440**	1398	
C-74-236	**203**	1629	
C-74-245	**321**	1479	
C-74-251	**840**	1453	
C-74-252	**839**	1453	
C-74-253	**218**	1454	
C-74-255	**1276**	1345	
C-74-257	**1225**	1345	
C-74-258	**1226**	1344	
C-74-259	**1278**	1345	
C-74-261	**912**	1307	
C-74-262	**786**	1458	
C-74-264	**110**	1441	
C-74-265	**510**	1441	
C-74-266	**960**	1328	
C-74-270	**851**	1095	
C-74-273	**921**	1328	
C-74-279	**1026**	1307	
C-74-282	**809**	Grave 288	
C-74-283	**1050**	1325	
C-74-286	**557**	1414	
C-74-287	**333**	1325	
C-74-289	**329**	1419	
C-74-290	**230**	1327	
C-74-294	**529**	1306	
C-74-296	**285**	1569	
C-74-297	**315**	1419	
C-74-298	**499**	1493	
C-74-301	**116**	1442	

Inv. No.	Cat. No.	Lot	Sherd No.
C-74-304	**548**	1328	
C-74-308	**533**	799	
C-74-309	**709**	1599	
C-74-310	**87**	1458	
C-74-312	**298**		
C-74-313	**500**	1420	
C-74-316	**113**	1599	
C-74-317	**910**	1469	
C-74-318	**890**	1465	
C-74-319	**223**	1070	
C-74-320	**929**	1307	
C-74-322	**939**	1307	
C-74-323	**1028**	1308	
C-74-330	**1233**	1345	
C-74-331	**1145**	1418	
C-74-332	**1227**	1334	
C-74-333	**1267**	1345	
C-74-335	**88**	1470	
C-74-342	**569**	1468	
C-74-343	**561**	Grave 295	
C-74-349	**567**	Grave 288	
C-74-354	**563**	Grave 281	
C-74-355	**562**	Grave 281	
C-74-356	**165**	1468	
C-74-357	**700**	1349	
C-74-363	**600**	1462	
C-74-370	**599**	1462	
C-74-371	**597**	Grave 271	
C-74-374	**564**	Grave 295	
C-74-380	**565**	Graves 295, 288	
C-74-387	**676**	1442	
C-74-411	**339**	1475	
C-74-411	**488**	1475	
C-74-414	**64**	1471	
C-74-417	**332**	1474	
C-74-420	**275**	1475	
C-74-424	**263**	1477	
C-74-426	**497**	1478	
C-74-428	**308**	1478	
C-74-430	**202**	1479	
C-74-433	**506**	1358	
C-74-435	**718**	1358	
C-74-436	**93**	1358	
C-74-440	**132**	1510	
C-74-441	**259**	1510	
C-74-444	**180**	1510	
C-74-445	**330**	1510	
C-74-449	**197**	1510	
C-74-451	**217**	1510	
C-74-453	**1146**	1511	
C-74-455	**843**	1099	
C-74-460	**838**	1501	
C-74-466	**208**	1418	
C-74-467	**1277**	1346	
C-74-469	**687**	1349	
C-74-481	**1133**	1416	

Inv. No.	Cat. No.	Lot	Sherd No.
C-74-482	**102**	1420	
C-74-483	**191**	1089	
C-74-484	**243**	1418	
C-74-489	**966**	1310	
C-74-491	**671**	1090	
C-74-494	**75**	1419	
C-74-496	**307**	1417	
C-74-501	**502**	1416	
C-74-502	**42**	1442	
C-74-503	**239**	1453	
C-74-505	**688**	1349	
C-74-506	**707**	1349	
C-74-507	**708**	1349	
C-74-508	**472**	1349	
C-74-509	**247**	1080	
C-74-510	**262**	1510	
C-74-516	**847**	1417	
C-74-525	**377**	1057	
C-75-001	**880**	Grave 310	
C-75-002	**897**	Grave 310	
C-75-004	**805**	Grave 308	
C-75-005	**1052**	1663	
C-75-007	**689**	1642	
C-75-011	**439**	1656	
C-75-012	**799**	1637	
C-75-015	**534**	1659	
C-75-018	**1289**	1656	
C-75-020	**428**	1659	
C-75-021	**1051**	1697	
C-75-022	**1099**	1636	
C-75-023	**1095**	1636	
C-75-026	**314**	1697	
C-75-027	**1027**	1697	
C-75-028	**492**	1645	
C-75-030	**299**	1798	
C-75-031	**264**	1800	
C-75-034	**177**	Grave 304	
C-75-036	**125**	1672	
C-75-037	**124**	1637	
C-75-038	**340**	1697	
C-75-040	**324**	1799	
C-75-044	**20**	1636	
C-75-047	**358**	1801	
C-75-049	**372**	1798	
C-75-050	**397**	1798	
C-75-057	**1047**	1697	
C-75-058	**1261**	1810	
C-75-059	**585**	Grave 309	
C-75-060	**155**	1636	
C-75-064	**72**	1683	
C-75-065	**106**	1662	
C-75-069	**552**	1662	
C-75-074	**998**	1676	
C-75-076	**424**	1770	
C-75-079	**206**	1703	
C-75-083	**386**	1801	

Inv. No.	Cat. No.	Lot	Sherd No.
C-75-084	**149**	1657	
C-75-087	**1147**	1673	
C-75-088	**328**	1846	
C-75-090	**209**	Grave 310	
C-75-099	**383**	1922	
C-75-100	**1240**	1657	
C-75-102	**623**	1657	
C-75-107	**726**	1636	
C-77-001	**480**	1939	
C-77-006	**723**	1959	
C-77-009	**387**	2076	
C-77-012	**1183**	1957	
C-77-019	**993**	1941	
C-77-060	**1169**	1958	
C-77-062	**1244**	2033	
C-77-063	**350**	1946	
C-77-070	**446**	1935	
C-77-071	**413**	1948	
C-77-073	**327**	1957	
C-77-078	**955**	1959	
C-78-001	**542**	2111	
C-78-006	**398**	2222	
C-78-009	**1031**	2350	
C-78-018	**1218**	2089	
C-78-027	**394**	2111	
C-78-029	**1232**	2111	
C-78-030	**421**	2111	
C-78-032	**443**	2112	
C-78-033	**537**	2228	
C-78-034	**638**	2206	
C-78-040	**300**	2208	
C-78-044	**1076**	2209	
C-78-045	**371**	2210	
C-78-048	**622**	2211	
C-78-050	**467**	2211	
C-78-052	**422**	2211	
C-78-058	**399**	2354	
C-78-060	**338**	2360	
C-78-061	**478**	2319	
C-78-062	**466**	2355	
C-78-073	**388**	2233	
C-78-075	**476**	2233	
C-78-076	419	2233	
C-78-079	**474**	2233	
C-78-086	**547**	2211	
C-78-088	**302**	2325	
C-78-090	**368**	2230	
C-78-091	**462**	2234	
C-78-093	**703**	2434	
C-78-094	**695**	2090	
C-78-096	**296**	2094	
C-78-100	**916**	2173	
C-78-101	**395**	2223	
C-78-102	**342**	2355	
C-78-112	**558**	2126	
C-78-118	**400**	2213	
C-78-120	**483**	2213	
C-78-121	**389**	2213	
C-78-123	**408**	2213	
C-78-125	**1251**	2213	
C-78-127	**964**	2213	
C-78-128	**431**	2213	
C-78-130	**353**	2213	
C-78-135	**1077**	2234	
C-78-138	**404**	2234	
C-78-144	**525**	2367	
C-78-149	**986**	2377	
C-78-154	**624**	2145	
C-78-155	**454**	2263	
C-78-156	**1249**	2263	
C-78-158	**53**	2302	
C-78-168	**1073**	2128	
C-78-170	**551**	2129	
C-78-172	**359**	2210	
C-78-197	**319**	2181	
C-78-200	**971**	2152	
C-78-212	**1025**	2236	
C-78-224	**390**	2186	
C-78-234	**631**	2281	
C-78-237	**346**	2385	
C-78-238	**301**	2236	
C-78-247	**427**	2307	
C-78-261	**409**	2405	
C-78-270	**460**	2218	
C-78-273	**391**	2347	
C-78-278	**414**	2407	
C-78-279	**362**	2407	
C-78-238	**361**	2407	
C-78-284	**679**	2408	
C-78-288	**530**	2382	
C-79-001	**375**	2455	
C-79-003	**373**	2581	
C-79-006	**453**	2581	
C-79-008	**370**	2581	
C-79-010	**549**	2537	
C-79-012	**444**	2581	
C-79-023	**704**	2604	
C-79-039	**702**	2581	
C-79-041	**420**	2581	
C-79-042	**402**	2580	
C-79-043	**396**	2579	
C-79-058	**392**	2581	
C-79-077	**469**	2588	
C-79-086	**360**	2604	
C-79-095	**470**	2604	
C-79-096	**448**	2581	
C-79-098	**475**	2605	
C-79-099	**423**	2581	
C-79-100	**457**	2581	
MF-74-147	**543**	1482	

INDEX

•

References are to text pages and to footnotes or to catalogue entries (**bold face**).

Aco workshop, 28, **96**, 38, **173**
Actium, 188
Adriatic region, 192–193; amphoras from, 89; as source of olive oil, 192
Aegean, 50, 53, 55, 61, 74, 98, 192, 193; amphoras from, 94, 191
African Red Slip imitations in local ware, 116, **911–915**, 117, **920–927**, 127, **1076**, **1077**
Alexander the Great (?), 80, **551**
amphoras, 193; stamps on, 93, 94; stoppers, 124
Ampurias, 13
applique decoration on pottery, 47, **248**, **253**, **254**, 48, **255**, **256**, **261**, **264**, **265**
Arezzo, 45
Asia Minor, gray wares, 10, 185, 189; imports at Stobi, 192, 193
Athenian Red Figure, 17, 22, **53**
Athens, 65, 89, 94
Augustus, xxv
Austria, 75
Axius river, see Vardar river

barbotine dot decoration, 36–37, **147**, **149**, 121
barbotine floral decoration, 41–43, 121
Basil II, xxii
Berenice, 89; amphora types: MR amphora 5, 94; MR amphora 7, 94; MR amphora 9, 95; MR amphora 16/17, 95; LR amphora 3, 96; LR amphora 8, 97; LR amphora 10, 96
Black Sea, 50
Brindisi, amphoras from, 89
Britain, 50, 66
bucchero, 13, 14, 23
Budius, Bishop of Stobi, xxi
Byzantium, 187

Campanian B imitations, 102, **731**, **732**, 103, **743**
Campanian C, 10
Çandarli, 23; imitations, 118, **934**, **935**, 125, **1027**
Carthage, 89; amphora types: LR amphoras 1, 2, 3, and 4, 96
Cnidos, amphoras of, 90, 94, **678**, **679**; plastic vases of, 78, **543**; as supplier of imports to Stobi, 185,n.7
Coan amphoras, 89, 90, 92, **654**, 94, **680**
Coela, xxi
coffins, 8
column bowls, 30, 33
cooking wares, 199
Corinth, 9,n.8, 65, 188; relief bowls from, 78, **542**
Cosa, 35
Crna river, xxii, xxvi, 3, 8, 10, 62, 184, 195, 197; floods of, xxvi, 192, 193; for transport, 193

Dacia, 65,n.8, 66, 75
Dalmatia, 90
Dardani, xxi, 14, 184
Delian bowls, 29–31
Demir Kapija, 8,n.5, 10, 190, 193
Dionysus, 34, 35, **145**, 79, **545**
Djevdjelija, 193
Dyrrachium, 187

early Bronze Age, 13
Egnatian Way, see Via Egnatia
Emporion, 23,n.27
Eastern Sigillata A imitations, 102, **729**, **730**, 109, **814**
Eastern Sigillata B imitations, 110, **830**, **831**, 118, **936–941**, 125, **1025**, **1026**
Erigon river (see Crna river)

Fabric Group 1, 9, 10
Fabric Group 2, 9, 10
Fabric Group 3, 10
figural scenes on pottery, 31–32, 58, **385**, 78–80
  animals: bucranion, 17, **19**; feline, 71–72, **482**; griffin, 32, **117**; lion, 58, **383**; lions' heads, 11; rabbit, 61, **416**; sheep, 80, **533**
  battle scenes: 31, **114**, 79, **548**, **549**
  erotic scenes: 80, **554–557**
  individual heads or figures: Alexander the Great (?), 80, **551**; head of woman, 77, **531**; head of youth, 78, **544**; nude youth, 22, **53**, 26, **72**
  mythological figures: Cupid, 80, **552**; Dionysus, 34–35, **145**, 79, **545**; Heracles, 78, **542**; Hippolytus, 32, **116**; Nike, 79, **546**, **547**
fish plates, 101
Florina, 18, 21, 188
Foliage bowls, 29, 32, 33

Gaul, 50; gray wares in, 61, 65,n.105
Gaza amphoras, 194
Germany, 75
Goths, 191

Gray Ware pottery tradition, 9, 10,n.9, 13, 14, 15, 23, 61–66, 184, 192, 194, 198–199, 202
Greco-Italic amphoras, 90–91
Greek pottery shapes, imitations of, 14

handmade pottery, 3,n.3, 14, 145,n.7, 184, 194, 199
Heraclea Lyncestis, xxii, 4, 65, 184, 188, 190, 193
Histria, 13
Hungary, 75

incense burners, 105, **766**, **767**, 108, **807–809**
Iron Age, 63
Istanbul, 94
Italy, as source of imports at Stobi, 185, 186, 188, 189, 195; kiln types, 195
Ivy-leaf bowls, 30, 33

Kumanovo, 14

Lapius workshop, 34
La Tène, 23, 39
Lesbos, 13, 23
Livy, xxi, 185,n.13, 188,n.17
Long petalled bowls, 29, 33
loomweights, 9, Table 2.1, 198, 199
Lot, explanation of, 6
Luna, 46
Lyon, 46

Macedonia, Aegean coast of, 194; amphoras in, 89; conquest of by Rome, 185–188; excavations in, 4; geology of, 197; kilns in, 194,n.47; production of olive oil, 192; regional ceramic production of, 194; *Salutaris*, xxi, 61; *Secunda*, xxii; transport of goods to, 194
Maedi, xxi,n.6
Magdalensburg, 23,n.33, 25
Marvinci, 4, 65, 190
Massilia, 13, 23,n.27
Megara Hyblaea, 13
Megarian bowls, 29, 30
metal vessels, imitations of, 13, 14, 29, 35, 63, 87
Metapontum, 23
middle Bronze Age, 13
Mica-Dusted Ware, 194
Minyan ware, 13
Modena, 46
Moesia, 65,n.105, 75, 187, 190, 192–194
moulds, 8, 11, 12, 29, 196

Naissus, 184
Negotino, 8,n.5, 10, 14, 62, 197
Nemesis as Nike, 79, **546**, **547**
Nerezi, 14
North Africa, as source of imports to Stobi, 192, 193
Noricum, 41

Ohrid, kilns in, 194, 195
Ostia, 89, 94
Ostrogoths, xxii

Paeonia, xxi, 14, 184
painted decoration on pottery, 74, **514**, 83, **566**
Palestine, 192
Palikura, 10,n.10
Pannonia, 41, 50, 65,n.105, 75, 86, 190, 193, 194
Pelagonia, 14
Pergamene pottery, 44
Pergamon, 23, 25, 53
Perseis, xxi
Perseus, King of Macedon, 185
petrographic analysis of pottery, 8
Philip V, King of Macedon, xxi
Philippi, 65
Phrygia, 13
pinecone decoration, 33, 38, 39
Pisa, 46
Pitane, 53
planta pedis stamps, 25, **69**, **70**, 26, **71**, 28, **104**, **105**, 46, 49, **291–293**, 50, **294**, **295**, 110, **833**, 120, **965**, 189
potters' stamps, 28, 46, 49–50, 51, 53
pottery, quantification of, 4
Po Valley, 46
Pozzuoli, 46
Prilep, 65

reduction firing technique, 9, 10,n.9, 14
Rhodes, amphoras from, 90, 93, **674–676**, 185

Samian ware, 24
Samos, 23
sanded decoration on pottery, 39–41, 74, 198, 201–202
Saraçhane, 88
Scupi, 4, 65, 194
Serdica, xxii
Sestius, P. and L., 89
Sirmium, 66,n.107, 184, 194
Skopje, 14
Slavs, 193
Spain, 50; amphoras from (?), 92, **657–661**, 95, **689**
stamped decoration, 26, 27, **84**, 61, **416**, **417**, 62–63, 77, **533–537**, 119–120, 190,n.34
stamps, 8, 11
Štip, 14
Stobi
- Acropolis, 3, 63,n.101, 65, 74, 88, 144
- basket, as documentation, 6
- brick production, 8
- Building A, 63, 192
- burial customs of, 81
- Central Basilica, 8, 14, 29, 34, 90, 144, 184, 195
- Christian churches, 3, 194
- Civil Basilica, 90

clay, 8, 10, 62, 197
coins, xxi,n.3, 144, 190; hoard of silver denarii, 19, **23**, 133, **1125**, 195
East City Wall, 63, 144
as emporium, xxi, 188
environment of, xxvi, 193
Episcopal Basilica, xxvi, 51, 63, 144, 194
excavations at, xxii–xxvi, 6
Fuller's House, 63,n.101, 88; 6th c. floor deposit, 87, **619**, 139, **1226**, 140, **1233**, 142, **1267**, **1276–1278**
geology of, 8
houses, 3
history of, xxi–xxii, xxv–xxvi, 3, 148, 185–195
Inner Wall West, 54, 74, 144
kiln, 8
kiln furniture, 11
Large Bath, 51, 74
literary references to, xxi–xxii
location of, xxii, 3, 184, 187–188, 193
mosaics, xxv, 3,n.7
Peristeria Court, graves in, 14, 147
pithoi, 9, Table 2.1, 199, 200, 201
population of, xxv–xxvi, 188
Potter's Workshop, 8, 34, 81, 194
pottery production, 194, 198–202
prehistoric period of, xxv, 3
prosopography, xxv, 190
residences, xxvi, 192
roof tiles, 8, 9, 10, 199
synagogues, xxvi, 63,n.101, 190, 192
transport of goods to, 193–194
theater, xxii, xxvi, 51, 63, 65, 144, 190
walls, xxvi
West Cemetery, 43, 51, 81, 185; Carbon 14 analyses in, 3,n.4, 144; Grave, 84, 20, **32**, **34**, 36, **147**, 82, 83, **566**
wine production at, 192, 193
Studeničani, 14
Styberra, 188
Switzerland, 75
Syro-Palestinian area, pottery from, 185

Tan Micaceous ware, 10, 194
Tarsus, 75
terra sigillata, imitations of, 10, 102, **729**, **730**, 104, **754**, 109–111, 113, 114; transport of to Roman military camps, 193
textiles, 192, 193
Thasos, 13
Theodosius I, xxi
Thessalonica, xxii, 63, 65, 184, 187, 193
thumb-impressed decoration, 42, **214**, **215**
Thrace, 13, 65, 184, 187, 190
Torone, 65
Tunisia, pottery from, 55; amphoras from, 95, 191

unguentaria, 9, Table 2.1, 196, 198

Vardar river, xxii, 3, 8, 14, 63, 190; for transport, 193
Via Egnatia, xxii, 184, 187, 193
Visigoths, 65,n.105
Vranje, 14

workshop production of pottery, 194, 198–199

Greek Words and Names

References are to text pages and catalogue numbers (in **bold face**).

’ΑΡΙΜΟ 26, **71**
’Αρχε]μβρότο[υ 93, **675**
ΓΑΙΟΣ 73, **496**
Δρακογ[τιδα] 93, **676**
’ΕΠΙΓΟΝΟΣ 72, **485–487**
’ΕΡΜΗ 72, **488**
[’Ευφρα]γορα 94, **679**
ΘΕΟΛ··ΟΥ 28, **102**
‘Ιππί[ας] 94, **680**
Κλε(υ)πολιος 94, **678**
[Κ]λευπολιος 94, **679**
Κνιδιον 94, **678**
[Κ]νιδιον 94, **679**
ΛΟΥΚ 28, **101**
ΛΥΣΥΣ 73, **493**
ΜΑΚΕΔΟΝΙΚΟΥ 42, **207**
]ΜΕ[79, **546**
]ΜΟΙ[72, **489**
ΜΡΛΥ 73, **492**
]ΝΕΜ[79, **547**
ΟΙΥΛΟΝ 72, **490**
Ρ·ΥΙΤΑ 28, **103**
ΤΕΡΤ 73, **495**
Τιμο[ξενος] 93, **674**
]τοντ[34, **141**
]τω[31, **116**
Φιλ[---] 93–94, **677**
ΧΝΕΓΡ 127, **1066**

Latin Potters' Names

References are to text pages and catalogue numbers (in **bold face**).

AFRI, 73, **498–501**
ANNIVS, 49, **287**
CAMVRIVS, 49, **293**, 50, **294**
GELLIVS, 49, **288**, 50, **295**
PERENNIVS, 49, **291**
PESCENNIVS, 49, **292**
TITIVS, 49, **286**
UMBRICIVS, 49, **289**
VIBIENUS, 73, **502**

PLATES

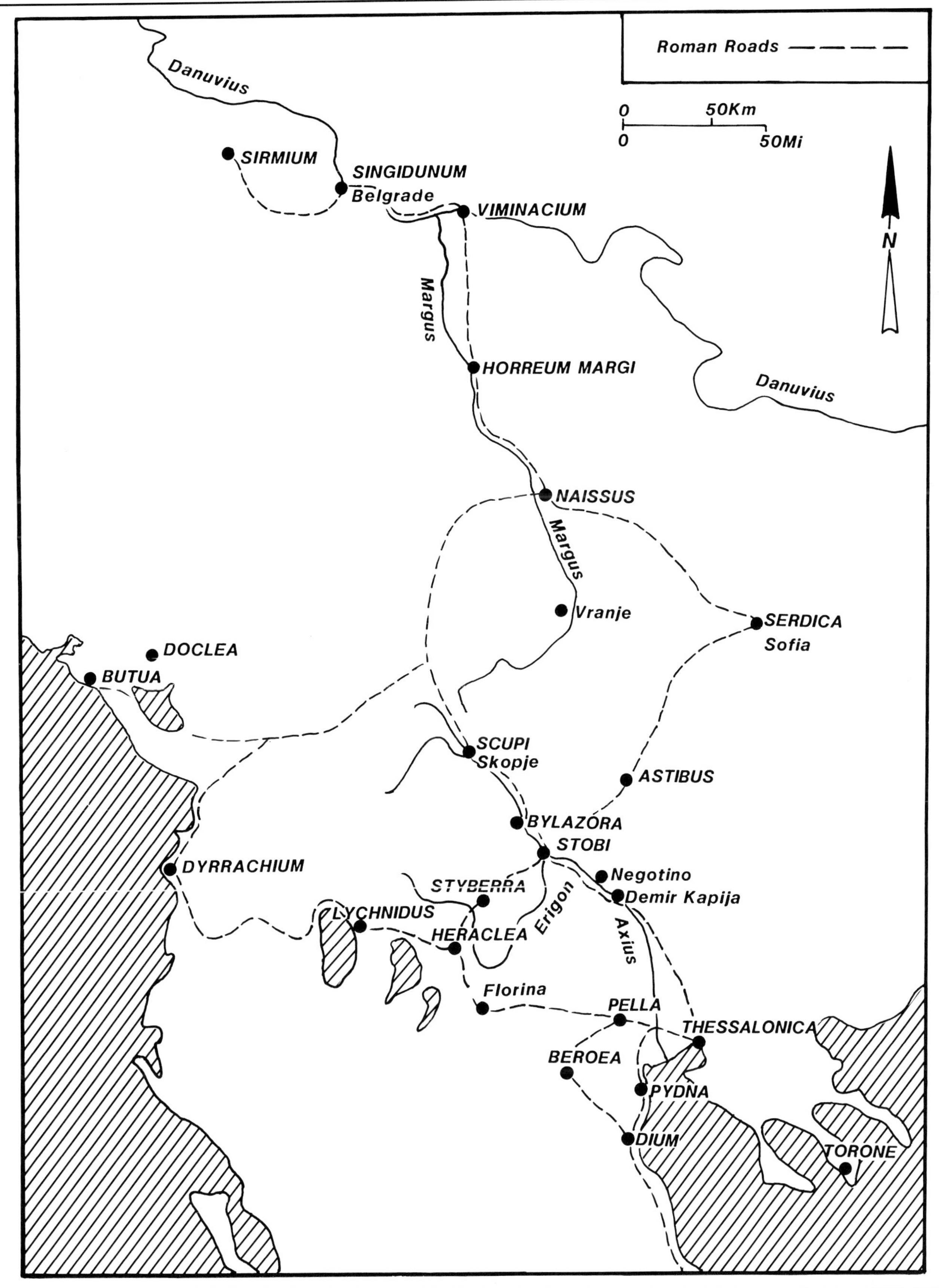

Plate 1. Map showing location of Stobi. By Dragan Stojanović and David Clayton. Names of ancient towns in capital letters

Plate 2. Map of Stobi

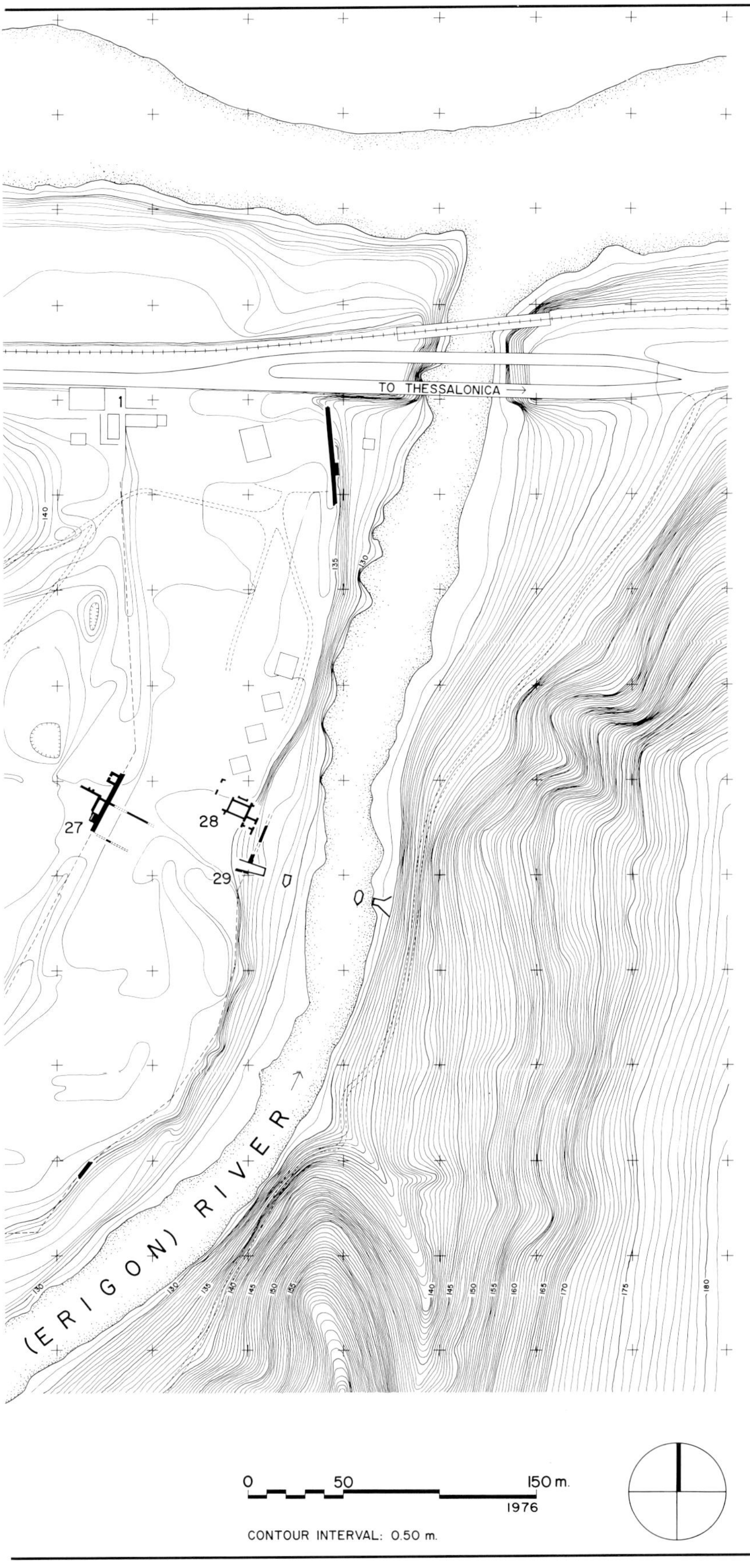

1. Museum
2. North Basilica
3. Small Residences
4. Civil Basilica
5. Little Bath
6. Central Basilica and Synagogues
7. House of Psalms
8. Central Fountain
9. Large Bath
10. Via Principalis Inferior
11. House of Peristeria
12. Via Theodosia
13. House of Parthenius
14. Theodosian Palace
15. Via Principalis Superior
16. House of the Fuller
17. Prison Area
18. Residence/Martyrium
19. Semicircular Court
20. Episcopal Basilica
21. Baptistery
22. Via Sacra
23. Porta Heraclea
24. Theater
25. Casino
26. Via Axia
27. Inner City Wall and Public Structure
28. Casa Romana
29. East City Wall and Turkish Bridge
30. West Cemetery
31. Cemetery Basilica
32. Palikura Basilica

The map was drawn by C. Salit, F. P. Hemans and E. Scull and is based on an earlier survey and drawing by Paul Huffman (1971) and David B. Peck (1972) with additions by Charles Ehrhorn (1973) and Hemans (1974).

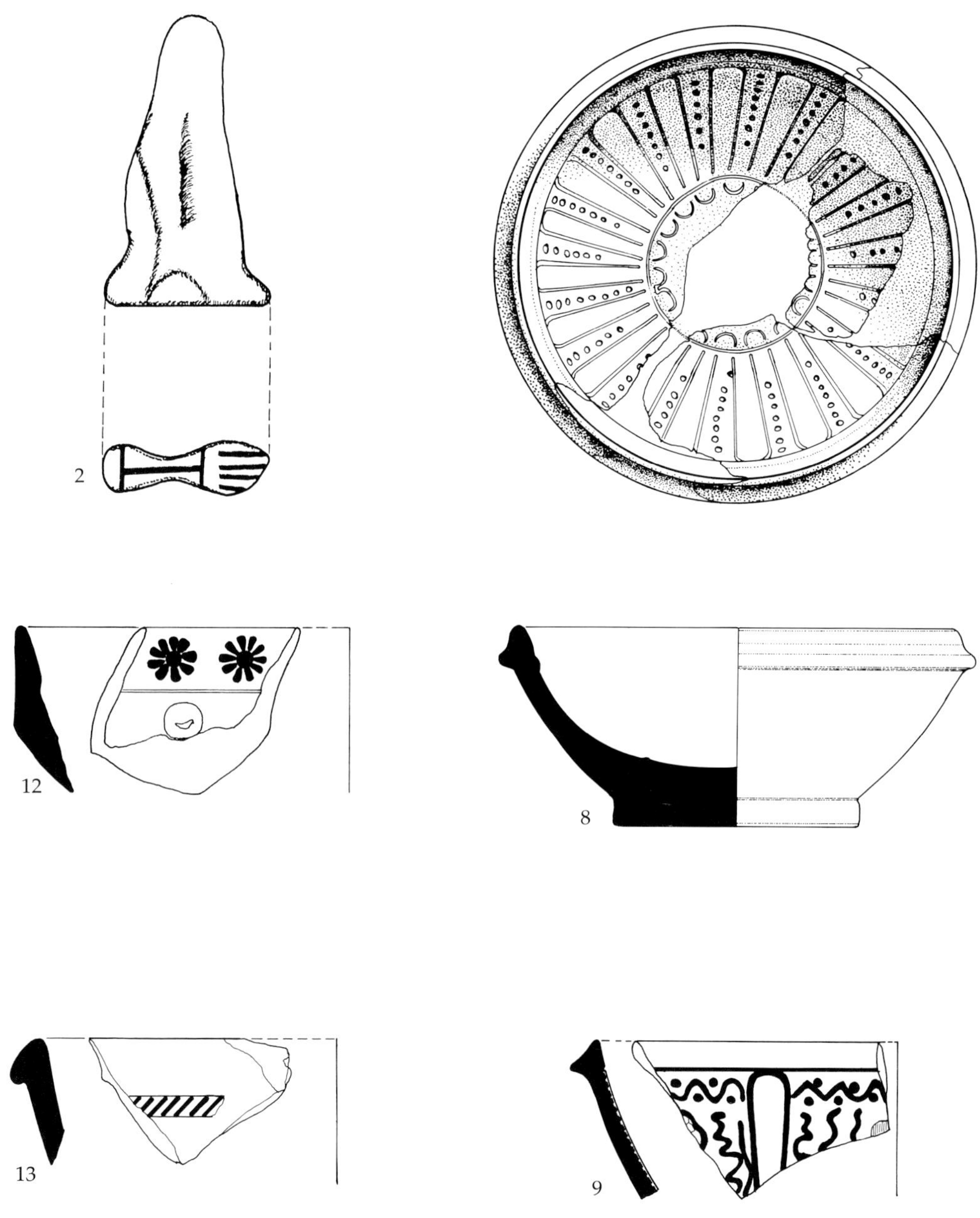

Plate 3. Pottery stamps and moulds (2, scale 1:1)

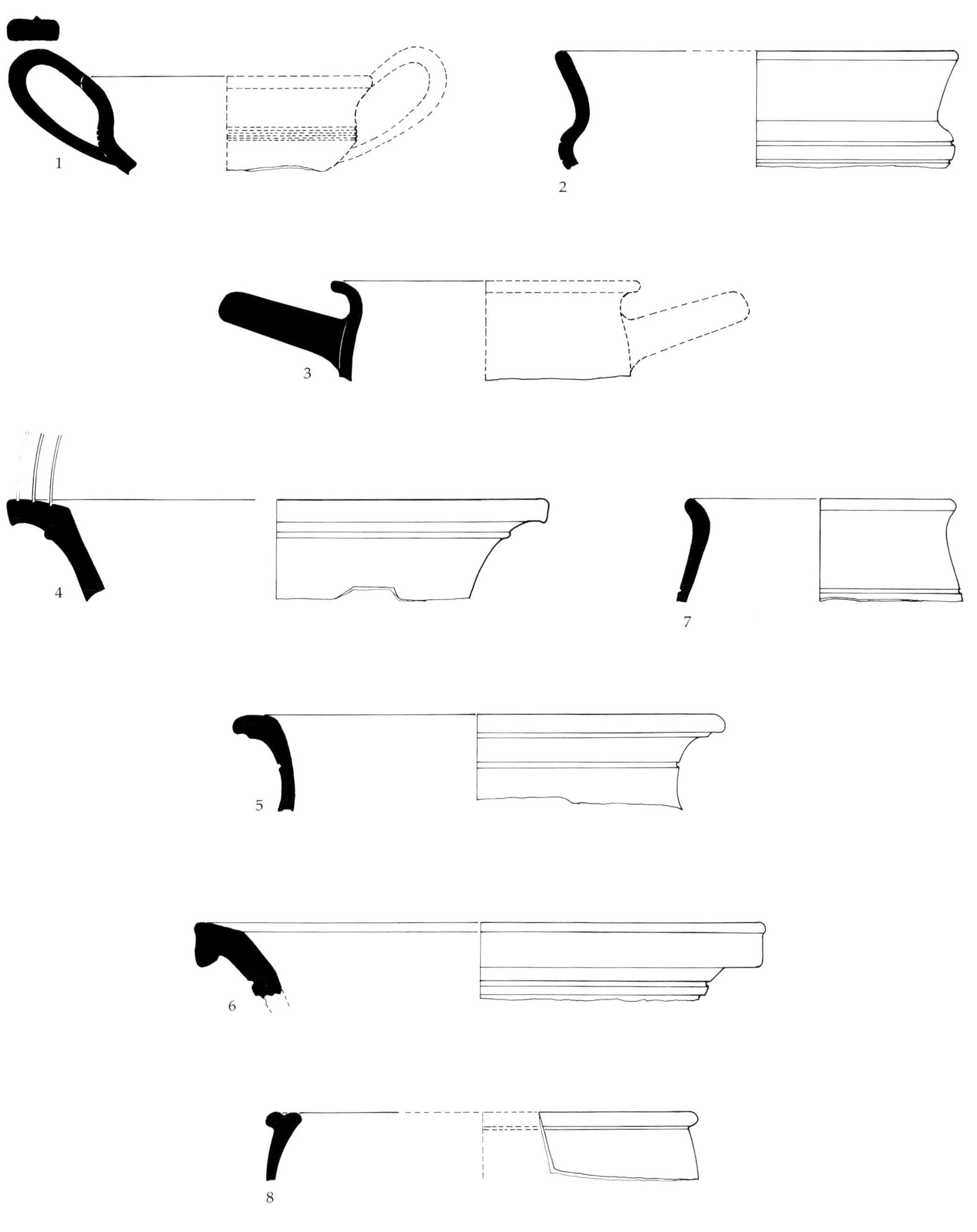

Plate 4. Early Hellenistic Wheelmade Gray Ware. Forms 1–5

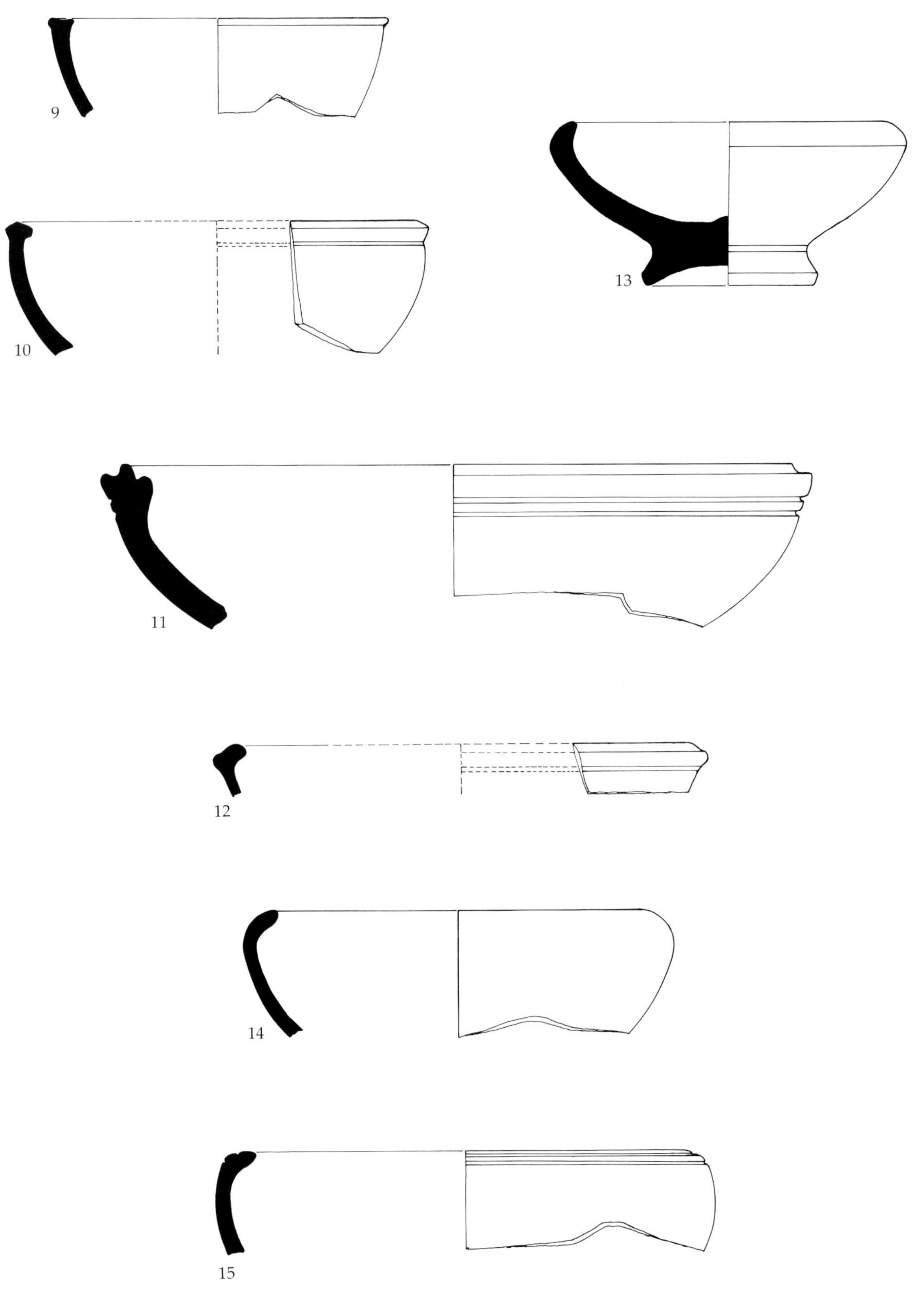

Plate 5. Early Hellenistic Wheelmade Gray Ware. Forms 6–10

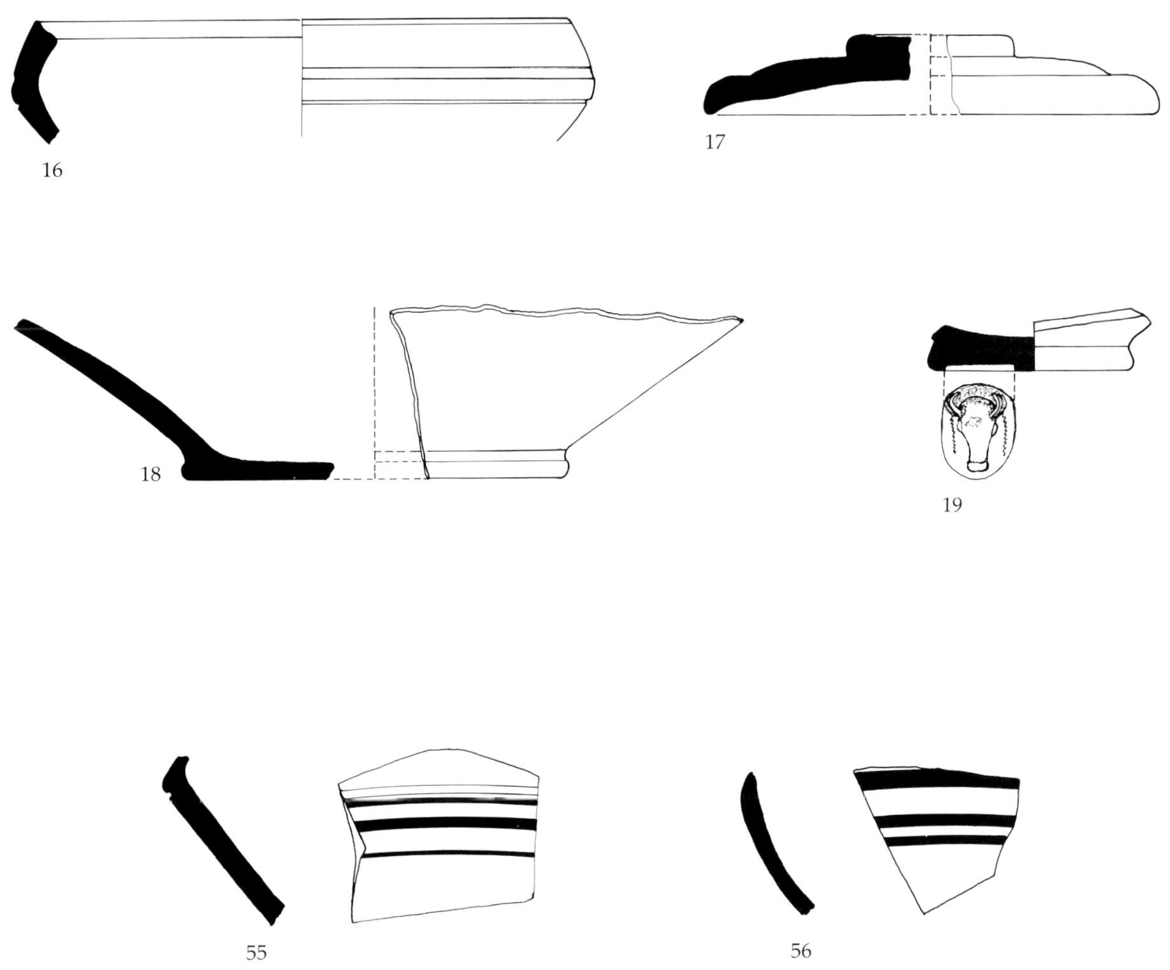

Plate 6. Early Hellenistic Wheelmade Gray Ware. Form 10, lids, bases. Lagynoi

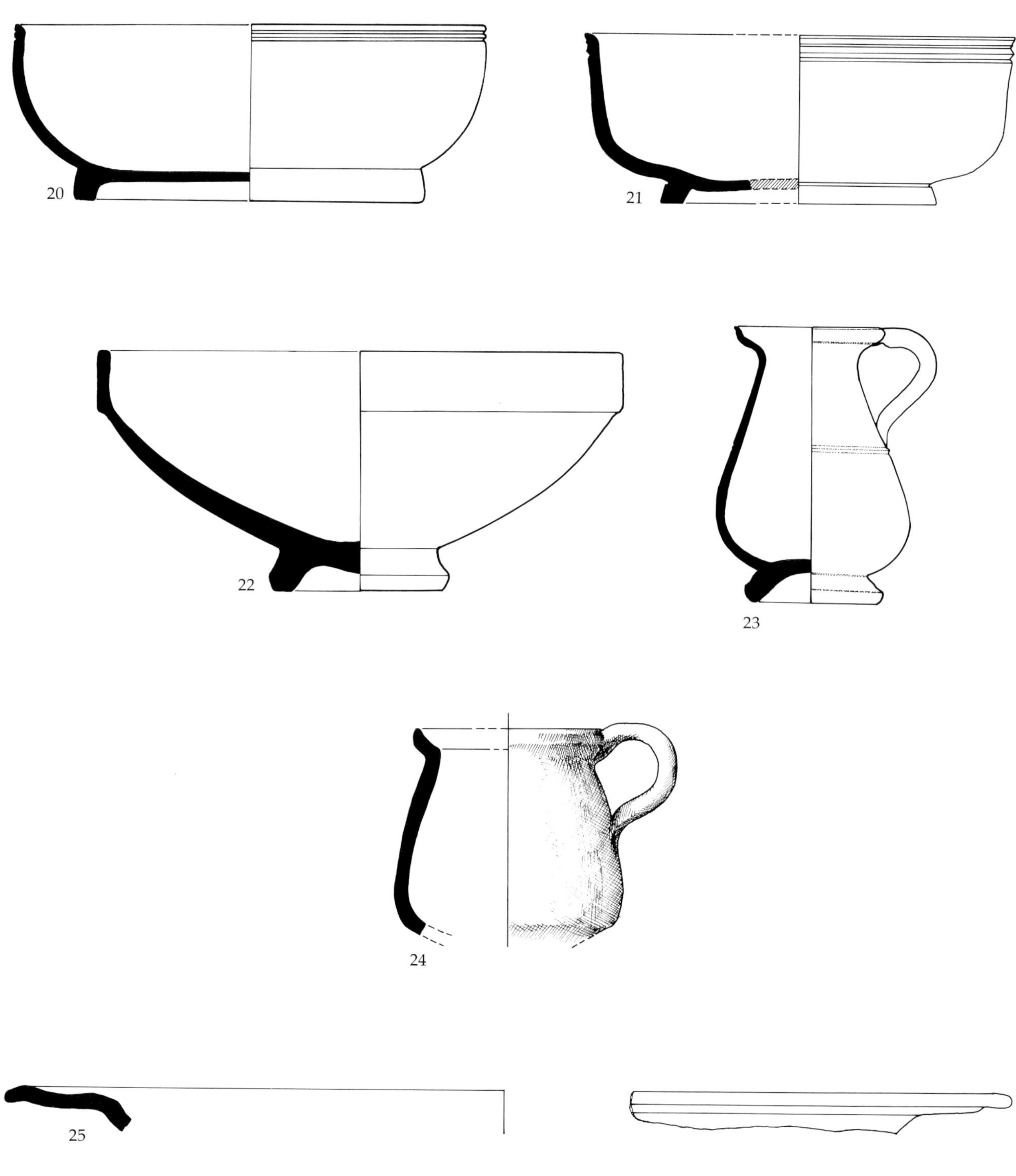

Plate 7. Black-Gloss Wares. Campanian A, B

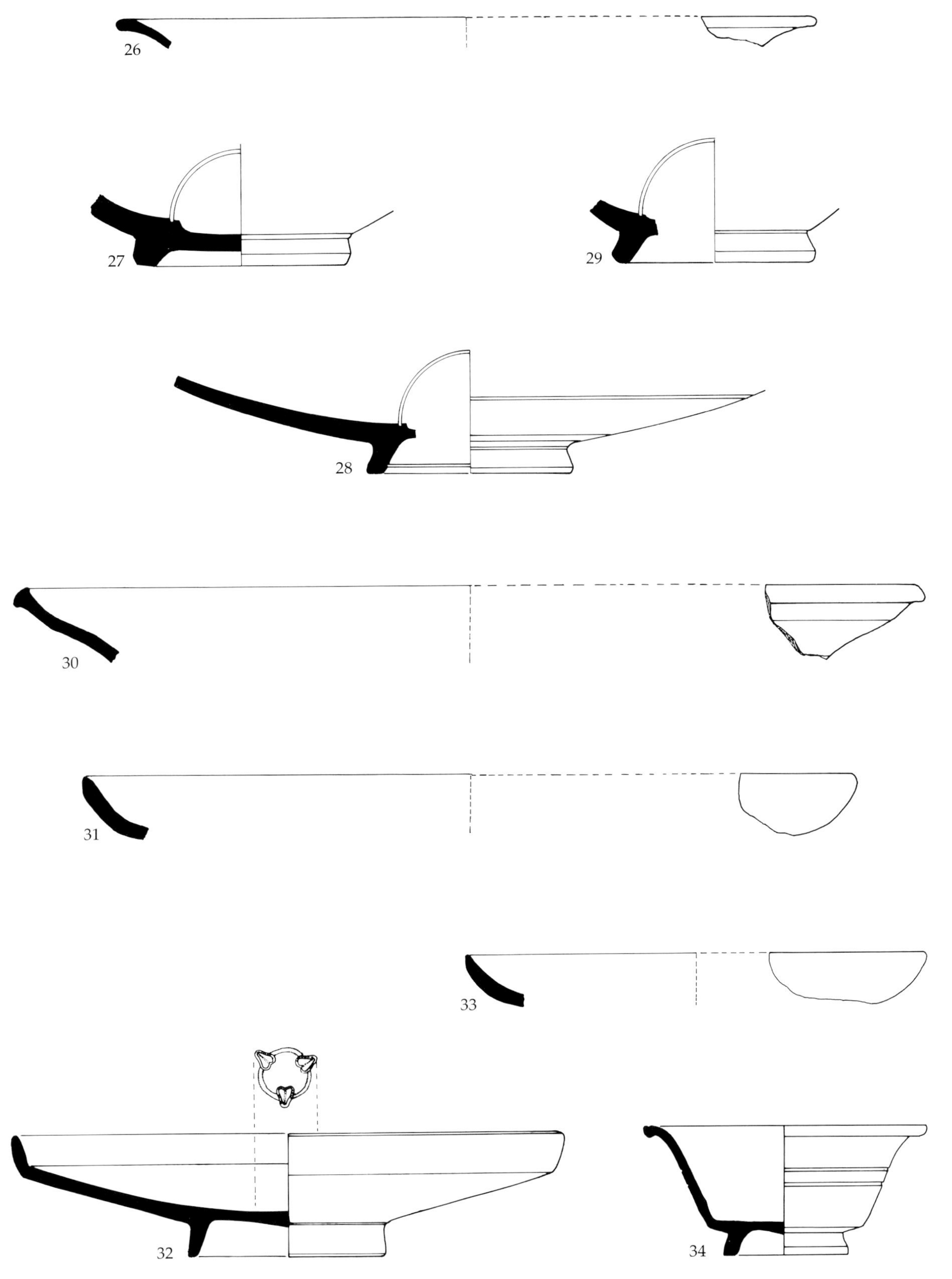

Plate 8. Black-Gloss Wares

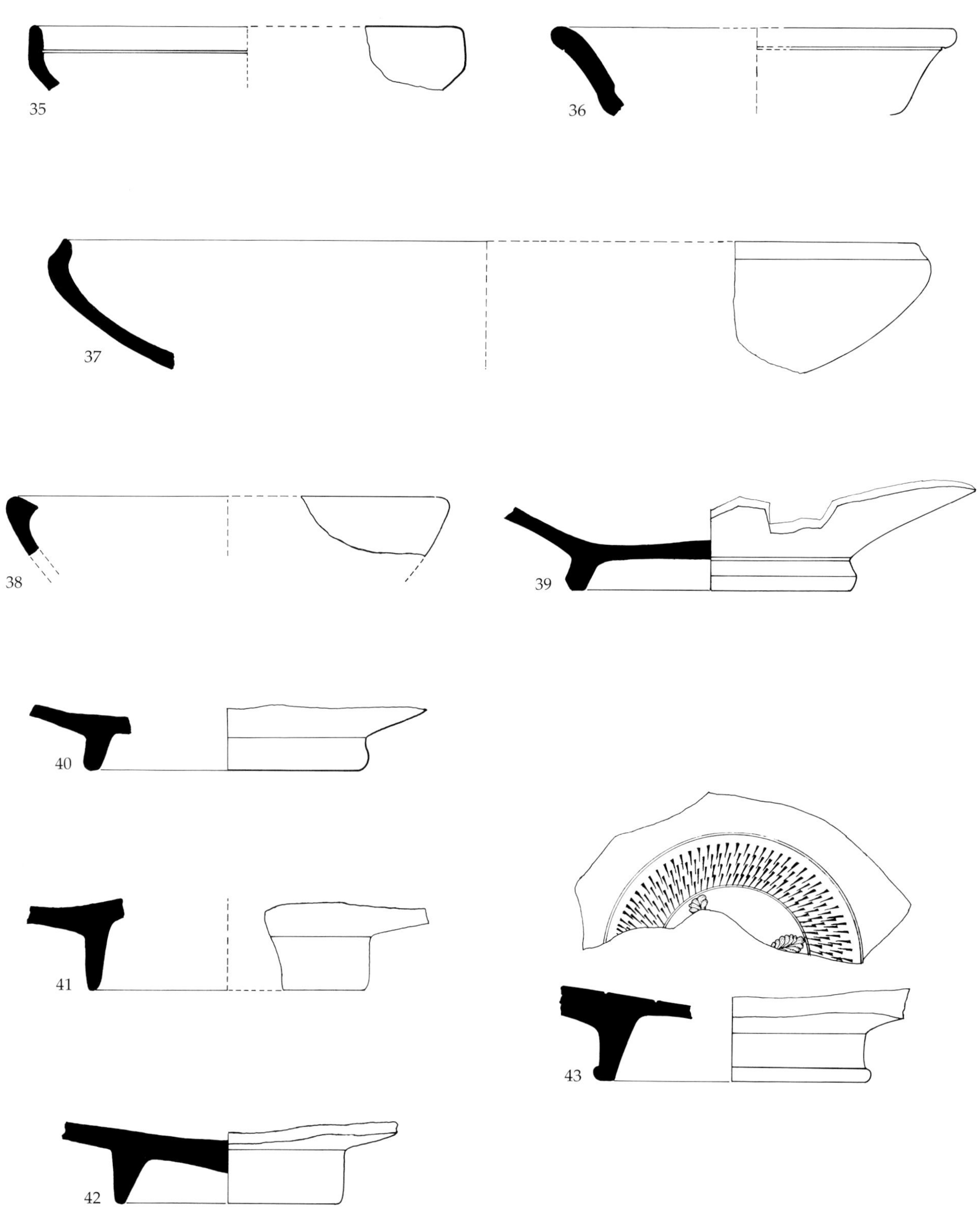

Plate 9. Black-Gloss Wares

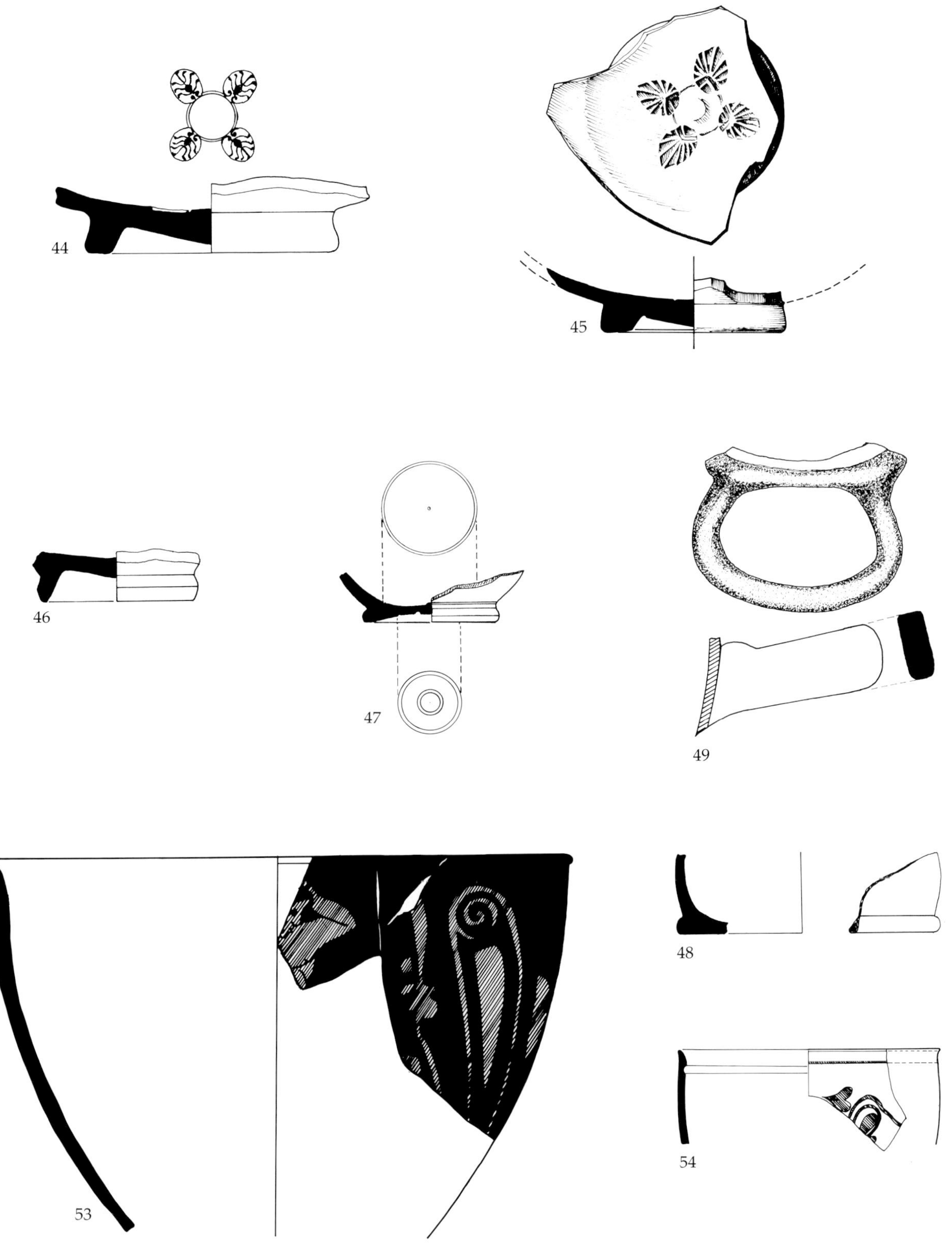

Plate 10. Black-Gloss Wares

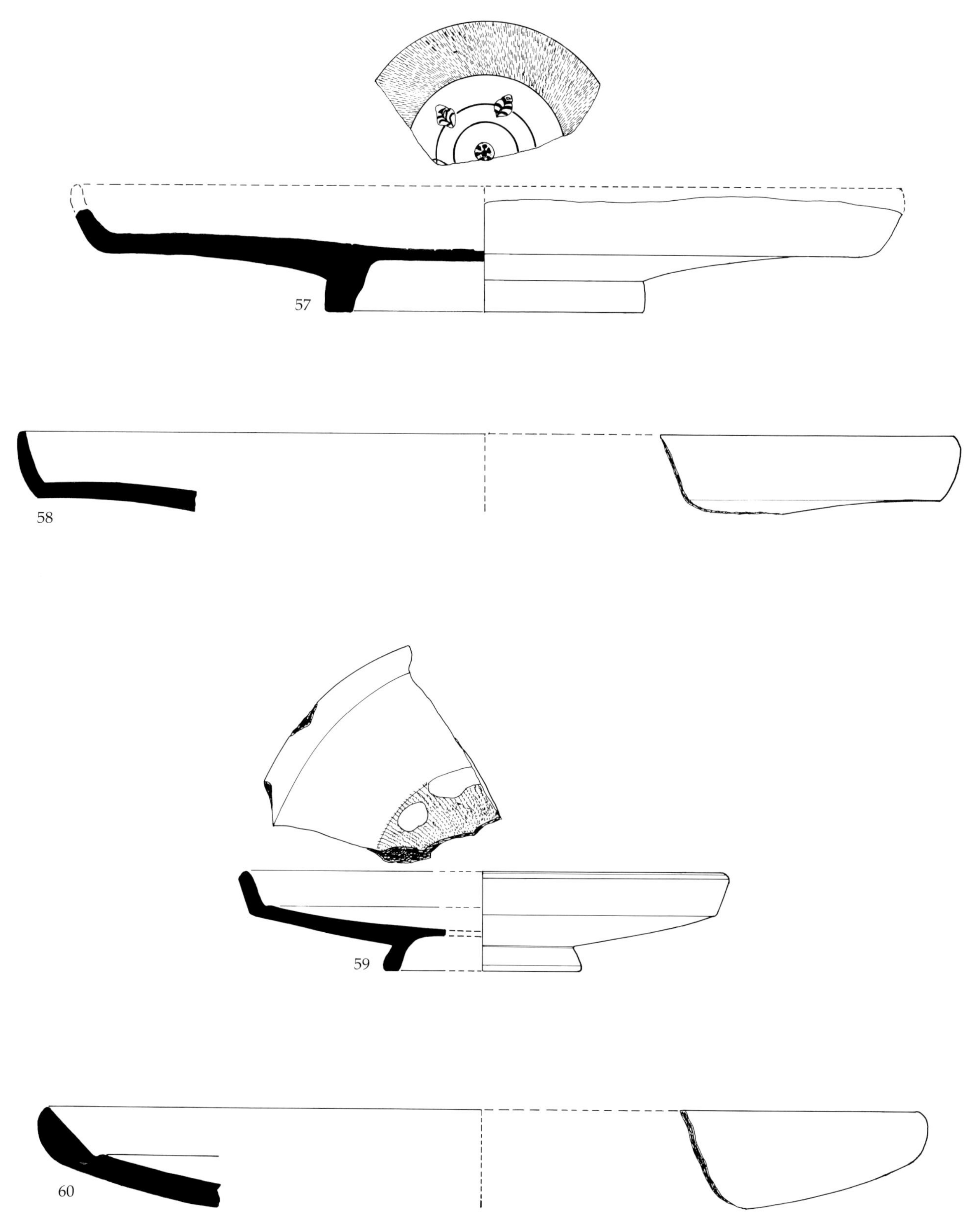

Plate 11. Black-Gloss Wares with Gray Fabric. Campanian C

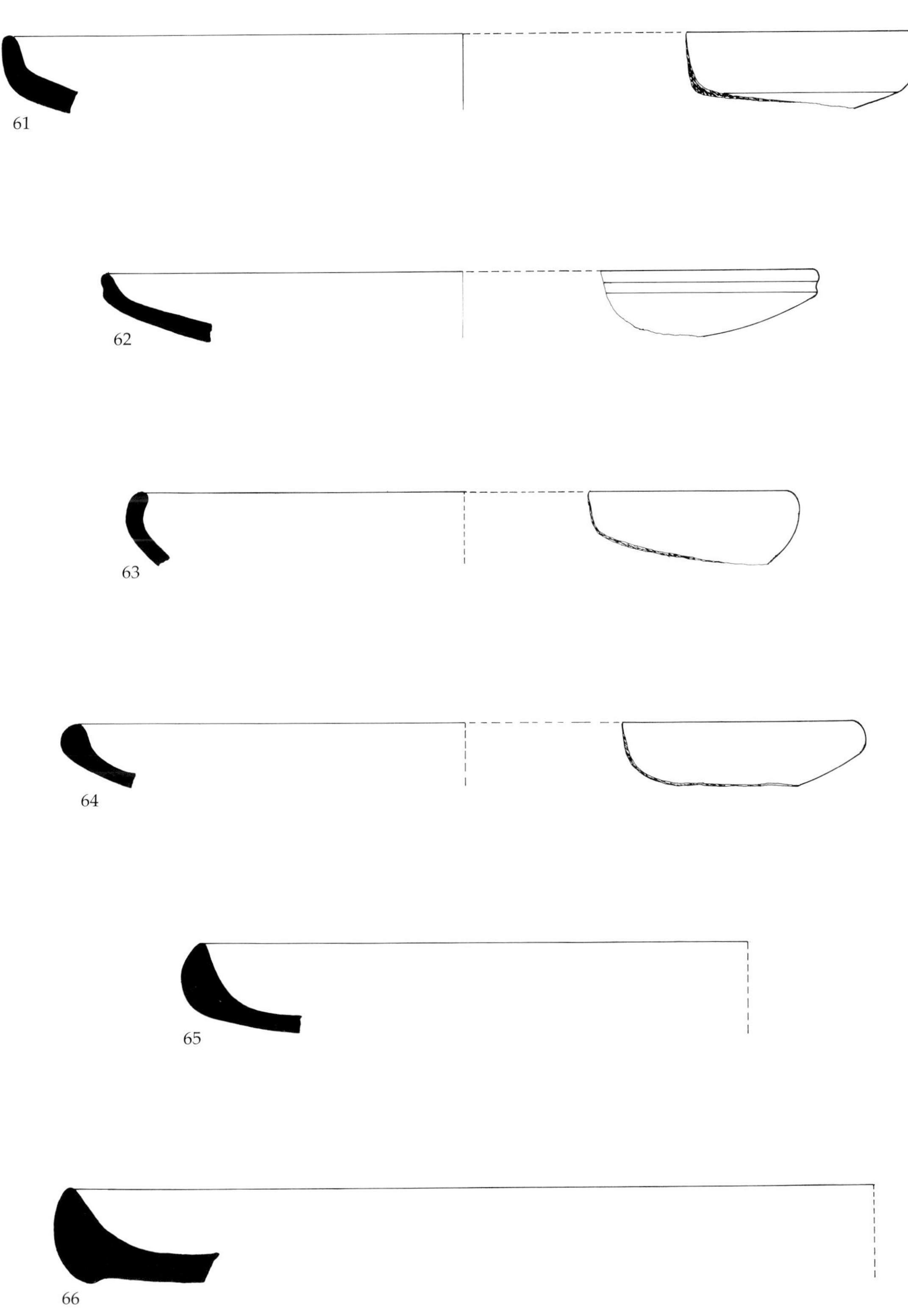

Plate 12. Black-Gloss Wares with Gray Fabric. Campanian C. Asia Minor Wares

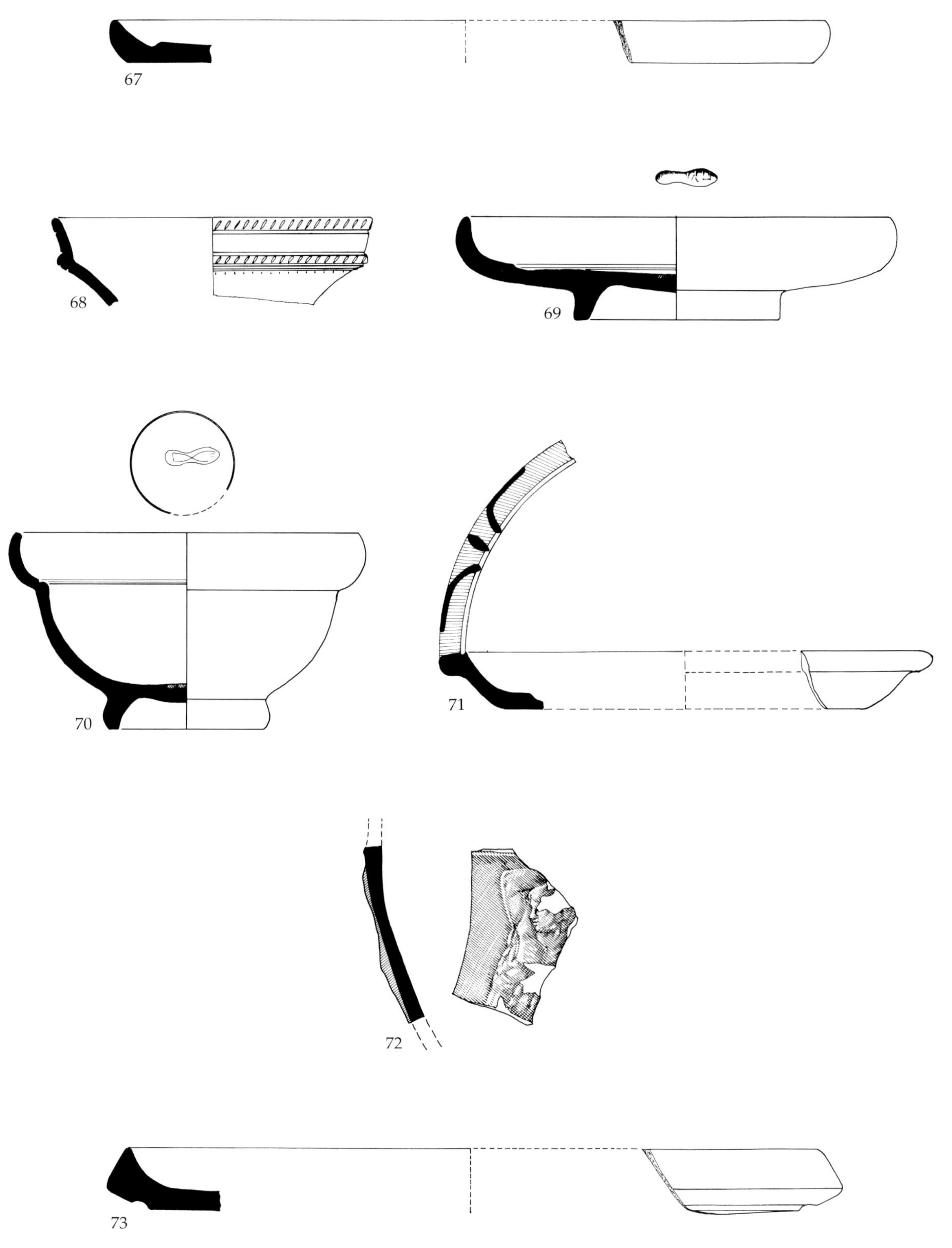

Plate 13. Black-Gloss Wares with Gray Fabric. Terra Sigillata Derivatives (67, 73, scale 1:3)

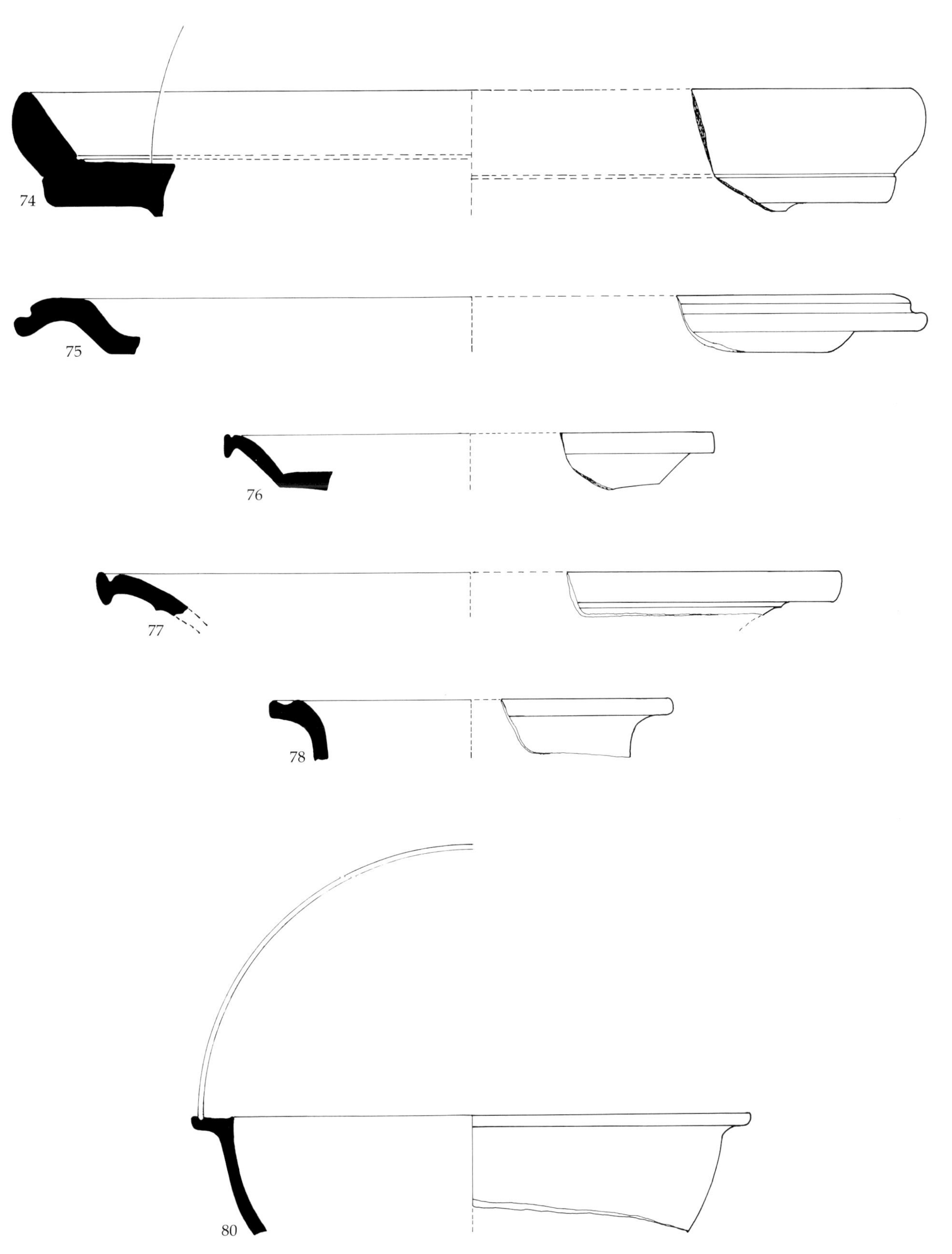

Plate 14. Black-Gloss Wares with Gray Fabric

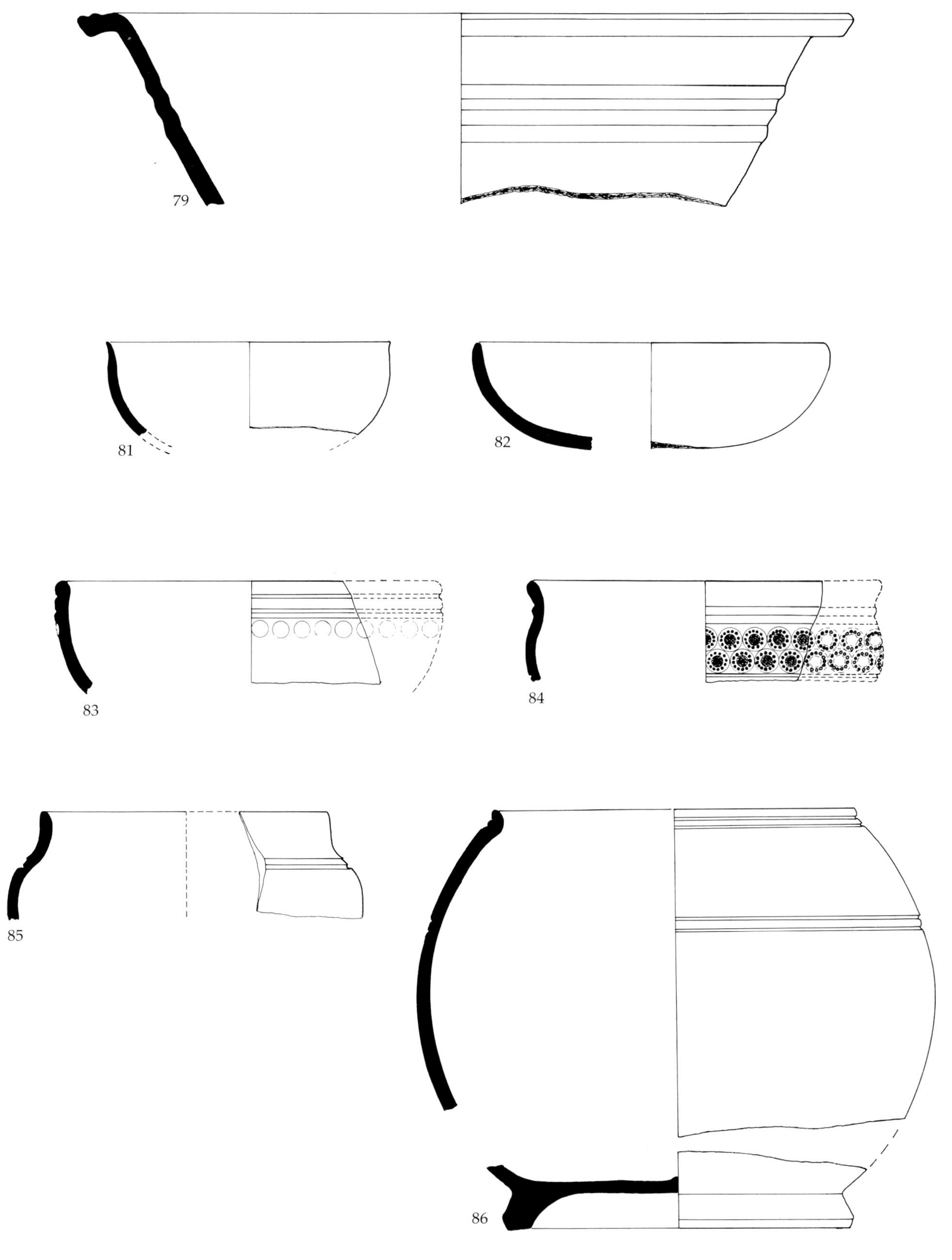

Plate 15. Black-Gloss Wares with Gray Fabric

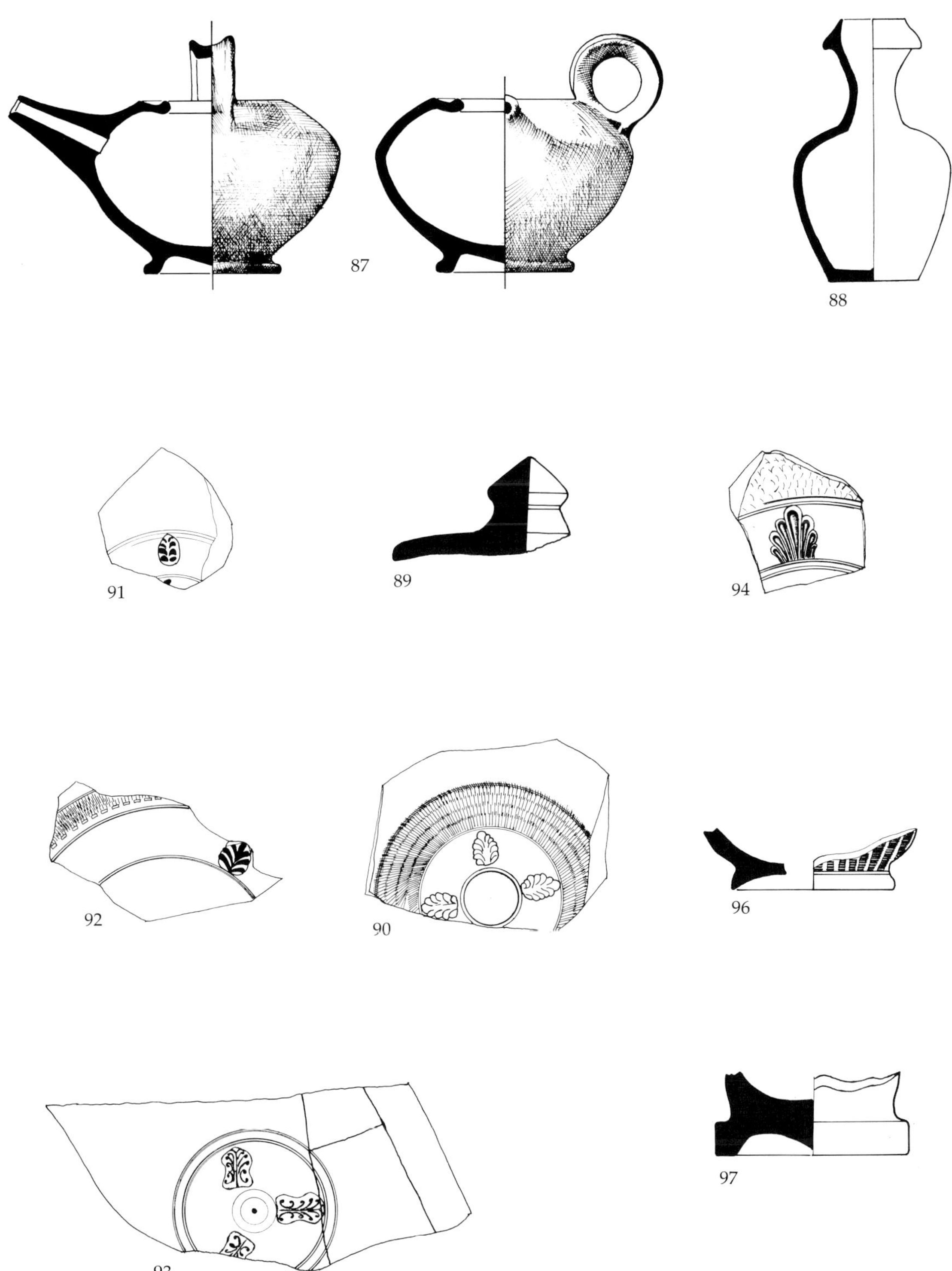

Plate 16. Black-Gloss Wares with Gray Fabric

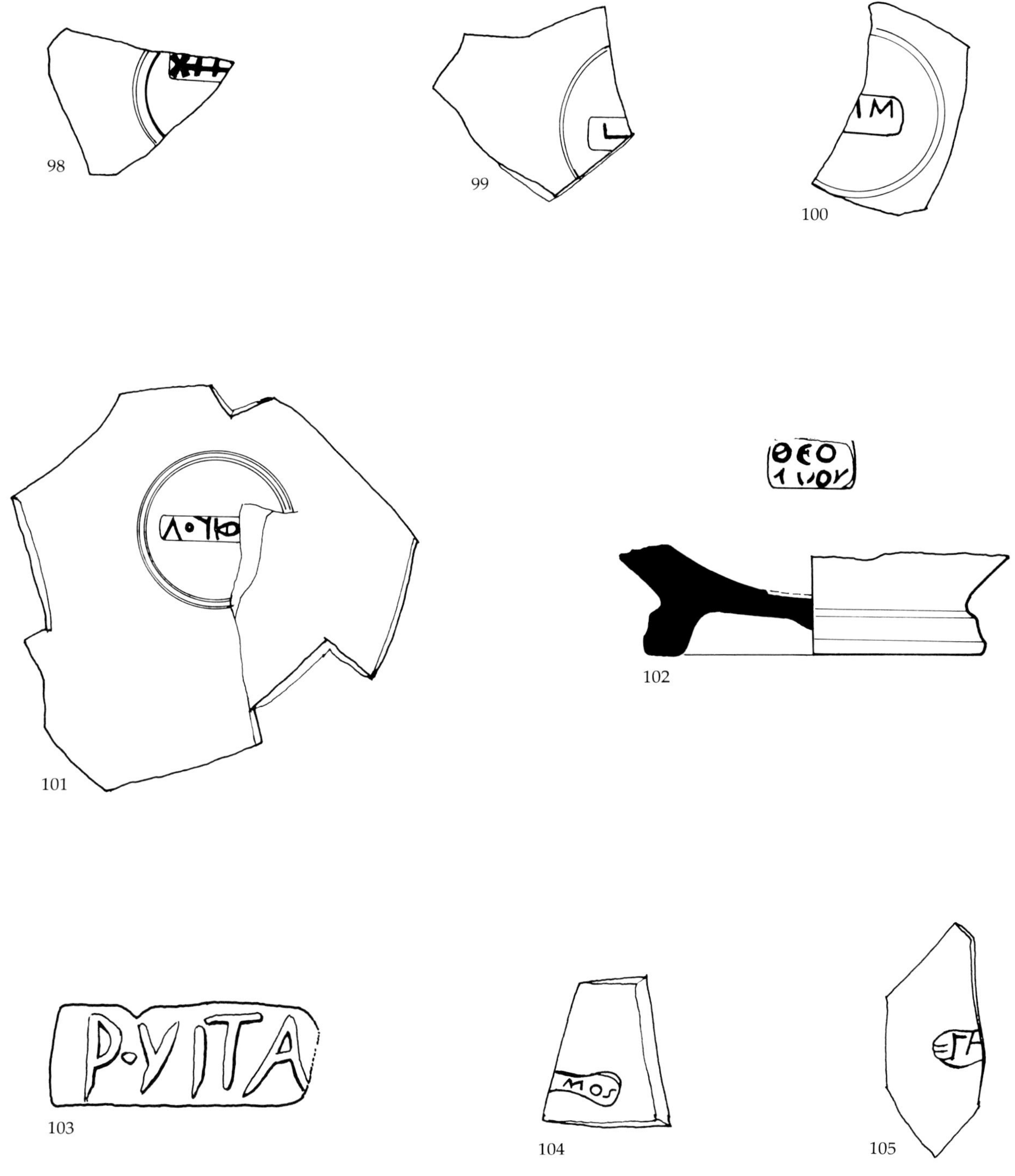

Plate 17. (scale 1:1) Black-Gloss Wares with Gray Fabric. Stamps

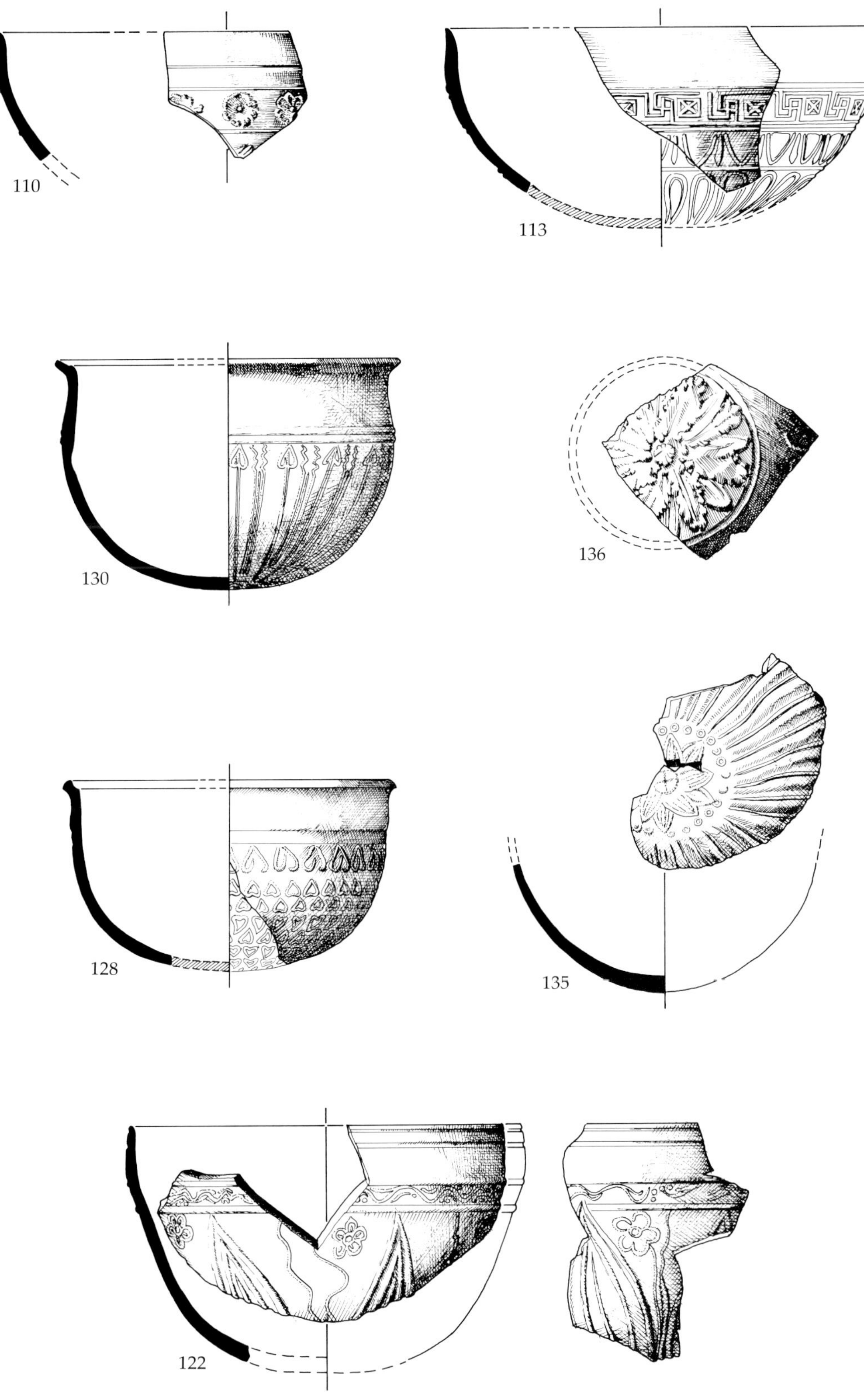

Plate 18. Hellenistic Moulded Relief Bowls

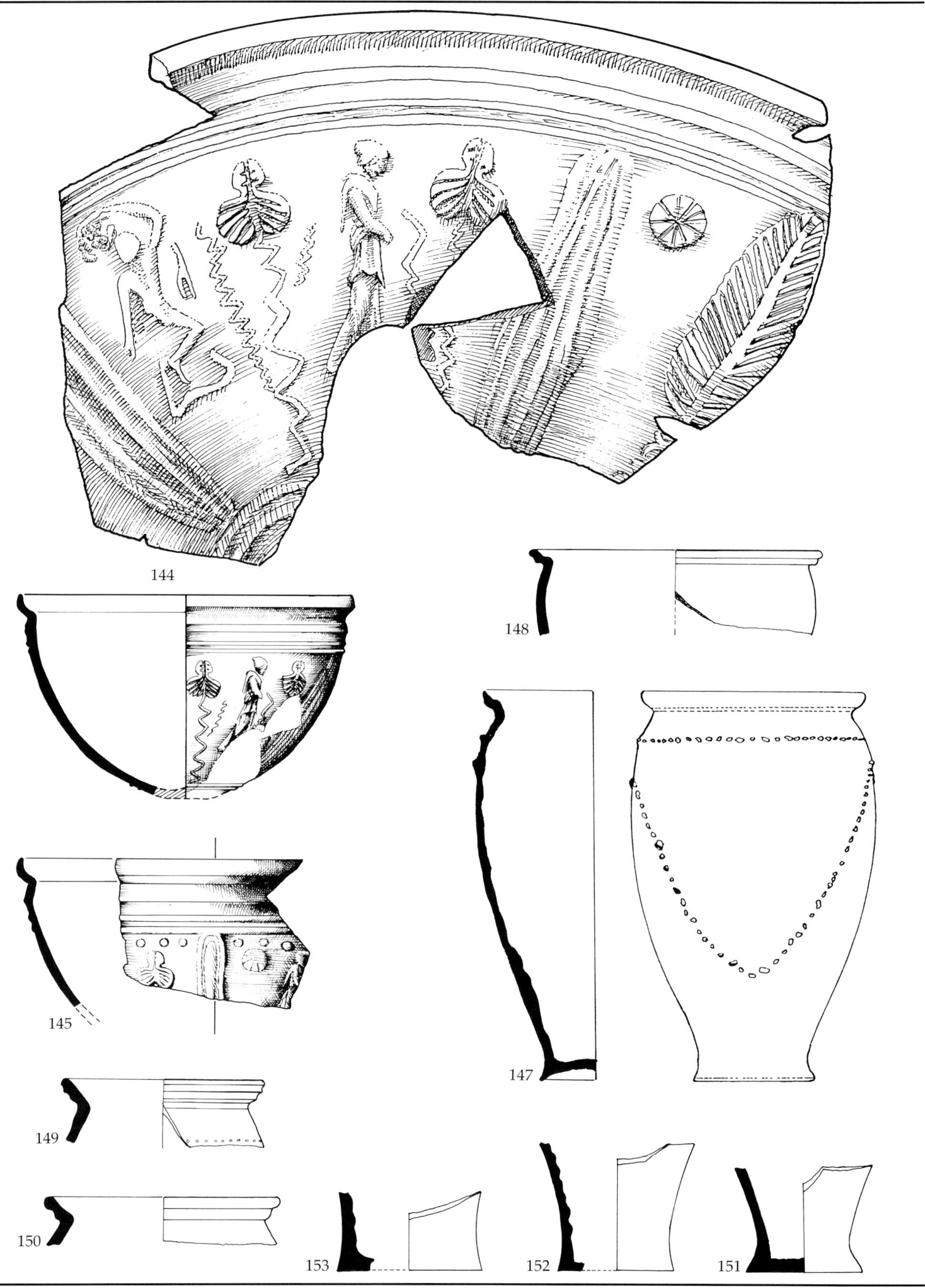

Plate 19. Hellenistic Moulded Relief Bowls, Local series. Thin-Walled beakers, Group I (144 top, scale 3:2)

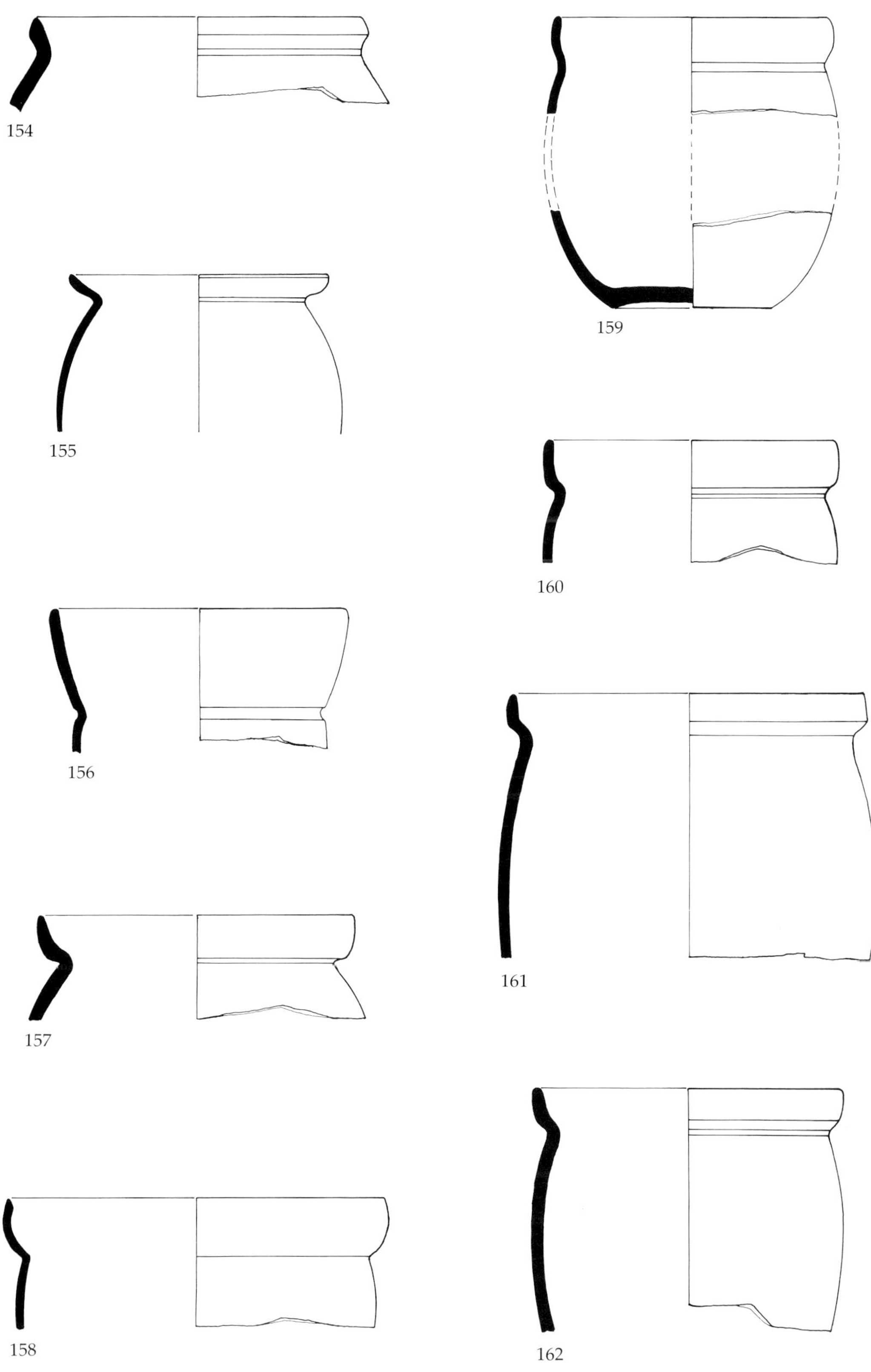

Plate 20. Thin-Walled Ware. Beakers and Jars, Group I

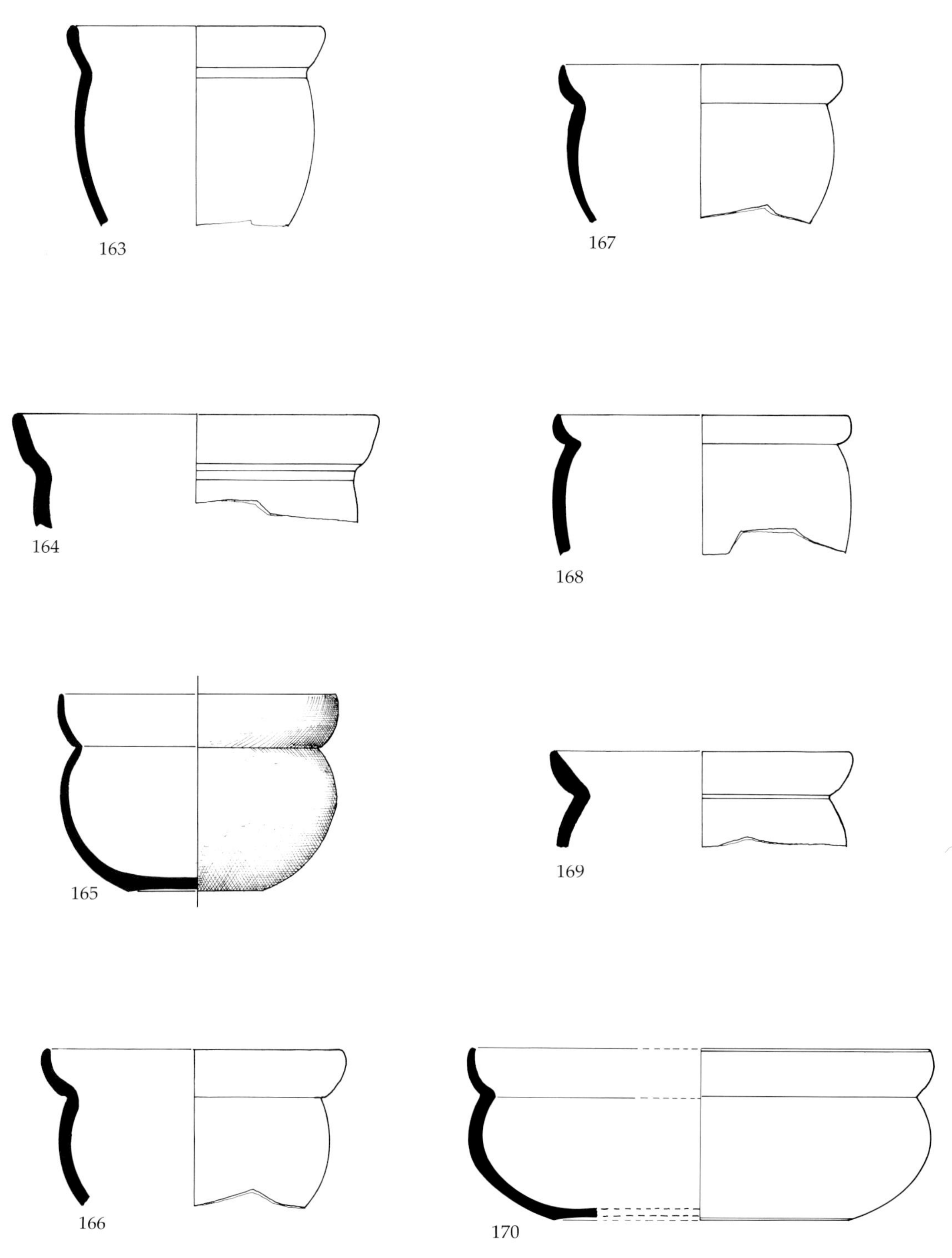

Plate 21. Thin-Walled Ware. Jars, Group I

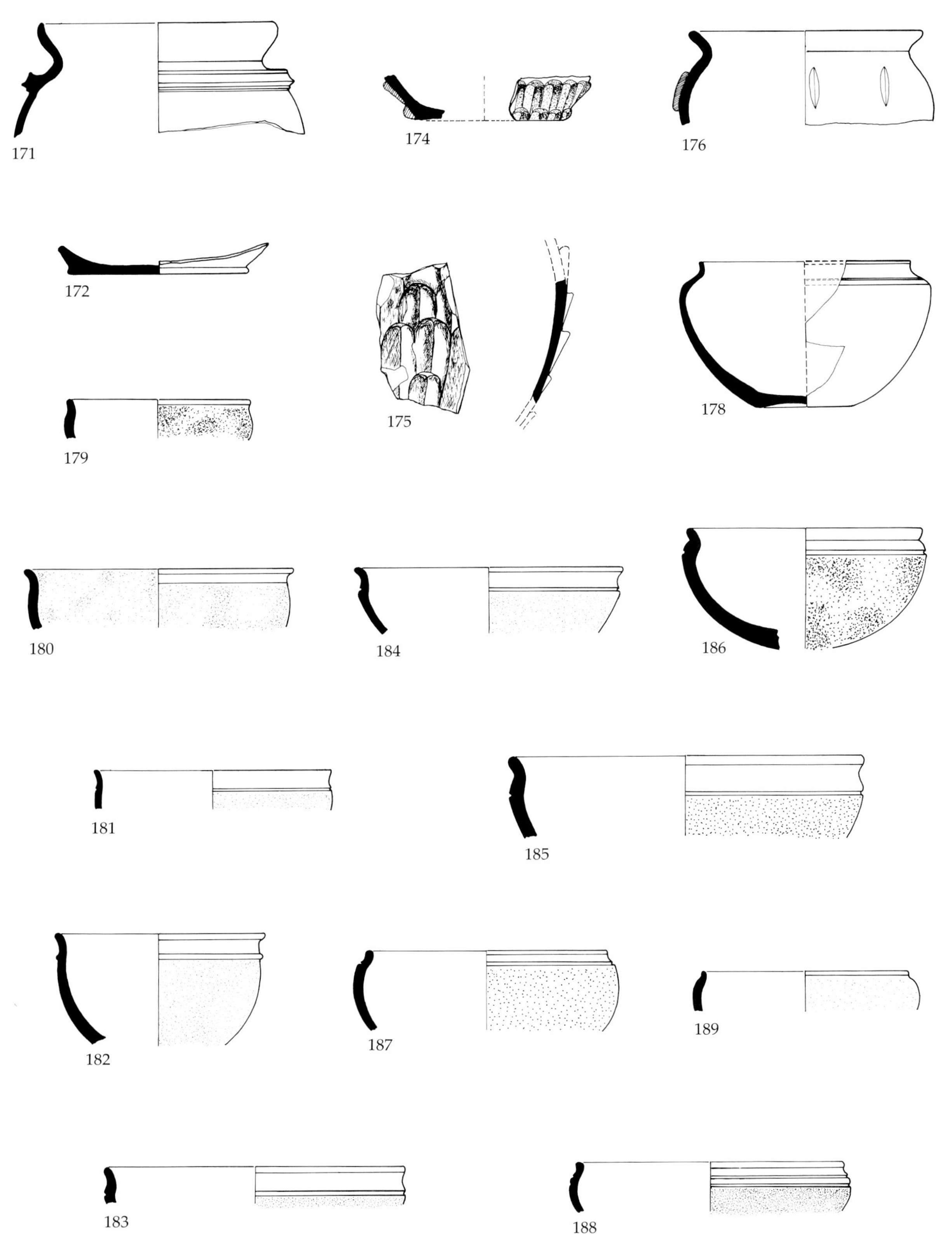

Plate 22. Thin-Walled Ware, Groups I, III, and IV

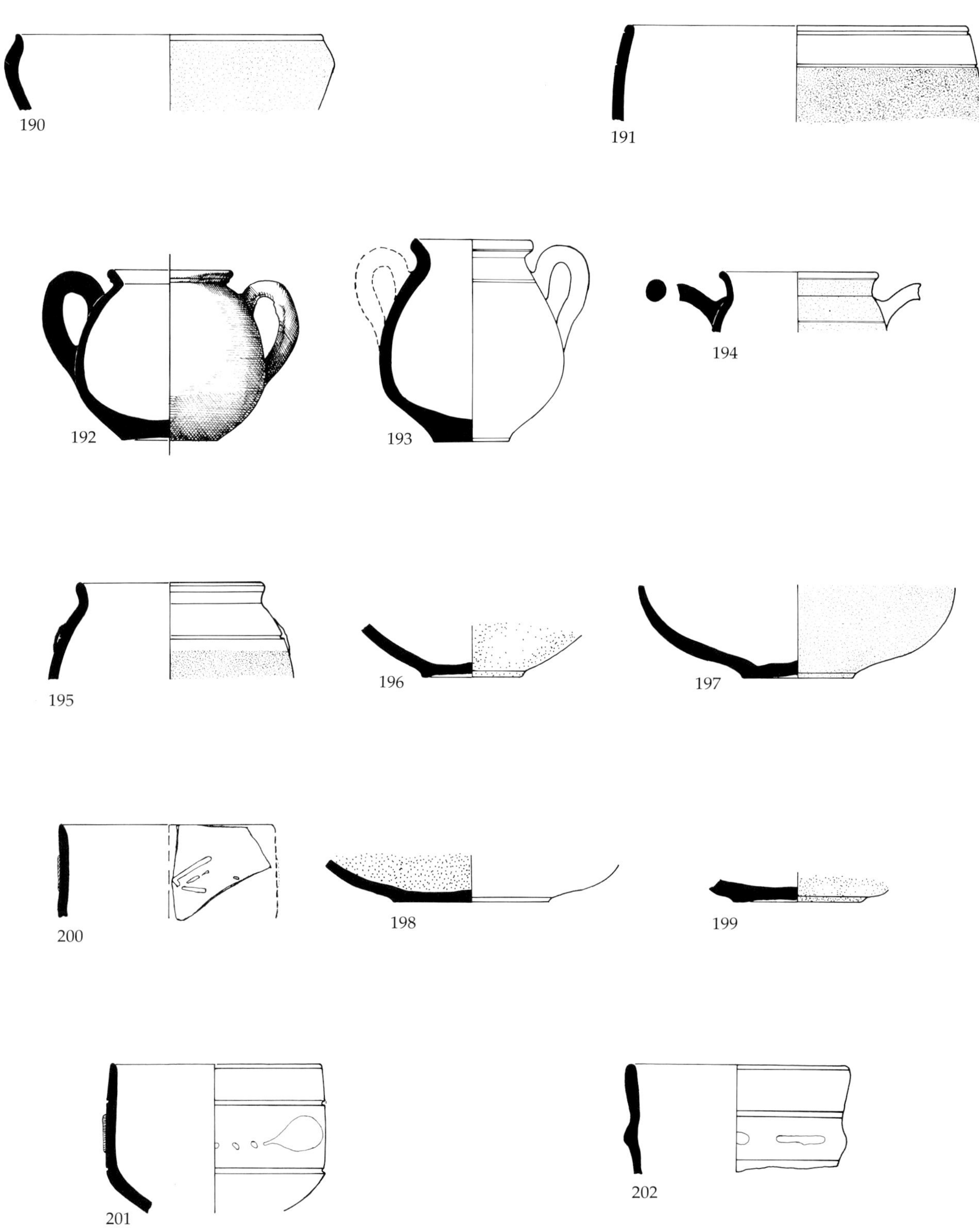

Plate 23. Thin-Walled Ware with Sanded and Barbotine decoration, Groups IV and V

Plate 24. Thin-Walled Ware with Barbotine decoration, Groups V and VI

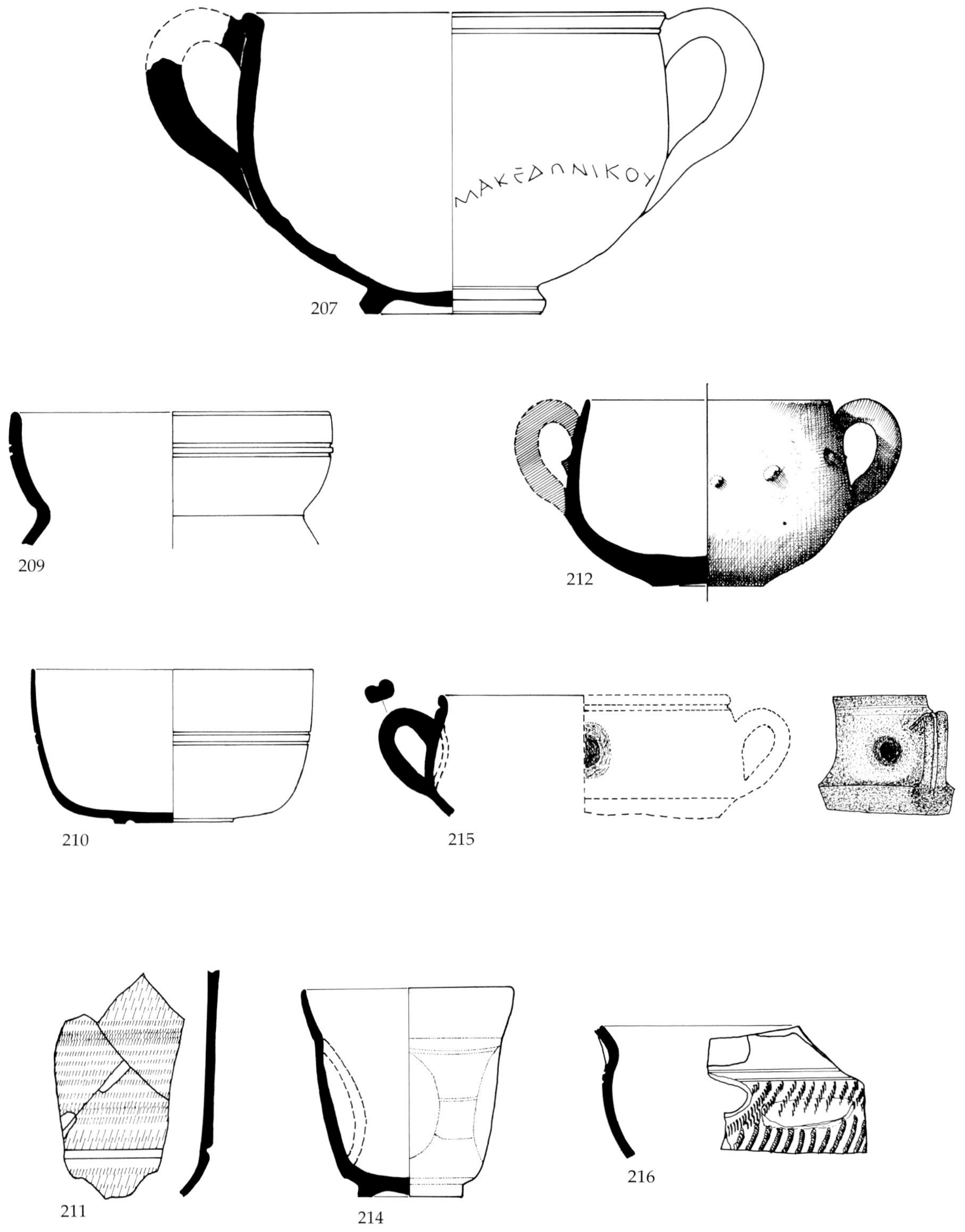

Plate 25. Thin-Walled Ware, Group VI and others

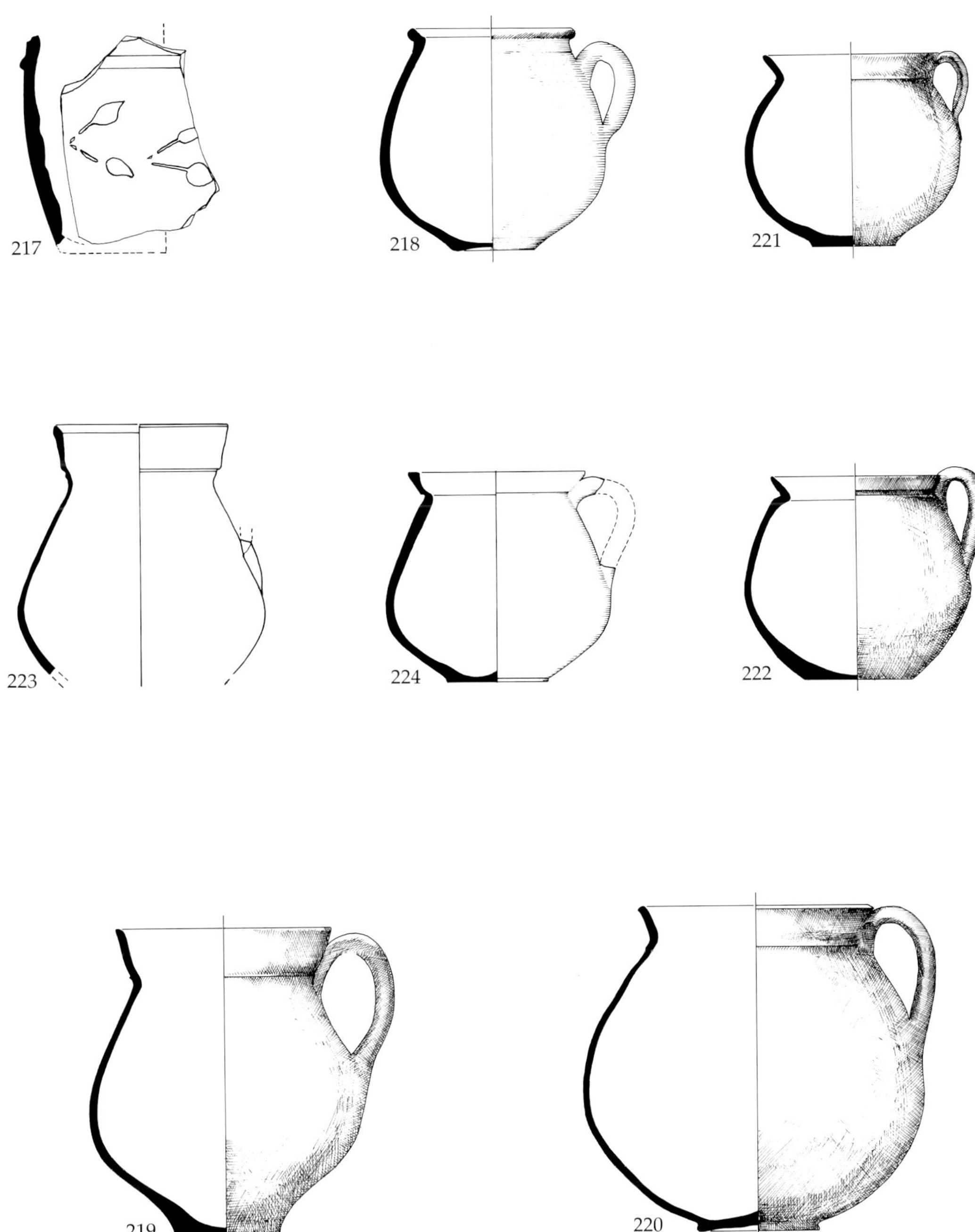

Plate 26. (scale 1:3) Thin-Walled Ware, Pitchers

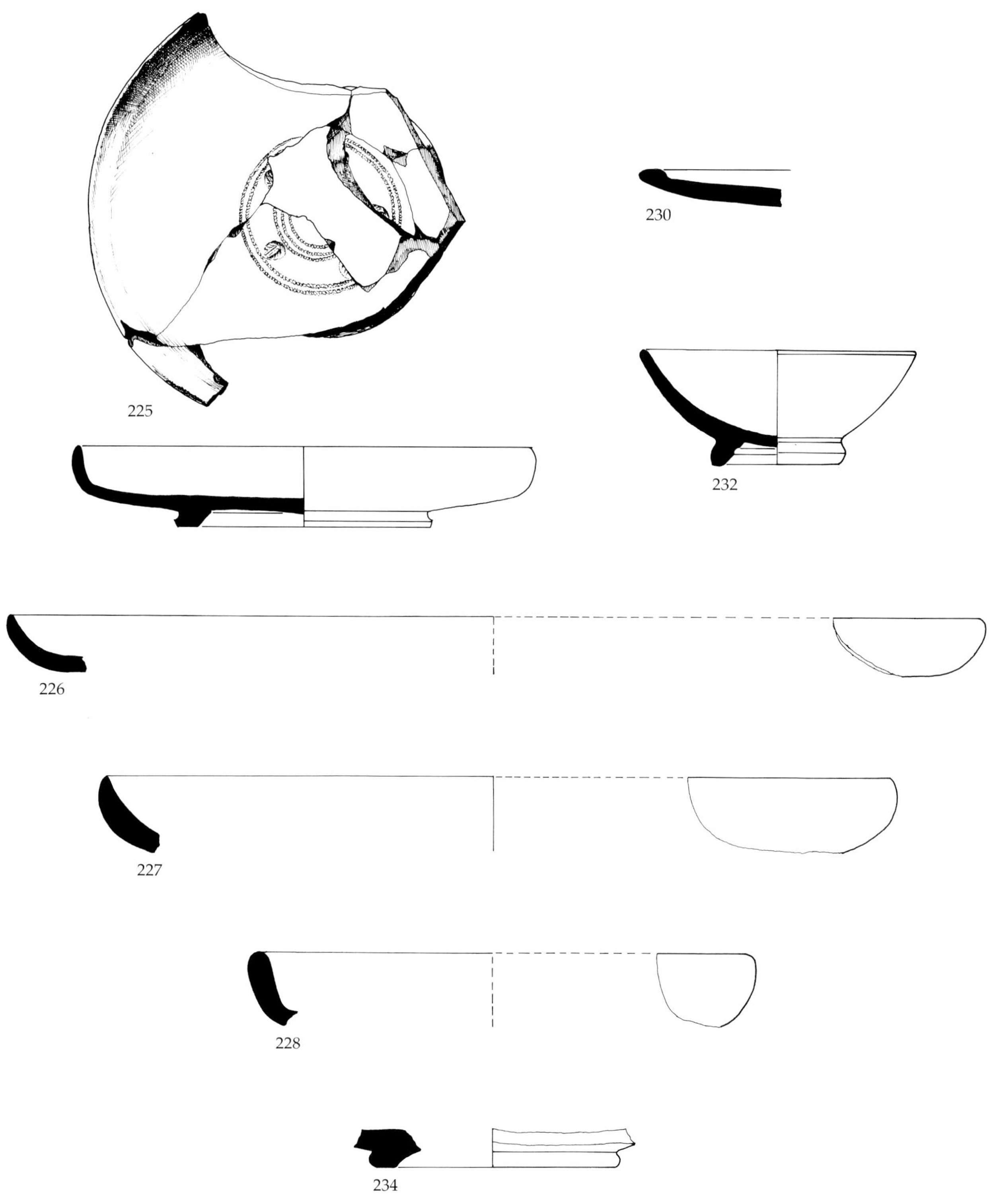

Plate 27. Eastern Sigillata A

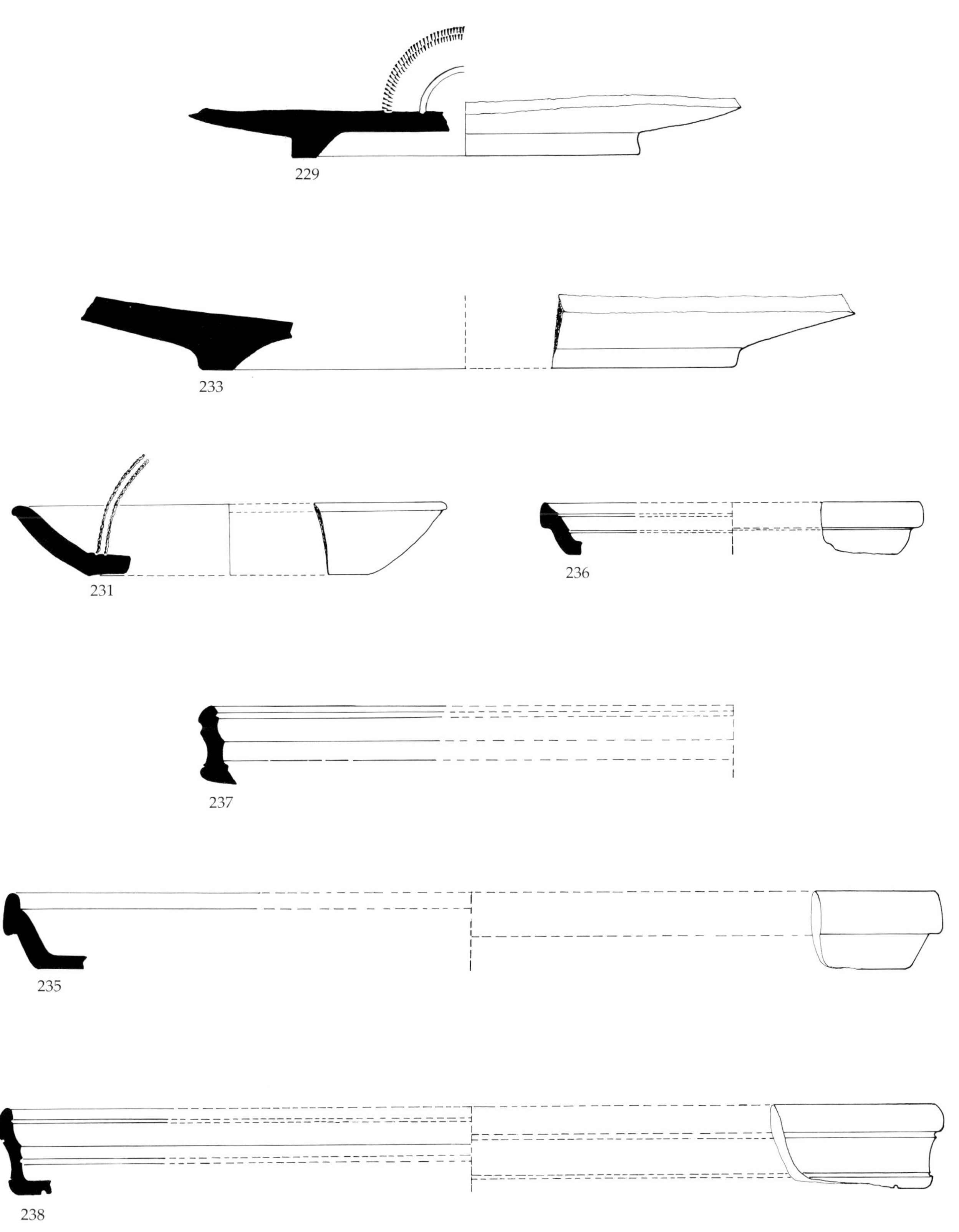

Plate 28. Eastern Sigillata A and Italian Sigillata

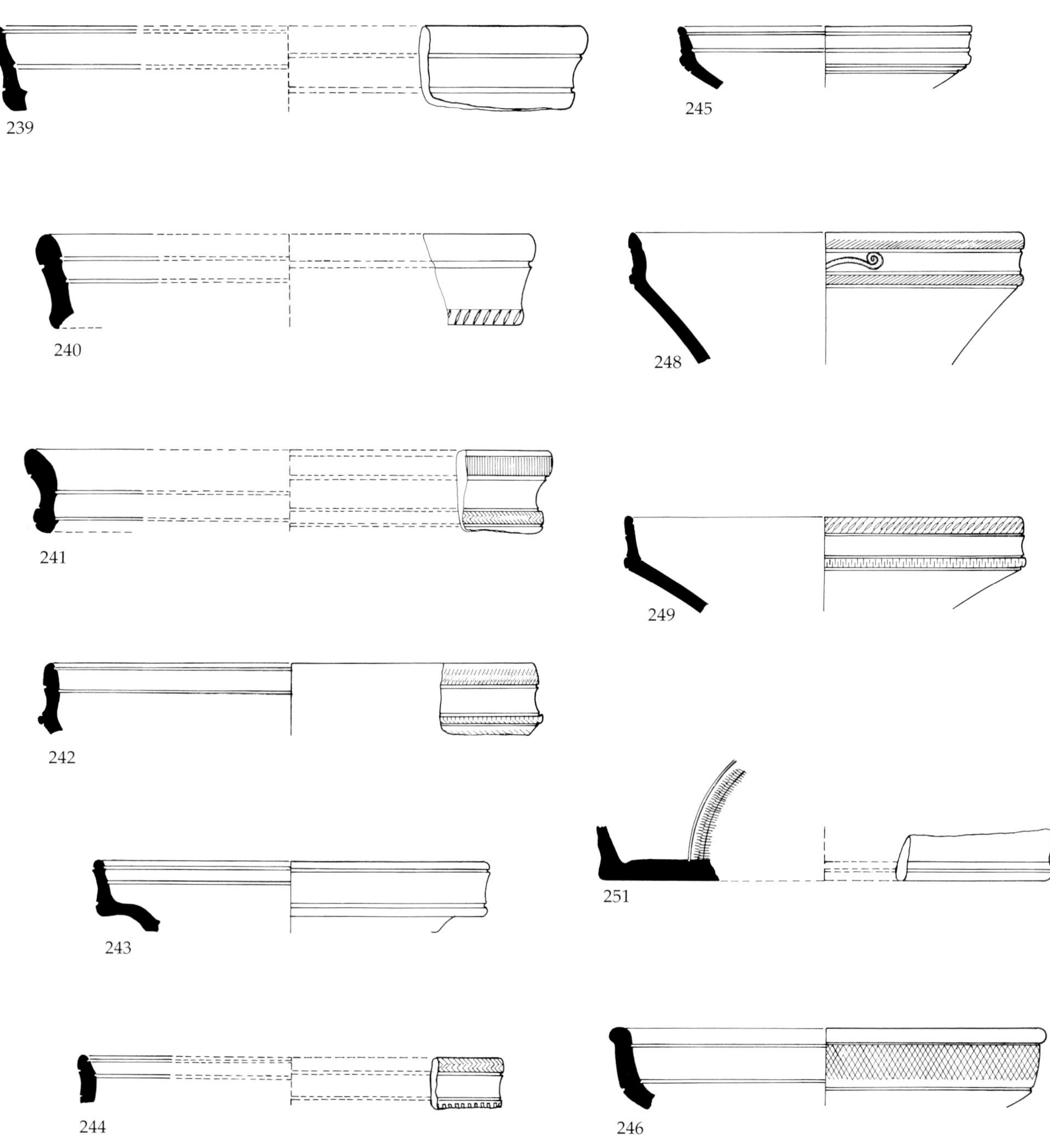

Plate 29. Italian Sigillata

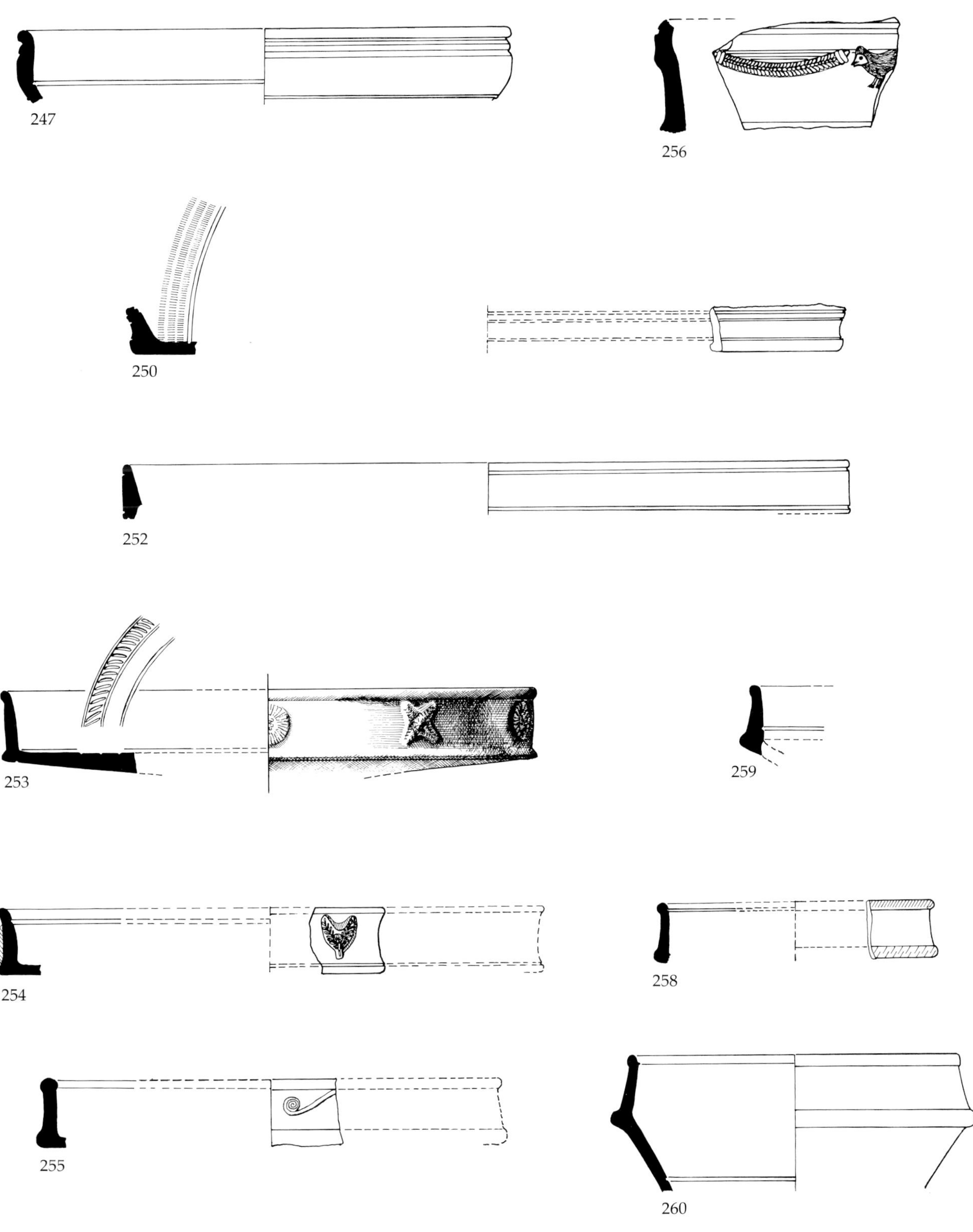

Plate 30. Italian Sigillata

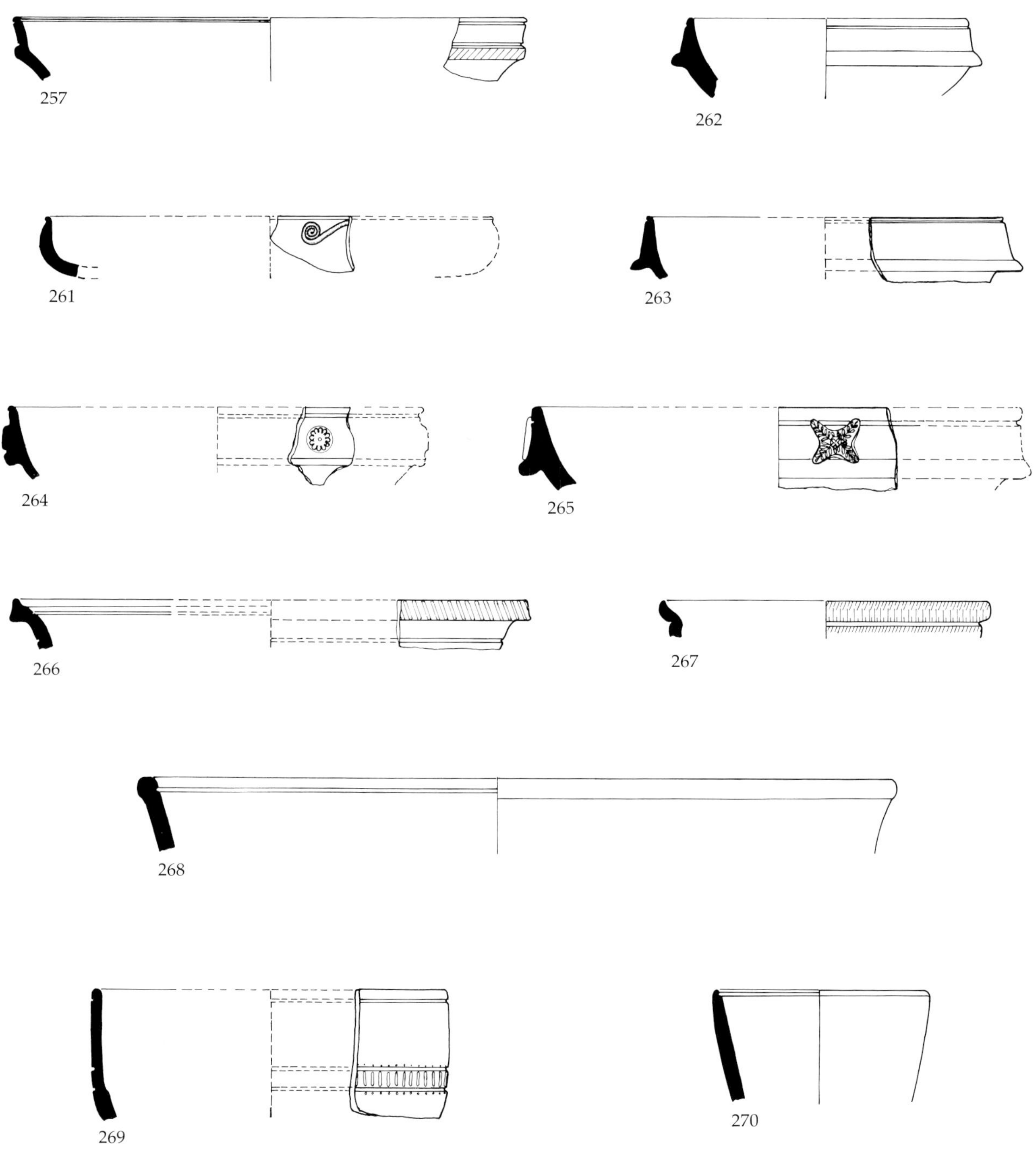

Plate 31. Italian Sigillata

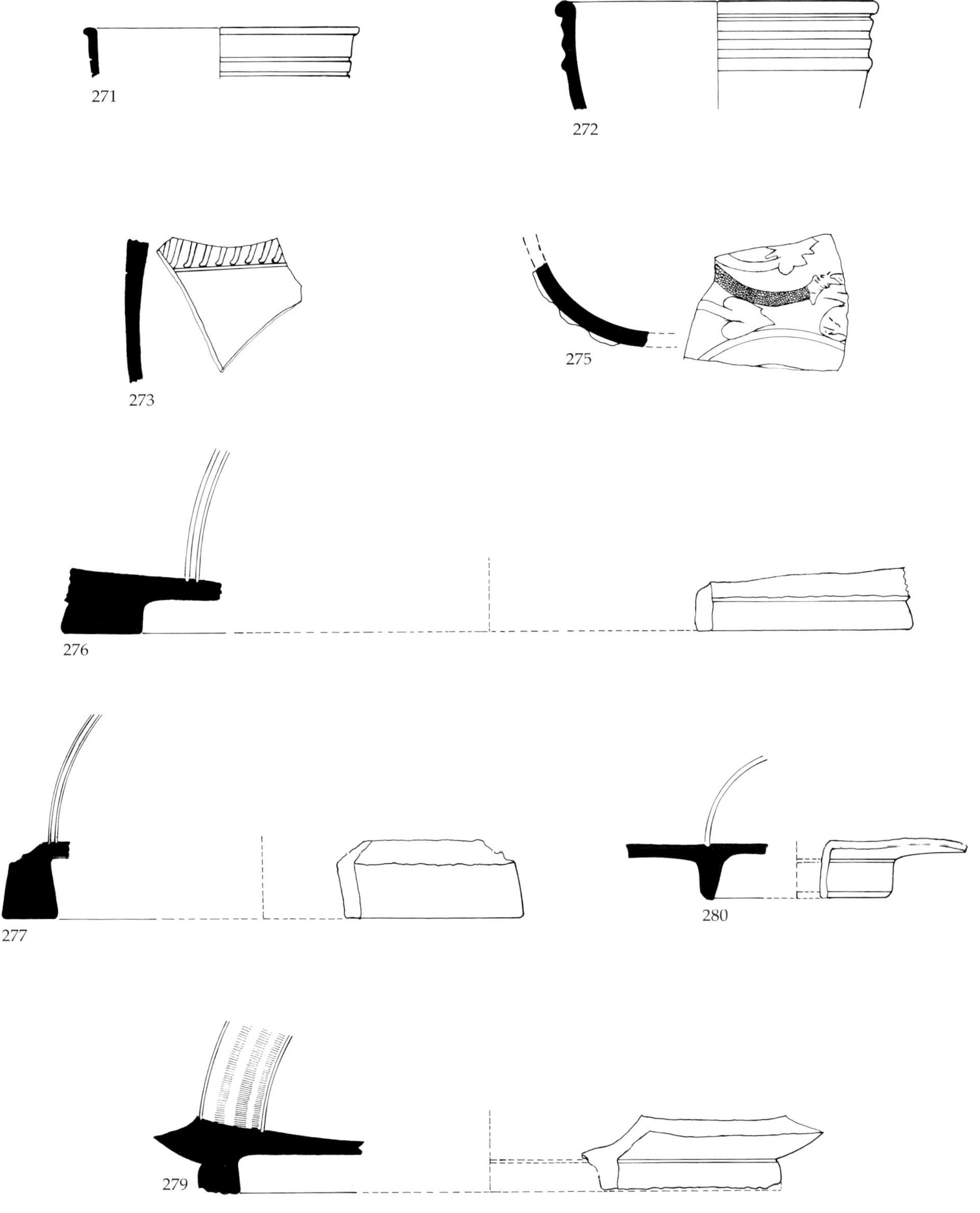

Plate 32. Italian Sigillata

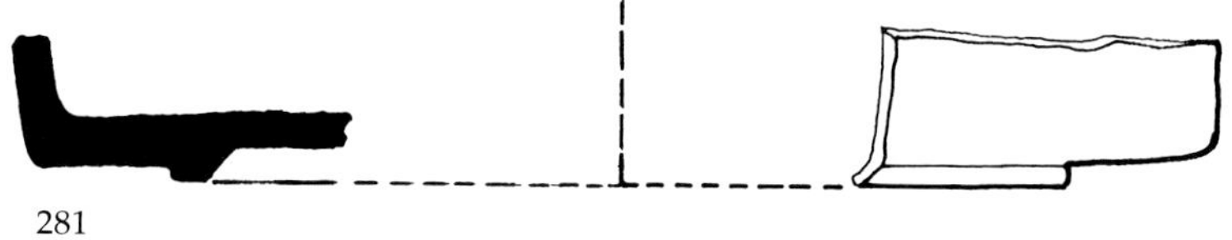
281

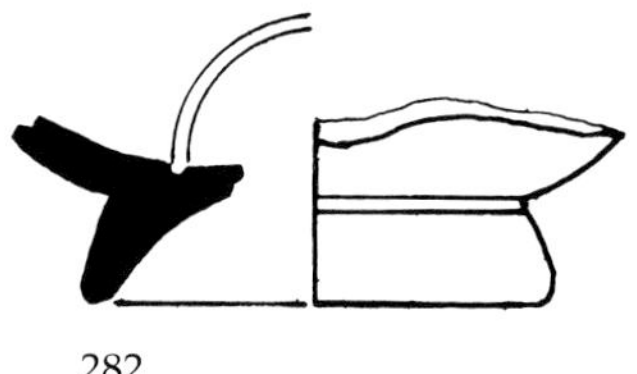
282

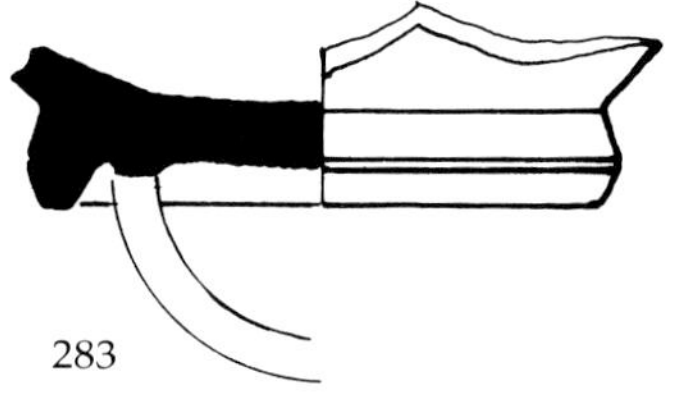
283

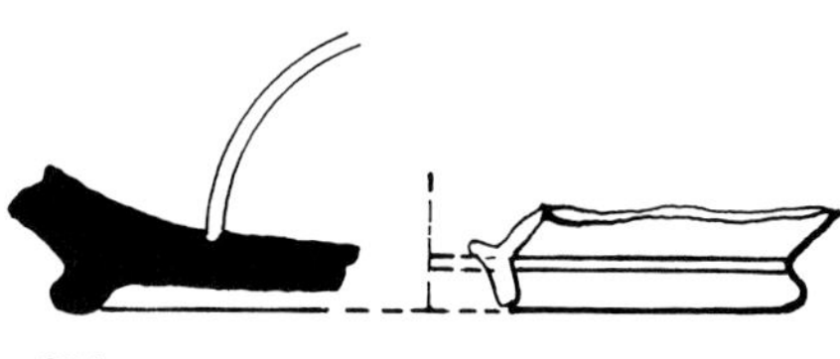
284

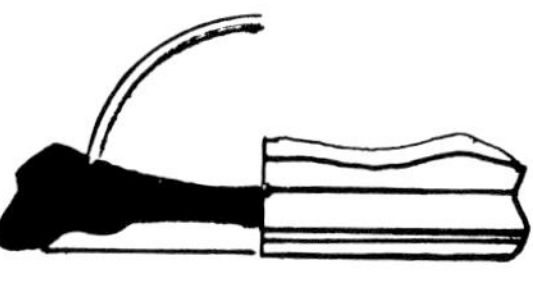
285

Plate 33. (scale 1:1) Italian Sigillata bases

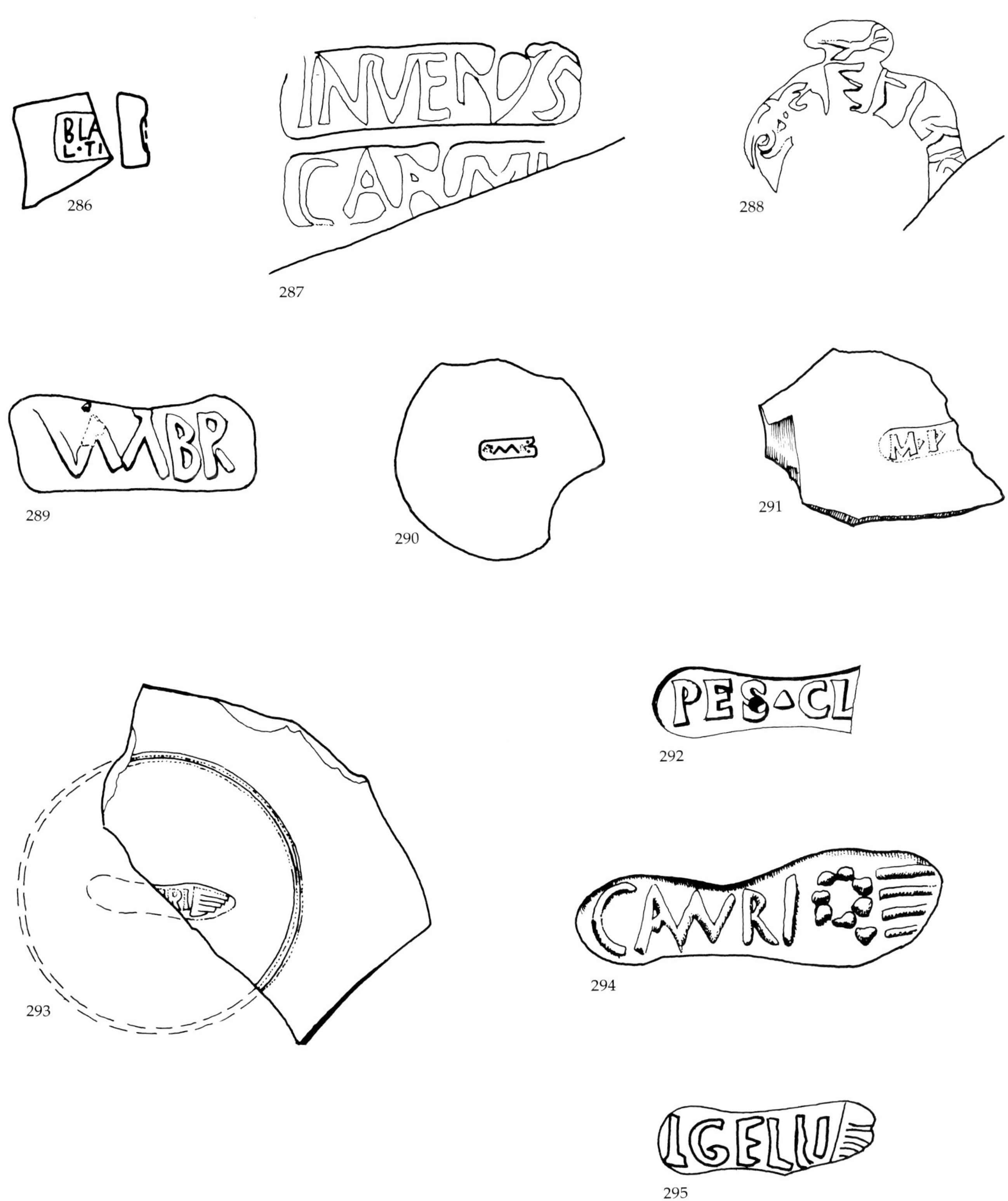

Plate 34. (scale 1:1) Italian Sigillata stamps (287, 288, 289, 292, 294, 295, scale 2:1)

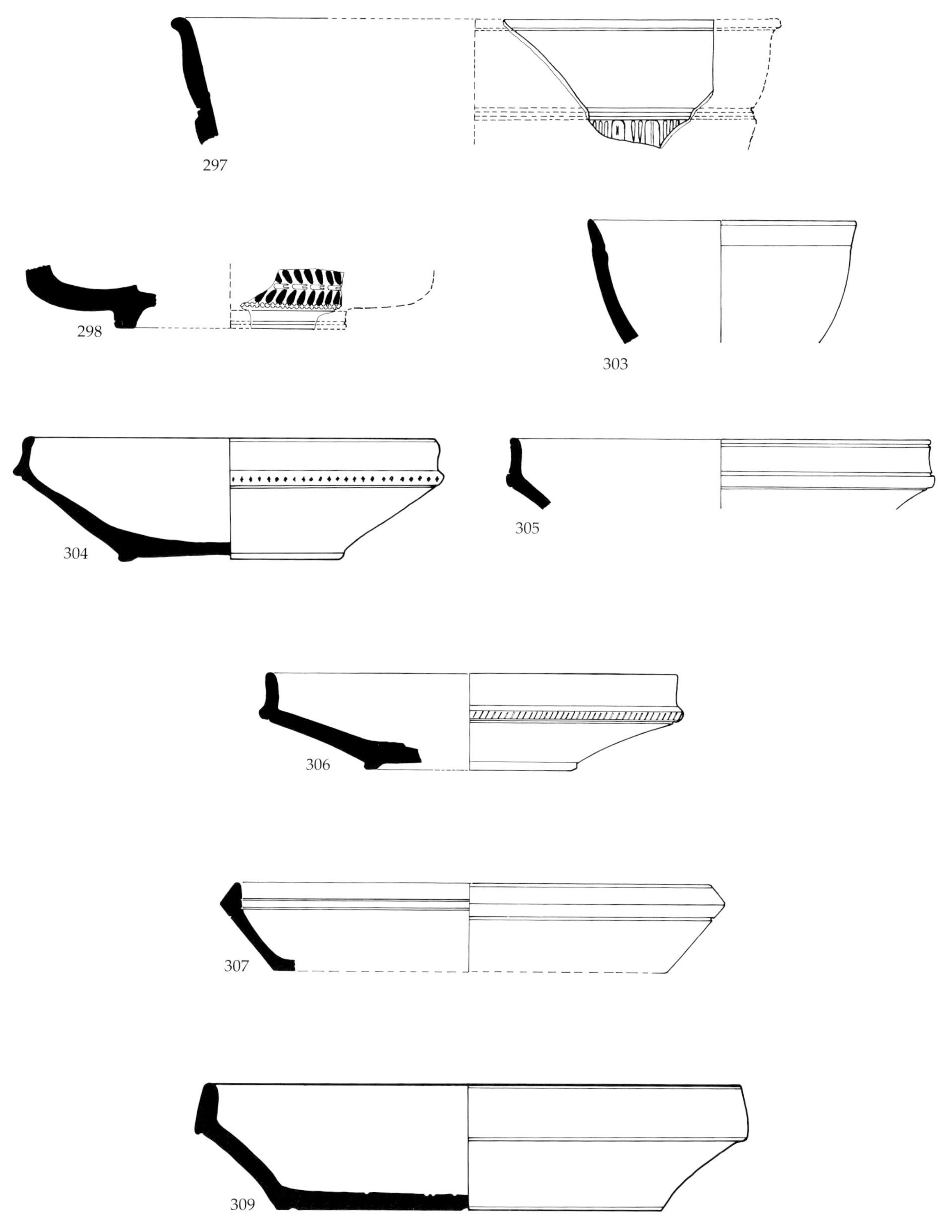

Plate 35. Other Western Sigillata and Eastern Sigillata B

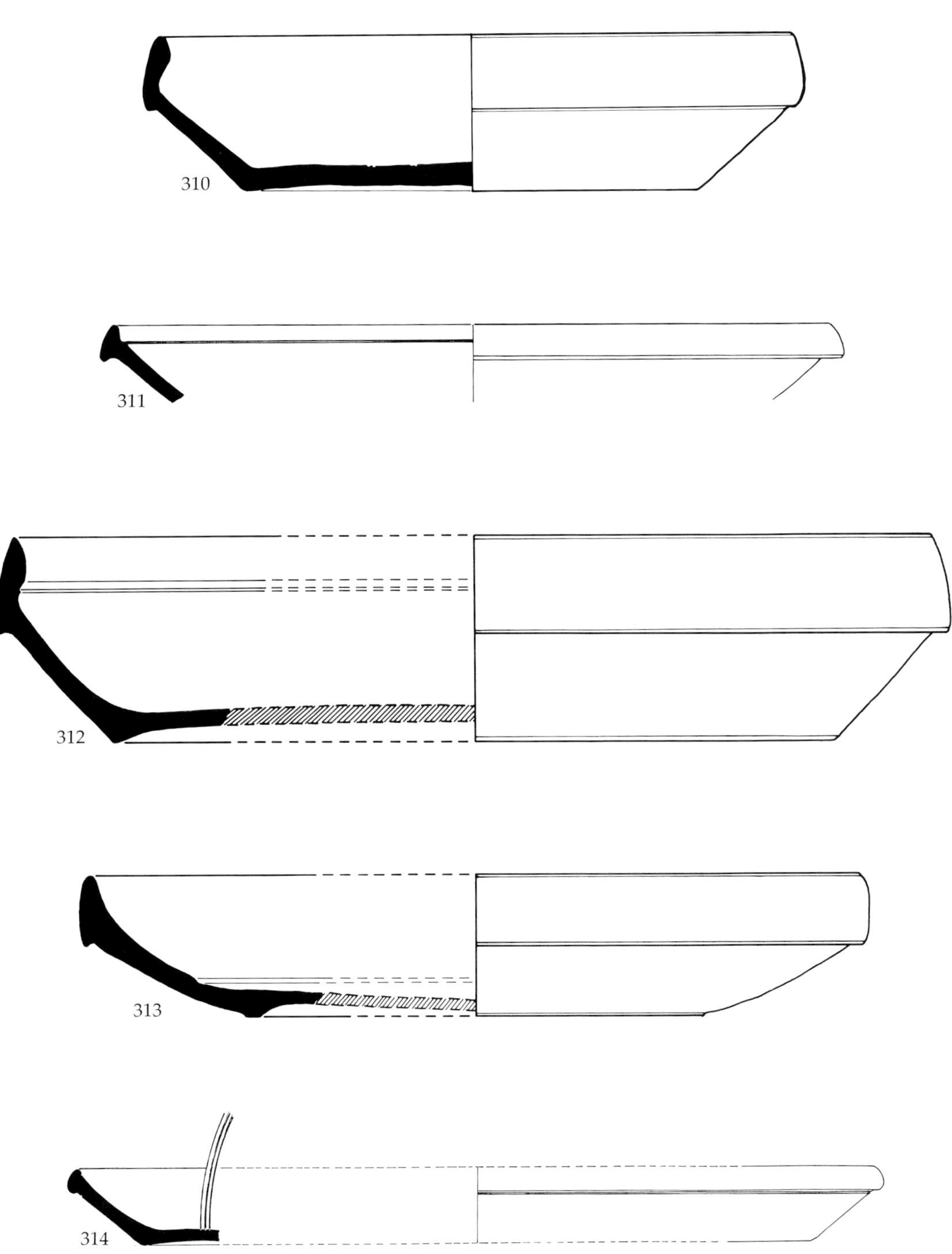

Plate 36. Eastern Sigillata B (314, scale 1:3)

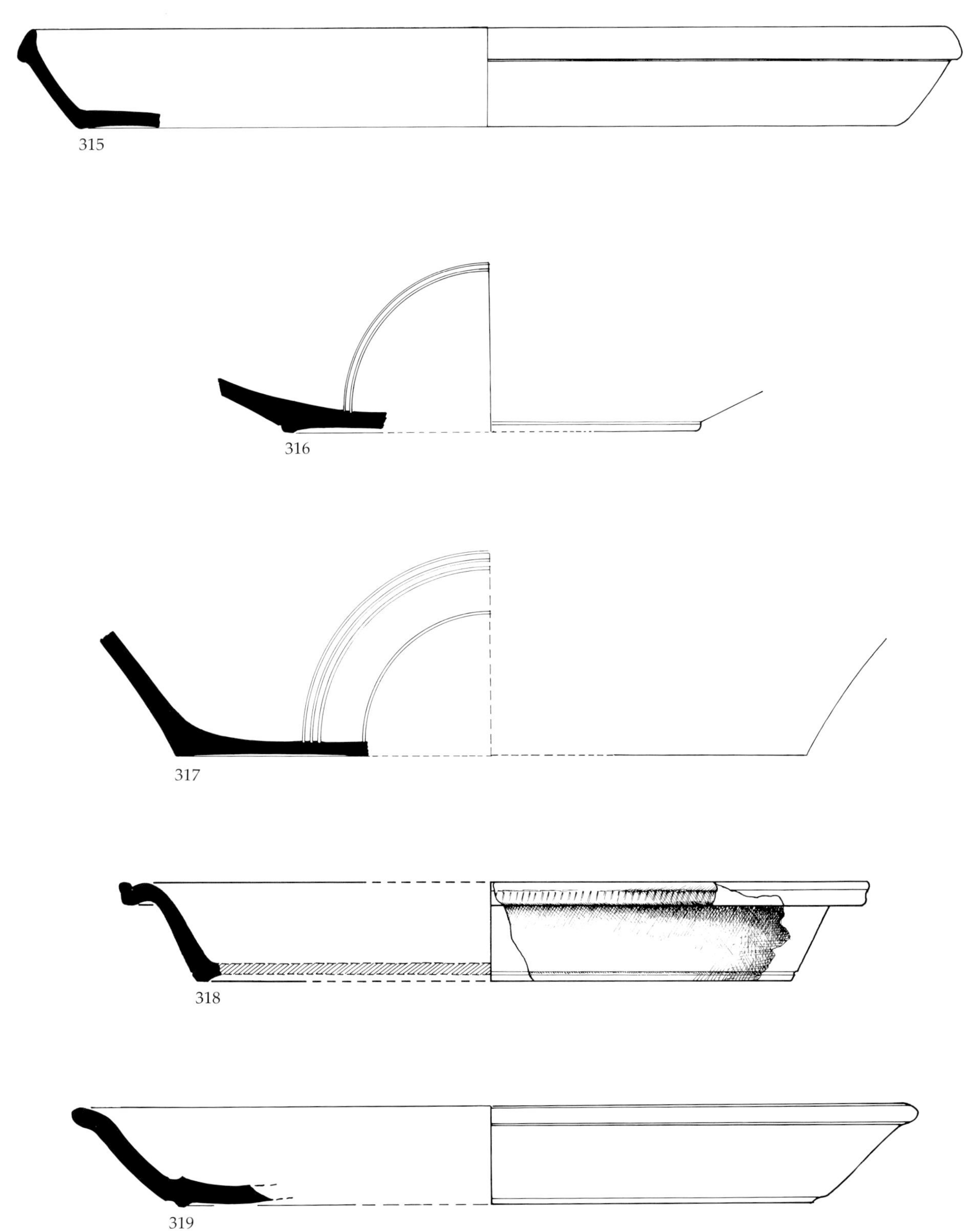

Plate 37. Eastern Sigillata B

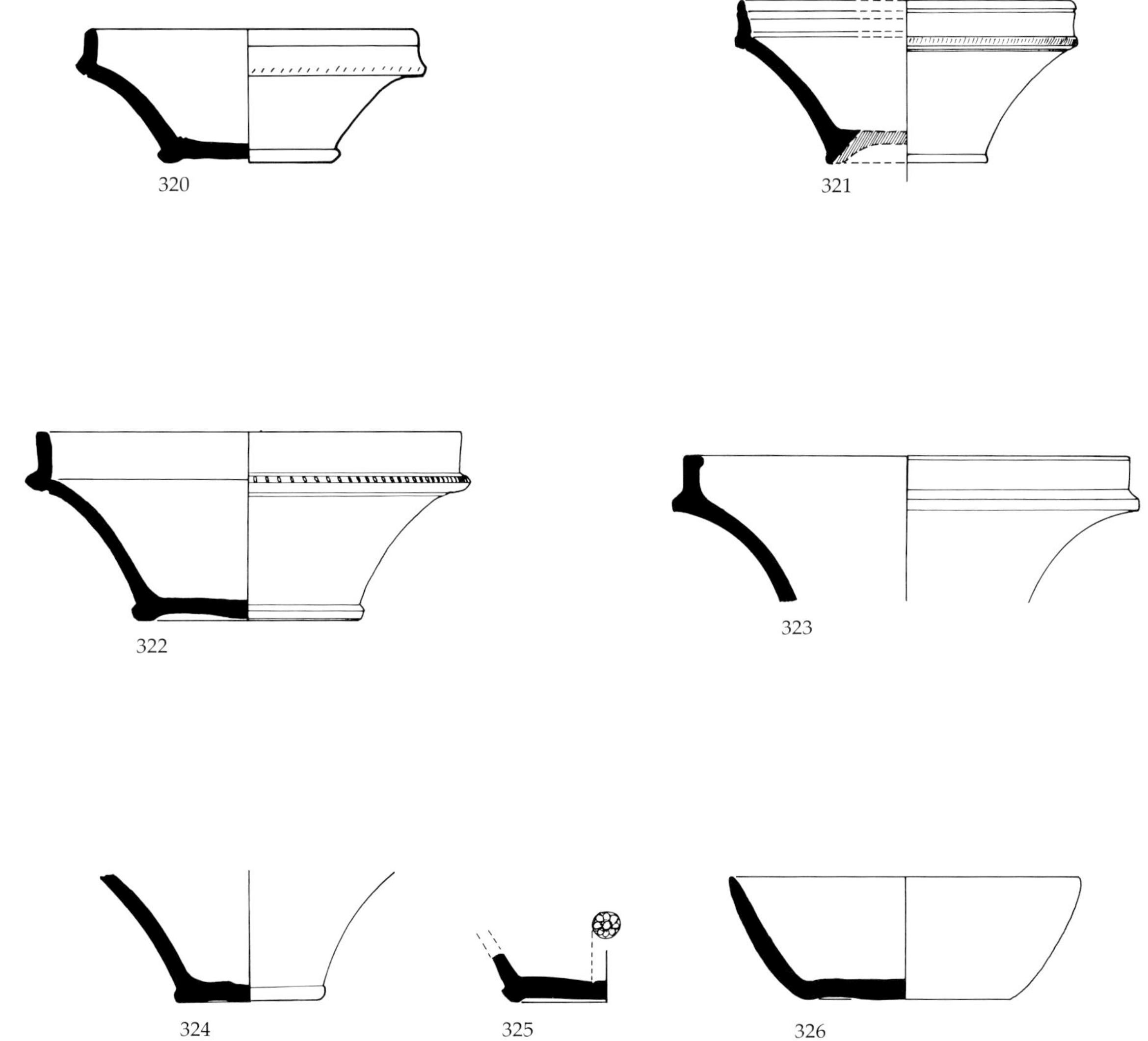

Plate 38. Eastern Sigillata B

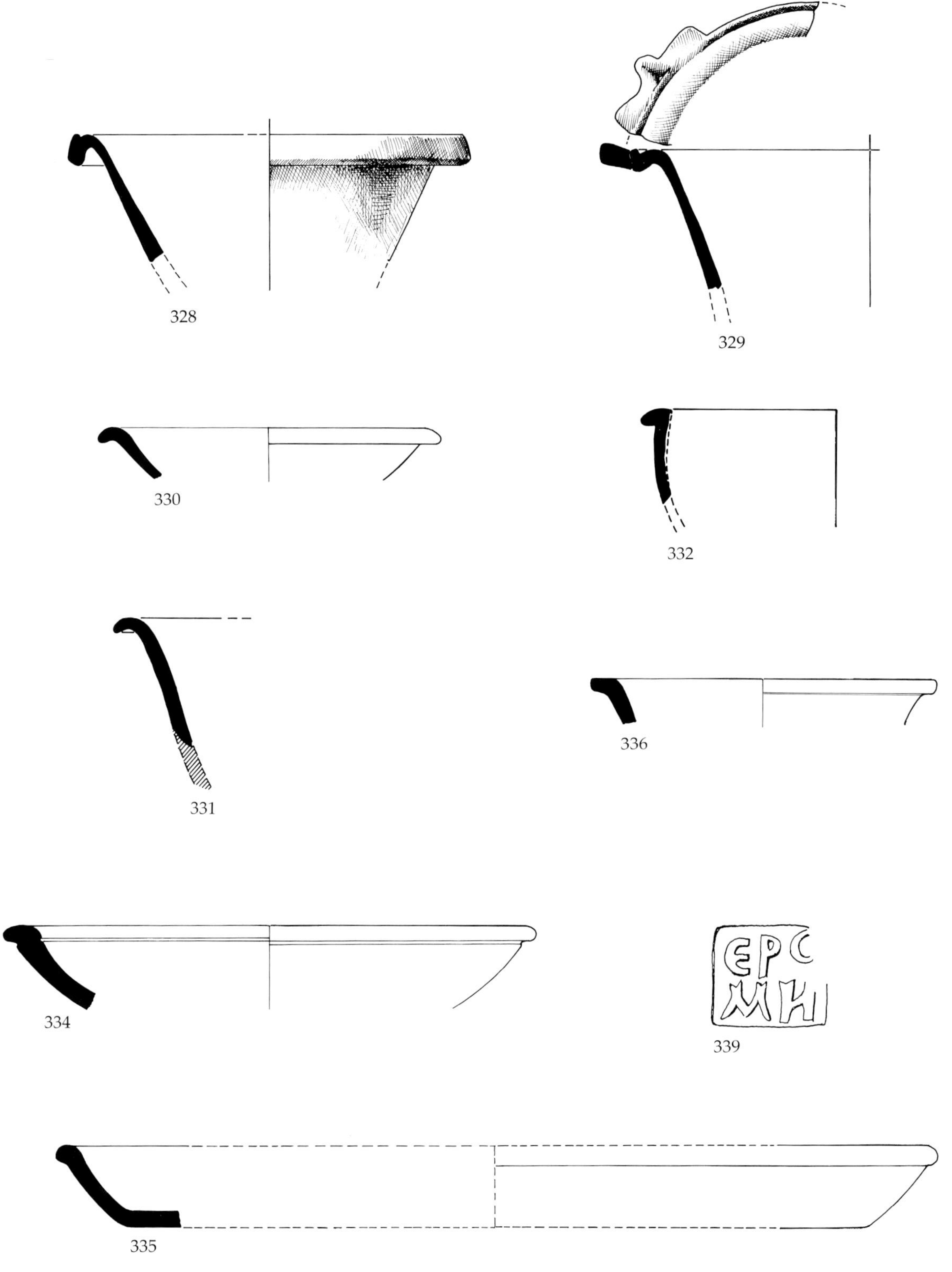

Plate 39. Eastern Sigillata B (339, scale 2:1)

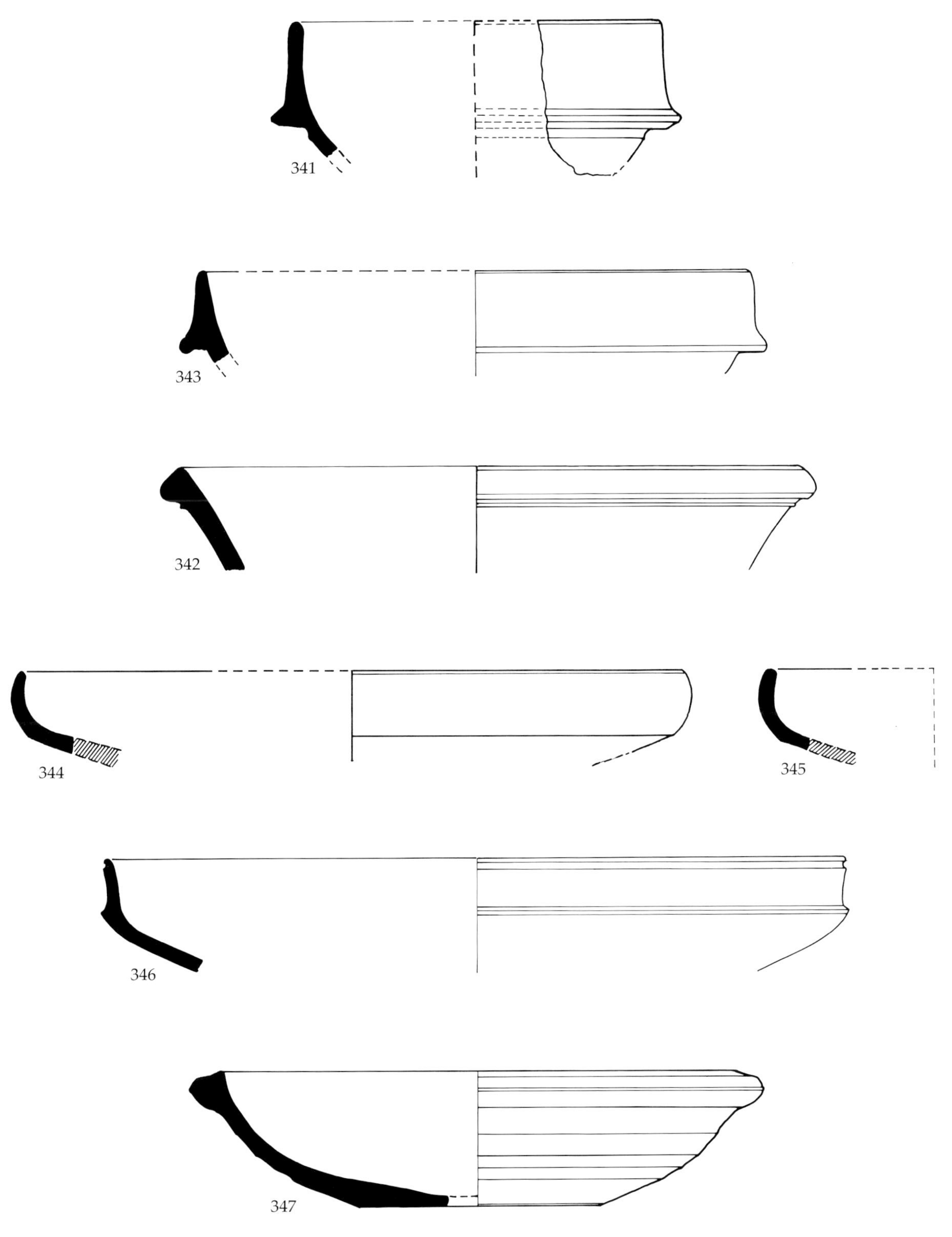

Plate 40. Çandarli Ware. Cypriot Sigillata. Cypriot Red Slip Ware

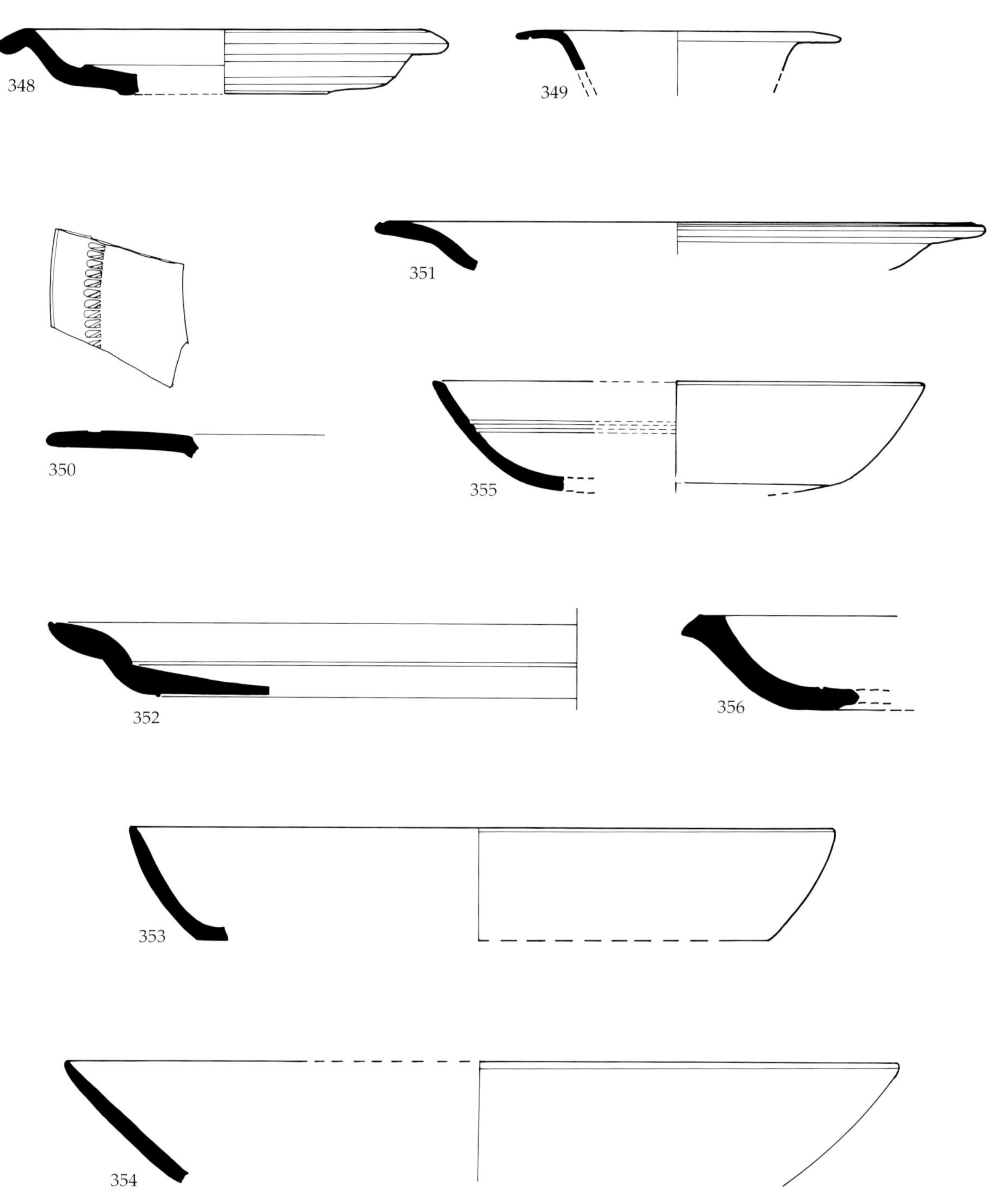

Plate 41. African Red Slip Ware

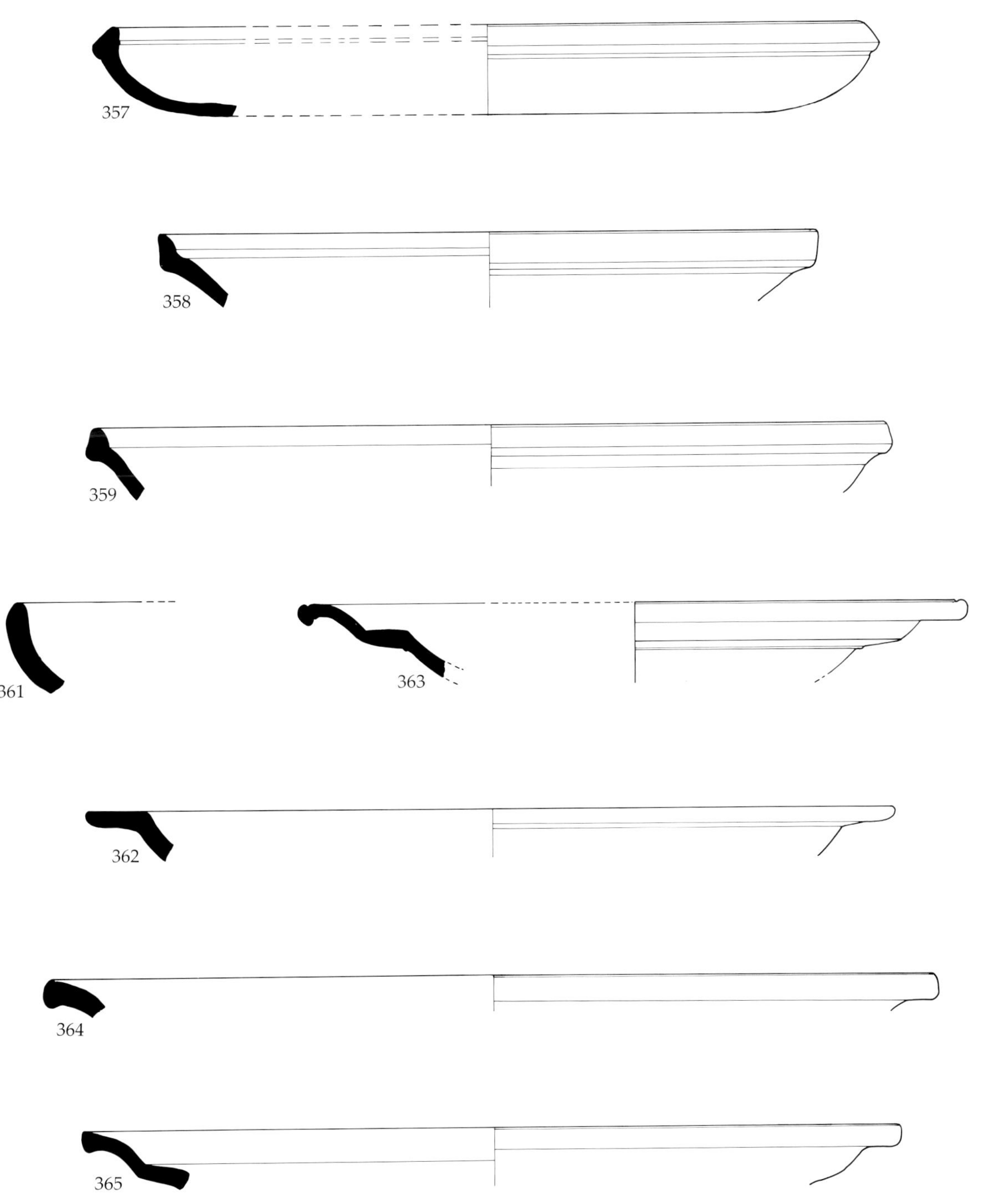

Plate 42. (scale 1:3) African Red Slip Ware

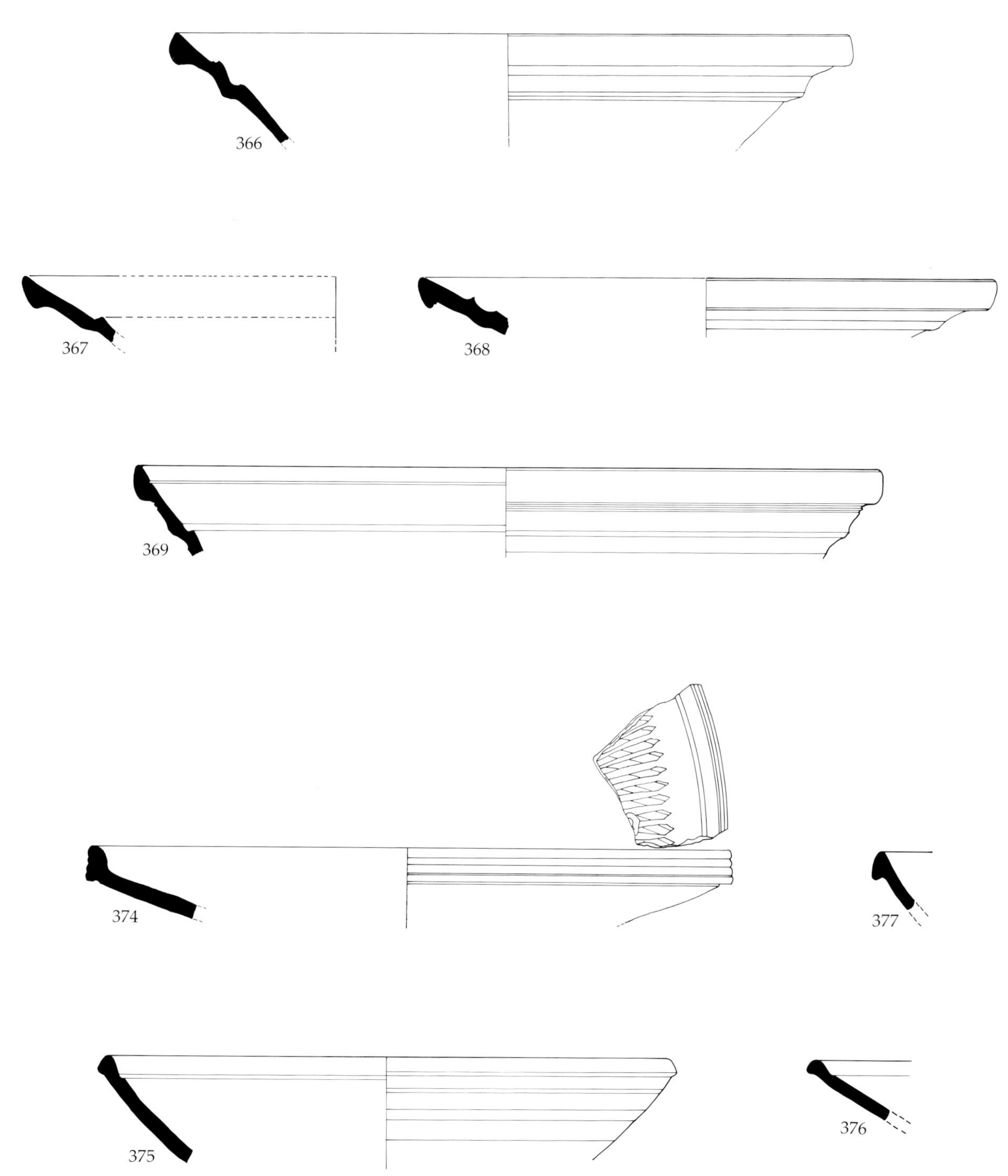

Plate 43. (scale 1:3) African Red Slip Ware

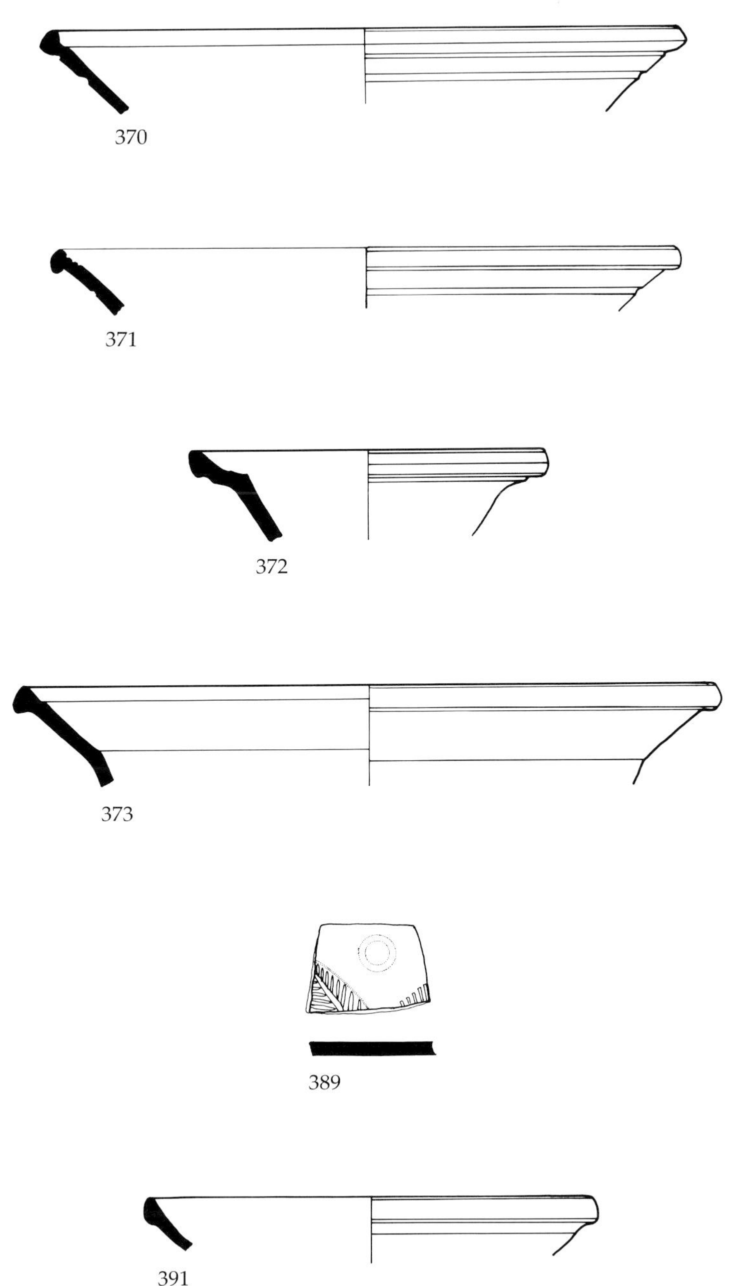

Plate 44. African Red Slip Ware

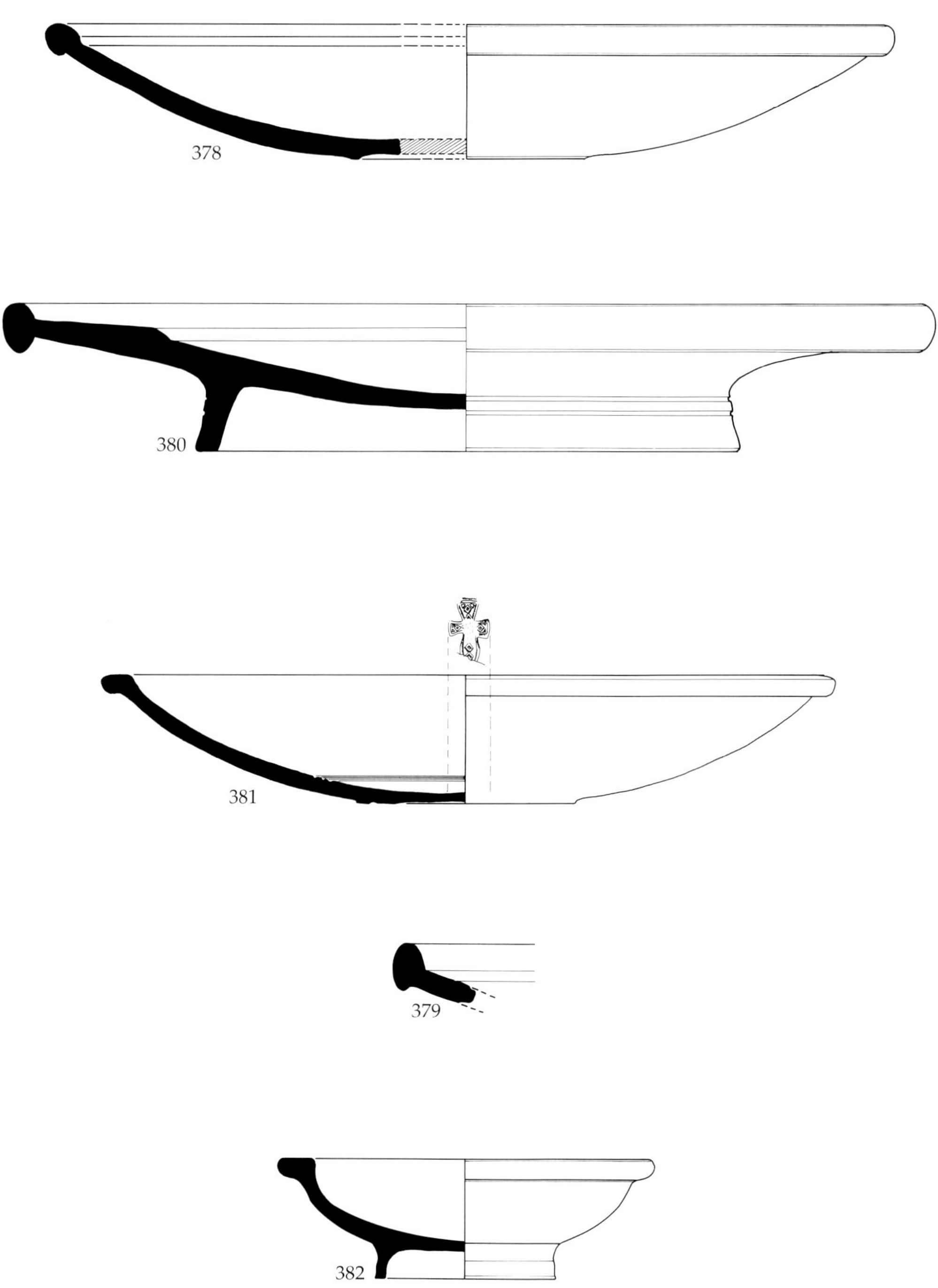

Plate 45. (scale 1:3) Phocaean Red Slip Ware

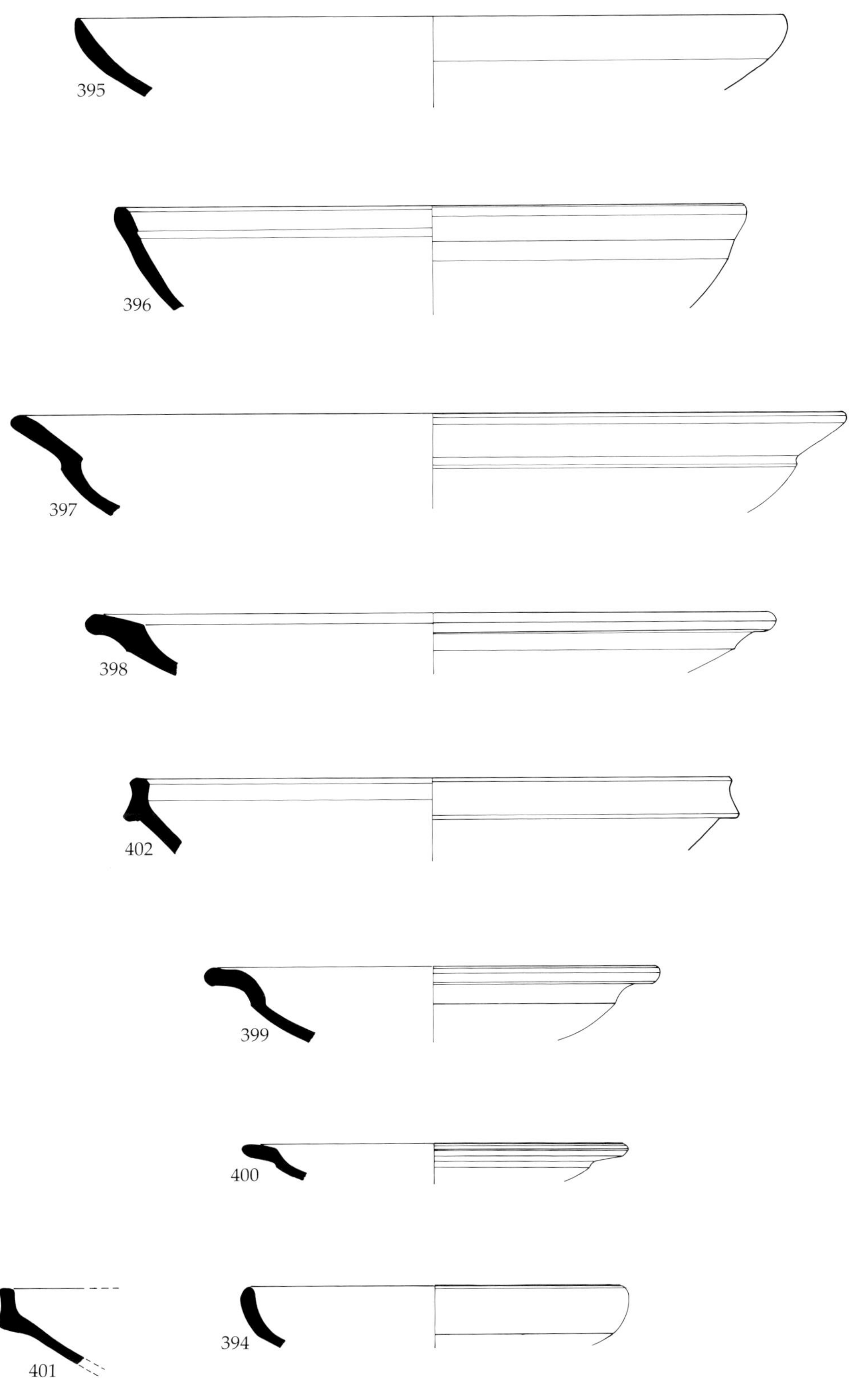

Plate 46. (scale 1:3) Phocaean Red Slip Ware

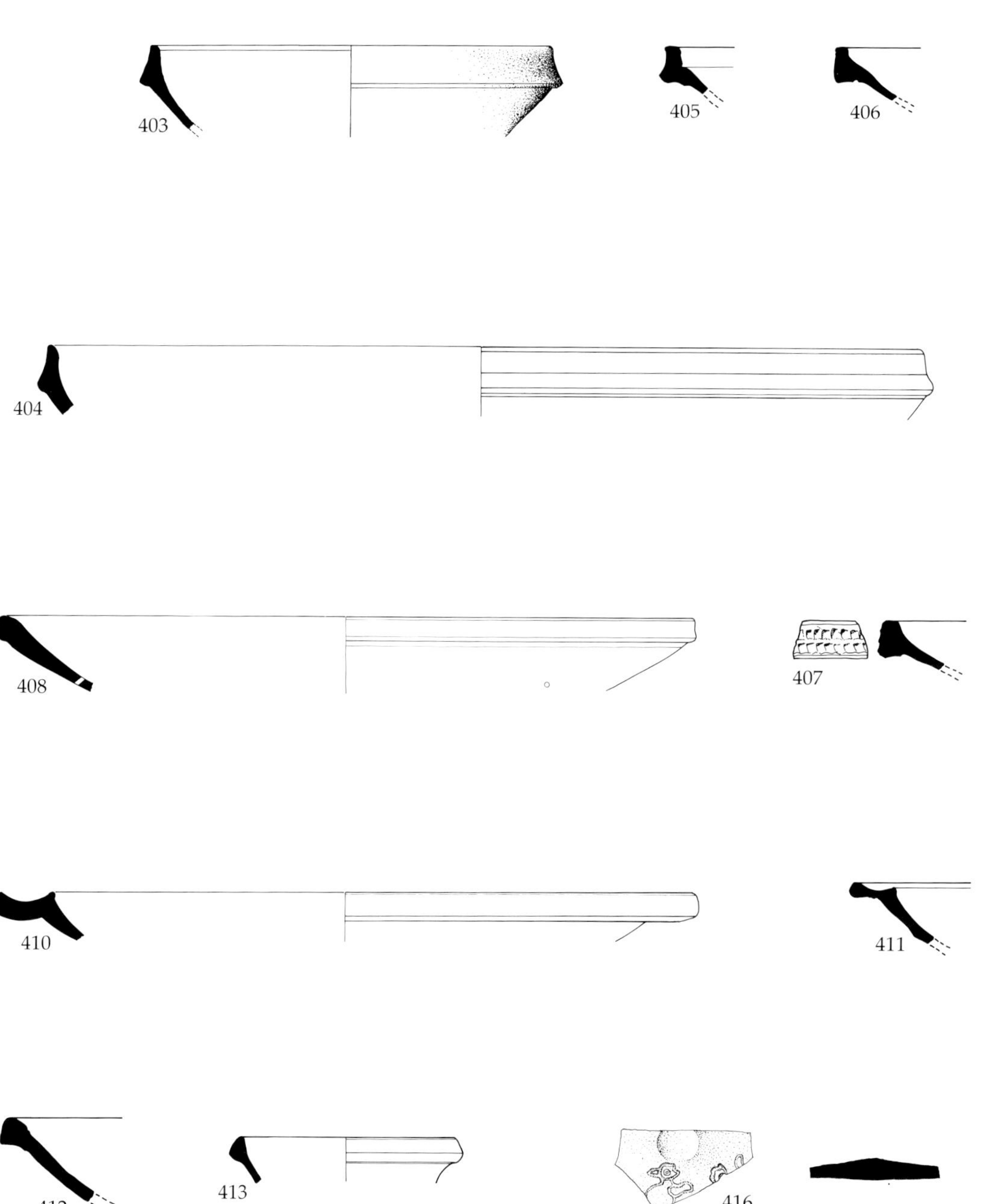

Plate 47. (scale 1:3) Phocaean Red Slip Ware

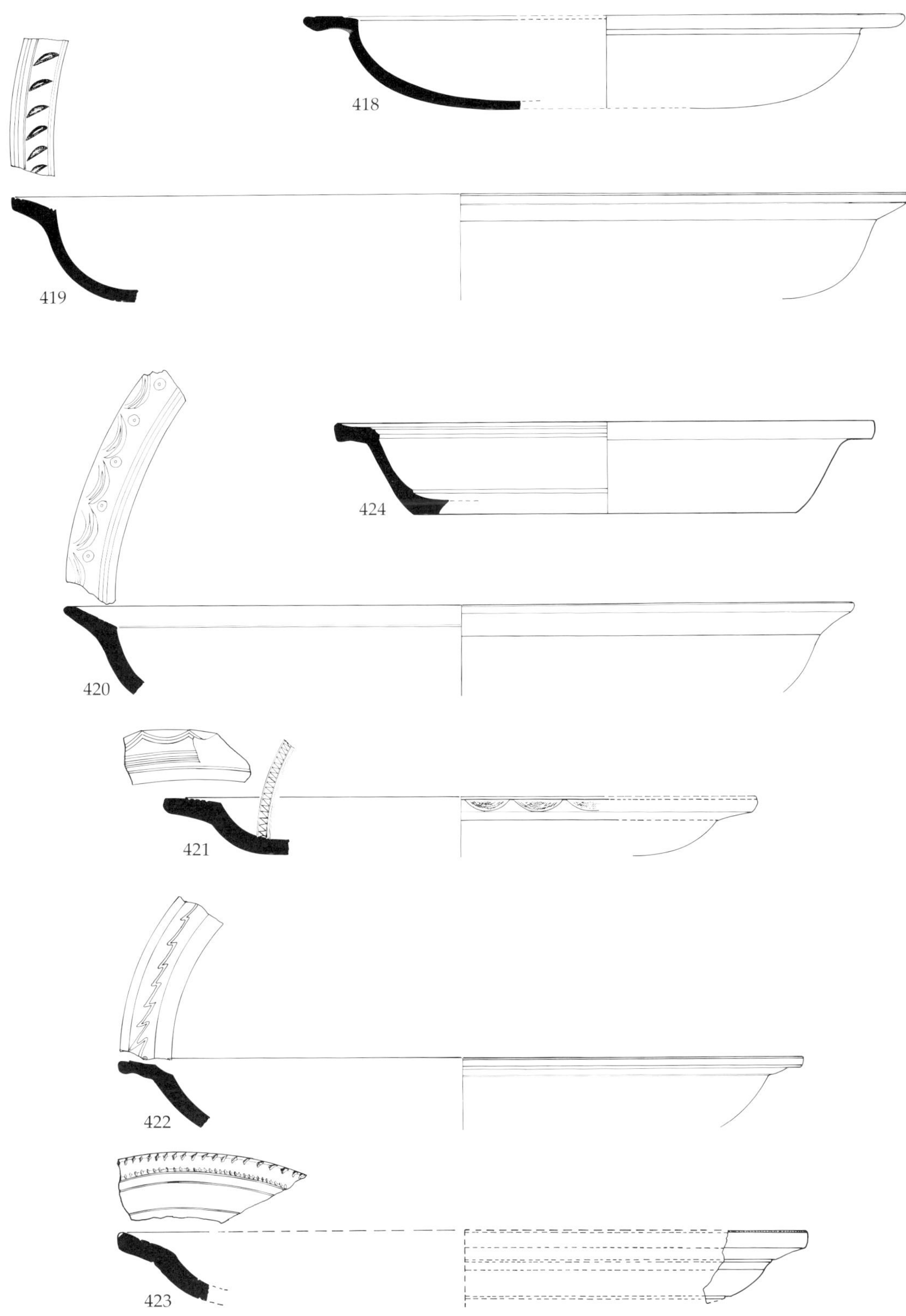

Plate 48. (scale 1:3) Macedonian Gray Ware. Form 1

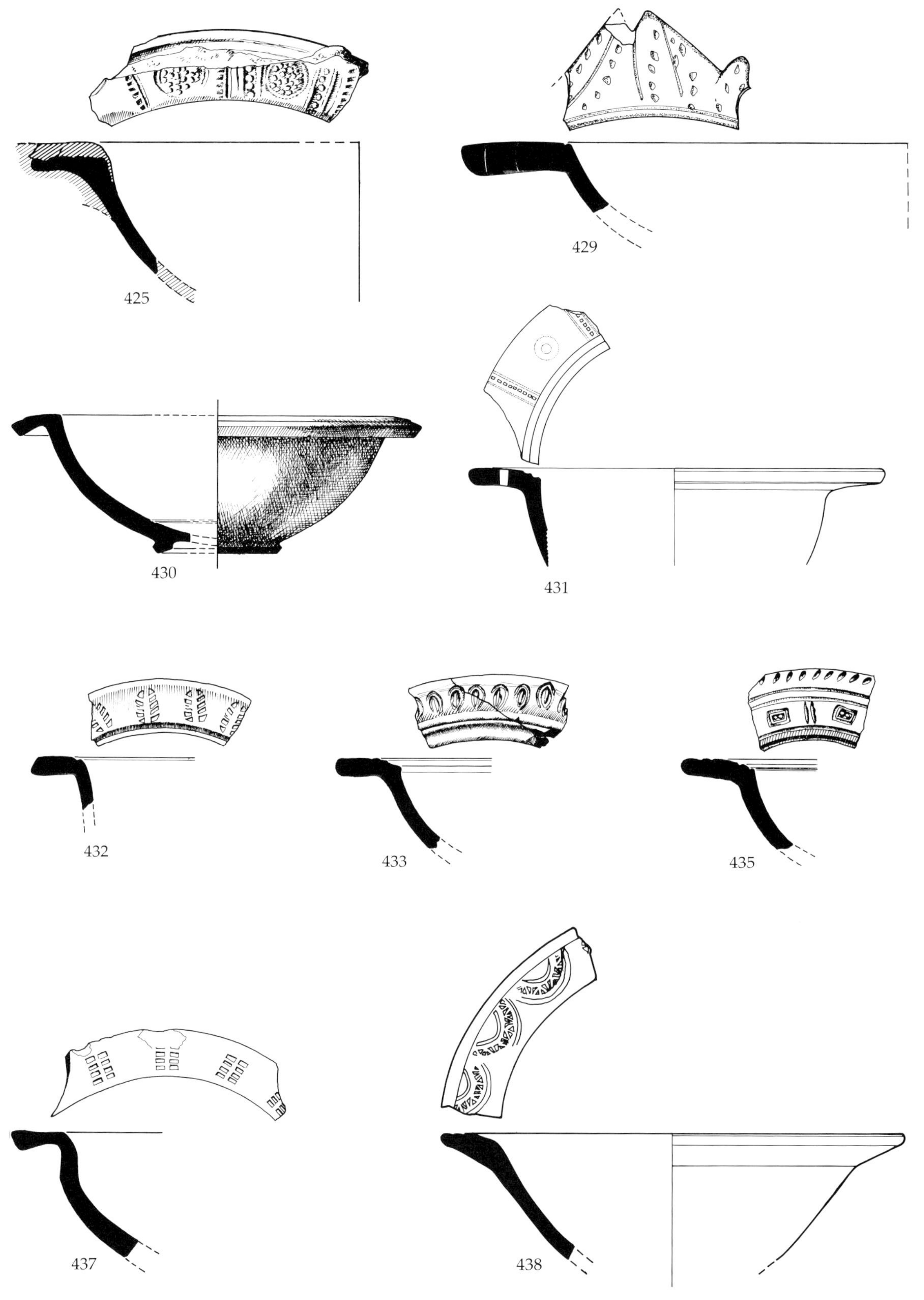

Plate 49. Macedonian Gray Ware. Forms 1 and 2

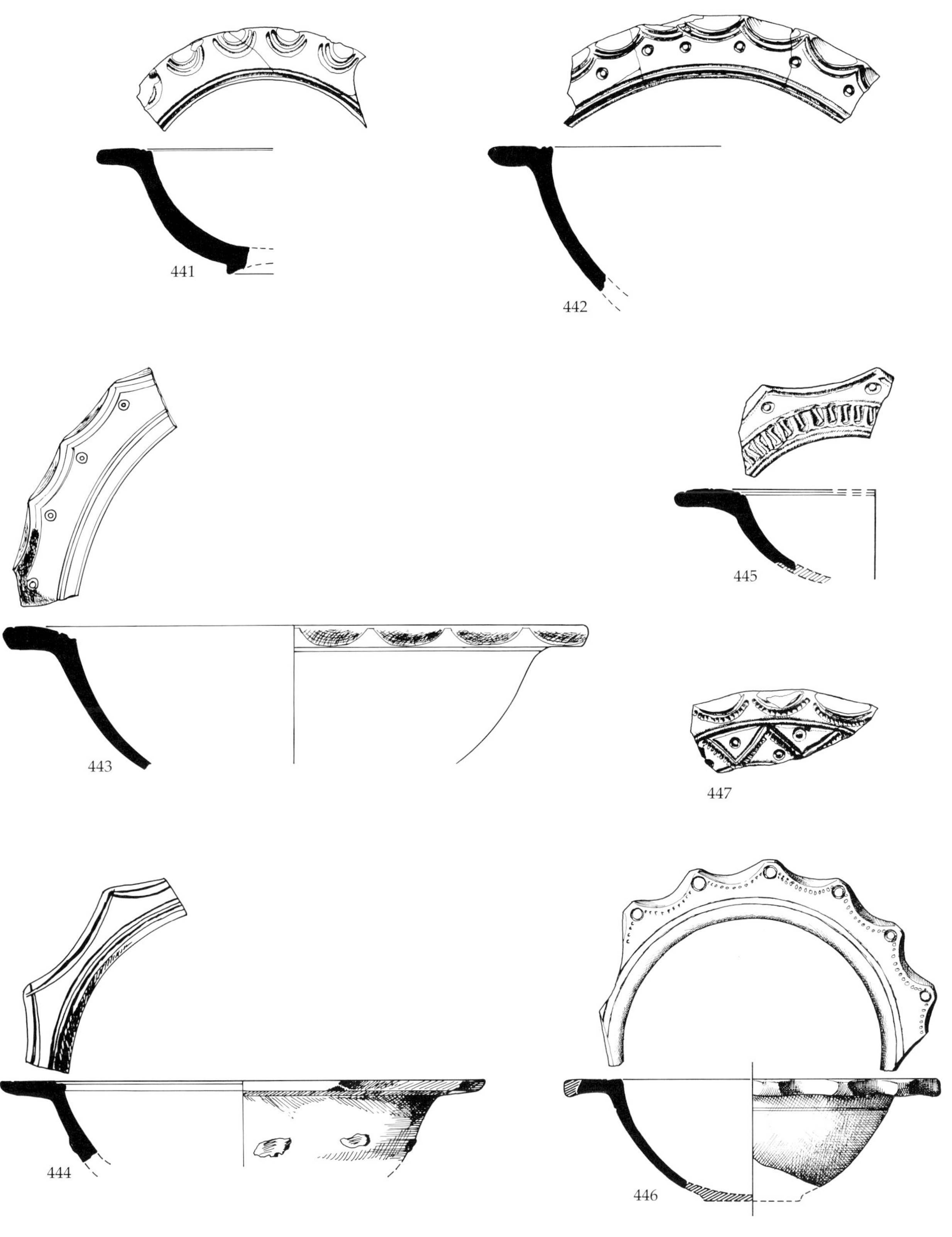

Plate 50. Macedonian Gray Ware. Form 2

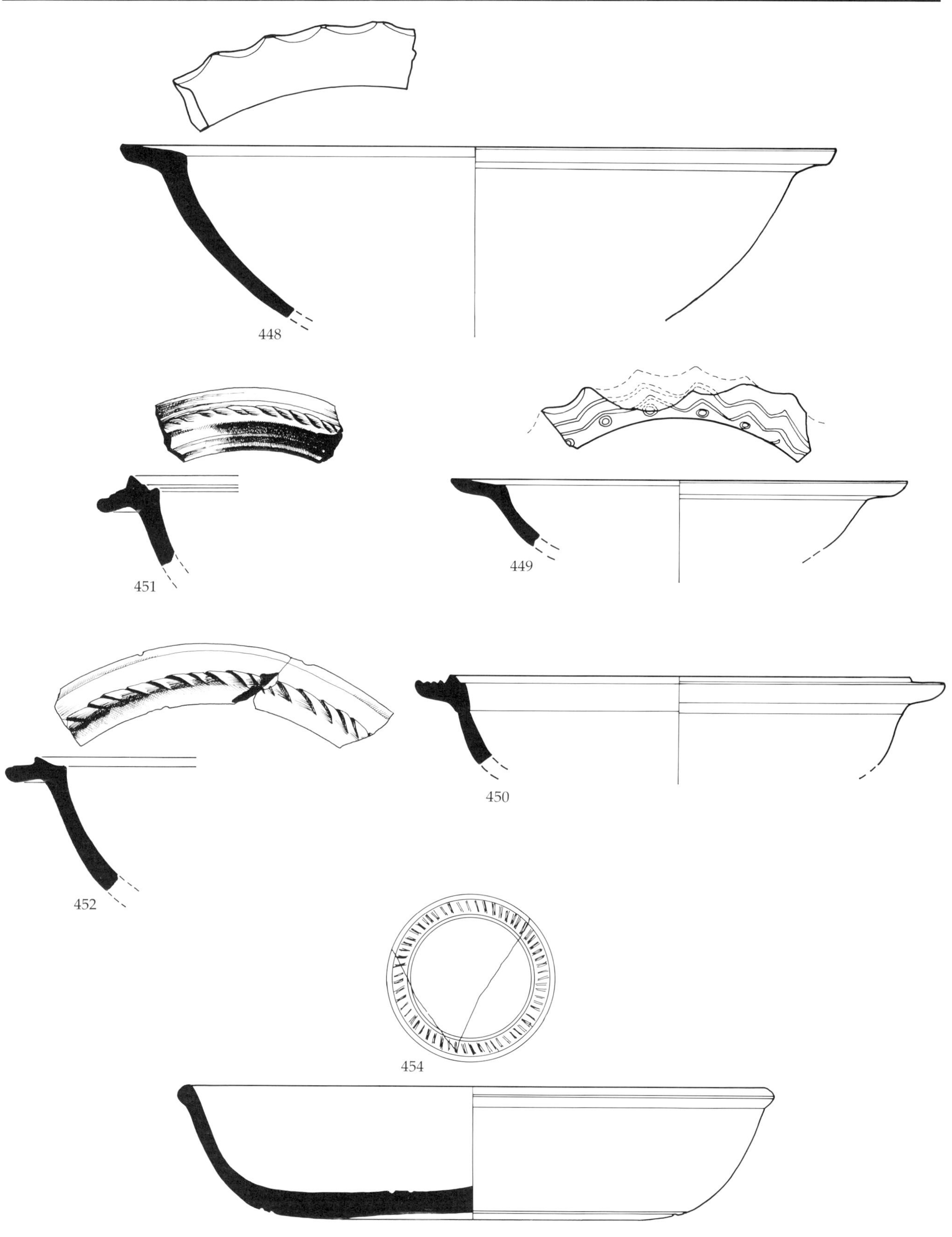

Plate 51. Macedonian Gray Ware. Forms 2 and 3

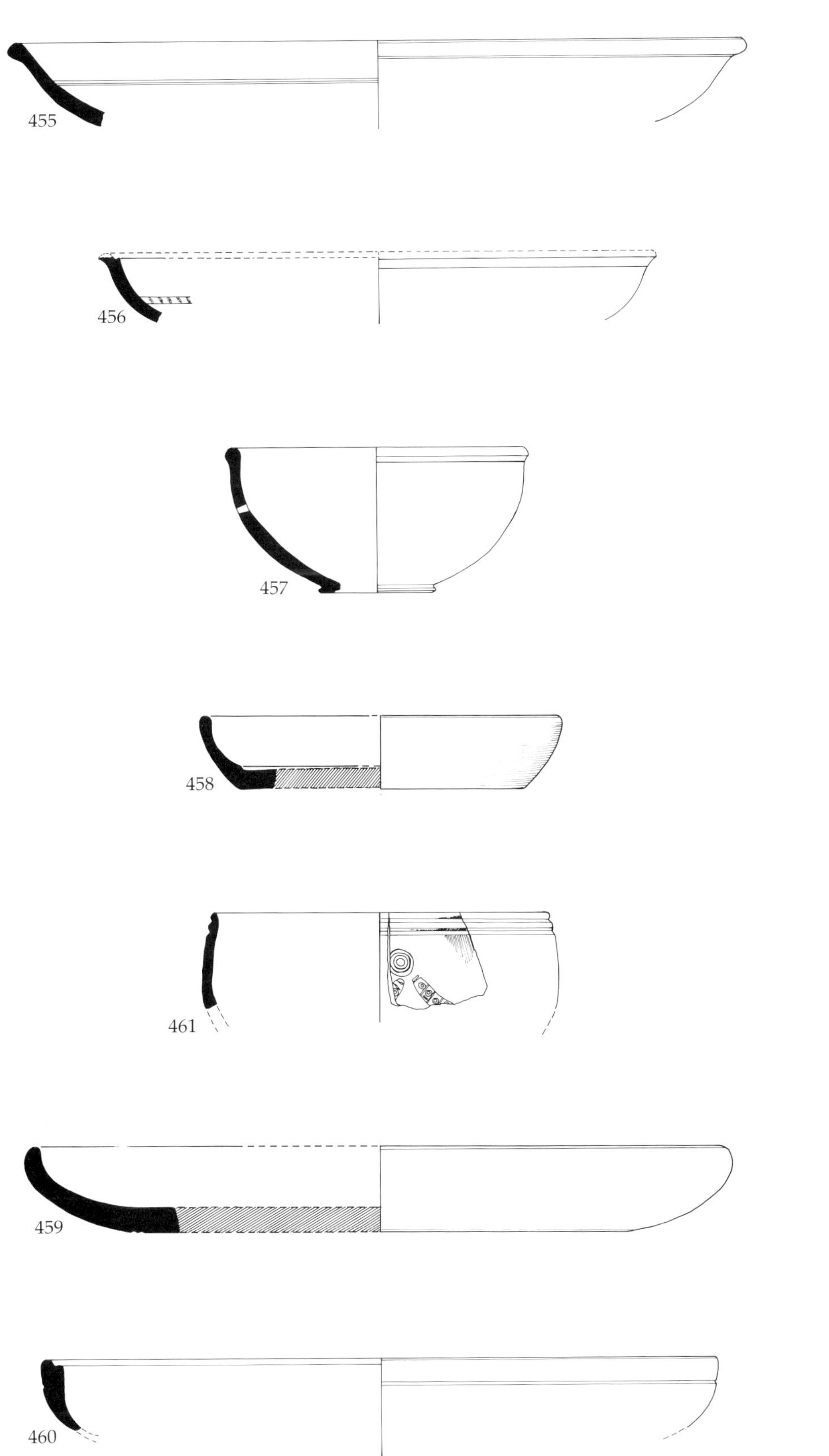

Plate 52. (scale 1:3) Macedonian Gray Ware. Forms 3, 4, and 5

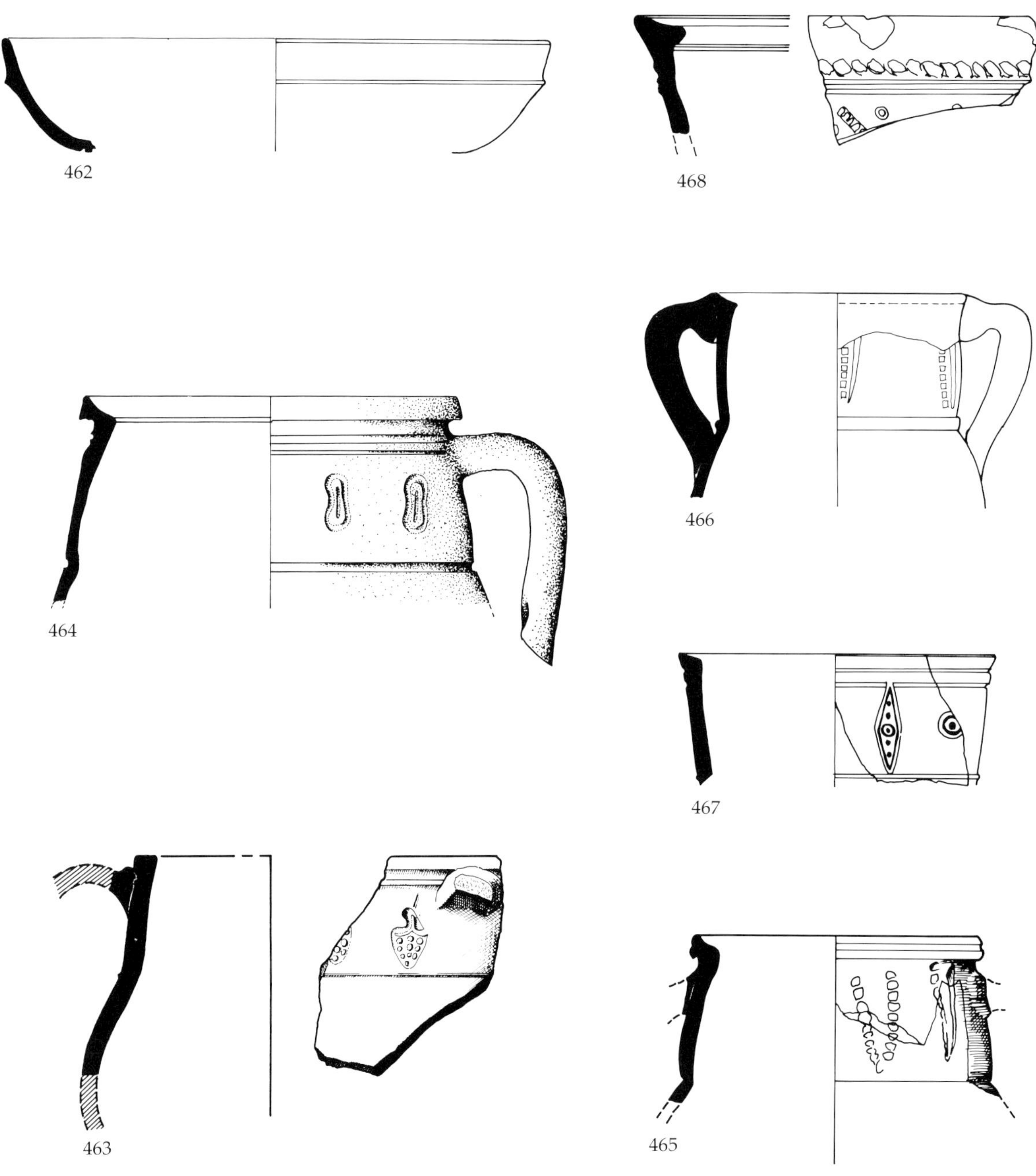

Plate 53. Macedonian Gray Ware. Forms 6, 7, and 8

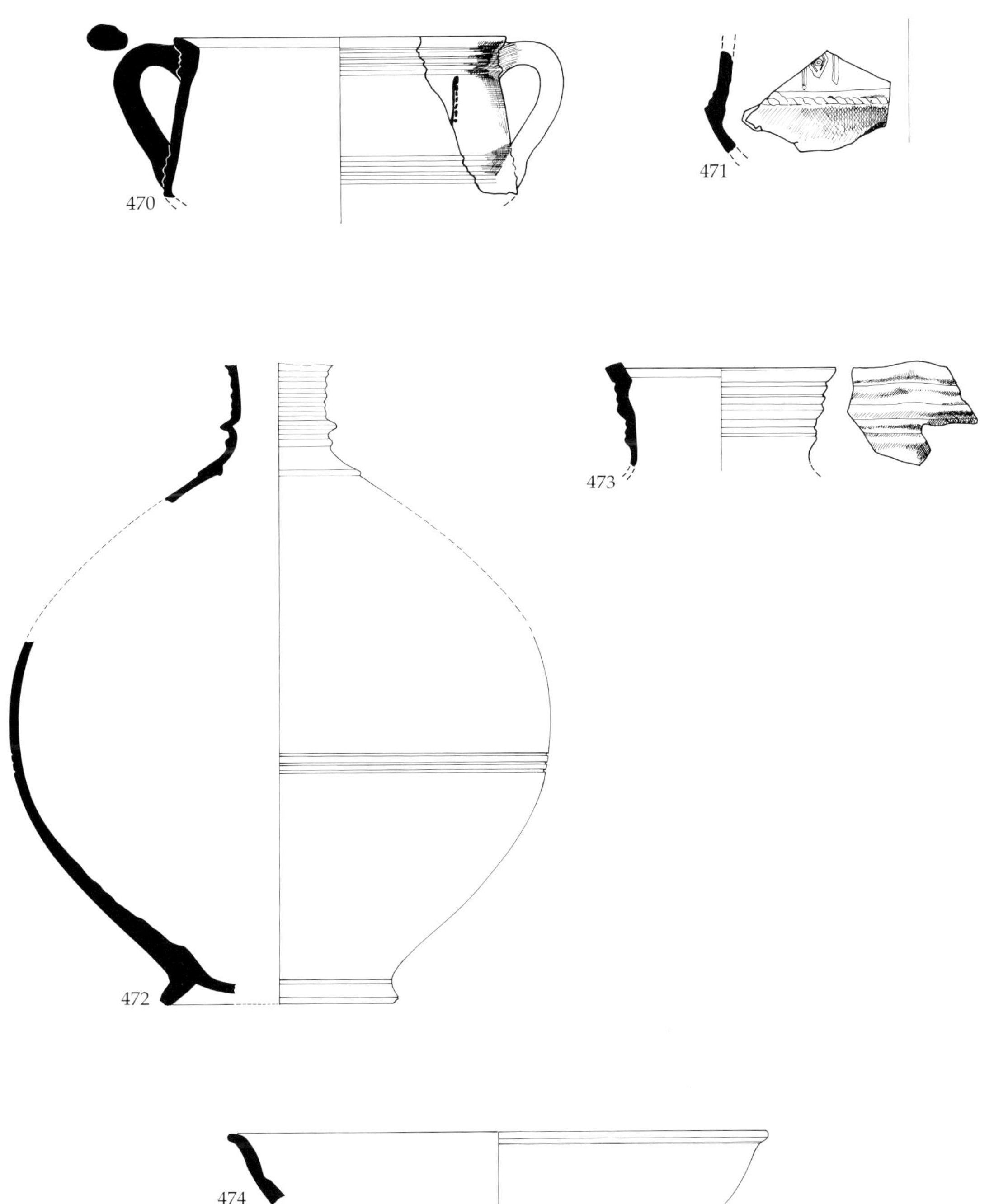

Plate 54. (scale 1:3) Macedonian Gray Ware. Forms 9 and 10

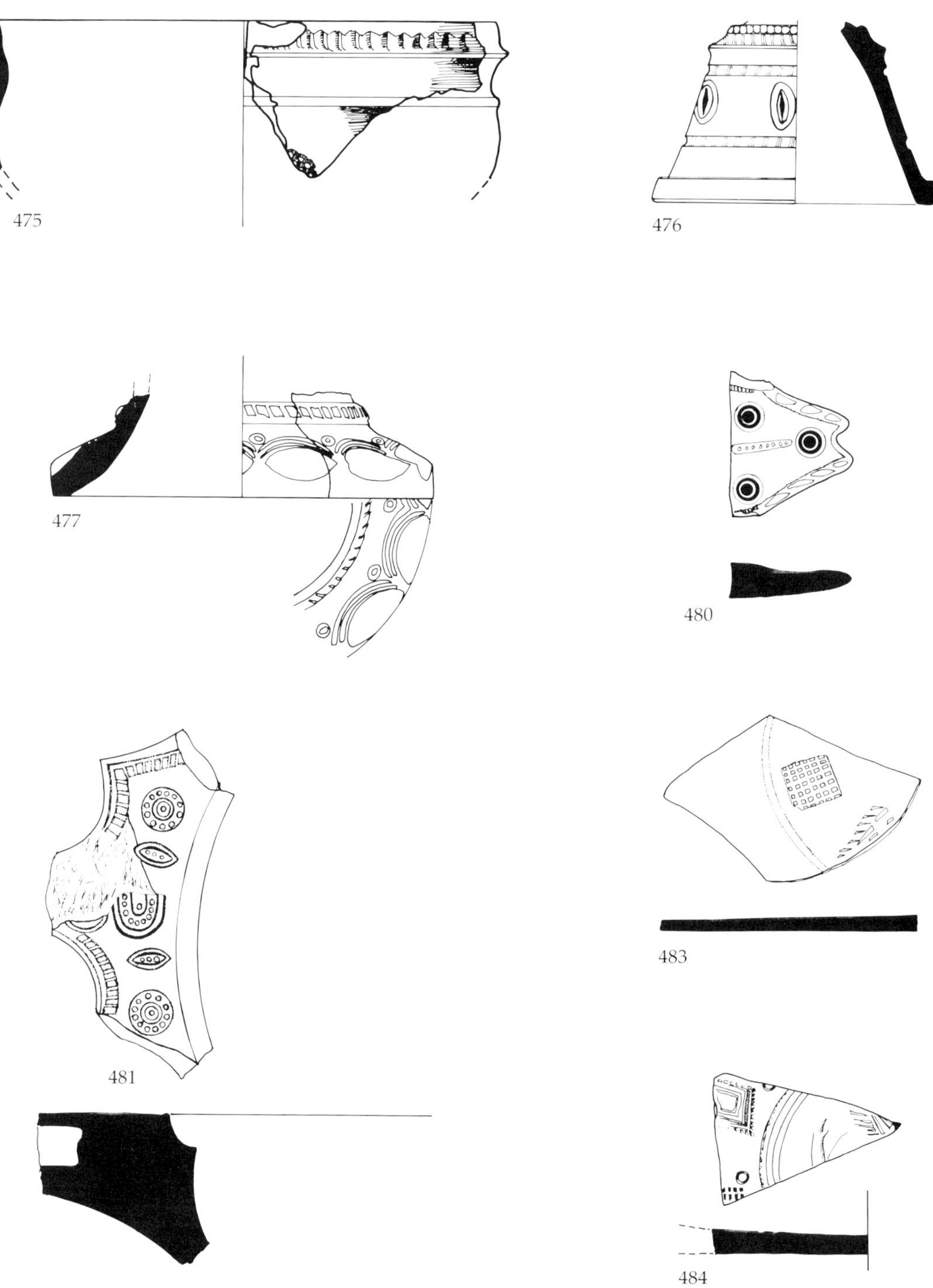

Plate 55. Macedonian Gray Ware

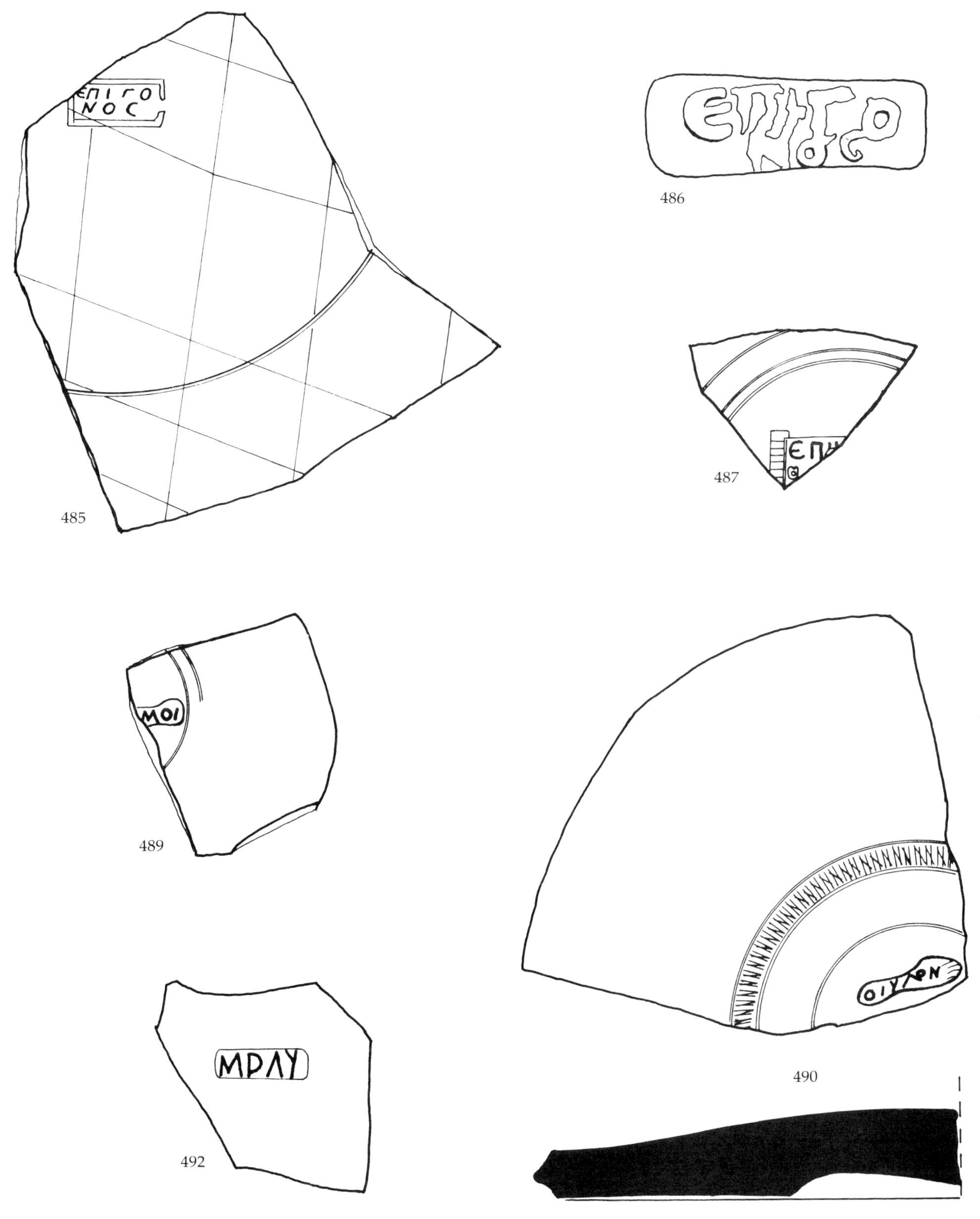

Plate 56. (scale 1:1) Potter's Stamps

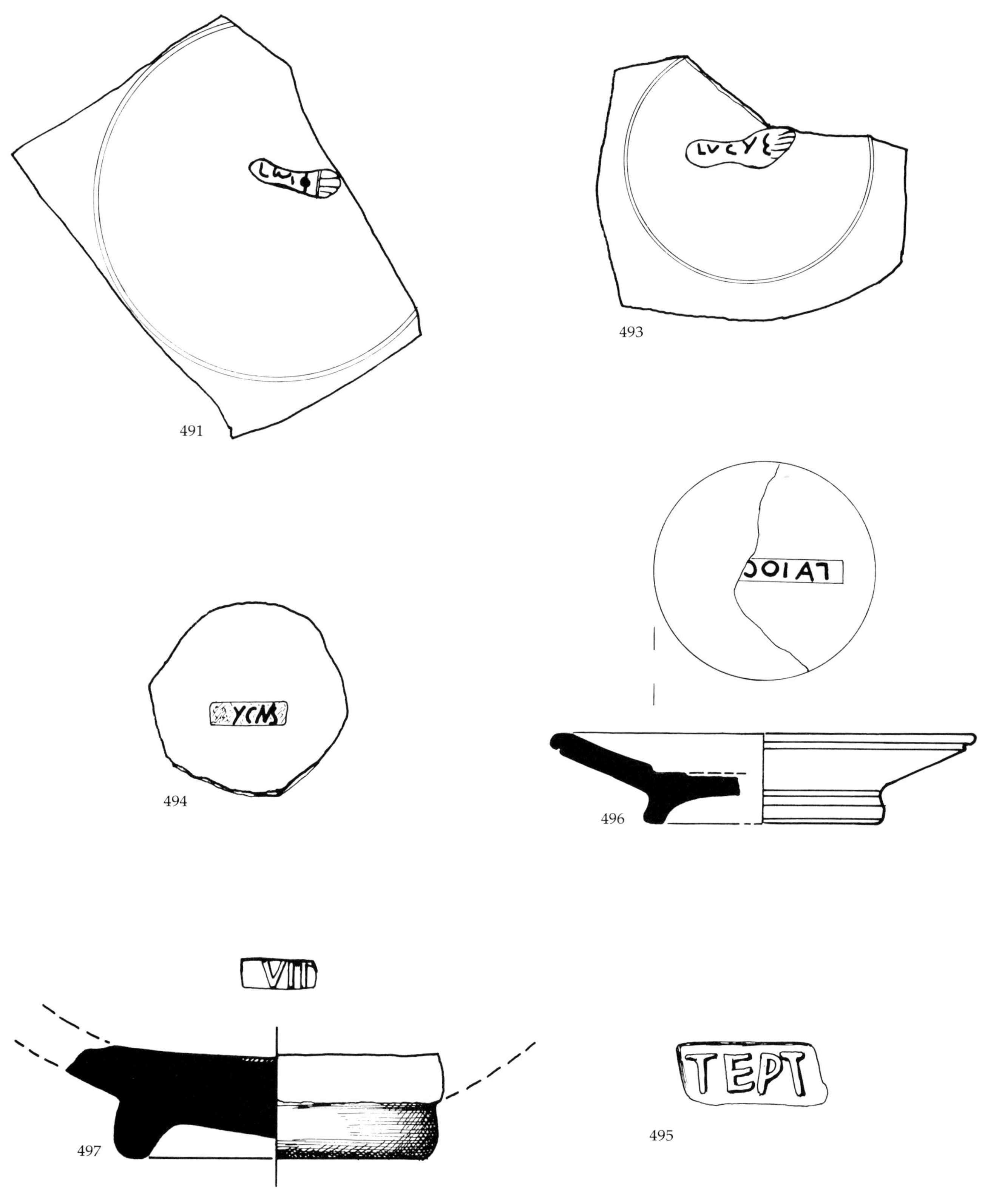

Plate 57. (scale 1:1) Potter's Stamps (495; scale 2:1)

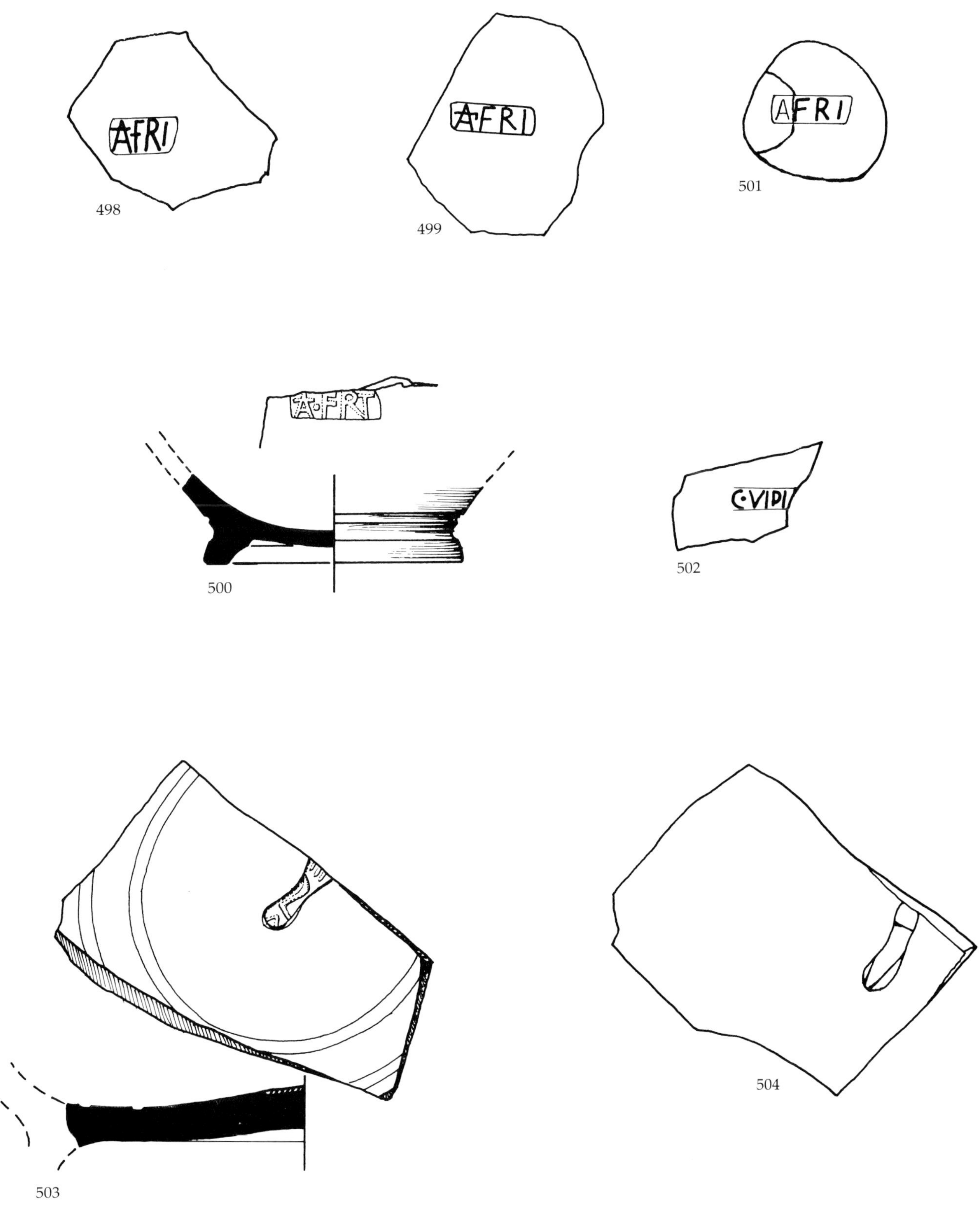

Plate 58. (scale 1:1) Potter's Stamps

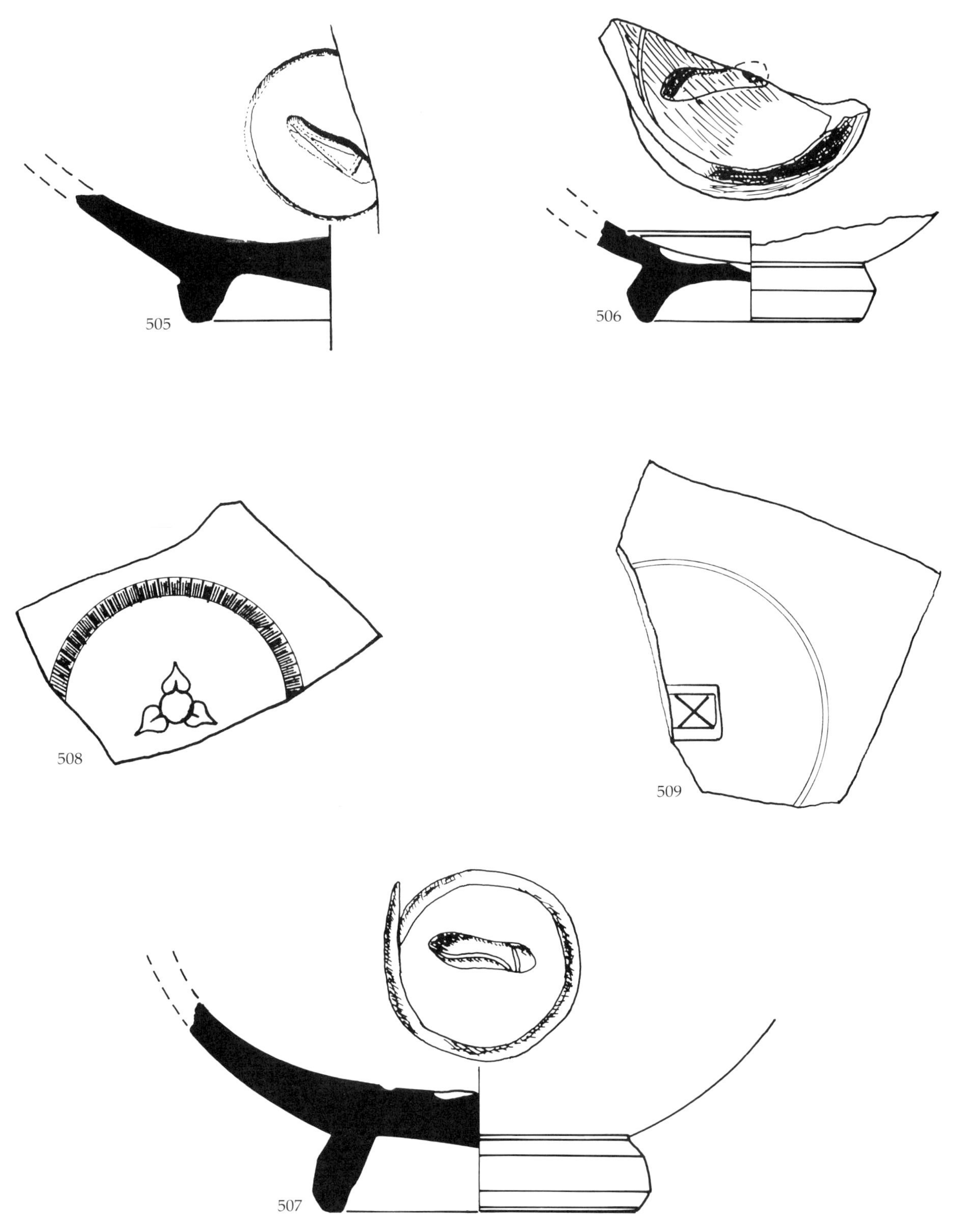

Plate 59. (scale 1:1) Potter's Stamps

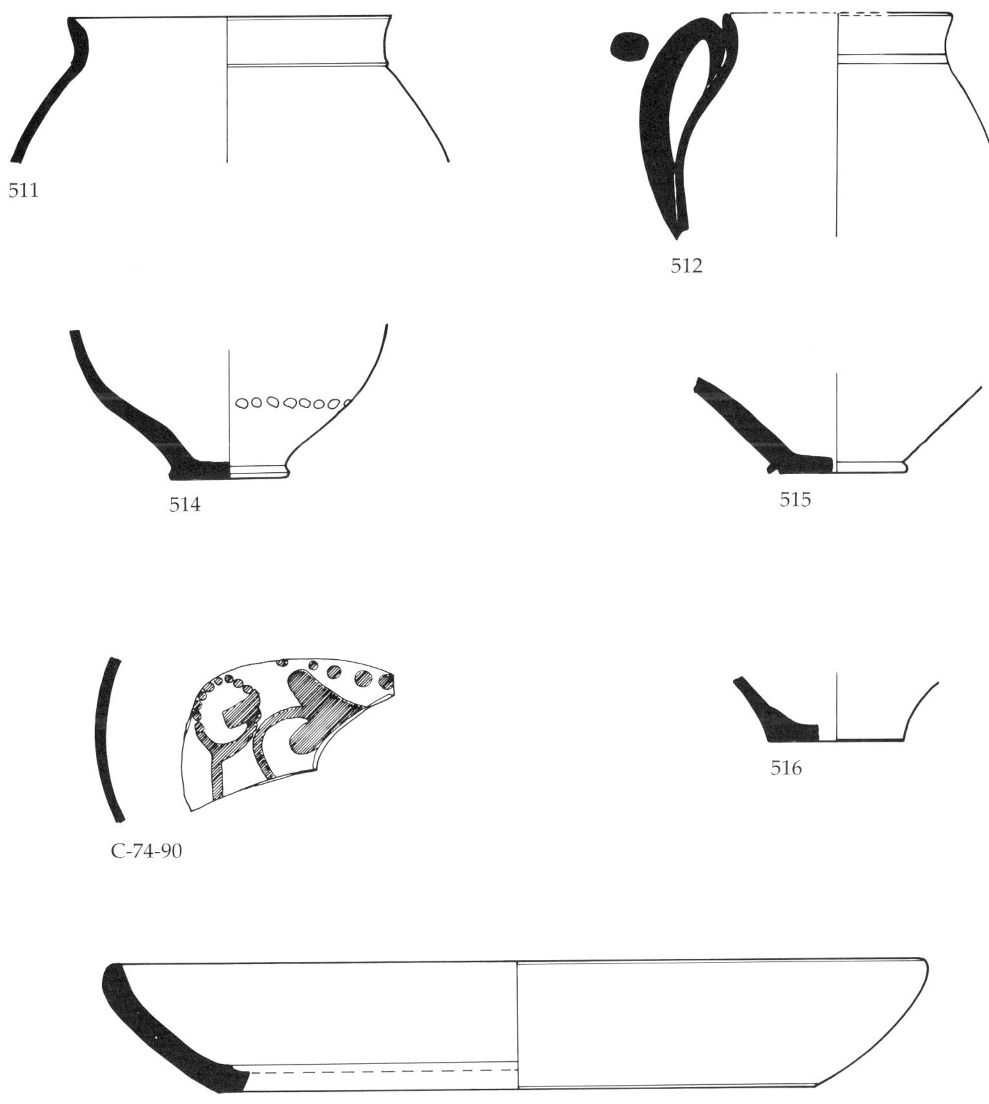

Plate 60. Italian Mugs. Marbeled Slip

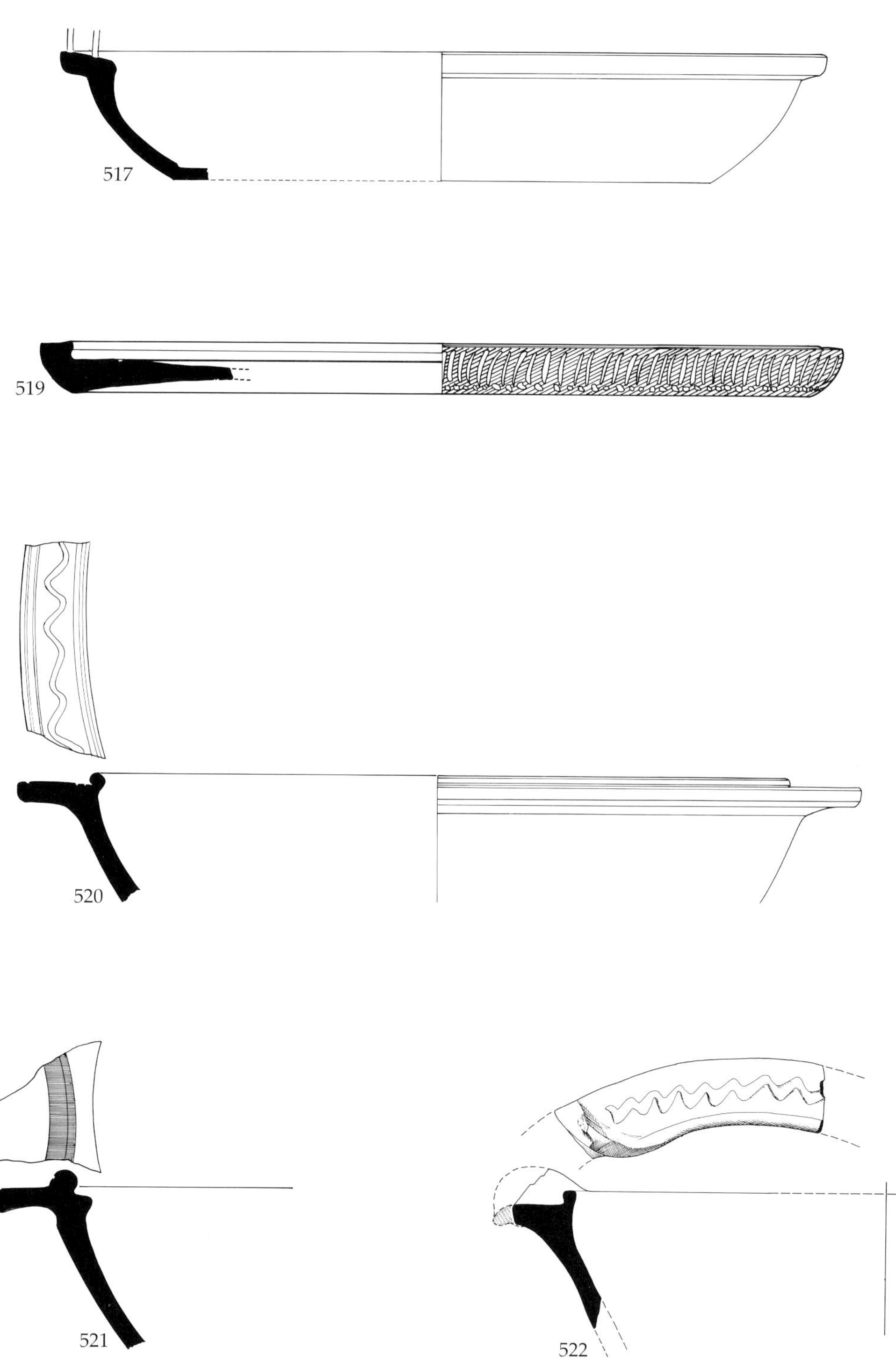

Plate 61. (scale 1:3) Marbeled Slip. Lead-Glazed Wares

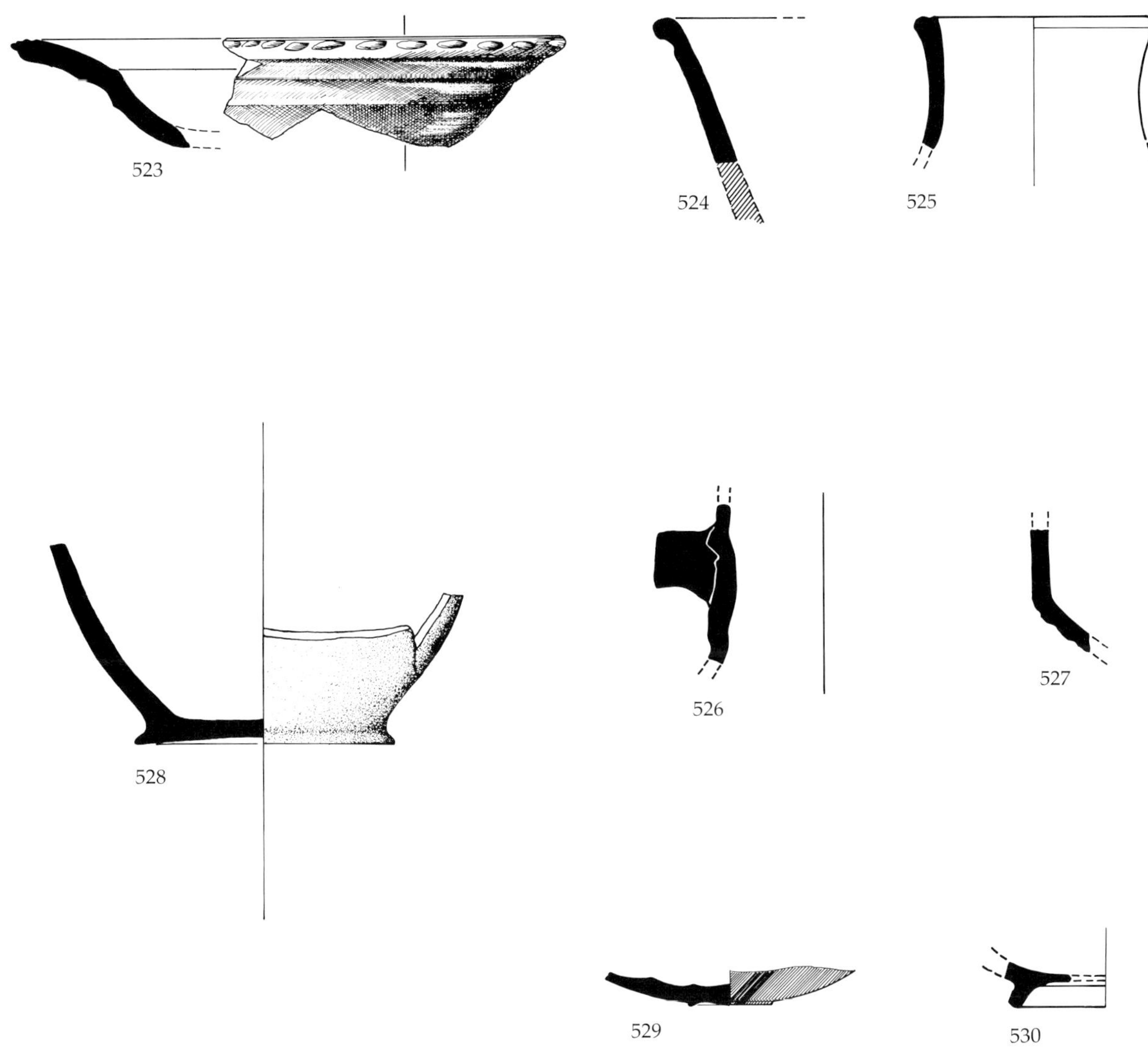

Plate 62. Lead-Glazed Wares

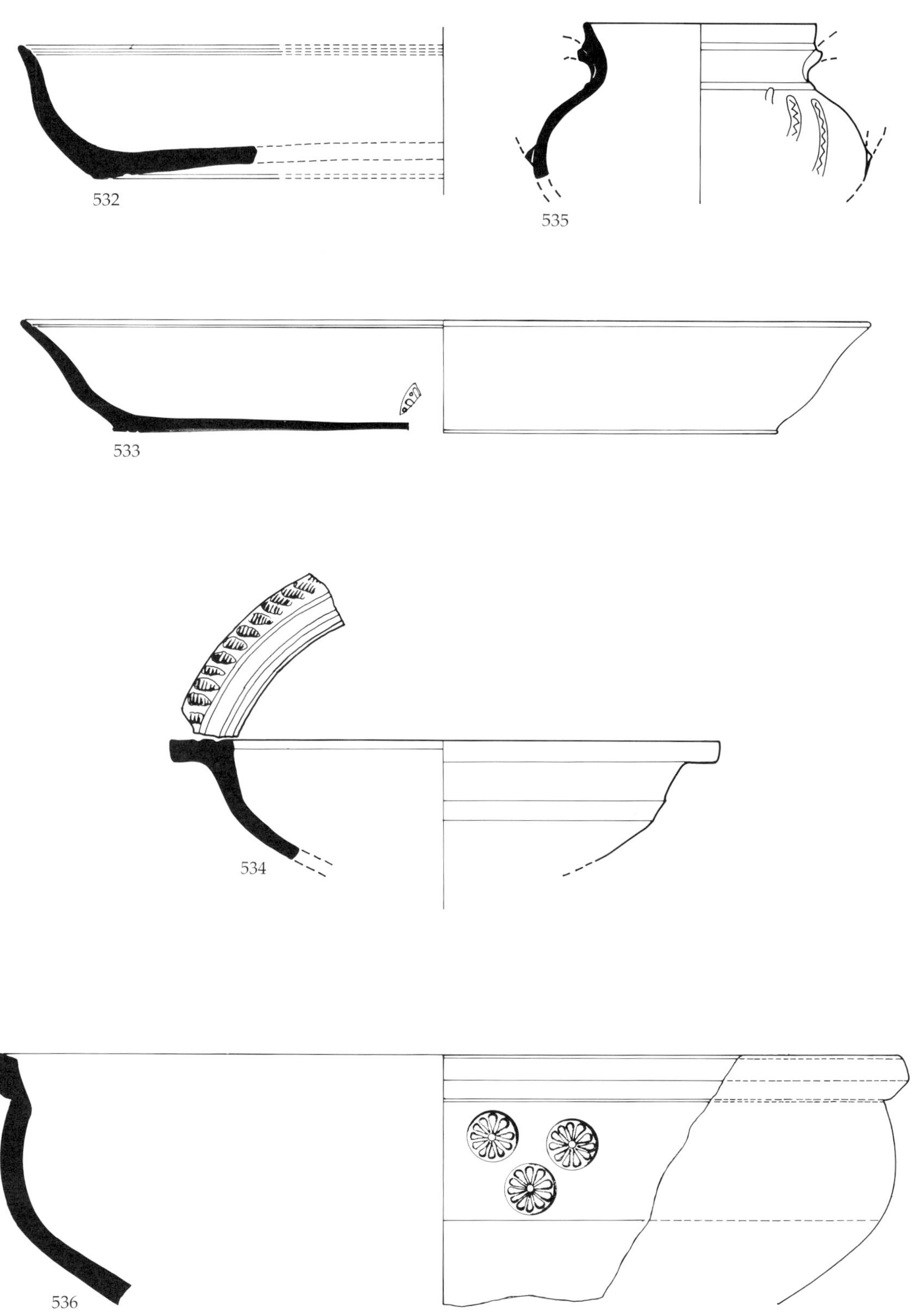

Plate 63. Miscellaneous Imports

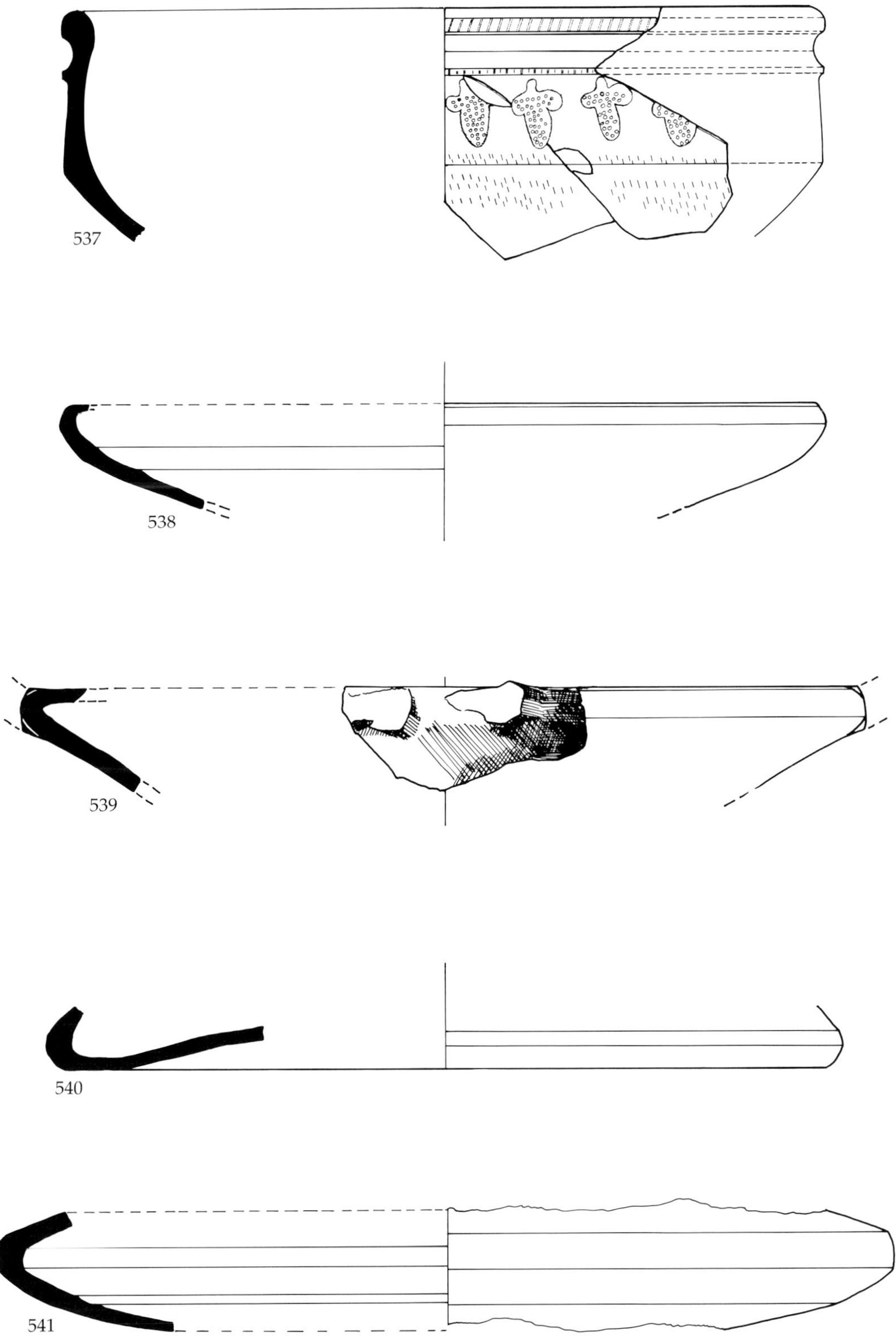

Plate 64. Miscellaneous Imports

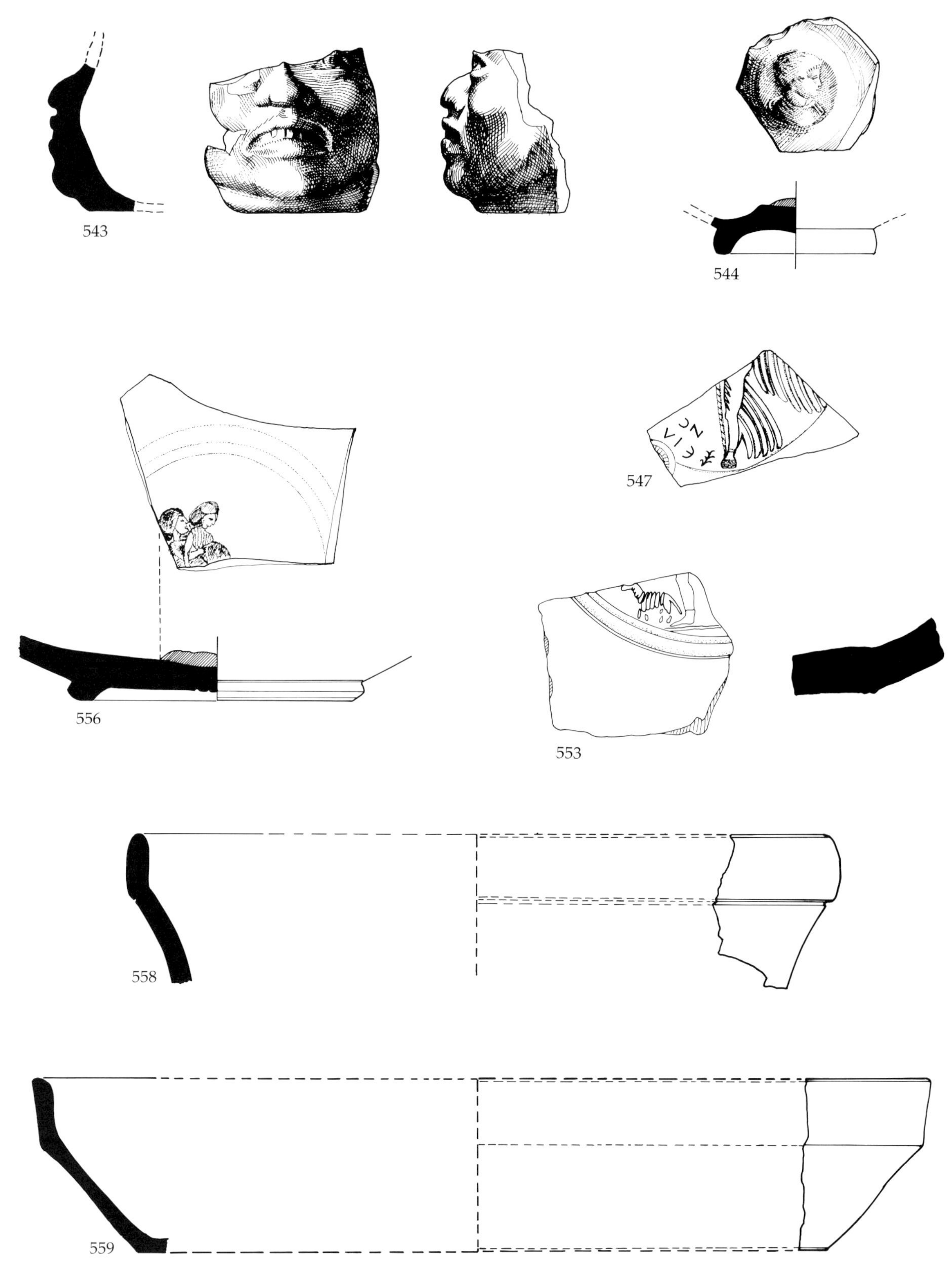

Plate 65. Miscellaneous Relief Wares. Imitation Çandarli Ware

Plate 66. Fusiform Unguentaria. Types A–C

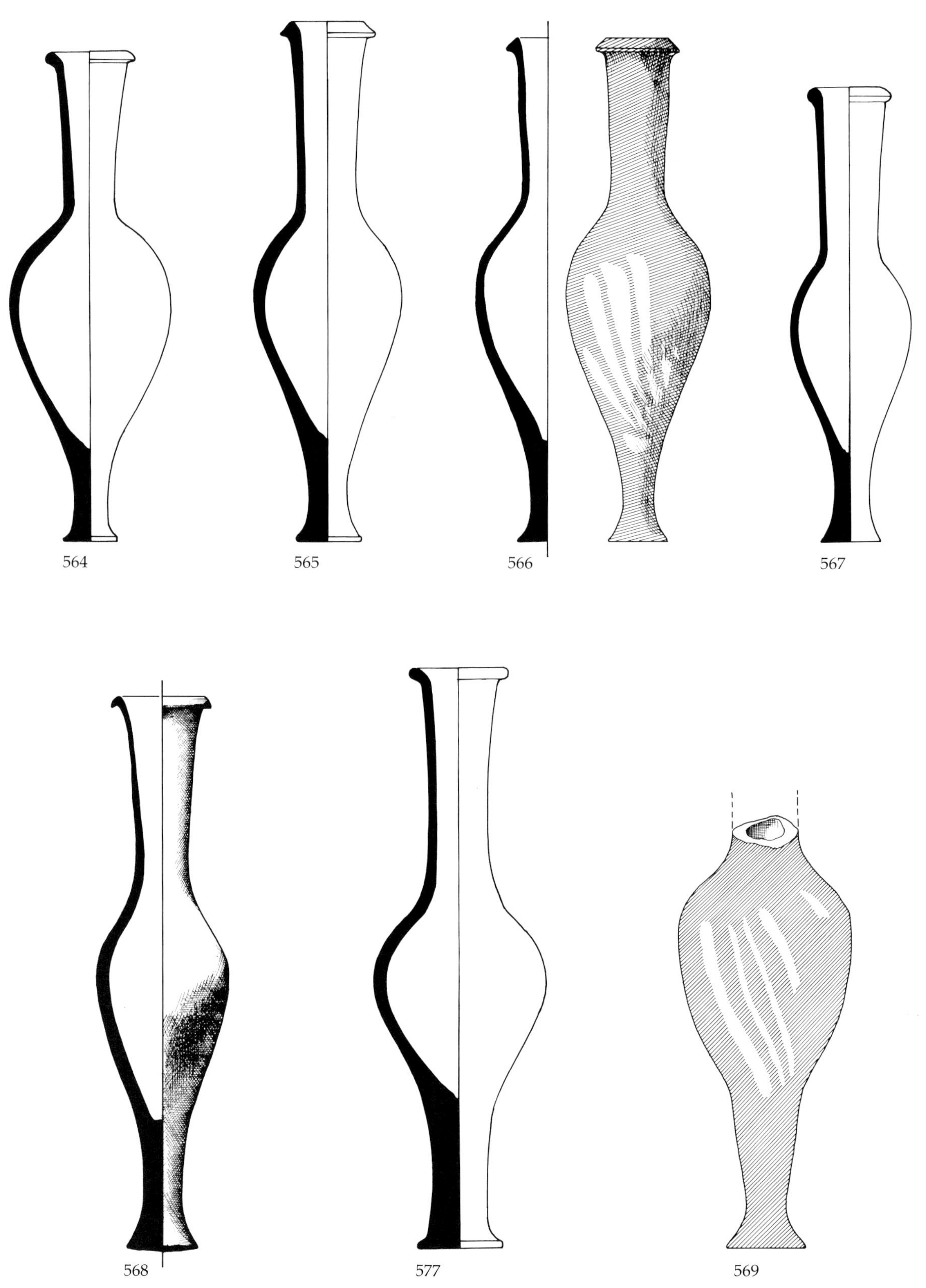

Plate 67. Fusiform Unguentaria. Types D, E, and G

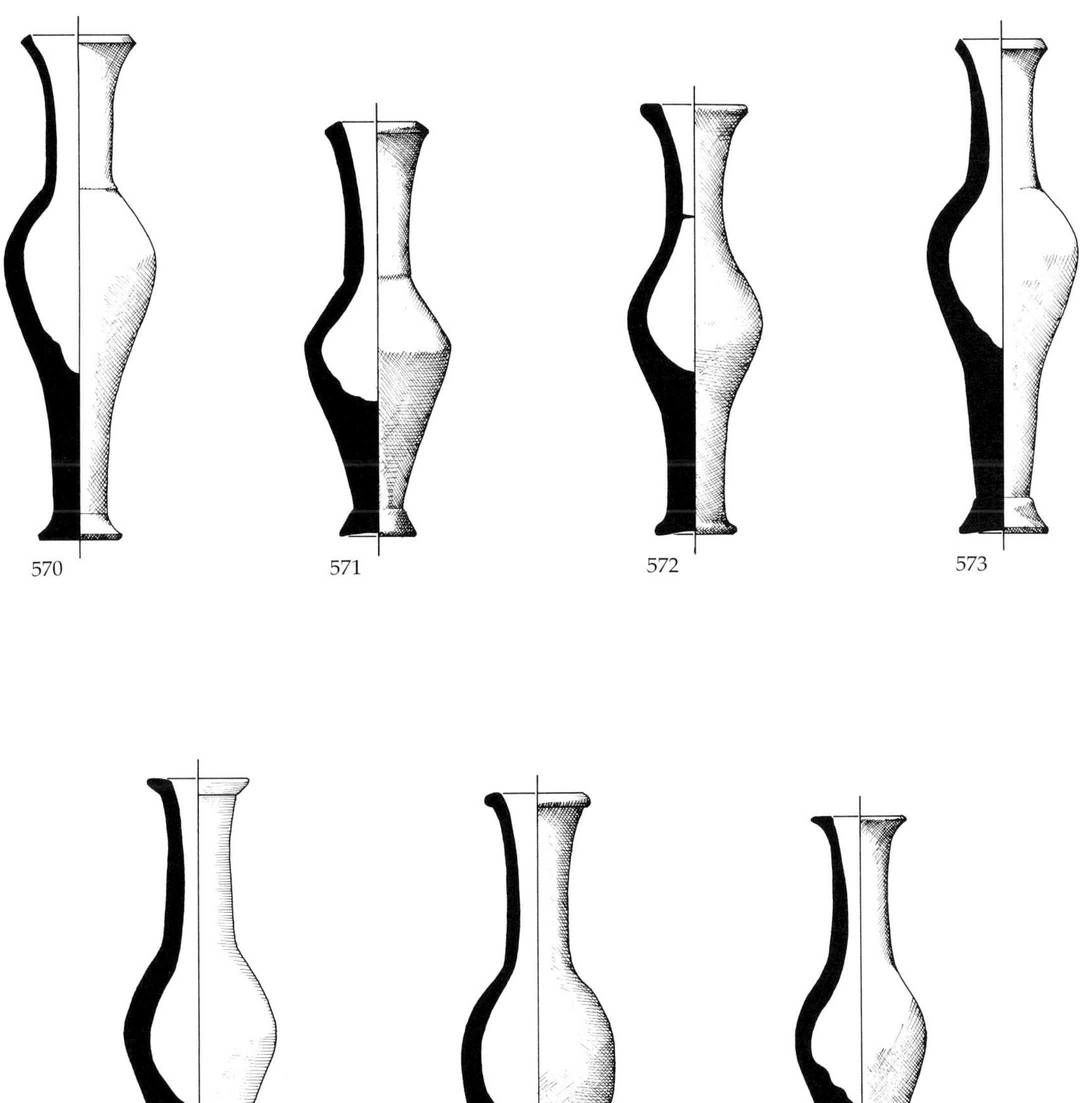

Plate 68. Fusiform Unguentaria. Type F

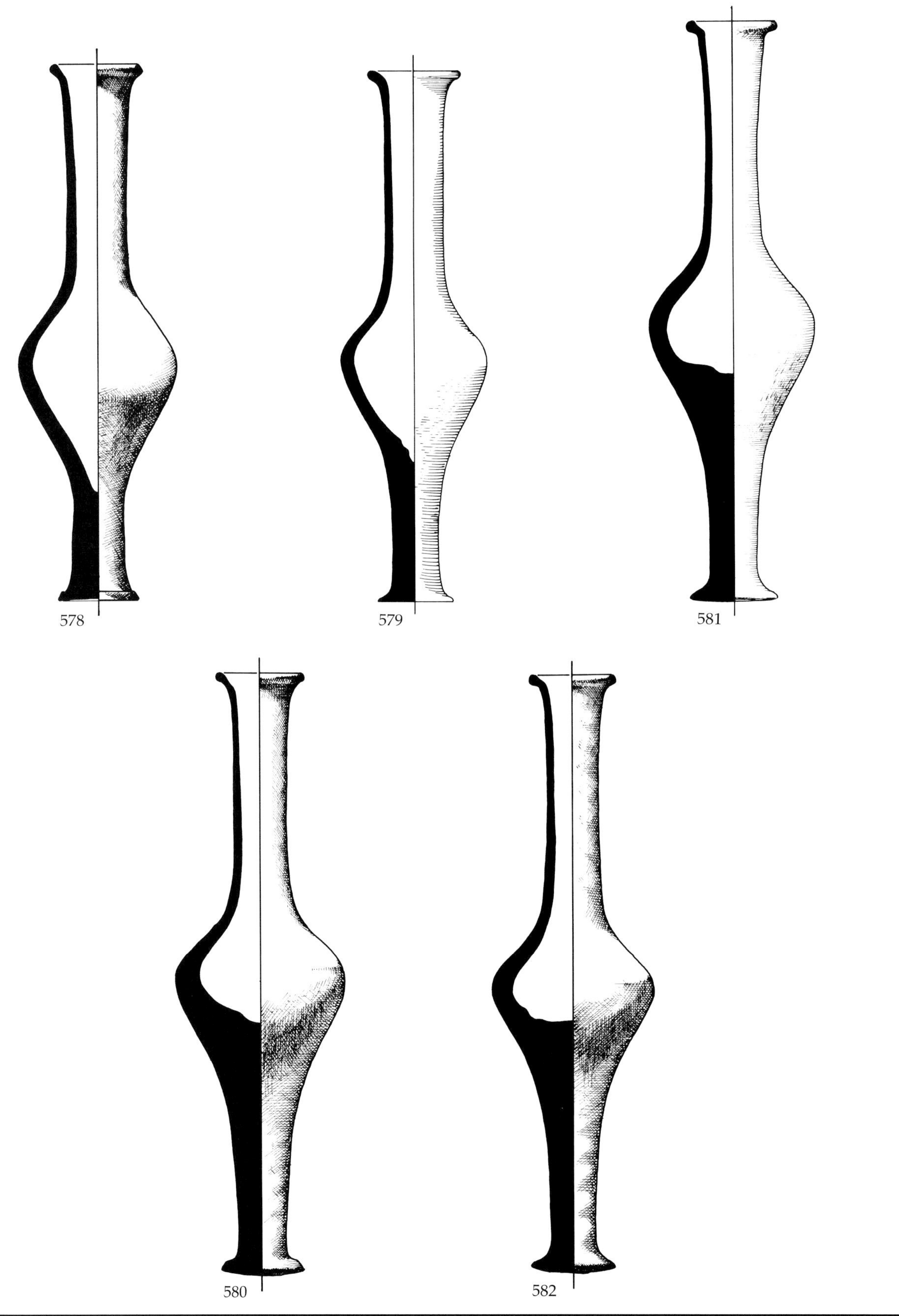

Plate 69. Fusiform Unguentaria. Type G

Plate 70. Bulbous Unguentaria. Types A–E

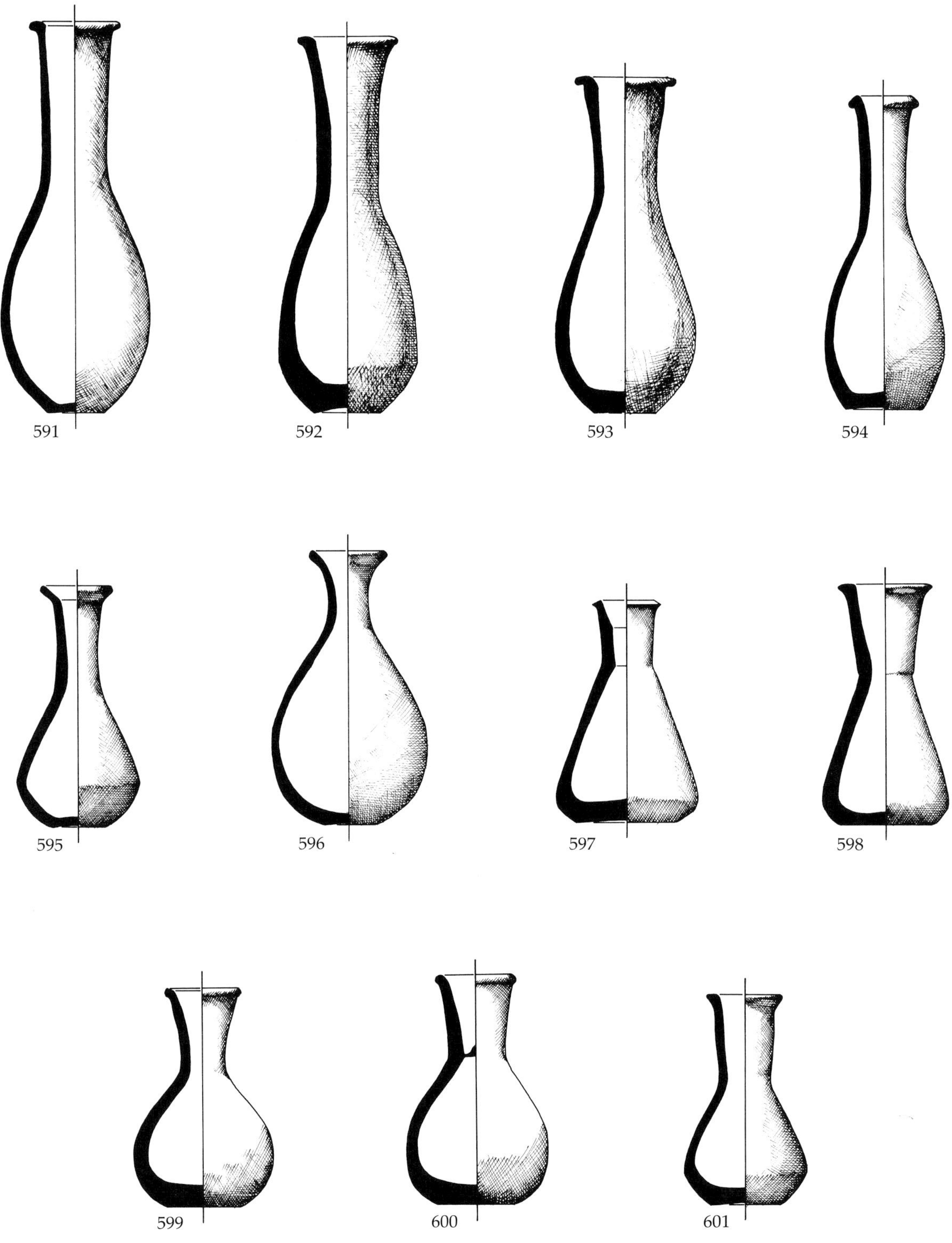

Plate 71. Bulbous Unguentaria. Types F–N

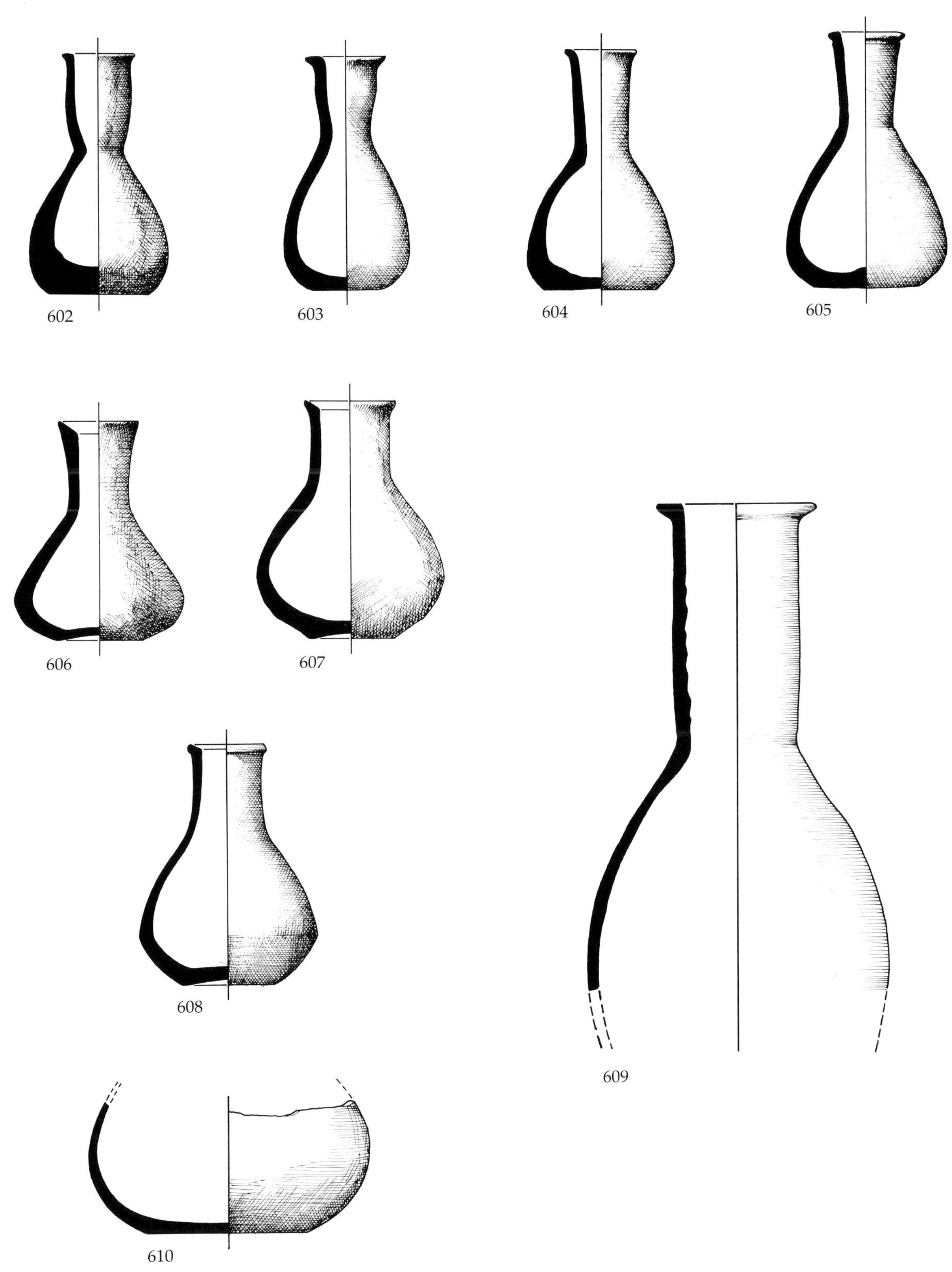

Plate 72. Bulbous Unguentaria. Types M–Q

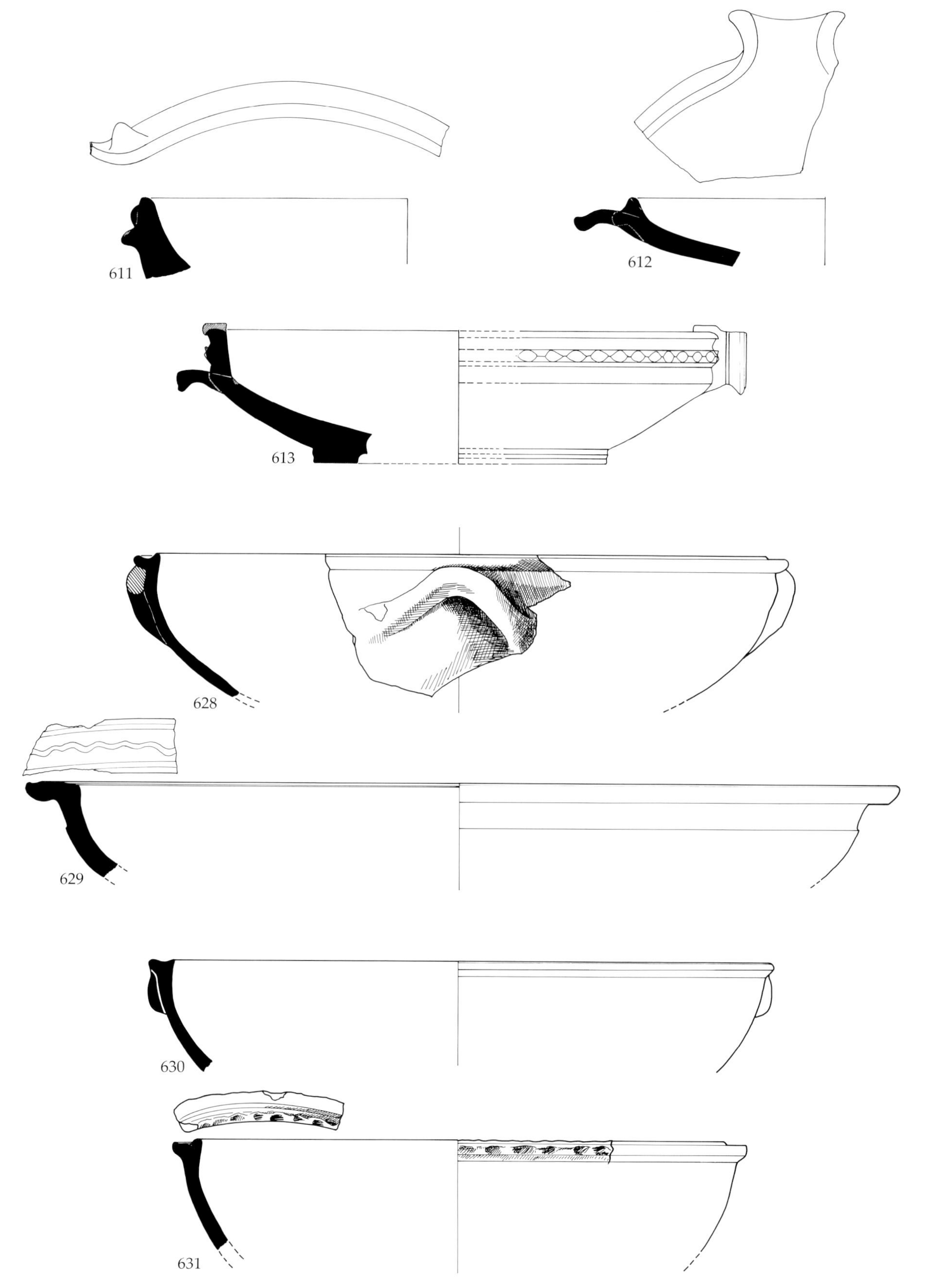

Plate 73. (scale 1:3) Mortaria. Red Micaceous Ware

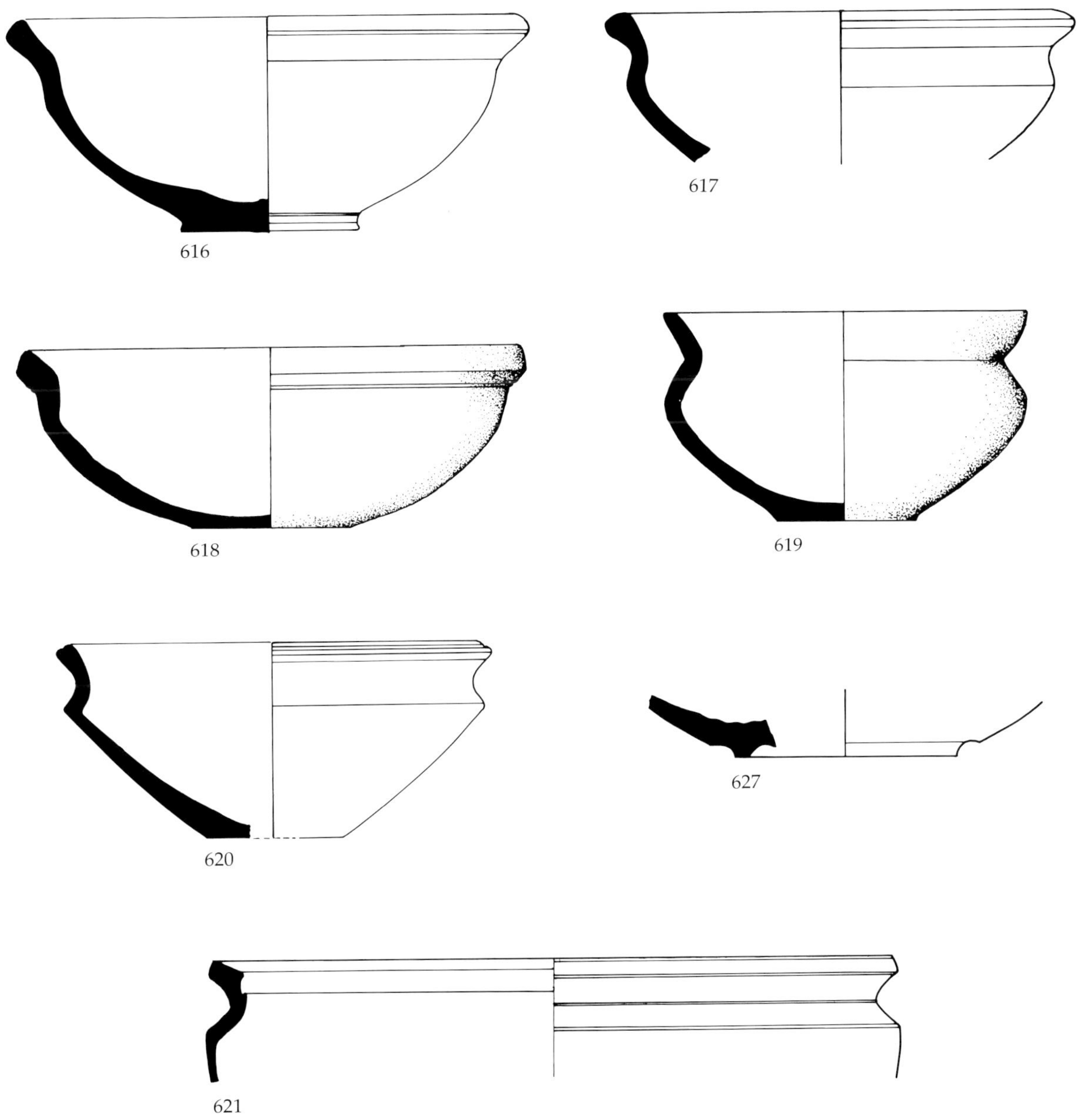

Plate 74. Tan Micaceous Ware

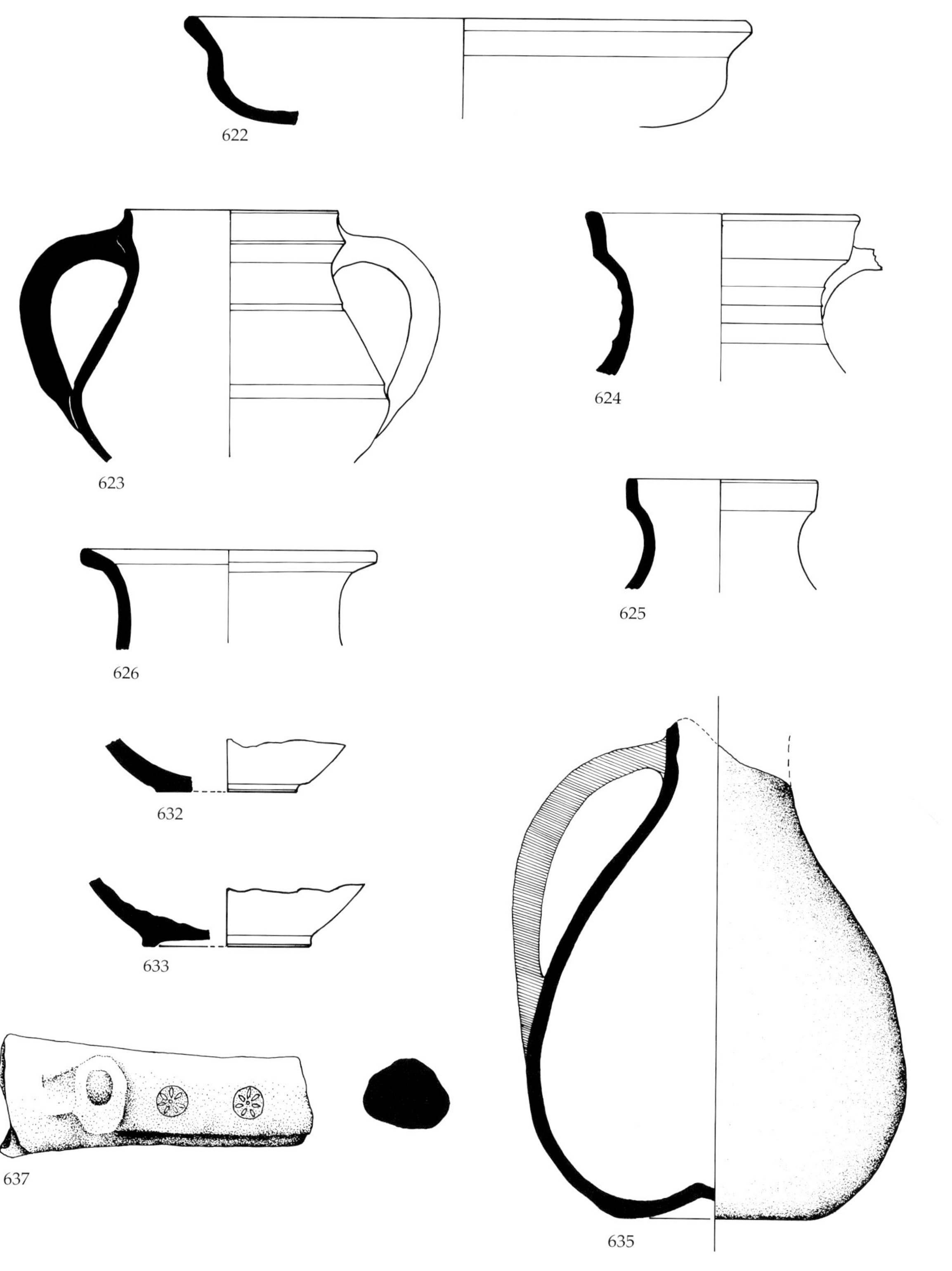

Plate 75. Tan Micaceous Ware. Mica-Dusted Ware

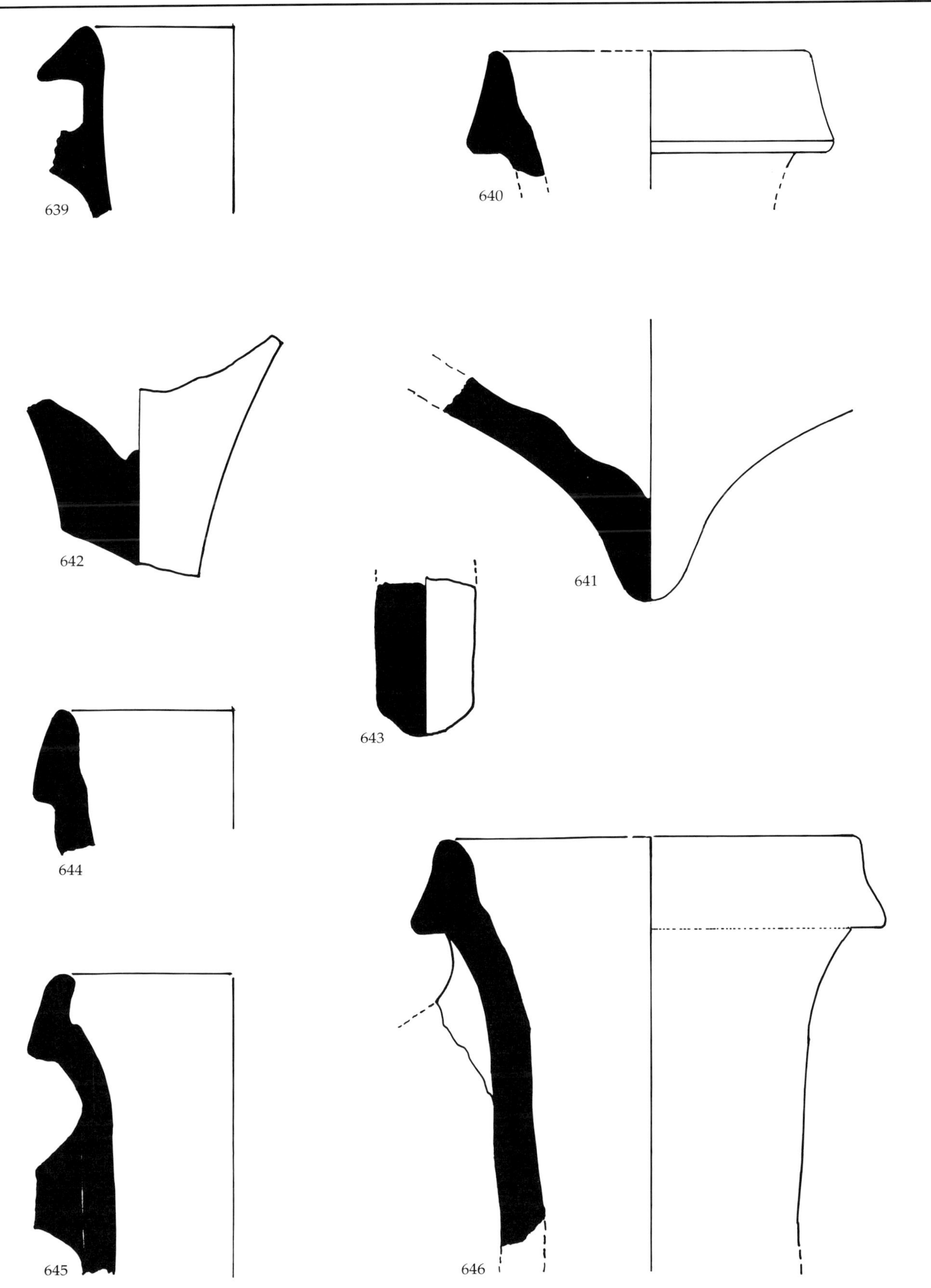

Plate 76. (scale 2:5) Amphorae. Hellenistic and Early Roman types

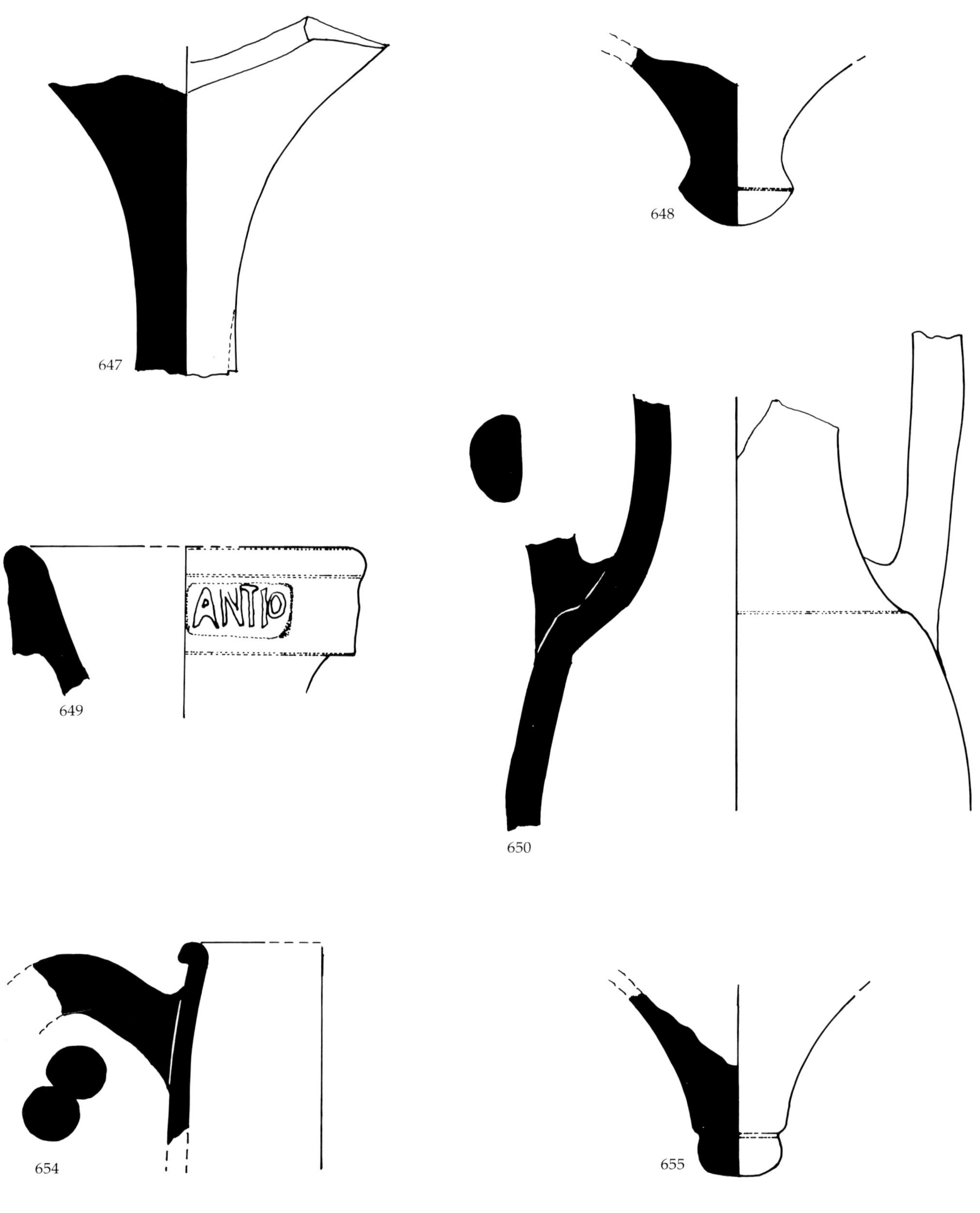

Plate 77. (scale 2:5) Amphorae. Hellenistic and Early Roman types (650, scale 1:4)

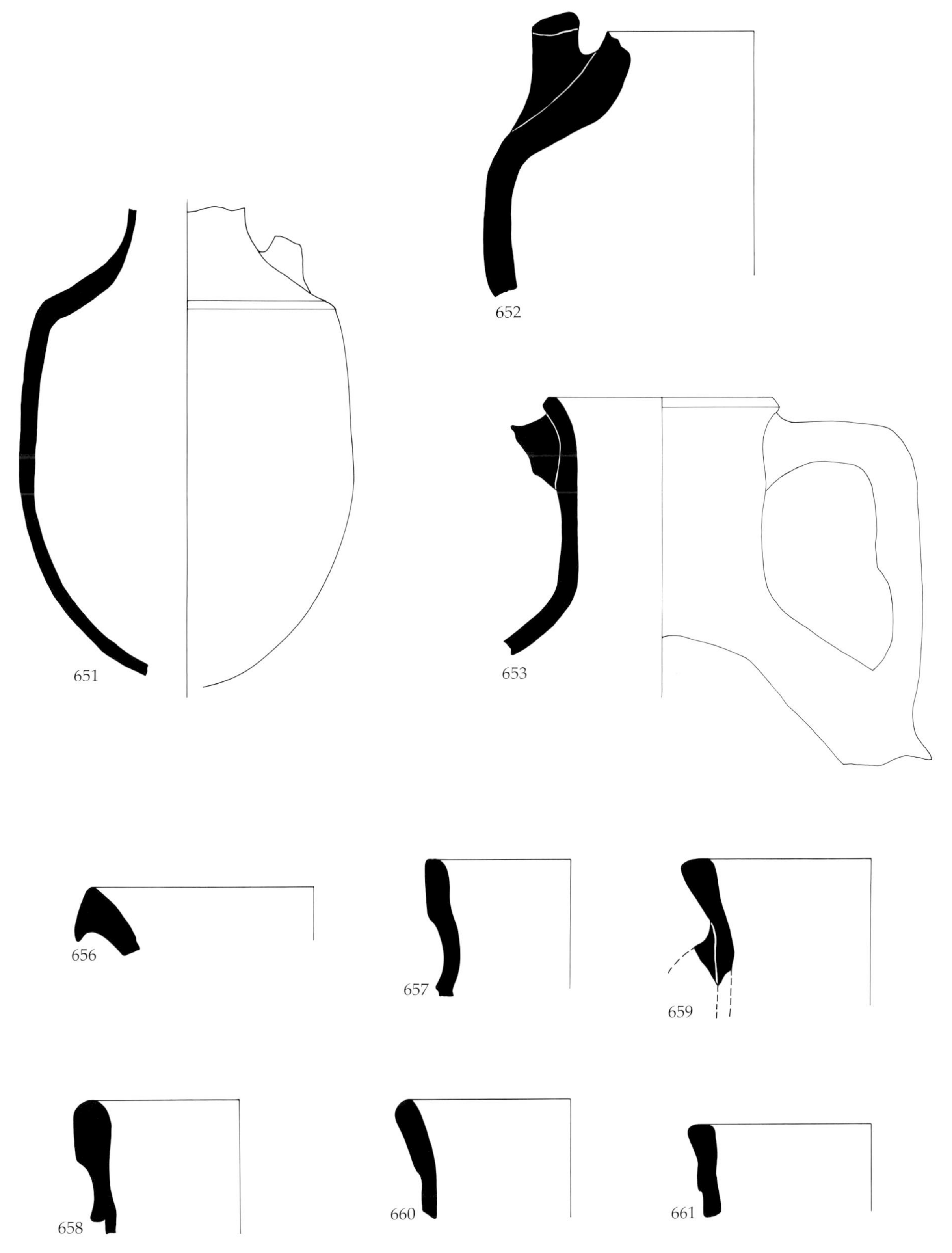

Plate 78. (scale 1:3) Amphorae. Hellenistic and Early Roman types (651, scale 1:6)

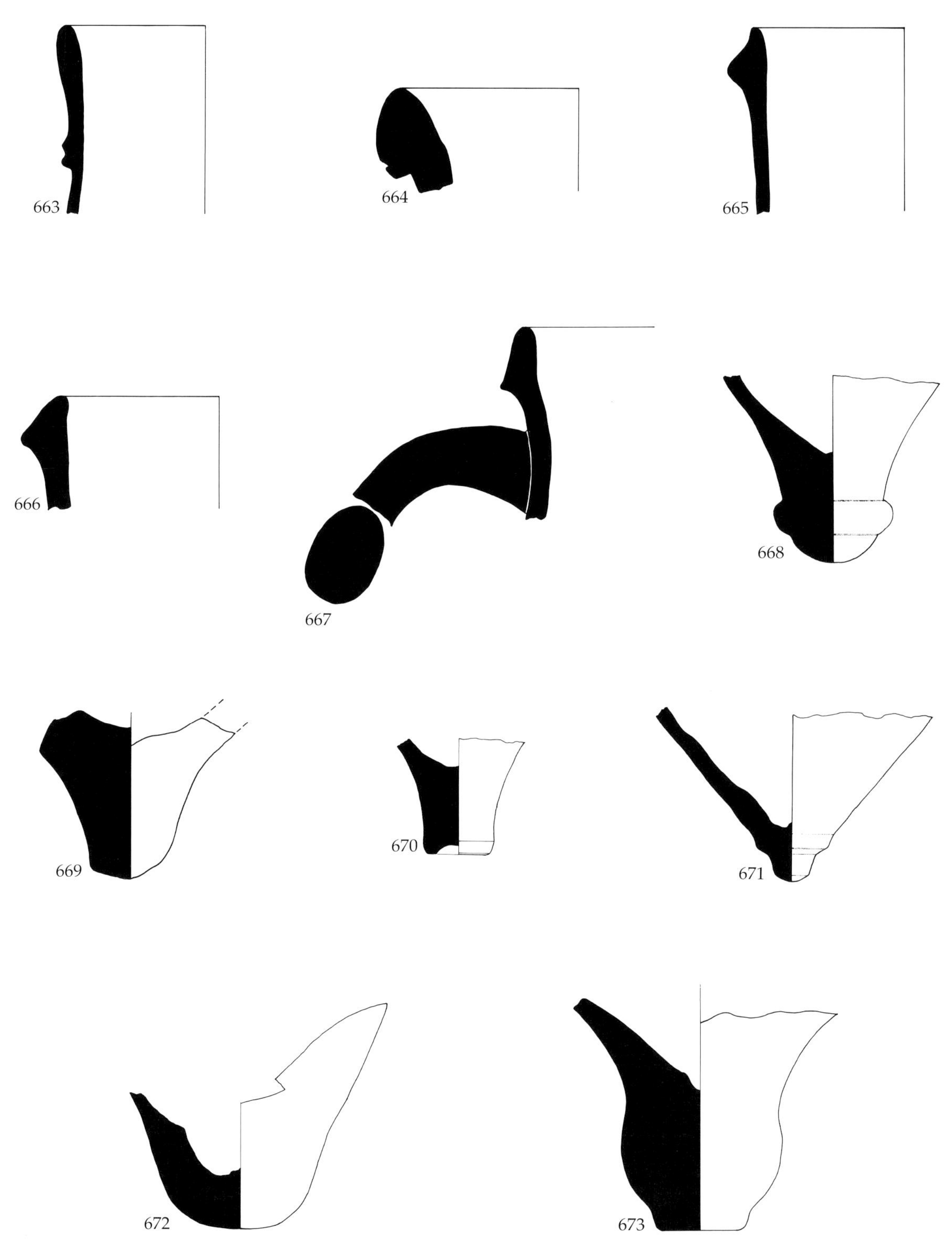

Plate 79. (scale 1:3) Amphorae. Hellenistic and Early Roman types

Plate 80. (scale 1:3) Amphorae. Middle Roman types

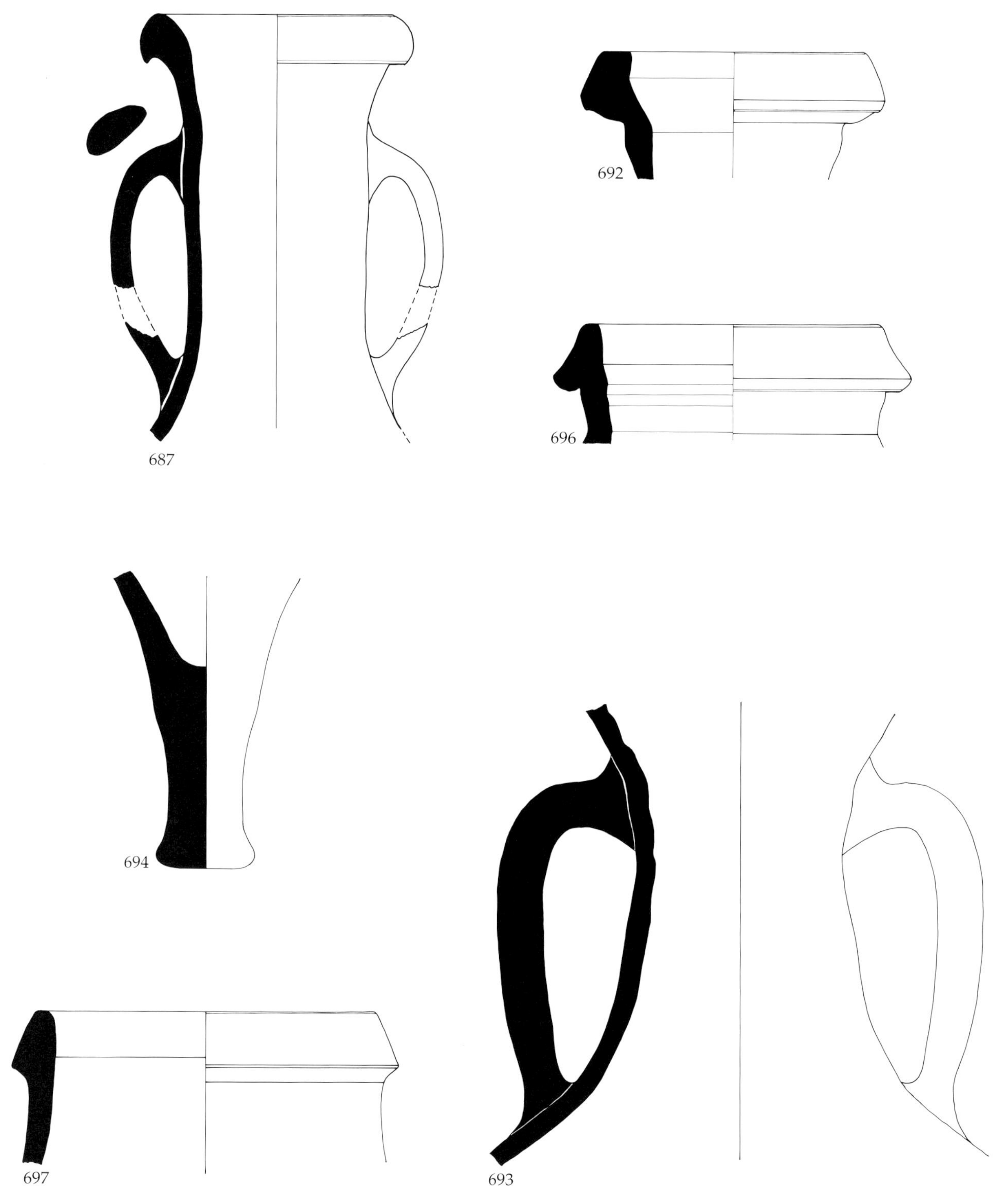

Plate 81. (scale 1:3) Amphorae. Middle Roman types

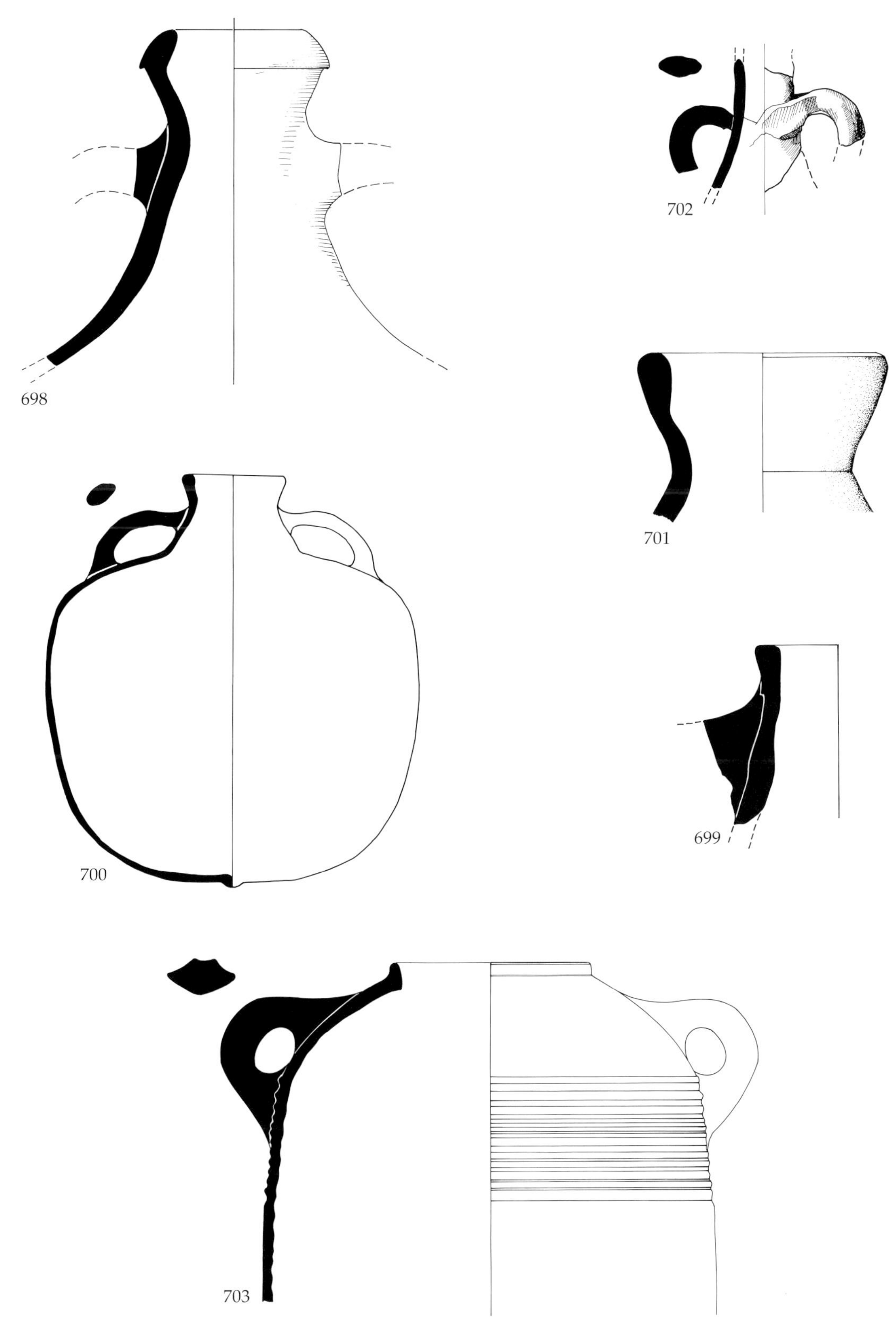

Plate 82. (scale 1:3) Amphorae. Middle Roman and Late Roman types (700, scale 1:6)

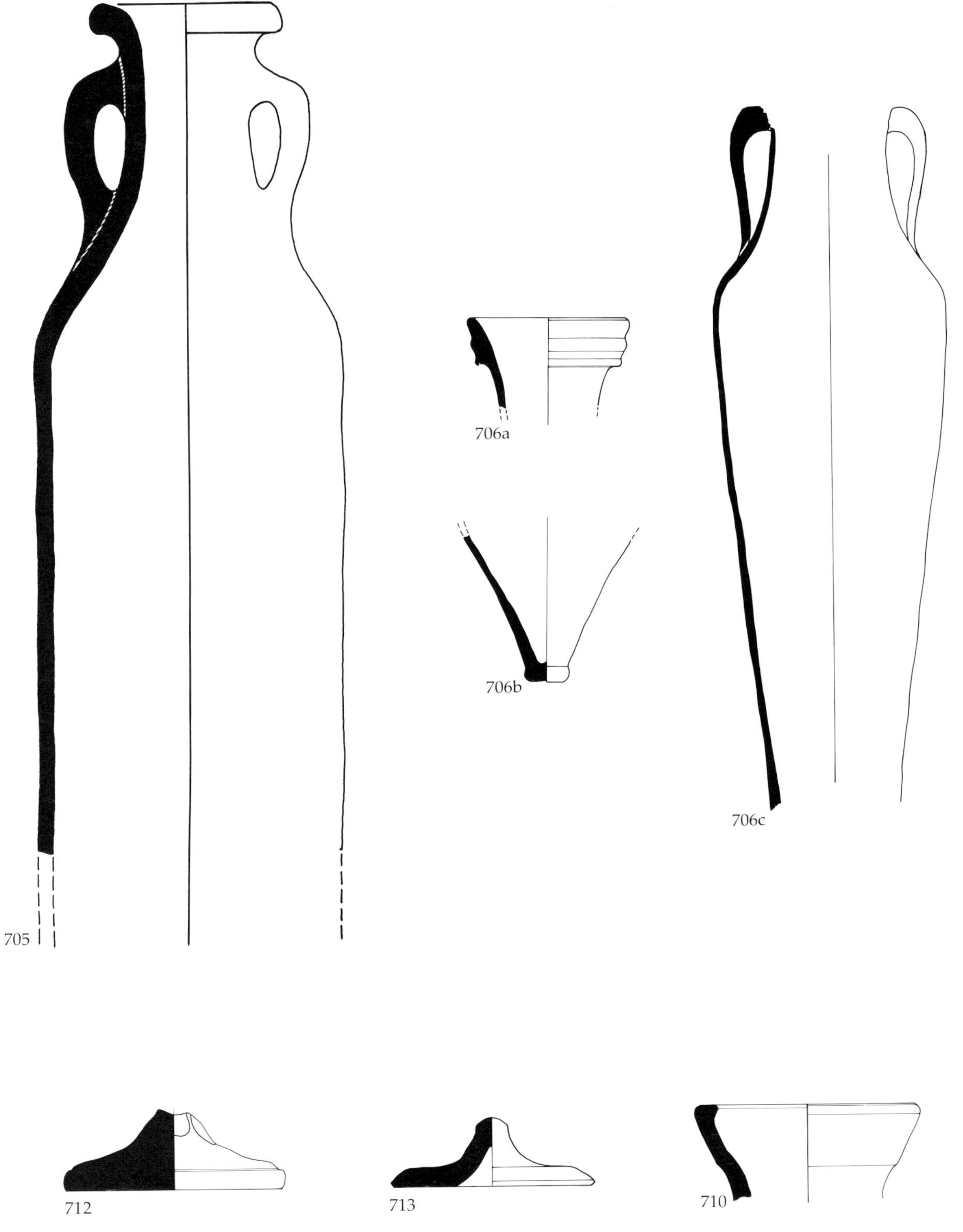

Plate 83. (scale 1:3) Amphorae. Late Roman types

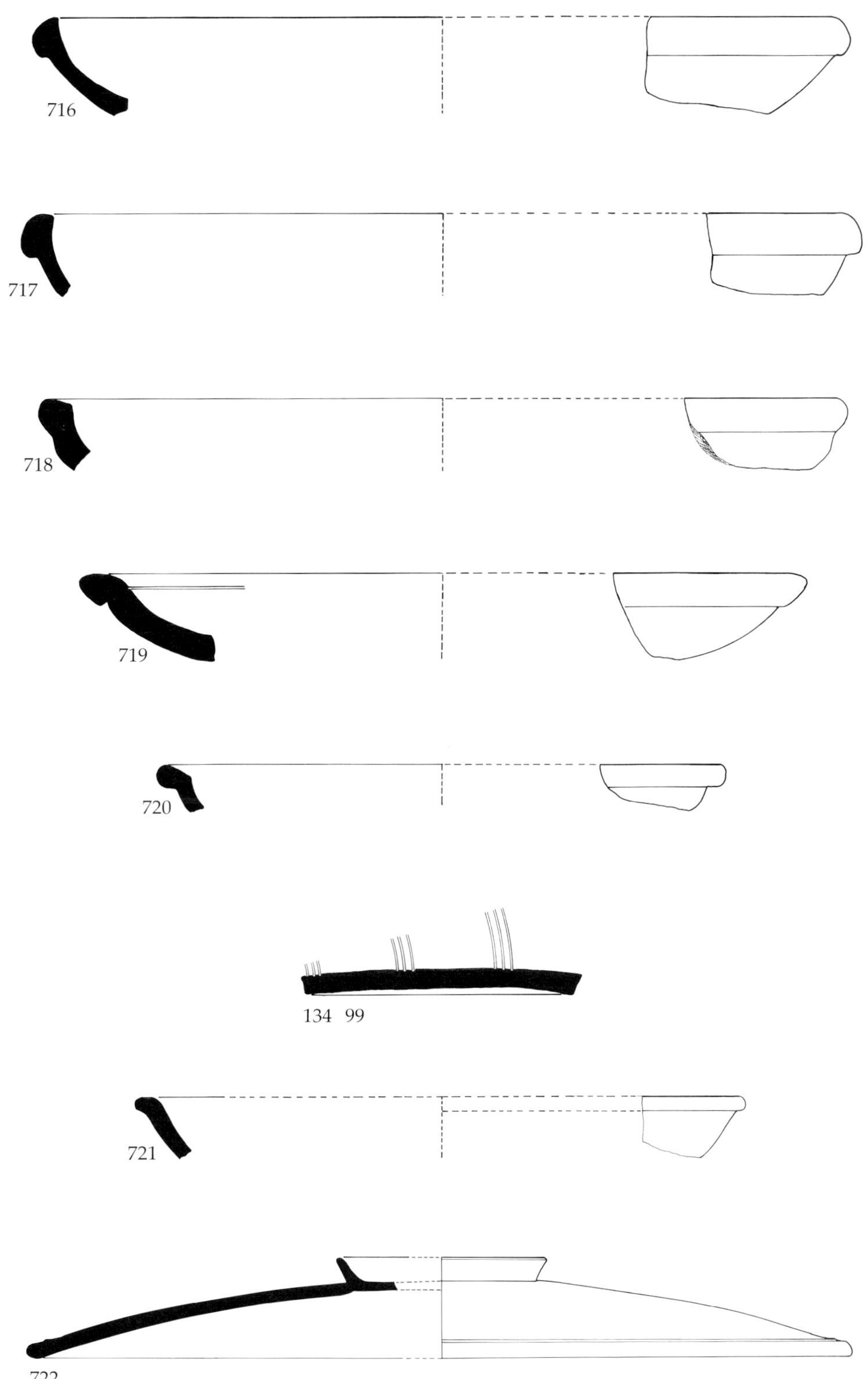

Plate 84. (scale 1:3) Pompeian Red Ware. Campanian Cooking Ware

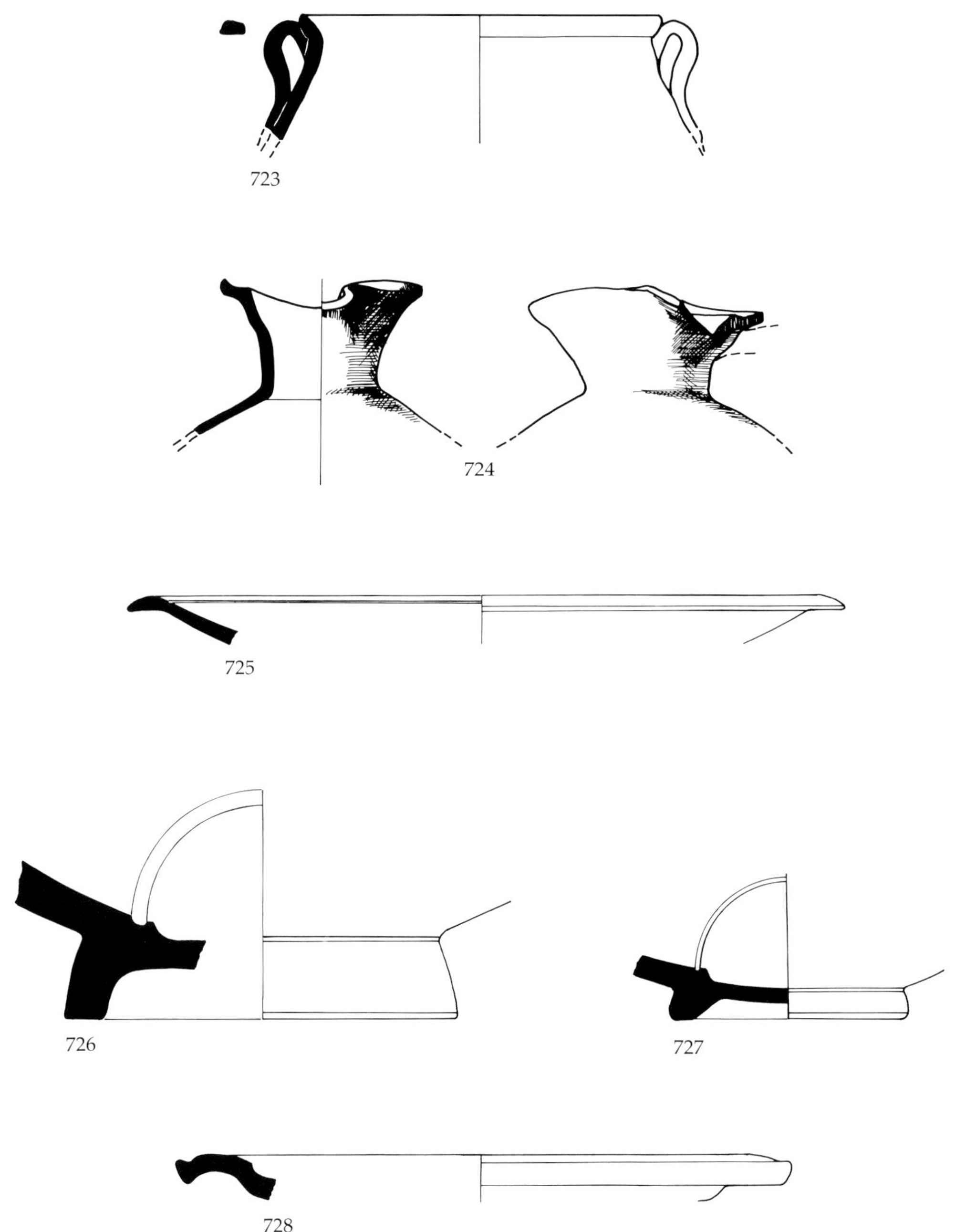

Plate 85. Aegean Cooking Ware. Hellenistic Color-Slipped Forms 1 and 2

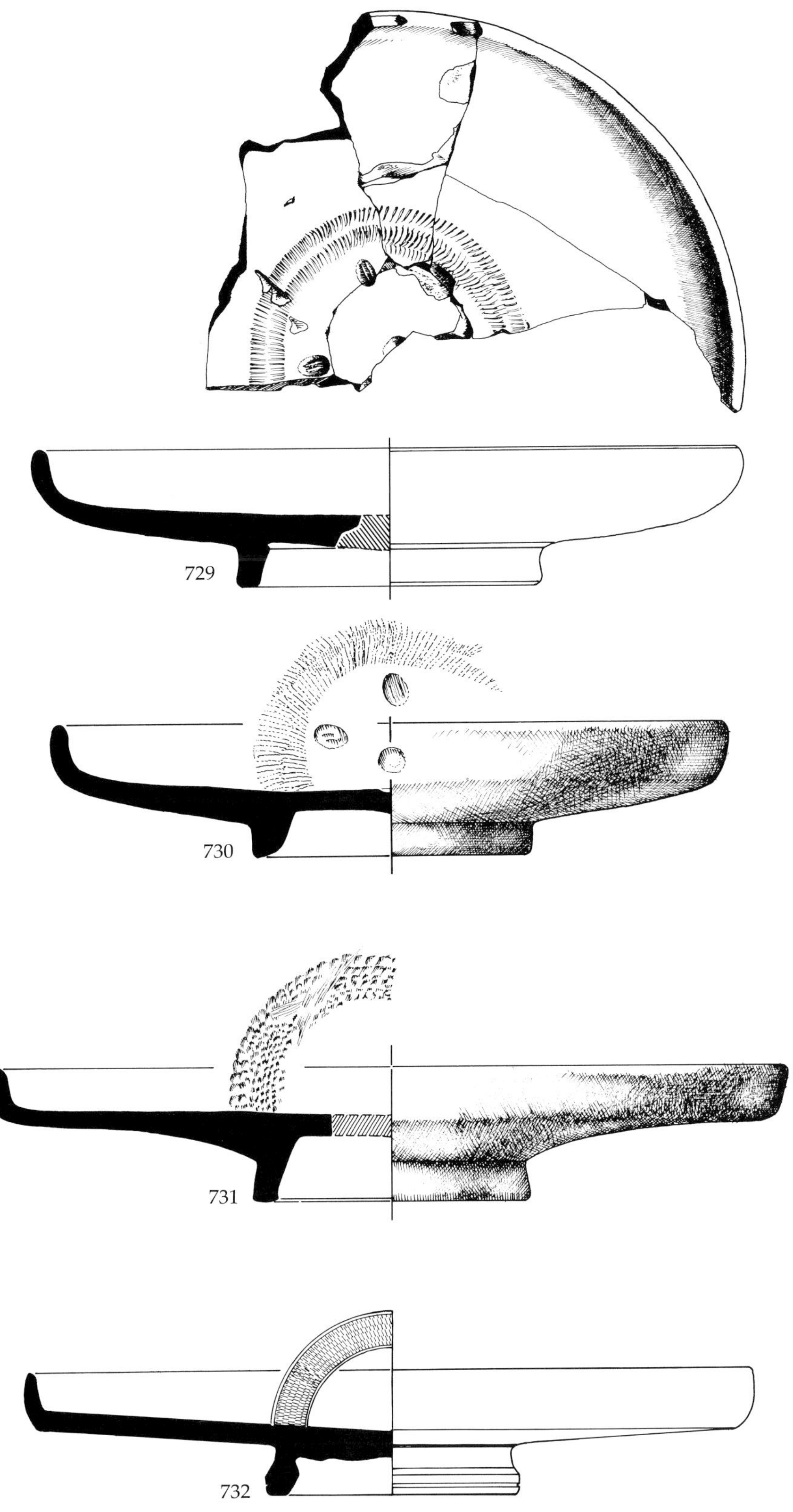

Plate 86. Hellenistic Color-Slipped Form 3

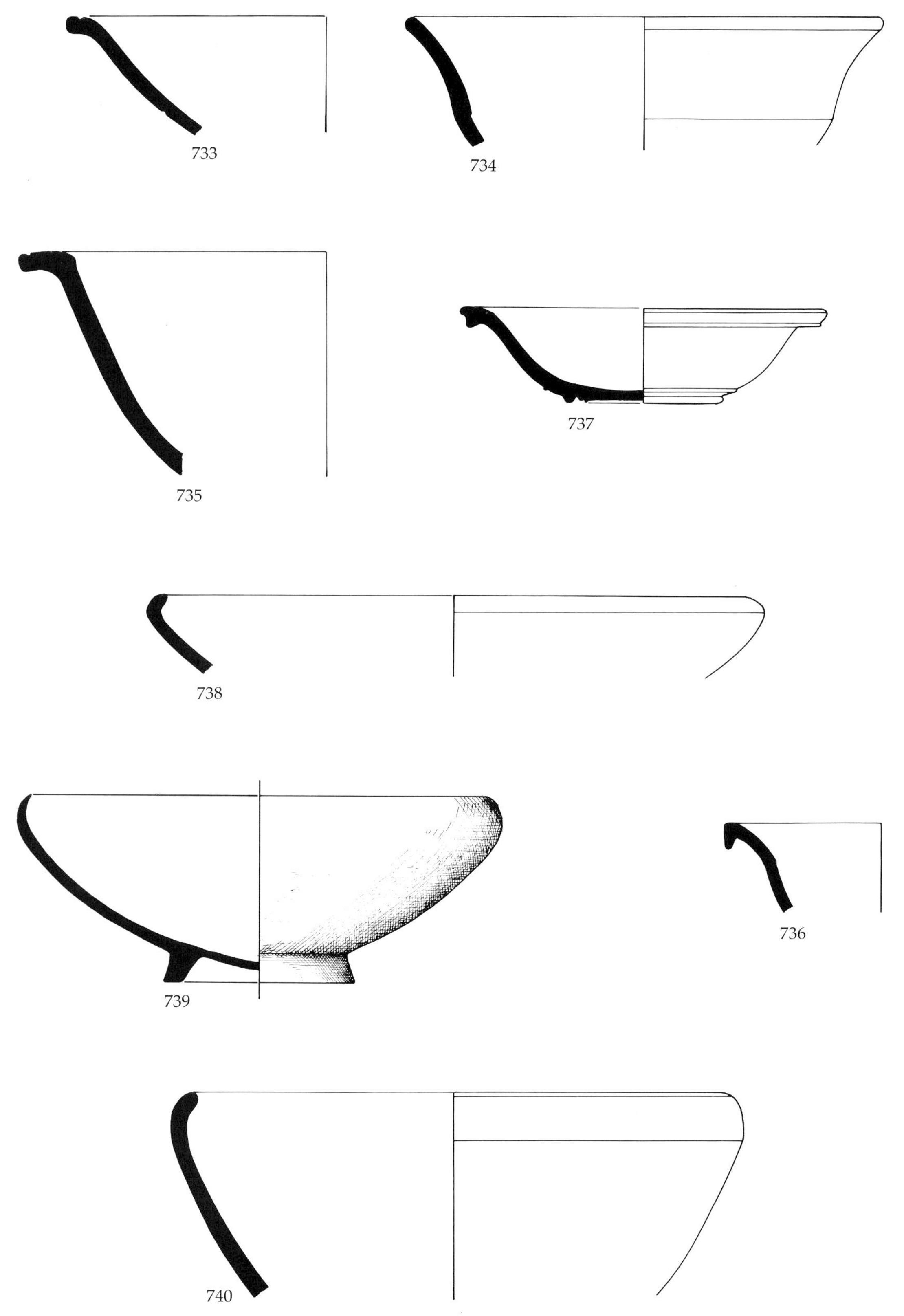

Plate 87. Hellenistic Color-Slipped Forms 4–8

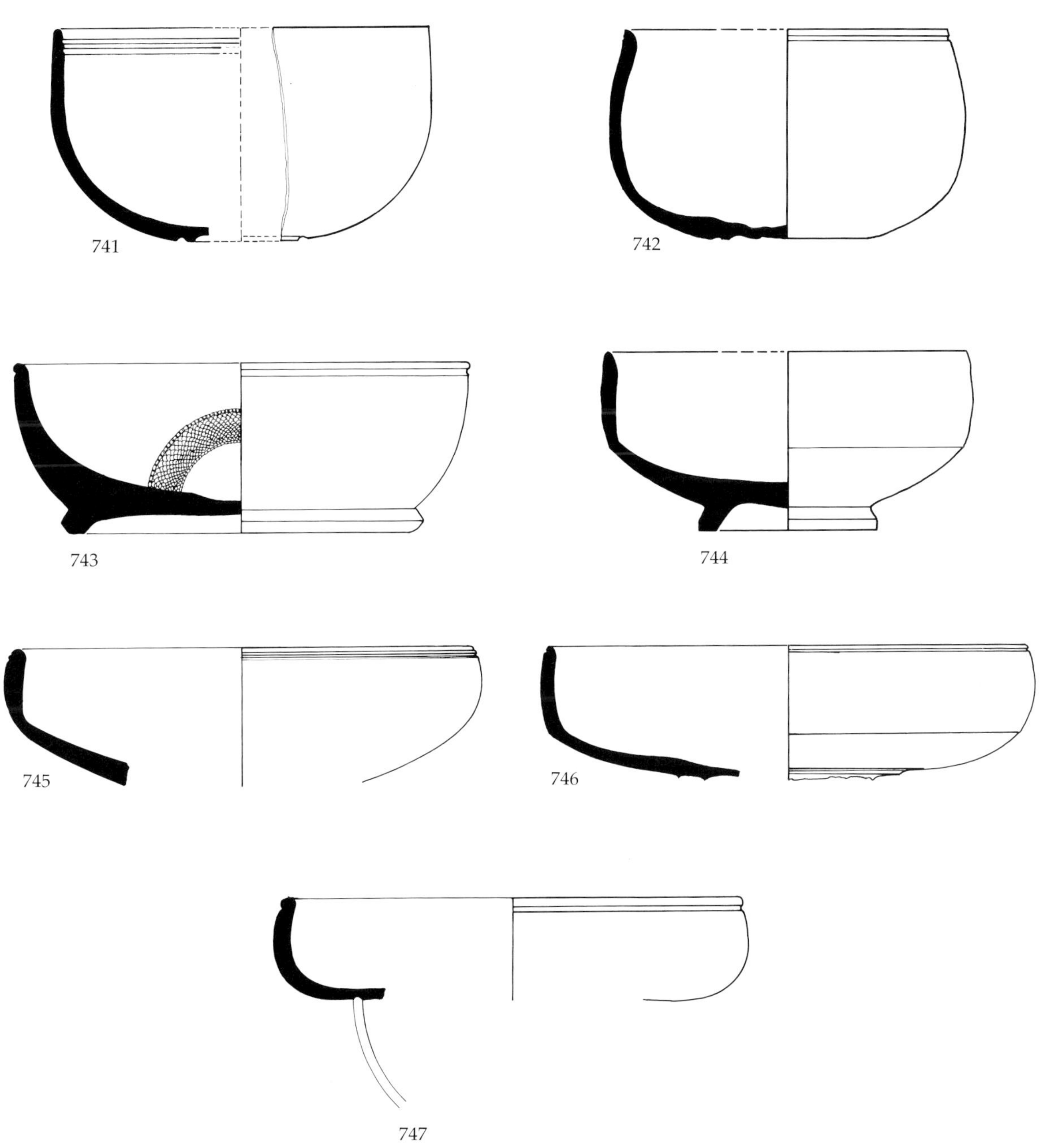

Plate 88. Hellenistic Color-Slipped Forms 10–12

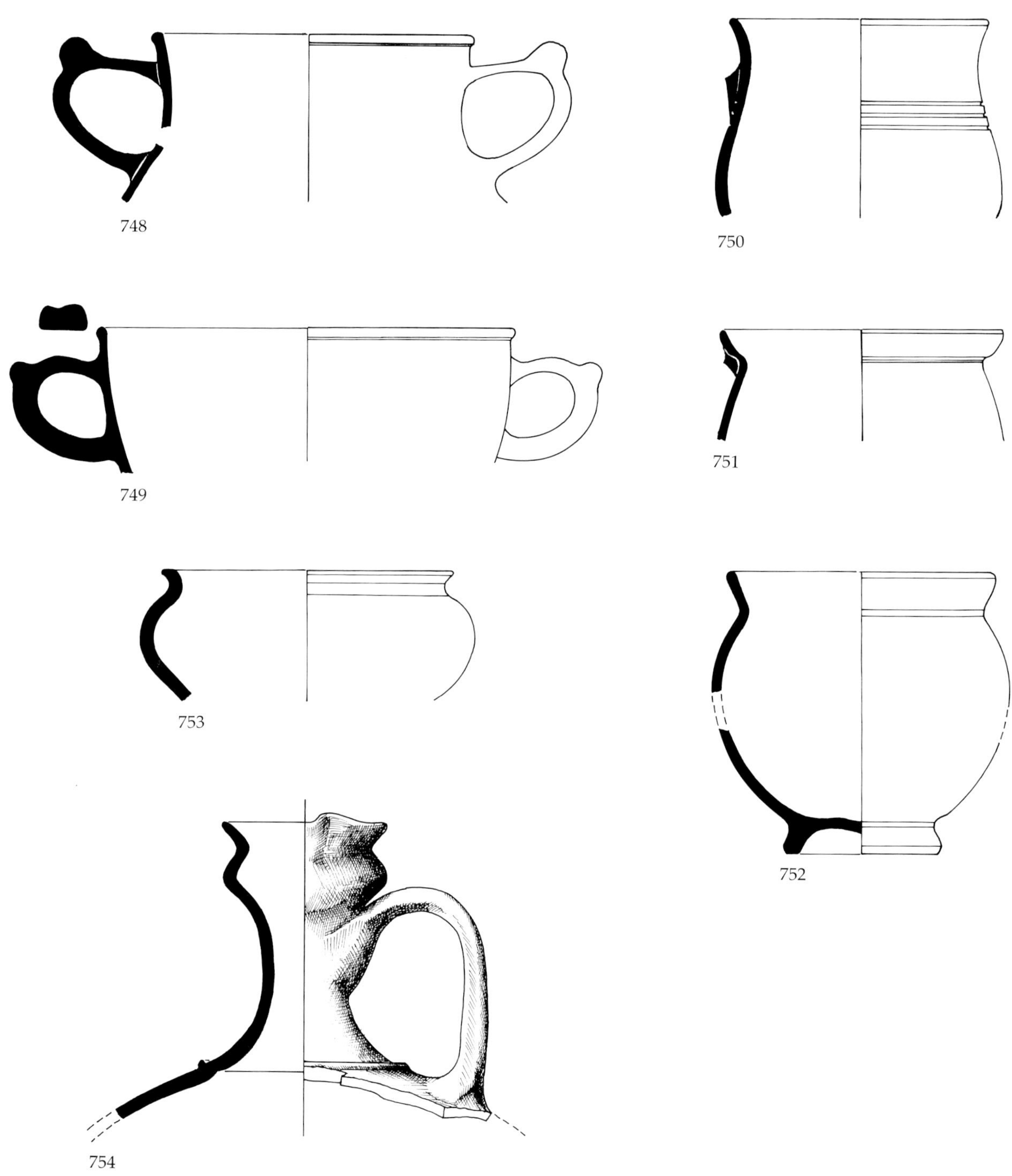

Plate 89. Hellenistic Color-Slipped Forms 13–17

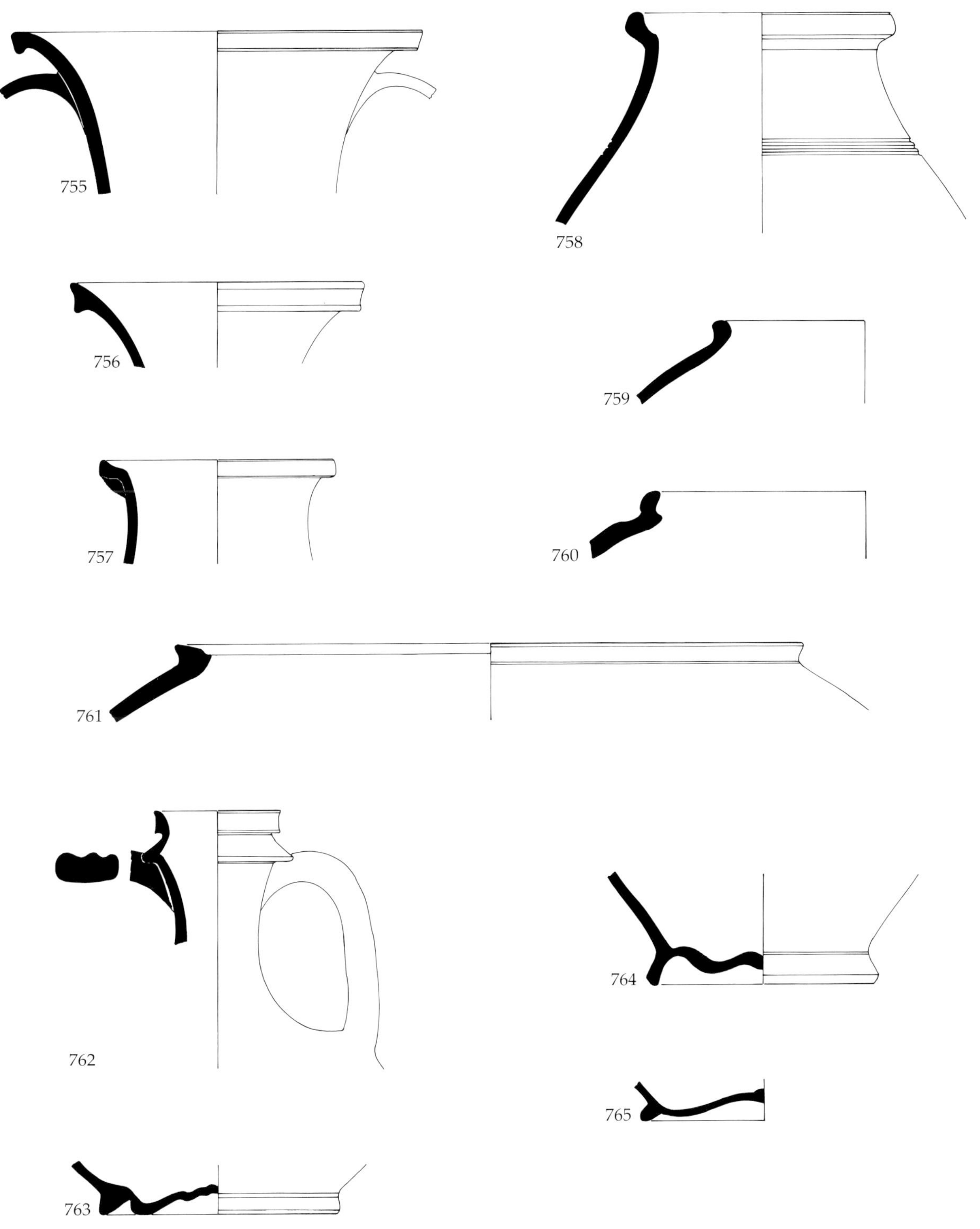

Plate 90. (scale 1:3) Hellenistic Color-Slipped and Plain Forms 18–22

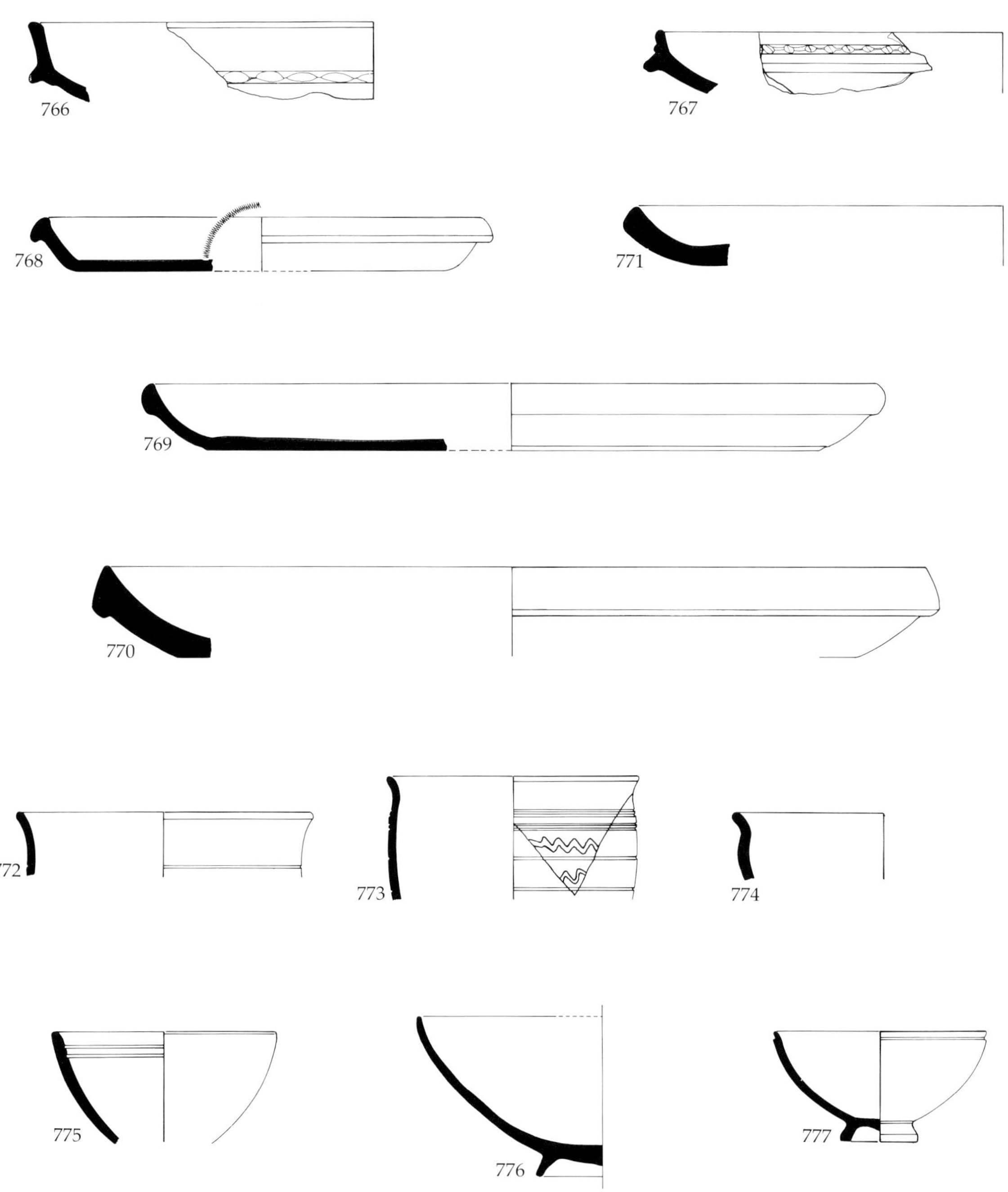

Plate 91. (scale 1:3) Hellenistic Color-Slipped and Plain Form 23 and Other Hellenistic bowls

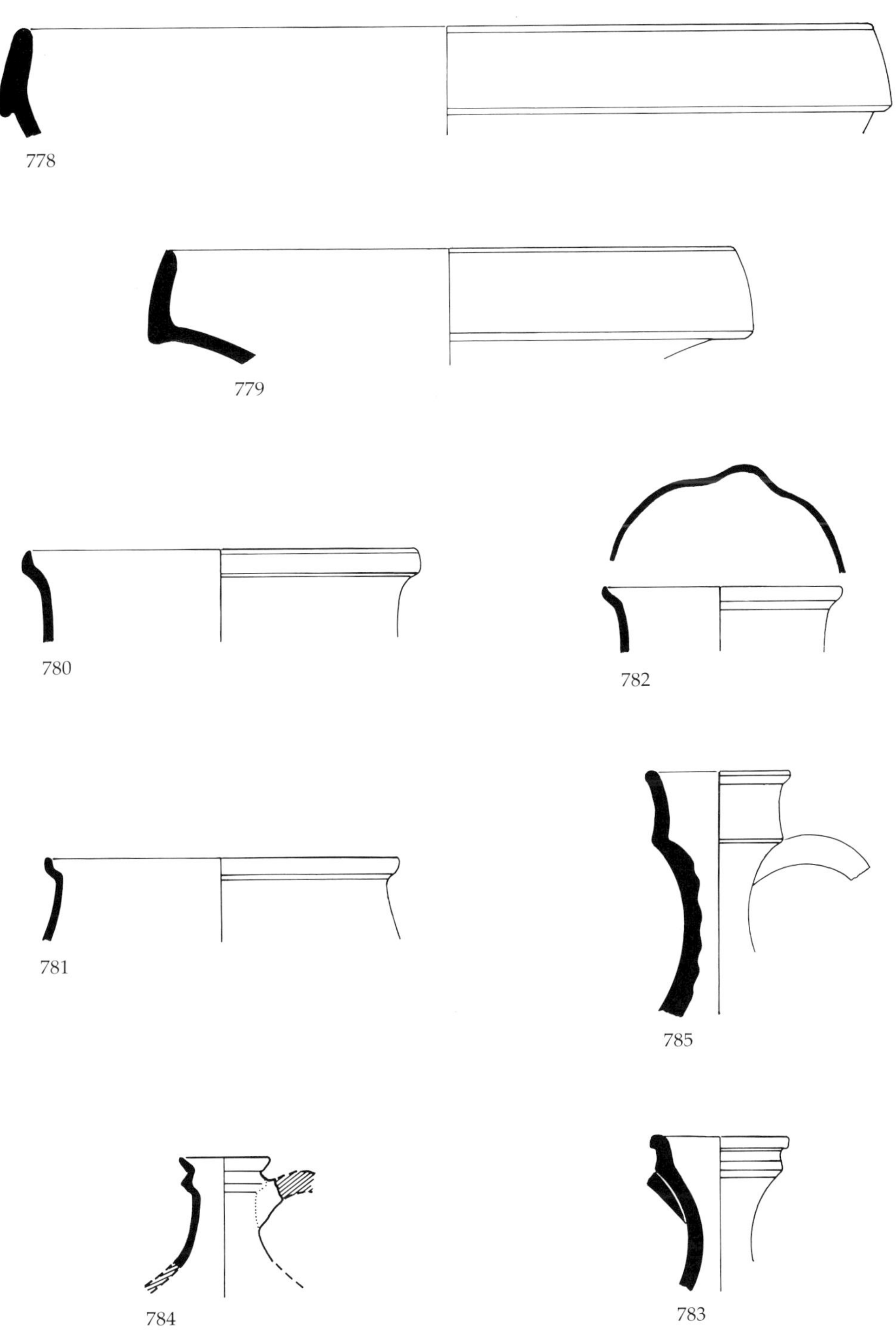

Plate 92. Hellenistic Color-Slipped bowls, jars, and pitchers

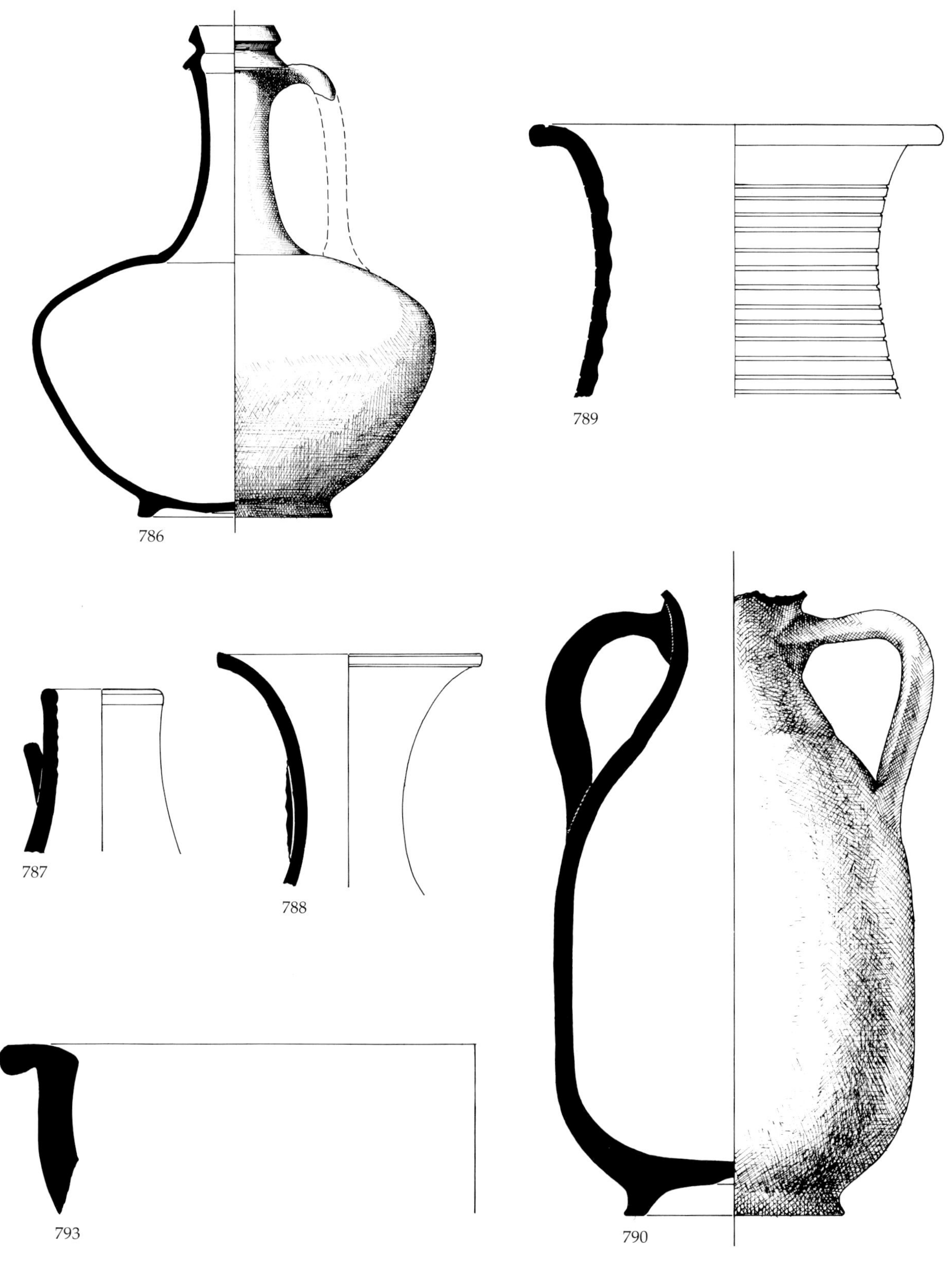

Plate 93. Hellenistic Color-Slipped and Plain pitchers, jug, and basin

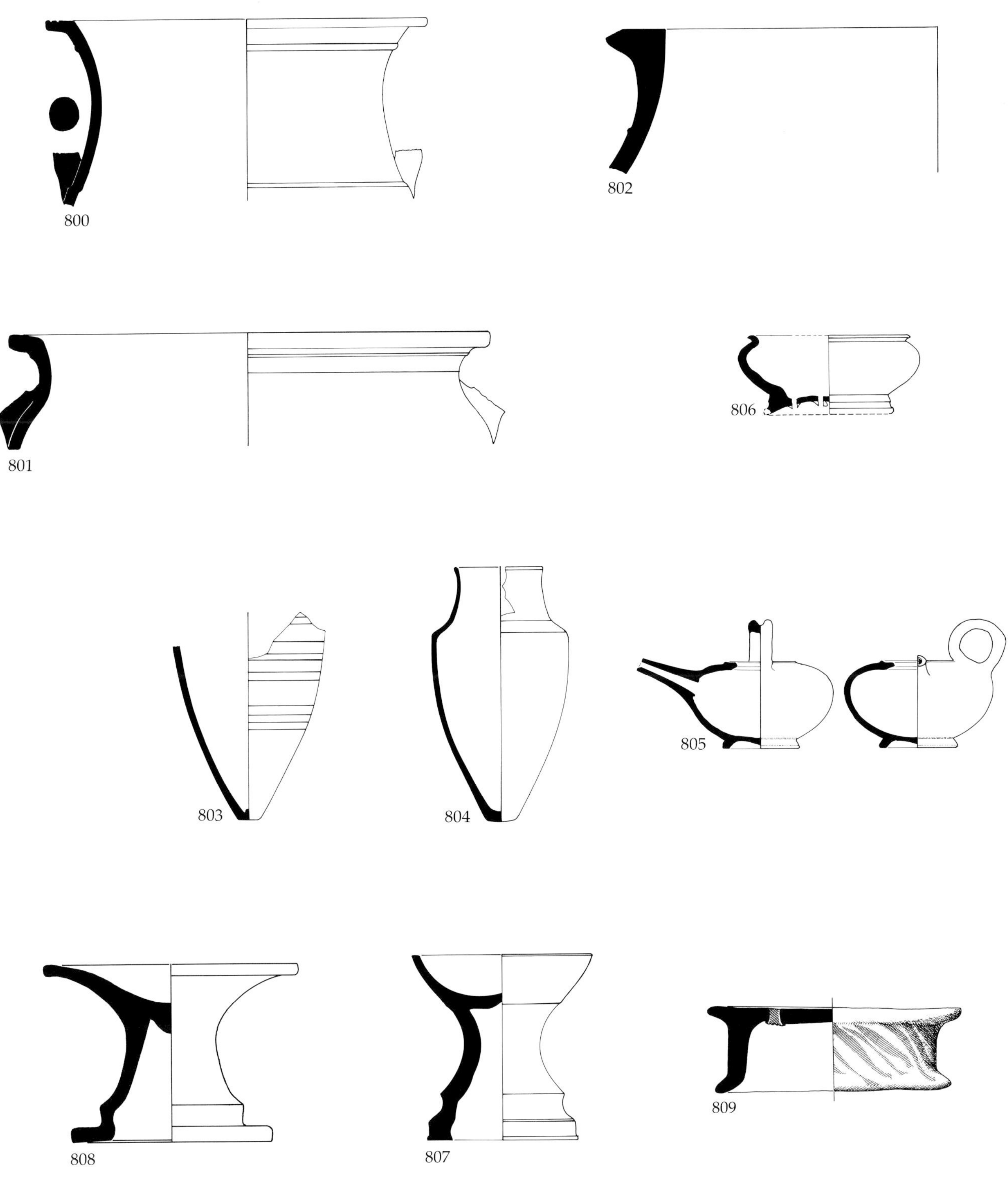

Plate 94. (scale 1:3) Hellenistic Color-Slipped and Plain kraters, jar, and other shapes

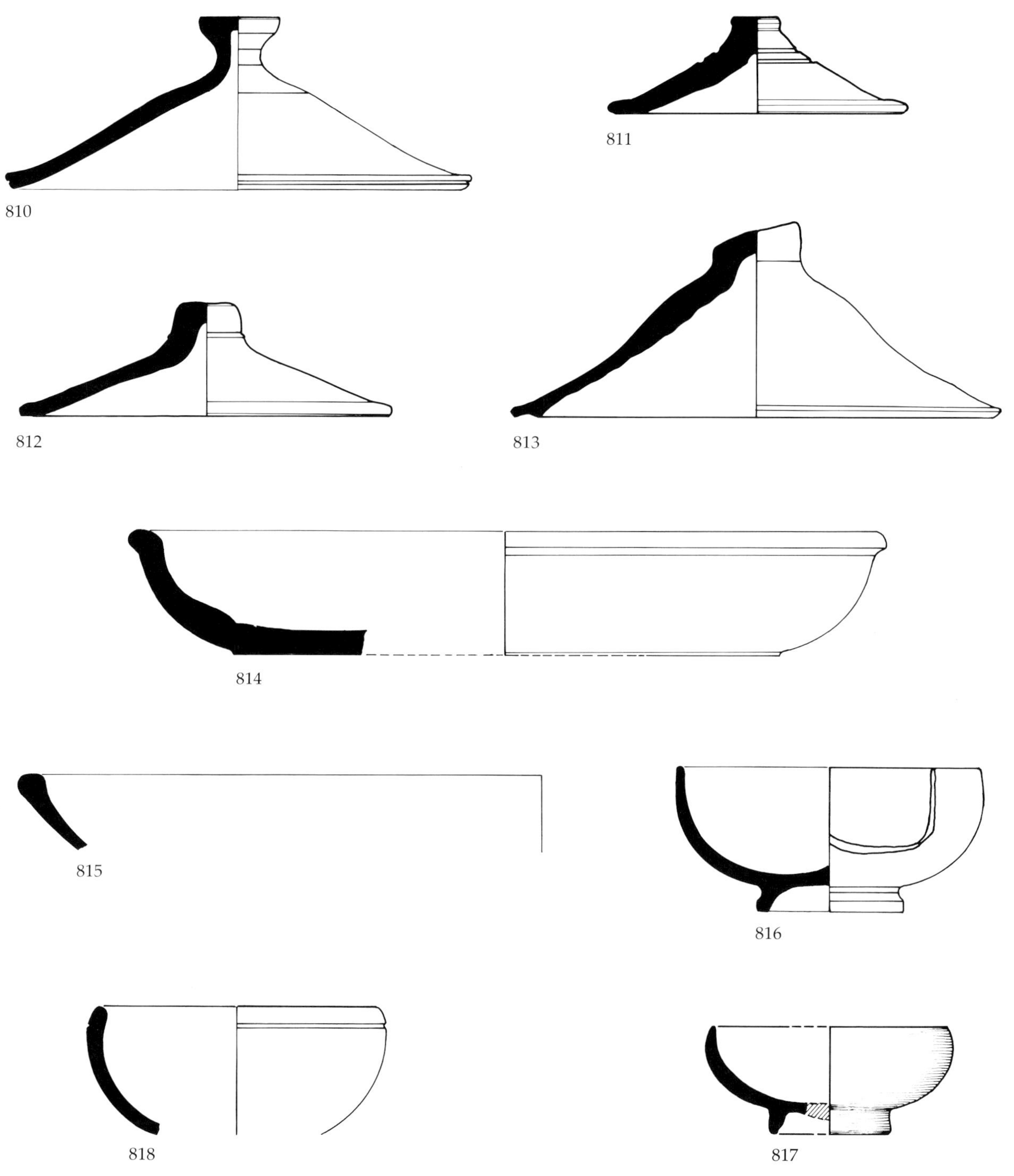

Plate 95. Hellenistic Lids. Early Roman Color-Slipped Forms 1–3

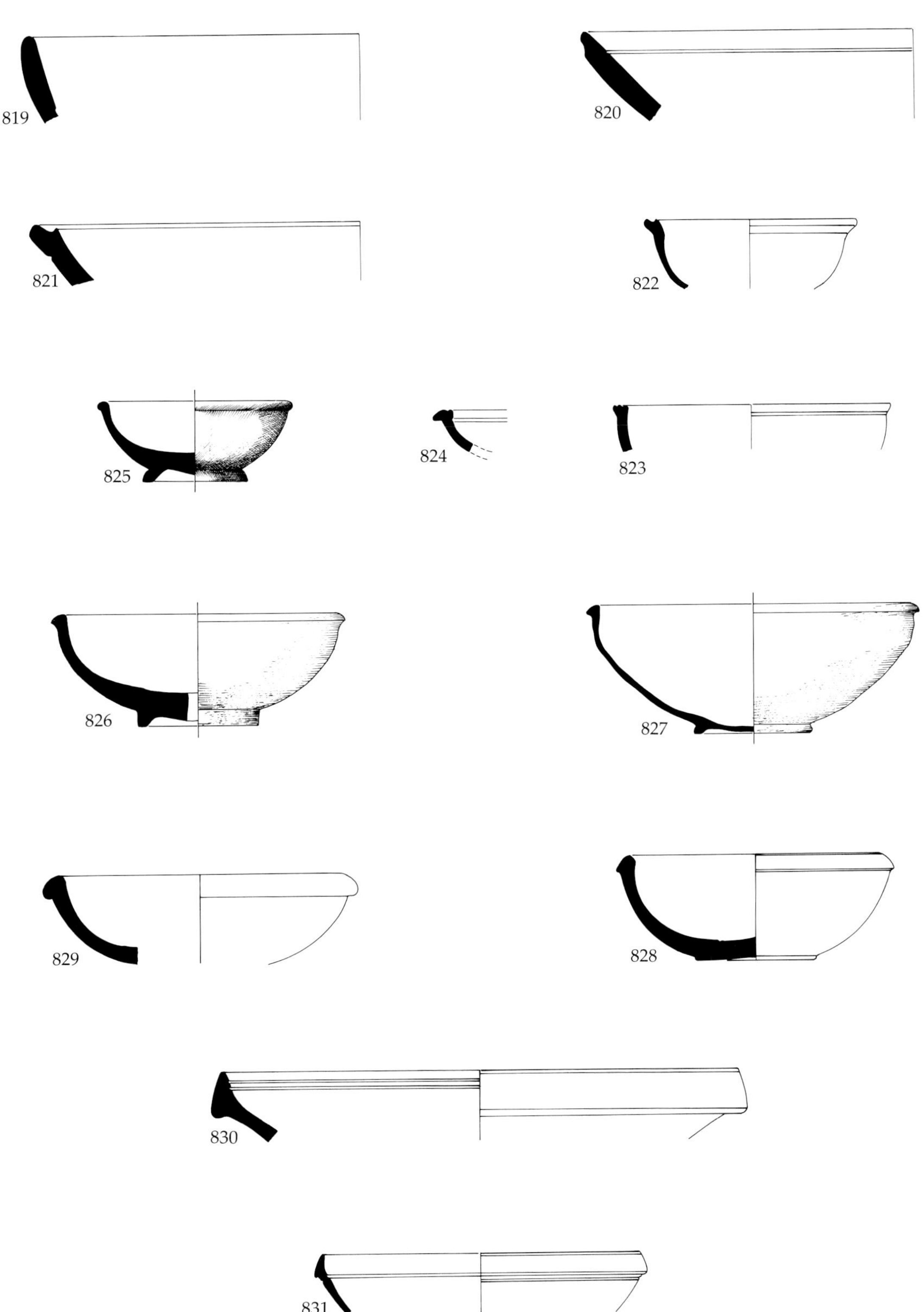

Plate 96. (scale 1:3) Early Roman Color-Slipped Forms 4–9

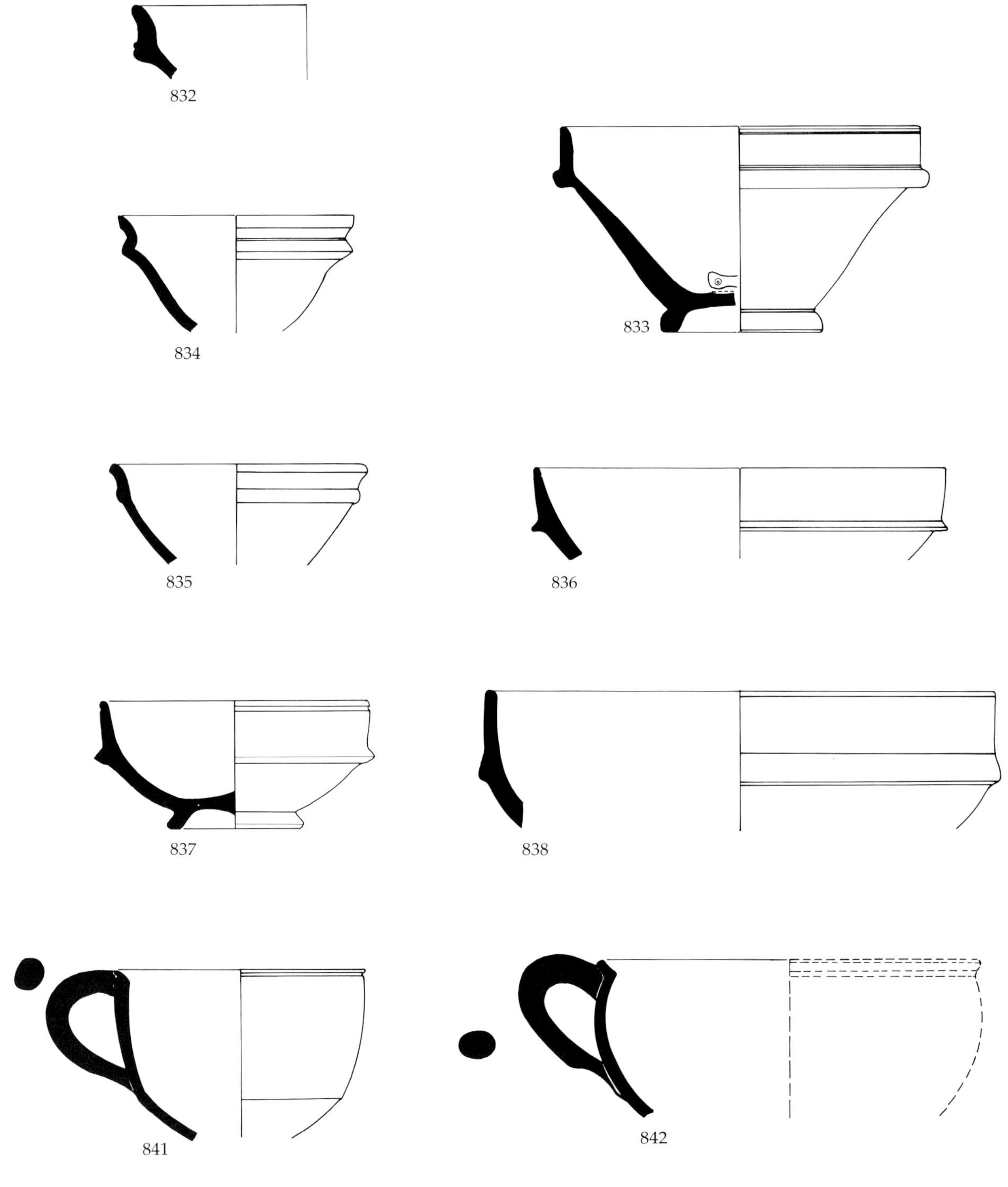

Plate 97. Early Roman Color-Slipped Forms 10–12

Plate 98. (scale 1:3) Early Roman Color-Slipped Forms 11, 13, 14, and 16

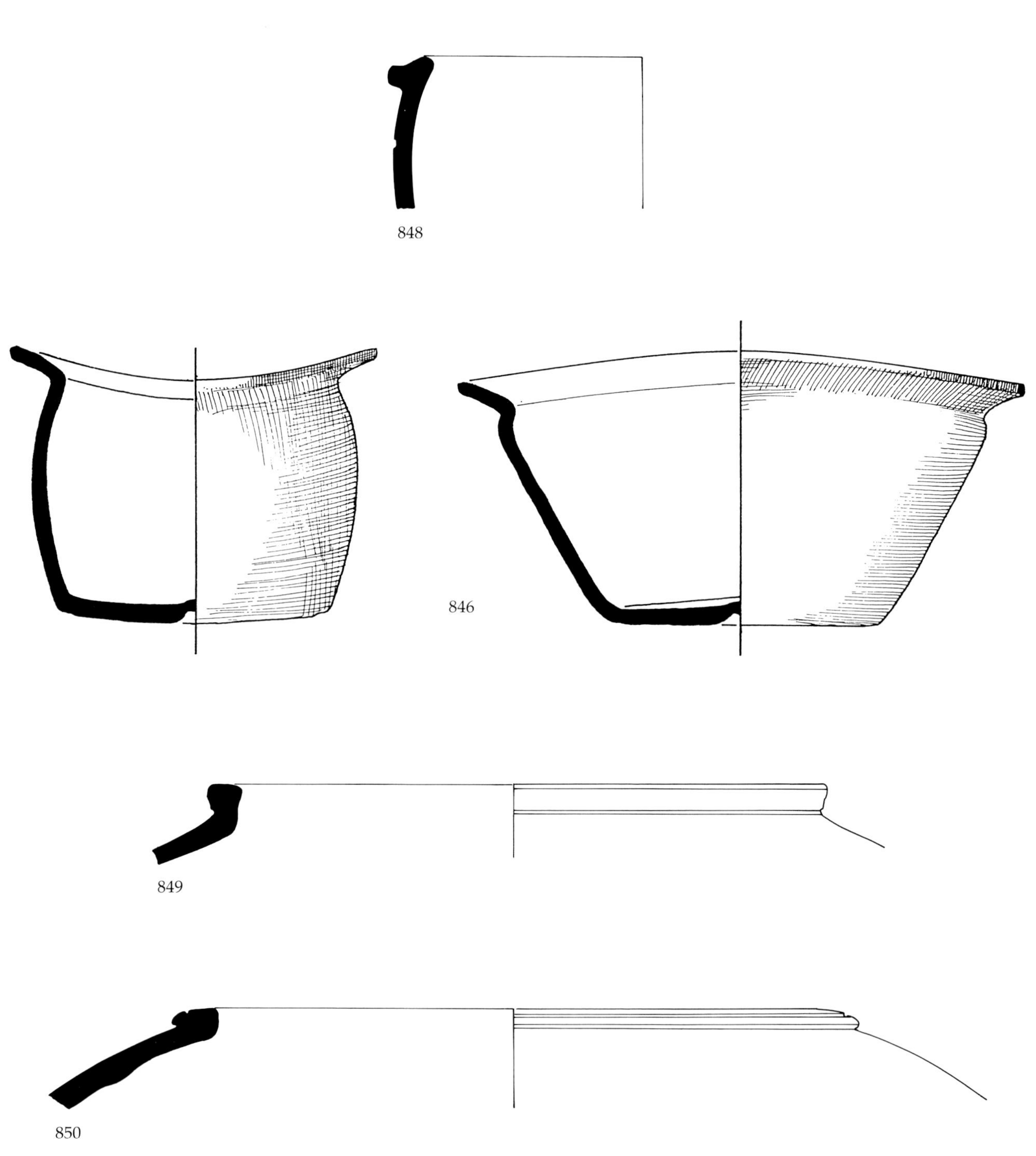

Plate 99. Early Roman Plain Forms 15–17 (846, scale 1:4)

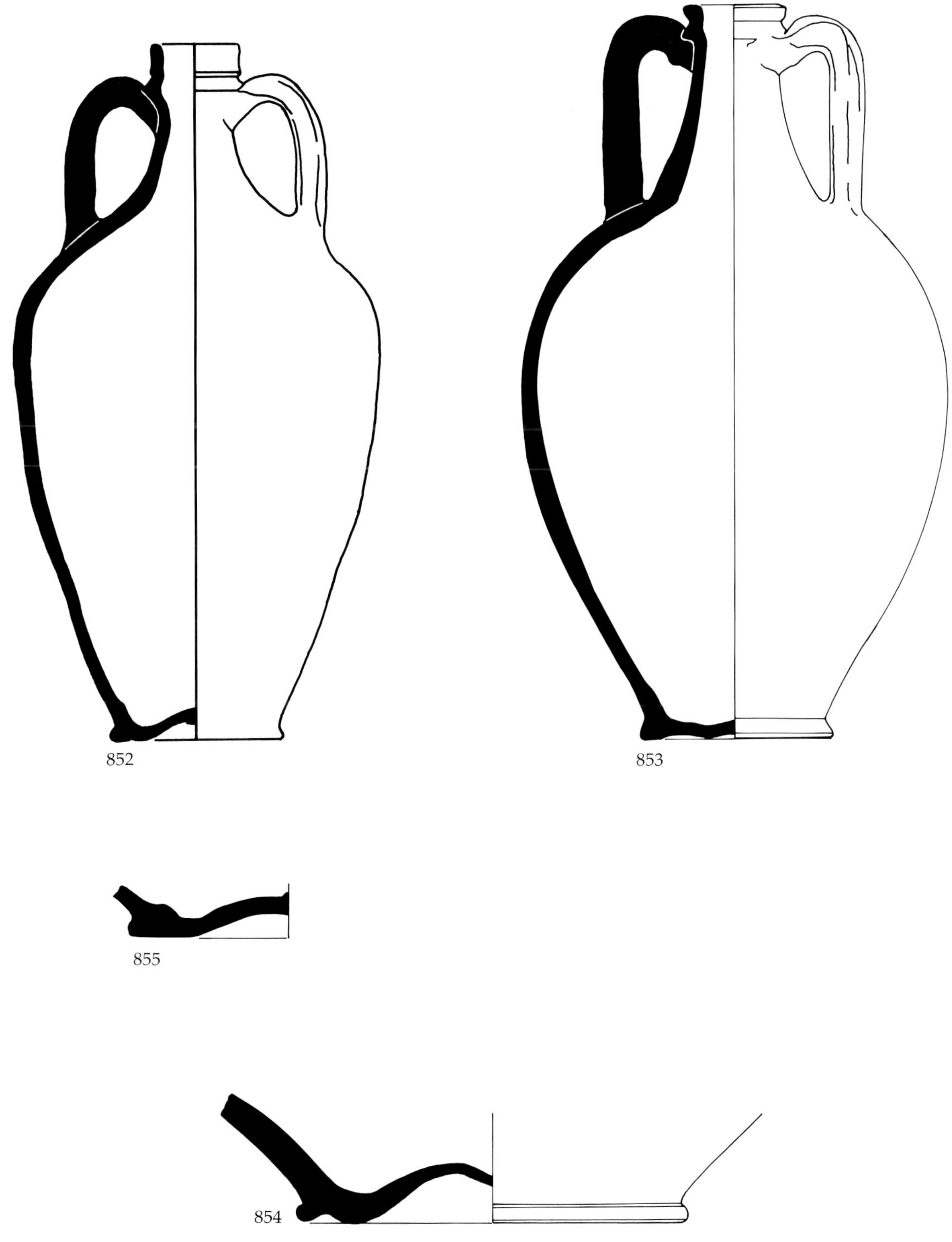

Plate 100. Early Roman Plain Form 18 (852, 853, scale 1:4)

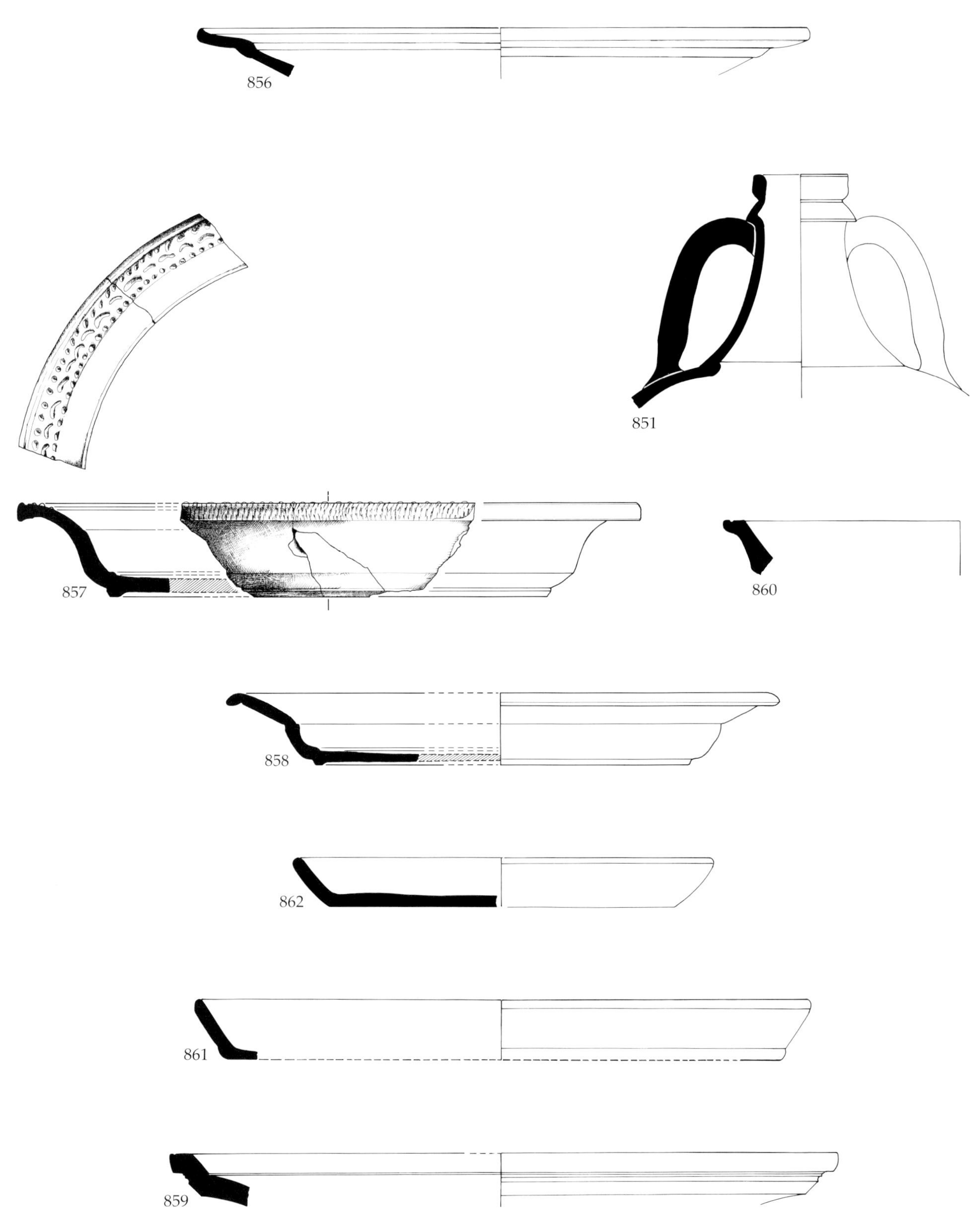

Plate 101. (scale 1:3) Early Roman Plain Form 18 and Other Color-Slipped dishes

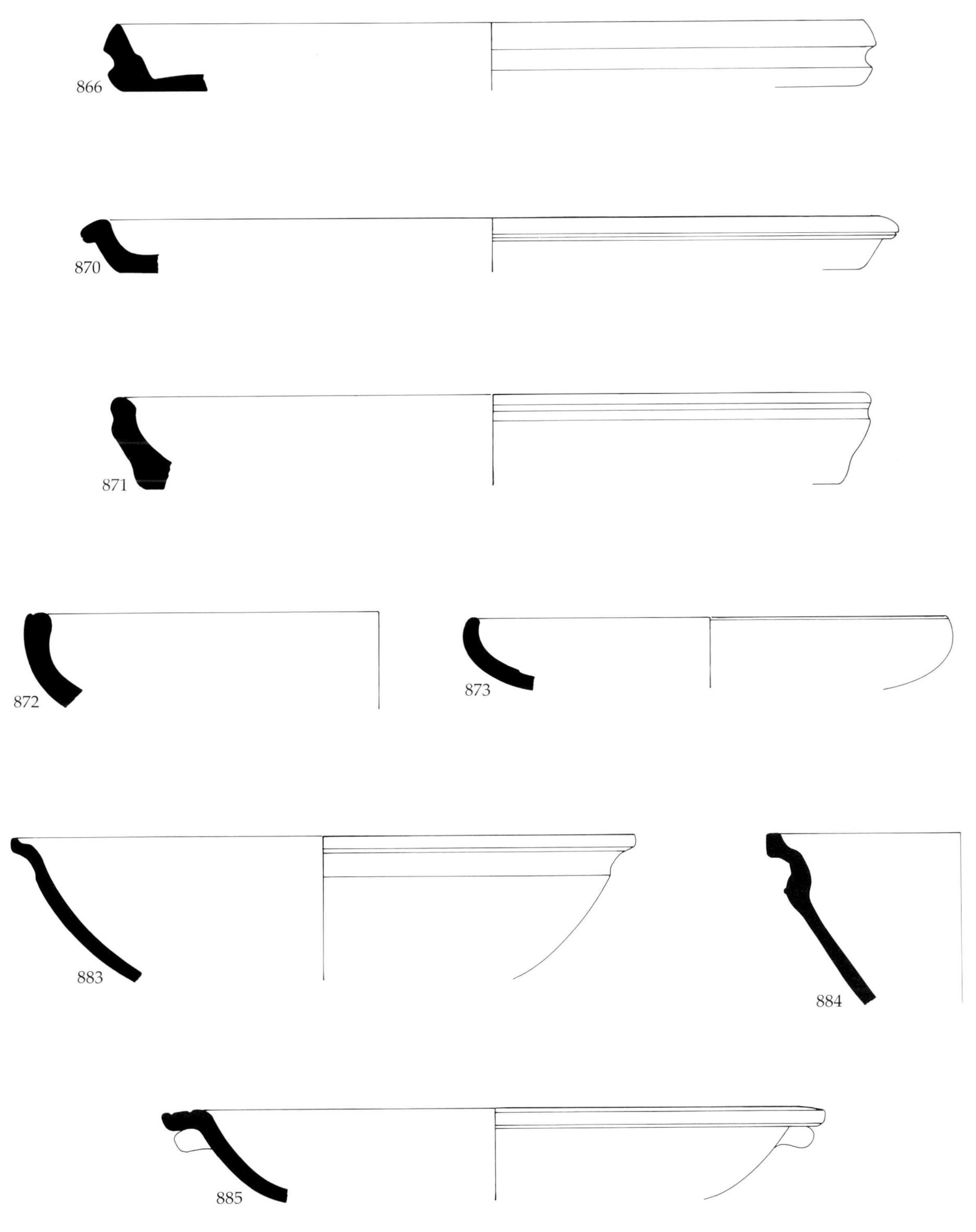

Plate 102. (scale 1:3) Early Roman Color-Slipped and Plain dishes and bowls

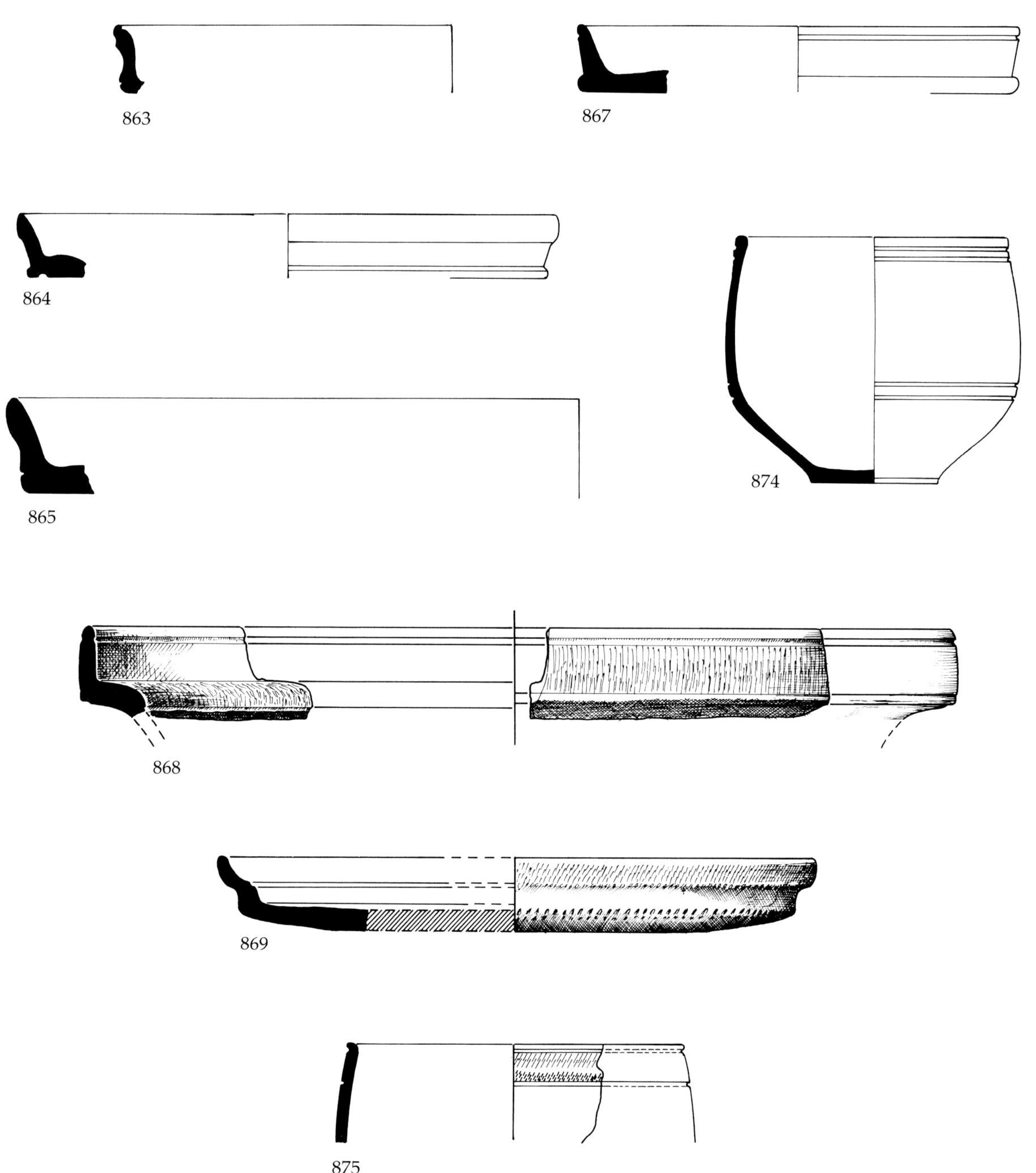

Plate 103. Early Roman Color-Slipped and Plain plates and bowls

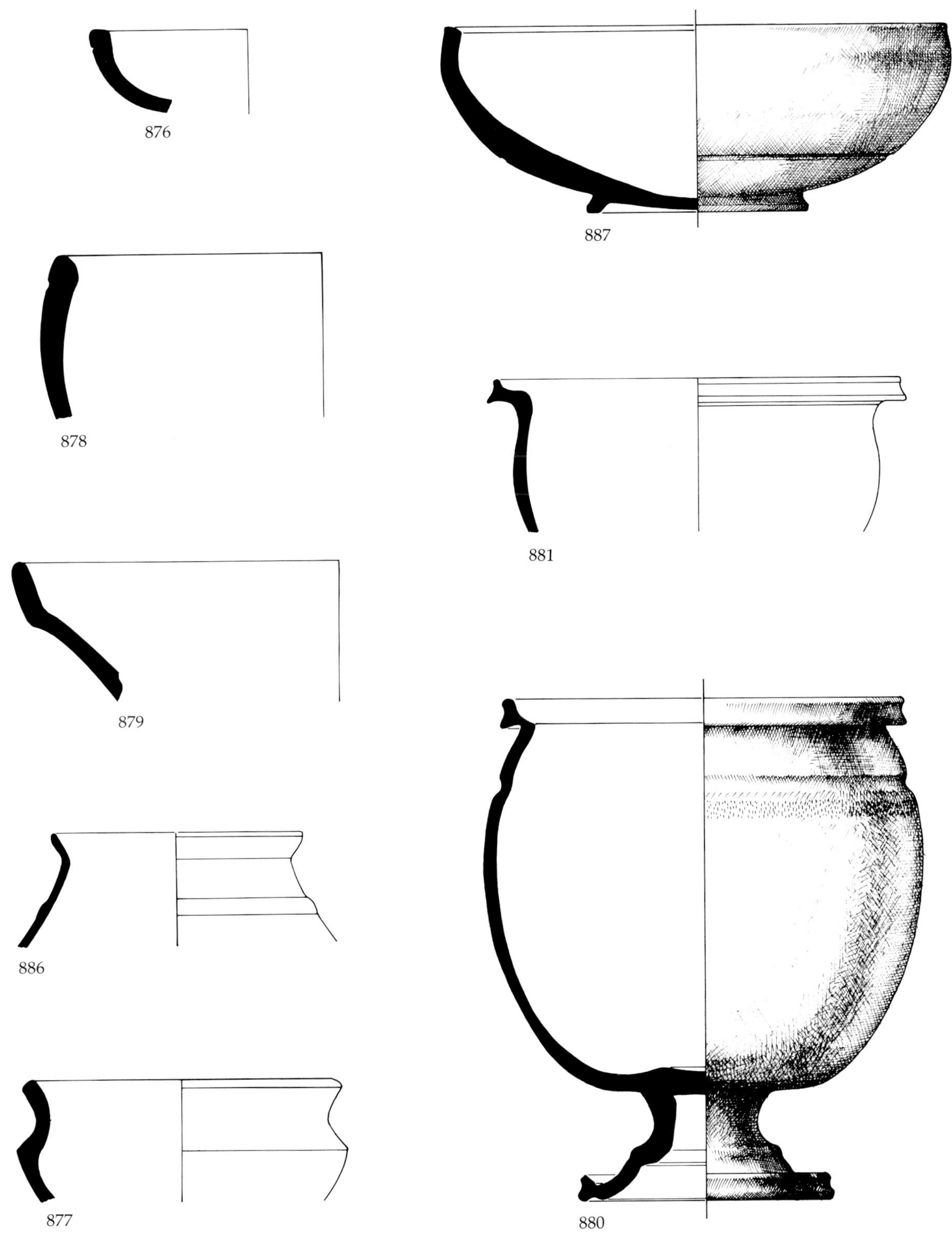

Plate 104. Early Roman Color-Slipped and Plain bowls and jars

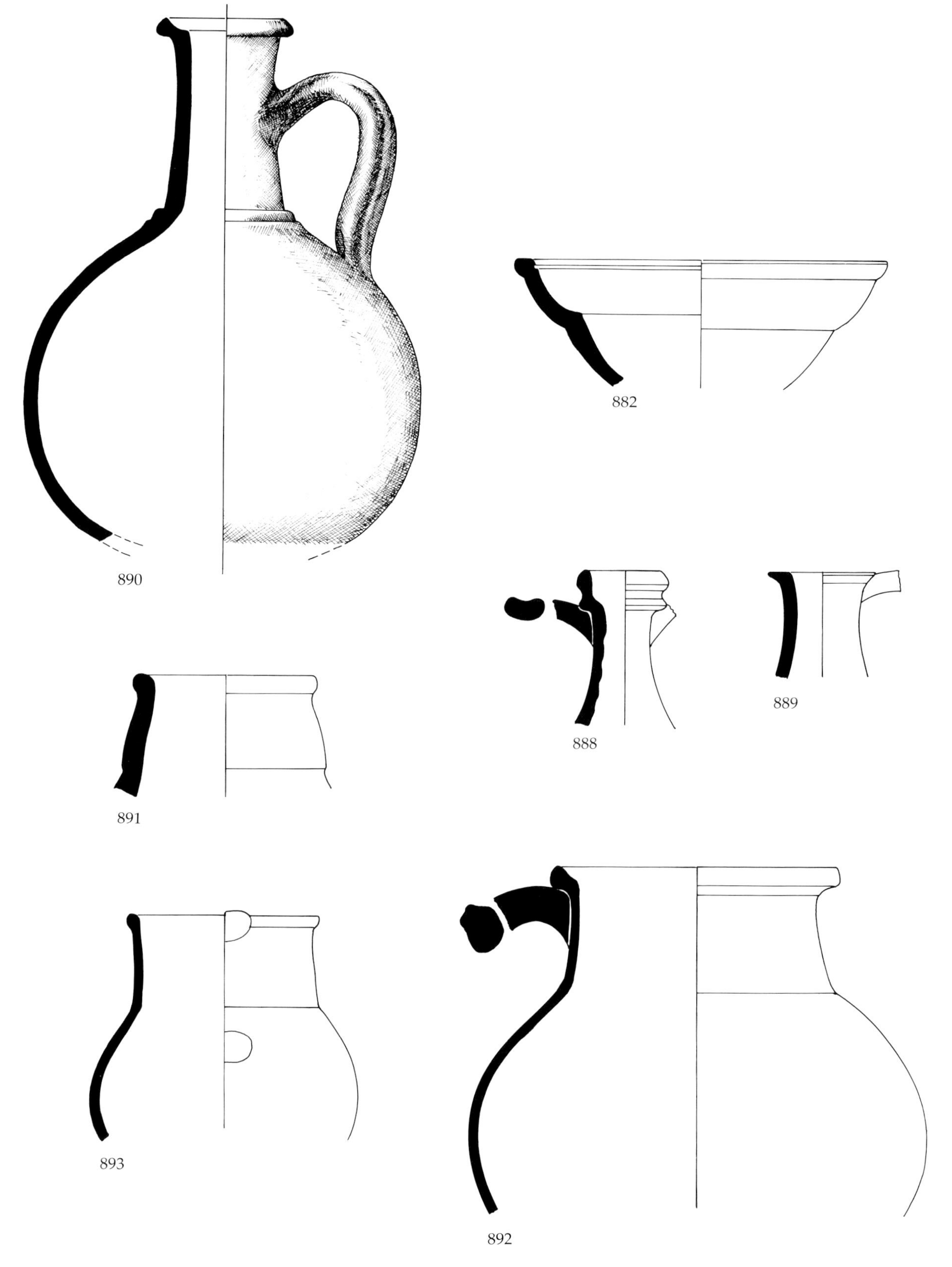

Plate 105. Early Roman Color-Slipped and Plain bowls and pitchers

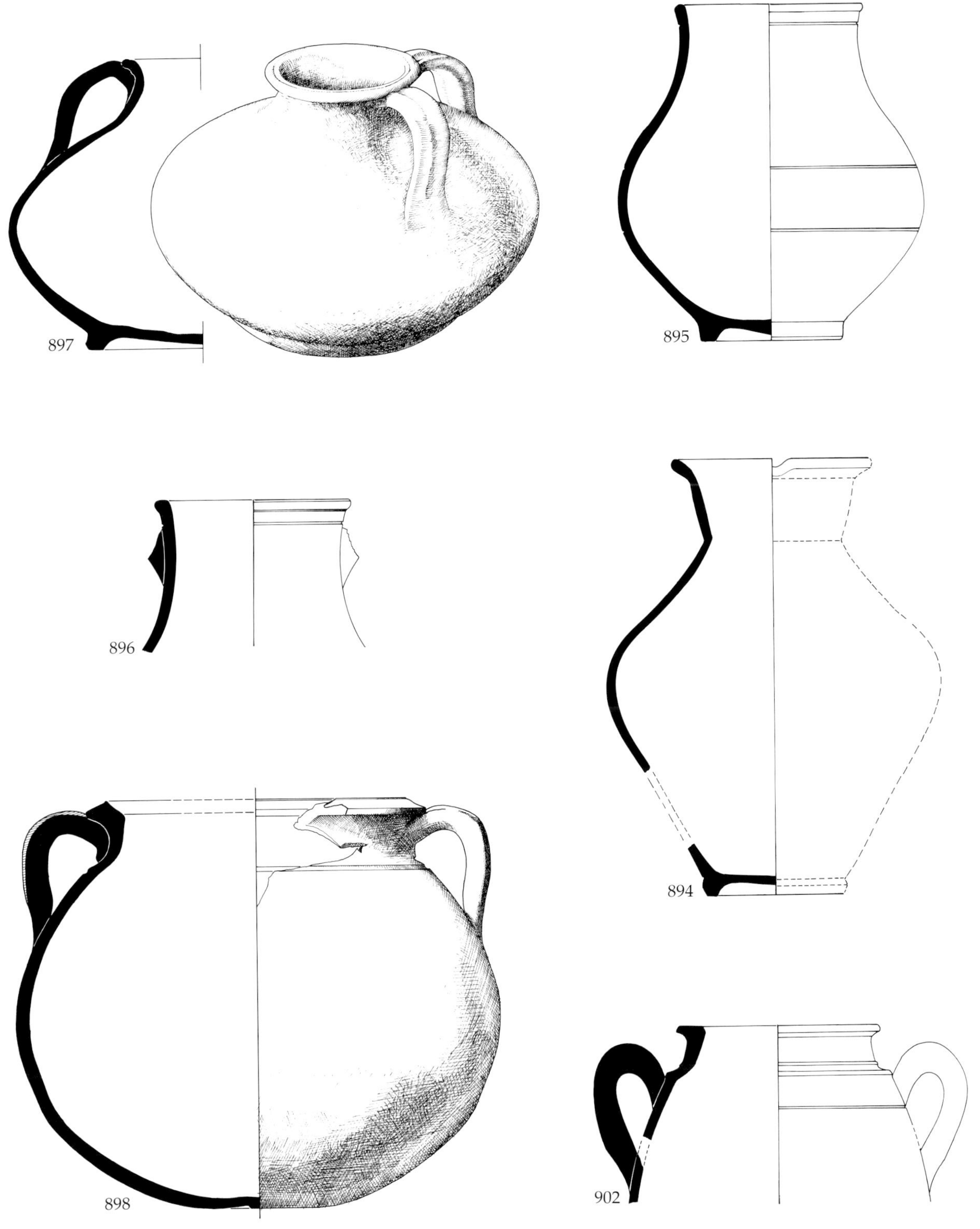

Plate 106. (scale 1:3) Early Roman Color-Slipped and Plain pitchers and jars

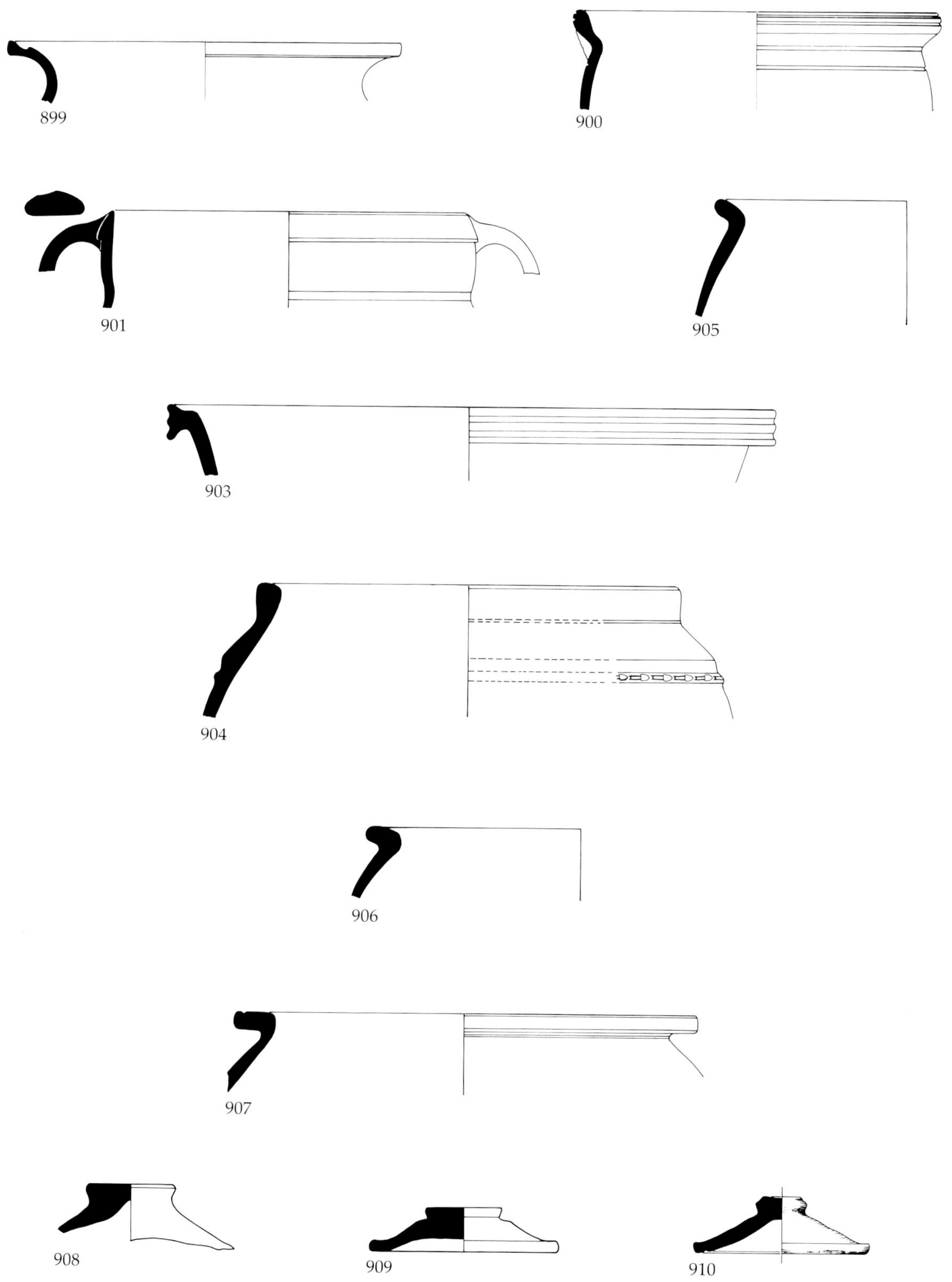

Plate 107. (scale 1:3) Early Roman Plain large jars and lids

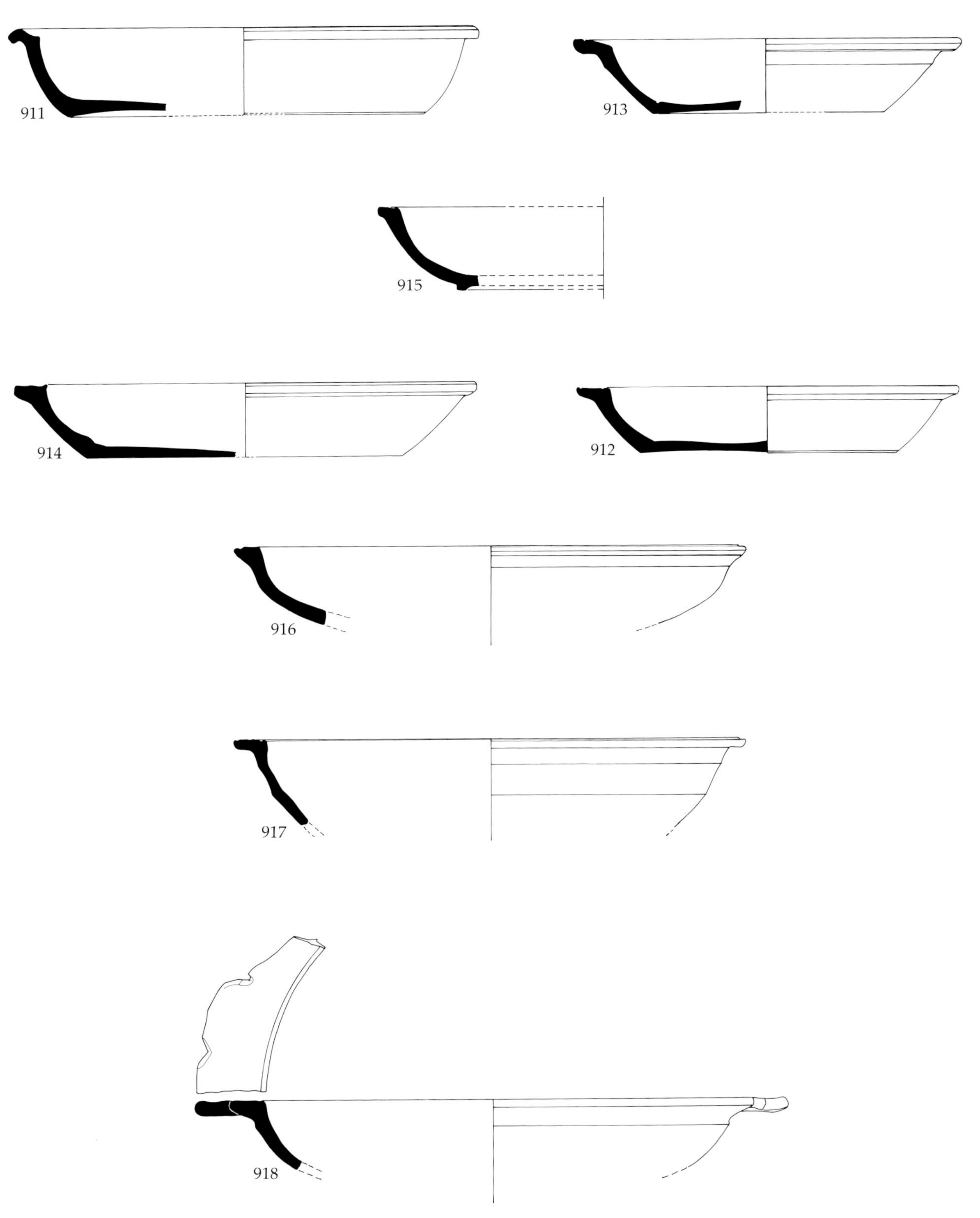

Plate 108. (scale 1:3) Middle Roman Color-Slipped Forms 1–3

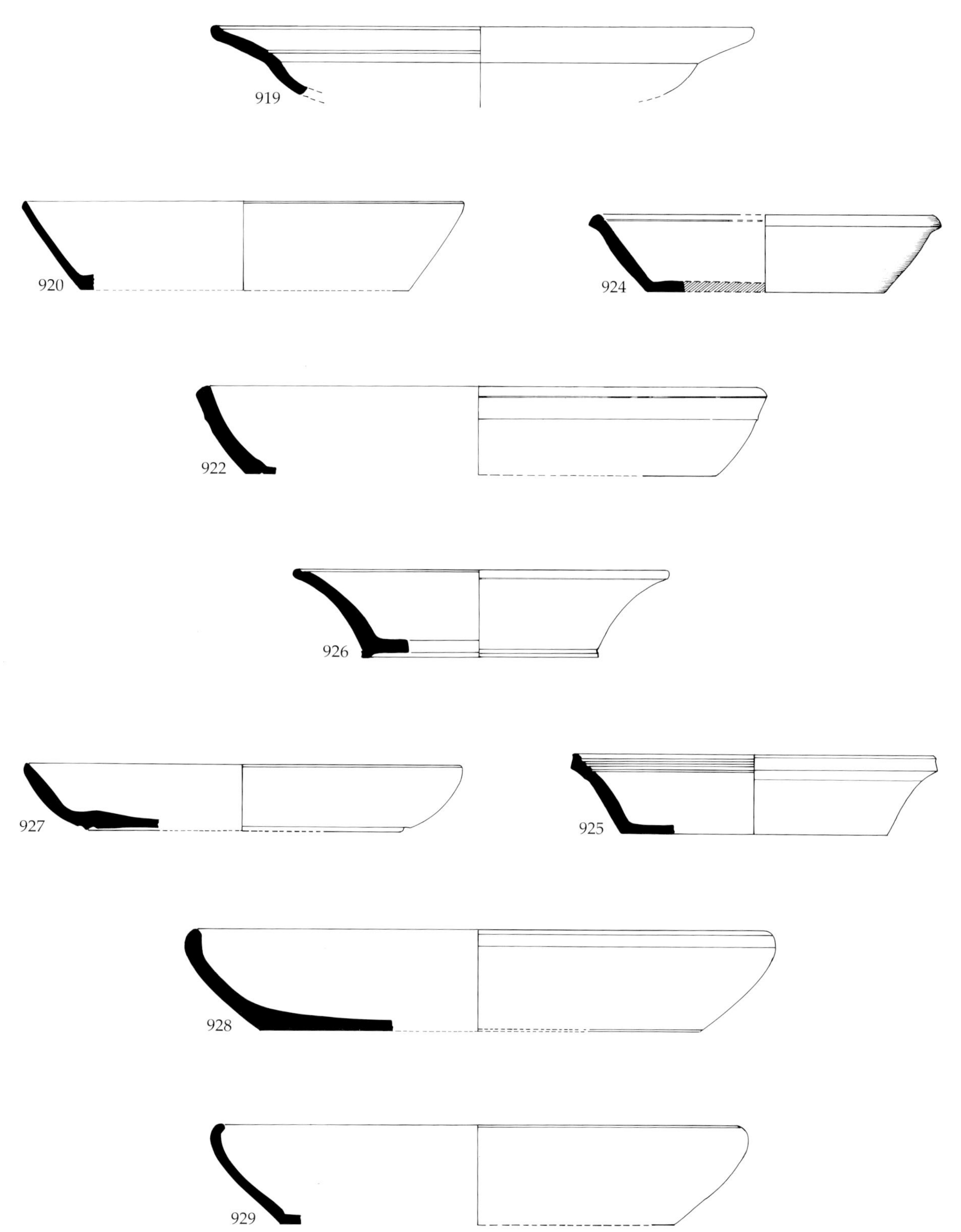

Plate 109. (scale 1:3) Middle Roman Color-Slipped Forms 4–6

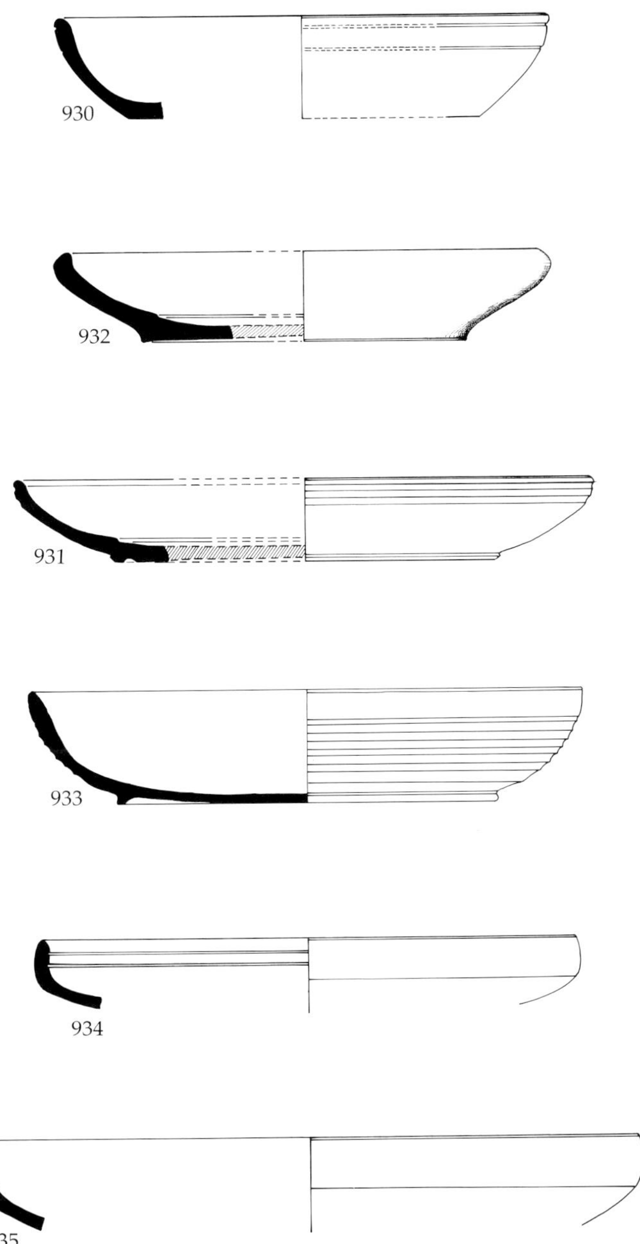

Plate 110. (scale 1:3) Middle Roman Color-Slipped Forms 6 and 7

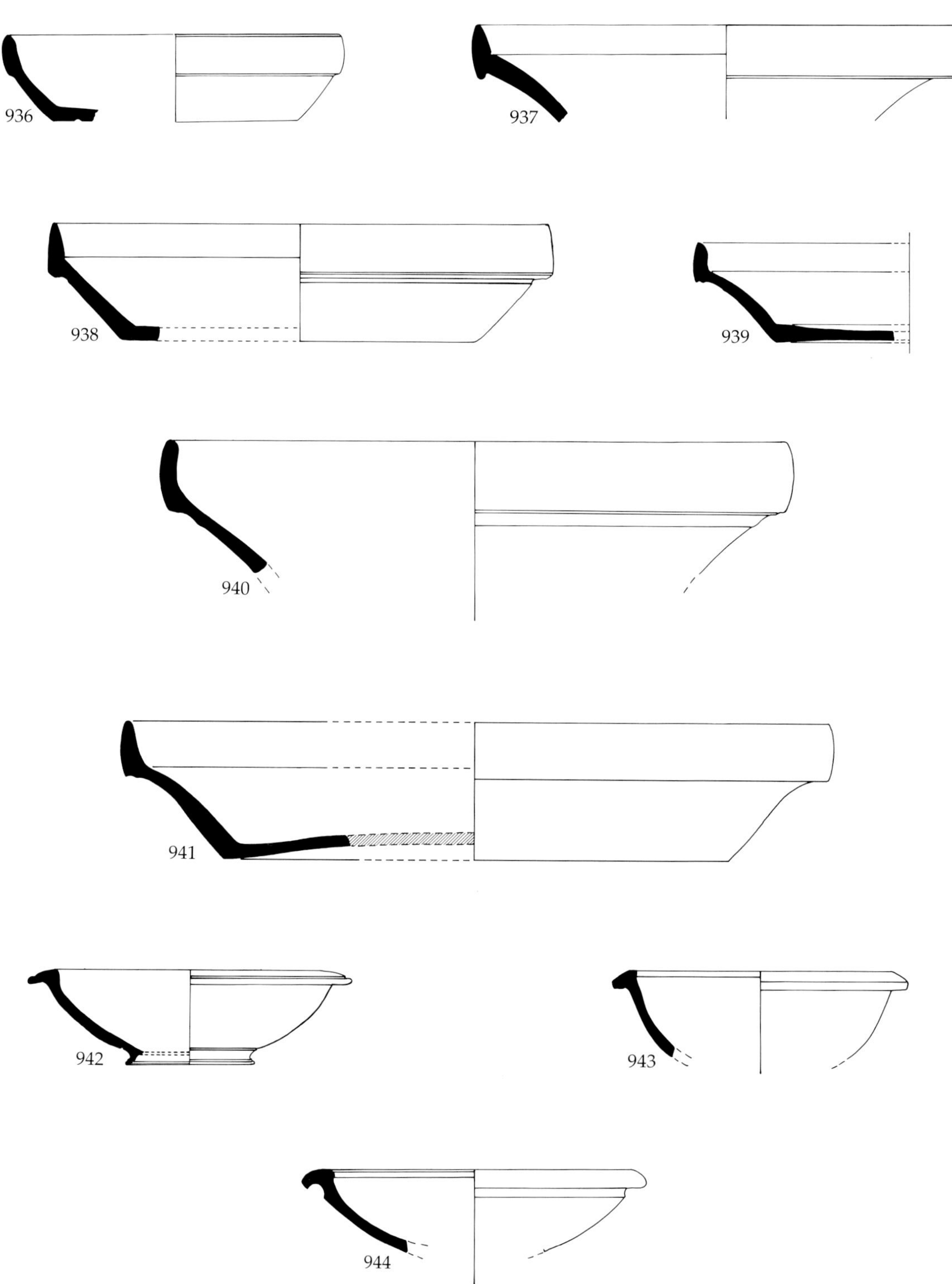

Plate 111. (scale 1:3) Middle Roman Color-Slipped Forms 8 and 9

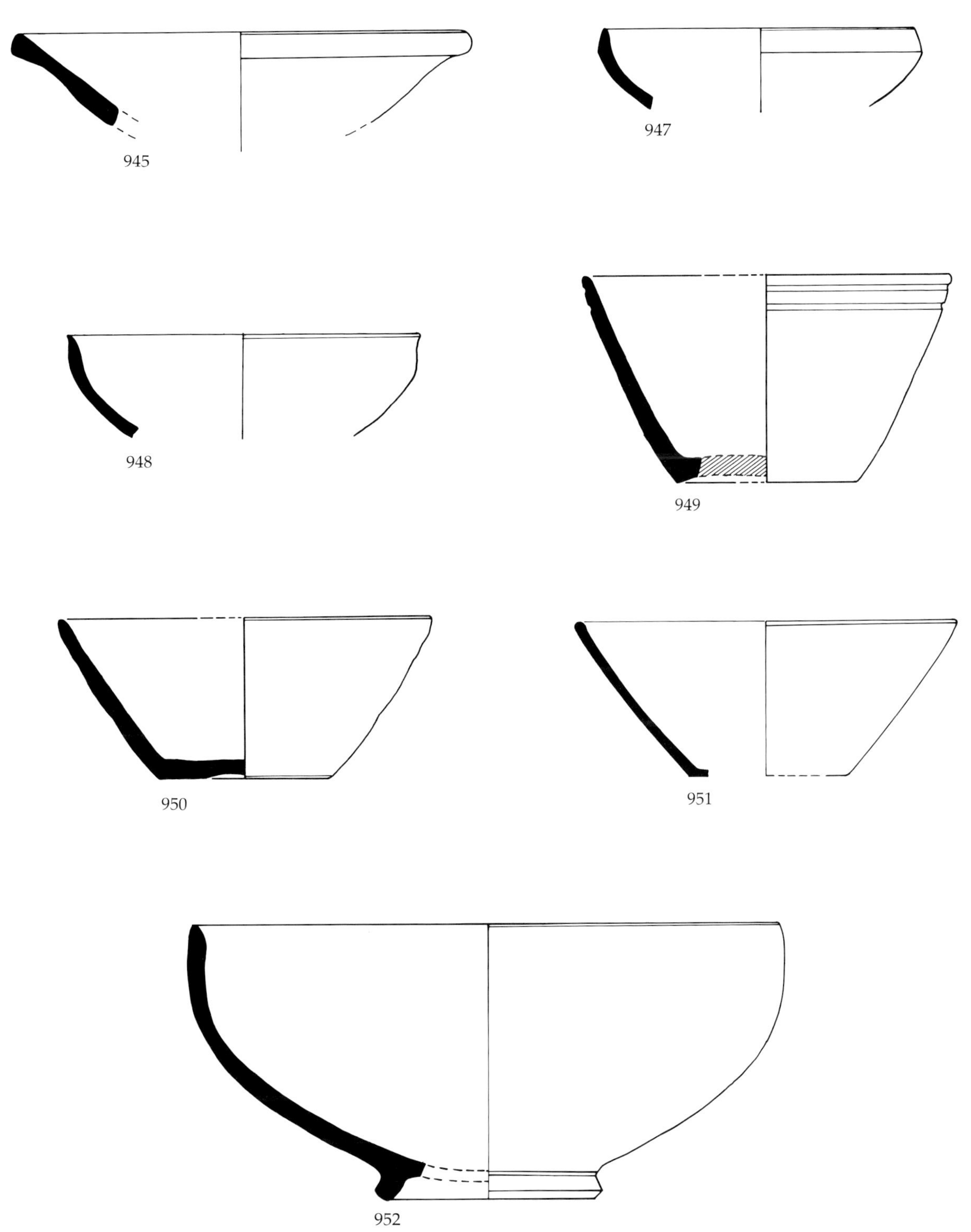

Plate 112. Middle Roman Color-Slipped Forms 10–13

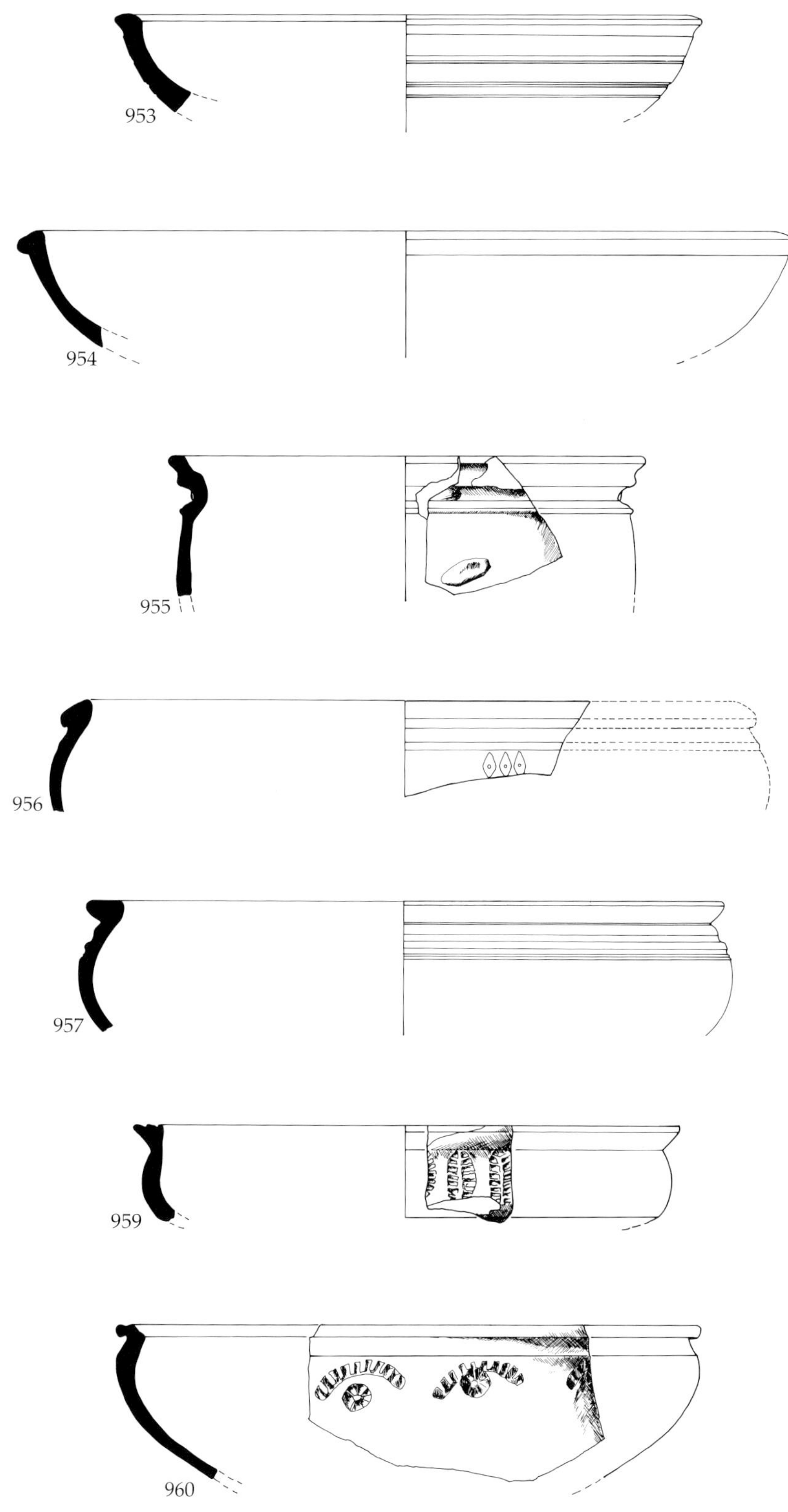

Plate 113. (scale 1:3) Middle Roman Color-Slipped Forms 13–17

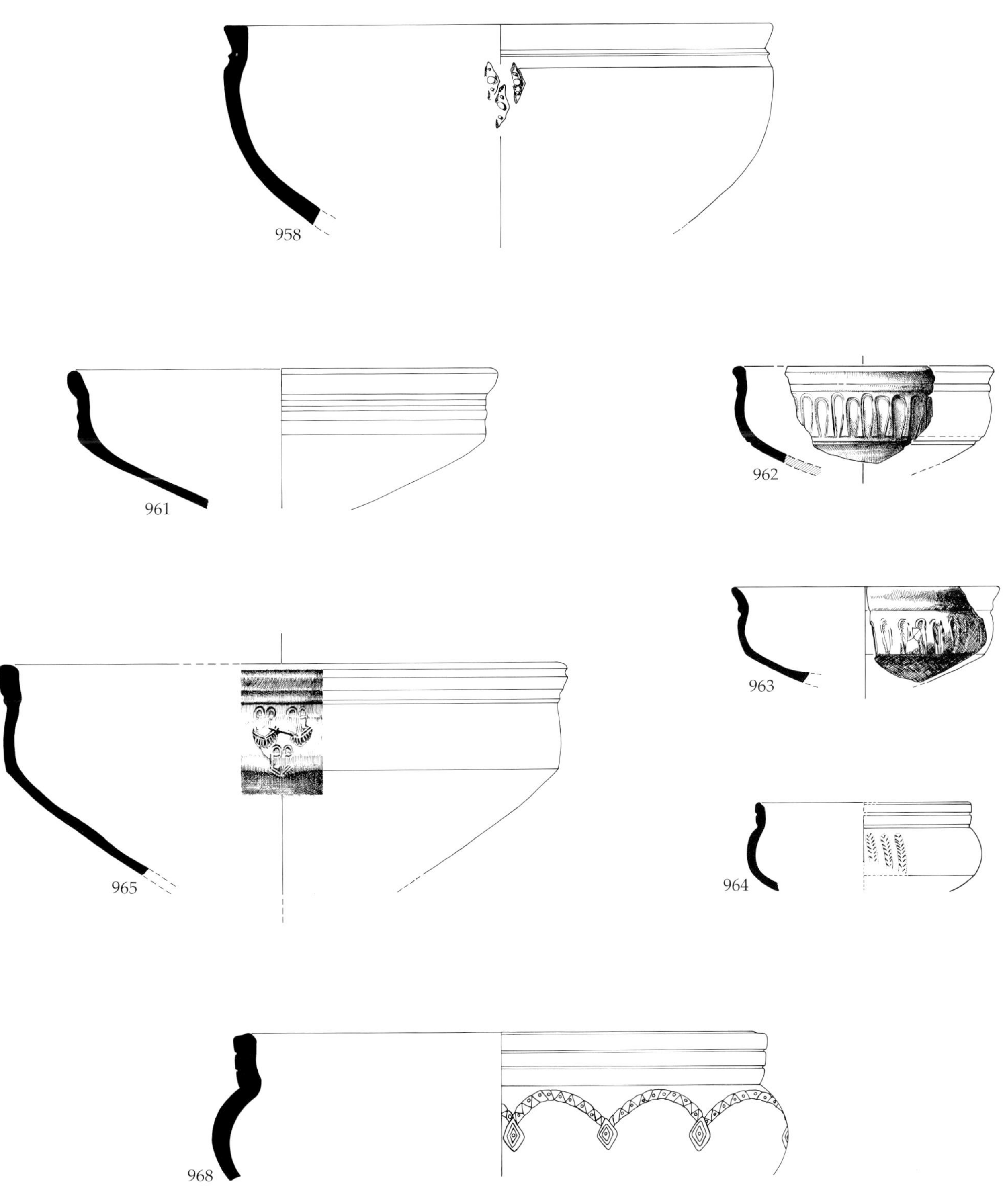

Plate 114. (scale 1:3) Middle Roman Color-Slipped Forms 17–19

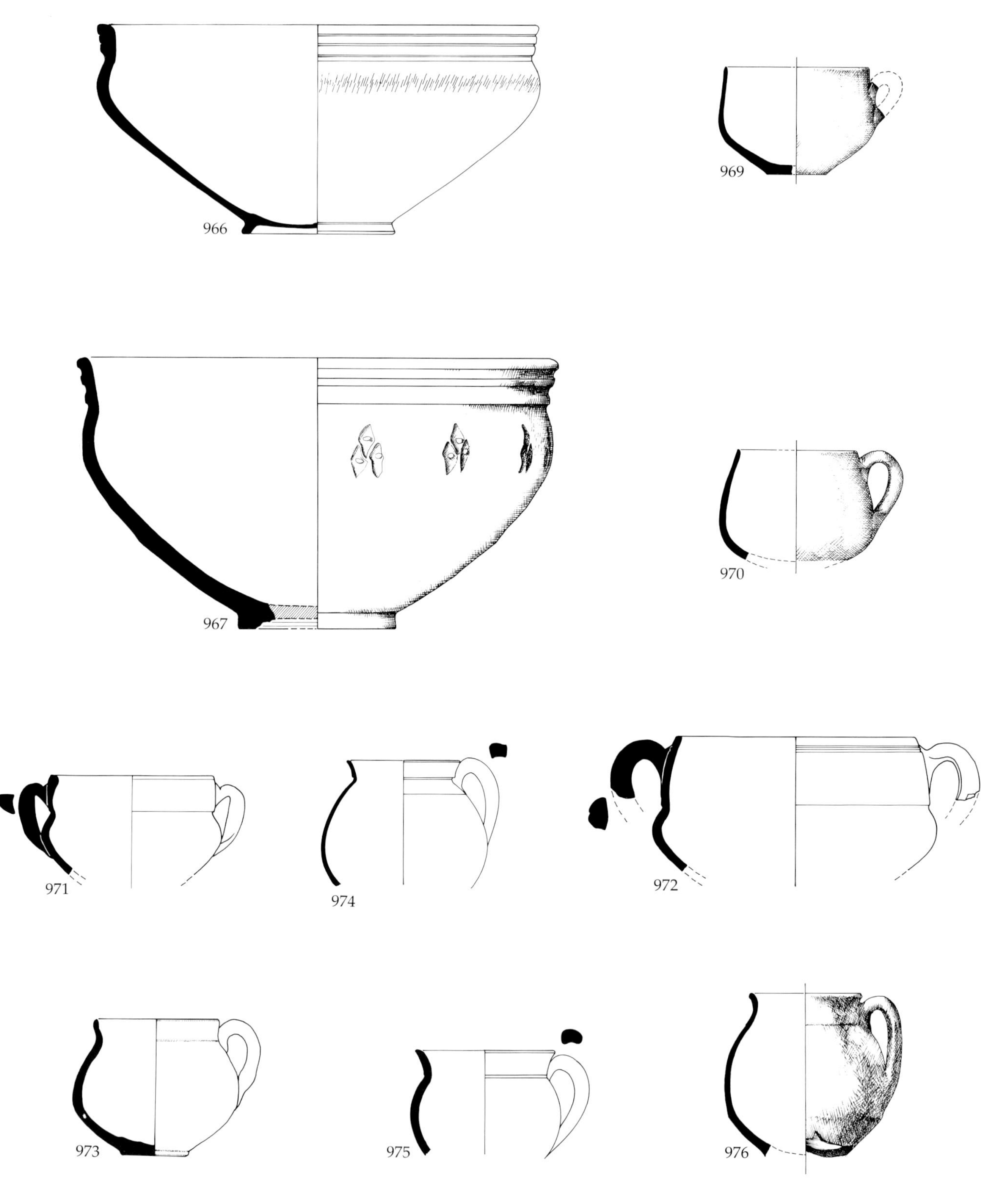

Plate 115. (scale 1:3) Middle Roman Color-Slipped Forms 19–22

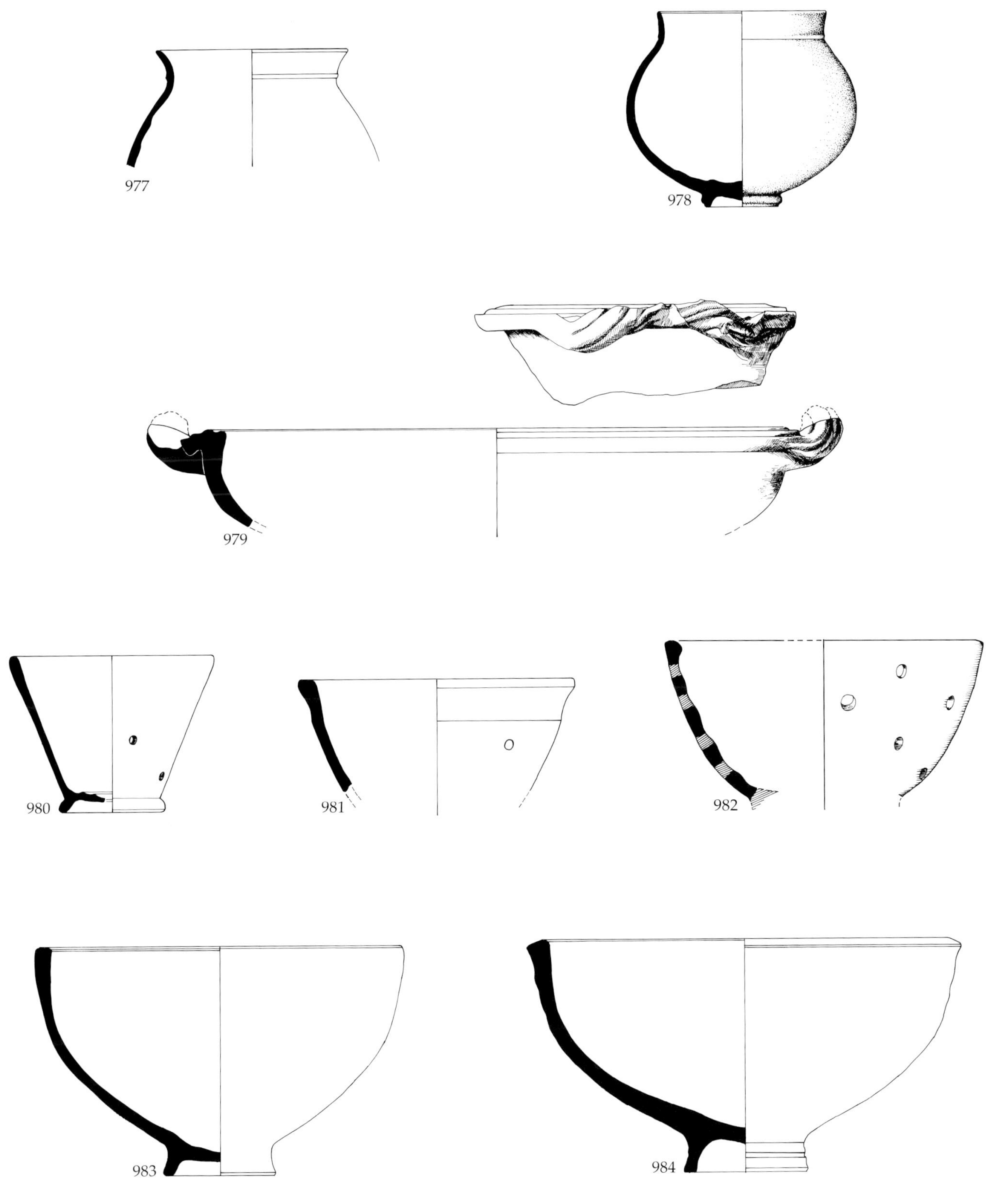

Plate 116. (scale 1:3) Middle Roman Color-Slipped Forms 22–25

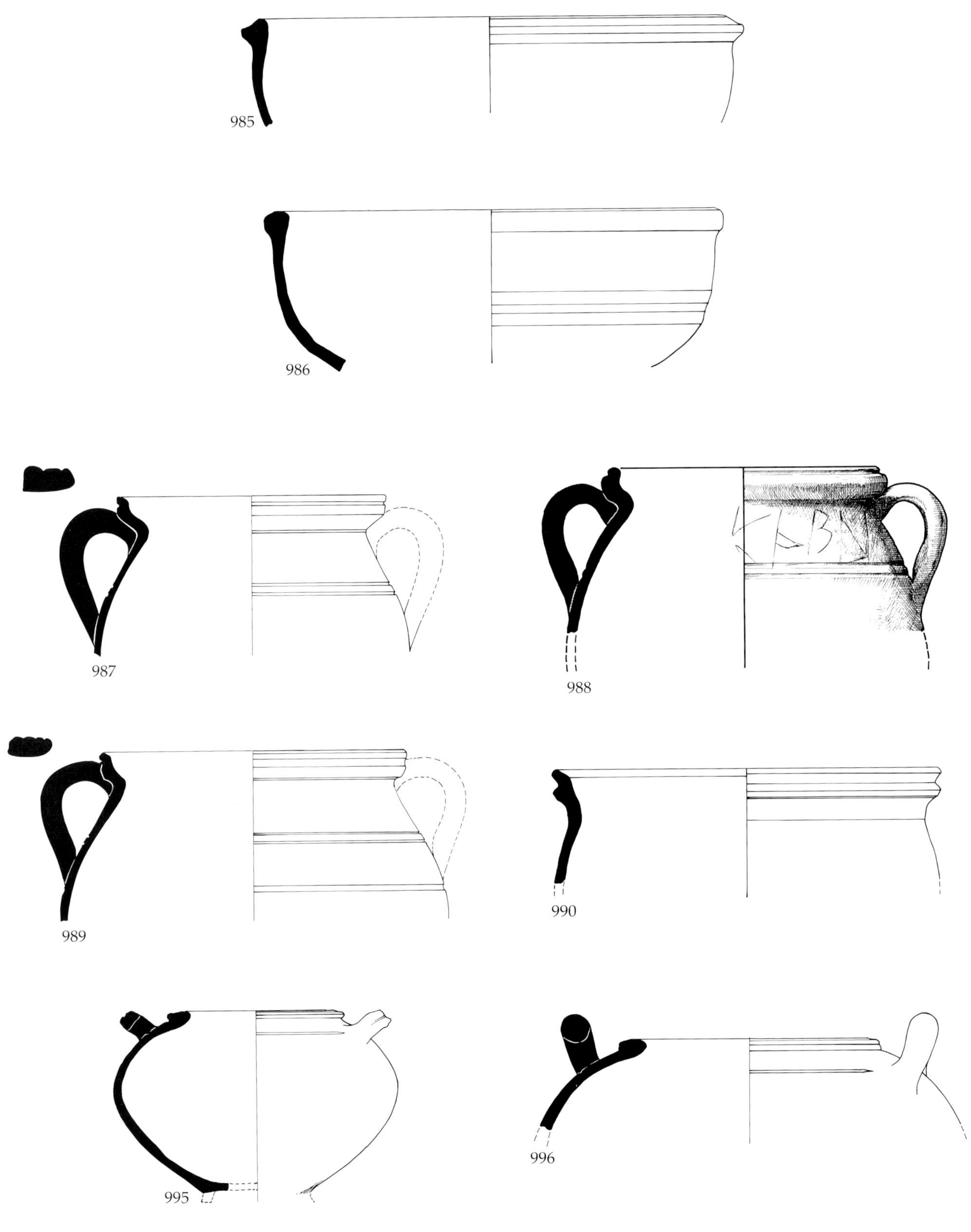

Plate 117. (scale 1:3) Middle Roman Color-Slipped and Plain Forms 25–27, 29

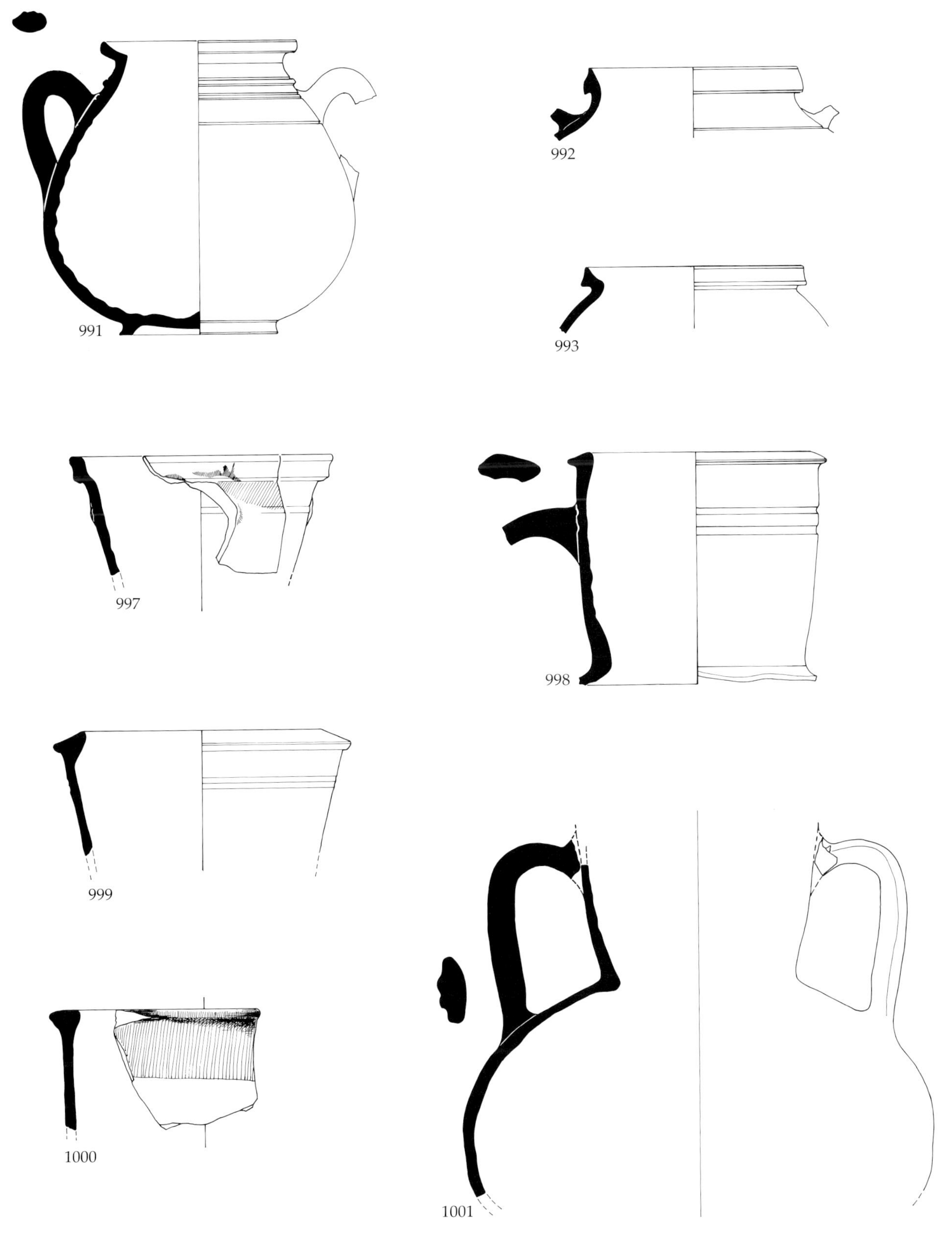

Plate 118. (scale 1:3) Middle Roman Color-Slipped and Plain Forms 28, 30, and 31

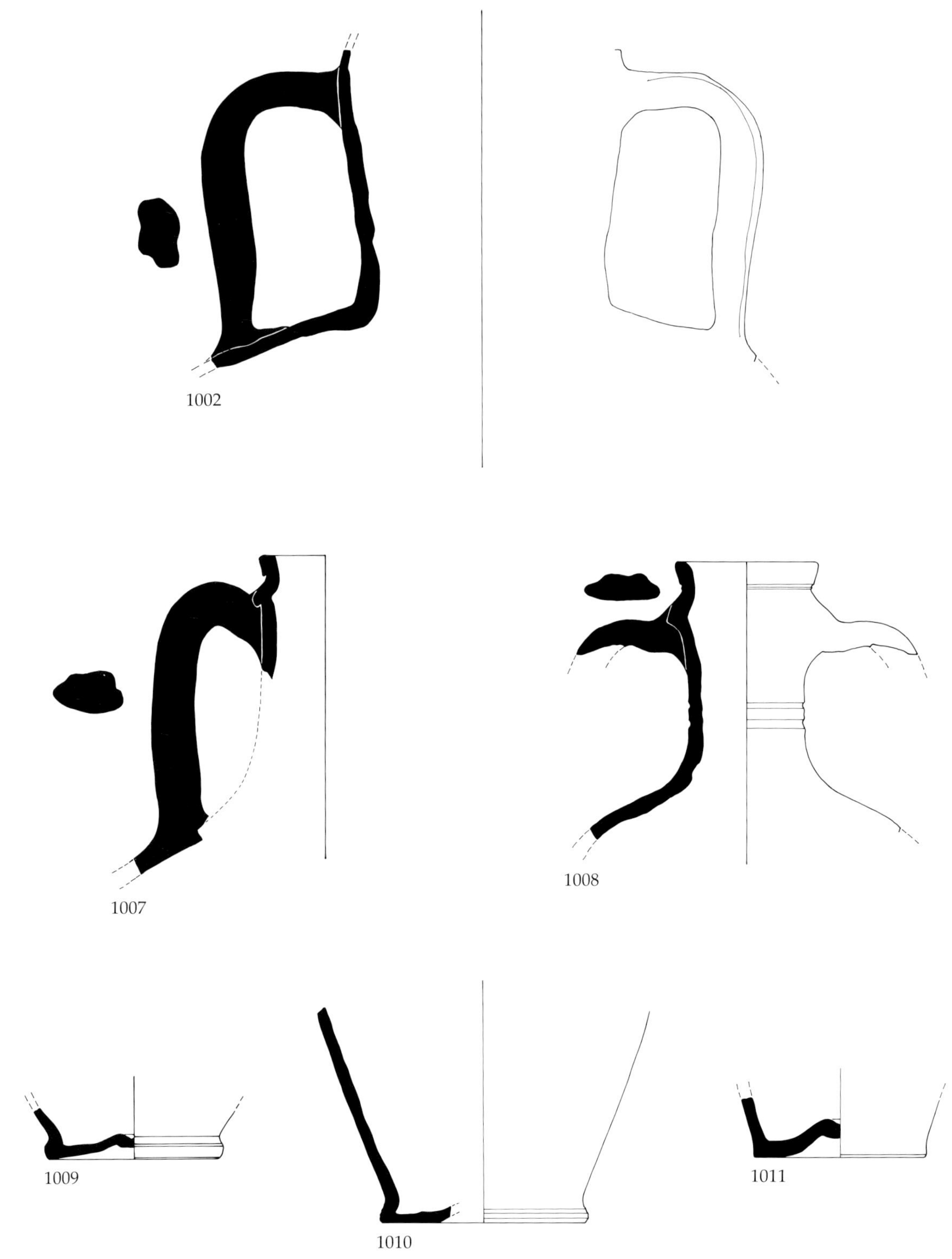

Plate 119. (scale 1:3) Middle Roman Color-Slipped and Plain Forms 31, 33

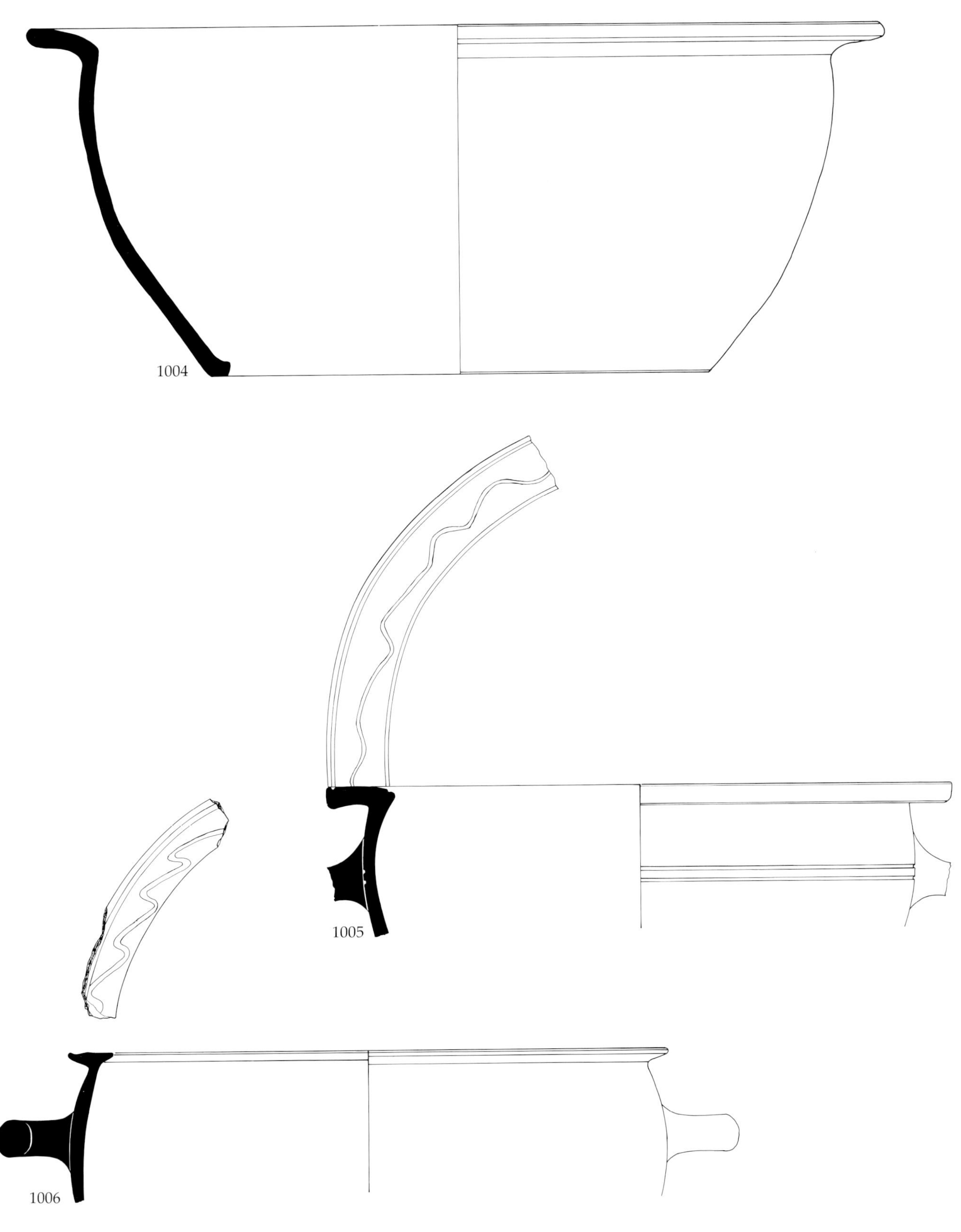

Plate 120. (scale 1:3) Middle Roman Color-Slipped and Plain Form 32

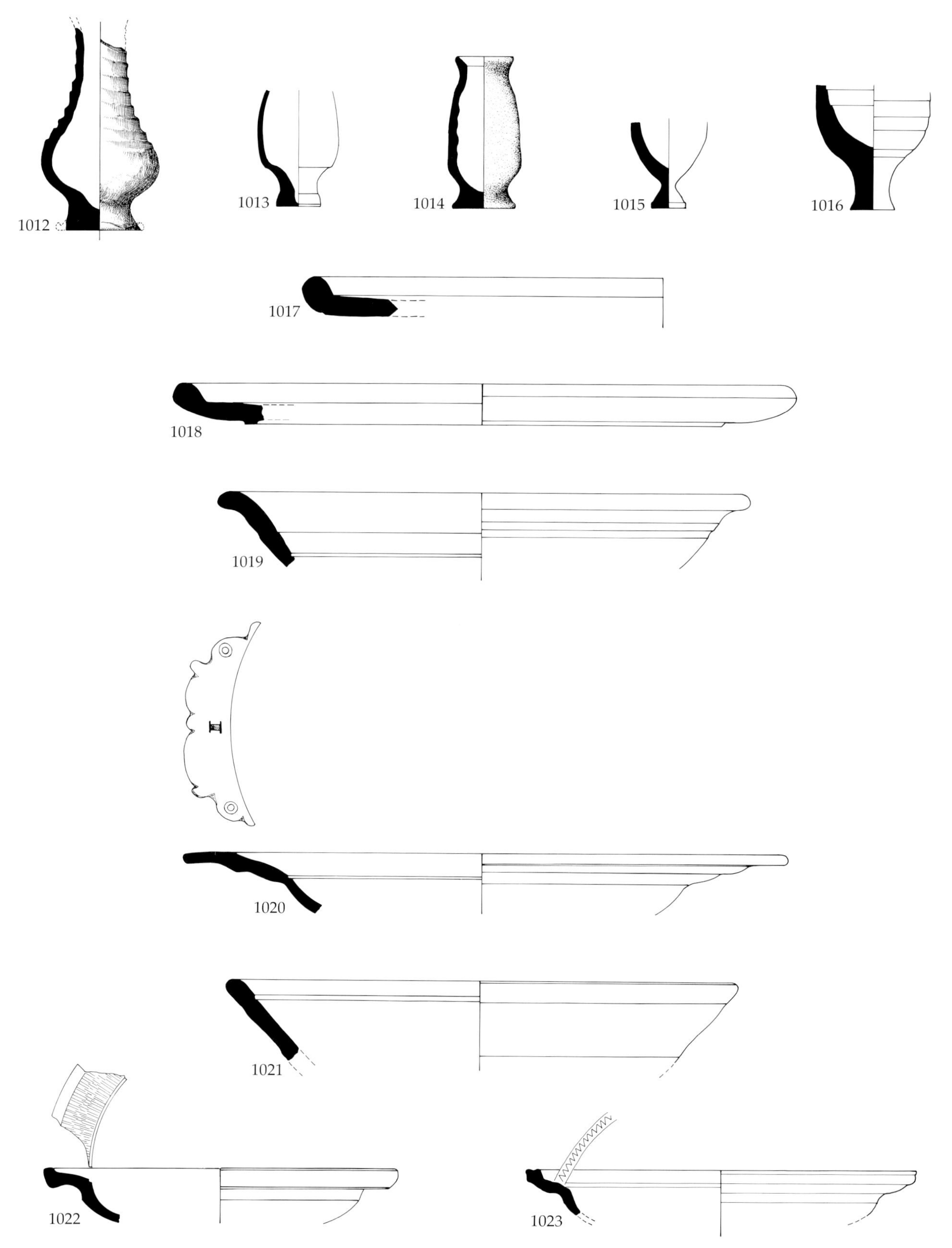

Plate 121. (scale 1:3) Middle Roman Plain Form 34. Middle Roman Color-Slipped plates and dishes

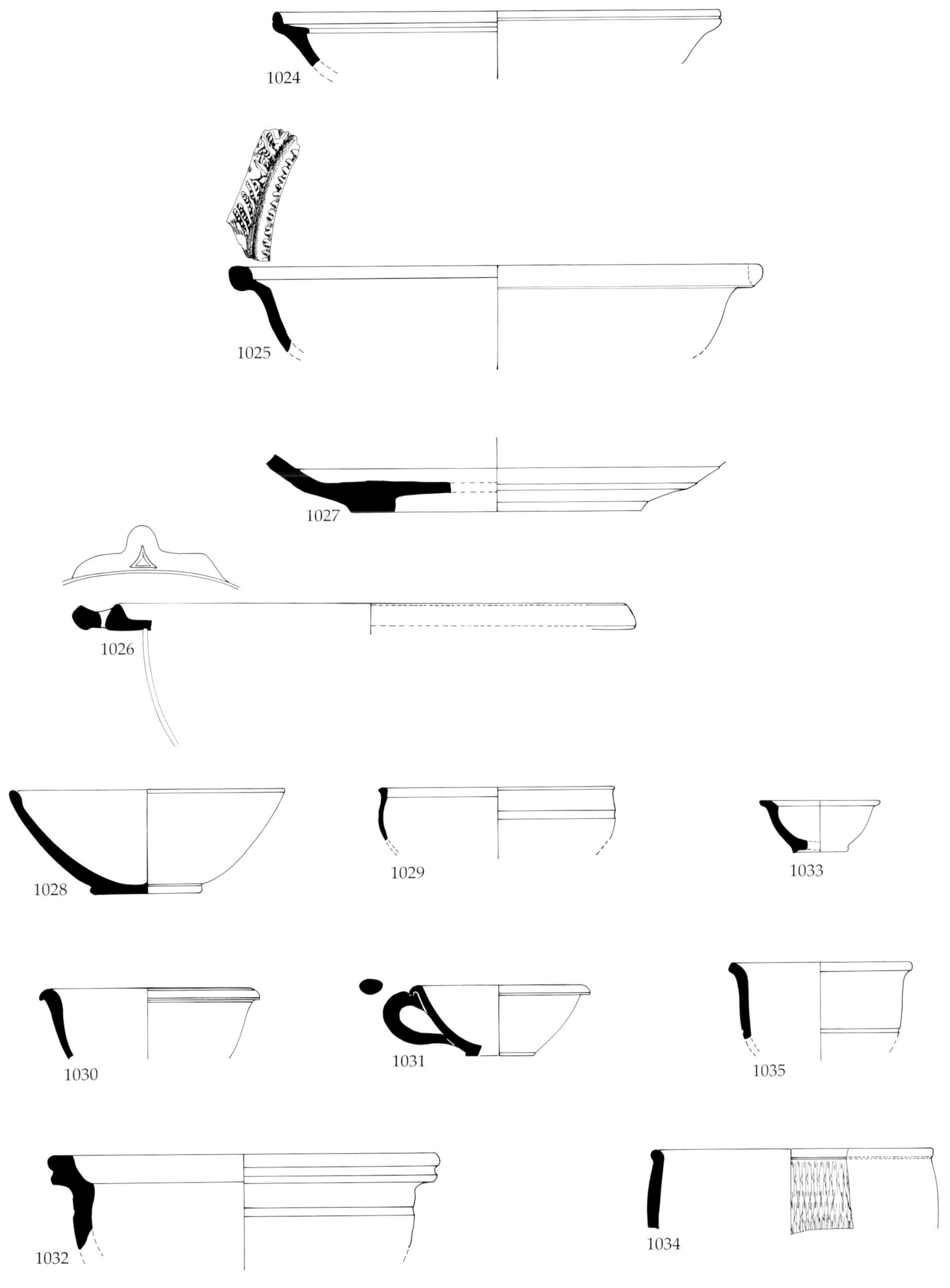

Plate 122. (scale 1:3) Middle Roman Color-Slipped dishes and bowls

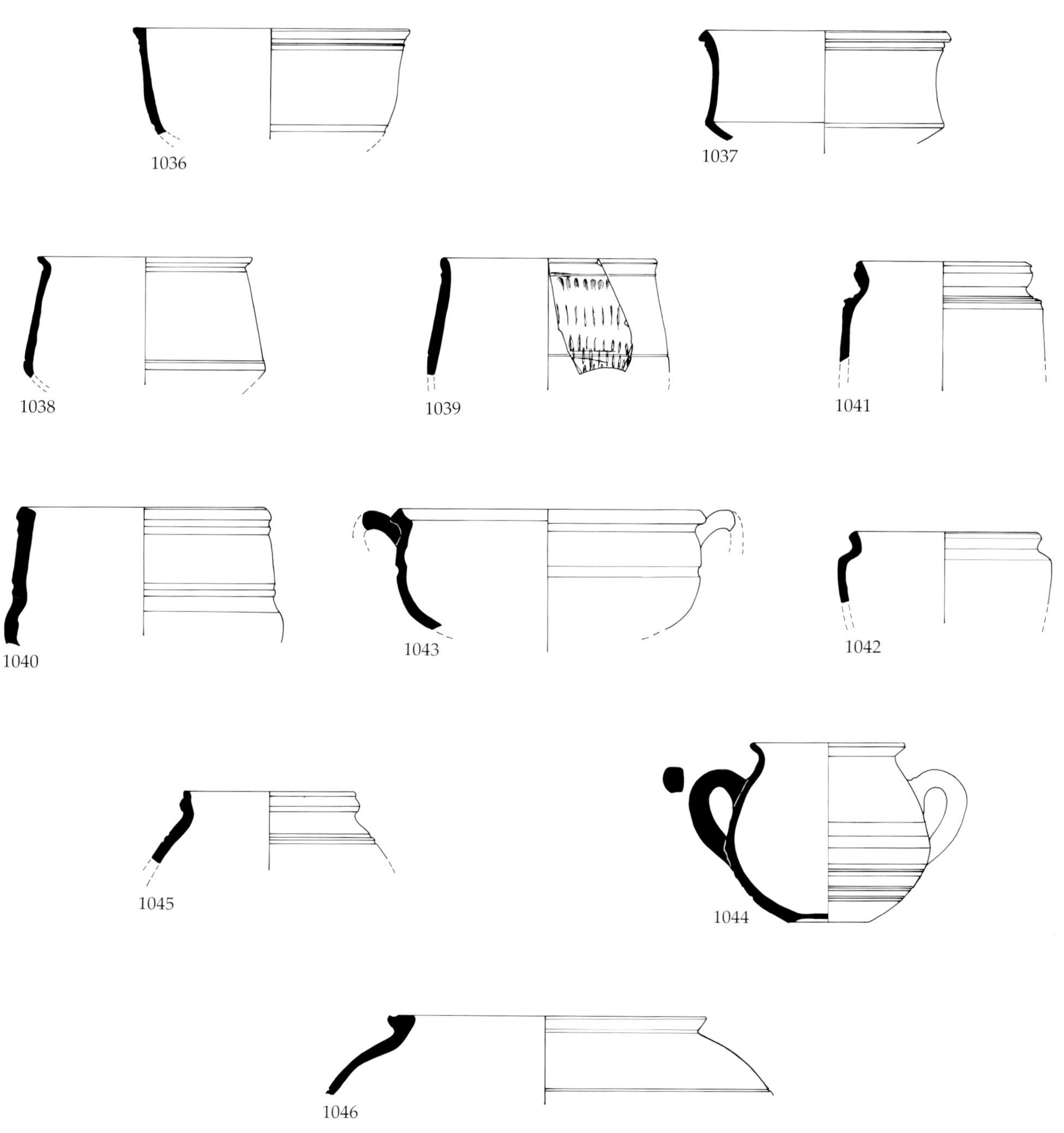

Plate 123. (scale 1:3) Middle Roman Color-Slipped bowls and jars

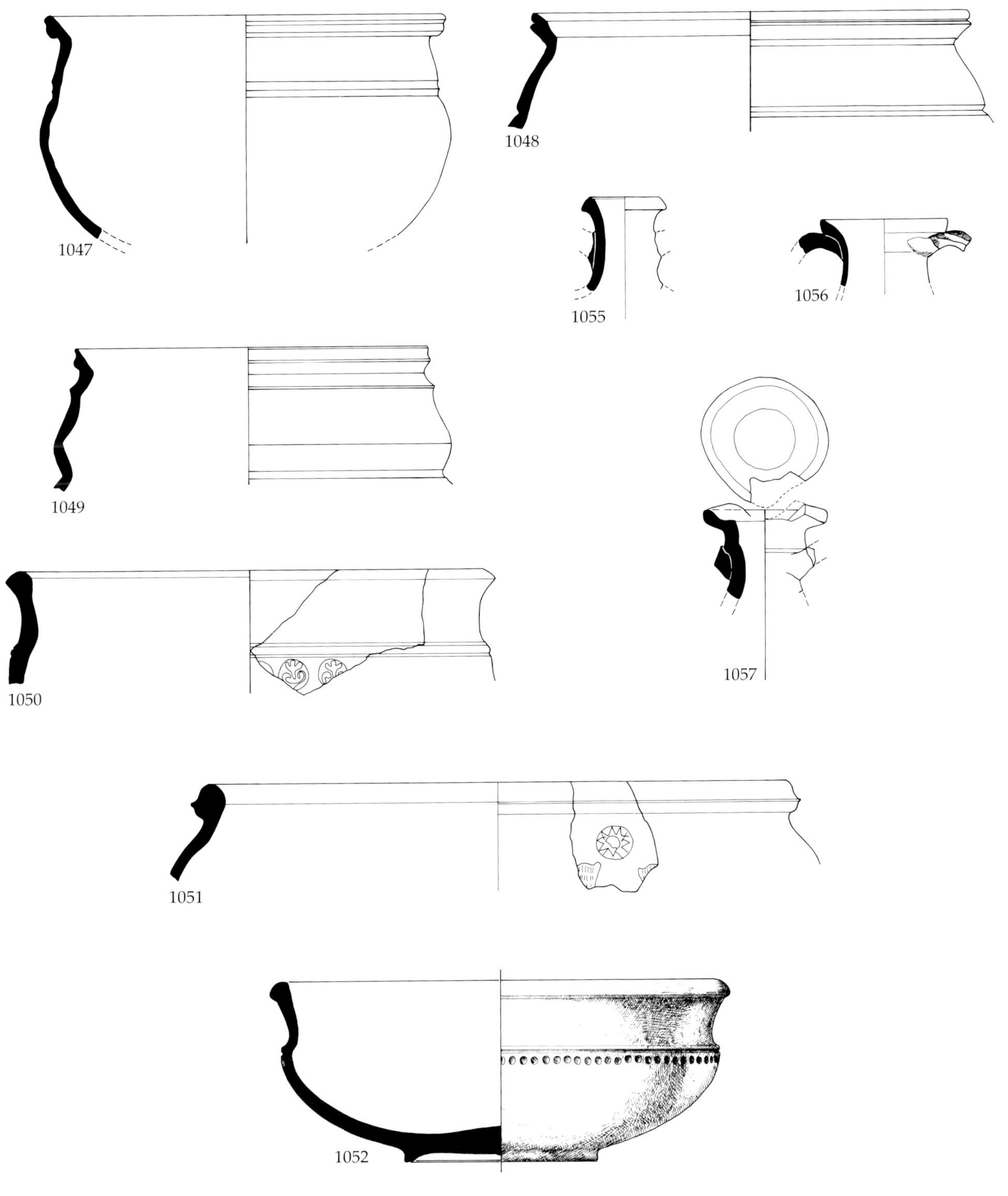

Plate 124. (scale 1:3) Middle Roman Color-Slipped jars and jugs

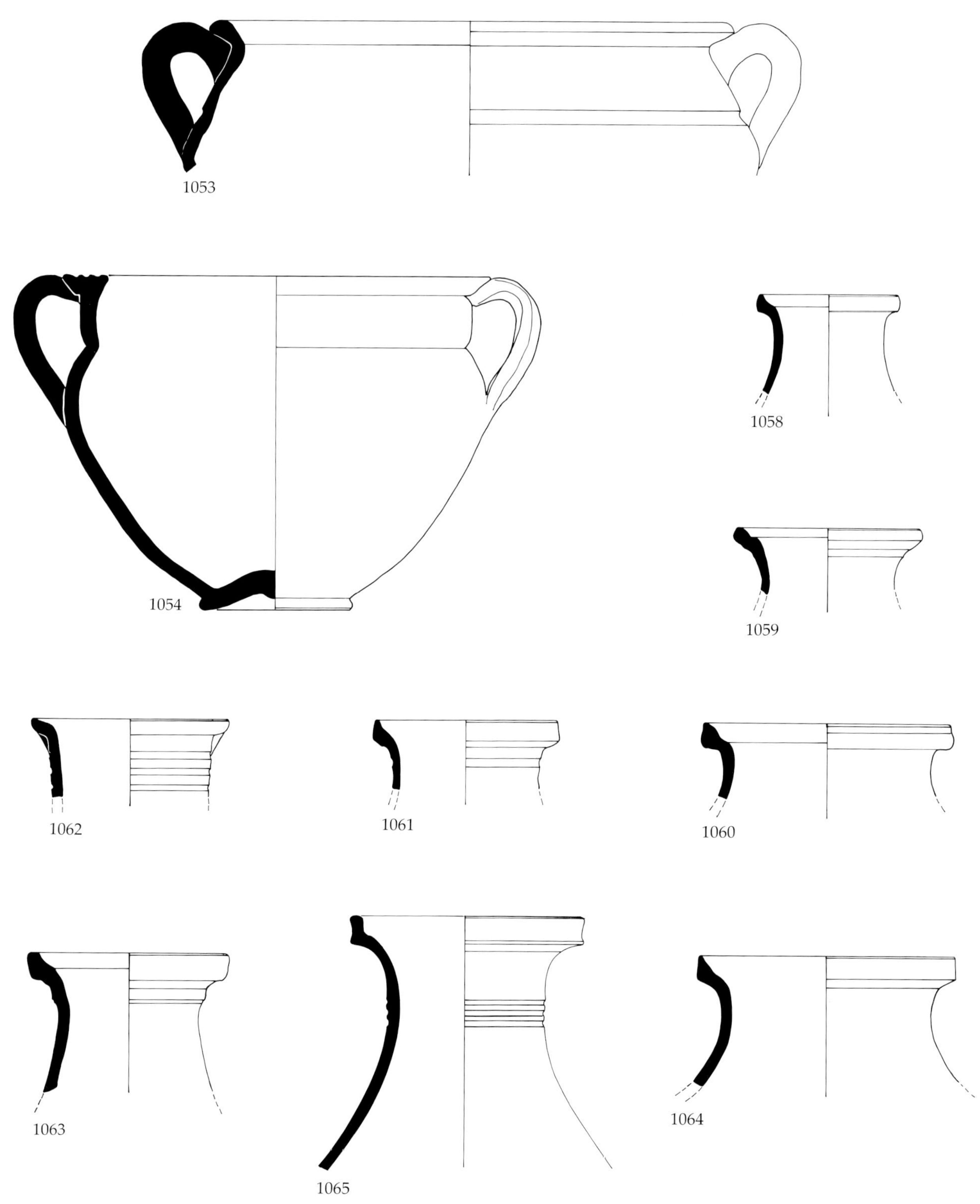

Plate 125. (scale 1:3) Middle Roman Color-Slipped and Plain jars, bowls, and jugs

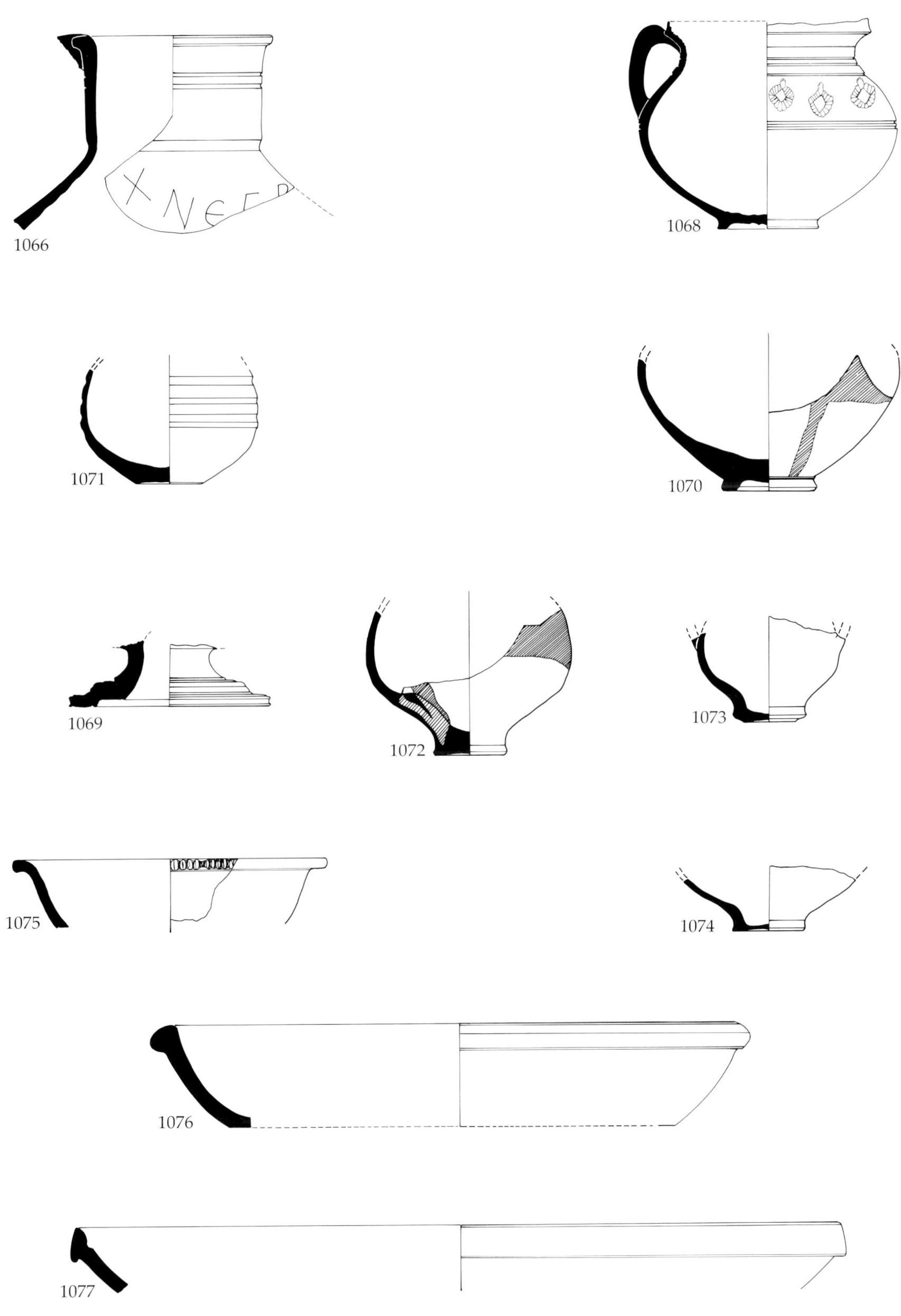

Plate 126. (scale 1:3) Middle Roman Color-Slipped and Plain jugs and bases. Late Roman Color-Slipped dishes

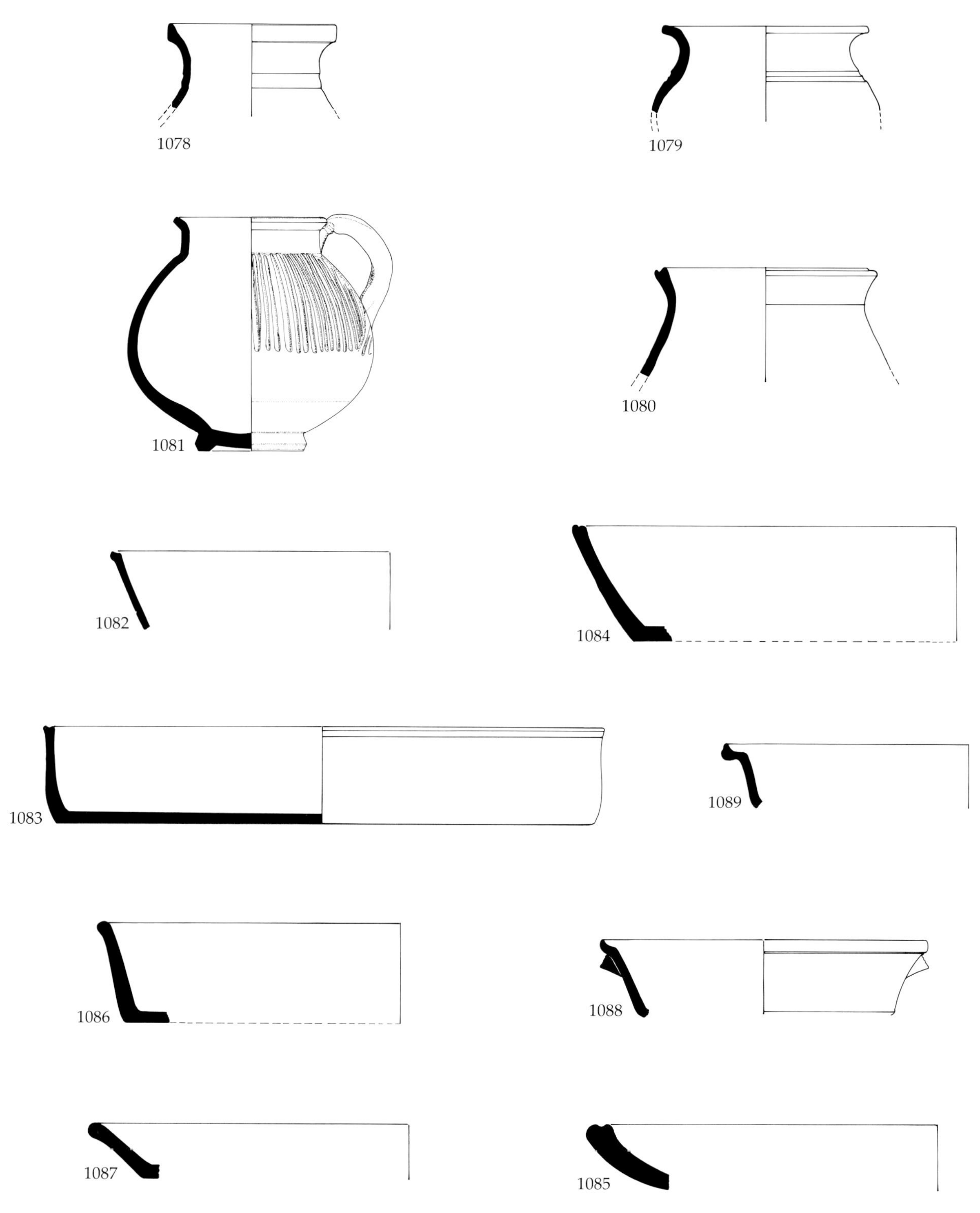

Plate 127. (scale 1:3) Late Roman Color-Slipped and Plain jars. Hellenistic Cooking Ware Forms 1–4

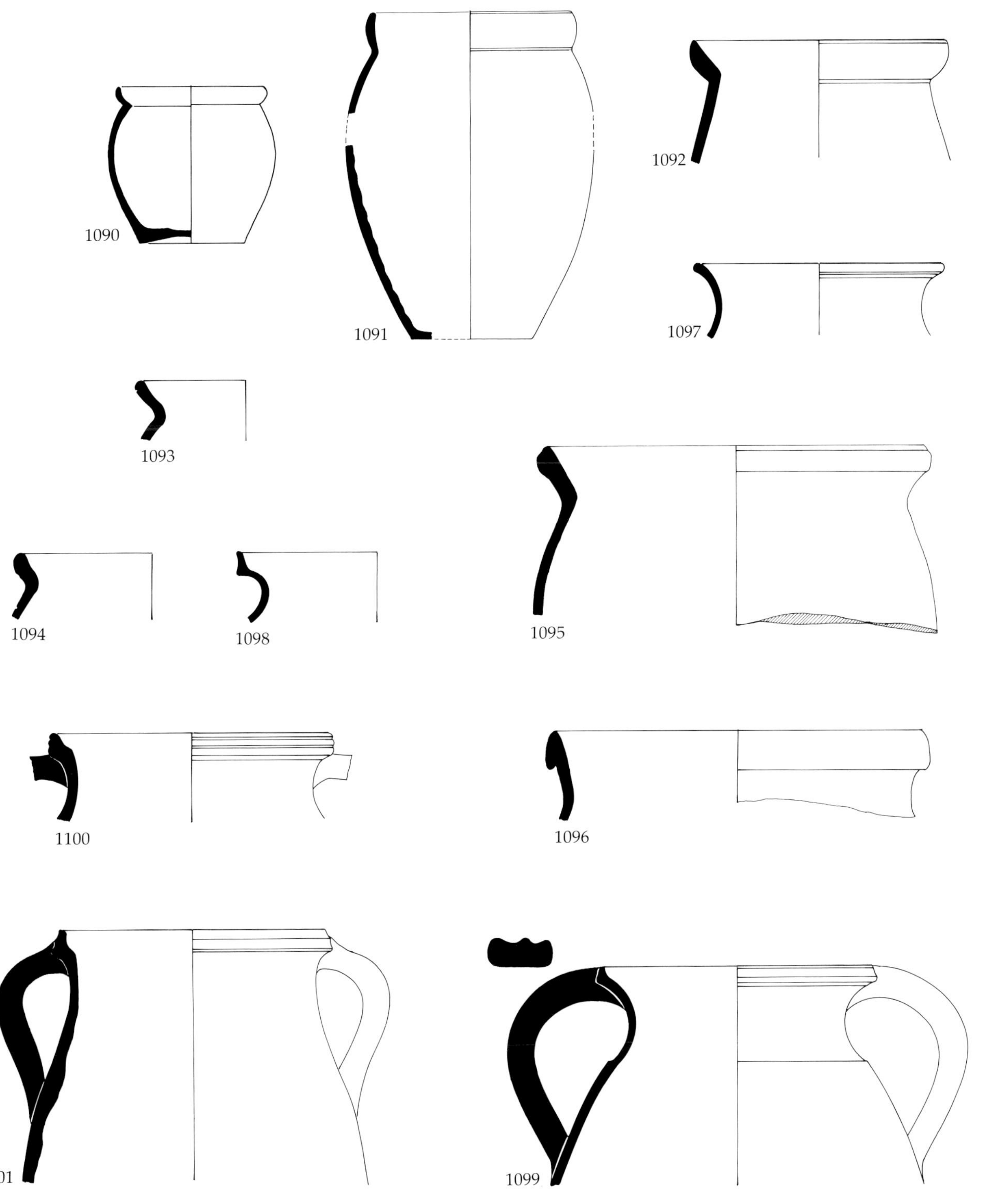

Plate 128. (scale 1:3) Hellenistic Cooking Ware Forms 5–10

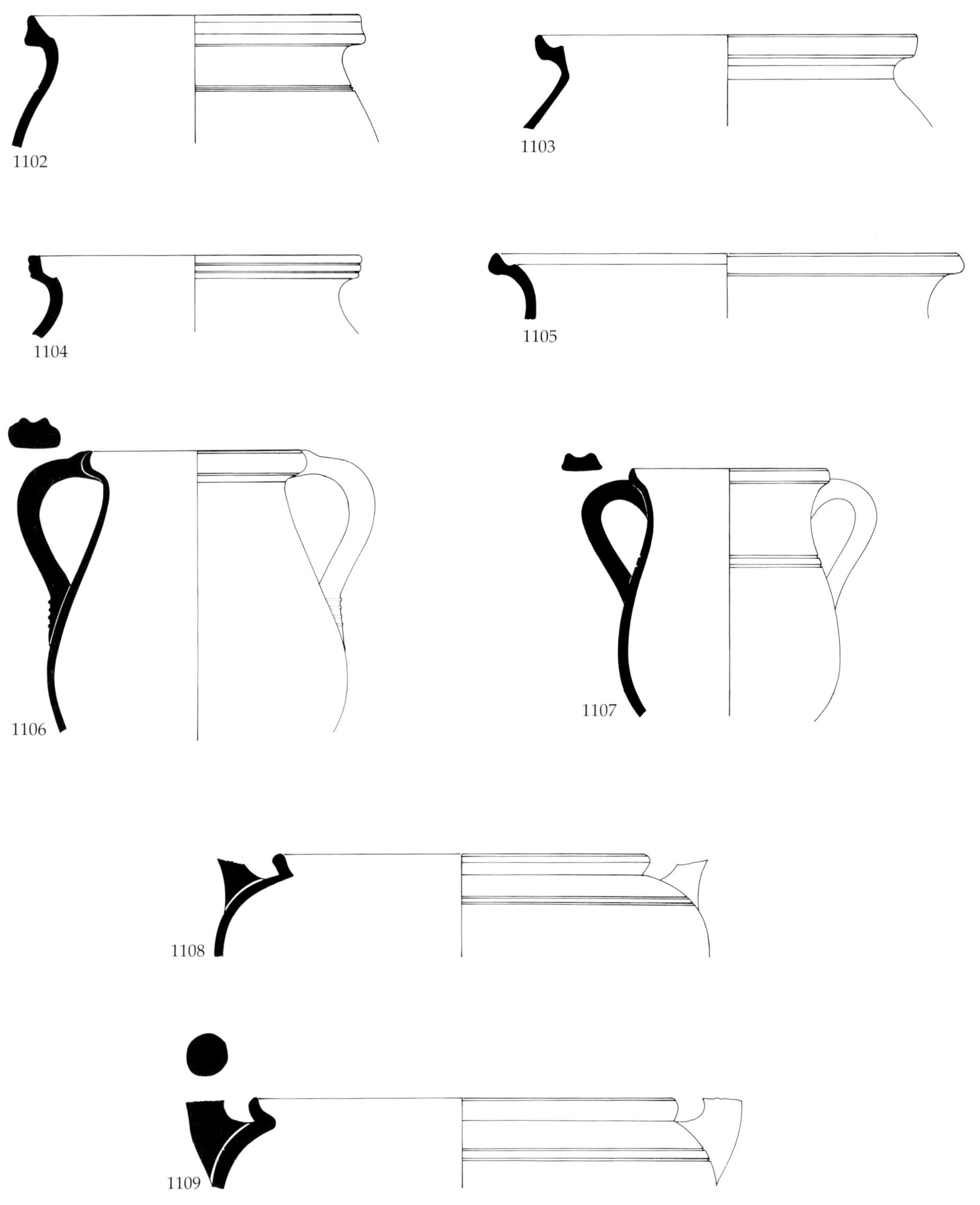

Plate 129. (scale 1:3) Hellenistic Cooking Ware Forms 10–13

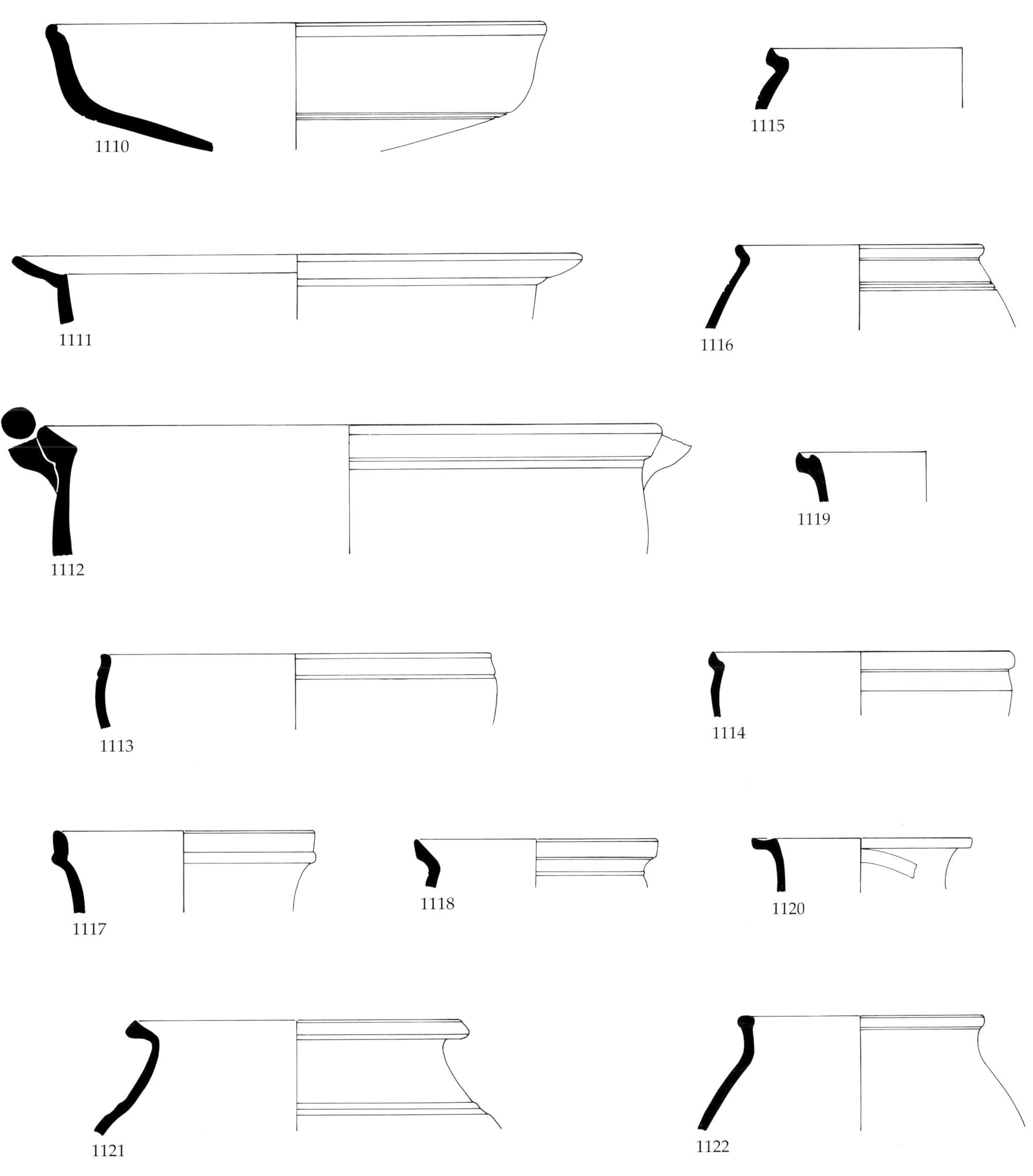

Plate 130. (scale 1:3) Hellenistic Cooking Ware pans, jars, and stewpots

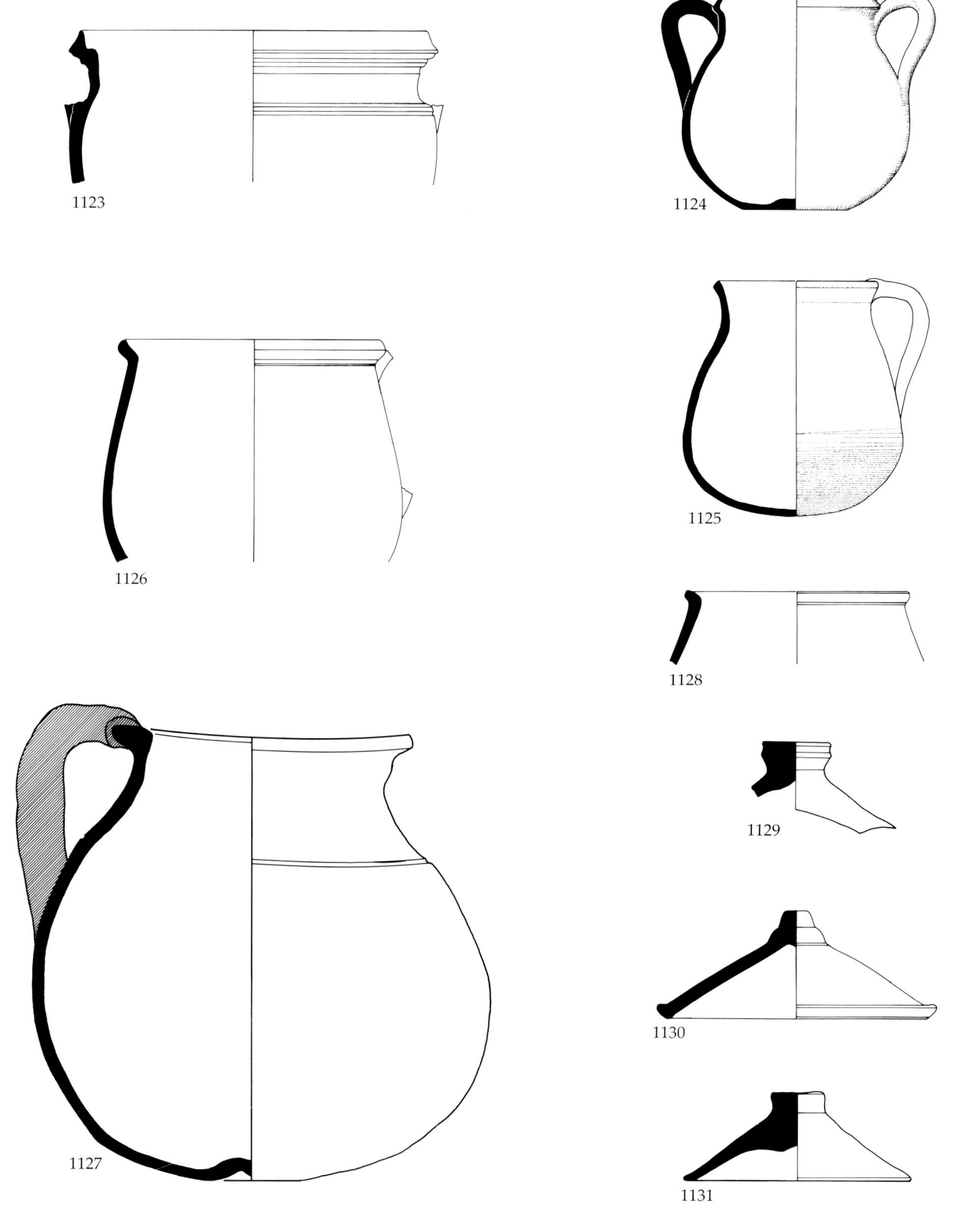

Plate 131. (scale 1:3) Hellenistic Cooking Ware stewpots and lids

Plate 132. (scale 1:3) Early Roman Cooking Ware Forms 1–6

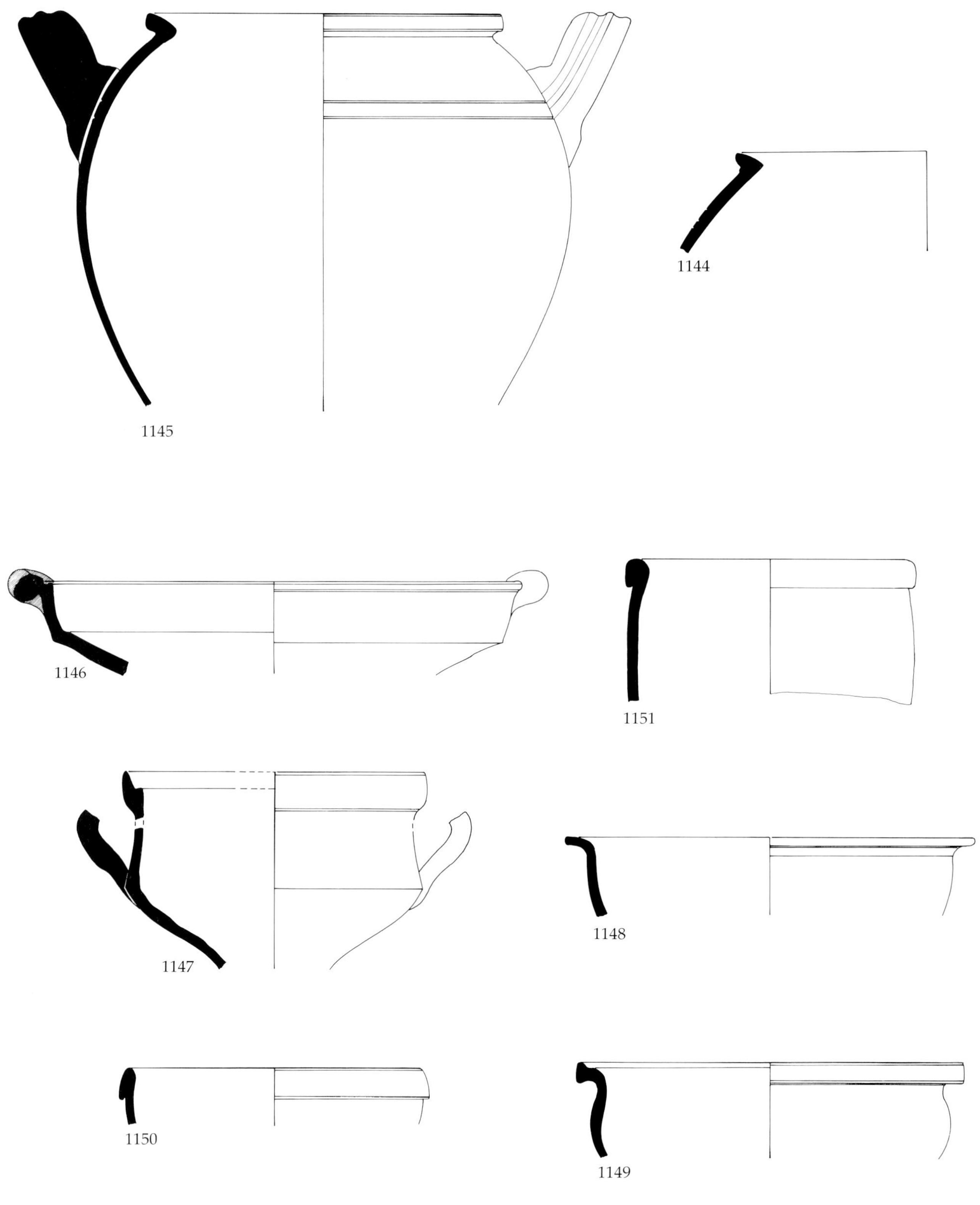

Plate 133. (scale 1:3) Early Roman Cooking Ware Form 7 and Early Roman Cooking Ware casseroles and jars

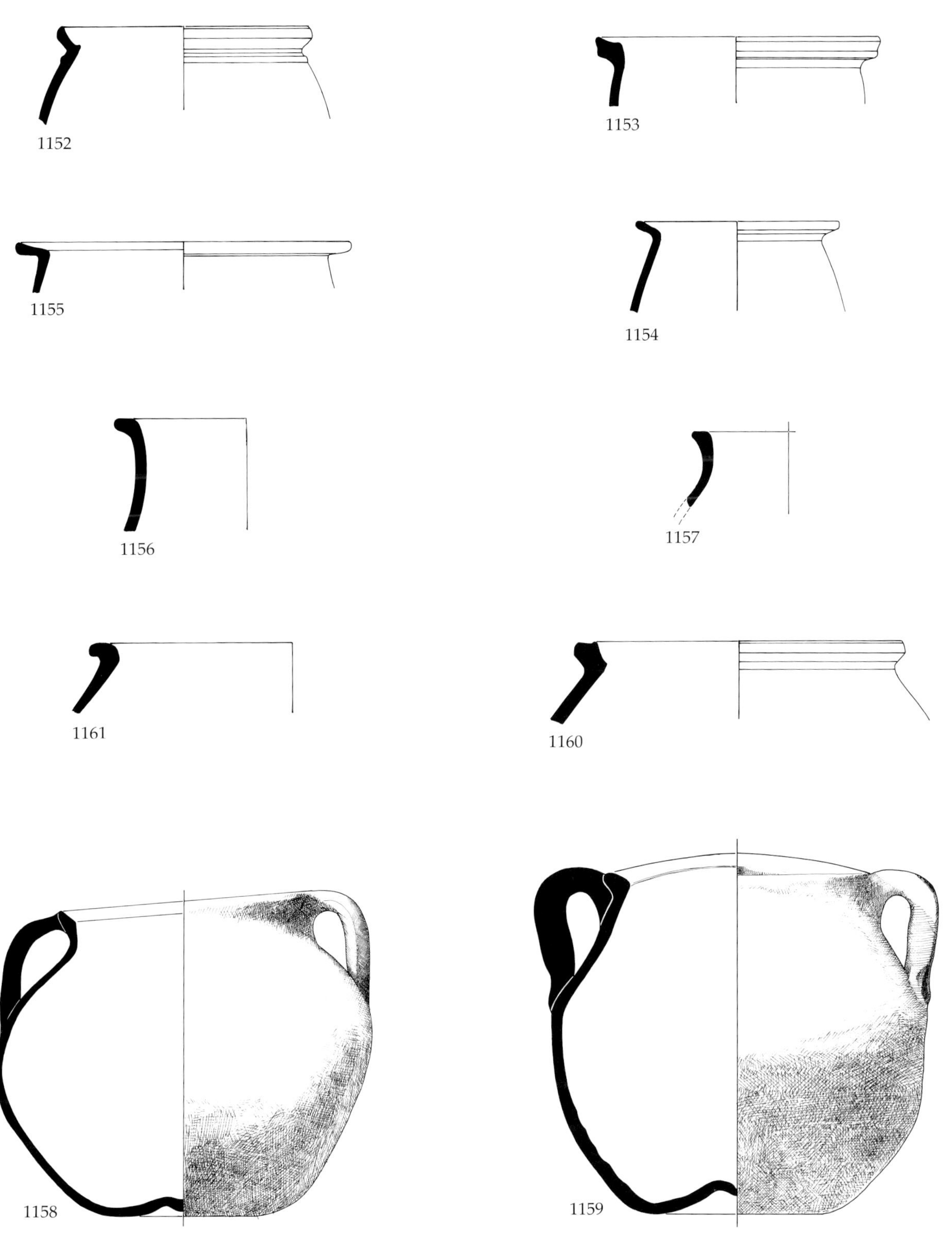

Plate 134. (scale 1:3) Early Roman Cooking Ware jars and stewpots

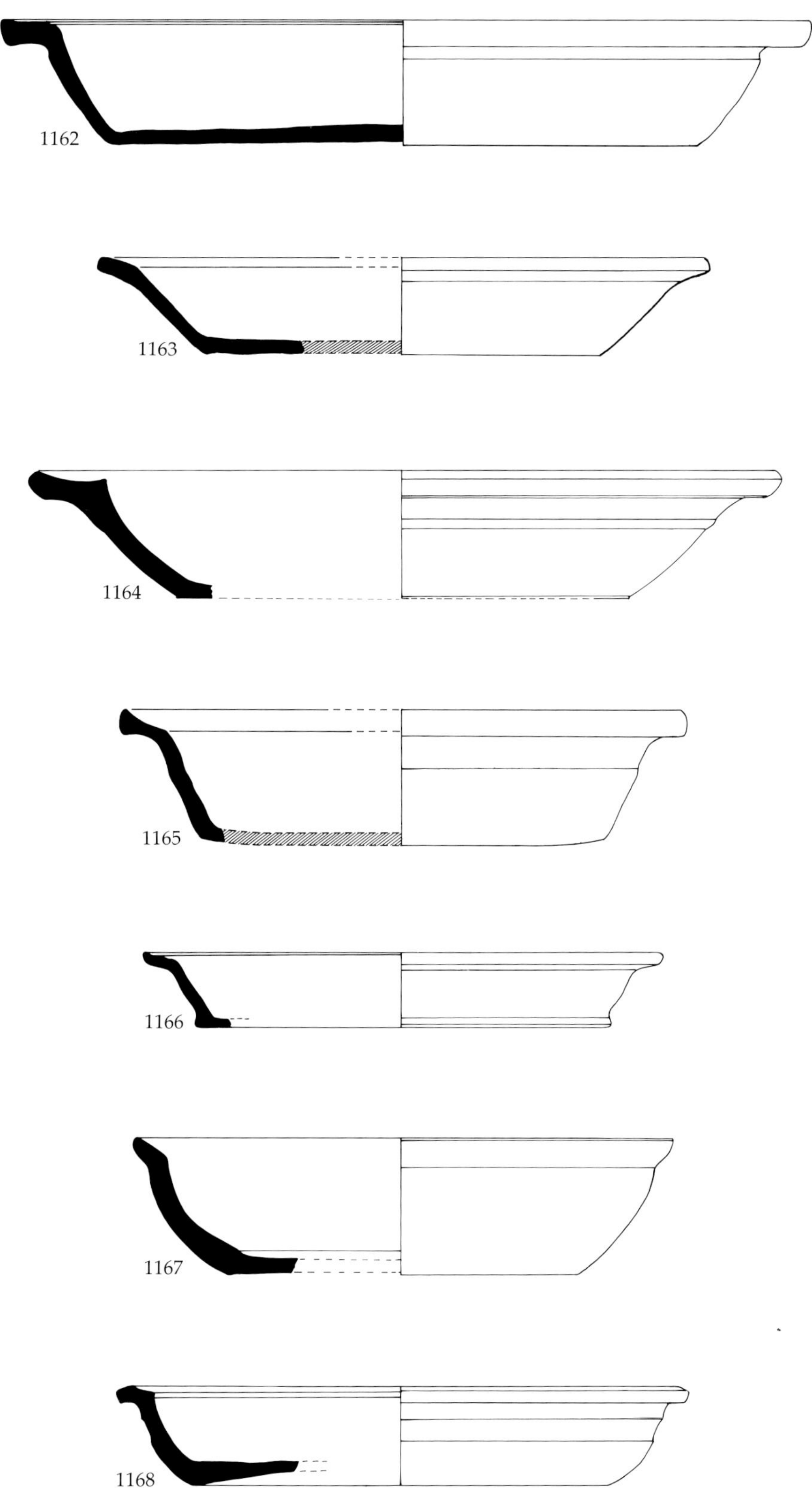

Plate 135. (scale 1:3) Middle Roman Cooking Ware Form 1

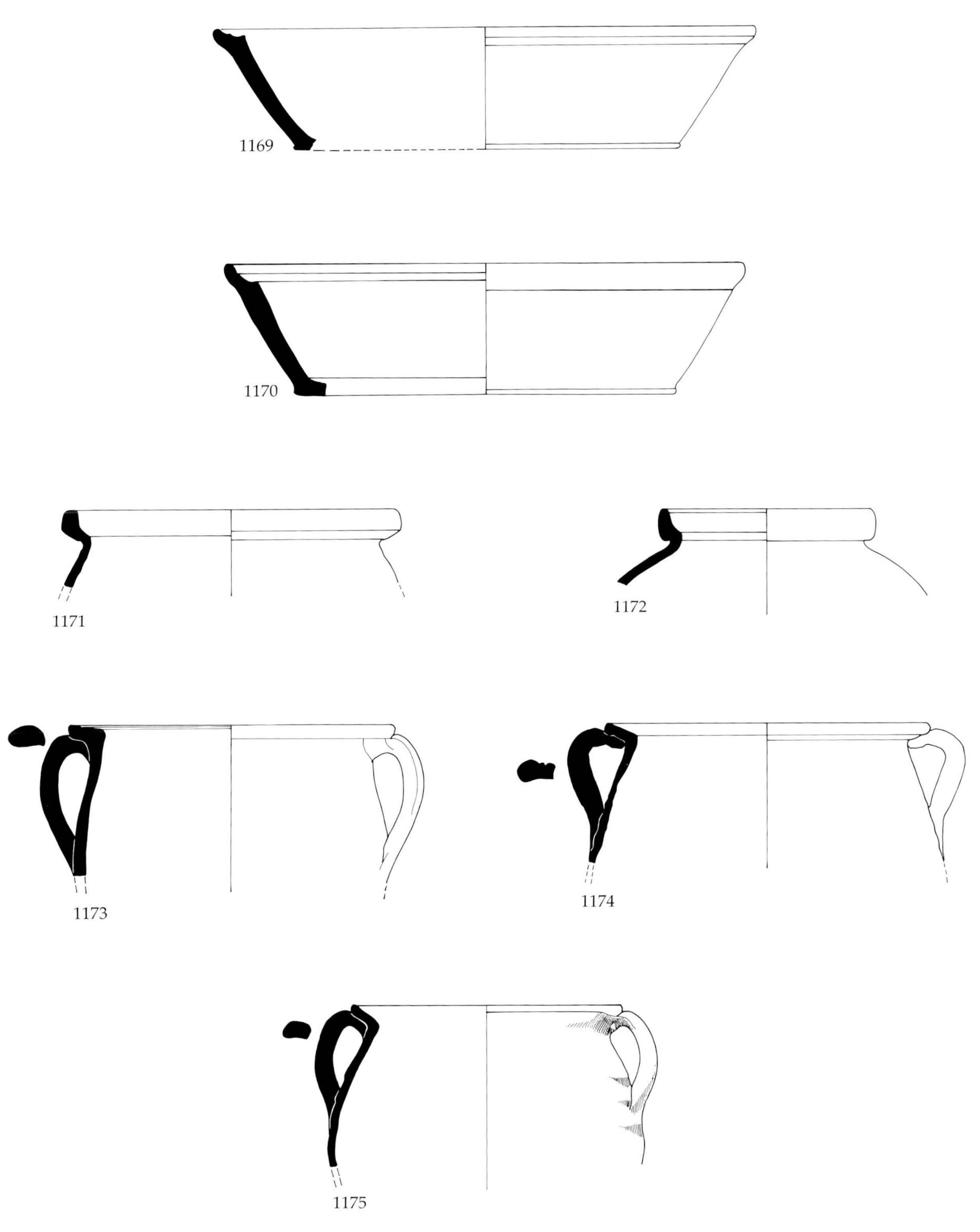

Plate 136. (scale 1:3) Middle Roman Cooking Ware Forms 2–4

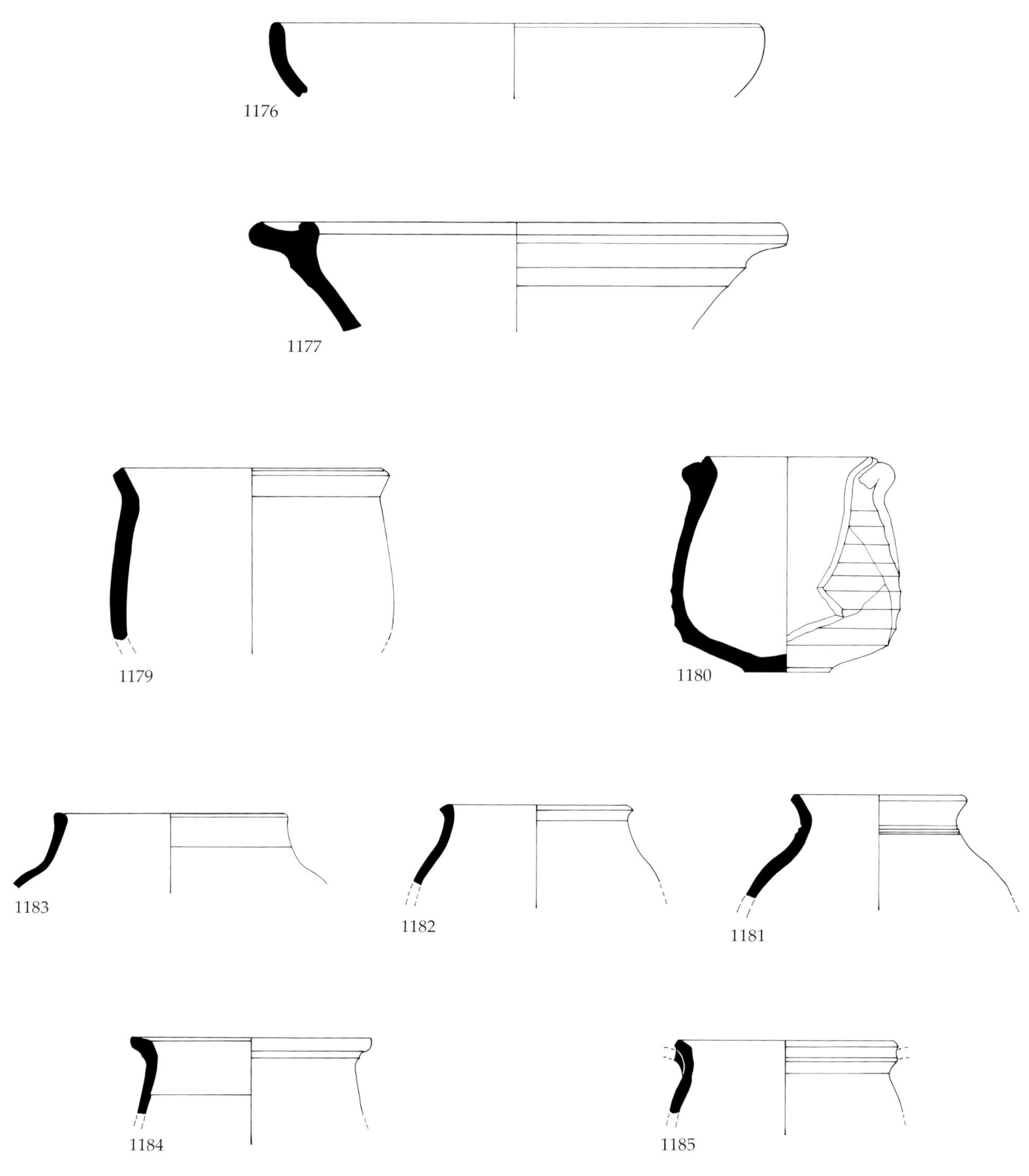

Plate 137. (scale 1:3) Middle Roman Cooking Ware dishes and jars

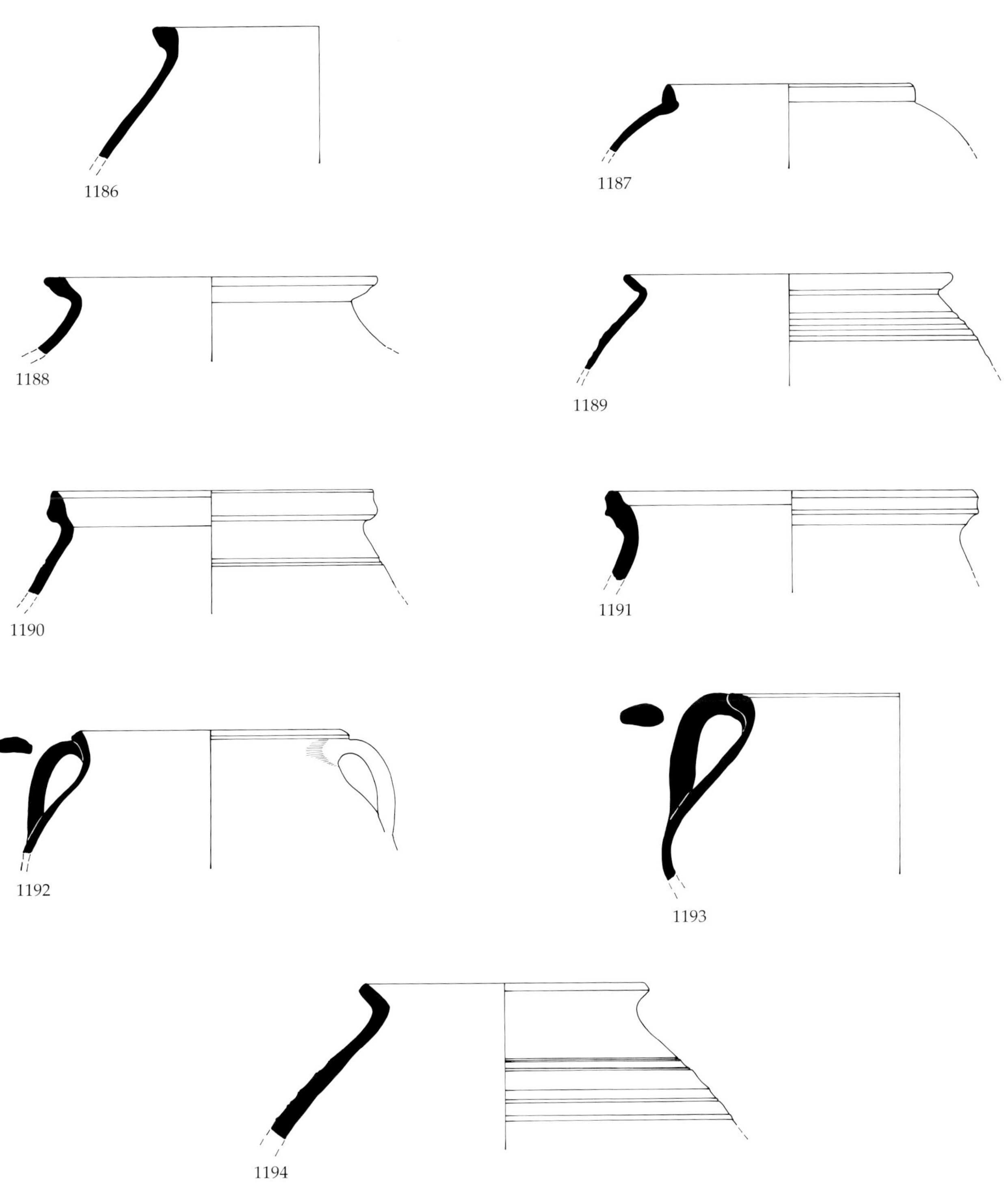

Plate 138. (scale 1:3) Middle Roman Cooking Ware stewpots

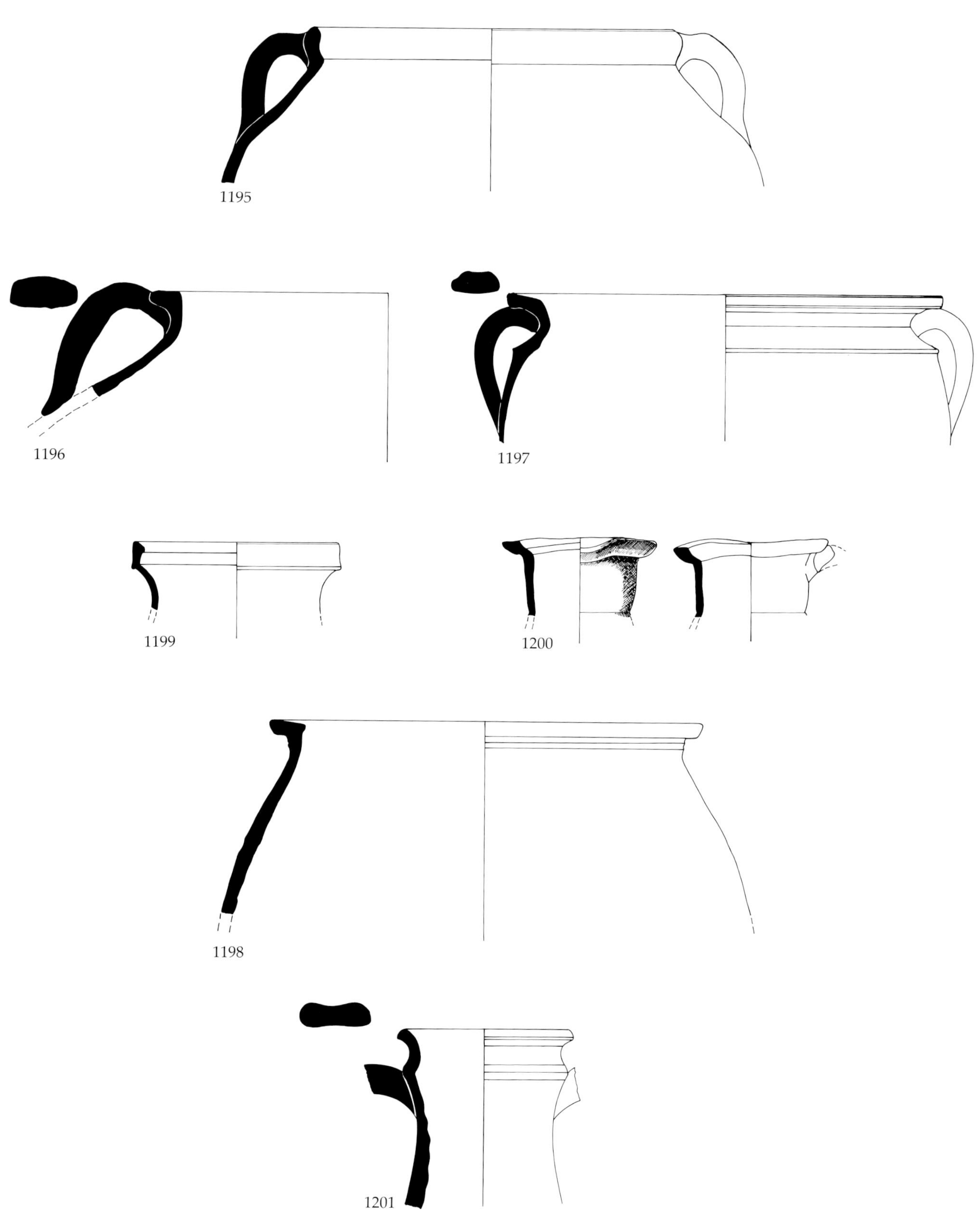

Plate 139. (scale 1:3) Middle Roman Cooking Ware stewpots, jars, and jugs

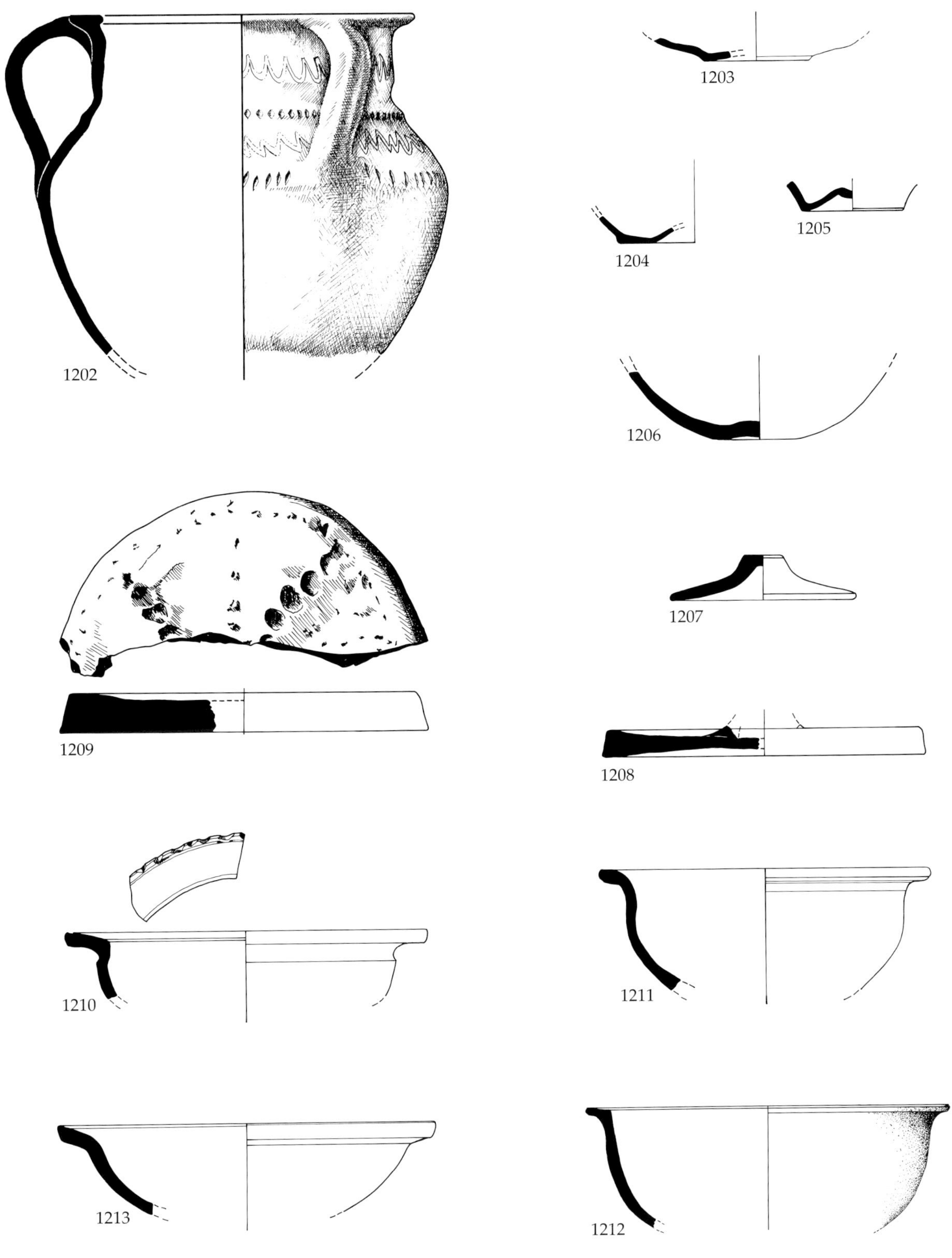

Plate 140. (scale 1:3) Middle Roman Cooking Ware stewpot, bases, and lids. Late Roman Cooking Ware Form 1

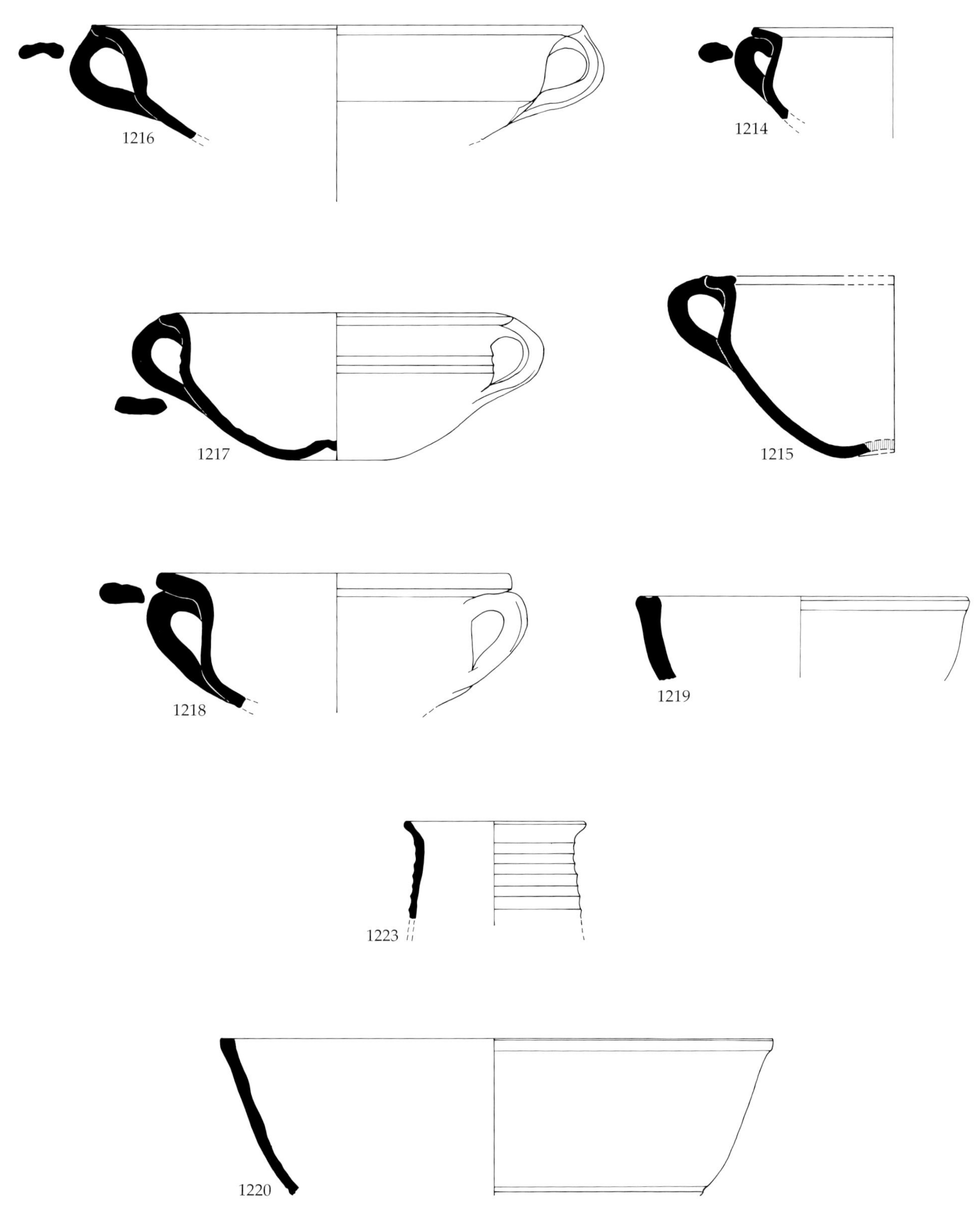

Plate 141. (scale 1:3) Late Roman Cooking Ware Forms 2, 3, and 5

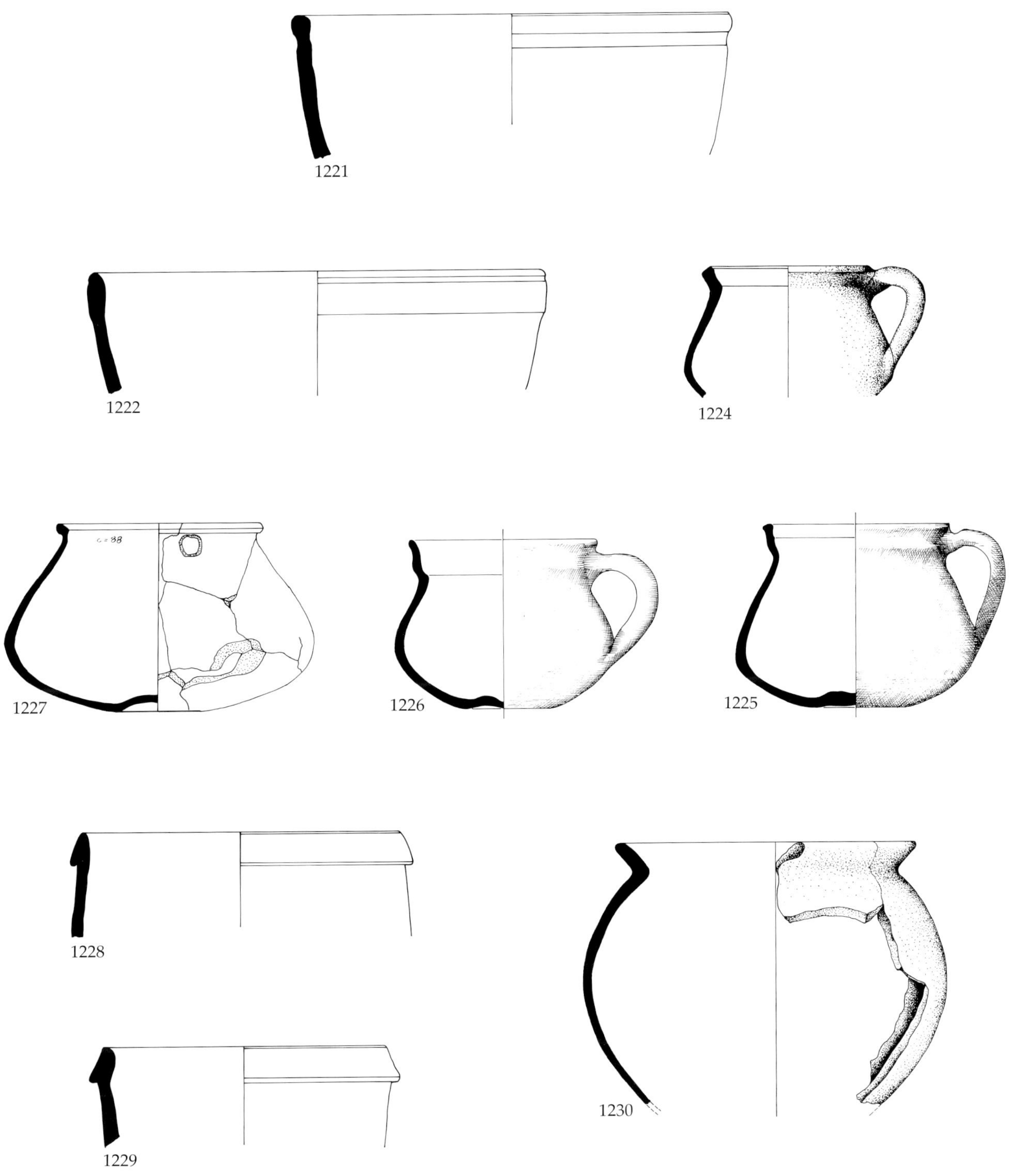

Plate 142. (scale 1:3) Late Roman Cooking Ware Forms 4–7

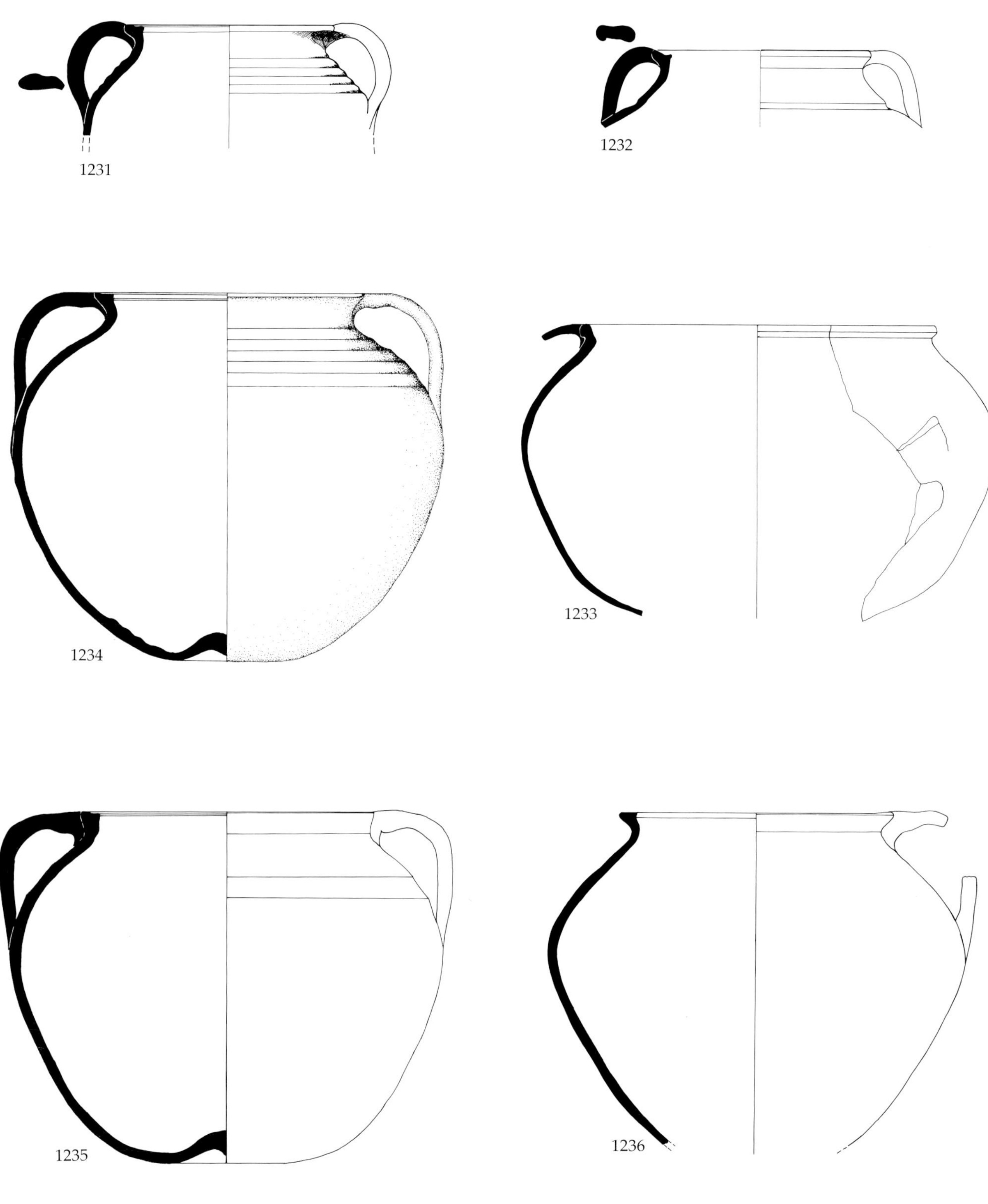

Plate 143. (scale 1:3) Late Roman Cooking Ware Form 8

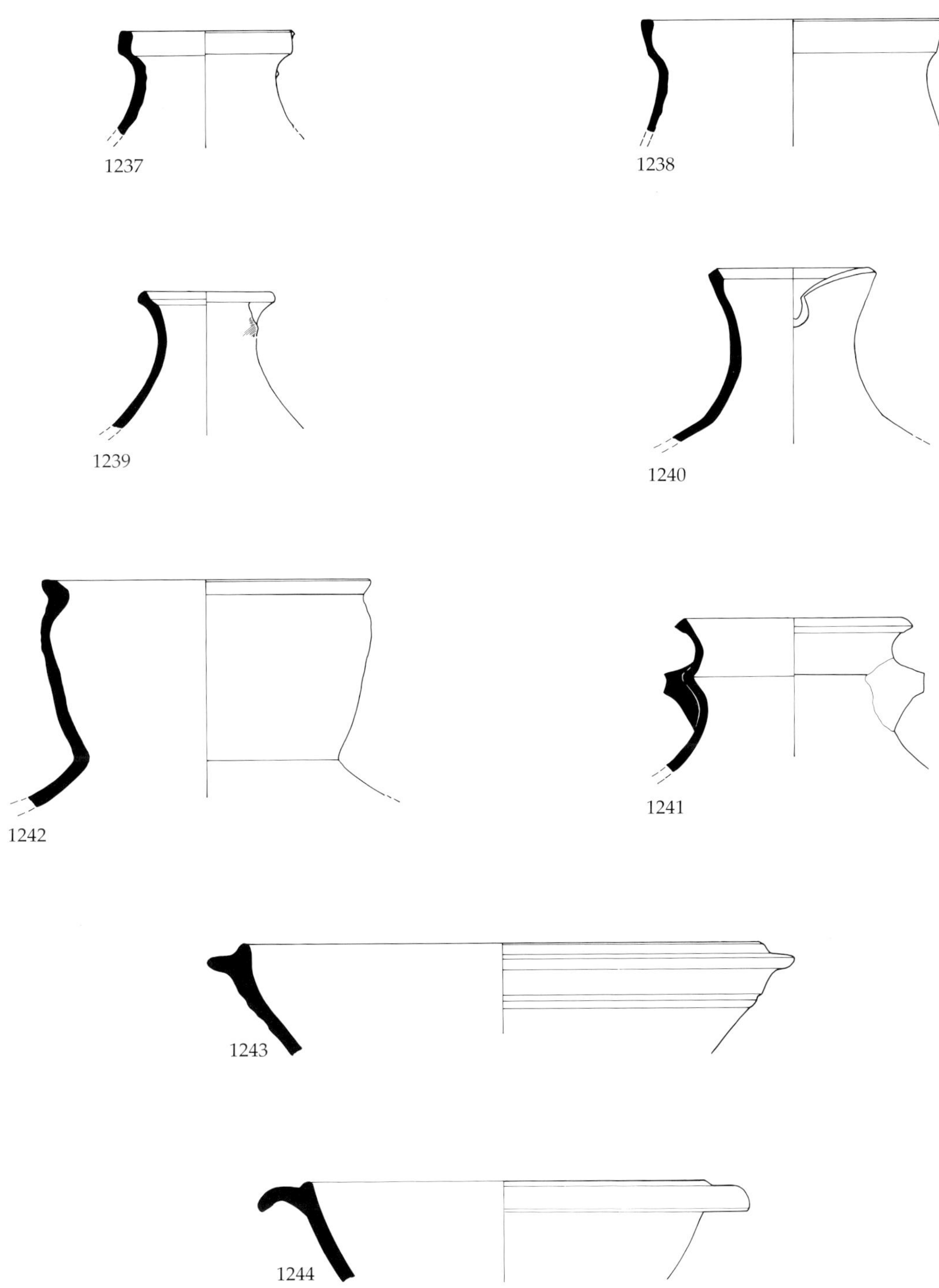

Plate 144. (scale 1:3) Late Roman Cooking Ware Forms 9–13. Late Roman Cooking Ware dishes

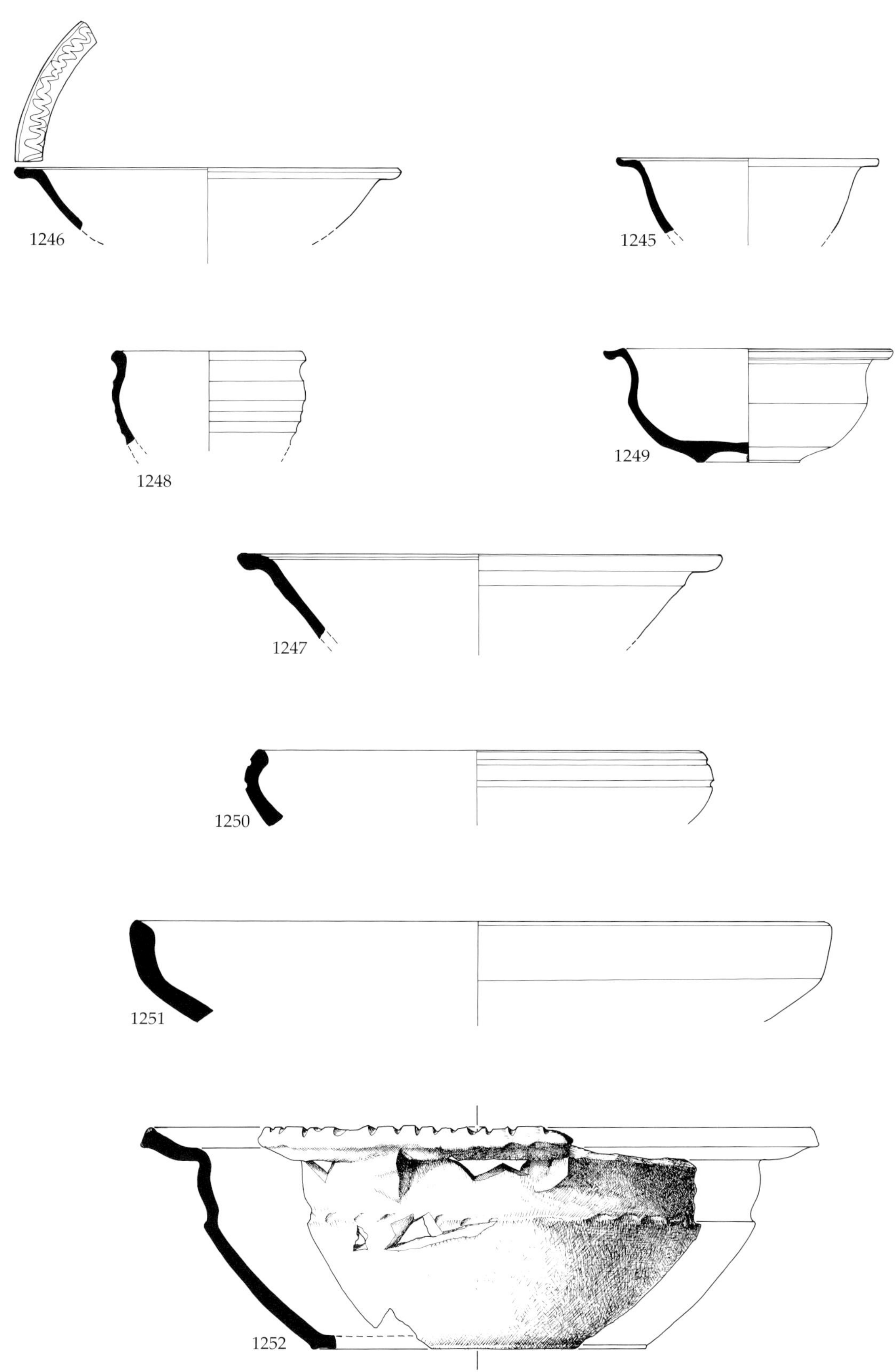

Plate 145. (scale 1:3) Late Roman Cooking Ware bowls and casseroles

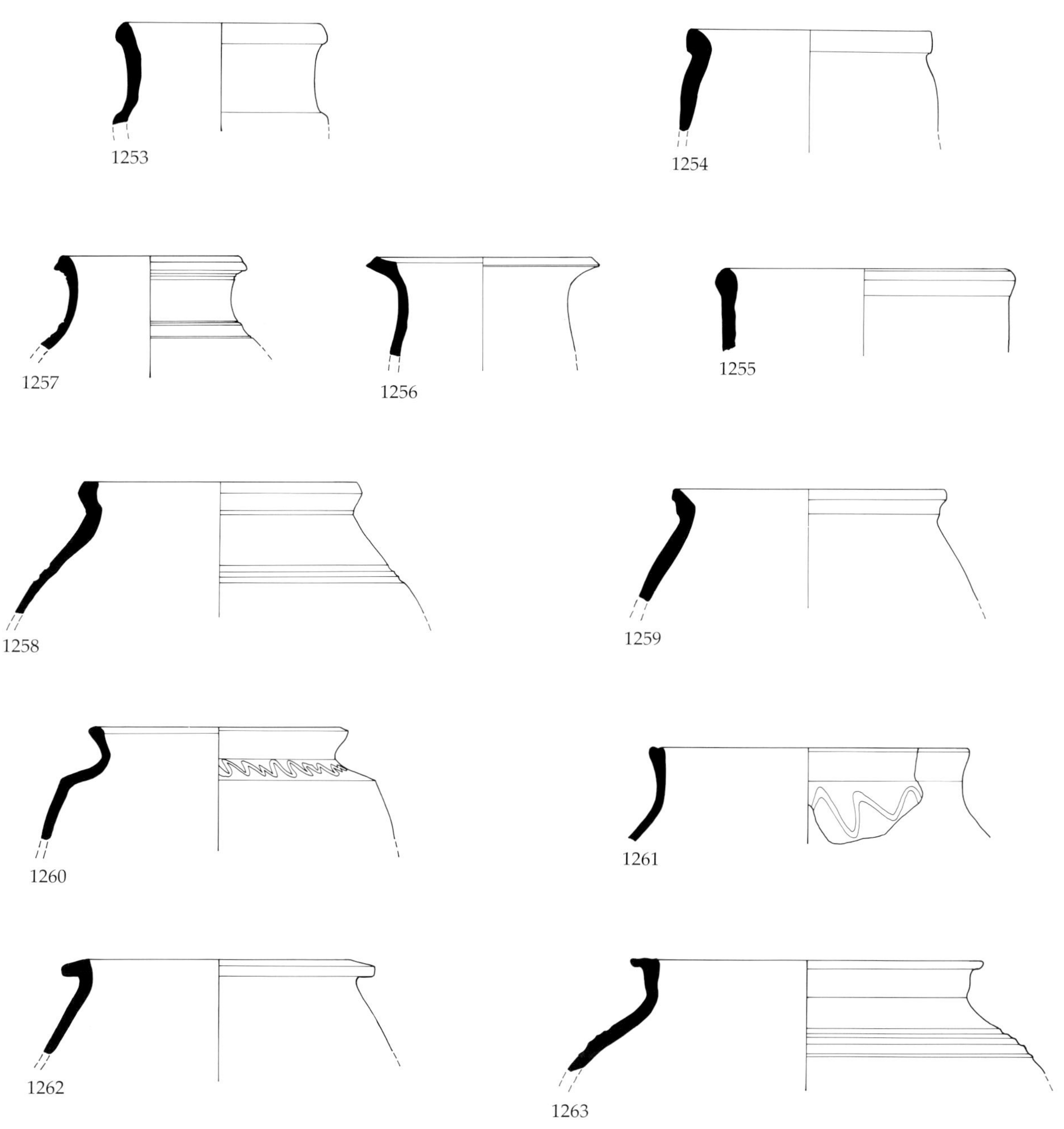

Plate 146. (scale 1:3) Late Roman Cooking Ware jars and stewpots

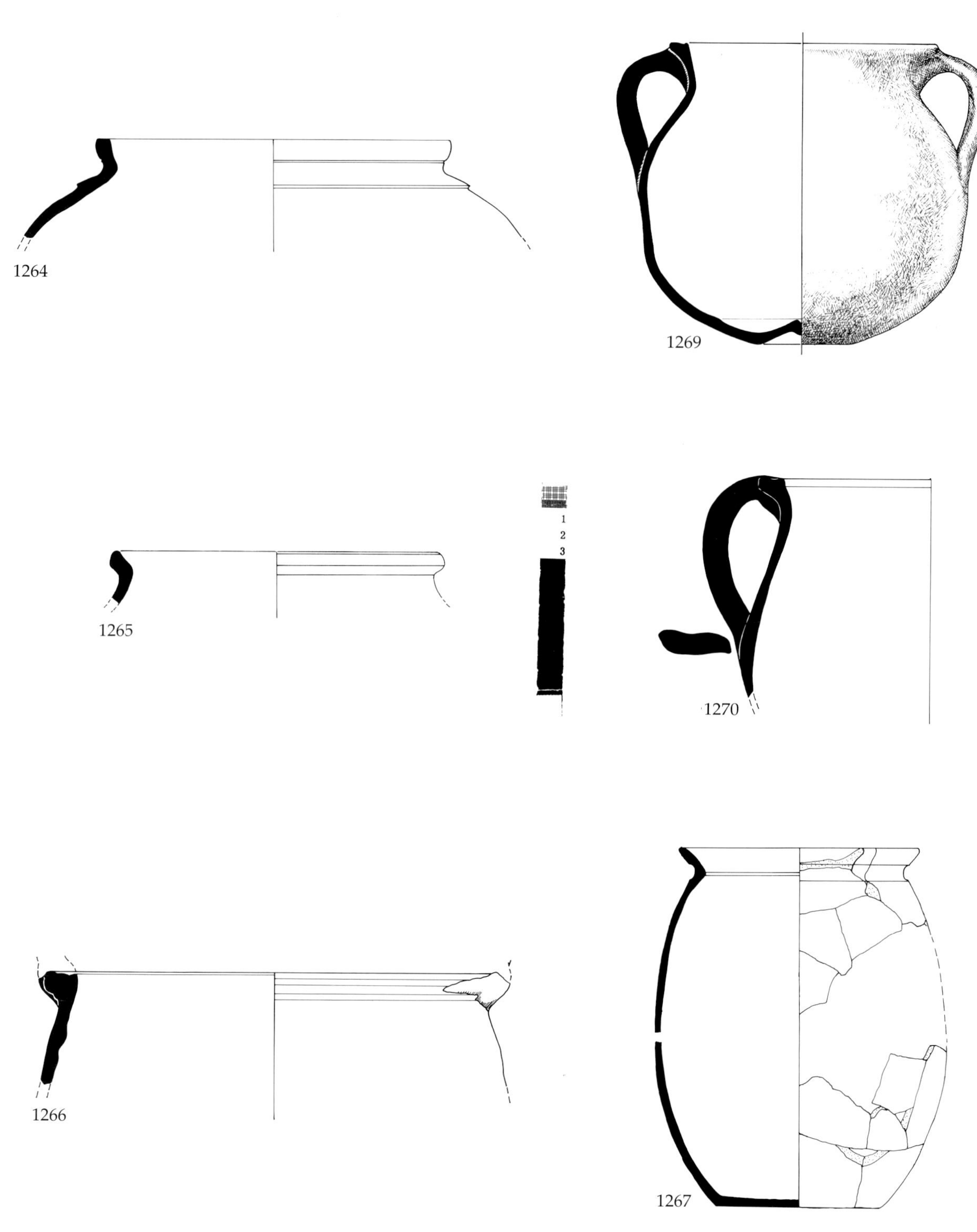

Plate 147. (scale 1:3) Late Roman Cooking Ware jars and stewpots

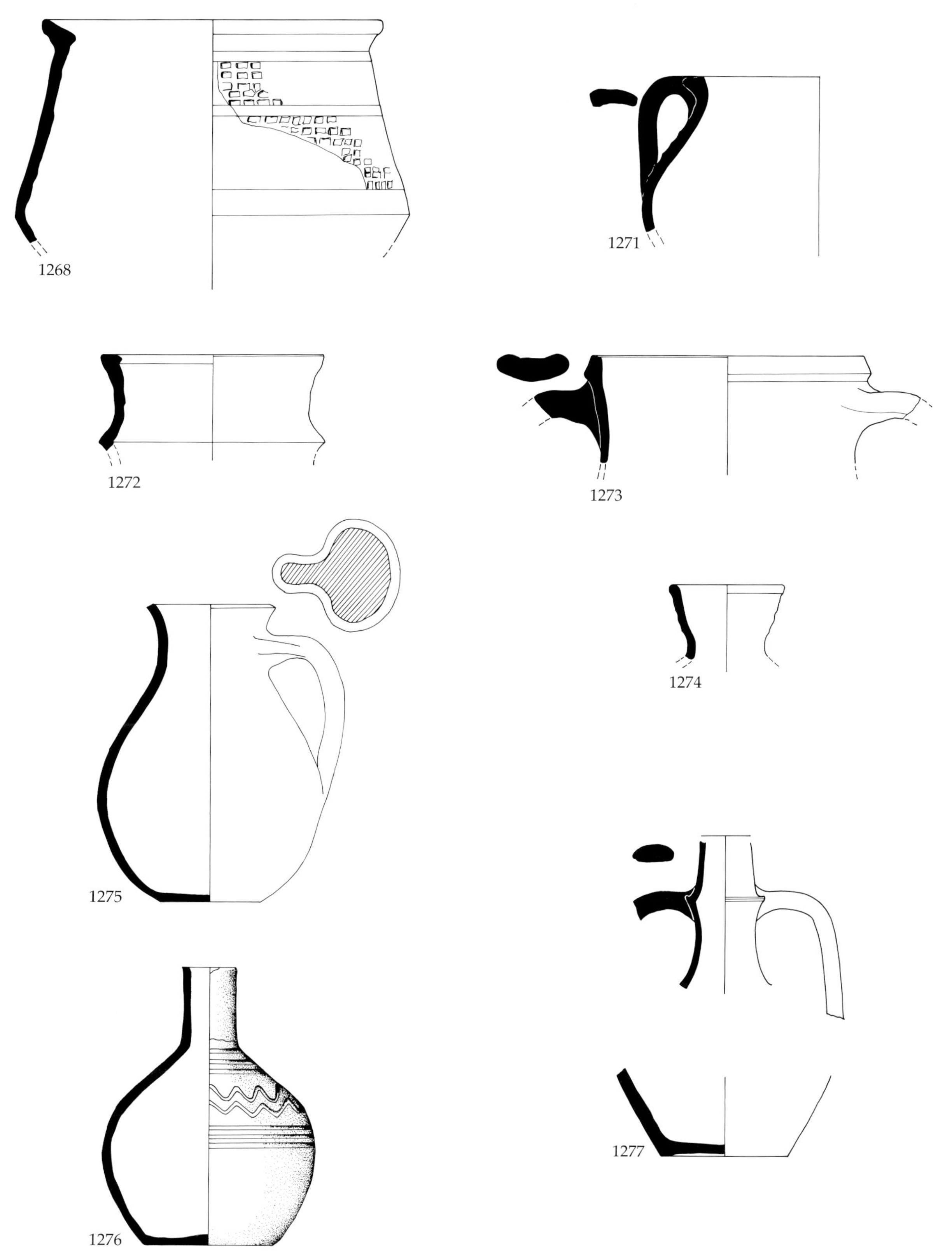

Plate 148. (scale 1:3) Late Roman Cooking Ware jars, stewpots, and jugs

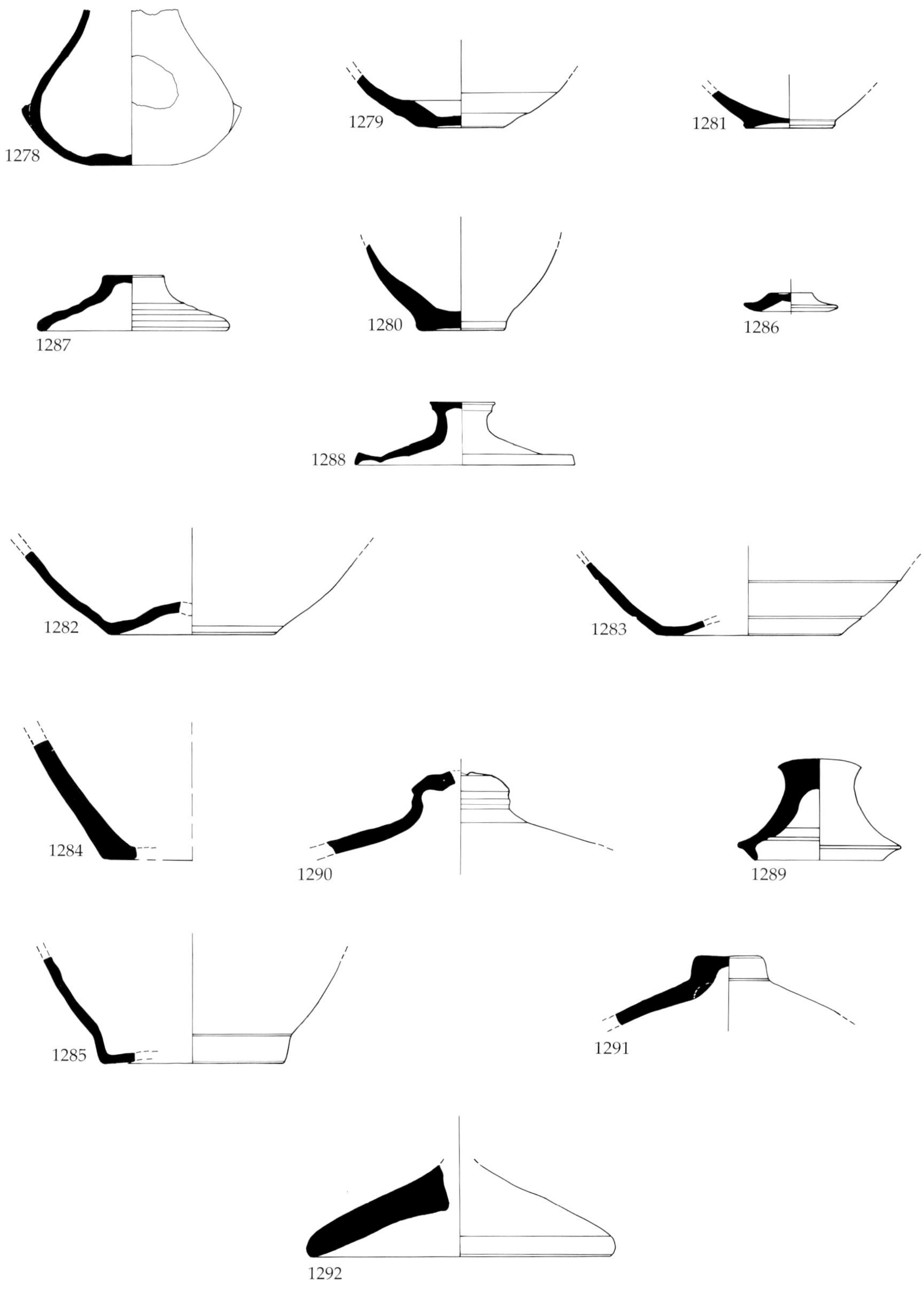

Plate 149. (scale 1:3) Late Roman Cooking Ware stewpot, bases, and lids (1288, scale 1:4)

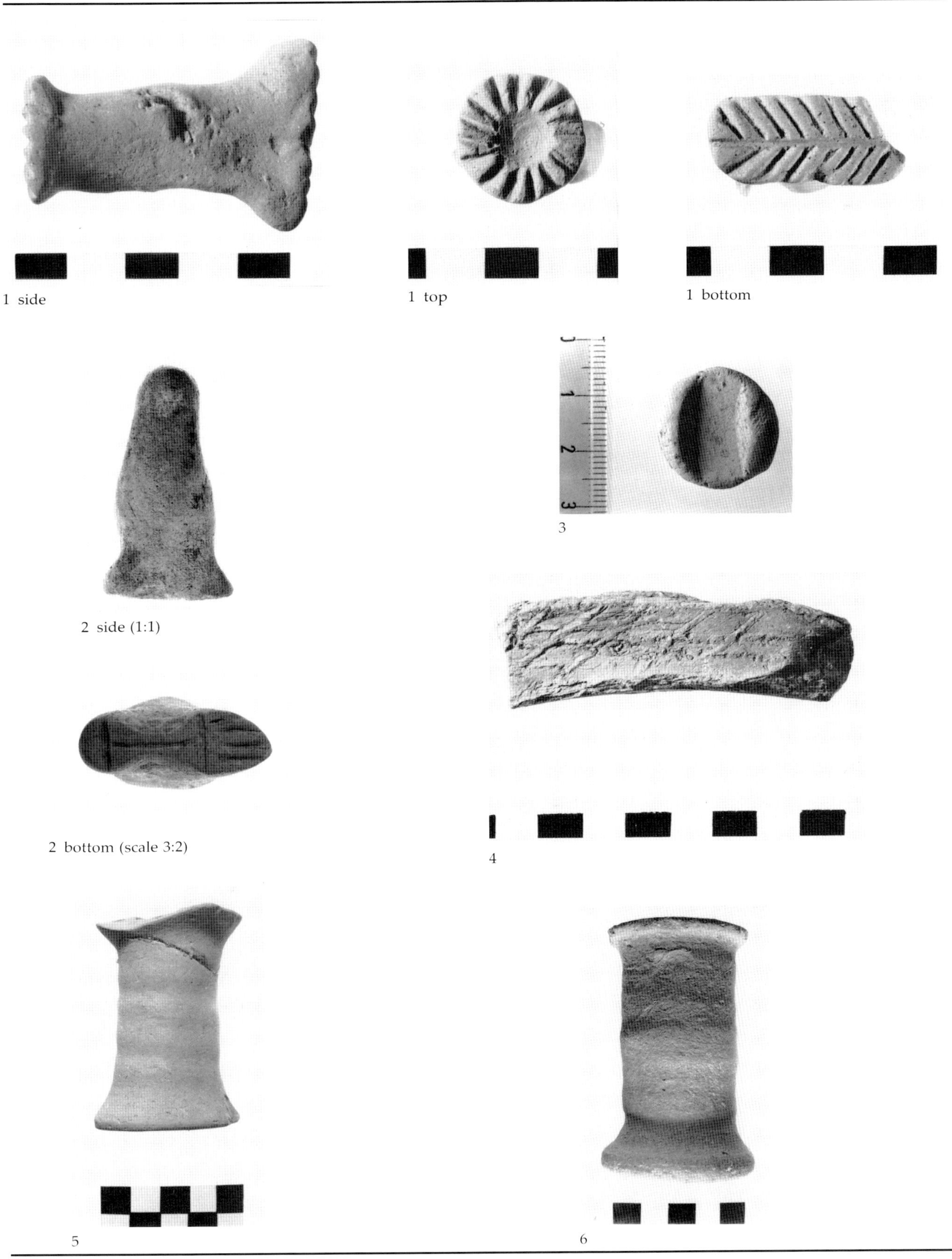

Plate 150. Pottery stamps and kiln furniture (2 side view, scale 1:1; 2 bottom, scale 3:2)

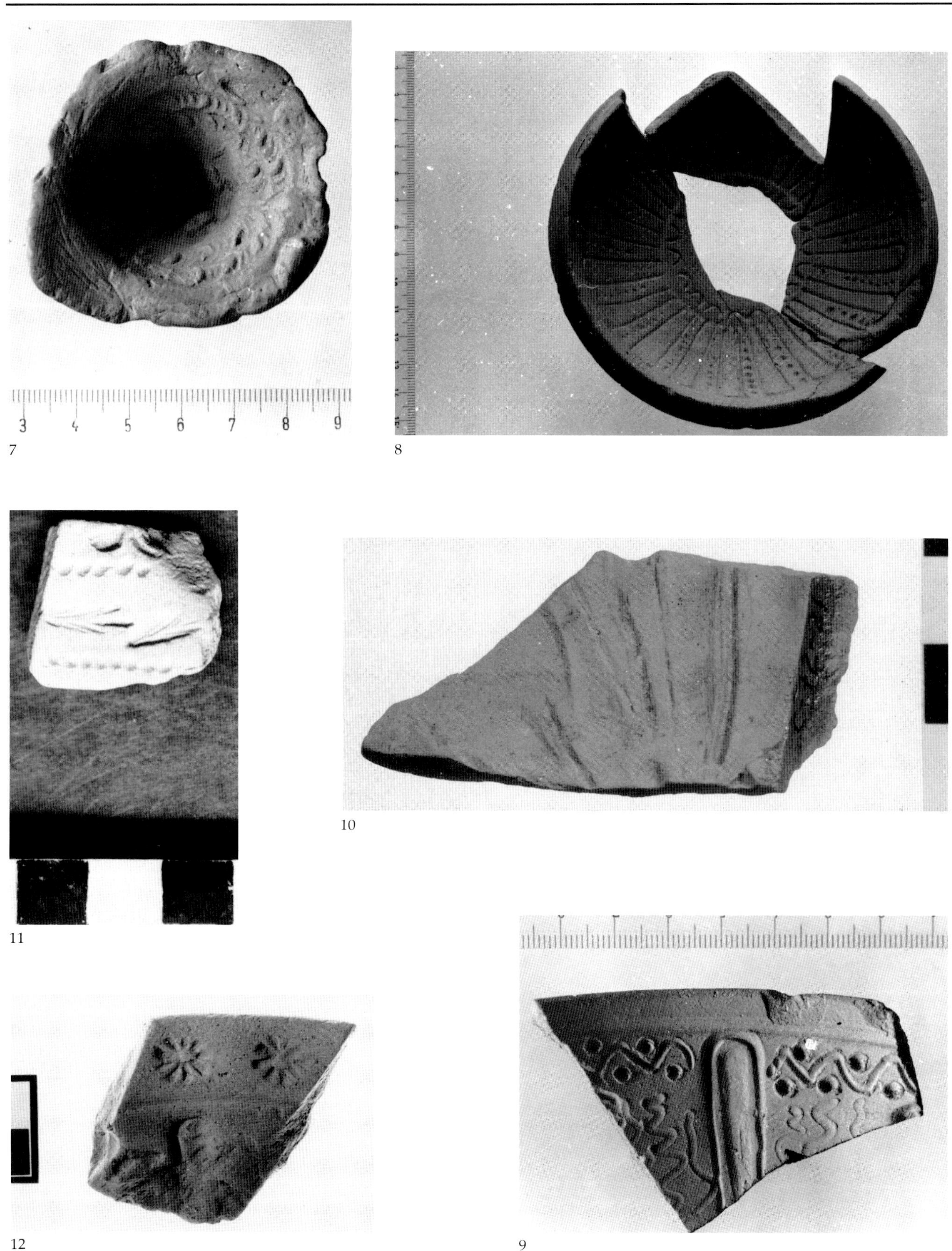

7

8

11

10

12

9

Plate 151. Lion's head mould and bowl moulds

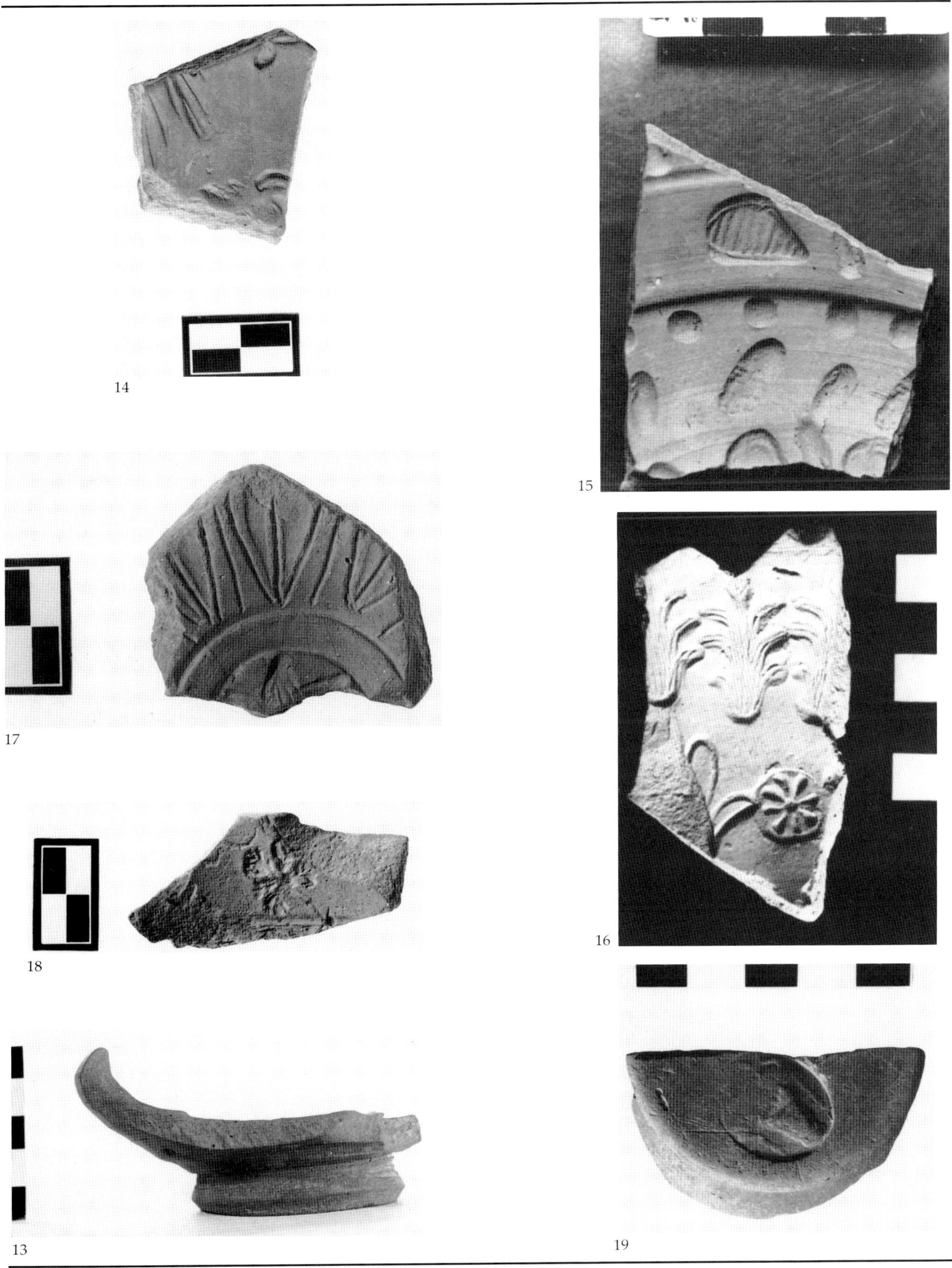
14
15
17
16
18
13
19

Plate 152. Bowl moulds, Early Hellenistic Wheelmade Gray Ware

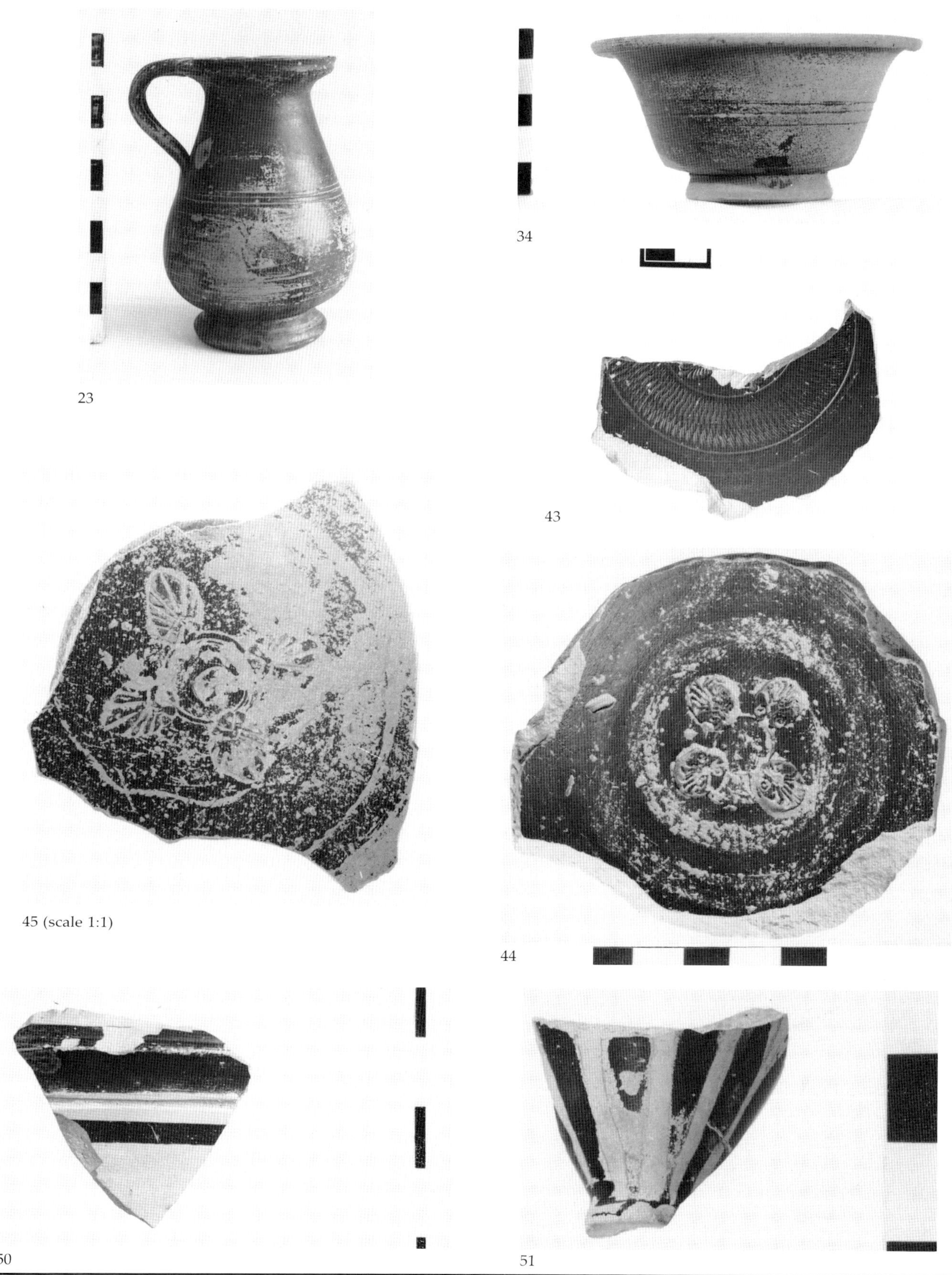

Plate 153. Black-Gloss Wares (45, scale 1:1)

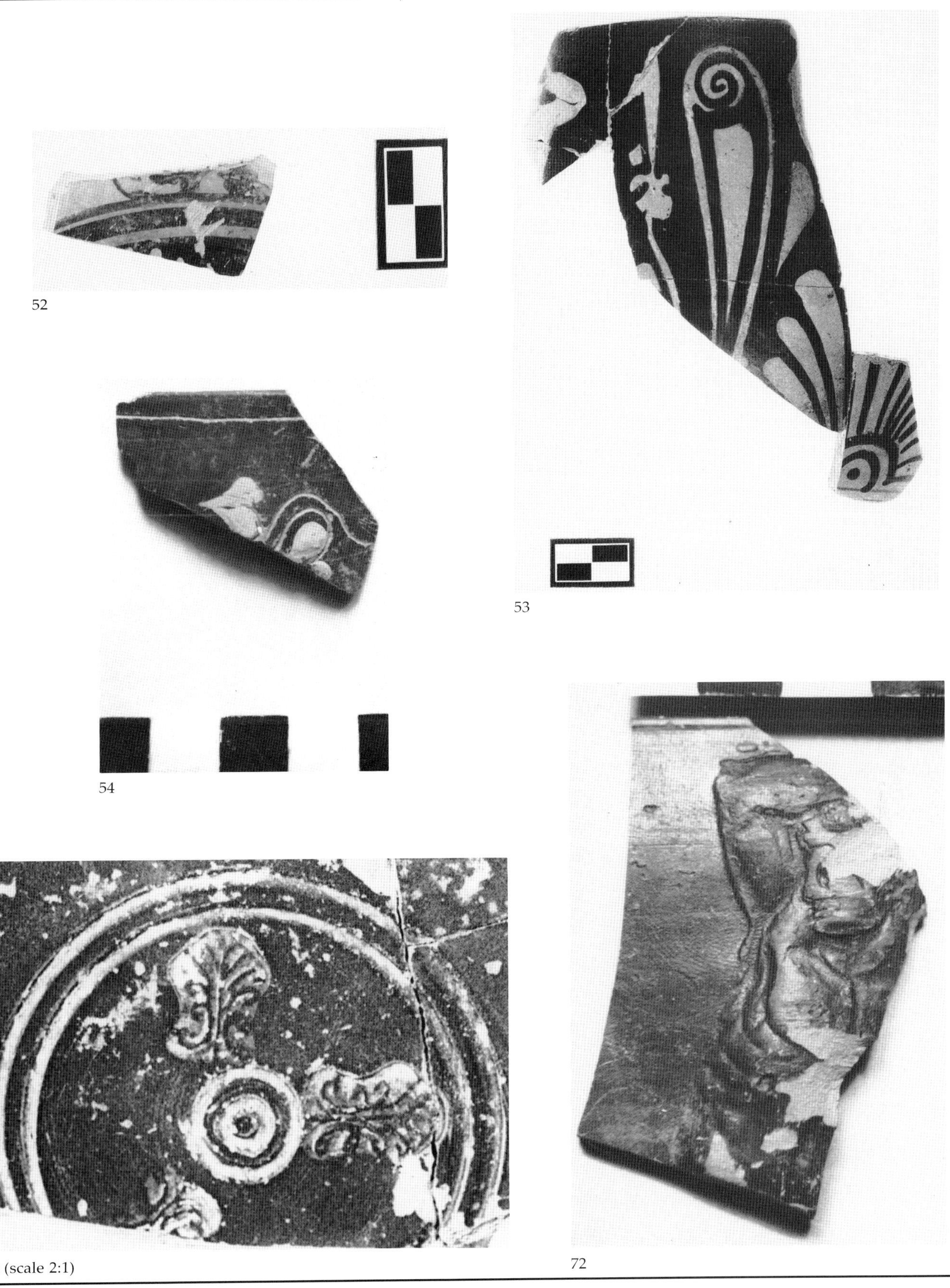
52

53

54

93 (scale 2:1)

72

Plate 154. Black-Gloss Wares. Black-Gloss Wares with Gray Fabric (93, scale 2:1)

101
110
102 (scale 1:1)
103 (scale 1:1)
111
106
109

Plate 155. Black-Gloss Wares with Gray Fabric. Hellenistic Moulded Relief Bowls (102, 103, scale 1:1)

108

114

112 (scale 3:2)

115

117

113 (scale 1:1)

Plate 156. Hellenistic Moulded Relief Bowls (112, scale 3:2; 113, scale 1:1)

116

119

118

120 (scale 3:2)

121 (scale 1:1)

Plate 157. Hellenistic Moulded Relief Bowls (120, scale 3:2; 121, scale 1:1)

122

123

124

125

126

127

Plate 158. Hellenistic Moulded Relief Bowls

128

129

130

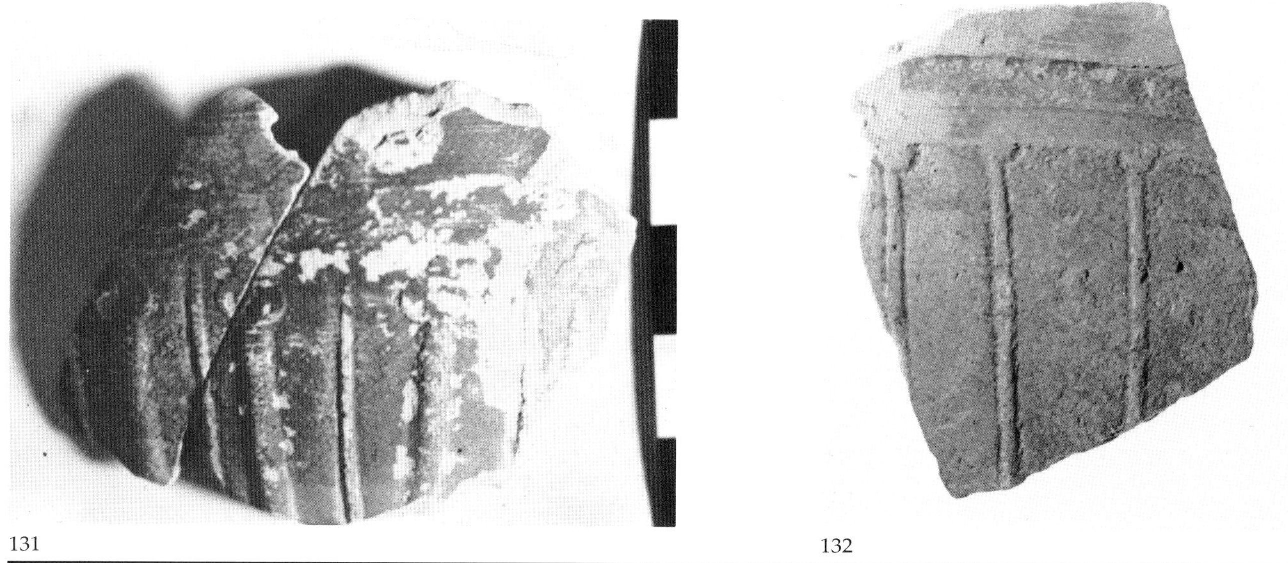

131

132

Plate 159. Hellenistic Moulded Relief Bowls

133
134
135
136
137

Plate 160. Hellenistic Moulded Relief Bowls

138

139

140

141

142

Plate 161. Hellenistic Moulded Relief Bowls

143

144

146

145

Plate 162. Hellenistic Moulded Relief Bowls

147
175
176
173
177
186
182
192

Plate 163. Thin-Walled Wares

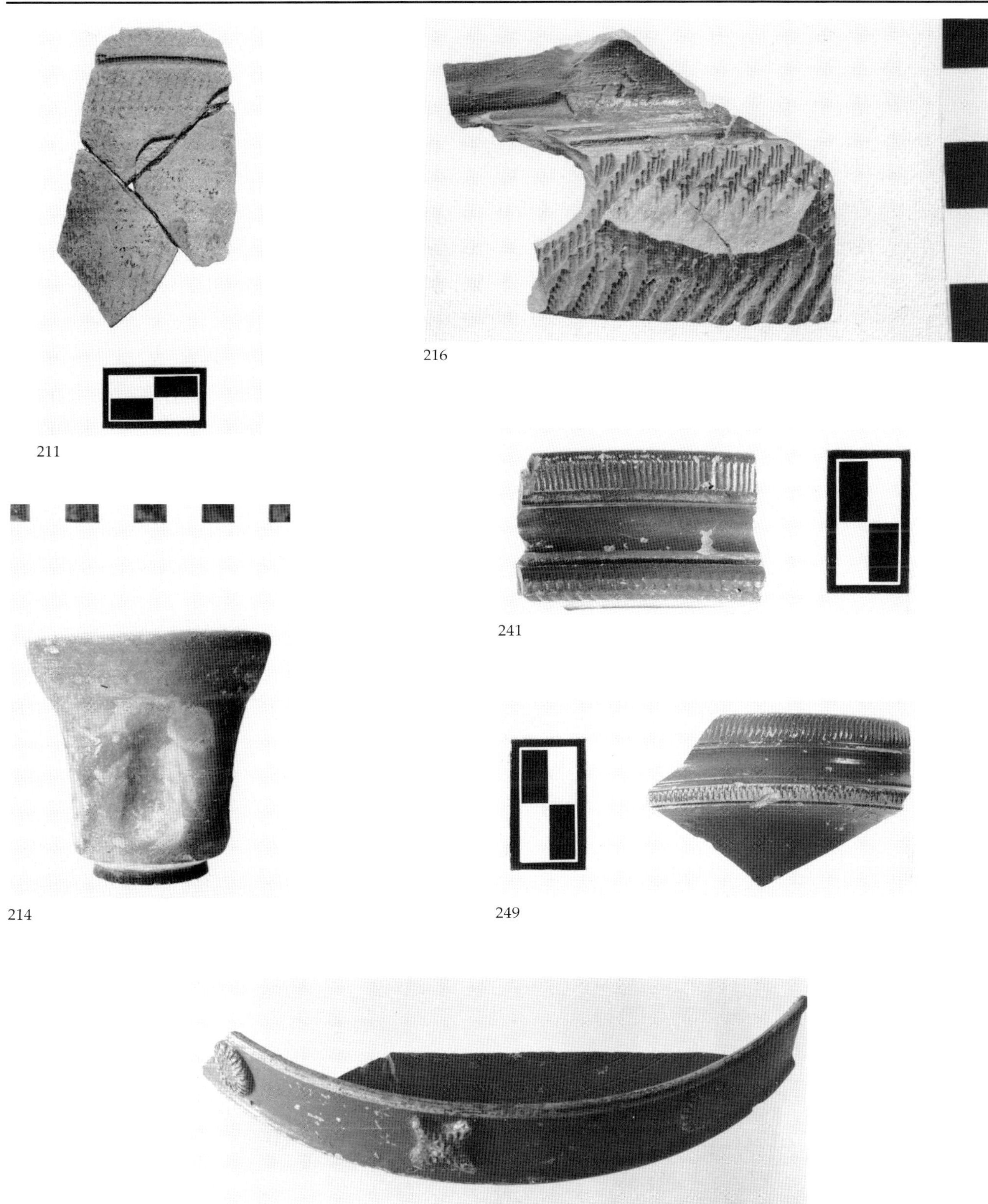
211

216

241

214

249

253

Plate 164. Thin-Walled Wares. Italian Sigillata

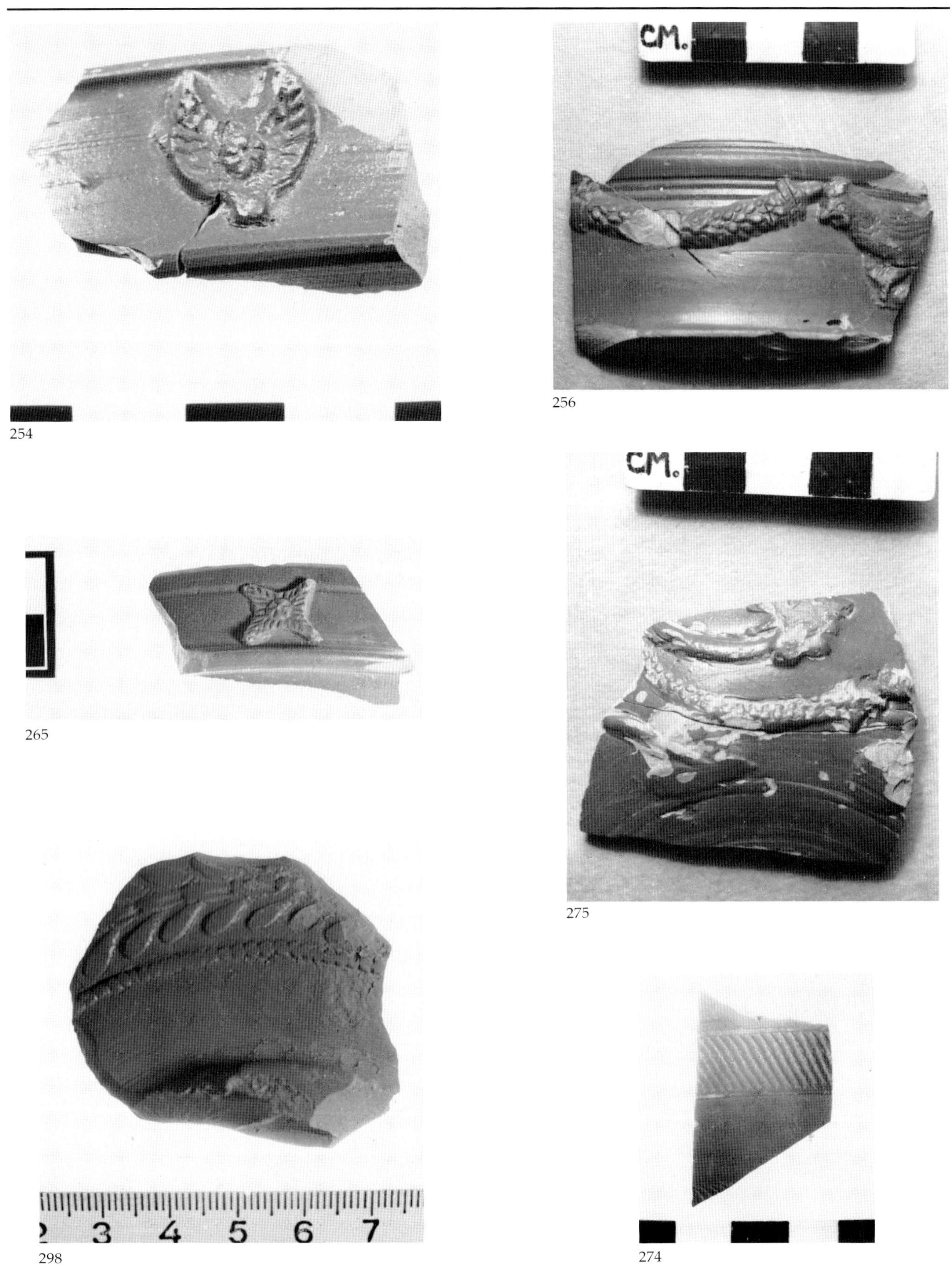

254
256
265
275
298
274

Plate 165. Italian Sigillata. Other Western Sigillata

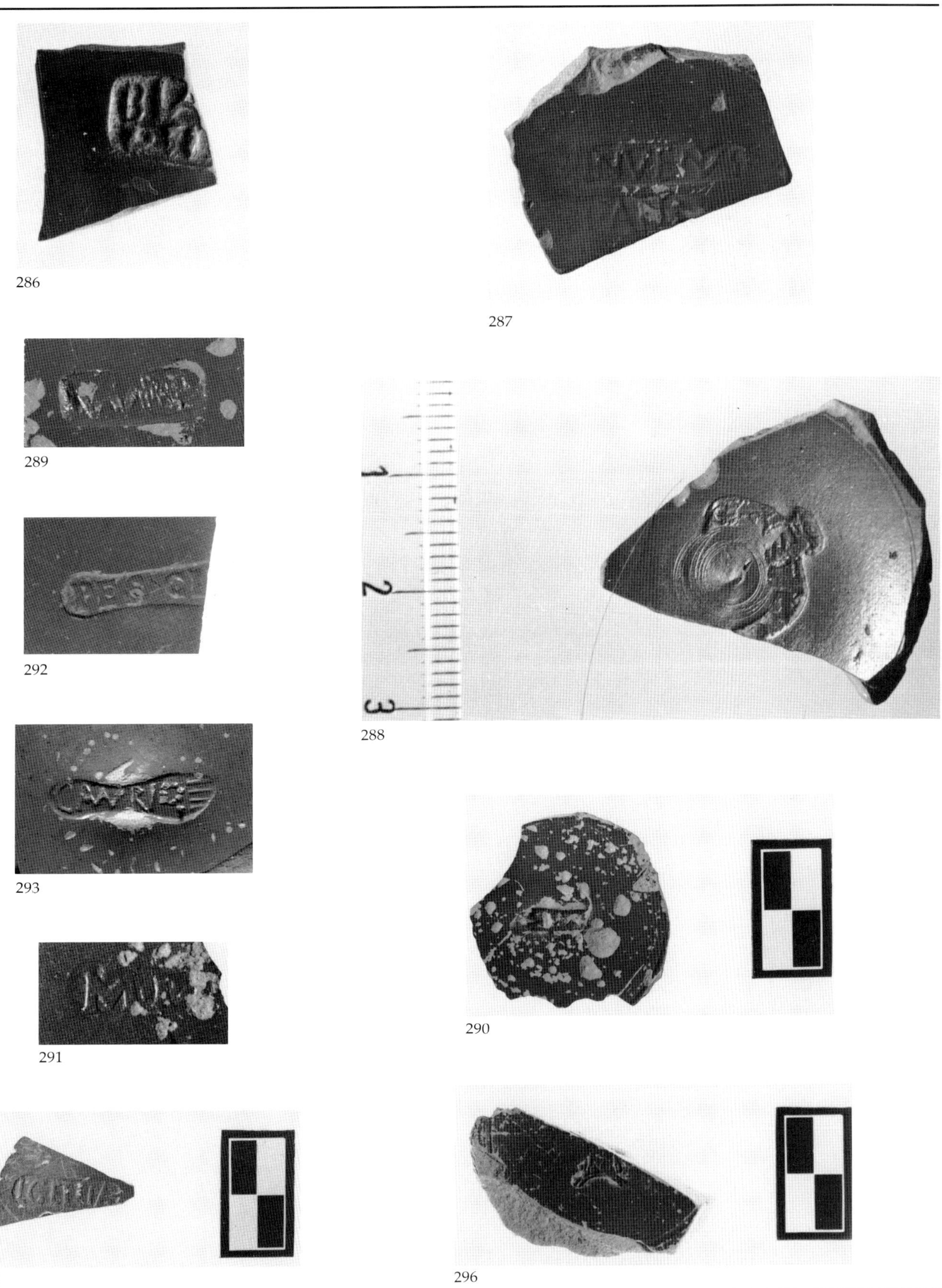

Plate 166. Italian Sigillata Stamps

Plate 167. Other Western Sigillata

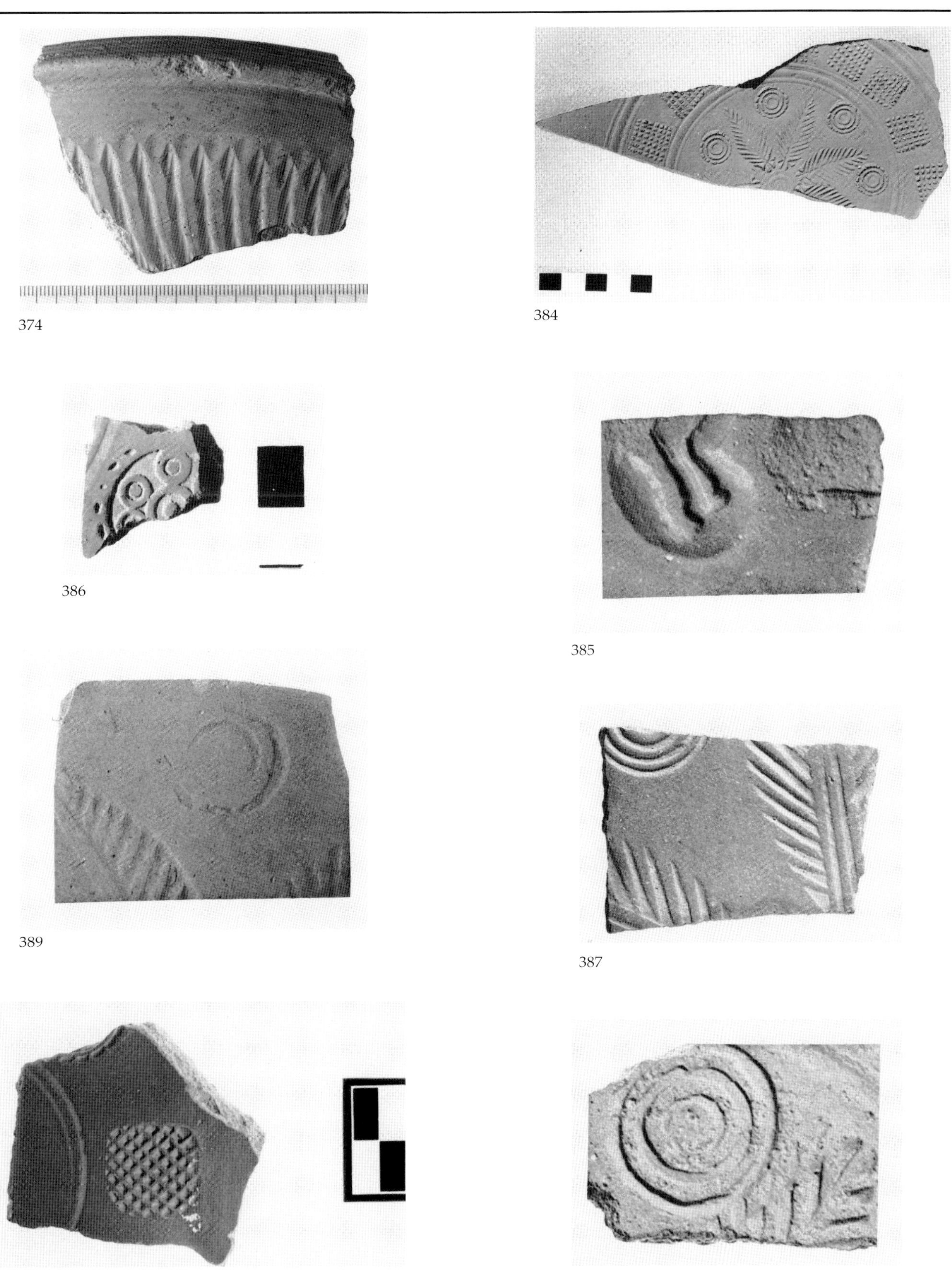

374

384

386

385

389

387

390

388

Plate 168. African Red Slip Ware

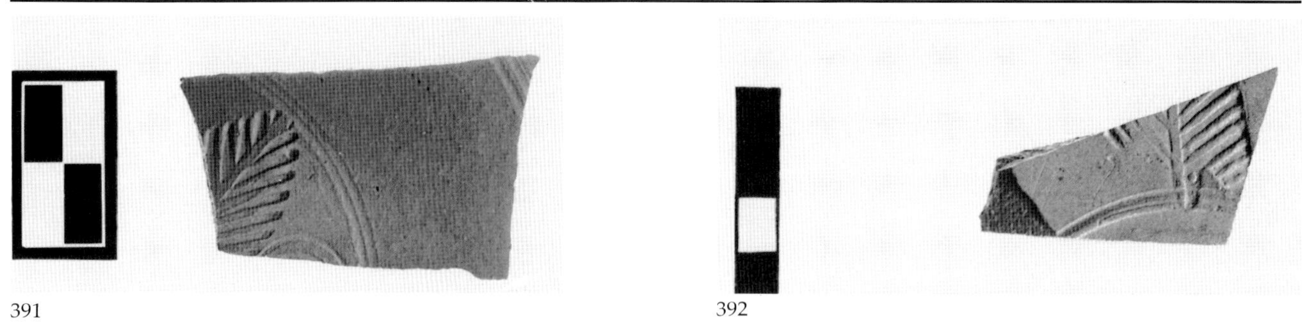
391

392

415

393

417

425

Plate 169. African Red Slip Ware. Phocaean Red Slip Ware. Macedonian Gray Ware

426

427

428

429

434

454

480

478

Plate 170. Macedonian Gray Ware

479 481 482 485 486 488 489 487 491 492

Plate 171. Macedonian Gray Ware. Miscellaneous Stamps

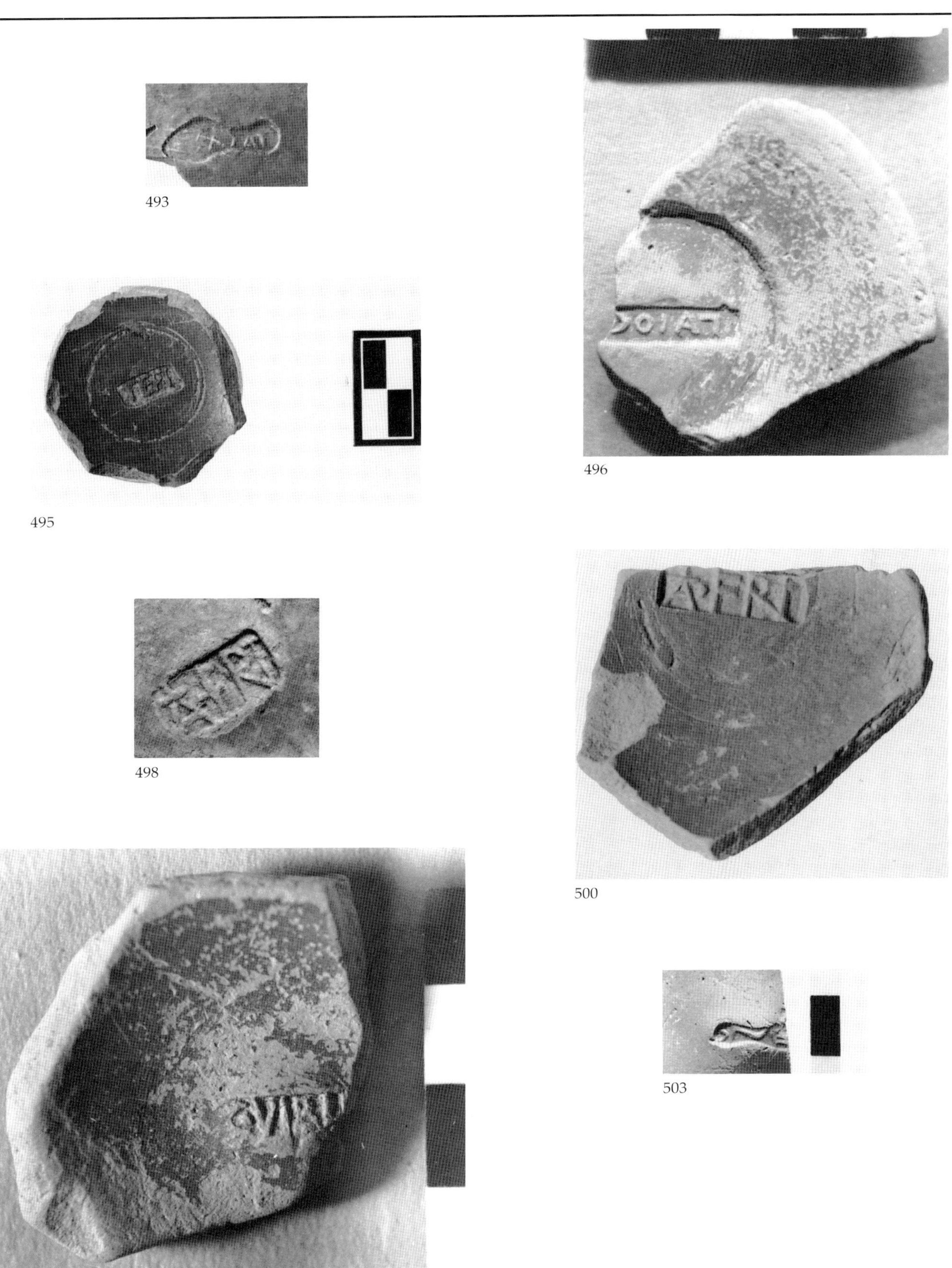
493

495

496

498

500

502

503

Plate 172. Miscellaneous Stamps

508

510

519

531 (scale 2:1)

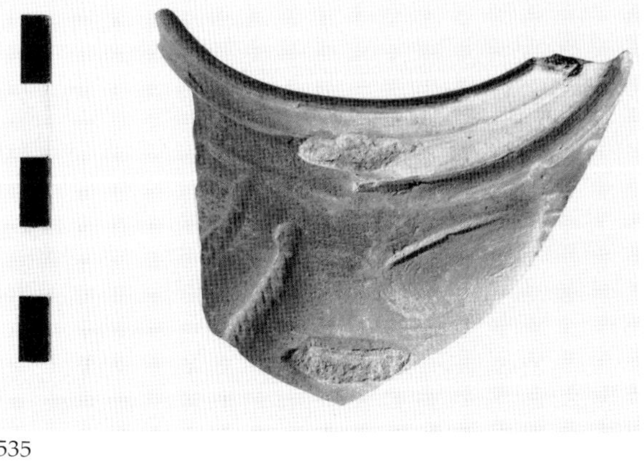

535

Plate 173. Miscellaneous Stamps. Marbeled Slip. Lead-Glazed Ware. Miscellaneous Imports (531, scale 2:1)

536

537

542

543

544

Plate 174. Miscellaneous Imports. Miscellaneous Relief Wares

545

546

547

552

548

550

Plate 175. Miscellaneous Relief Wares

551

549

554

553

556

Plate 176. Miscellaneous Relief Wares

555

560

557

561

614

Plate 177. Miscellaneous Relief Wares. Unguentaria. Mortarium

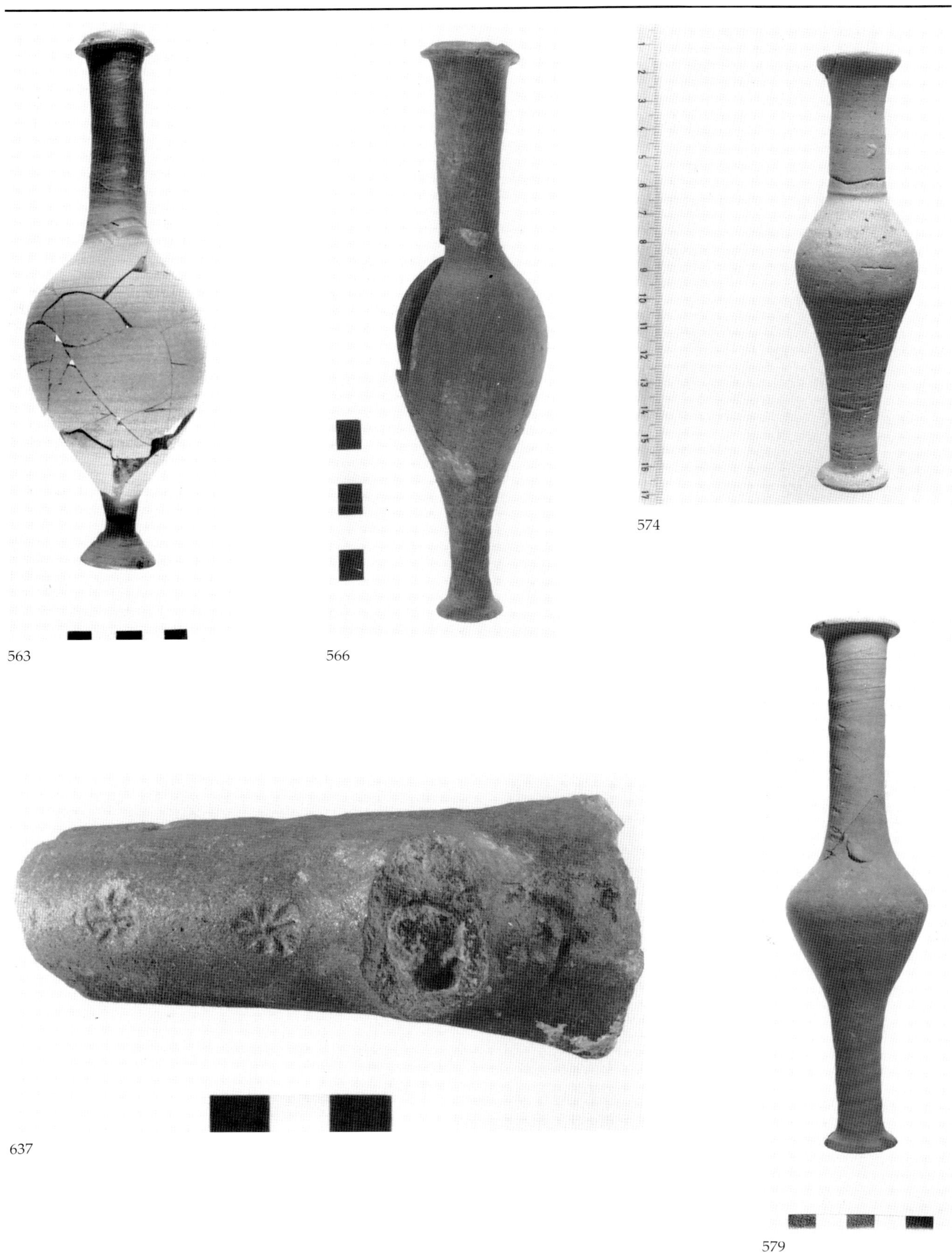

Plate 178. Unguentaria. Mica-Dusted Ware

583

585

607

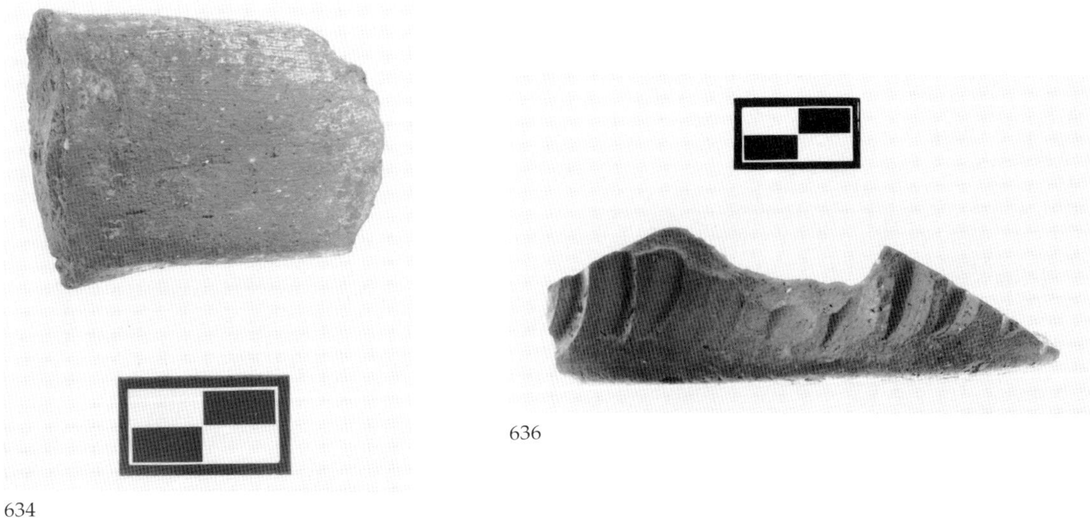

634

636

Plate 179. Unguentaria. Mica-Dusted Ware

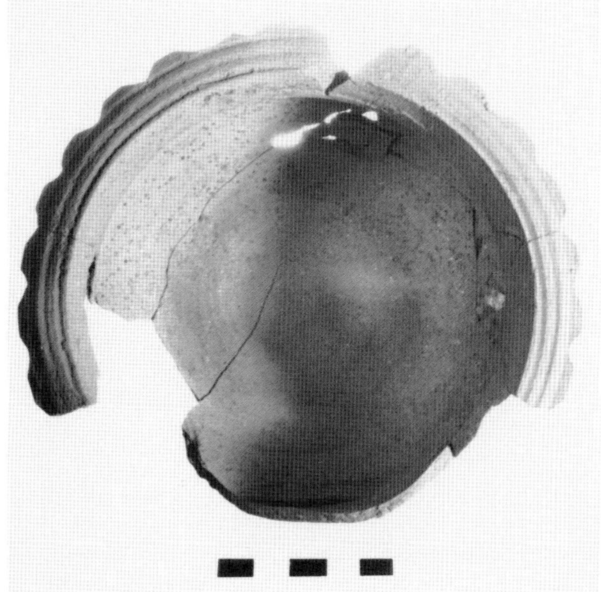

615

615

649

Plate 180. Tan Micaceous Ware. Amphora Stamp

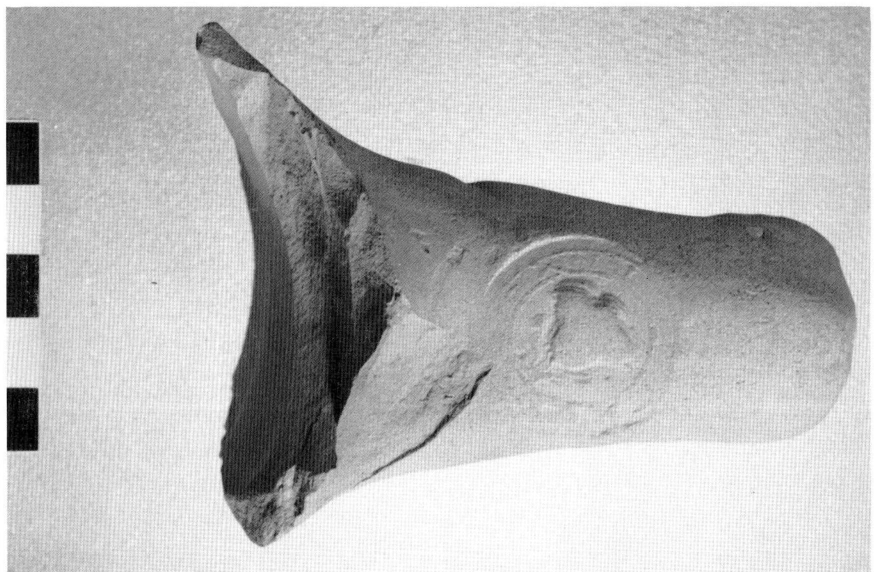
674

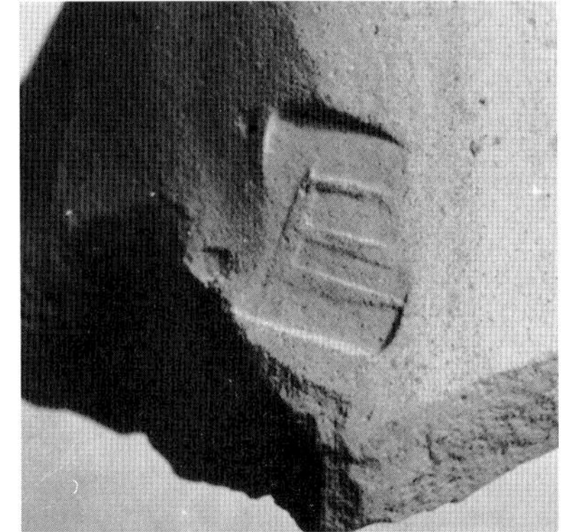
674

675

Plate 181. Amphora Stamps

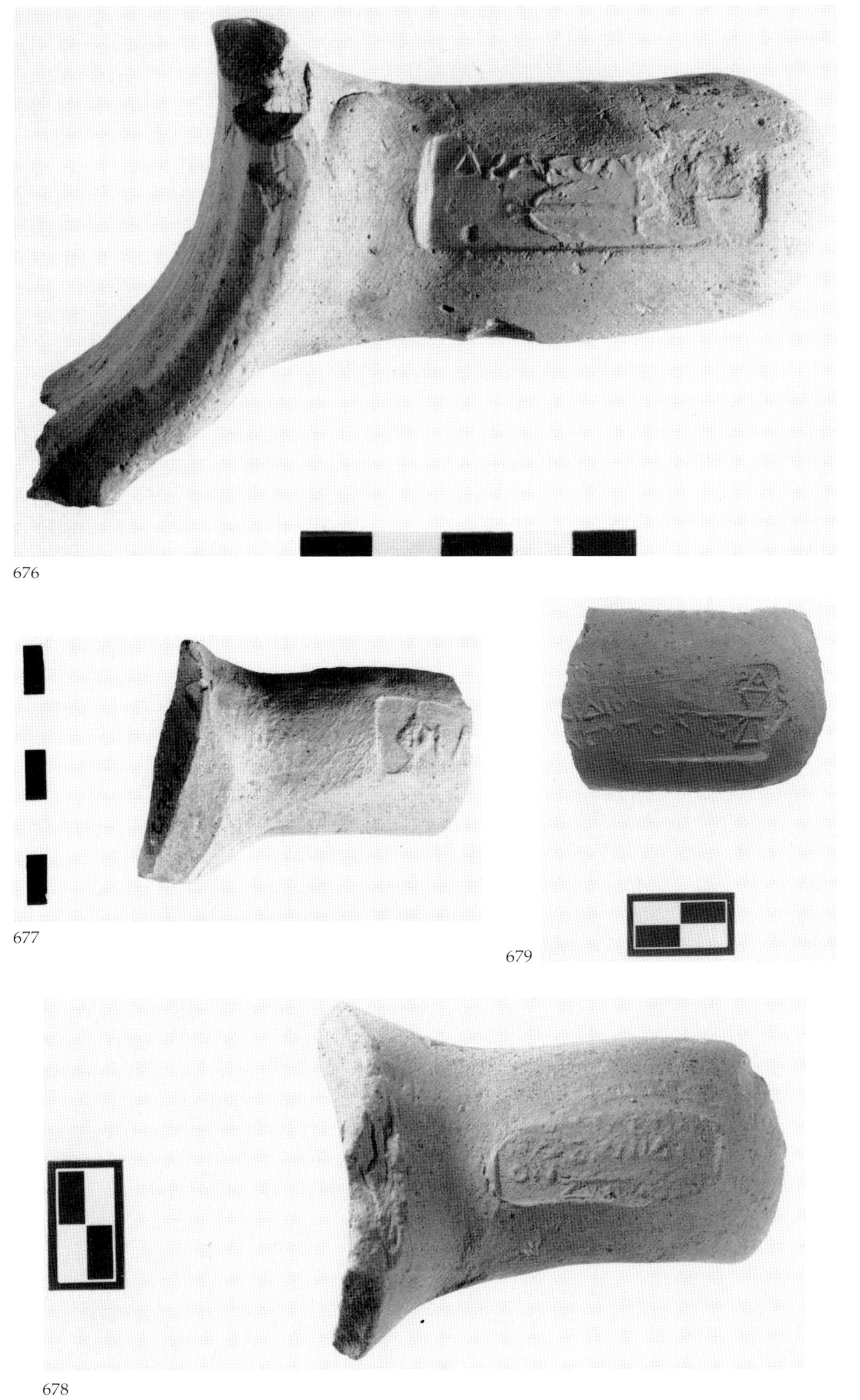
676
677
679
678

Plate 182. Amphora Stamps

680

681

688

695a

695b

Plate 183. Amphorae

689

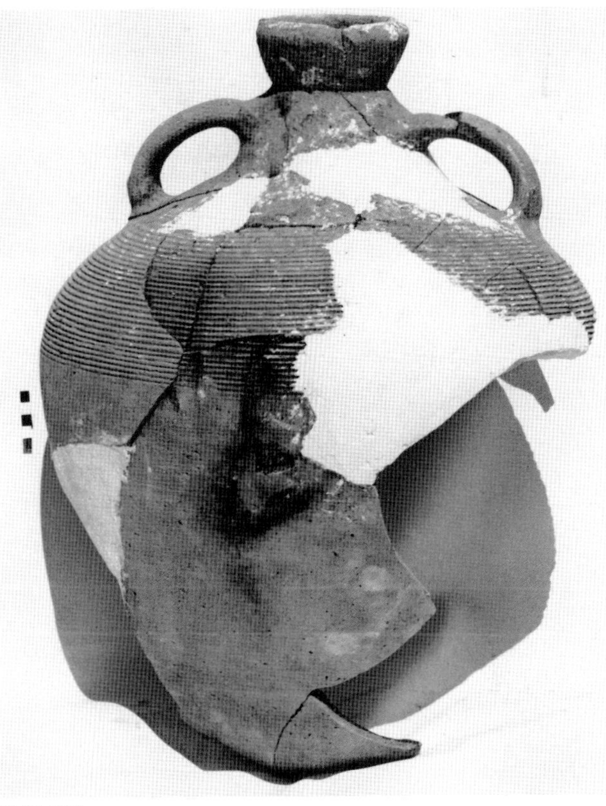
C-71-359

703

715

Plate 184. Amphorae

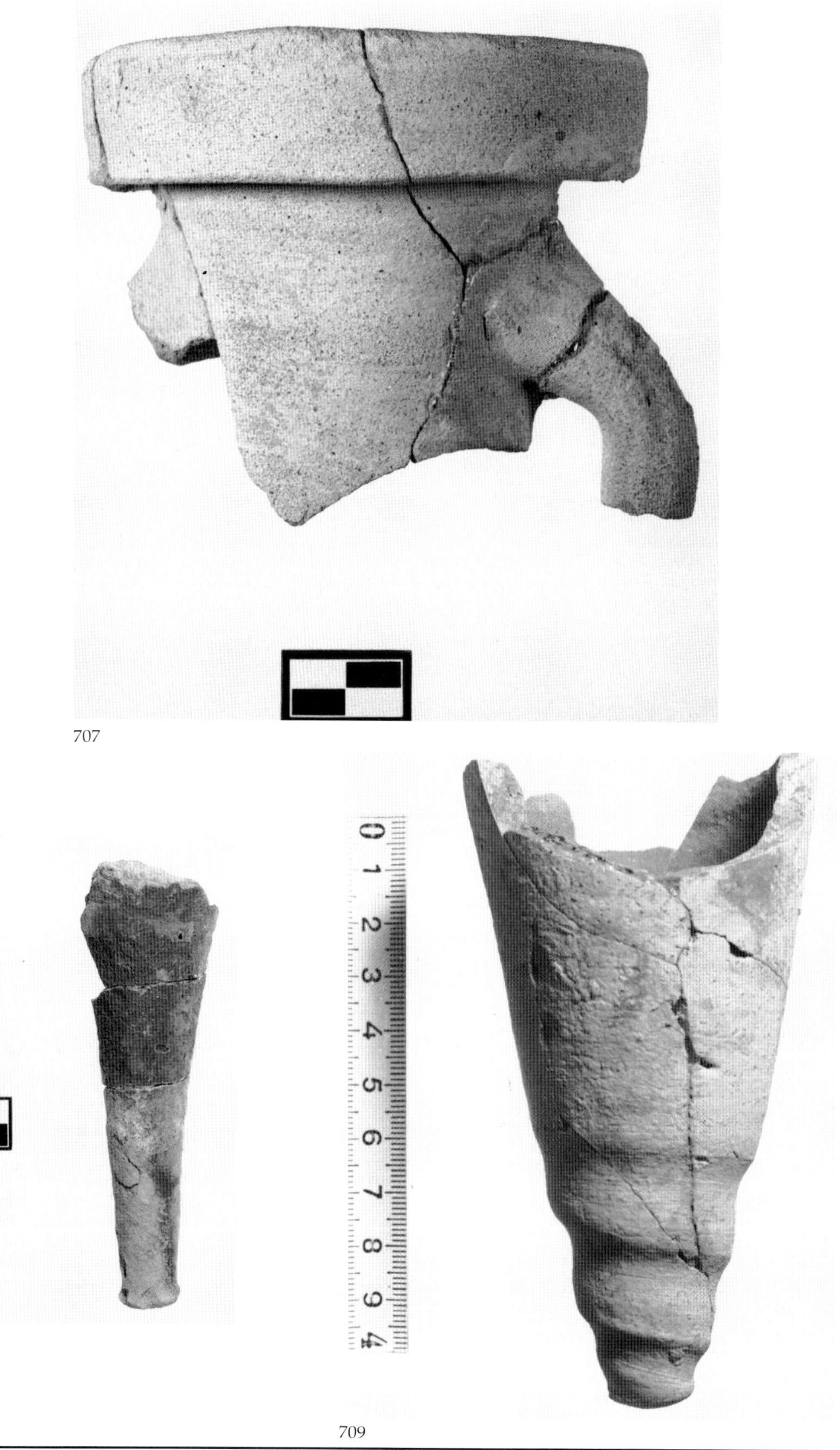

707

708

709

Plate 185. Amphorae

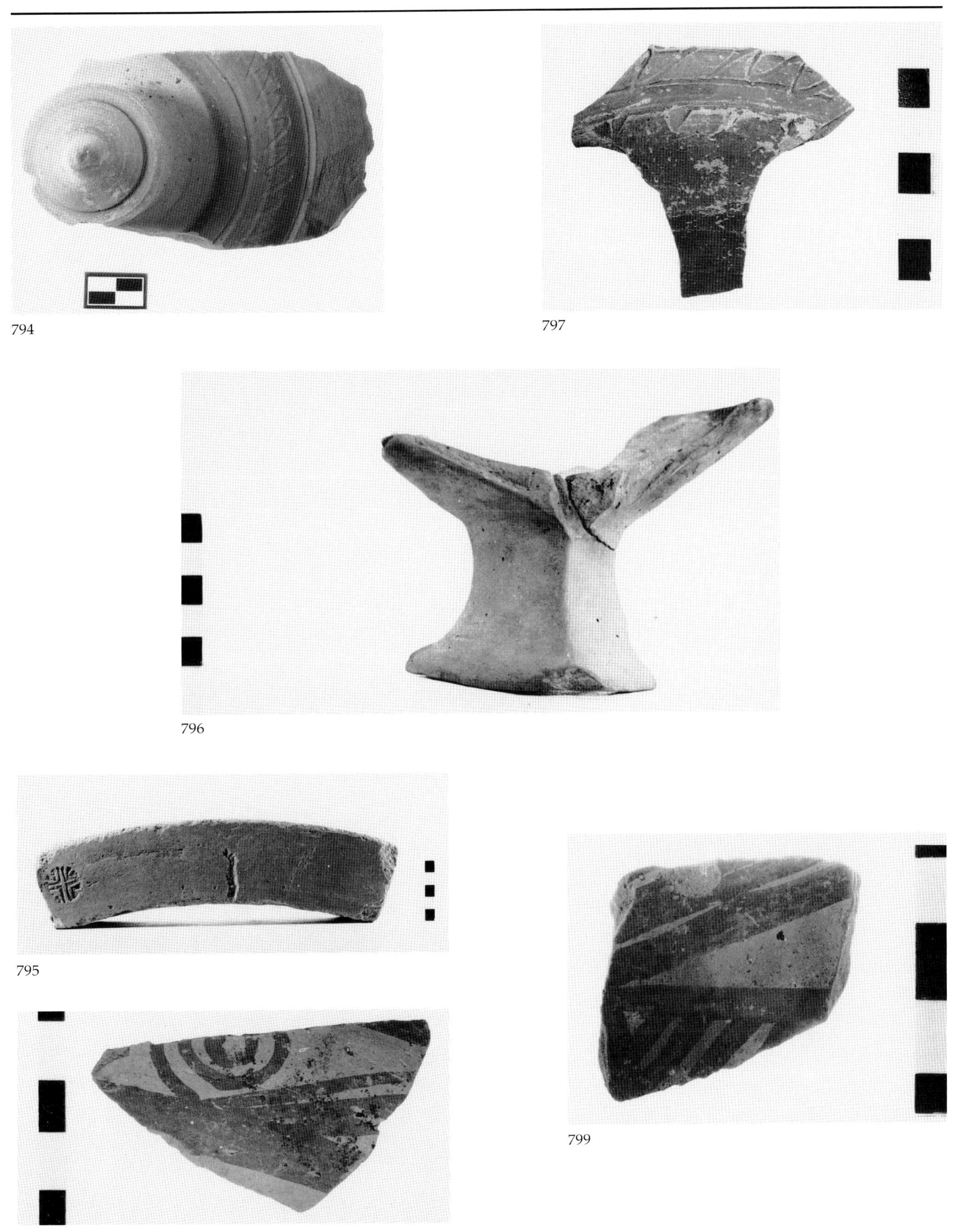
794
797
796
795
799
798

Plate 186. Hellenistic Color-Slipped and Plain Wares

840

880

1003

846

Plate 187. Early Roman and Middle Roman Color-Slipped and Plain Wares

963

965

1025

Plate 188. Middle Roman Color-Slipped Wares

Plate 189. Potter's Shop, a. (left) Walls 6 and 7, looking south and b. (right) Wall 7, looking north

Plate 190. Potter's Shop, a. (above) Wall 7, close-up of bricks, looking north and b. (below) Walls 6 and 7 with gravel in background, looking south

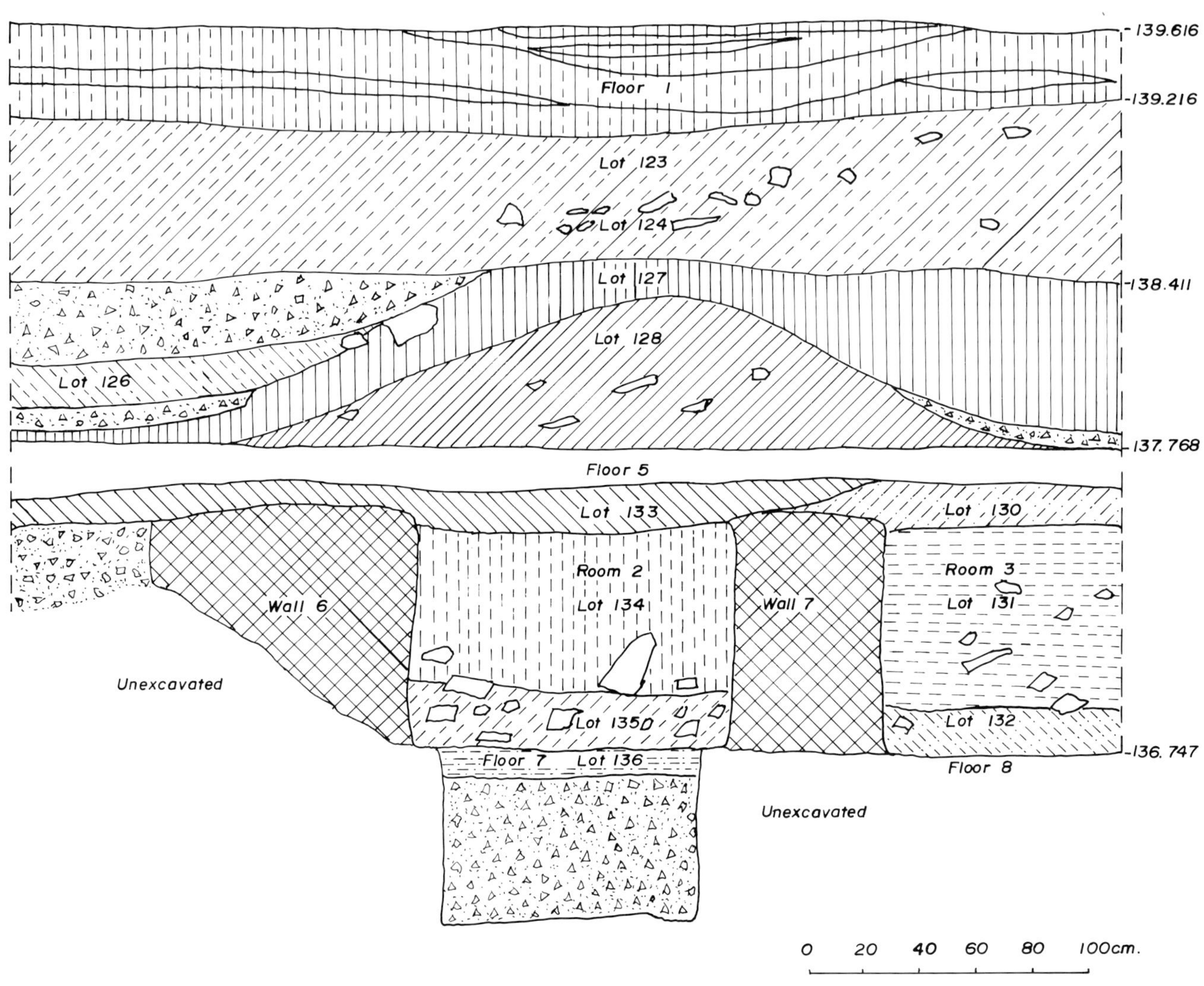

Plate 191. Potter's Shop. Deposits as seen in reconstruction of West profile of Central Basilica Narthex